KU-452-280

# ZULU RISING

## Other books by Ian Knight

The National Army Museum Book of the Zulu War

Brave Men's Blood

With His Face to the Foe:
The Life and Death of the Prince Imperial

The Anatomy of the Zulu Army:
From Shaka to Cetshwayo

Nothing Remains But To Fight:
The Defence of Rorke's Drift

Go To Your God Like A Soldier:
The Victorian Army on Campaign

A Companion to the Anglo-Zulu War

Zulu: The Battles of Isandlwana and Rorke's Drift

Great Zulu Battles

Great Zulu Commanders


*With Ian Castle*

Fearful Hard Times:
The Siege and Relief of Eshowe

The Zulu War: Then and Now


*With John Laband*

The War Correspondents: The Zulu War


*With Adrian Greaves*

Who's Who of the Zulu War (2 vols.)

IAN KNIGHT

# ZULU RISING

The Epic Story of iSandlwana
and Rorke's Drift

MACMILLAN

First published 2010 by Macmillan
an imprint of Pan Macmillan, a division of Macmillan Publishers Limited
Pan Macmillan, 20 New Wharf Road, London N1 9RR
Basingstoke and Oxford
Associated companies throughout the world
www.panmacmillan.com

ISBN 978-1-405-09185-5

Copyright © Ian Knight 2010

The right of Ian Knight to be identified as the
author of this work has been asserted by him in accordance
with the Copyright, Designs and Patents Act 1988.

The acknowledgements on page 698 constitute an extension of
this copyright page.

Every effort has been made to contact the copyright holders
of material reproduced in this book. If any have been inadvertently
overlooked, the publishers will be pleased to make restitution
at the earliest opportunity.

All rights reserved. No part of this publication may be
reproduced, stored in or introduced into a retrieval system, or
transmitted, in any form, or by any means (electronic, mechanical,
photocopying, recording or otherwise) without the prior written
permission of the publisher. Any person who does any unauthorized
act in relation to this publication may be liable to criminal
prosecution and civil claims for damages.

3 5 7 9 8 6 4 2

A CIP catalogue record for this book is available from
the British Library.

Map artwork by ML Design

Typeset by SetSystems Ltd, Saffron Walden, Essex
Printed in the UK by CPI Mackays, Chatham ME5 8TD

Visit **www.panmacmillan.com** to read more about all our books
and to buy them. You will also find features, author interviews and
news of any author events, and you can sign up for e-newsletters
so that you're always first to hear about our new releases.

*For Carolyn, Alex and Libby*

# Contents

# Contents

# Contents

# Contents

# Acknowledgements

This book has been over thirty years in the making, and it is impossible to acknowledge all the people who have helped to shape it with their opinions, ideas and knowledge. But some at least must be mentioned; my greatest debt still lies with that great old-time *fundi* on Zulu life and history, Sighart 'SB' Bourquin, whom I first met when I was visiting the country for the centenary in 1979, and who took me under his wing, taking me exploring in Zululand many times in the 1980s, often camping out on historic sites which host luxury lodges today but then were visited only by a trickle of the keenest of the keen – adventures which still burn bright in my memories. Without his enthusiasm and encouragement the history of the old Zulu kingdom would never have come to dominate my life as it has. *Ngiyabonga Makhandakhanda*.

Since then many people have taken up SB's burden – Professor John Laband, without doubt one of the finest scholars of the period, Dr Graham Dominy and his wife Anne, Gillian Scott-Berning in Durban and Graham Smythe during his tenure as curator at the museum at Rorke's Drift. Over the last fifteen years Eric Boswell and Ricky Crathorne have made Zululand accessible to me in a way I firmly believe no one else could, and I greatly treasure the time we spent driving down dusty roads among the hills exploring history and talking to people as the mood took us. My travels have brought me into contact with some remarkable people – John Aspinall, Dr Ian Player, Prince Gilenja Biyela, Barry Leitch, Pat Dunn – and many descendants of Zulu participants at iSandlwana, such as L.B.Z. Buthelezi, Chelmsford Ntanse, Mdiceni Gumede, Prince Michael Zulu, Paul Cebekhulu and particularly Lindizwe Ngobese, who has given me vivid insights into the life of his forebear, Mehlokazulu kaSihayo. My thanks are due too to Dr Tony Pollard who invited me to participate in the exploratory archaeological survey at iSandlwana in 2000 – which offered some fascinating material insights into the battle's controversies, and raised many more questions – and I owe a special mention to that remarkable American lady Pat Stubbs, whose adventures during the conception, building and running of Isandlwana Lodge I have followed closely, and who has been a charming and elegant host in the happy times I have spent there.

Many people in many libraries, museums and institutions have been unnaturally patient with me over the years, including the staffs of the Campbell Collections in Durban, the Local History Museums in Durban and the National Army Museum in London, Barry Marshall of Amafa KwaZulu-Natali, and successive curators of the Regimental Museum in Brecon, most recently Martin Everett and Celia Green. I have also benefited enormously over the years from the thoughts and advice of a handful of old friends with similar interests, who have proved by turn excellent travelling companions and a willing and mercifully irreverent sounding-board and who have always shared with me the fruits of their own research and collections. Prime among these are Ian Castle, Keith Reeves, Rai England, Bill Cainan, Mike McCabe, Ron Sheeley, Ian Woodason, Tim Day, Stephen Coan and Paul Marais. Many experts on the battle of iSandlwana have picked over the evidence with me, including Colonel Ian Bennett, Donald R. Morris and particularly F.W. David Jackson, whose own work on the subject has defined most subsequent study. Over the years I have also greatly enjoyed my association with Dr Adrian Greaves and the Anglo-Zulu War Historical Society and also the Victorian Military Society.

Most of all, my thanks go to my wife Carolyn and children Alex and Libby, who have sustained and encouraged me throughout.

## Note

Throughout the text I have retained original spellings and words in passages quoted directly. After careful consideration it was decided also to retain in such passages words which reflect contemporary racial attitudes, including those which are regarded as highly offensive today; this must be taken as an indication of nineteenth-century perspectives and does not in any sense reflect the opinions of the present author.

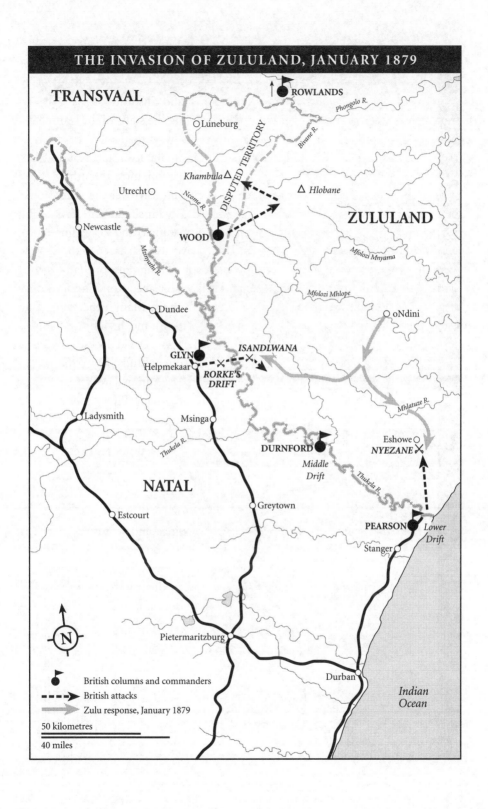

# THE INVASION OF ZULULAND, JANUARY 1879

TRANSVAAL

ROWLANDS

Phongolo R.

Luneburg

Bivane R.

DISPUTED TERRITORY

Khambula △

△ Hlobane

Utrecht ○

Ncome R.

ZULULAND

Newcastle ○

WOOD

Mzinyathi R.

Mfolozi Mnyama

Mfolozi Mhlope

Dundee ○

oNdini ○

GLYN

ISANDLWANA

Helpmekaar ○

RORKE'S
DRIFT

Mhlatuze R.

Ladysmith ○

Msinga ○

Thukela R.

Eshowe ○

DURNFORD

NYEZANE

Middle
Drift

NATAL

Thukela R.

Estcourt ○

Greytown ○

PEARSON    Lower
Drift

Stanger ○

N

Pietermaritzburg ○

● British columns and commanders

- - -► British attacks

➤ Zulu response, January 1879

50 kilometres

40 miles

Durban ○

Indian
Ocean

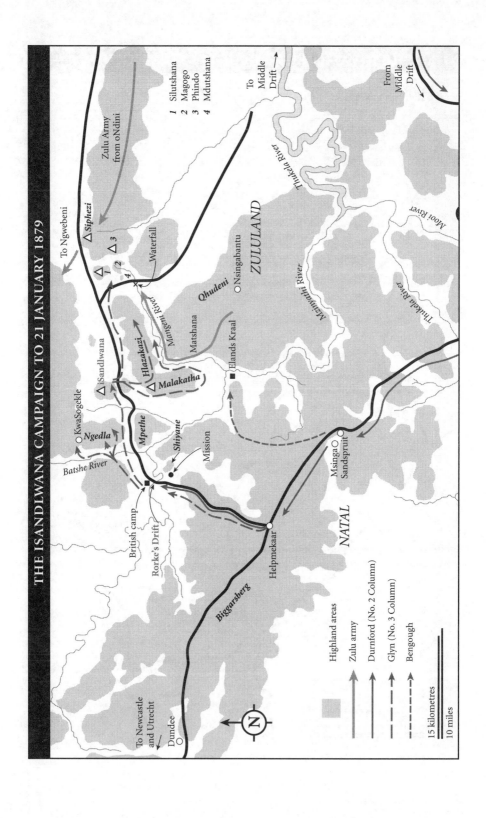

# THE ISANDLWANA CAMPAIGN TO 21 JANUARY 1879

1 Silutshana
2 Magogo
3 Phindo
4 Mdutshana

To Middle Drift

From Middle Drift

Zulu Army from oNdini

To Ngwebeni

△ *iSiphezi*

△ 3

△ 1 △ 2

4

Waterfall

Mangeni River

Thukela River

ZULULAND

*Qhudeni*

○ Nsingabantu

Matshana

■ Elands Kraal

*Hlazakazi*

△ *Malakatha*

△ iSandlwana

Mzinyathi River

Mooi River

Thukela River

○ KwaSogekle

*Ngedla*

*Mpethe*

Batshe River

*Shiyane*

Mission

Msinga ○
Sandspruit ○

British camp

Rorke's Drift

NATAL

Helpmekaar

Biggarsberg

To Newcastle and Utrecht

Dundee ○

**N**

| | Highland areas |
| → | Zulu army |
| → | Durnford (No. 2 Column) |
| → | Glyn (No. 3 Column) |
| → | Bengough |

15 kilometres

10 miles

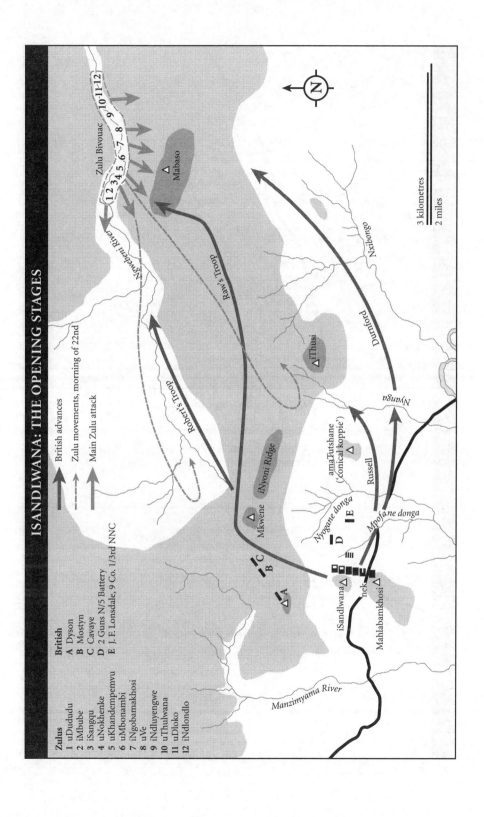

# ISANDLWANA: THE OPENING STAGES

**Zulus**
1 uDududu
2 iMbube
3 iSangqu
4 uNokhenke
5 uKhandempemvu
6 uMbonambi
7 iNgobamakhosi
8 uVe
9 iNdluyengwe
10 uThulwana
11 uDloko
12 iNdlondlo

**British**
A Dyson
B Mostyn
C Cavaye
D 2 Guns N/5 Battery
E J. F. Lonsdale, 9 Co. 1/3rd NNC

→ British advances
⇢ Zulu movements, morning of 22nd
→ Main Zulu attack

Zulu Bivouac

Ngwebeni River

Mabaso △

Raw's Troop

Nxibongo

Durnford

△ Thusi

Nyanga

Roberts Troop

iNyoni Ridge

amaTutshane ('conical koppie')

Russell

Nyogane donga

Mpofane donga

△ Mkwene

E ▮
D ▮

Manzimyama River

iSandlwana △    △
nek
Mahlabamkhosi △

3 kilometres
2 miles

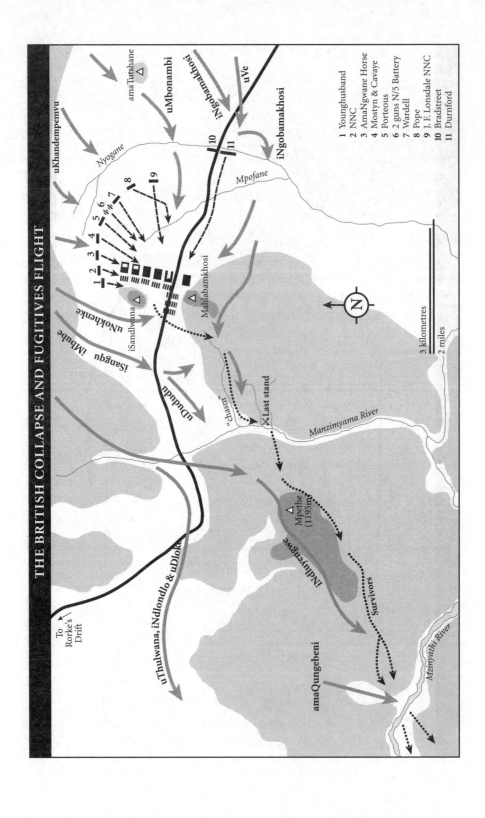

# THE BRITISH COLLAPSE AND FUGITIVES FLIGHT

amaTutshane

uKhandempemvu

uMbonambi

iNgobamakhosi

uVe

iNgobamakhosi

Nyogane

10
11

Mpofane

8
9

7
6
5
4

3
2
1

uNokhenke

iSandlwana

iSangu
iMbube

Mahlabamkhosi

uDududu

"chasm"

X Last stand

Manzimyama River

uThulwana, iNdlondlo & uDloko

To Rorke's Drift

Mpethe
(1195m)

iNdluyengwe

Survivors

amaQungebeni

Mzinyathi River

N

3 kilometres
2 miles

1 Younghusband
2 NNC
3 AmaNgwane Horse
4 Mostyn & Cavaye
5 Porteous
6 2 guns N/5 Battery
7 Wardell
8 Pope
9 J.F. Lonsdale NNC
10 Bradstreet
11 Durnford

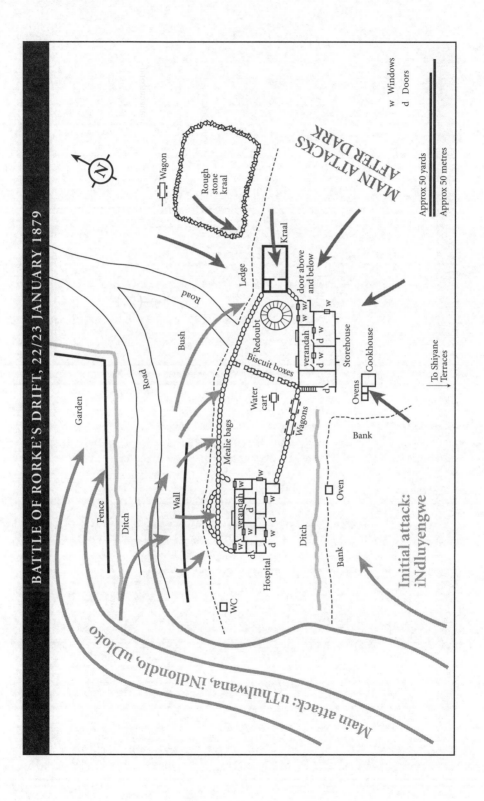

# BATTLE OF RORKE'S DRIFT, 22/23 JANUARY 1879

N

Wagon

Rough stone kraal

Ledge

Road

Bush

Road

Kraal

door above and below

**MAIN ATTACKS AFTER DARK**

Redoubt

verandah
w w
d w
Storehouse

Biscuit boxes

Cookhouse

Water cart

Ovens

Garden

Wagons

Bank

Fence

Mealie bags

To Shiyane Terraces

Ditch

Wall

Bank

Ditch

Oven

verandah
w d
w
d w d
Hospital

WC

**Initial attack: iNdluyengwe**

*Main attack: uThulwana, iNdlondlo, uDloko*

Approx 50 yards

Approx 50 metres

w  Windows
d  Doors

# Prologue

# 'The sun turned black'

When I had gone some way I turned and looked back at this lonesome, formidable hill standing there, a fitting monument for the multitude of death; immemorially stern, ancient and grand. The twilight was closing in, the sky was red, fading into grey. Over that savage crest trembled one star. Heaven's own ornament; near to it gleamed the faint but luminous bow of the new-born moon, that same young moon which once hung upon the slain on this forsaken field of blood. I walked a while picking my way over the stony ridge and dongas where the last stand was made against the roaring flood of foes and again looked back. Now the stark mount had become very black and solemn, the trembling star had sunk or vanished and of the following crescent of the young moon but one horn appeared above the hill. It looked like a plume of faint, unearthly fire burning upon Isandhlwana's rocky brow. This must be a quiet place for a man's eternal sleep. But the scene which went before that sleep![1]

Sir Henry Rider Haggard,
upon visiting iSandlwana for the first time in 1914

On 21 January 2007 – the day before the 128th anniversary of the battle of iSandlwana – I found myself, during the full fury of research for this book, perched uncomfortably on the stones which mark out the visitors' car-park on the battlefield. It was a typically hot Zululand summer's day with temperatures reaching nearly 40°C, much as they did on the day of the battle, and the landscape was enveloped in a drowsy stillness.

My companion, munching a packed lunch in silent reverie beside me, had travelled out from England specifically to visit the battlefields on the anniversary. Recently widowed in late middle age, he had come increasingly to draw comfort from a direct family connection with the powerful history that had taken place here – his great-grandfather had fought at Rorke's Drift.

Despite the growth in heritage tourism to South Africa in recent years, the battlefield was not busy, and small parties of visitors, staying at the luxurious nearby tourist lodges, were soon swallowed up in the quiet landscape. The words of their guides, evoking with familiar ease the names of long-dead participants in the battle such as 'young Charlie Raw' or Mehlokazulu kaSihayo, were soon lost with them among the boulders, leaving us in the comparative silence of the whispering grass. The car-park is situated uncomfortably in the centre of the killing fields, where the fight raged fiercely hand-to-hand, and in front of us iSandlwana hill, which witnessed it all, faced us blankly, bleached in the sunlight, offering no clues to the drama played out here.

I became aware, after a while, that we were not in fact alone. A small group of Africans was sitting perhaps 50 metres away from us, where the terrain drops away into the Manzimnyama valley behind iSandlwana, almost hidden in the long grass. We had not noticed them because they, too, were largely silent, their body language almost shy, as if they did not want to draw attention to themselves. After a while, however, three young men rose up from among the group and moved further off, walking slowly, their bodies hunched forward in the traditional attitude of respect. Two of them were carrying small rolled grass mats, the third a small green sprig of the *uhlalankhosi* thorn tree. They stopped, kneeling down, heads bowed, while the leader began speaking, addressing his comments to the empty valley beyond. I watched, intrigued, until at length they finished their deliberations, stood up, and returned to their companions, walking like men at a funeral. Only the man with the thorn sprig spoke, directing his words to the sprig in a soothing, reassuring tone. The group as a whole then made their way slowly back to their car, parked close to us.

The *uhlalankhosi* – 'the tree of the kings' – is associated with many traditional Zulu beliefs connected with reverence for the ancestors, and we had unwittingly stumbled upon a ceremony to return the spirit of a Zulu man, killed in the battle 128 years before, to the home of his modern family. The sharp thorns of the bush are said to catch the spirit of the deceased, enabling those who practise the ceremony to transport it to a more sympathetic environment, to familiar haunts where it may be properly honoured by living descendants. The bringing back of the spirits of people killed far from home is still common practice in Zululand, even for those killed in a battle so long ago. The practitioners are not generally allowed, during the ceremony, to talk to anyone but the spirit of the departed, although on this occasion one of the young men, seeing my interest, greeted me and volunteered the information that the ceremony had been carried out at the request of elders within his family. They were concerned that recent troubles within the family might have been due to their failure to give proper reverence to the ancestral shadow which languished, restless and unacknowledged, upon the battlefield. Their group, they said, had driven from Empangeni, over 100 kilometres away, and they were taking the spirit back there with them – a telling reminder of the fact that resistance to the British invasion in 1879 had been a concerted national response.

And this ceremony was by no means unique. Similar ones still occur regularly on dozens of battlefields scattered across this beautiful but blood-stained landscape, dating not only to the British conquest of 1879 but to great cycles of violence which began before the rise of the Zulu kingdom in the 1820s and which extended to a last forlorn struggle against European domination in 1906.

For me, the encounter was a forceful reminder of the impact of that violence today, not on a grand scale, upon political institutions or even upon the threads which bound together an entire way of life, but upon the lasting consciousness of ordinary people. If that one Zulu group was seeking expiation for today's woes by addressing the violence of the past, my friend, too, was linked to them by a legacy of participation on the other side. For both, the events of 1879 have offered a thread of continuity and identity – even of validation – and their presence on the battlefield, unintentionally together, seemed to me to have a deeper significance than the publicly orchestrated ceremonies of reconciliation which take place every few years on the anniversary.

My thoughts on the long-term impact of acts of extreme violence were given an added and shocking potency just a few days later, after I had returned to Britain. David Rattray, who lived at Fugitives' Drift, between the iSandlwana and Rorke's Drift battlefields, and who had made an international reputation as a pioneer of 'raconteur tourism', retelling the stories of the events of 1879, was murdered on 26 January 2007. His death was shocking in its suddenness and brutality; he was confronted by intruders in his home and shot down in front of his wife. I had worked for David years before, not long after he had first established his lodge, and he was very much a part of my own African journey; just how great his international standing had become since was brought home to me by the extraordinary media coverage his death provoked in Britain.

Underlying this reaction, however, I wondered if I discerned something which went beyond the justified horror at the pointless death of a much-loved public figure. There was an unease, it seemed to me, at the perception in Britain of our colonial past in Zululand, and an implicit questioning of the relationship between this one new violent death and that of so many for which the battlefields were famous. For the British today, of course, the invasion of Zululand is largely remembered for the heroism of the ordinary soldiers who took part. There are few things more profoundly pointless than attempting to apply contemporary morality to historical events, but it is nevertheless true that the policies and attitudes which produced the Anglo-Zulu War are deeply unfashionable in Britain nowadays, and uncomfortable truths are often buried uneasily beneath a veneer of Boy's Own derring-do, of stories of courage, self-sacrifice and Victoria Crosses awarded. If the British cause in 1879 seems reprehensible now, there are enough contemporary parallels, in Iraq and elsewhere, to suggest that no one, least of all politicians, learns from history. Even in the fashionable willingness to acknowledge the fighting qualities of the Zulu people, the noble opposition defending their home country, there is an element of romanticism which glibly avoids the true consequences of the war.

Yet the murder of David Rattray seemed to strip away the protective cocoon of history and expose the violence which lies at the heart of the story of iSandlwana and Rorke's Drift. Over 1,300 men died on the British side at iSandlwana, and their deaths were felt, weeks later when the news reached them, by bereaved families across the length of the British Isles. Several hundred of them were African troops, too, the NNC, whose allegiances were shaped by those conflicts which pre-dated the rise of the Zulu kingdom, and whose collaboration with the white invaders would have political repercussions into the twentieth century. Their spirits, too, remained on the battlefield, and require propitiation even today. At least 1,000 Zulus died in the battle, probably more; certainly many hundreds more were desperately injured and died on the long, agonizing walk home.

And the appealing stereotypes of brave redcoats and noble Zulu warriors exist without consequences only in the cinema. ISandlwana was but the costliest single event in a British invasion which cost the lives, altogether, of 2,500 British troops and their African allies and perhaps 10,000 Zulu men. The invasion was, moreover, part of a broader process of colonial penetration of Zululand which began with the arrival of the first white adventurers at Port Natal in 1824, lasted for the best part of a century, spanned a cycle of brutal wars, and which left the Zulu people dispossessed, without a voice in their governance, impoverished and economically exploited by their conquerors.

Many of the elements which have remained problematic in the otherwise apparently miraculous transformation of South Africa – political divisions, economic disparities, the stripping of the rural areas of human resources and consequent social dislocation and rootlessness – are the direct result of the complex conflicts of the nineteenth century, and have created between them a dark undercurrent that still profoundly affects life there today. In some marginalized sectors of society there remains a willingness to resort too quickly to violence as a means of resolving disputes, expunging resentments, or merely in pursuit of criminal activity. For Rian Malan, that most eloquent and unflinching observer of the darkness in the South African soul, there is no doubt that today's problems are shaped largely by historical factors. 'This cannot be how history ends in South Africa', he has said, 'this is an incredibly dramatic country. It can't end with an upbeat advertizing slogan.'[2]

In 'the Rainbow Nation' this recourse to violence is the unglamorous underbelly of the historic 'warrior tradition' of colonial interlopers and indigenous societies alike, of a society built on overlapping layers of conquest and dispossession. It continues to rob South Africa of rich lives, most of them anonymous by David Rattray's standards, yet in his death a cruel irony is apparent, for whatever the particular motives of his killers, he was in a sense consumed by the echoing tragedy that he had helped so vividly to articulate.

Perhaps the old Zulu heroes who fought in the great battles of long ago were correct in their assessment of the corrosive long-term effects of so much violence and division, for Zululand, it seems, has still to free itself entirely from the pain of old struggles – the stain of 'yesterday's blood'.

# 1

# Mehlokazulu's fury:
# The killing of MaMtshali

In Zululand in July the winter mornings can be bitterly cold. The days are often warm enough, but the heat dissipates quickly in the evening if there is no cloud-cover to retain it, and sometimes the clear, sharp air carries a chill borne by the wind off the icy peaks of the uKhahlamba mountains further inland. Snow is not an impossibility on the high, breezy ridges of the Biggarsberg range, which marks the western edge of the valley of the Mzinyathi river – the 'water of buffaloes' – and at dawn the brittle landscape is frequently dusted with frost. There is little joy in the ageless and bone-aching routine of abandoning the smoky fug of a hut to venture out, huddled in a blanket, into the dawn mist, to pad down paths trodden a thousand times before, winding between swathes of long wet grass and snagging thorn-trees festooned with spiders' webs, to fetch water, or to drive the cattle out from their overnight shelters to pasture.

Yet that time, called in isiZulu[1] 'the horns of the morning' – when the cocks crow and the horns of the cattle can first be seen against the greying horizon – was generally acknowledged as entirely appropriate for one activity: it was the time for killing.

Night was the greatest ally to enemies, raiders and execution squads, of course, not only hiding their movements but serving up victims taken by surprise, their minds foggy with sleep and their reactions dulled by that low psychological ebb that seems to come inevitably before the sunrise. So, too, was the mist, and the services of expert shamans, who could command the appearance of a good thick mist at will, were held in high regard by those who fancied themselves as warriors.[2]

If there was a mist on the morning of 28 July 1878, it must surely have added to the consternation of a man named Mswagele, who lived a few kilometres below that crossing on the Mzinyathi which the white settlers called Rorke's Drift. There, as the river snaked between steep, rocky ridges that folded impossibly over upon one another in jagged contortions, the Mzinyathi constituted the formal international boundary between the British colony of Natal and the independent kingdom of the Zulu. It was, in effect, the frontier of the British Empire in southern Africa – and Mswagele was a Border Policeman in the employ of the Natal authorities. His homestead, a collection of dome-shaped grass huts, lay only a few hundred yards from the river, and one of his regular duties was to observe the human traffic picking its way gingerly to and fro through a bad crossing that constituted the local ford or 'drift'. Occasionally an increase in numbers hinted at a subtle shift in the political undercurrents among the border population, and Mswagele duly reported anything suspicious to his superior, a white magistrate who lived a day's walk away.

In recent months this work had kept him unusually busy, for after more than fifty years of peaceful co-existence there had been a sudden rise in tension between Natal and Zululand, and a consequent increase in the number of people crossing the boundary. Most of the traffic had been innocuous enough, however, and nothing had occurred over the previous weeks to warn Mswagele of what was to happen that morning.

As he emerged from his hut, on his way, perhaps, to answer the call of nature, Mswagele suddenly became aware that he was not alone. Standing quietly in a ring beyond the palisades surrounding his huts were a large number of men – over 200 in all. Although in truth there was little to distinguish the physical appearance of the African communities on either side of the river, Mswagele knew at once, from the impressive array of shields and weapons that they carried, that these men were Zulus.

Their leaders, too were easily recognizable, not least because they were on horseback; Mswagele knew them to be prominent members of the family of Sihayo kaXongo Ngobese, the Zulu king's appointed representative on the other side of the river. An older man, distinguished by the polished ring of black gum around the crown of his head which marked him out as married and the head of his own estate, Mswagele realized was Zuluhlenga kaXongo, Sihayo's brother. Also present were two of Sihayo's sons, Tshekwane and Mkhumbikazulu, young men scarcely out of their teens.

What must really have concerned Mswagele, however, was the identity of the man at the head of the group. He, too, was young, still in his mid-twenties, but he carried himself with an air of easy authority, sitting comfortably on his horse and holding a white man's rifle with relaxed confidence. Mswagele had probably met this man before, and he certainly knew of his reputation, the way he was admired and respected along the length of the border by those who aspired to be warriors. He was *inkosi*[3] Sihayo's son and heir, Mehlokazulu.

Facing him, Mehlokazulu came straight to the point. Living at Mswagele's homestead was a woman, MaMtshali, a wife of *inkosi* Sihayo. Zulu society was polygamous and important men like Sihayo might maintain a household of twenty wives or more. MaMtshali, a senior wife and Mehlokazulu's mother, had abandoned Sihayo and crossed into Natal with a lover, taking refuge at Mswagele's homestead, trusting in his position as a representative of colonial authority and the security of the international border to protect her from the outrage she would cause. But she had fatally underestimated the strength of Mehlokazulu's fury and his determination to reclaim her.

To his credit, Mswagele appears for a moment to have considered resistance. He was, of course, absurdly outnumbered, but he had been joined by two or three fellow Border Policemen, who had been attracted by the commotion, together with several of his neighbours who had armed themselves with shields and spears and hurried over to investigate. Mswagele knew, too, that behind him stood the full weight of the British Empire. For a minute or two there was a stand-off, but then Mswagele's resolve crumpled: the simple, and inescapable, truth was that the Zulus were here in force – and the fabled red-coated colonial soldiers were not. What happened next, even allowing for the deliberate tone of cultivated outrage in the official colonial report, still has the power to shock 130 years after the event:

> Zuluhlenga, the brother of Serayo, was the first to enter [Mswagele's homestead]. He dragged the woman out of the hut. The other Zulus then seized her, some by the legs and some by the arms. They put a rein around her neck; they knocked out all her front teeth; they afterwards took the rein off her neck, and tied it around her waist, and so dragged her away along the ground.[4]

As Mehlokazulu's party moved off towards the river, watched by the helpless Mswagele and his followers, they struck up a war song. Somehow they bundled MaMtshali through the water, low at that time of year, and, back onto sovereign Zulu soil, then dragged her in the direction of kwaSogekle, *inkosi* Sihayo's principal homestead, which lay a few kilometres upstream. They had not gone far, however, when they reached the banks of the Cumbeza stream, and here MaMtshali paid the price for her infidelity and defiance. As the wife of an *inkosi*, she was entitled to a death without bloodshed; Mehlokazulu had no intention of further dishonouring his father's house, and so his men wound the leather rein once more around her neck, pulling the long ends taught – then they struck them with knobbled sticks. If MaMtshali was lucky, her neck would have snapped at once and she would have died instantly; if not, she would have been slowly garrotted to death. When she fell, Mehlokazulu's men gave a shout of exultation and fired their guns into the air in triumph. Then, still singing, they resumed their march home.

Nor was MaMtshali the only one to die. Her defection had encouraged a mood of defiance within Sihayo's household and another woman had also taken a lover. Her name was MaMthethwa, and when she had first been discovered, she had tried to suppress her husband's anger through witchcraft, infinitely compounding her crime. Mehlokazulu had found out and beat her but MaMthethwa escaped, following MaMtshali across the Mzinyathi. She had taken refuge with another Border Guard, Maziyana, whose post overlooked a minor crossing a kilometre or two below Mswagele's. Her flight didn't save her, either; a day or two after MaMtshali's death, Maziyana reported:

> . . . in the early morning, the sound was heard of horses approaching, and on going out Maziyana had found these to be ridden by Mehlokazulu and his brother Bekuzulu, and twenty or thirty other Zulus, who were then advancing towards the front of the hut. Another force numbering some forty or fifty, on foot and armed with shields and assegais, were seen advancing from the rear. Asked the cause of this visit, Mehlokazulu said he was in search of his mother, and thereupon ordered the men who were on foot to search for the woman in the huts. She was found there, dragged out and along the footpath and through the river by the ford called Nomavovo's. Another large body of Zulus was on the Zululand side of the river waiting.[5]

MaMthethwa was pulled and goaded along until the party was close to where MaMtshali's body must still have been lying out in the brown winter grass, and then she, too, was strangled.[6]

News of the first killing had spread through the communities on both sides of the river within hours, and their shock and horror at this second atrocity was infinitely compounded by the apparent ease with which Mehlokazulu had committed it. The white settler population was thinly scattered along the Natal bank of the upper Mzinyathi – a solitary missionary and a handful of farmers, with no military outposts to support them – and the incident aroused deep-seated fears about their vulnerability in the face of a robust and self-confident African neighbour. The fact that Mehlokazulu had been careful to state that he offered no insult or harm to Natal citizens counted for little in the face of Mswagele and Maziyana's obvious impotence, and Mehlokazulu's telling contempt at the prospect of reprisals. Worse still, the Border Guard's inaction hinted at a common settler paranoia – that, when it came to the crunch, black Africans in Natal would abandon their allegiance to white authority and form a common front with the Zulu.

Yet in fact the black community on both sides of the border was equally troubled by the events. There was little personal concern for the two dead women – they had, it was generally felt, brought their fate upon themselves – but the incident had thrown into sharp relief the ideological divide separating those on the two sides of the Mzinyathi River, the gulf which separated those who still lived under a free and independent traditional lifestyle and those who were constrained and limited by colonial authority. For fifty years African groups in Natal had passively accepted the reality of British rule, often because it provided a buffer against historic conflicts with the Zulu kings, yet many in Natal had become disillusioned with colonial rule, and for them the threat posed by marauding Zulu armies had receded as the Zulu kingdom assumed a nostalgic rosy glow as a bastion of African tradition and independence. Mehlokazulu's actions highlighted the uncomfortable but increasingly obvious fact that the British and Zulu could not readily accommodate one another – and that two very different cultures, fundamentally opposed to one another, were now in competition for the right to rule.

Which begged a disturbing question, one that seemed particularly pertinent to the communities straddling the political fault-line; if it came to an open conflict, who would win?

And if those living on the Zulu side pondered what those ragged volleys echoing briefly down the narrow valleys of the Mzinyathi portended, they were right to be concerned – for the gunfire heralded the death of more than MaMtshali and MaMthethwa. An act of ferocious domestic violence would prove the catalyst for a far greater international one, and although they did not yet know it, their own fate – and that of the entire Zulu kingdom – hung in the balance.

# 2

# Charlie Harford's luck

Lieutenant Henry Charles Harford's personal road to iSandlwana began in London one November morning in 1878 when he found himself, at nine o'clock sharp, in the ante-rooms of the War Office.

Harford's regiment, the 99th Foot, was based in Chatham, Kent, and Harford had been granted a day's leave by his commanding officer to seek an interview with Sir Martin Dillon, the British Army's adjutant-general. Harford had taken the precaution of arriving early, and was the first to be shown into Sir Martin's waiting-room. He had given his card to a porter, asking him to hand it in 'as soon as the Adjutant-General was disengaged'. He then sat down to wait, confident that whatever other appointments Sir Martin might have that day, he was first in line.

He was, however, to be sadly disabused:

> Officers of all grades, from Generals to subalterns, belonging to all arms of the Service, now began to pour in, and by eleven o'clock the waiting-room was simply crammed. There was scarcely standing room. Presently, the Adjutant-General began to receive the callers, and instead of my being ushered in as I had fondly hoped, having been the first to arrive, some of the senior officers were called upon. However, shortly before twelve noon Sir Garnet Wolseley arrived, followed by the Duke of Connaught, and until they had taken their departure no further interviews could take place. One o'clock, two o'clock struck, and still there was no sign of their moving, so a good many of those who were waiting went off. It was not until four o'clock that the Adjutant-General again became available for interviews.[1]

As a lowly lieutenant, Harford knew that he could not presume to take precedence over officers of a more exalted rank, but as the day passed he gave in to a flicker of frustration, the more so when the real reason he had been overlooked became apparent. When he had first given the porter his card, he had made a fatal breach of the unspoken etiquette which governed the waiting-room: he 'did not give him a tip, as I ought to have done'. The porter had his revenge; Harford was still waiting, alone in the empty room, at six o'clock that evening.

The situation was intolerable and, with no one left to witness his embarrassment, Harford set off to confront the porter: 'I walked out into the passage, and seeing the porter outside the Adjutant-General's room, said to him, in a fairly loud tone of voice, "Did you present my card to the Adjutant-General this morning? I gave it to you at nine o'clock, and asked you to give it in as soon as he was disengaged; and here I have been waiting ever since."' It was a stage whisper the porter could not afford to ignore, and he scuttled into the adjutant-general's office; at last the door was opened, and Harford was shown in.

Harford had been brought to London by news of impending troubles in southern Africa. It was rumoured that a confrontation with the Zulu king, Cetshwayo kaMpande, was imminent, and the British commander on the spot had issued a request for officers at home who were prepared to volunteer for 'special service' appointments. Such a request – which required officers to detach themselves temporarily from their regimental duties in order to take up a variety of staff posts in the field – was often a precursor to conflict, and it heralded a flutter of excitement among the young officers on garrison duty at home. At worst it would mean a break from the dreary routine of peacetime soldiering; at best, it offered a chance for adventure, and, if the shooting started in earnest, the thrill of combat and the possibility of realising dreams of distinction. In a system based strictly on seniority, nothing thinned the ranks and accelerated promotion like a good war. There was, moreover, always the chance to excel in the heat of battle, perhaps before the eye of an influential superior, with a healthy boost up the ladder of preferment as a result.

Charlie Harford, as he was generally known, had entered the 99th Foot as an ensign in 1870; he had been in the Army for eight years already, and had not seen a shot fired in anger. For much of his service the regiment had been based in Ireland, and by 1877 it had been due for a new posting. With British interests steadily expanding about the globe, Harford and his young colleagues must have entertained serious hopes of something a little more exciting. There was, for example, a fresh crisis brewing on the north-western frontier of India; the Amir of Afghanistan had received Russian envoys in Kabul, raising the spectre of a threat to Britain's influence in the 'Jewel in the Crown' of Empire.

Yet the 99th were not destined for the Afghan plains, nor even for the hot, dusty barracks of the frontier garrisons at Peshawar; instead, they were dispatched to Chatham, the ancient garrison town at the mouth of the Medway river, on the coast south-east of London, which was still regarded in the 1870s as strategically important despite the fact that the last time it had been threatened had largely passed out of memory.[2] Apart from the challenges of keeping their men out of trouble on their rare visits into the town – parts of Chatham, Gillingham and Rochester had an unenviable reputation for Dickensian levels of vice and depravity – most young officers had few enough duties in the daily grind of routine garrison work at home, and many were accustomed to taking long periods of leave, staving off ennui at the races or in fashionable clubs, or, for those who had country estates, passing their time hunting, shooting and fishing. It was a life not without its charms, but it was essentially a stagnant one, and those who were young enough still to hold ambitions longed for the promise of active service.

So when the request for volunteers for special service in Africa was posted, Charlie Harford had jumped at the chance. His application had, however, required some delicacy. Harford was adjutant of the 99th – one of the few posts that kept officers busy, even in peacetime – and he had, moreover, only held the appointment for a year. An efficient adjutant was essential to the running of the regiment, and appointment to the post was considered a mark of approval; by resigning it so soon Harford risked offending his commanding officer, turning his back on a confidence placed in him. In some regiments, where the colonel was of a certain temperament, that could lead to years of quiet retribution, of being passed over until the sin had been suitably expiated and the lesson thoroughly learned.

Fortunately, Harford had a trump card up his sleeve: he had spent much of his youth in southern Africa, and he had a good understanding of isiZulu. This was sure to make him almost unique among the special service applicants, and it gave him enough confidence to take his chance with the 99th's colonel, William Welman. Harford was in luck:

> Nothing could have been kinder than the manner in which the Colonel acceded to my request, and after discussing the matter with me at some length, and entering into the problem of my future prospects, being of the opinion that I would be certain to get a staff billet after the War, he advised me to resign the Adjutancy. This I did, and my application for special service was forwarded, with very strong recommendations.

Harford's luck held, too, when he finally found himself in Sir Martin Dillon's offices. It was difficult to argue with his credentials for the job, and, despite a long day of requests and entreaties, Sir Martin at once saw the merit in them:

'Sit down at my table, and I will dictate a letter for you.' This letter was, of course, to himself, which he then countersigned, passed in through a little window to an official in the next room, and gave orders for it to be attended to at once. He then questioned me about Natal, and asked me when I was prepared to start. 'Tomorrow morning, Sir,' I said, 'I'm going back to Chatham tonight.' 'Very well,' he said, 'the day after tomorrow you will get your orders', and bade me 'Good Night'. So, after all, my long wait had been a blessing in disguise; and I left the War Office in a true state of delight at my luck.[3]

It was the start of a few days of frenetic activity, and the beginning of an adventure which would prove, in many ways, to be the defining one of Charlie Harford's life.

To begin, there was the steam train back to Chatham, and the need to tell Colonel Welman of the outcome, to pass the adjutancy over to his friend, Lieutenant Arthur Davison and accept the good wishes and back-slapping of envious colleagues. Then uniforms and equipment had to be packed, and kit assembled, too, for the expected hardships of life in the wilds of Africa. Young officers about to go on postings to exotic parts of the Empire often had only the haziest idea of the conditions they were to encounter, and found themselves at the mercy of gentlemen's retailers keen to sell them the latest patented aids for travelling – anything from portable water-purifiers and one-man mosquito-proof tents, sand-goggles, anti-malaria vests and fever-belts, to a fearsome array of revolvers, hunting rifles and shotguns, each with its own allegedly unique capabilities. Harford's experience at least put him ahead of the game; when he encountered a naive young officer whilst shopping for kit in London he took him under his wing and advised him what to purchase. His list almost complete, Harford headed to Deans on the Strand to purchase two pairs of field boots. They didn't have a second pair in his size, but by a stroke of luck he managed to purloin a custom-made pair, reserved for another customer: of these, in due course, he would have a tale to tell.

His kit complete, Harford's next challenge was to be at the docks in time to catch the first boat to southern Africa. In the nineteenth century,

the British Government did not employ the Royal Navy to transport Army
personnel, the servants of Empire instead being dispatched around the
globe on regular civilian steamers. Harford had been booked a passage on
the SS *Edinburgh Castle*, and was expected to join her at Dartmouth,
Devon, her last port of call before leaving the British Isles. Having travelled
early from Chatham to Victoria Station in London, he was pacing idly
about beside his piled baggage waiting for a train to Dartmouth, when,

> . . . a porter appeared, and, having had a look at the baggage said, 'Is
> this your baggage, Sir?' I said, 'Yes.' 'I see it's labelled for Dartmouth',
> he said, 'You will never get to Dartmouth from here; you ought to
> have gone to Paddington!' 'Good Heavens!' I said, 'What on earth is to
> be done; I must get to Dartmouth by four o'clock today.' Then, taking
> out his watch, he said, 'There's a direct train leaving Paddington in a
> quarter of an hour. You may catch it if you look sharp.' Whereupon I
> said, 'I'll give you a half-sovereign and pay double fare for a cart, if
> you can manage it for me.' In an instant, he hailed a drayman with a
> two-horsed van in the station-yard . . . No fire-engine could have gone
> at a better pace than we did, we simply flew through the streets, which,
> luckily, were pretty empty. At Paddington, happily, there were plenty
> of porters, and my things, having already been labelled, were soon
> whipped off. Having paid the driver, I tore off to the ticket-office, and
> eventually jumped into the train just as it was moving off, the last of
> my packages being shovelled in while the train was on the move. It was
> a narrow squeak . . .[4]

In such ways did English gentlemen go to war in the winter of 1878.

Ironically, on his arrival Harford found the *Edinburgh Castle*'s departure had been delayed until midnight, 'and that a special late train was
being run from Paddington for the convenience of passengers to meet this
change; so really, I need not have hurried as I did'.[5] Nevertheless, he was
at least able to find his cabin and see his baggage taken aboard and stowed
away in daylight, unlike the latecomers, who blundered about on deck
throughout the early hours.

Harford was not the only officer on special service going out on the
*Edinburgh Castle*. A cluster of bright, hopeful young men joined from the
late train, the other successful applicants to the War Office request, most
of them, like Harford, looking forward excitedly to their first chance of
action. The majority were typical products of their class, the younger sons

of the minor gentry or of career soldiers; Harford found himself sharing a cabin with Horace Smith-Dorrien, a twenty-year-old lieutenant in the 95th Regiment – 'I don't know whether I ought to touch my cap to you or you to me', Smith-Dorrien told him – from Hertfordshire whose father was a colonel, and whose long face, lantern-jawed in later life, still then had a boyish softness about it. Among the others was the man Harford had met a few days before at Silver and Co., Lieutenant E.R. Courtenay of the 20th Hussars, Lieutenant Cecil Williams of the 58th Regiment, Captain E.J.H. Spratt of the 29th Regiment, and Lieutenant William Dundonald Cochrane of the 32nd Regiment.

At thirty-one, Cochrane was the oldest of the lieutenants on board, the slow progress of his career reflecting no lack of skill or enterprise on his part, but rather the grinding pace of promotion in the peacetime Army. Like Harford, he was returning to Africa, where his regiment had been posted at the Cape a few years before; his time there had coincided with one of the rare peaceful periods in the colony's history, however, and Cochrane, as much as the others, must have been hoping that this new posting would offer the chance at last for some real soldiering. He would be in luck; one way or another, the coming campaign would leave its mark on almost all of them.

Before the excitement of Africa, however, there was the dreary voyage out. It took between three weeks and a month for a steamer travelling from England to reach southern Africa, depending on weather conditions and stops along the way, and the first part was the most challenging for those not used to travelling by sea. Particularly in the winter months, conditions in the Bay of Biscay could be rough and unpleasant and many a soldier regretted, temporarily at least, the absence of still, dry ground beneath his feet. While the more adventurous wrapped themselves in oil-skin coats and tried to keep to a routine of invigorating walks about the decks, unregenerate landlubbers took to their cots and waited miserably for the bad weather to pass. 'I was awfully sick,' one young officer making the passage a few months later wrote breezily to his mother, 'in fact, so was everyone!'[6] Once past Portugal, however, there was a good chance that the weather would improve, and the possibility of a stop at Madeira, where the crew might take on coal, and lucky passengers run briefly ashore to marvel at the sight of the wooden sledges used to get up the steep cobbled streets. Then it was round the coast of west Africa, across the Equator and perhaps a distant view of St Helena, that most famous of the

British Empire's political prisons, where Napoleon Bonaparte had been
held captive until his death.

There was little enough to do on the way out, and passengers – soldiers
and civilians alike – had to pass the time as best they could. Amateur
dramatics and improvized shows were as popular on board as they were
at home, and concerts and theatricals, under Cochrane's direction, were
staged almost every day. A small charge was made, and 'at the end of the
voyage I think it was a little over £60 that was handed to the Captain for
charitable purposes'.[7]

For Harford, the journey into the tropics offered the chance to indulge
one of the great passions of his life. The natural sciences were something
of a fad among the Victorian gentry, a reflection of how the British perceived their role in the world during the great expansion of Empire. As
more and more obscure corners of the globe were painted red, so there
came the need to map, label, classify – and ultimately possess. The collection of exotic species of wildlife, to be brought home skinned, pickled or
in some other way preserved for the edification of science and the pursuit and betterment of Britain's knowledge of its imperial sphere, was an
essential part of the Victorian explorer's stock-in-trade. With the world
seemingly a far bigger, and largely unexplored, place then than it is today,
and the supply of species apparently inexhaustible, there were few who saw
the contradiction between discovering new creatures and killing them to
preserve them for study – and, indeed, many Victorian gentlemen already
enjoyed a close but somewhat ambivalent relationship with the natural
world at home. Outdoor pursuits were emblematic of life on a country
estate, where wildlife was appreciated and encouraged largely to fulfil its
role as sport or food for the table.

Charlie Harford enjoyed hunting, but he also had a genuine passion
for wildlife, and particularly for entomology; whenever he could, he looked
for rare and unusual insects, and when he found them he marvelled at
their beauty, killed them, and mounted them as specimens:

When off Cape Verde, about 150 miles [241 kilometres] out at sea, I
caught a number of little butterflies, 'Blues' of the family *Lycaenidae*,
and a few wasps. The former simply swarmed at the stern of the vessel,
fascinated, apparently, by churning up of the water by the propeller. It
was a lovely day, and very calm. Not withstanding the great distance
that they had flown out from the shore their flight was still very strong,

and they preferred to keep on the wing to settling anywhere on the vessel. Whither their instinct was leading them, it is impossible to say; but I am afraid they were doomed eventually to perish in the ocean.[8]

Nevertheless, despite such distractions, as Harford and his fellow officers were well aware, the voyage out was most likely the beginning of a period of active service, and most of them took the opportunity to hone their military skills. They brushed up their knowledge of signalling, while impromptu shooting practice was also popular. Sometimes the targets for this were made for the purpose and strung out on a line behind the ship, but often a passing gull or shark found himself on the receiving end of a badly directed shower of shot. Many officers were, of course, experienced shots with hunting weapons, and often took these on campaign with them; they were frequently less effective, however, with the revolvers that would constitute, along with their swords, their personal armament in any military campaign. Officers were required to equip themselves with privately purchased revolvers; there were no restrictions on the type or make, providing they were compatible with the .45 calibre of Government-issue ammunition. To many, revolvers lacked the practicality and familiarity of hunting weapons, or the glamour and heroic associations of swords, and those shots fired over the side of transports on the way to war were often their first. It was a neglect some of them would come in due course to regret.

It was common, too, for officers to mark their change to prospective combatant status by adopting a more warlike personal appearance. Queen's Regulations specified that Her Majesty's soldiers should grow moustaches where possible – it helped to create a manly and martial appearance – but that beards were not permitted except on active service.[9] The opportunity to make an early start on this was too good to miss, since the voyage to southern Africa offered the chance for the best part of a month's growth, and the daily comparison of their beardly progress became a part of shipboard ritual.

The *Edinburgh Castle* arrived at Cape Town without mishap, and most of the passengers took the opportunity to make a brief run ashore; Harford's married sister was living nearby, but he was disappointed to find that her husband's affairs did not appear to be flourishing, and that 'a more wretched, bare, bleak and uncomfortable-looking place than she was in, it would be almost impossible to find'.[10] Then the journey was resumed, around Cape Agulhas and into the Indian Ocean, hugging close to the shore and heading towards the British colony of Natal, to the north, which lay on the Zulu borders.

The *Edinburgh Castle* finally arrived off Durban, Natal's only viable port, on 2 December 1878. For newcomers, the approach by sea could be an unnerving one, since despite the best efforts of successive colonial engineers, the entrance to the harbour was as dangerous as it had been when the first settlers had arrived half a century before. The port consisted of a lagoon framed by two thrusting jaws of land – the steep, wooded Bluff to the south and the sandy Point to the north – with in between, across the mouth of the bay, a sandbar just feet below the surface. It was impossible for larger ocean-going ships to cross the bar without the risk of running aground or, in high weather, of being dashed to pieces; between 1845 and 1885 no fewer than sixty-six ships came to grief at the harbour mouth, with the result that all ships above a certain draught anchored sensibly offshore, and their passengers were landed by means of shallow steam tug-boats which plied between the open water and the rickety jetties alongside the Point. Once alongside the ships, their passengers – men, women and horses alike – had to be transferred to the tugs in baskets lowered over the side.

The arrival of the *Edinburgh Castle* brought an end to the cosy friendships forged on the way out. Neither Harford nor his companions knew what appointments lay in store for them, for they were entirely dependent upon orders from the commanding officer on the spot; whatever opinions they themselves might have formed of the unfolding political situation were already weeks out of date. Most waited only for their baggage to be safely put ashore before hurrying off to the colonial capital, Pietermaritzburg, 80 kilometres inland, to report for duty. Although Charlie Harford allowed himself the luxury of a day or two to visit old haunts, an air of expectation hung over Natal: the colony was alive with rumours of war.

# 3

# Snagged in the tree of the kings

## The land and its people

It had all begun – and within easy sight of the weathered outcrop called iSandlwana – more than sixty years before.

One unknown day in 1818, a group of elders of the Sithole people, who lived along the rugged flanks of Qhudeni mountain on the eastern bank of the Mzinyathi river, had gone up onto the grassy summit of the Hlazakazi ridge nearby to watch for signs of the momentous events that were unfolding nearby.

Hlazakazi is a good vantage point.[1] From the top one can look over kilometres of open country lying to the north of iSandlwana – sometimes, on exceptionally clear days, as far as the thin ribbon of the Zungwini and Hlobane hills on the far horizon. Further west, opposite the best crossing of the river for kilometres either side, lies the distinctive sugarloaf profile of Shiyane hill, and beyond it the distant wall of the Biggarsberg ridge. To the south, the wide valley narrows and the Mzinyathi is pressed in by hills on either side, vanishing and reappearing as it funnels through a series of twisting gorges, working its way round the jumbled ridges that tumble off the high shoulders of the grey bulk of Qhudeni.

The river was, and remains, a formidable feature, a resilient barrier to human movement, shaping by its few viable drifts the great human drama that unfolded along its banks over the course of more than a century. And in 1818, perhaps for the first time but certainly not for the last, war had come to the central Mzinyathi valley.

It was not a war in which the Sithole were directly involved – no doubt to their relief – although they were certainly concerned by the unnerving closeness to their borders of the fighting. Exactly what they could see from the top of Hlazakazi can never now be known, of course – the rising smoke from the burning homesteads of their neighbours, the amaChunu and amaThembu, perhaps, a drift of dust marking the passage of an army, an unusual glitter from the river as the sun glanced off spear blades held on high by men crossing the water – but it was more than enough to keep them there for a while, watching intently.

Presently they became aware they were not alone on the summit. Nearby was another group, also squatting in the long grass on the edge of the hill-top, also closely watching what was happening below. The Sithole did not recognize these strangers, but they appeared to be the retinue of someone of importance, an *inkosi*, for in among them was a young man whose authority was conspicuous, not merely because of the marks of rank he wore – a long tail feather of the blue crane in his head-dress, and twisted bunches of scarlet and green wing feathers from the purple-crested lourie – but by the exaggerated respect shown by his companions.

One of the Sithole group, a junior member of the royal house by the name of Jobe kaMaphitha, was deputed to approach the strangers and politely inquire after their interest. Jobe, it seems, was an affable man, and after the usual pleasantries, he struck up a conversation with the young *inkosi*. They chatted about unfolding events, no doubt exchanged snuff – an important social ritual among those who met on the road – and pondered whether the marauding armies below might be followers of the Zulu *inkosi*, Shaka, whose recent incursions against his neighbours were the subject of considerable anxiety locally. The Zulu territory lay a good distance away – 60 or 70 kilometres east of the Mzinyathi – but Shaka had already earned a reputation as a formidable warrior, a rising star in the spate of political turmoil which had recently convulsed the region, and it was rumoured he had been extending his influence steadily westwards.

Only an echo of that conversation has survived, passed down in oral histories, but it is testament to the way the world can turn on the serendipity of a moment. If Jobe and the stranger weighed up the merits of the warring sides, Jobe was astute enough not to be overly critical, and the two continued to chat until they were at last interrupted by a messenger struggling up, sweating, from the valley below. This man hailed the stranger by his *izibongo*, the long and mannered praise-poem by which the deeds of great men are still recognized in southern African society. And in that moment Jobe knew whom he had been so pleasantly conversing with that afternoon.

With some irritation, Shaka rose up and hurried away; the Zulu forces had been checked in the valley below, and the affairs of his kingdom were in urgent need of his attention. Yet he, like Jobe, would not forget that chance encounter on top of the Hlazakazi ridge, and from that moment the fortunes of the Sithole were steadily entwined with the fate of the Zulu royal house.

*

For thousands of years, the rolling grasslands and steep mountain ranges of southern Africa sustained the lives of numberless generations of a Stone Age people, the San 'Bushmen', who have left their enigmatic mark to posterity in their detritus – the abandoned stone tools which still turn up in unexpected places in the empty veld, and the extraordinary cave paintings which bear testimony to their intense spiritual ties with the landscape. It was only in more recent times, in the great centre of southern Africa – its heart – and in the well-watered coastal downlands to the east, that the San gave way to more robust cattle-owning societies, and retreated instead to the landscapes on the edges of the dry western deserts or into the inhospitable mountain uplands.

Quite when this happened is a matter of debate, for the origins of the black peoples of southern Africa are by and large lost to us. Europeans, arriving late on the scene, preoccupied with defining, classifying and controlling, fondly believed that native Africans were only recent arrivals, with scarcely more claim to the land than themselves. Yet archaeologists have dated Iron Age sites in some areas to at least the second century AD, and it is now generally accepted that there is a direct and continuous line of descent from the people of that time to the African population of South Africa today. In the eastern coastal strip, between the uKhahlamba and the sea, sites dating to AD 800 reveal strands of a lifestyle which bind them intimately to more modern peoples. But, in truth, cultures are never static, being best defined – if at all – by constraints of time and place, and there was, over the years, a fluid movement of peoples, some of it dramatic and confrontational but much of it gradual and interactive. Traces of language or cultural practice overlapped and intermingled to leave complex residues which emerged unexpectedly, generations later, and often in defiance of easy categorization.

By the end of the eighteenth century, however, the eastern seaboard was populated by African groups which are broadly identified today, according to their language and culture, as the northern Nguni. There were subtle variations of custom and dialect across the region, but there was sufficient in common for groups to communicate, interact and recognize patterns of mutual belief and behaviour. Further south, where the coast of Africa begins its great curved sweep westwards towards the extreme tip of the continent, there lived a related people, the southern Nguni, whose language was similar but whose material culture was noticeably distinct. Across the mountains, the Sotho- and Tswana-speaking groups inland were markedly different.

Nguni culture, north and south, was centred largely upon cattle. In much the same way that the buffalo had come to play a central role in the lives of the Native Americans of the Great Plains, cattle fulfilled a role among the Nguni that was at once practical, symbolic and spiritual. Whereas the movements of the great herds of buffalo provided Plains Americans with a nomadic lifestyle, the Nguni lived and moved at the more sedentary pace of their cattle, and their patterns of habitation were defined by the need for good grazing and a reliable access to water. Cows provided food and clothing, were an essential element in religious ritual, and offered a means of assessing wealth and status. Although beef was only eaten on special occasions and festivals, sour milk curds were a food staple, while hides were used to make cloaks and *reims* – long strips of hide used as ropes – or cut into shields for protection; horns could be used for signalling or to make pipes to smoke cannabis, and bone was fashioned into ear-plugs or snuff-spoons. With no other form of storable wealth, cattle were the main currency, governing familial relations through the *ilobolo*, the giving of cattle from the groom's family to the bride's during the marriage contract, a vital guarantee of her good standing and future welfare. The sacrifice of a beast was crucial, too, to most religious ceremonies, the means through which the spirits of long-dead ancestors could be addressed and placated.

More than that, however, the Nguni deeply loved their cattle. Though lacking any form of written communication, they reserved some of their most intense poetic expression for their animals, evoking the beauty of the natural markings on an animal's hide. Every possible combination of spots, flecks and patches, of light hairs overlaid on a dark background, or dark on a light, or the two intertwined together, had a specific and richly eloquent name, the imagery reflecting the way in which the Nguni perceived the world around them. A white beast with flecks of black hair on its sides, for example, was known as *inkomo imasenezimpukane*, 'flies in sour milk', while a dark beast with white legs and belly was known as *inkomo bafazibewela*, 'a wife crossing the river', conjuring up the image of a married woman hitching up her heavy leather skirt to reveal the pale complexion of her untanned legs.[2] Conversely, the appearance and character of cattle provided the Nguni with a reference point for analogies and metaphors with which to describe the landscape around them – the hill that looks like a bull, the mountains of the calves, the stream that looks like a tail – or even the time of day.

And it was the rich and fertile land of the coastal belt which of all the varied ecosystems of southern Africa was among the best cattle country – something which, for the Nguni, was to be their enduring tragedy. South of the Zambezi river the African continent rises slowly from the west coast, reaching a peak near its eastern edge where, as the great geological plates tilted, the upper crust broke to produce the fracture line of the uKhahlamba, falling again steeply on the eastern side in a series of rugged terraces towards the shore of the Indian Ocean. In the summer, wet winds blow inland from this warm sea, seething thermals carrying heavy moisture-laden clouds high over the escarpment. Eons of heavy downpours have created major rivers, the most impressive of which, like the Thukela, are born in thin, shining cascades on the uKhahlamba mountain face, bubbling through the foothills to carve twisting and tortuous gorges. Nearer the sea, the landscape becomes milder and the rivers empty into the sea through pleasant meandering valleys.

Over the centuries, these same rains have stripped many hills to a skeleton of boulders, bleeding away the earth, only to deposit it again where the rivers meet the incoming tide of the ocean. Ancient dunes mark the shoreline, only broken where the rivers, from great lagoons on the landward side, have forced their way out through narrow passages; passages almost closed off, for most of the year, by sand-bars lying just below the waves' surface. Only during flash floods, under pressure from a roaring torrent of water and debris are the sand-bars washed away, their inexorable reconstruction only to begin again as soon as the flood subsides.

Despite the erosion, a variety of grasses grew here throughout the year and the area once supported a high density of ruminating wildlife and the carnivores that preyed on them. But with the heavy influx of Man the game retreated from the open slopes and plains into the thick bush in the valleys, and the primordial forests on the ridge-tops. These grasslands framed the life of the Nguni, for they settled wherever their cattle would thrive, shifting occasionally as their herds demanded, or when an area of settlement became degraded.

The Nguni lived in family units, each one the home to a man – the family head or *umnumzana* – his wives and dependants, and comprising a cluster of dome-shaped huts. The physical design of the homestead reflected not only the Nguni's complex personal relationships but also the central role of their cattle. At the centre was a circular cattle-pen surrounded by stout upright posts, while the huts around it were positioned according to the standing of each of the wives and their offspring, each wife having her own hut. The *umnumzana* had perhaps two or three wives, for a commoner – many more for a person of power and influence – and moved between them, sleeping where the fancy took him; only the wealthiest homestead head might boast a hut of his own.

The huts were skilfully and neatly made of thatch fastened to a framework of saplings, cool in summer, warm in winter and dry in the rain. The floors were made by crushing termite heaps and mixing the powder with water to form a 'concrete' that baked hard in the sun. In better homes this was smeared with a mulch of cow-dung and polished with a smooth stone to give a subtle bottle-green glaze. Most huts had a hearth in the middle of the floor for a fire but there was no chimney, the smoke making its way out through the thatch where it could. It often hung a foot or so off the floor in a great fug, catching the thin streams of light that speared through narrow gaps in the thatch. The smoke helped preserve the thatch, of course, keeping insect infestation to a minimum, but even so a quiet, dry clicking from the roof and walls provided a nightly accompaniment to sleep. Over the years, too, the smoke coated the interior with a thick, greasy deposit of soot, so that the scent of wood smoke permeated the fabric of Nguni life.

Theirs was a life lived close to a landscape which could be stunningly beautiful but which was also at times harsh and unforgiving, and the hard physical labour necessary simply to survive was organized strictly along sexual lines. Although there are suggestions that in the early days, among some groups, both men and women worked in the fields, growing corn (maize) and pumpkins, by the nineteenth century this had come generally to be regarded as women's work. Women also had the arduous duty of walking to the nearest stream at dawn each morning to fetch water in large clay pots, of harvesting and grinding the corn, and of preparing food and cooking. To men fell the general duty of protecting the homestead, of mounting occasional hunts, and – most important of all – of tending to their cattle.

Of all the many rites of passage which governed life among the Nguni, marriage was the most important, and it was this, rather than physical maturity, or the onset of sexual relationships, that marked the true attainment of adulthood. Until they were married, Nguni males, no matter their age, were regarded as *izinsizwa*, youths, a part of their father's homestead with no mature responsibilities of their own; on marrying they left the huts where they had grown up and built a new homestead in which to raise a family of their own. Now they were accorded a new level of respect as *abamnumzana*, head of the family. The transition in status was marked in both sexes by a transformation in their physical appearance. On the eve of their first marriage, north Nguni men put on the *isicoco*, a circle of animal sinew bound neatly into the hair which was then plastered with black resin and polished with wax. The *isicoco* was permanent, never being removed, except perhaps by baldness in old age, and it conferred on the wearer a very public recognition of status, and with it dignity and respect. Many men neatly trimmed or shaved the hair around the ring to make it all the more conspicuous. Married women, too, adopted a top-knot, the *isicholo*, shaving their heads apart from a single tuft of hair which was teased up and coloured, in the early days of the Nguni, with red ochre.

Despite the chill that sometimes blows off the mountains in winter, and the heavy rain of the summer months, the northern Nguni did not trouble with complicated clothing. A thick cloak of animal hide might serve to ward off the worst excesses of the weather, but for the most part the solution to days of rain and cold was to stay indoors by the fire as much as possible. The basis of male dress was the *umcedo*, a small sheath of banana skins worn over the penis, often with a loin-covering of animal skins. For men related to the ruling lineage the square of skin covering the buttocks might be made of a spotted cat skin – civet, genet or, for the most exalted, leopard skin. Unmarried girls wore little more than a girdle of twisted strings, and married women a heavy goatskin skirt. On ceremonial occasions, however, men wore a more lavish and complex costume, resplendent with bushy white cow tails stitched to thongs fastened below the knees and above the elbows, and a necklace of thick bunches of cow tails, which completely obscured the upper body. Headbands made from otter or spotted cat, stitched into a tube and filled with bullrushes to make a neat roll, formed the foundation for ornate headdresses of ostrich, lourie, finch and crane feathers.[3]

Life's responsibilities began early for both sexes. Even as young boys, five or six years old, Nguni males were expected to join their elder brothers herding the cattle. They grew up in a natural outdoor environment, accustomed to its pleasures as well as its risks, discovered which wild fruits could be eaten with relish and which were poisonous, learned to be on their guard for signs of the green mamba in the tree-tops and the long, relentlessly aggressive black mamba in the grass, the spitting cobra among the rocks, or the puff adder on footpaths, all the more dangerous for its habit of lying still and unseen underfoot. They became familiar with the signs that warned of the presence of heavy game – elephant, buffalo and rhino – which still teemed in the thickest bush, with the occasional cough of the lion or growl of the leopard after dark, and with the lurking threat of crocodiles which infested the rivers. And as boys they learned to hunt small game – rock-rabbits and lizards – by hurling sticks at them, graduating in due course to the small buck they sometimes surprised, rietbuck, duiker or dik-dik. For sport they rolled fleshy tubers down the hillsides as moving targets and hurled sharpened sticks at them, or fenced with each other. At first they used switches cut from branches with the leaves still on for this, but progressed as they grew older to long sticks, bearing the swollen knuckles and cut heads they received as a result as a badge of their emerging manhood. Lacking any form of transport beyond their feet, both men and women were accustomed from childhood to walking long distances and they could move through their world in a way which amazed and frustrated later European travellers. It was a life that left its mark physically on them, on foreheads scarred from stick-fighting, in the thin lines raked into the skin by thorns and the thick hard skin on the soles of their feet.

If the Nguni grew sick or were badly hurt, however, there were specialist herbalists to treat them, who applied a wide variety of native herbs which had both physiological and psychological properties. Broken limbs were bound, dislocations reset, deep wounds washed with water and stitched up with sutures made from animal sinew; swellings were treated with poultices and fevers with medicines scratched into the skin with needles made from porcupine quills. If the rates of recovery were influenced, inevitably, by an element of the survival of the fittest, it at least meant that as a people the Nguni were hardy and possessed of a degree of stoic resilience. Necessity had taught them to endure levels of pain which often astonished European observers.

When they were old enough, boys were entrusted with spears, an example of one of the most sophisticated elements of their indigenous technology. In common with many African societies, the forging of iron was regarded as a mystical act among the Nguni, and smiths with a degree of awe that set them apart from ordinary society. The ore itself was collected from surface deposits and heated in clay forges worked with goatskin bellows. The molten metal was poured into a rough mould cut into the hard ground – the shape of a spear blade, axe or hoe – and then, as it cooled, beaten with rocks with an extraordinary degree of skill. When finished, it was passed over to a different specialist whose art lay in fixing the blade to a haft, drilling a hole to set the iron tang into the wood and fixing it with natural glues made from roots and resins, and then binding it tight with a wet tube of hide, from a cow tail, which shrank tightly as it dried.

For the Nguni, the everyday world they saw about them was but one dimension of a world that stretched beyond the present into a shadowy infinity populated by the spirits of their dead ancestors. These ancestral spirits, the *amadlozi*, although by and large invisible, kept a watchful eye on the affairs of the living, intervening occasionally to bring good luck and fertility, or to offer blight and misfortune when they were displeased. Almost every untoward event in everyday life could be traced to the disequilibrium between the living and the dead, and it was the job of the diviner to to decide the reason why this was and offer a solution. The diviner was the priest of Nguni society, called to his – or her – profession by dreams and visions, and trained by a long period as an apprentice to an established practitioner. When people were troubled by bad luck, by signs and portents or by prophetic dreams, they appealed to them to speak directly with the spirits on their behalf. The diviners' communciation with the ancestors was heightened by the performance of rituals, dancing and inhaling the smoke from herbs burned on potsherds. Sometimes they read the answers from bones and other nostrums spilled onto a mat, and the solutions they offered required little more than the sacrifice of a goat or cow, or abstinence from some daily habit. Sometimes, however – in the most serious cases, when someone was found to be the victim of deliberate witchcraft – they would 'smell out' the evil-doer, and the penalty was invariably death.

To the first Europeans who encountered them it was axiomatic that the beliefs of the black inhabitants of southern Africa trapped them in a state of physical and psychological bondage. The affectations of the diviner seemed so patently absurd to whites raised in an essentially Christian tradition – be they British, Dutch, French, German, Portuguese – that it exacerbated their innate feelings of cultural and racial superiority and encouraged them to think of Africans as naive or intellectually stunted. It did not, of course, seem that way to the Nguni themselves, who remained throughout the period of inter-racial contact remarkably attached to their religious and political institutions. Arthur Bryant, a missionary and avid collector of Nguni oral traditions in the 1920s, who himself displayed much of the cultural, imperial and religious arrogance of his time, was yet moved to observe that,

> The gloomy old yarn, so often trotted out, about the pitiable conditions under despotic chiefs and the perpetual nightmare of superstitious dread in which the [Nguni] lived, is mostly 'bosh and bogey', conjured up by Europeans whose 'knowledge' of Native life is the product solely of their own imaginations. Hardships and injustices there were (from our point of view); but to them they were the normal state of affairs, to which they were accustomed from birth. Other conditions simply did not exist, as unknown. In [traditional society] law-abiding tribesmen, who knew how to live on friendly terms with their chief and their neighbours, had no more fear than we have from the police or terrors of our own 'religious' beliefs.[4]

Not that tensions were unknown within Nguni society – far from it. Political rivalries were common, and so too were disputes over land and family wrangles over cattle. Moreover, inter-generational conflicts were endemic. Nguni society was essentially hierarchical and respect accumulated along with age and authority, and many elders insisted on full recognition of this from younger family members; while unmarried sons equally resented their exclusion from the world of wives, cattle ownership and influence. Effective management of the group often depended on the ability of a leader to find positive outlets for these frustrations.[5] Nor should the role of women be overlooked, for although they were superficially subservient in a male-dominated patriarchal society, their personal prestige and influence grew, too, with age and the enlargement of the family, giving them an increasingly respected voice within the management of their personal homesteads.[6]

When an *umnumzana* died, he was buried at the head of his cattle-pen, inside his homestead and, if he were an important man, the settlement was broken up and his family taken in by his brothers and close relations. The graves of significant individuals were marked by planting on them the *uhlalankosi* bush, 'the tree of the kings', whose sharp thorns are thought to snag the deceased's spirit, or *amadlozi*, binding them to the familiar places of their earthly lives. Grave-sites of ancient ancestors were remembered for generations and were regarded with a reverence bordering on sanctity. This created a sense of an ever-present past and gave the Nguni a deep spiritual attachment to their land. Time was a long river, stretching back into the undefined past and on again into the future, and the one constant in the present was the group, and its physical place in the world. Land was owned in common, and the right to live upon it, to exploit it and ultimately to be buried in it, came with belonging to the group. Use of the land might be given to outsiders by the group leader, but the land itself was inalienable. This was a concept radically different to the pragmatic attitude of the first European settlers, for whom land could be bought and sold like any goods and chattels, and for this difference much blood would in time be shed.

The political structures of the northern Nguni were essentially those of the family homestead writ large. Groups defined themselves by shared descent from the followers of a particular ancestor and the senior man in the dominant lineage of each group ruled it under the title *inkosi*. Some groups were large enough to be divided into sections, each ruled over by an *inkosi* of its own, their relative positions dictated by their status within the family as a whole. The *amakhosi* had considerable power over their subjects, deciding foreign policy, participating in religious ritual, judging disputes and criminal cases and commanding the services in particular of young, unmarried youths who had no adult responsibilities of their own. These young men were required to attend the *inkosi* at his command, staying at his homestead (at his expense) for days or weeks at a time and carrying out whatever duties he allotted them. They might serve as a member of an army or police force, take part in occasional mass hunts or in national religious ceremonies, herd the *inkosi*'s cattle, repair his huts or hoe his fields. Laws among the group were few but commonly understood, and transgressors were likely to be fined in cattle or, in extreme cases, put to death; the Nguni had little concept of imprisonment, and regarded European punishments, when they encountered them, as unnecessarily prolonged and cruel. In the case of malefactors accused of witchcraft, the death sentence also applied to their immediate family, who were guilty by association.

Yet the powers of the *amakhosi* were not unlimited. All major decisions were made in conjunction with an advisory council, consisting of elders drawn from the most significant and influential sectors of the chiefdom. Ordinary *abamnumzana* also had a voice in the political debate, but decisions, once made, were binding on the group as a whole. Administration was carried out by a tier of officials appointed by the *amakhosi* and known as *izinduna*. An *induna*'s (pl. *izinduna*) responsibilities might be regional – he acted as the local mouthpiece for the *inkosi*'s instructions – or specific – he might be appointed to a command in the military forces, as a messenger, or as a functionary in the *inkosi*'s household.

The attachment of people to their *amakhosi* was an aspect of Nguni life that constantly surprised Europeans. It went far beyond the personal charisma of the individuals themselves – there were good *amakhosi* and bad across the ages, of course – for the person of the *inkosi* represented much more. He was the touchstone which validated the sense of identity and belonging of ordinary members of the group, the embodiment of the inherited tradition, law and lore which defined an individual's existence, as well as a powerful conduit for the acknowledgement and propitiation of the ancestors. The most important rites in the chiefdom's calendar – the rituals which ushered in the new harvest, or the ceremonies to bind together and purify the community in a time of trial – could not be performed without the central participation of the *inkosi*, and any threat to the person of the *inkosi* was regarded as a threat to the community as a whole.

The *inkosi*'s relationship with his people was a reciprocal one; if they were prepared to serve and fight to protect him, he was in return expected to shelter them from dangers – not only from the potentially hostile world around them, but from a hostile universe. And at the end of the eighteenth century, the universe of the northern Nguni suddenly became very hostile indeed.

*

It remains difficult to disentangle the story of the rise of the Zulu from that of the man who undeniably had the greatest impact upon it.

The personal history of Shaka is so central to that of his age, and to the emergence of the Zulu kingdom itself, that his life has become the stuff of legend, and it is almost impossible, now, to tease out the truth about him from the mythology. Moreover, in modern times, his image has been manipulated and exploited by his adherents and his enemies alike, to such an extent that his true personality has been largely obscured. Shaka has become cast in a rich array of often conflicting archetypes, a warrior hero and a ruthless tyrant, a symbol of both political unity and division, a visionary, a military genius and capricious killer, at once exalted for his nobility and damned for his savagery.[7]

Which is a shame, because, for all that, he remains one of the most important southern African figures of his day. The political changes associated with his name – the sudden sharp rise to prominence of the Zulu kingdom – were stupendous, and they shaped the response of the peoples of the African seaboard to the greater challenge that the advent of European settlement would bring. Even as Shaka fought to extend the influence of the Zulu among the Nguni, great events were under way hundreds of kilometres distant which were destined to bring them sharply into contact with the wider world, and create a nexus for two centuries of bitter and destructive power struggles. And it would be the political and military systems perfected by Shaka which would define that conflict, not just in framing the means of resistance but – more darkly and damagingly – generating fractures within the African community which would work to the detriment of them all.

Shaka was born about 1787. His father, Senzangakhona, was *inkosi* of the amaZulu – 'Zulu's people', named after a long-dead forebear – who lived along the pleasant valley of the Mkhumbane stream. The Mkhumbane drains off the eastern edge of the Mthonjaneni uplands and is a tributary of one of the major rivers of the northern coastal strip, the Mfolozi Mhlope,[8] and the Zulu – a small group of a few thousand souls – had lived there for several generations with little to distinguish their history. The graves of Senzangakhona's ancestors can still be seen today, shaded by their *uhlalankosi* bushes, within a sacred kilometre or two of each other in an area still known as *emaKhosini*, the place of the kings.

Yet during Senzangakhona's lifetime the ageless world of the Nguni began to change. At some point in the late eighteenth century, beyond the far-off hills that limited the Zulu horizon, and for reasons which remain largely obscure, the northern Nguni chiefdoms began to grate upon one another. It might have been due to the *Madlathule*, a period of drought at the end of the eighteenth century remembered as 'Let Him Eat What He Can and Say Nothing', which dried up traditional pastures and created competition for natural resources, or to the disruptive influence of a small

European trading enclave in Mozambique, or perhaps a combination of both. What is certain is that by about 1790, at the northernmost end of the coastal strip, the Nguni groups had began to fight with one another.

The process was probably already under way in 1787 when Shaka was born. The circumstances surrounding his birth are contested, but it is generally agreed that his mother, Nandi of the eLangeni people, was one of Senzangakhona's minor wives, and that at some point in his childhood Shaka's parents separated. He grew up among a neighbouring people, the Mthethwa, who lived further east, south of the lower reaches of the Mfolozi Mhlope, and who were at that time emerging as the centre of a coalition of local chiefdoms. At such times young men were a valuable resource, and it was among the Mthethwa that Shaka first established a reputation as a warrior of note – an *iqawe*, a hero. At a time when battles consisted of an exchange of thrown spears, Shaka was one of a handful of hard men who preferred to wear their personal aggression as a badge of honour, and who chose to fight at close quarters with a stout-handled, broad-bladed spear. He soon found himself given an appointment as an *izinduna* in the Mthethwa army.

When, around 1816, *inkosi* Senzangakhona of the Zulu died, the Mthethwa interfered in the succession, overthrowing Senzangakhona's appointed heir and setting their own candidate, Shaka, upon the Zulu throne. It was a defining moment in the history of the Zulu people, and it is difficult not to feel that with Shaka's return to the grassy slopes of the Mkhumbane an old order passed away and a new one – undoubtedly more dangerous, but possessed of an exhilarating potential – began. If nothing else, Shaka brought with him an awareness of the great events unfolding around him, and ambitions to match. Within a year he had begun to establish himself as a competitor in the regional power struggle in his own right, and over the following decade he rose to eclipse all his rivals, including his former patron, the Mthethwa.

Despite myths to the contrary – many of them fostered by the colonial need to legitimize white authority by denigrating what went before – Shaka built his new kingdom as much through alliances as by the use of force. He invited neighbouring *amakhosi* to join him, sometimes sealing the bargain by offering members of his extended family as brides, and affording them a privileged position within a greater kingdom and a united front against the threat from outsiders.[9] This meant acknowledging Shaka as overlord, of course, and for many *amakhosi*, with proud traditions of their own, this was a hard choice to make; but the alternative was to risk a Zulu attack, and although Shaka's military accomplishments have perhaps been exaggerated over the years, the fact remains that he conquered many – and was never conquered himself. Those who refused his advances faced the prospect of a swift regime change. Not all submitted – many were able to exploit natural strongholds and resist for years, while others preferred to move away from the cause of the trouble, though abandoning the graves of their ancestors. Nonetheless, by the early 1820s, a new political structure was beginning to emerge, and the pattern of political power within it has shaped allegiances in Zululand to this day.

Shaka's Zulu kingdom was essentially a conglomerate of local groups under their pre-existing traditional leaders with a new layer of Zulucentric state administration imposed over it. This state system was centred upon the person of the king himself; it was Shaka who now presided over the great national ceremonies, who promulgated laws, and above all who took to himself the right – traditionally enjoyed by local *amakhosi* – to raise *amabutho*. These *amabutho* were the apparatus through which the service of young, unmarried men was organized on behalf of the group. Every three or four years the young men of the kingdom, the *izinsizwa* – all those who had reached their late teens since the last call-up – were gathered together from across the kingdom. Assembling first at their nearest royal homestead for a period of training, they were then called together nationally and formed into a guild, an *ibutho* (pl. *amabutho*). Senior officers were appointed by the king, and junior ones selected from among those who had distinguished themselves by their courage and initiative in training. The *ibutho* was given a name, and its members were either directed to build a new royal homestead to serve as their barracks and headquarters, or attached to an existing one where the current *amabutho* was dwindling through old age. They were given a token gift of feathers and furs by the king, to form the basis of a distinct ceremonial uniform, and a herd of carefully matched royal cattle from which they took hides to make war-shields.[10]

From the time of their enrolment until the time the king granted them permission to marry, the *amabutho* were required to work at the king's behest whenever he called upon them to do so. Although they served as the state labour gang and police force as well as the army, there was not enough work to keep them permanently occupied, nor food available to feed them for long periods when assembled; instead, most young men only mustered with their *amabutho* for a month or two each year, when they were needed, and they lived the rest of the time at home in their fathers' homesteads.

By taking the power to raise *amabutho* into his own hands, Shaka effectively monopolized the most powerful resource within the greater kingdom – its manpower. Although service in the *amabutho* would only ever be a part-time affair, it gave the king control of thousands of young men, their loyalties honed by complex rituals designed to exaggerate their sense of belonging, who could be used to ward off outside enemies and suppress internal opposition.

In the space of a few short years, his reach had extended far beyond the confines of the Mkhumbane valley. With the subjugation of major rivals like the Ndwandwe, he pushed the boundaries of Zulu influence north towards the Phongolo, and east down the length of the Mfolozi towards the sea, then south towards the natural barrier of the Thukela.

And he had turned west, too, towards the valley of the Mzinyathi. Rising as it does from the northern spurs of the uKhahlamba mountains and draining into the mighty Thukela, the Mzinyathi provides a natural fault line. Its open upper reaches provide a highway towards the mountains and across into the interior, while the rugged drifts in the wild country further downstream give direct access to central Natal. This fact had become unnervingly apparent in the early days of the disturbances, when groups retreating before the escalating violence had blundered through the valley's upper reaches, dislodging those living there and largely depopulating it – and the lesson was not lost upon Shaka.

Control of the Mzinyathi valley offered effective command of the western approaches of Shaka's emerging Zulu kingdom – and it was this that brought Shaka to his opportune meeting with the Sithole Jobe kaMaphitha that day in 1818 on the Hlazakazi ridge.

*

Shaka's campaign in the Mzinyathi valley had been directed against the amaThembu and the amaChunu, the two most powerful groups living along the central Mzinyathi, and both had put up a fight, contesting not merely the river-crossings, considerably delaying Shaka's advance, but stubbornly conducting a fighting withdrawal as they retreated down the western bank. The amaThembu, in particular, had rallied below the Biggarsberg heights, near the modern village of Pomeroy, and had checked the Zulu advance, buying enough time for both groups to retire south in good order. For the amaChunu the campaign marked the beginning of a long resentment of the Zulu royal house – one which would one day set them on the road to iSandlwana – but for Shaka the campaign was nonetheless a success. He had driven out potential rivals on his sensitive western borders, creating a local power vacuum which could be filled by Zulu loyalists.

A few weeks after the campaign ended, Zulu messengers arrived at the homestead of Shaka's new friend Jobe kaMaphitha of the Sithole bearing a surprising offer. Shaka invited Jobe to be the guardian of the Zulu kingdom's western marches.

It was, of course, an approach entirely in keeping with Shaka's broader political programme – overturning an established order, and raising up a minor group whose elevation was entirely dependent upon his patronage – and he was astute enough to recognize the value of an established knowledge of local conditions and affairs. Nonetheless, it must have come as a considerable surprise to Jobe, for it was an appointment quite beyond his own importance in Sithole affairs: it would mean a sudden rise in personal power, prestige and wealth, as well as the protection of the Zulu army in these unsettled times. Jobe does not seem to have hesitated overmuch in his response. He accepted, and sometime in 1819, at Shaka's insistence, he led the bulk of the Sithole across the Mzinyathi river, abandoning their old homelands along the slopes of Qhudeni mountain, to establish new homes on the opposite bank.[11]

The Sithole now provided a buffer of Zulu influence on the western bank of the Mzinyathi, and their new location was bordered by some impressive and highly strategic geography. Above them, to the north, lay the great long Biggarsberg ridge, while below, to the south, lay a district of spectacular broken country known as Msinga. Msinga remains a place of fierce and austere beauty, a dry moonscape of high, stony hills slashed by the great meandering valleys of several major rivers, notably the Mooi and the Thukela. It was a difficult area in which to scrape a living, and a notorious one to police (and remains so, even today), but the very difficulty of the country served to channel the passage of those seeking to enter or flee from Zululand – and the Sithole settlements now lay across the obvious routes.

And Jobe seems to have been good at his new job. The caves and hidden valleys along the western bank of the Mzinyathi were infested with the wretched survivors from the groups displaced by the passage of successive armies, some of whom had resorted to cannibalism to survive. Jobe extended Sithole control over them, offering protection and rehabilitation to those who submitted, and hunting down and destroying those who did not. Within two or three years of making the move, he controlled one of the most powerful African groups on the Zulu borderlands.

In that, he was very much a representative of a new order. From about 1820, Shaka had looked increasingly south across the Thukela river, keen to extend his influence over the rich and powerful chiefdoms there. Yet despite the fact that his last royal homestead, kwaDukuza, was established south of the Thukela, he never really succeeded. Many groups resisted him, and were simply too far away, or too secure in natural strongholds, to be defeated, while others, as the amaThembu and amaChunu had done, moved beyond his reach. Even those who remained, and who acknowledged Shaka's leadership, were never fully incorporated into the Zulu kingdom, which remained at its most cohesive north of the Thukela. Instead, Shaka's influence south of the Thukela was largely dependent upon local allies, proxies like the Sithole who were committed to Zulu interests, but who retained a good deal of administrative independence locally.

It was a position which made Jobe and those like him powerful individuals and their followers wealthy in cattle and security – but it would leave them dangerously exposed when the borders of the Zulu kingdom contracted. And even before King Shaka's death in 1828, and at the very height of Zulu prestige and influence, would come a new element, so quietly and insidiously at first that the northern Nguni were unaware of the enormity of the threat it posed, a challenge to their way of life itself.

# 4

# 'When I am gone'

## The vision of King Shaka

Since the first European voyager to the region Bartolomeu Dias had edged gingerly round the southern tip of Africa in 1488, there had been a steady trickle of carracks and caravels up the eastern coast. Yet, while some had been forced to risk a brief landfall to replenish water supplies, most had been content to sail on, put off from any serious attempt at landing by the forbidding breakers, and by the ubiquitous sand-bars that denied the endless succession of river mouths the advantages of a natural harbour. Even so, it was to these first brittle contacts that the region's enduring name is due. On Christmas Day 1497 Dias's fellow Portuguese, Vasco da Gama – the first man to lead an expedition directly from Europe to India – noted in his log the existence of the eastern coast-line, and called it Terra Natalis in honour of Christ's birth. And on European maps Natal it became.[1]

For more than 300 years, despite occasional attempts to chart the coastline, the outside world passed resolutely by. Although the Portuguese had discovered the existence of the Rio da Natal – the Bay of Natal, the shimmering lagoon that would become the site of modern Durban – they had preferred to establish a settlement further north on the more sheltered offshore islands of Mozambique.

Yet Europeans were not unknown to the northern Nguni, even in the long years before their presence became an established one. Whites were cast up now and then – mostly dead, and sometimes scarcely recognizable after the sharks and crabs had been at them – by the crashing surf that breaks relentlessly upon the open beaches, and because of this the Nguni imagined them to be a manifestation of the profound mysteries of the ocean, a pallid and rather fragile sea creature, which they came to call *abelungu*, rumoured to live beneath the waves and scarcely able to survive when exposed to the open air of dry land.

Even after the Dutch built a large way-station on the shores of Table Bay at the Cape in 1652 – the largest permanent European settlement in southern Africa at the time – to service their fleets on the long haul to the East Indies, there remained little to tempt whites into Natal. Not until the great shift in the balance of European imperial rivalries which followed the upheavals of the Revolutionary and Napoleonic Wars, and the ultimate eclipse of the French after Waterloo, did the situation change. Then, in May 1824, an ex-Royal Navy lieutenant, Francis George Farewell, risked the lives of a small group of adventurers by leading them across the bar at the mouth of the Bay of Natal, and into the pristine wilderness of the lagoon beyond. The British Empire had come to Natal.

Ironically, it had been the great international struggle against Napoleon that had brought Britain to southern Africa in the first place. Despite a long and tangled history of conflicts between them, the British and Dutch had been allies for much of the eighteenth century, and this had allowed British fleets to call safely at the Cape en route to Britain's expanding empire in India. Old rivalries resurfaced briefly at the end of the century, however, after the Prince of Orange was driven out of the Netherlands in 1795 by Napoleon. The establishment of the pro-French Batavian Republic in Holland had deeply concerned British imperial strategists. The Netherlands' colonial possessions had also passed, inevitably, under French influence, and control of the Cape might allow Napoleon to use it as a base from which to cut off the maritime highways upon which so many British interests depended. In 1795, therefore, a British expedition landed on and occupied the Cape, brushing aside light resistance, only to be forced to give it back a few years later under the terms of the Treaty of Amiens. The peace, however, proved short-lived, and with a fresh outbreak of hostilities the British returned in force: in 1806 they wrested the Cape permanently from Franco-Dutch control after a land battle fought out, bizarrely, close to the open beaches and within sight of Table Mountain.

Britain was to remain the dominant European power in southern Africa for the next century. Occupation of the Cape had been a move embarked upon by the Government of the day with the severe reservation that its control should not lead Britain deeper into Africa by that debilitating and expensive process today categorized as 'mission creep' – yet that is, of course, exactly what happened. The Dutch had held sway over a small but well-established settler community which had long since assumed an

expansionist dynamic of its own, and which paid little regard to the British
takeover. Dutch-speaking farmers in the borderlands were already creeping
slowly along the fertile eastern coastal downlands, clashing sporadically
with the African groups they found living there. Whether its new masters
liked it or not, Europe was already pushing into Africa by way of the Cape,
and the price of policing it would be paid, as it so often was, with the
blood of the long-suffering redcoat.

There were other motors for change too, ones the British brought with
them, and Francis Farewell had typified them. With the long war against
France at an end, Britain had emerged as an unrivalled world superpower
and was expanding its international interests on the backs of thousands of
adventurous young men whose promising service careers had been cut
short by the outbreak of peace. Farewell's mission in 1824 was part of that
organic process of imperial growth. There was nothing official about it,
despite his Navy associations; a consortium of Cape merchants had heard
rumours of the emergence of a powerful and – more to the point – wealthy
African kingdom just up the coast from Natal, and Farewell had been
commissioned to investigate. His brief had been to establish a profitable
trading concession from the Zulu kings.

That Farewell succeeded was not due so much to his undoubted
enterprise as to the open arms with which he was welcomed by the Zulu
King Shaka. The whites had arrived at a fortunate moment – in 1824 Shaka
was in the process of consolidating the rapid expansion of the Zulu
kingdom, and for him Farewell represented an unexpected and lucky
contact with a new world of exotic trade goods and powerful new weapons.
Farewell's party hastily threw up a ramshackle settlement of wattle and
daub huts among the dunes above the beach, and over this King Shaka
extended his protection.

The whites enjoyed all the prerogatives of state officials of the Zulu
kingdom, hunting and trading and running their own affairs – free from
the interference of far-off British laws, and confident in the royal patronage
they enjoyed. They shot elephant for tusks and buffalo for hides and horns,
shipping these out in occasional boatloads to traders back in the Cape and
importing in return beads and trinkets which they exchanged for cattle
with the Zulu, making them wealthy to their eyes. They enjoyed a gloriously
anarchic lifestyle, scheming and quarrelling among themselves, presuming
upon Shaka's name to bully and intimidate their neighbours whenever it
suited them, and taking African wives – many of whom they were later to

set aside when the settlement inclined to respectability. They accumulated followers, too, most of whom were survivors fleeing Shaka's military expeditions or political refugees from the Zulu kingdom itself, who saw in the white enclave something of a safe haven. And in truth, if it was often a happy life, it was also frequently a dangerous and a short one. Farewell and his men were at the mercy of an exotic array of diseases, and at risk when the animals they shot or attempted to slaughter – at ranges of just 30 or 40 metres, with cumbersome and inaccurate flintlock muskets – turned on them. They were at the mercy of King Shaka, too, but he proved a remarkably tolerant host, allowing their eccentricities free rein as long as they provided the services he required of them – and this, as with all the other groups under his benevolent patronage, undeniably included occasional participation in his military campaigns.

In return for Shaka's generosity, the traders betrayed him in a way which seems particularly pungent in the light of all that came after. They quite deliberately damned his reputation, and that of the Zulu people, to posterity. Many of those first whites were illiterate adventurers, of course, unemployed sailors and runaway soldiers, the flotsam of the taverns of the seas, but their leaders were educated men who fully understood that they were in the vanguard of momentous events. Farewell and his cronies tried their best to manipulate colonial opinion at the Cape and even in London, playing on the vulnerability of the settlement at the hands of an African host whom they portrayed as capricious and ruthless, hoping to tease out support in Government circles and laying a powerful trail of commercial promise to tempt investors. Between them they controlled the written record and in it they conspired to demonize Shaka and to obscure their own questionable agenda; and the extent of their duplicity, and its insidious lasting effects, is only now becoming clear.

It is to this unlikely beginning that all later British interests in Natal were due. Ironically, Shaka's own extraordinary career – so significant, yet so much an enigma to modern historians – came to a sudden and violent end in September 1828 when he was assassinated in a palace coup orchestrated by members of his own family. Ambushed outside his private huts at his kwaDukuza homestead, he was repeatedly stabbed. As he fell, he turned to his assassins to make a last dying prophecy. 'Sons of my father', he said scornfully, 'you will not rule when I am gone, for the land will see the white locusts come.'[2]

In the years ahead, the Zulus as a people would come ruefully to reflect upon the truth of his words.

*

Almost exactly fifty years separate the death of Shaka and the arrival of Charlie Harford and his colleagues on the *Edinburgh Castle* in 1878. The demographics of Natal had changed immensely in that half-century. Nevertheless, the pattern of authority connived at in Natal by Shaka and Farewell – in which a small number of Europeans had an undue degree of influence and control over a much larger African population – remained its defining political characteristic. In the immediate aftermath of Shaka's assassination, his successor – his brother and murderer Dingane – abandoned the southern settlement at kwaDukuza in Natal, and built himself a new royal homestead in the heart of the Mkhumbane valley, the old Zulu country. This allowed him to consolidate the transition of power in the Zulu heartlands, but it marked a retreat in Zulu political influence south of the Thukela. In effect, it was an abandonment of Shaka's uncompleted programme of extending control over the remaining chiefdoms in Natal, leaving it to those allies already established there to oversee Zulu interests on the king's behalf.

Among these were both the Sithole chiefdom and the British trader enclave at Port Natal. Ironically, both had found themselves subject to a new influx of refugees claiming protection – the regime change in Zululand had led to an inevitable exodus, both among Shaka's supporters and those groups who had never been fully reconciled to Zulu rule – and this had added materially to their power base. Yet, as King Dingane recognized, there was a danger in this, since the growth in power and influence of the Natal client chiefdoms was achieved largely at the expense of his own. He pressed the Port Natal traders, in particular, to return a number of important political refugees, but when they – flexing for the first time their fledgling political muscle – refused, the king found he could not act directly against them without compromising his own commercial and political interests.

For many of the older chiefdoms scattered throughout the rolling hills, too, those who had eluded or survived Shaka's attempts to coerce them into the kingdom, the growth of the white community, in particular, offered a shield against possible renewed Zulu expansionism. As a result, they strove to maintain good relations with the traders, tacitly acknowledging their privileged status – but in doing so, over the next half century, they sowed the seeds of their subjugation.

For a decade, during the 1820s, the traders lived at Port Natal respecting no laws but their own and, sometimes, those of the Zulu kings. Farewell's attempts to invite the intervention of the British authorities fell largely on deaf ears; the British Government was embarrassed by the traders' actions, and was in any case set against further expansion into southern Africa. That it later reversed this policy was due in the end not to lobbying on the part of the settlement, but rather, as it so often was, to a new threat to British strategic interests. And this came through an entirely unexpected sequence of events.

*

When the British arrived in the Cape, this time to stay, in 1806, the settler population there had already assumed distinct characteristics of its own. The original Dutch burghers established by the East India Company had been swollen in pulses over the years by religious refugees expelled from Europe, mostly French Huguenots and German Lutherans. Cut off from the currents of the great intellectual movements that had spread throughout Europe during their absence, many of them had turned increasingly away from the outside world, and looked instead toward the African interior. Hardy and self-reliant, they lived isolated lives close to the hard and unforgiving soil in small frontier villages or on great farms they had carved themselves from the wilderness. They spoke a dialect which mixed their original Dutch with phrases borrowed from European latecomers and words and concepts appropriated from Indonesian slaves imported to the Cape and from the African communities among whom they travelled. With language came a sense – hazy at first, but honed by shared hardships over the coming century – of a distinct identity. Most of these people were farmers by occupation, and they are best known even today by the Dutch term for countryfolk – *boere*. To outsiders they were the Cape Dutch, or Afrikanders – white Africans – and in more recent times Afrikaners.[3]

It had become clear early on that the Afrikaners resented the arrival of the British. There were certainly specific grievances which burned sorely among them – a perceived failure of the British to protect frontier settlements against African resistance, the abolition of slavery in British colonies in 1833, and the cumbersome and impractical structures set up to award financial compensation for the value of the slaves they had lost – but underlying it all was a deep ideological difference. From the Cape, British administrators looked out towards the wider world – to the metropolitan hub in far-away London, and to the expanding empire of which they were a part. What mattered to the Afrikaners, in contrast, was the hard reality of life on the African land, with all its fierce insecurities, and the strong religious faith and ingrained sense of racial superiority that sustained them. Occasionally the Afrikaners resorted to violence to express their frustrations, and the willingness of the British to respond in kind convinced the Boers that their different ways of life were profoundly incompatible. So, in the mid-1830s, whole sectors of Boer frontier society simply decided to remove themselves from British influence – to sever, in effect, their remaining links with the European world and to give themselves up to Africa in the hope of finding a new home in the limitless wilderness beyond colonial boundaries.

Hundreds of Boer families packed their possessions into their tented ox-wagons, rounded up their livestock, sold or abandoned their farms and set off into the unknown. Most set out from the Eastern Cape, travelling in straggling groups linked by ties of family patronage, moving initially into the interior, skirting the western spurs of the uKhahlamba mountains, and crossing the great Senqu river. Once into the grassy highveld, they pushed up through the very centre of southern Africa itself. The movement – the *trek* – was never a cohesive one with clearly defined objectives; it was driven by individual needs and riven with personal animosities, and *trek* parties travelled together or fragmented according to the personal relationships of their leaders. Many of the less venturesome settled where the fancy first took them, content to have placed a good distance between themselves and the *'verdommed Englse'* – the damned English. The most free-spirited, however, the most hardy, together with those who nursed the fiercest hate for the British in their devoutly Christian hearts, kept going until they had crossed the River Lekwa (Vaal). Here and there small settlements sprang up along the way, some of which thrived briefly as the centre of an optimistic new republic, full of hope and heady promises of freedom, only to collapse in due course when they proved economically unviable.

The Boer tragedy lay, however, in the fact that the interior of southern Africa was not an empty landscape. Parts of it had sometimes seemed so, because of the physical constraints imposed on African societies by the necessity of locating themselves near water and avoiding areas of fever or

insect-borne parasites, and the ravages wrought by political conflicts, yet
almost every corner of the land was claimed by somebody or other, and
the progress of the Boer diaspora was characterized by constant friction. It
remains a bitter irony of the movement as a whole that in seeking no more
than the freedom to live on the land according to their cherished beliefs
and traditions, the Boers inevitably denied this right to others who had
been there first.

Nor did the simple fact of removing themselves from British boundaries free them of their entanglements with British authority. If the British
could not prevent them physically from leaving, they nonetheless refused
to recognize the Boer right to act independently, treating them instead as
wayward citizens whose actions might impact upon British interests inter-
nationally, and whose excesses therefore needed to be curbed. The result
was a series of skirmishes between British troops and Boer citizen militias
fought out in remote places scarcely marked on European maps, the first
faltering steps in a protracted struggle which would intensify as the century
wore on. Fought initially to secure or deny political influence, these
struggles became, as the settler economies of southern Africa grew, a contest
between two radically different forms of colonialism, each competing for
control of the land and resources which drove European expansionism.
Underlying the rhetoric of the warring parties in the last, most protracted
and bitterest of the struggles – the Second Anglo-Boer War of 1899–1902 –
is a common ideology of racial supremacy and conquest which suggests
that at its heart the struggle was essentially a civil war between opposing
poles of a shared settler vision.

That early struggle of the Boer people, the saga of the astonishing
individual hardships they endured in the 1830s and the extraordinary
journeys they accomplished, is conflated together and remembered today
as the Great Trek. As a history it has been sadly compromised in recent
times, exploited by Afrikaner nationalists in the twentieth century to
provide an ideological framework for apartheid and discredited as a result;
as a human drama it deserves to be celebrated, however, for in its way it is
no less epic than the great westward movement of Europeans in America
in the nineteenth century.

It was towards the end of 1837 that the first Trekker scouts crossed into
Natal from beyond the mountains, and it was immediately obvious to the
African population living there that these were a very different people to

the traders at Port Natal. They spoke a different language, of course, and whereas the British had arrived dripping on the beach at Port Natal in little more than the clothes they stood up in, clutching their guns and their bundles of trade beads, the Boers had come with rolling homes, bringing with them not only their wives, children and servants, but their entire herds. They were mounted on horses and bristled with weapons, and the intimidating impression they created is confirmed by the stories which trailed in the wake of their clashes with the Africans on the highveld. The English traders' firearms might have triggered a subtle shift in the balance of power in Natal, yet the men themselves were not perceived by the Africans as being fundamentally in competition with them and their lifestyle. The English were hunters and traders, not farmers; but if ever a people were seeking a new land for themselves, it was the Boers. The question was, whose land?

King Dingane soon answered that question to his own satisfaction. The Voortrekkers, or more commonly Trekkers, visited him to beg permission to settle in Natal; Dingane at first tried to fob them off but when they proved to be both dangerous and persistent,[4] he decided simply to destroy them. In February 1838 the Boer leader Piet Retief and sixty of his followers – together with about thirty of their servants (who often get left out of the story) – were surprised and seized as they attended Dingane's eMgungundlovu royal homestead, ostensibly to negotiate. Overwhelmed by weight of numbers, they were dragged away to the Zulu capital's place of execution and beaten to death with sticks. Dingane then dispatched his army to attack Boer encampments scattered along the foothills of the uKhahlamba mountains. The attack caught the Boers entirely by surprise and although the noise of the slaughter of the first settlements provided some warning for those further behind, many families were simply wiped out. Nearly 400 old men, women, children and servants were killed in a night of fire and blood which has seared itself into the folk memory of the Afrikaner people.

It was the first of a series of catastrophic conflicts between Africans and Europeans in Natal, a defining moment which brought to a head the underlying tensions that had been slowly and subtly festering since the British traders had first arrived. It was a war which laid down the tactical ground rules for greater battles to come, pitching the mobility, courage, numbers and fieldcraft of the Zulu *amabutho* against the horses, guns and wagon-circles of the Boers. And for the Zulus, the lessons for the future proved to be ominous, for despite King Dingane's *coup de main* he singularly failed to drive the Trekkers out of Natal.

The plight of the survivors, clinging on in cramped and insanitary *laagers* – camps fortified by the simple expedient of drawing their wagons into a circle – caused fellow trek-leaders in the highveld to set aside their personal differences and rally to their aid. Renewed fighting spluttered on throughout 1838 until, on 16 December, a strong fighting commando, led by an experienced commandant from the Cape frontier, Andries Pretorius, won a bloody victory over Dingane's principal *amabutho* on the banks of the Ncome river, a tributary of the Mzinyathi. Pretorius pressed on in the hope of capturing Dingane himself, but the king had set fire to his eMgungundlovu palace and fled before the Boers arrived. Pretorius's men found the remains of Piet Retief and his men on the slopes of the hill where they were executed, and buried them there; lying beside Retief, so they claimed, they found a leather pouch containing a deed ceding Natal to the Trekkers, which the king had signed moments before ordering the slaughter.

Although the strategic impact of the Battle of Ncome – known to the Boers as *Bloedrivier*, Blood River, from the gory state of the waters after the protracted slaughter – has certainly been exaggerated, it undoubtedly had the effect of further reducing Zulu influence in Natal. King Dingane built a new royal homestead further north, beyond easy reach of Pretorius's horsemen, while the Boers returned to the comparative safety of their settlements in the uKhahlamba foothills. A great swathe of country lying between them became something of a no-man's-land, a political vacuum over which neither side was able fully to extend its authority. For the African inhabitants, it marked an uneasy interregnum in which the bonds that had bound them to the Zulu kings were tested against the possibility of greater independence and sense of menace afforded in equal measure by the presence of the Voortrekkers.

This dilemma weighed particularly heavily upon those groups in Natal who, since the assassination of King Shaka a decade before, had represented the voice of the Zulu kings there. This included not only African groups like *inkosi* Jobe's Sithole, but the British community at Port Natal: the war had offered them both hard choices.

In truth, the traders at the Port Natal settlement had already begun to tire of the obligations placed upon them by the Zulu kings, and had found it easy to decide their new loyalties along racial lines. When the war broke out early in 1838 they had allied themselves to the Trekkers, repaying the hospitality invested in them by Shaka and Dingane with armed raids against outlying Zulu settlements. Although they had justified themselves with a heady rhetoric complaining of Dingane's murderous attack on the Trekkers, the traders' forays were no more than cattle-rustling expeditions designed to take advantage of the Zulu army's preoccupation elsewhere. In this the traders' judgement had seriously erred, however, for they were destined to receive a brutal reminder of where – conflict with the Trekkers or not – the balance of power in Natal still truly lay.

In April 1838 a party of traders, supported by an army recruited from among their African followers – some of whom they had armed and trained in the use of muskets – crossed the lower Thukela and began looting Zulu homesteads there. Here they were surprised by a Zulu army under the command of Dingane's brother, Prince Mpande kaSenzangakhona, surrounded, and after a stiff and bloody fight outmanoeuvred and largely wiped out.[5] A dozen traders were killed – including at least one who had first arrived in Farewell's party a decade before – together with hundreds of their African retainers, and the survivors fled back towards Port Natal with the victorious Zulu army in pursuit. While the traders and their families took refuge on schooners anchored in the bay, the Zulus razed the settlement to the ground.

The sacking of Port Natal, so richly deserved in Zulu eyes, brought an end once and for all to the cosy illusion that the objectives of the British and the Zulu could accommodate one another. For twenty years the commercial benefits of the settlement had obscured the fact that their interests were fundamentally opposed to one another, that a nascent capitalist economy could only thrive by subverting the communal traditions and economic self-sufficiency upon which so much of African society was based.

Once the Zulu amabutho had retired, the surviving traders went ashore once again, picking through the smoking ruins to salvage what they could to rebuild their lives. These later settlers were profoundly different to the white men Natal had known in the past, those pathetic souls who had been thrown upon the shore by shipwreck, and whose greatest wish had been to find a way back home. These abelungu were here to stay.

*

For African groups like the Sithole the situation was, if anything, worse. Tied by a common culture and by shared history to the Zulu kingdom, they now found themselves in a very real sense on the front line between two colliding worlds, torn by their loyalty to their former patron, yet dangerously exposed to the newcomers, to the Trekkers' military might and their profound disregard for African sensibilities.

This had become apparent to the Sithole representative Jobe kaMaphitha even before the climactic battle on the banks of the Ncome. Riding out from their camps in the mountain foothills, Andries Pretorius's commando had opted for the most direct route towards Zululand, avoiding the long detour necessary to advance by way of the well-used crossing near the mouth of the Thukela river, and striking north-east instead, aiming for the crossing over the Mzinyathi river. In this he was following in the footsteps of the warring armies of Shaka's time – exactly that route which the Sithole had been set in place to block. Such was the efficiency of the Zulu intelligence system that King Dingane knew about Pretorius and his commando even before they had passed through the Msinga hills on their way to the Mzinyathi, and so he sent instructions to Jobe to prevent their passage.

This had, of course, been Jobe's principal duty since Shaka's time – the basis of the Sithole's elevation to power and prestige – and it was perhaps the greatest test of his loyalty since he had taken up his duties. Yet, with the Boers now pressing towards them and the fate of the Zulu kingdom clearly hanging in the balance, Jobe faltered. The Trekkers were on his doorstep – several hundred of them, armed to the teeth with heavy hunting muskets and ships' cannon mounted on improvised carriages dragged by oxen – and King Dingane's *amabutho* were not. Instead of attacking them Jobe opted to appease them, greeting the Boers with a dance of welcome – the site where it took place is still remembered today by the name Danskraal – and then let them pass by.

The Trekkers' victory a week or two later at Ncome not only confirmed their position as a major new power in Natal, it broke the bonds of trust which had linked the Sithole and the Zulu royal house, cutting the Sithole adrift in a dangerous and unpredictable new world.

*Inkosi* Jobe, revealing the same political astuteness which Shaka had first recognized in him, took the precaution of shifting his principal homesteads to a more defensible position. It was about this time that he moved from the open country below the Biggarsberg deeper into Msinga proper, establishing himself near the foot of the iLenge mountain (subsequently known to the settlers as 'Job's Kop'), a position which afforded him some protection against the suspicion of the Trekkers – and the wrath of his spurned patron, King Dingane. After he moved, the Boers steadily crept across the country behind him, marking out farms across the Biggarsberg,[6] poised to spill for the first time into the valley of the Mzinyathi beyond.

The cold war between the Trekkers and King Dingane could not last indefinitely, however, and the manner of its resolution reveals the extent to which defeat at Ncome had weakened Dingane's prestige among his followers. In late 1839 Dingane's brother, Prince Mpande, crossed the Thukela river with thousands of his followers and offered his allegiance to the Boers in Natal. Mpande has been the most consistently underrated of all Senzangakhona's extraordinary sons, largely because he successfully cultivated an air of Claudian indolence and disinterest, the assumption of which had allowed him to escape Dingane's suspicion in the purges following Shaka's assassination. In fact he was an astute and subtle political survivor and in due course would prove a patient and able administrator, and his defection proved – as perhaps he knew it might – the end for Dingane's regime. It was a move which both acknowledged the reality of the military power possessed by the Trekkers, and gave an air of legitimacy to their vendetta against Dingane. The Boers offered to install Mpande as king in Dingane's place in return for confirmation of their territorial claims in Natal. In early 1840 an army of Mpande's followers crossed back into Zululand with Boer support, and the fate of the royal house was decided, Zulu against Zulu, in the first of the country's bloody civil wars. Those *amabutho* who remained loyal to Dingane met the invaders at the Maqongqo hills near the Mkhuze river, but after a sharp fight an air of defeat seemed suddenly to sweep through the king's army and their defence collapsed.

Dingane, with the remnants of his court, retreated to the far north of Zululand. Here he built a new royal homestead on the edge of the Hlatikhulu forest, on the very crest of the Lebombo mountains, a remote and inaccessible spot which vouchsafed him breathtaking views across the hazy Maputland flats and the Swazi borders. But an embarrassed and defeated Zulu king could only be a source of suspicion and resentment to his new neighbours, and in March 1840 a group of assassins infiltrated his homestead, stabbed Dingane as he emerged from his hut at dawn one morning, inflicting a deep gash in his abdomen, and fled leaving him to bleed to death.

The death of Dingane was a watershed in the separation of Natal and the Zulu kingdom. For the Trekkers it was a triumphant end to the bitter struggle which had begun with the death of Piet Retief two years before, and it left them the undisputed masters of the field. They installed Mpande as king of the Zulu in Dingane's place, and celebrated his apparent compliance by demanding thousands of head of cattle and great swathes of land as a reward for their support. Freed now from any significant African challenge to their authority, they declared Natal a Trekker republic, and set about dividing up the land, apportioning the best of it for white settlement and clearing off the African population they regarded as surplus – as many as 80,000 were dispossessed in the first year. Cut off from ancestral lands they had occupied for generations, these people were simply required to move away and find land in those areas the Boers did not want. Msinga, with its hot, narrow valleys and steep hillsides, held little appeal for the Trekkers and it began to fill up with the Africans, the genesis of an overcrowding that has defined its problems into modern times.

And if this process at least added to the widening of the support-base of chiefdoms already established there, like the Sithole, there were mortal dangers in this, too. With Natal carved up to suit their needs, the Trekkers began to eye with some suspicion those African groups who retained a degree of prestige and authority. They targeted each in turn, manufacturing complaints over missing cattle or alleged disrespect to the new administration and punishing them forcefully, burning huts and carrying away herds to bolster their newly established farms. For all *inkosi* Jobe's practised fence-sitting, the privileged role the Sithole had enjoyed at the centre of nearly twenty years of fluid frontier life was clearly at an end. Jobe's tacit support of the 1838 Ncome expedition had not been enough to save him from a demand in 1840 that he more clearly demonstrate his loyalty; he had supplied a contingent of men to support Mpande's forces, but in the aftermath he found himself accused of appropriating too great a share of the looted cattle. It was a charge typical of those trumped-up by the Trekkers against the Natal *amakhosi*, and when Jobe appealed to Mpande for support he discovered just how far his earlier actions had compromised him in the eyes of the Zulu royal house. Astute as ever, Mpande had noted how all too often Jobe had switched sides at the crucial moment, and he refused now to save him; late in 1840 a Boer commando rode into Msinga, attacking Sithole homesteads and looting cattle.

Jobe survived, but the attack left him impoverished and humiliated. A lifetime's association with the Zulu kings was finally broken and the Sithole found themselves stranded on the wrong side of the Mzinyathi, abandoned to the tender mercies of the white 'wild beasts'. It would be left to Jobe's descendants to discover the full extent to which they had traded the frying pan for the fire.

*

The enthusiasm with which the Trekkers redrew the political map of Natal came as something of a shock to the remaining trading community at Port Natal, who soon found that their white skins and support in the recent fighting had earned them no particular influence in the new order. Zulu authority under Shaka's protection had been irksome enough, but it seemed particularly irritating to have unsympathetic whites now meddling in their affairs, distorting the passage of free trade in accordance with their own agendas. The traders' response was to appeal to the British authorities in Cape Town to intervene on their behalf. This was a ploy they had tried in the past and it had never succeeded, but ironically the Trekkers' ascendancy had led to a distinct shift in official British attitudes towards Natal.

Two things worried London. First, the Trekkers announced their intention to resettle Natal's surplus African population – those people recently dispossessed by the appropriation of their land for farms – in the extreme south of the country. For the British this was a sensitive area, lying as it did not far north of their own borders on the Eastern Cape. The Cape frontier was notoriously volatile, and the British feared that an influx of Africans might destabilize the brittle peace which prevailed there. Worse still, the passage of a solitary American brig across the bar and into Port Natal had raised the uncomfortable possibility that the Trekkers might try to establish international relations with a rival world power, and in an area the British already regarded as their strategic back yard.

These insecurities had prompted the British to look again at the claims of the traders, and it suddenly seemed that Francis Farewell's dubious attempts to persuade King Shaka to recognize a Union flag run up above the dunes might provide a legal pretext for Britain acting to isolate the port. In late 1838 the British had gone so far as to send a detachment of troops by sea to establish an outpost on the sandy spit of the Point, but once it became clear that they were unable to influence affairs and powerless to intervene in the worsening conflict between the Boers and the Zulu they were withdrawn. In March 1842, however, Britain acted with rather more resolve. A Major Thomas Charlton Smith was dispatched from the Eastern Cape to march overland to Port Natal at the head of 300 men, including two companies of the 27th Regiment.

It was a bizarre expedition, a slim little column of ox-wagons and men in bright uniforms traipsing through the virgin bush or marching heavily along the sand of the open beaches, flanked by the endless crashing breakers of the Indian Ocean. At one point they marvelled at the skeleton of a whale, stranded on the beach, and their passage was made tedious by the need to ford the scores of rivers which crossed their path. Several of the soldiers took their wives with them – a common enough practice in the Napoleonic Wars, a generation before – and two babies were born along the way. And on 30 April, a Private Devitt of the 27th succumbed to exhaustion on the banks of the Mkhomasi river – the first of many hundreds of British soldiers who would die during the long struggle to secure Natal for the British Crown.

Smith arrived at Port Natal on 3 May 1842. It had taken him 33 days to cover 420 kilometres, an epic journey largely forgotten today. But if the traders at the bay were delighted to see him, the Trekkers assuredly were not. Testy negotiations soon gave way to open hostility, shots were exchanged, and Smith resolved to take decisive action. He planned to mount an ambitious attack at night on the Boer encampments which had now been set up at the bay, advancing by way of the sandy beach, but the Trekkers were alerted by the clanking of the wheels of his gun-carriages and ambushed him from the cover of a line of mangrove trees. Raked with close-range fire, Smith's column disintegrated and his men scattered in disarray back to their camp.

Yet the Boers could not drive him from the earthwork fort Smith hastily threw up, and instead Smith found himself completely surrounded, a tiny dot of British scarlet in the green and hostile sub-tropical wilderness of the south-east African coast, a pin-prick flag in the map of some far-away imperial strategist. The Boers sniped at his outposts and riddled his position with musketry day and night, percolating his tents and forcing his men to live in a warren of shelter-trenches. With his food supplies dwindling and the nearest help hundreds of kilometres away, surrender seemed inevitable. It would doubtless have happened, too, had not one of the Port Natal traders – Richard King, a survivor of the disastrous Thukela expedition four years before, as tough as nails and equally resourceful – slipped through the Boer lines one night with his African servant, Ndongeni. The pair swam their horses across the bay by moonlight, then set out to ride 960 kilometres to the nearest British garrison, Grahamstown on the Eastern Cape. Ndongeni, who was riding bareback, had to give up along the way but King arrived ten days later, and his news galvanized the Grahamstown command. Troops were embarked on the first available ship, and on 24 June 1842 a schooner ran across the bar towing long-boats full of troops into the bay of Port Natal. As it did so, a warship, HMS *Southampton*, provided covering fire from the deep water beyond – a ship of Nelson's line, firing broadsides at a handful of farmers sheltering in the cover of the African bush.

Of such absurdities are empires made; the landing was hardly contested. The Union Flag had come at last to Port Natal.

The arrival of the British in force was a bitter blow for the Boers. Some would not countenance living under the British yoke again, but preferred simply to turn their back on the sea, and on Natal, the land which had brought them so much bloodshed and heartache. They would, as one Trekker's irate wife told British officials, rather walk back barefoot over the Drakensberg than suffer to live under the damned English again. Many did just that, loading up their wagons once more and braving the mountain passes to return to live among more congenial company in the Trekker republics beyond. By the end of 1843 there were scarcely 500 Afrikaner families left in Natal. Many of those who remained chose to move as far away from the centres of British metropolitan authority as possible, and some obtained a concession from the Zulu king Mpande to settle territory nominally under his control along the northern uKhahlamba foothills.

*

It took a while to establish the mechanics of the new colonial adminis- tration, and longer for the settlement itself to assume its distinctive British character. Natal was officially declared a British colony in 1843, and cobbled on a couple of years later as an administrative adjunct to the Cape. Only then did the first British lieutenant-governor arrive, setting up office, ironically, in Pietermaritzburg, the village the Trekkers had built to serve as the capital of their republic. Nor, despite various commercial schemes launched in Britain designed to promote the delights of life in the sunshine

to prospective immigrants, did the new colony fill up particularly fast with
settlers. It was not until the 1850s that a thin line of ox-wagon tracks began
to cleave perilously through the rocky hillsides, threading through the
scatter of villages which constituted the most conspicuous sign of European
occupation. For the most part the land they settled in was unforgiving,
ploughable only along the broad valley floors, and only profitable to those
cattle ranchers whose holdings were large enough to allow a disproportion-
ate area to sustain their herds.

Many of these early settlers bolstered their fragile income by the 'native
trade', taking time out for three or four months a year to run goods across
the border into Zululand and return laden with cattle or hides. Only the
coastal strip, where the climate was more suitable, enjoyed something of a
boom, when it was discovered that sugar-cane thrived in the mellow coastal
soils. To their intense irritation, those early English – and Scottish, Irish,
even German – pioneers struggled to persuade Natal's Africans to shoulder
the burden of the hard manual labour necessary to work the sugar fields.
They solved the problem, however, by a piece of typically imperial thinking,
importing indentured labourers from Britain's Indian colonies – with the
result that South Africa today has the largest population of Indian descent
outside the subcontinent itself.

In fact the settlers' relationship with Natal's African population was
infinitely more precarious than their mere failure to imbue them with the
spirit of capitalist enterprise and the dubious advantages of the Protestant
work ethic. The white population was outnumbered many times over by
the African groups who had been living on the land before either the
Trekkers or the British had arrived. The overwhelming presence of these
people had hardly registered in the grand imperial fretting which had
prompted the British to intervene in Natal, nor had the British at first
troubled themselves unduly as to what the African population thought
about becoming so arbitrarily subjects of the 'Great White Queen'. Very
soon, however, it became clear that the colony's survival would depend on
the effective management of the majority of its population for the security
and economic benefit of the small settler elite.

The British approach to governing Natal, especially in those early years,
was entirely pragmatic. Even by 1871 the white population of the colony
was no more than 18,000, compared to 300,000 Africans, prompting one
observer to comment that Natal was 'a British colony, so-called, but in

truth a native territory scantily occupied by Europeans'.[7] With British commitments increasingly stretched around an expanding empire, there was little hope that sufficient troops could be deployed to secure the colony properly; the military garrison usually consisted of a single battalion of British infantry – 800 redcoats, at full strength – or at the most two. Indeed, for the first twenty or thirty years of the colony's life the administration of its population – black and white – fell to just a handful of British officials. Governance of Natal was therefore largely by means of bluff – an assumption of power and control which the British could not in fact enforce. For this reason it was necessary that the African population continued to live under the illusion that it had the power to influence its own affairs wherever possible, lest it recognize that the British wardrobe of administration largely comprised the emperor's new clothes.

The British had certainly been quick to recognize the withdrawal of Zulu influence from the region. Delighted that the British victory had freed him from his onerous obligation to the Trekkers, King Mpande readily agreed to allow the physical barrier represented by the line of the Thukela and Mzinyathi rivers to serve as the boundary between Zululand and Natal,[8] and the official retrocession of Zulu claims further south reassured those African communities who had never been incorporated into the Zulu kingdom. Many of these began to emerge from their places of temporary refuge and return to their ancestral lands. Often, however, they found their old territories barred to them, for the British administration made no effort to overturn the patterns of land ownership established by the Trekkers. The best farmland was to remain in the hands of the Europeans – Natal's African population would have to be content with what remained. The British at least formalized the arrangement, marking out a series of reserves – known as 'locations' – into which Natal's blacks were shovelled, sometimes without much ceremony. Among the largest of them, hemmed in by the new settler village of Ladysmith to the west, by the Biggarsberg to the north and by the Zulu border to the east, was Msinga, the hot, rugged, dusty and overcrowded home of the Sithole and their neighbours.

Even so, for most of Natal's Africans, it was to be decades before the impact of European rule became truly apparent. For many, living far away from the centres of the new administration, who seldom saw a passing white trader and never a colonial official, there appeared to be no perceptible change in their ancient patterns of life. They nurtured their cattle and struggled to raise crops, honoured their ancestors, married, intrigued and quarrelled among themselves and with their neighbours, just as they had always done – failing to notice as they did so that the earth had moved inexorably beneath their feet.

# 5

# 'Better move before them'

## The Sithole return to Zululand

Theophilus Shepstone towers over the early history of colonial Natal almost as much as Shaka bestrides the age before. He was born near Bristol, England, in 1817, the son of William Shepstone, a Wesleyan parson. In 1820 William accepted a place on a sponsored scheme intended, optimistically, to populate troublesome parts of the Eastern Cape frontier with British settlers. Young Theophilus had grown up on the frontier during its most expansive phase, when the new wave of British immigrants had vied with established Afrikaners and the Xhosa for the land, and his exposure not only to a disparate mix of peoples, to hardship and the threat of violence, but also to the tentative and hesitant realization of the imperial vision in Africa profoundly shaped his character. By nature tough-minded and self-reliant, Shepstone's taciturn manner concealed an astute political mind which grew increasingly labyrinthine and purposeful with the years. He was fluent in Afrikaans and Xhosa, and understood something of the complexities of both societies – of their needs and limitations, and how both might be manipulated in the service of British interests.

In 1835, when still a young man, Shepstone served as an interpreter on the British military staff during one of the interminable wars against the Xhosa,[1] and the experience gave him a taste for the practicalities of imperial administration in the field. In 1838 he accompanied the abortive British military expedition that briefly occupied Port Natal, and on his return to the Cape he took up a post as a border official. When, in 1845, Natal became a British colony Shepstone was ideally placed to seize the opportunities it offered adventurous civil servants like himself. His knowledge of language and custom suited him ideally to a position in the Native Affairs department – the first step in a lifetime's association with the management of Natal's African affairs, initially as Agent to the Native Tribes, then Captain-General of Native Levies and finally, from 1853, as Secretary for

Native Affairs. With the last position came a seat on Natal's legislative council, and by then such was Shepstone's fabled insight into 'the African mind' that few in the new colonial elite were informed or interested enough to challenge his opinions or his policies. For much of his career Shepstone was responsible to no one but the lieutenant-governor,[2] his immediate superior, and the Colonial Office in London; since neither troubled to look too closely at his actions, he ran Natal's African affairs largely without interference. In that he was aided and abetted by no more than a small trusted circle of relatives, among whom was his lugubrious-looking walrus-moustached younger brother, John Wesley, and in later years his own sons.

Shepstone learned early in his career to give away little of his thinking. In his youth, like many settler lads, he took at least one African lover, but as his authority and reputation grew he set her aside and adopted instead that deliberate distance from the people he administered which is so often a part of the psychology of colonialism. Instead, he cultivated an air of paternalistic authority, adopting when among Africans the name Somsewu – a rather cumbersome amalgam of various indigenous words which loosely translates as 'father of whiteness' – and deliberately created a persona which was at once both stern and commanding, yet apparently sympathetic. Indeed, there is a good deal of evidence to suggest that Shepstone thought of himself as a natural successor to Shaka in his relationship with Natal's black population – a Shaka shaped by Christian belief and shorn of his supposed bloody excesses, a benign despot, but a despot nonetheless. To most in the settler population the mystique which accrued around Shepstone made him an aloof figure, made distant by the mysteries of his administration, a solitary bastion which stood between them and the alien and unfathomable world that surrounded them.

Beneath Shepstone's patriarchal manner there lay in fact no great sympathy for the African way of life. He submerged himself in its intricacies not because he admired or respected it, but rather to discern the best ways to control it, to shape and govern the African population in accordance with his personal belief that Natal's role in the British imperial mission in Africa was a central one. He saw Natal as a conduit through which British ideologies and trade might expand into the limitless human pool of central Africa beyond, and the African population of both Natal and the independent territories as the raw material to be shaped to that end.

His approach to managing Natal's black population was nothing if not pragmatic; under the 'Shepstone system', which dominated the colony's administrative approach for more than half a century, the *amakhosi* were transformed from autonomous rulers into a layer of colonial government. They appeared to govern their people according to traditional law and custom, but in fact had been through a subtle and profound shift of power; their dictates were now subject to the approval of the Natal legislature, and their authority remained unchallenged only so long as it did not conflict with the broader policies and attitudes of the colonial regime. To Shepstone, it was an approach that offered some ready parallels with the Zulu system across the river – in which the local *amakhosi* were subject to control by the apparatus of the Zulu kings – and by maintaining a façade of traditional power structures it minimized the risk of African dissent. It was also cheap for the imperial exchequer as it required no great colonial bureaucracy. In reality, of course, it meant that, once the system was fully established, every *inkosi*'s position was dependent ultimately – and almost solely – upon Shepstone's goodwill and patronage. With few enough checks to his own authority, it was Shepstone who provided the frame of reference by which their actions would be judged good or bad, by which they would be left to administer in peace or be called to account. He was free to reward his favourites, to manipulate demographics by creating artificial chiefdoms where none had previously existed, from among those dispossessed by Shaka's wars or by land clearances – and to choose the men to rule them – and to depose and punish those *amakhosi* who offended him.

The contradictions of their new position only slowly became apparent to the *amakhosi* as the nineteenth century wore on. While their own objectives remained rooted in the traditional aspirations of their people, they had in fact now become an integral part of a system fundamentally hostile to the traditional way of life. The colonial administration imposed taxes upon its African population, not merely to bolster its revenues, but to force African society away from self-sufficiency and into the developing cash economy – an economy intended solely for the settlers' benefit.

Faced with taxes levied upon them, the *amakhosi* were compelled to send their young men away from home for long periods to work as migrant labourers, and in so doing unwittingly found themselves cast in a compliant role as the colony's labour masters. Sometimes the colony employed more direct methods, a direct levy, known as the *isibhalo*, which forced the *amakhosi* to raise work gangs for road-building and other public projects – again, principally for the settlers' benefit. This brought with it subtle pressures of its own, for the absence of so many young men for months at a time inevitably had an impact upon the bonds of family life which bound Nguni society together. The Government also required the *amakhosi* to host not only magistrates, who supervised their affairs, but missionaries, whose presence foreshadowed a sustained attack upon traditional religious practice, which damaged communication with the ancestors, and long-established customs.

It was only when their people became discontented with their lot, unsettled by the burdens placed upon them and troubled by the insidious erosion of their age-old way of life, that the *amakhosi* came fully to recognize the bind in which they found themselves: that their own position was in fact dependent upon the very people, the colonial administration, about whom their followers were complaining. The *amakhosi* faced a stark choice: to betray the needs of their people and accept a role as a Government lackey, or to make a stand on behalf of the ways of their ancestors – and resist.

This was the dilemma in which the Sithole now found themselves – and, as they discovered, the consequences of even the mildest expression of dissent could be terrifying indeed.

*

Jobe had died sometime in the 1840s, and with him the golden age of the Sithole. By then he had been patriarch of the Sithole for over twenty years, and, venerated and respected, he went to his ancestors in the manner of his forefathers, buried at the head of the cattle-pen in the middle of his homestead on the slopes of iLenge mountain – the spot is marked by an *uhlalankhosi* tree to this day.

Jobe's heir was his son Mondise, who did not long survive him. Mondise's son, Matshana, was still too young to assume the role of *inkosi*, and for several years the Sithole were ruled by a regent, Mondise's brother Mveli. In 1850, however, Matshana came of age and claimed the throne from his uncle. The transition of power within Nguni society was often fraught with pitfalls, particularly when an older generation was reluctant to give up its power and prestige, and on this occasion Mveli was not reconciled to the succession. Matshana's response was a traditional one – Mveli was 'smelt out' for witchcraft, and he and his family were put to death.

It is unlikely that this incident caused much concern among the Sithole, as the ruthless removal of a handful of disaffected was often better for a group in the long run than the cancer of protracted dissent. Yet, to Matshana's surprise, the death of Mveli provoked a stern reaction from the Government authorities, for whom deaths associated with witchcraft would remain a sensitive issue. Although it was the prerogative of the *amakhosi* in Natal to try their subjects for crimes committed among them, the colonial administration refused to accept on ideological grounds the existence of witchcraft, and regarded any manifestation of it as improper or illegal. Shepstone also tended to regard those who ordered executions for witch-craft as clinging too determinedly to a state of political autonomy which had now passed. It was an issue which threw into sharp relief the gulf between the assumptions of power held by the *amakhosi* and the reality of their position; required by the Government to administer their people on traditional lines, they could find themselves bewilderingly out of favour on occasions when they did so.

Matshana himself was tried for the murder of Mveli, but the authorities took a lenient view in the light of his youth and he was allowed to retain his position as *inkosi*. His card was marked nonetheless, and when, towards the end of 1857, another death occurred among the Sithole, Shepstone decided to act firmly. One of Matshana's supporters, a man named Mtwetwe, had died under suspicious circumstances, and Matshana had once again staged a cleansing ceremony to unite and purify the people – and to 'smell out' the cause of the evil which had befallen Mtwetwe. A man named Sigatiya – an associate of Mveli – was denounced, and Matshana had sent men to arrest him. These had treated Sigatiya so badly on the road that he died. A few days later, Sigatiya's wife had made a complaint to the local white magistrate.

To Shepstone it seemed that Matshana was wilfully challenging the constraints placed upon him by the Government, and messengers were sent to demand he come and give an explanation. This was a development that seemed to take Matshana by surprise and, instead, he sent an apology and offered to surrender the men who had killed Sigatiya. But at the very least Shepstone demanded a public act of contrition, and Matshana's reluctance to act on the summons only deepened his guilt in Government eyes. Twice John Shepstone rode out to Sithole territory, quite probably intending to trap Matshana, for he later complained that he had been unable to inter-view the *inkosi* on these occasions without a large retinue being present. The meetings had therefore been tense and inconclusive. Taking fright,

Matshana had moved into hiding in the broken country along the flanks of the iLenge mountain. This had merely increased the Government's frustrations, and the nascent colonial militia – only recently established from among the settler population for the colony's defence – had been dispatched to the location to confiscate Sithole cattle by way of punishment.

Now, for a third time, Matshana had been summoned, and it was clear to him and his councillors that this was a last chance to placate the authorities before a complete rift ensued. Yet the summons itself was deeply ominous, for the British had a well-known history of using ostensible parleys to arrest their targets – or worse. In 1836, on the Cape frontier, the Xhosa King Hintsa had met with the British general Sir Harry Smith, only to find himself detained; and when Hintsa try to escape, colonial troops had mercilessly hunted him down and shot him dead. More recently, and in Natal, the Government had begun its ruthless deposition of the Nhlangwini *inkosi*, Sidoyi kaBaleni, with such a summons. No one was too strong for the Government summons to topple, and its power had already become proverbial – '*Ibizelo ladl'ikhondekazi*', it was said, 'the summons ate up the big baboon'.

Nor were the Sithole reassured that it was John Wesley Shepstone who attended the meetings. Employed as an enforcer by his brother Theophilus, it was John who had spearheaded the attack on Sidoyi.

The spot appointed for the third meeting in April 1858 was on neutral ground, on the boundary of the Sithole location. The Sithole had been told to attend unarmed and Matshana had emerged from hiding nervously, accompanied by his attendants. They were escorted, however, by a large crowd of younger men in defiant mood, carrying shields and spears and singing war-songs, and vowing that they would not allow their *inkosi* to be insulted as Sidoyi had been.

John Shepstone and his entourage had arrived early at the rendezvous, and the advantage of picking the site had fallen to them – they had chosen an open space with clear views of the approaches but with a low ridge close behind. A large leopard-skin – a symbol of royalty and authority among the Nguni – was spread out as a rug, and Shepstone sat in state upon it; next to him, in a nod to normality, sat his wife. Behind Shepstone squatted several African *izinduna* in the service of the authorities. Shepstone himself appeared to have come unarmed to the meeting, but there were others among his escort who clearly were not; a small party of Europeans with rifles were positioned on horseback nearby, while standing further back were groups of Africans carrying conspicuous shields and spears. These men were amaHlubi, followers of the *inkosi* Langalibalele who lived in the uKhahlamba foothills, who were then – ironically, in the light of later events – trusted allies of the colonial government.

As the Sithole approached the meeting, the bravado of the younger men began to evaporate and they reluctantly allowed themselves to be persuaded to leave their spears behind – 200–300 metres from the rendezvous, they slipped them into the long grass as Matshana went forward hedged by his councillors. After the formal greetings, Matshana squatted down in front of Shepstone and his wife and his councillors fell in behind him.

The agenda was much as the Sithole had feared. Shepstone outlined the Government's grievances – that Matshana had allowed a man to be executed for witchcraft, and had failed to attend when summoned to explain himself. His words heightened the air of unease which had settled over the Sithole. As Matshana leaned forward to respond, however, a sound drifted across the veld from behind the low ridge to the rear of Shepstone's party – the clatter and jangle of horses on the move. Shepstone heard it and suddenly leaned back, breaking the intimacy of the conversation, and called out to an African servant-boy behind him to bring him a drink.

And in that moment all hell broke loose. One of the Government *izinduna* suddenly stood up, rushed out from the ranks behind Shepstone and lunged towards Matshana. Someone heard Shepstone call out '*Bambani abatagathi!*' – 'Seize the evil-doers!'[3] – but Matshana sprang to his feet and in one lithe movement leapt backwards, passing clean over the heads of several of his own councillors sitting behind. The Sithole had been right to be suspicious – the meeting was a carefully laid trap, and with his call for a drink Shepstone had sprung it. Even as Matshana hit the ground, the collective tension burst in shouts of anger and surprise as the Sithole struggled to their feet. Shepstone's amaHlubi rushed forward, pushing men out of the way with their shields in an effort to reach the *inkosi*. By this time a fresh party of horsemen had emerged into view from their hidden position behind the ridge. They were white men, and armed, and they rode forward trying to surround the Sithole, cutting off their line of retreat and trying to get between the fighting men and their secreted weapons. Mrs Shepstone – who was clearly a formidable lady – reached under the leopard-skin rug and dragged out a double-barrelled shotgun, while Shepstone himself pulled two hidden revolvers from his pockets. He fired after Matshana, but in the confusion the bullets missed their mark and one struck a Sithole named Deke in the leg. The sudden crack of the gunshots, cutting through the hubbub, and the glimpse of splashing blood provoked angry cries from the Sithole and several young men broke away to retrieve their spears. Pulling them out from the long grass, they rushed back to the mêlée, aiming towards Shepstone himself. One of them drew back a spear to throw it but before he could do so was intercepted and stabbed to death by one of the amaHlubi. In the noisy excitement, some of the whites on horseback began shooting indiscriminately into the crowd. A wounded Sithole fell at Mrs Shepstone's feet; just a few seconds before she had been prepared to cut men down with her shotgun but now, with that curious mix of robustness and compassion that characterized so many Victorian adventuresses, she bent down to examine his injuries. She was too slow – the wounded man tried to reach for his spear and an amaHlubi killed him on the spot.

Shepstone himself had managed to struggle free from the throng to reach his horse. Looking up, he saw a group of Sithole in the distance, hurrying away, their heads bent low; among them he recognized Matshana. He hauled himself into his saddle but had only ridden a few yards when he felt a sudden sharp blow beneath his arm. He looked round and saw a Sithole, a man named Mdemude kaMasimbana, standing next to him who had just stabbed at him – the point of the spear had been deflected by the belt of Shepstone's ammunition pouch. Shepstone turned his revolver at Mdemude, who stepped back out of the way, tripped, and fell sprawling in the grass. Before Shepstone could intervene, several amaHlubi surrounded Mdemude and one of them crushed his skull with a knobbed stick. By the time Shepstone was able to look back again, Matshana had disappeared.

The scrimmage was soon over. With Matshana safely away, the Sithole began to disperse, retreating towards iLenge mountain. The settler volunteers and amaHlubi went after them, however, shooting at them, riding them down and spearing stragglers, and by the time Shepstone called a halt to the pursuit and the smoke had cleared some thirty Sithole bodies lay strewn across the grassy slopes.

When they regrouped in the hills under cover of darkness that evening, the Sithole considered the catastrophic blow that had befallen them. With the death of several of Matshana's senior advisers, and also of his uncle Sondlovu, a man considered one of the Sithole's heroes for the part he played in destroying the cannibal bands the Sithole had encountered on their arrival in Msinga,[4] they can hardly have failed to recognize the collapse of an old and venerated order. And with it they saw, too, beyond the benign façade presented by the colonial regime, the ruthless heart of the new world which had replaced it – and realized the terrible danger to which they were now exposed.

There was no doubt that John Shepstone had delivered a severe punishment to the Sithole, and he followed up the attempted capture by sweeping through Sithole territory. Colonial militias and the amaHlubi rounded up cattle and burned homes, and shot out of hand those who resisted. Yet it was hard not to recognize that the attempt on Matshana's life had been botched, and there was a feeling of unease in Government circles that far from reinforcing the administration's authority the Shepstones had brought it into disrepute. The punishment they had inflicted was out of all proportion to any disrespect displayed by Matshana, and the *inkosi* himself had in any case got away. A missionary in Msinga commented privately that both Shepstones would have lost their jobs had full details of the incident become known. John Shepstone squirmed uncomfortably as reports spread, at first claiming that the skirmish had never taken place, then denying that he had tried to gun down the unarmed Matshana, and finally justifying his actions on the grounds that he had proof Matshana had been preparing to ambush *him*.

The Shepstones' embarrassment was, however, cold comfort to Matshana. After disappearing with the survivors of his entourage into the deep valleys near iLenge, where they regrouped, a number of his people rallied to him, and here they considered their future. Msinga was lost to them now – and the door into the wider world which Shaka had opened for them half a century before had now swung shut with a vengeance.

Instead, there was the border country. The far bank of the Mzinyathi was independent territory, where the ancient customs of the Nguni still ruled unchallenged, and where the ancestors of the Sithole from the time before Jobe still lay buried: Zulu country.

But that, too, was not without its challenges – for the Zulu kings had notoriously long memories, and to claim sanctuary there from the fury of the white man, Matshana would have to beg forgiveness for their past lapses. It was scarcely an ideal choice – but by that stage Matshana really had no choice at all.

*

The Zululand that Matshana found on his arrival there in the winter of 1858 was very different to the confident, expanding kingdom which had dispatched Jobe as an agent to Natal forty years before. It had been damaged almost to destruction by the war with the Voortrekkers and by the costly struggle between Dingane and Mpande. Not only had the fighting consumed several thousand Zulu lives and seen the country's cattle resources plundered, but power had slipped effortlessly away from the centre towards the regional *amakhosi* who had traded their support for the warring factions in return for greater independence in their affairs. King Mpande had devoted his reign to reversing this tendency, but in 1856 the country had once again been convulsed by a bitter internecine struggle within the royal house which had threatened to rip Zululand apart.

Unlike Shaka and Dingane – neither of whom produced surviving heirs – King Mpande had many wives and fathered twenty-nine sons and twenty-three daughters in all. More than astute enough to recognize that between them they constituted both the nation's future and a formidable threat to his own security, he had deliberately avoided, as his sons grew up, nominating an heir. The Boers had tried to force the issue as early as 1840, even before Mpande had taken the throne, being keen to protect their long-term investment in the Zulu royal house. To keep them happy Mpande had appointed Cetshwayo, his son by his 'great wife' Ngqumbazi, as his successor. The Boers had clipped a piece out of Cetshwayo's ear, marking him like a prize heifer so that he could not avoid their claim upon him later, but there is no evidence that Mpande regarded the incident as binding. Indeed, while Cetshwayo grew to manhood convinced that the throne was his birthright, Mpande shifted his favour between his other sons as the mood took him. By the 1850s he was widely rumoured to favour Prince Mbuyazi, whom he had fathered by a woman given to him from his household by the great Shaka himself.

The two princes had conceived an intense rivalry for one another, and although Mpande separated them, placing them in royal homesteads at opposite ends of the country, they had begun to build factions about themselves. Mpande refused to intervene decisively, merely remarking that 'two bulls cannot live in the same kraal', and by late 1856 it was clear that a clash was imminent – and that Mbuyazi had failed to secure widespread support within the kingdom. Privately, the king had urged Mbuyazi to repeat his own road to the throne – to leave Zululand and seek the support of the whites. In November 1856 Mbuyazi had gathered up his followers –

some 7,000 fighting men and as many as 13,000 dependants – and made a dash for the border.

He had misjudged his moment. When he arrived at the lower Thukela crossing he found the river in flood, a slick brown sheet of water 400 metres wide. And he found, too, that the British were not of the same mettle as the Trekkers a generation before; the solitary colonial official guarding the crossing on the Natal bank was appalled by the prospect of such an exodus, and the British steadfastly refused to intervene in the divisions between the rival Zulu factions.

Mbuyazi was still there on 2 December when Cetshwayo caught up with him at the head of 12,000 armed followers. The ensuing battle was the bloodiest in Zulu history – Mbuyazi's followers were quickly overrun and a panic-stricken mob fled towards the Thukela, only to be brought up short on the river's edge. In the heat of the moment Cetshwayo's men drove into them, killing fighting men, women and children alike. Hundreds preferred the fragile hope of the roaring torrent to the cold certainty of Cetshwayo's stabbing spears and threw themselves into the river. Most drowned or were taken by crocodiles, their bodies carried away downstream only to be washed up on beaches for kilometres either side of the Thukela mouth over the following days – a grisly flotsam gnawed by sharks and crabs and left to rot at the high-water mark. Mbuyazi himself was killed, together with six more of Mpande's sons and as many as 14,000 of his followers.

The battle had spectacularly secured Prince Cetshwayo's claim to the throne, but it had undone much of his father's work in restoring the bonds which tied the kingdom together. Like Mpande in 1840, Cetshwayo had bought much of his support in 1856 by promising a greater degree of autonomy to Zululand's great barons, the most powerful of the *amakhosi*, and so long as his father still lived a protracted political struggle of intrigue and influence was inevitable. Mpande clung to his support among the established order, and to the ceremonial power vested in the king; Cetshwayo, inevitably, sought to cultivate a new order of his own.

It was into this tense environment that Matshana walked to an uncertain welcome with the tired and dusty remnants of the Sithole in May 1858. He had every reason to be nervous of the king's reaction; Jobe had undeniably failed in his loyalty to Dingane in 1838, and Mpande had exacted his revenge by failing to support Jobe against the Trekkers in 1840. Furthermore, while Jobe had been part of the new elite raised up by Shaka, Matshana was not – he was an outsider, born in Natal, who had never been an integral part of the Zulu establishment. In a dismissive phrase current in Zululand at the time, Matshana was a *khafula* – one 'spat out' by the true kingdom and tainted by his association with the whites.[5]

Yet whatever King Mpande thought of him, what mattered, in 1858, was Cetshwayo's opinion. At a time when the prince was seeking to build his power base among a younger generation of *amakhosi* uncommitted in the recent fighting, Matshana's return was timely. It afforded Cetshwayo not only the support of the head of a lineage which owed its ascendancy to the intervention of Shaka himself, but allowed him to pose as the public champion of ancient traditions threatened by the unsympathetic colonial administration on the far side of the river. Cetshwayo not only offered Matshana the opportunity to return and reclaim the old Sithole lands on the slopes of Qhudeni mountain, but gave him two of his own sisters in marriage into the bargain. It was far more than Matshana can have expected, and he was quick to accept – and if King Mpande objected, he was wise enough to keep his views to himself.

And so Matshana kaMondise had returned towards the end of 1858 to the old lands his grandfather Jobe had left in 1819. For Matshana it must have been a bitter-sweet moment, his delight in his homecoming tempered by the painful awareness of just how nearly the Shepstones had come to destroying not only himself but his entire people.

It was a feeling he did not hesitate to express as his followers built him a new royal homestead at Nsingabantu. Like an African Paul Revere, his warning to his neighbours among the border community was simple enough: the British are coming. Shaka had been right to warn of them – the *abelungu* were voracious. They bore no respect for the traditions of the ancestors and the *amakhosi*, and they devoured everything that lay in their path. No one was safe; in a matter of years, Matshana said, if the Zulus were not careful the British would have 'advanced over the whole of the western portion of Zululand, and they had better move before them'.[6]

*

It was a warning that fell on open ears. The vulnerability of the western border had troubled King Mpande since he had first agreed his boundaries with British Natal in the 1840s. The formidable natural barriers of the Thukela and Mzinyathi rivers had provided an obvious and incontrovertible point of demarcation along the central and lower reaches of the boundary, but further north, along the upper reaches of the Mzinyathi, the line was less geographically precise. At the beginning of the century this area had been occupied by two major groups – the amaHlubi and amaNgwane – together with a number of smaller ones like the Sithole's old neighbours, the amaThembu and amaChunu. Most of these had been driven out in the fighting that followed, leaving a great slice of territory straddling this strategic crossroads largely depopulated. It was partly to secure the western marches, of course, that Shaka had moved Jobe and the Sithole across the Mzinyathi to provide a buffer on the far bank, and to shore up the northern reaches he had built a royal homestead, ebaQulusini, on the slopes of the Hlobane and Zungwini hills. By the 1850s, the descendants of those attached to this homestead were beginning to form a distinct group of their own, the abaQulusi, who were fiercely loyal to the royal house, and who were administered by appointed *izinduna* rather than by hereditary *amakhosi*.

Along the middle reaches of the Mzinyathi, however, the situation had been complicated by the intrusion of a new group pressing forward from the western banks – the Boers. Although the Zulu kings considered their authority to extend all the way up the Mzinyathi to the uKhahlamba foothills, there were in fact few people living on the open, breezy uplands, so that when, following the British annexation of Natal in 1845, disillusioned Voortrekkers who wanted to remove themselves from British jurisdiction had appealed to Mpande for land, he had granted them permission to graze this area. The loss to the Zulu kingdom had been minimal, since much of this region was caught in an ecosystem of its own, a combination of sandy soils and rain shadow which left its grasses unusually impoverished and made it mediocre cattle country.[7] In any case, Mpande later claimed, – and it was probably true – in allowing the Boers seasonal grazing rights he never intended to give away his claim to the land in perpetuity, but rather to allow them the use of it at his discretion. The deed once done, however, had proved remarkably difficult to undo without the serious risk of a further open confrontation with the whites. The Boers first built shacks to shelter themselves when tending their herds, but, with time, these inexorably turned into more permanent structures. In 1854 the farmers had combined to build a small village, Utrecht, in a fold in the twisting course of the Mzinyathi – they optimistically proclaimed it the centre of a new republic although it was too small to prove economically viable and it was eventually subsumed as no more than an administrative district of the more robust Transvaal Republic across the mountains.

The Utrecht district grew slowly – even by 1878 there were only 1,352 whites living in the area, of whom just 375 were adult males, and only 248 of these lived in the village itself – but it profoundly altered the dynamic of the western borders. Furthermore, as the Utrecht community grew, so it assumed a fresh expansionist urge; driven in part by the inadequacy of the pasturage, the Boers had started to creep slowly eastwards in search of the better grazing to be found in Zululand proper. The Boers first spilled into the large 'V' of territory that lay between the Mzinyathi and its confluence with the Ncome – and then tentatively edged across the Ncome itself.

These areas, too, were thinly populated – but the Zulu kings regarded them as decidedly their own, and they watched the Boer movements with growing concern. As Anthony Durnford, a British soldier whose own future would hang in the balance of the unfolding friction, was to put it, displaying a degree of sympathy unusual among the white community at the time:

> One thing is clear, that the white man wanted the black man's land – that he got leave from the black to graze cattle in the first instance, then came over and put up a shanty, then a house. Then more Boers came, and so on, until, as the Zulus told us, the Boers were like a toad that comes hopping and hopping until it hops right into the middle of the house.[8]

As early as 1850 – eight years before Matshana kaMondise returned to the ancestral lands of the Sithole – King Mpande had tried to limit Boer encroachment along the lower Mzinyathi. He had directed a new group to occupy the area, the followers of a carefully chosen royal favourite, whom he ordered to settle the country north of the Malakatha and iSandlwana hills, and to monitor the movements of both the Boers upstream and the British settlers directly opposite.

These people were known as the amaQungebeni, and they too were part of that elite established in Zululand by King Shaka. The amaQungebeni ancestral lands lay at Ntabakuzuma on the Mfolozi Mhlope, not far from the old Zulu territory, and Shaka had forged an alliance with Xongo kaMthinthisi Ngobese, raising him up as *inkosi* of the amaQungebeni. Xongo's family had remained on good terms with the royal house after Shaka's death and throughout the upheavals that followed. When Xongo died around 1850, Mpande had conferred the succession upon his son, Mfokozana, and at the same time appointed him *induna* of the western borders. Mfokozana had uprooted his followers and settled along the Batshe valley, close to the iSandlwana hill, with the Mzinyathi in front of him and a chain of hills at his back. It was a spot which effectively commanded the entry points into the kingdom along the central reaches of the river, and in recognition of its strategic importance Mpande himself is said to have conferred a name upon Mfokozana's hills. They were, he said, the nation's *isiNquthu*, its 'eyes in the back of the head',[9] and Mfokozana and the amaQungebeni must be his watchmen.

Ironically, fate intervened to prevent Mfokozana fulfilling his duties for long – he died about 1852. As Mfokozana had no heirs, Mpande confirmed Mfokozana's younger brother, Sihayo kaXongo, as *inkosi* of the ama-Qungebeni, and passed over the duties that that entailed. Those early 1850s were golden years for Sihayo and his family, for shortly after his ascendancy he fathered a son and heir. There is nothing in the historical record to suggest that the boy's birth and childhood was in any way different from thousands of other young Zulu of his time. He was born at his father's kwaSogekle homestead – 'the cock's comb',[10] so called because it nestled at the foot of a horseshoe curve of cliffs crested by a distinctive jumble of rocks – in the Batshe valley, scarcely 10 kilometres from iSandlwana, some time in 1853 or 1854.

In a polygamous society the ranking of the wives of a great man was of enduring importance, and the child was the first male born of Sihayo's 'great house' by his senior wife, MaMtshali. So, no doubt, when MaMtshali first recognized the pangs of labour she retired to the privacy of her hut in the usual manner, prompting the family elders – led perhaps by Sihayo himself – to assemble and form a ring around it outside, walking around it slowly and chanting incantations to the ancestral spirits. When labour began in earnest, however, the men would have been shooed away by three or four mature women who hurried into the hut to serve as midwives. The hard clay floor was carpeted with a matting of grass cut specially for the occasion, and onto this the child would have been born, one of the midwives quickly cutting the umbilical cord with a sliver of sharpened reed. Then the boy was washed in an infusion of herbs, believed to secure the ancestors' blessings, and both the mother and child were smeared with red clay. A belt of plaited grass was bound tightly around MaMtshali's stomach to help her recovery, and the soiled grass bed was scooped up, taken outside and carefully burned to prevent any trace of body fluids falling into the hands of the ill-disposed. Then the *impepo* herb was sprinkled into the smouldering fire and as the sweet-smelling smoke rose to the spirits the placenta and cord were buried a foot or so beneath the clay floor. Only when these precautions were complete was Sihayo allowed in to see his son, and word of the safe delivery passed through the homestead and into the community beyond. The child was named Mehlokazulu – 'eyes of the Zulu' – and there was never any doubt at whom he was supposed to be looking.

For the first years of his life MaMtshali would have kept Mehlokazulu close to her. He suckled at her breast until he was two or three, and slept beside her in her private hut. Motherhood permitted no evading of the family chores, however, and when MaMtshali rose to collect water or firewood in the early dawn light, or hoed the fields or crushed corn kernels in the grinding-stone, she carried Mehlokazulu with her, slung in a bag of animal skins held fast across her body by hide ropes. Or perhaps, as most Zulu mothers did, she passed him over now and then into the care of another woman's child, a girl older than Mehlokazulu, whose own duties included the role of childminder.

Once they could walk, Zulu children were allowed the run of the homestead, toddling about among the huts, teasing the chickens and tormenting the lizards that emerged from the dark crevices to sun themselves on the hot midday rocks, while family members kept an eye on them to ensure that they didn't trip into the fire or stray too close to the cattle. Like all other boys, Mehlokazulu would have served his apprenticeship, when he was old enough, by milking the family cows at daybreak each morning and accompanying the older boys in the daily round of driving the cattle to pasture and watching over them. He grew up comfortable in the landscape which framed his home, the pleasant, fertile sweep of the Batshe valley as it winds its way along the spurs of the isiNquthu hills towards its confluence with the mighty Mzinyathi – the open country which characterizes the course of the Mzinyathi upstream, and the sudden crowding of hills which forces it through a series of gorges below. He knew intimately, too, the stubby nub of iSandlwana to the east. In fact it is said that the outcrop was originally known to those living locally as iFenu, and that it was *inkosi* Sihayo himself who bestowed the name iSandlwana. The meaning of the newer name is complex, but like a good many Zulu allusions it reflects the profound hold exercised over the people's imagination by their cattle. Literally, iSandlwana means 'it looks like a little hut', a reference to the grain store on stilts in the family homestead. But the hut in question was a common metaphor for a portion of a cow's entrails – to

Sihayo, it seems, that rocky stub looked rather more like the second stomach of a cow and with the ascendancy of the amaQungebeni the name iSandlwana stuck.

iSandlwana pointed the way towards the Zulu heartland, and the tracks which led past it to the great royal homesteads of the Zulu kings. Even as a child, Mehlokazulu passed down those tracks many times, and he was assured from an early age of the place his family held in the world of the Zulu. It had always been apparent, of course, that his father was an important man, for he had seen Sihayo communing with the elders of the amaQungebeni on an almost daily basis. Once he was old enough, however, Mehlokazulu was called upon to carry his father Sihayo's rolled sleeping mat and carved wooden head-rest on the 80- or 90-kilometre walk to the capital on those occasions when his father was summoned to the royal homesteads at kwaNodwengu or oNdini across the Mfolozi Mhlope.

He was, perhaps, even required to attend his father when he sat on the royal council, that inner circle of great and powerful men who advised the king on affairs of state. As a boy Mehlokazulu would have been proscribed from addressing or even openly gazing upon the king or his councillors, but instead would have squatted respectfully behind his father's right hand, waiting to offer him a pinch of snuff, a drink or, on particularly hot days, to pour water over his father's *ingxotha*, the brass armband which the king bestowed on his favourites, and which had always to be worn in his presence, regardless of how uncomfortable it became in the naked sun.

Later, as a young man, Mehlokazulu was chosen as one of four youths selected to attend Cetshwayo when he performed ritual ablutions at the time of the great national ceremonies, and who took it in turns to fetch water from a pure spring which flowed from the slopes of the Hlopekhulu mountain, a few kilometres from the royal homestead. Since anything that touched the king's person was a source of great spiritual power – hardly to be surpassed, in the wrong hands, as a means of bringing misfortune upon the kingdom as a whole – only those from the most trusted families were invited to perform such intimate duties, and it is no coincidence that of the remaining attendants two were the sons of *inkosi* Mnyamana Buthelezi, the king's most senior councillor.

Only in that regard – in his exposure to the innermost private workings of the Zulu state – was Mehlokazulu's youth different from that of any other young man who was raised in the traditional lifestyle during all the greatness and power of the Zulu kingdom. And yet Mehlokazulu grew up knowing, more than most, that the ancient timeless rhythms which had shaped his forefathers' lives were changing, imperceptibly but inexorably, and that the world into which he had been born was already irrevocably altered from the one that his father had known as a boy. No longer was the universe defined by the language and culture of his people alone; and the Zulu kingdom, itself no more than a generation or two old, was already confined and constricted, pressed into shape by a new and powerful agent of change. Mehlokazulu understood that agent – its presence had, after all, been directly responsible for his family's rise – for he gazed out towards it every day of his life, and saw it manifest in a growing trickle of passers-by. He had known, since he was old enough to know anything, that the Mzinyathi marked the western limit of the writ of the Zulu kings, and that on the far bank, across scarcely a hundred metres of muddy brown water, lay a very different world – Natal, the country where the white men, who had come there first as Shaka's guests, now ruled, and where the black *amakhosi* acknowledged as their masters not great African kings but European colonial governors.

It is likely that from early childhood Mehlokazulu shared that wariness of the white world articulated by Matshana kaMondise on his return to the neighbouring Sithole country downstream in 1858. Mehlokazulu was part of a rising generation which had grown up familiar with contact with the European world, who lacked the exaggerated respect for whites which King Shaka had encouraged among the older generations, and who saw little allure in the European world beyond the material benefits it offered. Nor did he always trouble to hide his lack of respect for European affectations; even as a young man his unwillingness to be cheated earned him a bad reputation among border traders as 'an irreclaimable scamp, and many a bit of sharp practice is laid to his account'.[11]

Yet, as the traveller Bertram Mitford recognized, underlying this growing resentment among young Zulus of the airs the whites adopted, was a robust self-confidence in their own traditions and values which made them unwilling to deal with Europeans except upon their own terms:

> I believe that, save in actual war time, any Englishman may go all over Zululand alone and unarmed with perfect safety providing he is friendly and courteous towards the natives; in short, provided he behaves like a gentleman ... But the 'Jack and baas' style of intercourse with the

colonial natives [i.e. that which prevailed in Natal] does not go down [well] among the Zulus.[12]

\*

The whites had first come to the western bank of the Mzinyathi during the brief interregnum of the Voortrekkers. Pretorius's commando had passed that way during the Ncome expedition in December 1838, and a year or two later the Vermaak family had claimed farms stretching across the open, grassy heights, but it was the British annexation of Natal which led the first settlers into the valley itself. In 1847 an Irishman, James Alfred Rorke,[13] bought a farm of 1,619 riverside hectares from Crown agents and built himself a home at the foot of Shiyane hill, less than a kilometre from the stony drift across the river. Rorke's was a Spartan home built in typical frontier style – two long, low single-storey buildings, the exterior walls made of squared-off local stone and interior partitions of sun-dried mud brick, with big, airy verandas and thatched roofs – which commanded a fine view up the valley and served him as a house and a store. From there he eked a precarious living as a hunter and trader, a tough life and a lonely one, even after he married a Voortrekker's daughter, Sarah Strijdom, and one that clearly left its mark on Rorke in the fierce glint which shines from his eyes, seen in his surviving portraits. There were still, in the 1840s, a few of the buffalo which had given the Mzinyathi its name to be found in the area, and even an elephant or two, and Rorke shot them for their tough hides, horns and tusks, which continued to be in demand as the settler economy slowly expanded. But this was an unpredictable and dangerous profession, and Rorke supplemented his living by trading 'in the Zulu'; like many other border settlers he loaded his wagon with blankets, beads, brass wire, gin and trinkets – and perhaps even the odd illicit firearm – and crossed into Zululand by the ford at the edge of his property. It was a way of life that left his wife to fend for herself for days or weeks at a time, but it was usually profitable, and it was common for such traders to return with empty wagons but driving a herd of cattle which they had bartered in exchange. The profits could be spectacular – in 1856 a group of twenty-one traders had the misfortune to be trapped between the warring factions of Princes Cetshwayo and Mbuyazi on the banks of the Thukela. They escaped with their lives but not with their cattle, and after the battle assessed their losses at a staggering 5,000 head, or 238 each.

Even by the time Mehlokazulu was born, around 1853, Rorke's store was a well-known feature of Zulu life, and where he had pioneered others followed. A precarious track soon snaked down the Biggarsberg towards the drift, and a trickle of passing traffic became commonplace, hunters and traders stopping off at Rorke's store on the way to or from Zululand to pick over his stock or enjoy a glass of gin in his makeshift canteen. Among the African communities on both sides of the border the store had already become a landmark, '*kwaJim*', Jim's place, and his crossing became universally known to the whites as Rorke's Drift.

Those tented wagons, with a heavily bearded white man dressed in the ubiquitous yellow corduroy sitting on the box, their long spans of lowing oxen urged on by the great cracking whips, the whistles and cries of the black drivers walking beside them, were the spearhead of change for the African communities on both sides of the border. Whereas once African groups like the amaThembu and amaChunu had sought to defend the river-crossings against Shaka in order to resist the expansion of the Zulu kingdom, so now a spider's web of wagon tracks ensnared them slowly from the opposite direction. Rorke's Drift was becoming a portal through which an enticing, exotic, alien and ultimately dangerous and destructive new world had begun seeping in to eat away at the very fabric of traditional African life.

The amaQungebeni were by no means immune to its allure. As the first community of power and influence on the Zulu bank, most passing whites stopped off to pay their respects at kwaSogekle, and *inkosi* Sihayo, no less than many others, succumbed to the temptation to buy the latest fashion in beads for his wives, to buy woven European blankets to replace cloaks of animal skins, to buy everything from cast-iron hoes made in Birmingham to horses, gin – universally known in Zululand with a perceptive touch of melancholy as 'The Queen's Tears' – and even the best of any firearms that were on offer.

Mehlokazulu himself grew up familiar with horses and guns – and knew well enough how to use both. At a time when whites themselves were still a novelty in Zululand, possession of their artefacts conferred on Zulu owners an air of cosmopolitan worldliness, that prestige and status that came with the demonstrable proof that they were players on more than a parochial stage and champions of the new. Sihayo himself grew increasingly at ease in white society, sometimes wearing European clothes, entertaining white visitors cordially, and more than capable of deporting himself appropriately at a missionary's table. The traveller, Bertram Mitford, was to meet him in decidedly straitened circumstances in 1882, yet Sihayo's delight in white company remains obvious enough:

> ...an urbane, jovial-looking old Zulu [came] to meet me with an outstretched hand, and grinning from ear to ear. Looking at him I thought of the West African potentate, described as in full dress in a cocked hat and a pair of spurs. His South African brother, however, was less aspiring, and rejoiced in a head-ring and a pair of boots (of course not omitting the inevitable 'mutya'[14]), for the pedal extremities of this worthy were cased in a huge pair of bluchers,[15] which, he being a great sufferer from gout, seemed about the worst line of adornment he could have struck out in. The old fellow lumbering along (he is enormously fat), with a barbed assegai in his hand, and trying to look as if he were not on hot bricks, cut a slightly ridiculous figure.[16]

Yet at the same time, from the comfort of 'the cock's comb', Sihayo could see, too, the tangible proof of the impoverishment of his country in the herds driven across the border into Natal. There was a widespread unease in the community at large as to what the coming of the whites portended for the future of the African way of life – a growing awareness that the traders were at the vanguard of a movement which was steadily rolling up Africa, pushing into each African society which lay across its path in turn, dragging in its wake a heavy baggage of violent conquest and the destruction of ancient and venerated traditions.

With the return of Matshana kaMondise to the border in 1858, the Zulu were granted a direct insight into the reality of life across the great divide. And Matshana would be proved right in his warnings – there was certainly far worse to come, and his old nemesis, Theophilus Shepstone, would again be right there at the centre of events.

# 6

# 'The power to control the Zulus'

## Shepstone crowns a King

Some time in September or October 1872, old King Mpande died. He had grown enormously fat in his later years – so much so that his attendants had wheeled him about in a small hand-drawn cart – but although physically impaired his mind had remained as sharp as ever and he had managed to retain some semblance of authority until he finally succumbed to old age, the only one of Senzangakhona's extraordinary and tempestuous sons to do so.

News of his death was kept from the population until the burial ceremonies had been properly done – and until his successor had secured his grip on the reins of power. Mpande's body was drawn into a sitting position and bound tight with leather *reims*, wrapped in a fresh bullock's hide and left, with the head exposed, in his hut. There it was watched over for days by his senior councillors and female attendants – who survived their ordeal by blocking their noses with sweet-smelling herbs – until it had desiccated. Then his closest attendants dug a grave at the top of the great central enclosure at his favourite homestead at kwaNodwengo, a large pit with one side hollowed out where the body was carefully propped in place. The king's personal possessions were placed into the grave – his spears were broken so as to prevent his spirit wreaking havoc from the afterlife – and then, at the last minute, two of Mpande's wives and one of his body-servants were swiftly and efficiently killed, grabbed from behind and their necks twisted so sharply that they snapped cleanly. As was customary, their bodies too were placed in the grave, to attend their master among the spirits.[1] The grave was then filled in and fenced off with stout wooden posts – and the whole of kwaNodwengu abandoned. Cetshwayo would later build a new complex of the same name two or three kilometres away but the old one could not be defiled, now that the king was dead, by the living, and the huts – over a thousand of them – and the

great surrounding palisades were simply allowed to collapse and rot away
with time.

The last decade of the late king's life had been characterized by a subtle
power struggle with his son Cetshwayo. Since Cetshwayo's victory over his
rival Mbuyazi in 1856, no serious challenger to the succession had dared
declare himself inside Zululand, but a number of his remaining brothers
had taken advantage of the confusion to place themselves safely out of
Cetshwayo's reach across the border. Mpande maintained a clandestine
communication with them, and used them to retain the last vestiges of his
control over Cetshwayo, tweaking his son's ambition by hinting that he
might yet bestow his official support upon first one, then another. It was a
situation which had further corroded the central authority of the state as
both the king and his would-be heir manoeuvred to secure support among
the country's powerful regional barons, buying allegiances at the price of
granting increased local autonomy. It exaggerated the national tendency
towards friction between the generations, too, as Mpande appealed to the
innate conservatism of elderly *amakhosi* who had enjoyed their power and
privilege since Shaka's day while Cetshwayo worked to build up his power
base among young and hungry men of his own age.

More dangerously, both parties flirted with the settler states on the
Zululand borders, jockeying to achieve support from the Governments of
Natal and the Transvaal. Although there was widespread lingering resentment within Zululand at the means by which Mpande had secured the
throne, the fact remained that where the whites had played kingmaker once
they might undeniably do so again. To the irritation of traditionalists, both
the king and his would-be successors had little choice but to tacitly
acknowledge a harsh political truth – that the affairs of the Zulu royal
house were no longer, as they had been in King Shaka's day, entirely the
prerogative of the Zulu alone. But in coaxing and wheedling white support,
in knowingly trying to play on the European hunger for land, trade and
labour to their own advantage, the competing players unleashed complex
and variable elements which they could not hope to fully control.

In 1856, shortly after the battle on the Thukela, Princes Mkhungo and
Sikhotha had slipped across the border into Natal. Cetshwayo had indignantly pressed for their return, but Shepstone had recognized their value
as hostages to the future fortunes of Zululand, and had refused. Mkhungo
was a mere lad at the time, and Shepstone had spotted an opportunity to
inculcate in him an appreciation of British imperial ideology. He gave him

into the care of the head of the Anglican Church in Natal, Bishop John Colenso.

Colenso himself had not been in southern Africa for long, but he was already developing a searching interest in its affairs, including those of the neighbouring Zulu kingdom. A Cornishman, born in St Austell in 1814, Colenso's early life had been characterized by hard work and a dogged determination to overcome misfortune. The family assets had been ruined when the sea flooded a tin mine in which his father had invested heavily, and Colenso had been obliged to pay his own way through Cambridge University by working as a private tutor. After graduation he had taken up teaching, and had written successful mathematical textbooks before turning his diligent and rigorously inquiring mind to theology. In 1846 he had entered the Anglican Church, and seemed destined for a quiet career as a country parson in a Norfolk village until a chance meeting with Robert Gray, the Bishop of Cape Town, led to an invitation to become the first Bishop of Natal. Colenso had arrived in the colony in 1853, trailing his wife Frances and their young family in his wake, and had established a home at Bishopstowe, outside Pietermaritzburg.

Unwilling, in contrast to many missionaries, to distance himself from the life of his potential converts, Colenso had found himself re-examining his Christian doctrine through African eyes. In time he would become a forthright and steadfast critic of imperial policies towards the black population in both Natal and Zululand, but in 1856 he had not yet discerned the ruthlessness which lay beneath Shepstone's paternalistic mask, and had been willing enough to accept the tutelage of Mkhungo:

> If ever the British Government interferes, as I imagine some day it must, in the affairs of Zululand, a youth like this, civilised, and (may God in His mercy grant it) Christianised, would surely be the person whose claim would be most likely to receive our support, more especially as he is even now regarded, both by friends and foes, as the rightful successor to Panda's authority.[2]

That Mkhungo was openly spoken of as 'the rightful successor' in Natal had intensified Cetshwayo's frustration, the more so as both Mkhungo and Sikhotha had drawn a number of their followers into exile after them. The Natal authorities had settled them in one of the locations, and over the years their community grew as each political crisis in Zululand produced a new trickle of refugees. While they had left Zululand for varied reasons, these people shared a common antipathy to Cetshwayo's succession, and they formed a significant body of dissent living beyond his control, yet worryingly close to the border. They maintained a distinctly Zulu identity and kept themselves aloof from the Natal chiefdoms and, ominously, identified themselves by the name of Prince Mbuyazi's defeated faction in the struggle of 1856 – the iziGqoza. Their potential for mischievous intervention in Zulu affairs was not lost on Cetshwayo – nor upon Theophilus Shepstone.

Mkhungo's presence at Bishopstowe also threw an unexpected political highlight upon the activity of white missionaries in Zululand. The history of mission activity in Natal was almost as old as white settlement at the port, and in the 1830s an American mission society had established a station inside Zululand itself. It had not lasted long – chased out by Dingane's war with the Voortrekkers – and Mpande had been initially cautious in allowing missionaries to return. His attitude had changed after the war between the princes in 1856, however, and he had allowed a number of Norwegian Lutheran and British Anglican missions to build stations, although he had been careful to place them in districts already exposed to white traffic. He had no interest in their teachings, of course, but their presence was a connection to the white world, and a subtle reminder to Cetshwayo that the elderly king still had the ability to influence the aspirations of his sons in exile. In 1869 Mpande had gone so far as to allow Germans from the Hermannsburg Mission Society to settle the slopes of the Ncgaka mountain, near the Phongolo river. This was a long way from the centre of royal authority, way up on the northernmost point of the contested border where the claims of the Zulu royal house overlapped those of not only the Transvaal Republic but of the neighbouring Swazi kingdom. By granting the Germans permission to settle there, Mpande had not only established his own authority in the region but had effectively established a door to the wider world beyond.

For the most part, while the missionaries seem to have accepted Mpande's goodwill at face value, they were well aware of their position at the sharp end of the conflict between African and European value-systems. Cut off among the rolling hills, small islands of European belief in a traditional landscape, they would win few converts. The Zulu people proved too attached to their beliefs, to the links which bound them to their ancestors, and too sceptical of the cultural changes that came with conversion – the setting aside of polygamous marriage, the wearing of European clothes, the adoption of the principles of the capitalist economy – to willingly embrace Christianity. Frustrated, many missionaries allowed themselves to become embroiled in politics, accepting the hospitality of their Zulu hosts while at the same time urging their sponsors in Natal to intervene to reduce the power and influence of the Zulu kings, to weaken the Zulu sense of pride and self-reliance and so make them more receptive to alien teachings of salvation.

Prince Cetshwayo – and many young Zulus like Mehlokazulu kaSihayo, who took their cue from him – instinctively understood the threat that the missionaries posed, and resented them for it. A traditionalist himself, Cetshwayo recognized their role in the advance across southern Africa of the British Empire – 'first comes the trader', he is supposed to have said, 'then the missionary. Then the Red Soldier.'[3]

In 1861 the flight of two other of Cetshwayo's bothers – this time to the Transvaal – almost brought about a war between Zululand and its neighbours. Princes Mthonga and Mgidlana had suddenly made a dash for the western boundary. As soon as he heard the news, Cetshwayo sent word to Sihayo instructing him to muster his fighting men to intercept them. Sihayo successfully blocked the Rorke's Drift route but the two princes had struck further north, slipped past him, and reached the Boer settlement at Utrecht in safety. For several days Sihayo's men had lingered in the hills nearby in the hope that the Boers might be frightened into giving up the fugitives. The Utrecht burghers went into a *laager* and rumours swept down the border into Natal that either Cetshwayo was preparing to invade the Transvaal – or Natal, or both – or that the Boers, in concert with Theophilus Shepstone, were preparing to invade Zululand. In the event, Cetshwayo was forced to recall Sihayo and endure a public rebuke from his father, but the princes remained in Utrecht.

In order to secure their return Cetshwayo had then embarked on a dangerous course which complicated the already tense situation in the disputed territory. According to the Boers, he offered territorial concessions in return for the surrender of Mthonga and Mgidlana. The exact nature of the negotiations was hotly contested afterwards, and indeed any promises made by Cetshwayo were never ratified by the king and his council, but the discussions had strengthened the resolve of many in the Utrecht community to push their claims further east into Zululand itself. In the end, the two princes had become too hot for the burghers to handle and they were finally returned to Zululand. This success would, however, buy Cetshwayo little lasting comfort. Although Mgidlana renounced his claim to the succession and would remain in Zululand, Mthonga was destined to escape again a few years later.

The Boers had also felt emboldened enough to press their claim. In 1864 they had marked out what they considered to be the border by erecting a chain of stone beacons. This incorporated not only much of the country between the Mzinyathi and the Ncome rivers, but a slice of land lying further east, including a swathe of country Mpande had given to the amaQungebeni. Sihayo himself had been obliged to walk the Boers up onto the top of the Nquthu hills and point out to them where, in his opinion, the true border lay.[4]

All of this had served to create in the minds of a good many Zulus, not just the border communities but those at the centre of power, something of a siege mentality, a feeling that they were permanently under threat from neighbours whose motives they could neither fully understand nor trust.

For Cetshwayo, the death of his father in 1872 had brought little immediate reassurance. He was now in the prime of life; in his forties, he had a pleasant, open face and the typical upright carriage and strong thighs of the sons of the royal house. He was considered a good-looking and attractive man despite a rather taciturn manner and a temper which, though seldom unleashed, could be fierce and intimidating. King Mpande had delayed longer than usual permission for Cetshwayo's *ibutho*, the uThulwana, to marry, fending off for as long as possible public recognition of his son's manhood, but he had not been able to delay the inevitable indefinitely and Cetshwayo was already married to the first of his wives, and wearing the head-ring, by the time of his accession.

But if he was young, vigorous and good-looking, he remained troubled by the nagging fear that, even at the eleventh hour, a fresh challenge might emerge to cheat him of his birthright. The émigré princes beyond the border posed the most obvious threat, but it was even rumoured that Prince Mbuyazi had survived the slaughter on the banks of the Thukela all those years before, and had been living secretly in Natal under Shepstone's wing, waiting for the right moment to return.[5]

Cetshwayo's insecurities were compounded by the uncertain political landscape within Zululand itself. Many of the powerful regional barons had grown used to running their own affairs and it was difficult to calculate where their loyalties lay. In particular, in the northern reaches of the kingdom, along the foothills of the Lebombo mountains, lay the territory of the Mandlakazi, a section of the Zulu royal house who traced their descent from Senzangakhona's father, Jama. Blood relatives of the king, the Mandlakazi *amakhosi* regarded themselves as allies rather than subjects of the Zulu state. In Mpande's time the head of the Mandlakazi, Maphitha kaSojiyisa, had been one of the most influential men in the kingdom, and Mpande had seldom acted without first securing his support. Maphitha had recently died, and Cetshwayo had intervened to secure the succession for Maphitha's young, thrusting and ambitious son Zibhebhu. Even so, it was not entirely clear whether Zibhebhu could be relied upon to return the favour.

There was, moreover, at least one other potential claimant within the kingdom. King Mpande had fathered a son, Prince Hamu, who was raised as the heir to the estate of Mpande's dead brother, Nzibe. As such, Hamu was technically debarred from contesting the succession, but he was a powerful man who maintained an impressive court of his own, and was widely known to resent Cetshwayo's ascendancy. Hamu lived in the north, where his territory bordered that of the Mandlakazi – together, if they so chose, they could provide a powerful axis of opposition.

Faced by a nightmare scenario in which his exiled rivals might combine with colonial supporters and internal dissidents to overthrow him, Cetshwayo took an extraordinary decision as he began to plan the ceremonies that would install him as king. He decided to invite Theophilus Shepstone to attend on behalf of the Natal government.

This was certainly a bold move – it would turn Shepstone from a potential opponent to a very public supporter, harnessing the European factor to Cetshwayo's cause and effectively cutting the ground away from under the feet of his rivals, but even as he made it Cetshwayo knew it was also a risky one. He risked the alienation of many of his most senior councillors, men who had served Mpande and even Dingane before him, men for whom the idea that the Zulu kingship needed validation by outsiders was anathema. And in any case, if Shepstone were to accept, it posed a clear and dangerous question – what exactly would he hope to gain from the exercise in return?

*

The Zulu deputation arrived at Shepstone's offices in Pietermaritzburg on 26 February 1873. 'The Zulu Nation', it complained, 'wanders', and it begged Shepstone to intervene to establish a sense of order 'wanting among the Zulu people'.[6]

For a man who thought of himself as a benign Shaka, a kingmaker adroit enough to interfere in the affairs of sovereign states and manipulate them to Britain's advantage, it was an appeal too ripe with possibilities for him ever seriously to contemplate refusal. In the years since the Matshana affair, Shepstone had grown more confident in his position, managing not only Natal's African affairs but cultivating diplomatic contacts deep into the heart of independent southern Africa, advising, suggesting, and shaping the policies of African rulers who as yet had had little other contact with imperial Britain. And his vision had grown along with his reach, for while he still saw Natal as Britain's gateway to Africa, he had begun to recognize both the Transvaal Republic and the Zulu kingdom as obstacles to this and to ponder how they could be outmanoeuvred. It had, by 1873, become increasingly clear that his earlier dalliance in Zulu affairs had not been entirely successful. So far from proving a compliant stooge, Prince Mkhungo had distanced himself from Bishop Colenso, and his continued presence in Natal, along with several of his brothers, had largely cost Shepstone any influence he might have enjoyed over Cetshwayo. The coronation invitation, however, offered him an unexpected opportunity to place himself at the very centre of Zulu affairs, and with the new king firmly in his debt. With this greater prize now in view, Shepstone was content to drop his support for the émigré princes. In a telling remark which hints at something of his broader vision, he admitted that the invitation gave him the chance to achieve 'a good deal of additional influence and real power, not only over the Zulus, but over all the other native powers of South East Africa, for the power to control the Zulus includes that to control all the rest'.[7]

It is debatable whether his position, even under its broadest remit, sanctioned so blatant an interference in the affairs of a sovereign state, but while the Colonial Office in London was wary of any commitments which might flow from it – Shepstone was refused permission to take an escort of imperial troops, and strictly admonished not to try to win territorial concessions from Cetshwayo – it did not forbid it, and there was a significant undercurrent of support within settler society from those who aspired to access to Zulu labour and markets.

The coronation ceremonies were fixed for the beginning of September 1873 – a year after Mpande had died. They were to take place both in the emaKhosini valley – the place of the kings, where Shaka's ancestors lay buried – and at the eMlambongwenya royal homestead, east across the Mfolozi Mhlope, not far from the ruins of kwaNodwengo. It seems that Cetshwayo saw no need for Shepstone to be present for the most powerful and potent part of the ceremony, the propitiation of the ancestors at emaKhosini; instead the two were to meet at eMlambongwenya.

When Shepstone crossed the border at the lower Thukela drift on 8 August, he was accompanied by an escort from the settler Volunteer Corps (or Volunteers) with two light field-guns drawn by the Durban Volunteer Artillery. And on his staff was one imperial officer, Anthony William Durnford, whose complex and enigmatic personality would be at the heart of the iSandlwana drama.

Anthony Durnford was born into a distinguished military family on 24 May 1830 at Manor Hamilton in Leitrim, Ireland. His father, Edward William Durnford, was then a lieutenant in the Royal Engineers attached to the Ordnance Survey. The Durnfords had a long association with the Royal Engineers – there had been a member of the family in the corps since 1759 – and it is unlikely that Anthony ever seriously considered an alternative career. He was educated in Ireland before being sent, like many sons of the minor gentry of the day who had cosmopolitan aspirations, to a private school in Germany. In September 1846, at the age of sixteen, he entered the Royal Military Academy at Woolwich. While the leading graduates each year traditionally elected to join the Artillery, Anthony Durnford's ambitions were never in doubt: on 27 June 1848 he was commissioned as a second lieutenant into the Royal Engineers. He was then posted to their barracks at Chatham for specialist instruction, where his commanding officer astutely noted the personality traits which would define his professional career – his 'intelligence, abilities, zeal and high principles'. It was, of course, far too soon to observe another enduring characteristic – a perverse and damaging streak of bad luck that would seem to dog him throughout his life.[8]

Despite this early distinction, Durnford's career had quickly become humdrum. On leaving Woolwich, Durnford had been posted first to Scotland and then, in October 1851, to Trincomalee in Ceylon (Sri Lanka). Here he devoted his professional energies to civil engineering projects, including improving the colony's roads, and his spare time to the rather boyish and repetitive pursuits which passed for social life among the colony's introverted and predominantly male-ruling elite:

'Twas our custom to dine with each other in turn, every man bringing his own dinner, there being no mess ... One of the most common dinners was mulligatawny soup, roast foul and plantain fritters ... On moonlight nights as the midnight hour drew near we often had our tables set outside in the grassy quadrangle and there with converse and cheroots, whiled away the time till nearly daylight when we all retired, the lazy ones to lie in bed till 9 or 10, the active ones for an hour or so till dawn, when a brisk gallop on horseback round the inner harbour followed by a bath, braced one up a little to encounter the intense heat of the day.[9]

There were some racier distractions. It was in Trincomalee that Durnford first developed a taste for gambling that would continue throughout his life, a passion which reveals a hint of recklessness not altogether compatible with Durnford's own view of himself as a man of impeccable integrity. Even at this early age, it seems, he was not able to sublimate entirely a curious lack of judgement, a character trait which would mature in time – and under a burden of bitter experience – into a streak of self-doubt and loathing.

It was in Trincomalee, too, that Durnford married. On 15 September 1854 he wed Frances Catherine Tranchell at St. Francis's Church. It was, by the standards of the day, a good marriage for an aspiring career soldier, since Frances was the youngest daughter of a retired lieutenant-colonel in the Ceylon Rifles; yet it is a truism of Army life that the combination of a heavy workload, a deeply unsettled lifestyle and uncertain prospects militated against the success of an early marriage. 'Lieutenants may not marry, Captains should marry, Colonels must marry' ran the saying, and Durnford's haste to the altar while still a lieutenant in his twenties perhaps offers a further glimpse of his impatience. If so, he was to pay a hard price for it, for the marriage was not to last.

In 1854 Great Britain embarked upon its one great conventional war of the Victorian era – the campaign to reduce Tsarist Russian influence in Asia, waged on the Crimean peninsula alongside curious allies – the French,[10] the Turks and the Sardinians. It was immediately obvious to officers of Durnford's generation that this was perhaps a once-in-a-lifetime opportunity to test their professional skills – and, equally to the point, their personal courage and sense of honour – in the crucible of modern warfare. There was a rush of applications from around the Empire for active

postings, and Durnford was among them. In November 1855 his application was approved and he was ordered to proceed to Malta, where the
British reserve was assembled; here his family connections may have served
him well, for he was appointed adjutant to his father, who was commanding
the Royal Engineers there. Yet not for the last time in his career fate was to
thwart Anthony Durnford; his departure was delayed by a bad bout of fever
contracted in Ceylon, and it was not until March 1856 that he finally
reached Malta. It was a misfortune that cost him his chance of a baptism
of fire, for the war was almost over and he would never reach the front. It
was a bitter disappointment, no doubt made worse by the realization that
no less than six of the twelve lieutenants who had received their commis-
sions alongside him in 1848 had managed to see active service. Experience
of such a war would not only shape the attitudes of those who took part in
it, but frame friendships, alliances and mutual understandings which would
deeply affect future career paths – and Anthony Durnford was certainly
astute enough to realize this, and the nature of the club from which he had
been excluded.

This professional setback was mirrored by a deeper personal tragedy. In
1856, while stationed at Malta, Frances Durnford gave birth to a baby boy
who died shortly afterwards. While Durnford appeared to be reconciled to
the loss, he felt a sense of private despair, a profound disappointment at
the blows life had dealt him. Despite the birth of a daughter – named after
her mother – the following year, the strain took its toll on the marriage,
and Anthony and Frances began to drift apart. A spell of active service
might have distracted him and restored his sense of self-worth, but while
many of his colleagues were involved in fighting to suppress the Indian
Mutiny, or trying to open China to British influence at the point of the
bayonet, Durnford was sent back to England. When, in 1860, Frances bore
a third child, Julia, and she too died, the marriage finally collapsed. Their
separation was not made public and the couple were never to divorce.
Durnford took the route well known to successive generations of Army
officers trapped in unhappy marriages, seeking overseas postings, and that
same year was sent on a four-year mission to Gibraltar.

If this new job offered some hope of a fresh start, it also served to keep
him away from a new wave of conflicts in the 1860s – the wars against the
Maori in New Zealand, and the first of the interminable series of entanglements on the North-West Frontier. Undoubtedly frustrated, Durnford took
matters into his own hands when the Gibraltar posting ended, applying for

and receiving permission to sail to China, apparently to join his fellow Royal Engineer Captain Charles George Gordon who had taken a commission from the Chinese Emperor. Once again, however, fate was to intervene, as Durnford was struck down with heat exhaustion en route and had to be hospitalized in Ceylon. By the time he recovered, Gordon's campaigning was drawing to a close and the moment had been lost. Durnford returned to England.

Then, at the end of 1871, Durnford was finally offered the appointment he had wanted for so long. There was a vacancy for a Royal Engineer officer in the Cape Colony, and Anthony Durnford grabbed it with both hands.

When he arrived at Cape Town in January 1872 there was outwardly much about him to impress a colonial society at the Cape which was no less introverted and self-conscious in its way than that of Trincomalee. He was forty-one years old, and physically in his prime – tall, upright, with sharp features and a set of side-whiskers running to a moustache impressive even by the standards of the day. He seemed at ease socially – only a rather cynical edge to his humour betrayed anything of his personal disappointments – and he wore about him an air of honour and integrity which greatly appealed to Victorian sensibilities. In his most widely published photograph – the one chosen to accompany eulogies after his death – he seems benign and self-assured, a man at ease with himself. Yet this was far from the truth, and in other, less guarded, images the mask slips, revealing something of the flint in his personality beneath.

For all that, Durnford quickly found that Africa suited him best of all his postings. His duties soon took him to the Eastern Cape, where the open big-sky country allowed him to revel in a physical lifestyle – riding over long distances, camping out, testing his impressions by seeing people and places for himself – which provided an antidote for a while to his internal woes. It was his first experience of a black African society, and he found much to admire in the Xhosa he met there, judging them 'honest, chivalrous and hospitable . . . Thoroughly good fellows'.[11] This was a view which was not shared, on the whole, by settler society, the first hint of damaging gulfs to come.

In May 1873 Durnford, recently promoted major, was posted to Natal to join the imperial garrison at Fort Napier in Pietermaritzburg, and his life now entered its most significant phase. Natal society was, if anything, even more claustrophobic than that at the Cape, and curiosity about the rather dashing new arrival allowed Durnford to mix freely with the handful of individuals who wielded power and influenced colonial opinion. He was immediately attracted to Shepstone, whose vision, energy and paternalistic approach towards the colony's African population Durnford admired. He was impressed, too, by Colenso whose controversial views challenged the many widespread assumptions held in settler society about the role of Christianity in British Africa.[12]

In many ways these two men, Shepstone and Colenso, reflected two distinct – and, as it turned out, conflicting – aspects of Durnford's own personality. Durnford was a Christian who accepted implicitly the essential righteousness of the British Empire, who believed that the expansion of British interests meant the furthering on a grand international scale of the public school ideology of duty, service to others, fair play and standing up for the underdog. It was the imperialist in him which responded to the vision espoused by Shepstone of an Africa dominated by British virtues, of African societies shorn of their perceived excesses, introduced to the self-evident benefits of capitalism and the Protestant work ethic, and managed in a fatherly manner and for their own good by British overlords. And it was Durnford's shared faith which drew him to Colenso too, and which led him to respect Colenso's readiness to expose the darker realities of imperial control, and in particular the way in which good governance seemed to be distorted by the settler need to appropriate land, exploit African labour and suppress African voices of dissent. Colenso held fast to the view that manifest injustices were not the inevitable consequence of British rule but were rather aberrations, the result of failures of principle perpetrated by flawed or self-serving individuals, and that these needed to be publicly challenged wherever he found them.

Shepstone, of course, knew better, but the gulf between their views was by no means obvious to Durnford when he arrived in Natal. The public stance adopted by both Colenso and Shepstone was a similar one, and the personal relationship between them was then amicable enough. Experience would soon disabuse all three, however, and over the next few years Durnford would vacillate uncomfortably between the two poles, sublimating his instinctive view – that Colenso's suspicions about practical imperialism in Natal were essentially correct – beneath his faith in the Crown and his obligation to serve it. 'Duty is duty,' he wrote, in the manner of a man long used to shutting away private pain and doubts, 'that is all that is clear to me.'[13]

*

When Shepstone set out to attend Cetshwayo's coronation ceremonies in August 1873 – he had already taken to himself the right to 'crown' the new king – Durnford was invited to join his staff on the pretext that as a Royal Engineer he was to map the route into the Zulu heartland.[14] It was just the sort of adventure he had come to enjoy, and he was delighted to accept. Allowed to ride about freely to survey the landscape, he was able to observe the Zulu lifestyle and to mix with the people, and he discerned in them a freedom of spirit which was in marked contrast to that displayed by Natal's black population. Most ordinary Zulus, he noted, greeted passing whites with open curiosity and good humour, and he saw no trace of subservience in the manner of the *amakhosi* he met. The Zulu, it was clear enough even to a committed imperialist like Durnford, were kings in their independent country, and the pretensions of settler society cut no ice there. He found it rather refreshing.

It took Shepstone's party a fortnight to reach the Mthonjaneni heights, the great high ridges overlooking the valley of the Mfolozi Mhlope where the Zulu kingdom had first been born. In that time, though Shepstone did not know it, Cetshwayo had already been proclaimed king by traditional rite. Cetshwayo had been living at the oNdini homestead, and from there he had made a grand ceremonial procession to the *emaKhosini* valley accompanied by his attendants and assembled *amabutho*. He had delayed there for several days, performing ritual cleansing ceremonies while he waited for the northern *amakhosi* to join him. There had been a tense moment when Zibhebhu and Hamu, accompanied by thousands of their followers, had come into sight, and Cetshwayo's men had nervously shuffled into a battle formation, but to everyone's relief the northern barons had come in peace. By this time Shepstone had reached the appointed rendezvous at eMlambongwenya, but Cetshwayo's councillors fobbed him off for several days until the last of the traditional ceremonies had been completed. Already, when Shepstone and Cetshwayo finally met on 1 September, many of the crowd had begun to disperse.

Shepstone's 'coronation' of King Cetshwayo is one of those bizarre moments that were occasionally thrown up in the heyday of British imperial pretension. Against a background of golden winter hillsides, Shepstone, dressed in full diplomatic regalia, placed a theatrical crown – made specially for the occasion by a military tailor in Pietermaritzburg – on Cetshwayo's head while a Durban photographer recorded the scene for posterity. Shepstone then delivered a long lecture on the theme of good government

– later he would claim it outlined binding conditions upon which British support for Cetshwayo would depend, but at the time it seems that Cetshwayo merely thought it a lesson to his *amakhosi* and subjects on how they should behave.

In private Shepstone and Cetshwayo fenced about each other in the confines of the eMlambongwenya homestead as Shepstone sought to exact promises from Cetshwayo regarding the role of missionaries in Zululand and settler access to Zulu labour. Freed from his official duties, Durnford took the opportunity to explore the complex in the company of Bishop Hans Schreuder. A man of formidable intellect, many accomplishments – he bolstered a classical education with a mastery of carpentry and black-smithing – and a notoriously strong will, Schreuder had cultivated the friendship of King Mpande and had secured permission to establish a station at eNtumeni as long ago as 1850. A Norwegian Lutheran, he was perhaps the most prominent of the Zululand missionaries and his under-standing of Zulu affairs was such that Shepstone had invited him to join his escort as an unofficial political adviser – something which was not lost on Cetshwayo. Schreuder explained to Durnford the significance of the *isigodlo* – the king's private quarters, where outsiders were prohibited on pain of death – and introduced Durnford to members of the royal family. Durnford witnessed the assembly of the *amabutho* and was struck by the grandeur and solemnity of the occasion. 'They sang a war-song,' he wrote, 'a song without words, wonderfully impressive as the waves of sound rose, fell and died away again, then rose again in a mournful strain, yet warlike in the extreme.'[15]

At the climax of the ceremony Shepstone's party fired a seventeen-gun salute from the two light field-guns his escort had brought with them, and in response Cetshwayo's men struck up a loud rhythmic ritual challenge by drubbing their shields sharply with their sticks and spears. Shepstone's escort were dismounted, and the sudden brittle cacophony startled the horses which reared and plunged, struggling to break free from the horse-holders, and it was a few minutes before order was restored. Durnford noted the incident. He would return to Natal with two distinct impressions of the expedition: that the Zulu were a formidable people, and that the Natal Volunteers could not be compared to regular troops in discipline and training.

In the final analysis, Shepstone's coronation jaunt had proved to be something of a political stand-off. While both Shepstone and Cetshwayo had secured immediate goals, both had hoped for something more, and both were to remain disappointed. A small incident, inconsequential in itself, took place which perfectly parodied the hollow posturing that lay beneath the encounter. Shepstone, in accordance with his sense of public dignity when attending African events, maintained on his staff his own praise-singer. One morning the royal homestead woke to the sound of a noisy altercation; it was the custom, when the king was in residence, for the royal praise-singer to announce the new day by reciting his praises, and on this occasion Shepstone's man had felt obliged to challenge the right. Within a few minutes,

> ... each [was] yelling out the string of praises of their respective Chiefs ... and trying to outdo each other. At last they got so excited, being urged on by the crowd of whites and blacks who had formed a ring about them, that they were very nearly coming to blows. Seeing the matter was getting serious, I stepped in and separated them by taking Cetywayo's [sic] man away. The scene had indeed been highly diverting. The lively and extraordinary grimaces and the other visual contortions of the men must have been very edifying to anyone who had never witnessed such a scene before ... .[16]

When the ceremonies at last finished, a crowd of thousands started to disperse, and long lines of people began threading through the hills on the long walk back to their homes in the far corners of the kingdom. Even as Shepstone and his party returned to the Thukela, the new king turned his attention to practicalities. On the undulating plain just a few kilometres from his father's grave, in sight of the crumbling ruins of kwaNodwengo, Cetshwayo pointed out a patch of gently sloping ground above the Mbilane stream, and instructed his followers to build him a new royal homestead there. Young men were sent out to cut saplings and women to gather grass, and work began on a complex that, by the time it was complete, numbered as many as 1,200 huts. Cetshwayo named it oNdini, after his homestead near the coast,[17] and it was perhaps the largest and most impressive of all the great Zulu royal homesteads, rivalling even King Dingane's fabled eMgungundlovu in its splendour. In that, it reflected not only Cetshwayo's personal optimism for the future, but his sense of the grandeur and power of his people.

Back in Pietermaritzburg, Shepstone proclaimed the expedition a great success. He had, he claimed, secured a lasting influence over the affairs of the Zulu kingdom, though this was greeted with considerable scepticism. Even among a colonial society wary of Zulu power and economic independence, there were those who found the image of Shepstone draping Cetshwayo in a coloured mantle and placing a tinsel crown upon his head as absurd as it seems to modern sensibilities. 'The tin-pot coronation of Cetewayo is laughed at everywhere,' wrote one observer, 'except where the farce has been used to make capital of.'[18]

Just what capital would be made of it remained to be seen, but no sooner was Shepstone back in Natal than his handling of the colony's African affairs was plunged into a new and desperate crisis, one which would not only expose the true nature of his administration, but which would have bitter personal consequences for Anthony Durnford, and foreshadow the greater calamity that waited in the wings for the Zulu kingdom itself.

# 7

# 'Will no one then stand by me?'

## The blooding of Anthony Durnford

If Shepstone's coronation expedition had failed overly to impress Natal's white settlers, its effect on one of the most powerful and prestigious of the colony's black chiefdoms was, by contrast, little short of startling. In 1873 the amaHlubi people were living in a location at the foot of the central uKhahlamba mountains, south-west of the settler village of Ladysmith. Their history had been a chequered one which fully reflected the coastal strip's complex and entrenched rivalries. Originally a Sotho-speaking group from west of the mountains, they had crossed east at some indeterminate point in their past and settled along the upper Mzinyathi valley. They were, however, one of the first groups to be dislodged by the violence of the early nineteenth century, being driven out even before Shaka had scoured the riverbanks around Hlazakazi and Malakatha further downstream.[1] When their *inkosi* was killed, they had broken into groups and scattered into Natal or across the mountains into the interior, and it was not until after the death of Shaka that they had begun to gravitate home again, begging the protection of King Dingane. Dingane had allowed them to return to their ancestral lands under their young *inkosi* Langalibalele kaMthimkhulu. Langalibalele was an *inyanga* – spirit doctor – of note, accredited with the awesome ability to conjure rain, and after Dingane's fall his successor, Mpande, gradually became wary of Langalibalele's influence. In 1848 Mpande had sent a Zulu army to attack the amaHlubi, but Langalibalele's followers managed to avoid the worst of the onslaught. Realizing that their position had once again become untenable, Langalibalele had sent an urgent message to Shepstone begging for sanctuary in Natal. Shepstone had agreed, and for the second time in their history the amaHlubi had abandoned their homes and emigrated to safer pastures. Shepstone had apportioned them a strategic slice of land along the foothills of the mountains where they might serve as a buffer to protect the white farming community from opportunistic cattle raids by the Sotho peoples inland.

For many years Langalibalele had managed to remain on good terms with colonial authority. Several times during the 1850s he had supplied contingents of men at Shepstone's request to assist in various punitive campaigns – including, ironically, the botched attempt to capture Matshana kaMondise. At the same time, however, Langalibalele had been able to retain a good deal of traditional autonomy; he had held the annual ceremonies that ushered in the harvest each year, had reinvigorated the bonds between the people, their *inkosi* and the ancestors, and had even been allowed to raise *amabutho* from among his young men. His standing had grown among the black population on both sides of the border, to the extent that even King Mpande had been prepared to set past enmities aside and send to him on occasion to beg for rain.

It was this very prestige enjoyed by Langalibalele and his followers that increasingly made his white neighbours wary of him, however, a situation which was exacerbated in the early 1870s when the amaHlubi found themselves ideally placed to profit from a sudden and dramatic change in the economic fortunes of southern Africa.

In 1866 a bright pebble had been found on a farm belonging to the independent Griqua people, near the confluence of the Lekwa and Senqu rivers north of the Cape Colony; it turned out to be a 21.25-carat diamond, and when, in 1871, an even bigger one had been found on the neighbouring farm of the De Beers brothers, the world had rushed in. Thousands of hopeful prospectors staked their claims to a few crowded square metres of hard, dry soil, digging down in the hope that some small part of what would prove one of the world's richest diamond pipes might lie beneath their feet. The discovery of diamonds had galvanized British thinking about the Cape, for the first time wrenching the attention of imperial theorists away from the idea that the southern tip of Africa had no value beyond its strategic control of the maritime highways, and raising the intoxicating possibility that it might contain natural wealth of its own. The independence of the Griqua did not last long – the British adroitly redrew their political boundaries, narrowly beating the neighbouring Boer republic of the Orange Free State, and the diamond fields became a British possession. Within a decade their presence would tease the British into redefining their policies across the region as a whole, sending political shockwaves into communities far away from the diggings themselves.

As the bizarre chequerboard of open cuttings descended steadily into the ground, the ramshackle tents of the early prospectors gave way to a shanty town christened – with an inappropriate sense of grandeur – Kimberley, after the Secretary of State for the Colonies. By 1873 Kimberley had already become the second largest town in southern Africa. Yet even then its African population heavily outnumbered the European, for while the first diggers had been content to swing pickaxes and heft shovels themselves they had soon found it preferable to hire black workers to do it for them as the work had become more labour-intensive. There were too few workers to be found locally – the semi-arid landscape did not maintain a large population – but the profits to be made at the diggings soon attracted African workers from as far away as the Pedi kingdom in the northern Transvaal – and Natal. Gangs of migrant workers, sometimes organized in groups according to age, were dispatched by their *amakhosi* to work at the mines for months at a time, returning home laden with the blankets, clothes and manufactured utensils which constituted their wages – if they weren't robbed along the way.

Most prized of the exotic European luxuries given them were firearms. Paying for labour with guns was illegal, of course, but it was widely practised, the more so because the diggers could obtain poor-quality obsolete weapons for a fraction of the value of the labour for which they might be exchanged. As new economic highways began to emerge, fragile tracks which funnelled towards Kimberley from far distant centres of African population, so a trickle of labour moved in one direction, and European weapons in the other, passing to communities along the way which would one day use them to defend themselves against more forceful forms of European expansion.

Positioned with their backs to the mountains, the amaHlubi had perhaps been the chiefdom best placed in Natal to engage in the diamond industry, and to reap the profits in return. By 1873, however, the prevalence of guns among the amaHlubi had begun to alarm the Natal authorities, picking at that old and deepest of settler sores, the dread that the majority African population among whom they lived might secretly be arming in the hope of one day driving the white man back to the sea. In fact, there is no evidence that Langalibalele harboured any hostile intent towards either the authorities or his individual white neighbours, and the possession of stocks of firearms had more to do with the prestige they conferred than with any immediate plan to use them for military purposes. But the resident magistrate among the amaHlubi, the inflexible and disciplinarian John Macfarlane, was concerned that the accumulation of guns was an expression of dissent in itself, an assertion of independence that was entirely inappropriate in colonial Natal, and he began to press Langalibalele to surrender the weapons. Langalibalele, caught – as so many would be in the years to come – between the aspirations of his followers and the demands of colonial authority, squirmed and prevaricated but did nothing.

Macfarlane, of course, had passed his suspicions on to Theophilus Shepstone, and it was only a matter of time before messengers were sent to Langalibalele with the inevitable and dreaded summons. Langalibalele remembered only too well what had happened to Matshana kaMondise in similar circumstances – his own men had been there. Frightened that the messengers might be secretly armed, Langalibalele ordered them to be stripped and searched. The likely Government response to such provocative action was obvious enough – and when the messengers had left for Pietermaritzburg Langalibalele sat back to watch nervously for any signs of official retribution.

When troops were mustered near Ladysmith a few weeks later he interpreted this as the action to come, though it in fact had nothing to do with his own burgeoning crisis. Shepstone had called out the colonial Volunteers to accompany him on his expedition to Cetshwayo's coronation, but Langalibalele's spies had jumped to the conclusion that they were in fact mustering to attack them. The amaHlubi promptly hid their cattle among their neighbours and Langalibalele gathered his followers to hold a cleansing ceremony to ward off the looming evil. The reports of bodies of armed men making their way to his homestead only further aroused the fears of his neighbouring settlers that they were about to attack. By the time Shepstone returned from Zululand in the middle of September, a confrontation seemed inevitable. It seemed to him that Langalibalele and the amaHlubi had embarked on a deliberate course of defiance, and even before any illegal act had been committed, he confided to the Lieutenant-Governor of Natal, Sir Benjamin Pine, that he was ready to make an example of them. 'The whole tribe, it seems to me, must be removed from where it is, and dispersed among the farmers.'[2]

Throughout October the Government drew up plans to surround and contain the amaHlubi location. During that time, no attack was made by the amaHlubi on the neighbouring white farmers or anybody else, and at last the Government received information that in fact Langalibalele was not planning an invasion – in fact he was preparing to migrate, once again, with his entire following. As he well knew from Matshana's experience, there was nowhere safe for him to go in Natal; instead, this time he intended to move over the uKhahlamba mountains, and seek refuge in the independent kingdom of BaSotholand beyond.

It is doubtful, in hindsight, whether BaSotholand ever really offered the sanctuary Langalibalele sought, for the kingdom had lost much of its power and independence in a series of wars in the 1850s, and it was now under a good deal of influence from the neighbouring Cape Colony. But the move would, at least, place Langalibalele beyond the immediate reach of the vengeful Shepstones, and by adopting an essentially passive resistance Langalibelele hoped to avoid the worst of the authorities' wrath. In fact, there was nothing in the Natal statutes – either under European law or the rather more convoluted and ambiguous assumptions of 'native law' – to define mass emigration as an illegal act. Nevertheless, it was a significant affront to the dignity of the colonial administration, and one that set an uncomfortable precedent. While it was common in African societies for groups to express their discontent by placing themselves beyond the reach of an unpopular overlord and seek the protection of another, it was not a concept the British administration – which ideologically believed itself to be superior to indigenous forms of government – could afford to accept, and when he heard of the plan Pine directed that troops should be deployed prevent the amaHlubi from escaping.

And therein lay the first problem. The mountains consisted of by far the most difficult and inhospitable terrain in the colony, and any strategy of containment was bound to be hampered not merely by a shortage of troops – there was, typically, only one regular infantry battalion stationed in Natal at the time – but by inadequate mapping. The mounted Volunteer Corps maintained by the Natal authorities had the advantage of mobility and an understanding of local conditions, but the vast majority of its members had no more experience of practical soldiering than their annual training camps. Its numbers were tiny, too, and it would need to be supported by any African auxiliaries who could be procured from Shepstone's 'loyal' *amakhosi.*

The senior military officer in Natal was Colonel Milles of the 75th Regiment, and, on arrival in Natal, Anthony Durnford had been offered a post on his staff as Colonial Engineer. Durnford had more understanding of local affairs than Milles, and as a Royal Engineer he was thus the obvious choice to draw up the plan of campaign. Durnford himself was delighted at this unexpected turn of events, which promised, at long last, to give him his first taste of active service.

Initial reports suggested that the amaHlubi would leave the colony by the most direct route. The Bushman's river bisected their location and it was possible to follow its course upstream to its source, a cleft on the very top of the mountains dignified with the name of the Bushman's River Pass. Preventing them passing through was problematic; if the British troops pushed into the location from the neighbouring white farms downstream on the Bushman's, there was a real danger that they would merely hurry the amaHlubi away from them and over the pass. Instead Durnford proposed sending light flying columns up other passes which flank the Bushman's, to converge on the summit and block Langalibalele's escape route.

It was a strategy which should certainly give Government forces the initiative, but it would depend for its success on rapid movement, good coordination of the units, and a mastery of the terrain at least equal to that enjoyed by the amaHlubi on their home ground. In the event, none of these elements would be forthcoming.

The troops – woefully inadequate, in retrospect, for the purpose – duly assembled towards the end of October in the foothills on either side of Langalibalele's location. To the north – flanking Langalibalele to the right – a force of African auxiliaries raised by a local magistrate, Captain Allison, was to ascend by means of a pass marked on the inadequate maps as the Champagne Castle Pass. To the south, below the Bushman's river, a detachment of Natal Volunteer Corps troops were to ascend the Giant's Castle Pass. These were given to the command of Anthony Durnford.

It was a moment Durnford had waited twenty years for – at last he held an independent command in a battle under a plan of his own devising. He must have looked forward to it all the more eagerly because there was a distinct possibility that he would need considerable mettle to accomplish his objectives – in Pietermaritzburg all the talk was that the troops would have to face 'a real army of bloodthirsty rebels'.[3]

At the last minute, however, Lieutenant-Governor Pine issued an order which would severely compromise Durnford's freedom of action. Fearful that an open clash with the amaHlubi might provoke a much wider African rising, Pine ordered Durnford to try to assert the Government's authority without appearing the aggressor; he was ordered to use force only as a last resort and, in particular, not to fire the first shot. This was an entirely unrealistic demand in the circumstances, and one which was largely responsible for the debacle which ensued.

The mission was further complicated before it began by the selection of the troops placed under Durnford's command. Considering that the amaHlubi *amabutho* were thought to number several thousand men – armed with their Kimberley guns – his detachment was ludicrously small, just fifty-five men selected from the Natal Carbineers, the oldest of the Natal Volunteer Corps units. Formed of two troops, based at Pietermaritzburg and Karkloof, the Carbineers were mostly the sons of wealthy settlers who could ride and shoot. They looked smart enough in their dark blue uniforms with white facings and forage caps but, with the exception of a few former professionals, they had seen no shots fired in anger. Some, indeed, had been among the men present at Cetshwayo's coronation whose horses had panicked at the menacing sounds of the Zulu *amabutho*.

The white troops were bolstered by some of Shepstone's most reliable African supporters, twenty-five auxiliaries led by a young *inkosi*, Hlubi kaMota of the Tlokoa, a Sotho group originally from beyond the mountains which had sought refuge decades before in Natal.[4] The Tlokoa had been neighbours of the amaHlubi, and indeed Hlubi's name had been chosen by his father to honour the association between the two groups. Yet the Tlokoa had close links, too, with a community held in altogether higher regard by the authorities, the Edendale Christian mission settlement outside Pietermaritzburg.

The Edendale mission had been founded by Wesleyans in the 1840s, and most of its converts had been newcomers to Natal – Sotho, like the Tlokoa, or Swazi drawn to Natal by Wesleyan mission activity in Swaziland. The Edendale community had turned its back firmly on African traditional values, and had allied itself not merely with the authorities politically, but with the European way of life and values. As such, Shepstone had conferred on it a favoured status, and often relied upon it for support in return. Knowing that Durnford spoke no isiZulu, Shepstone offered to lend him Elijah Nkambule, a prominent Edendale elder who was employed by the authorities as an interpreter. With Nkambule went another Edendale man, Jabez Molife, a Tlokoa, and it was Molife who had suggested that his kinsman Hlubi might make a worthwhile leader of auxiliaries. Knowing that the Tlokoa shared the Sotho mastery of mountain ponies and were perfectly at ease in the high, rocky terrain where the campaign would be fought, Shepstone had readily agreed. The Tlokoa turned out dressed in European clothing – the ubiquitous hard-wearing yellow corduroy jackets and trousers which were commonplace among the farming community – but most carried traditional weapons and only a few had firearms; no one, Durnford included, seems to have thought to issue them with a supply of powder.

Durnford's force set out from the field headquarters on the borders of the amaHlubi location at 8.30 on the evening of 2 November 1873. Durnford planned to climb the Giant's Castle Pass overnight – a difficult enough task in the dark at the best of times – and arrive at the head of the Bushman's River Pass to rendezvous with Allison's party soon after daybreak the following morning.

Things went badly wrong from the start. A heavy, chilling drizzle descended over the foothills, and in the twilight the party began to wander from the track. The inadequacy of their intelligence soon proved painfully obvious; their maps were inaccurate, Hlubi's Tlokoa had only a hazy knowledge of the route, and Durnford had been in too much of a hurry to stop and interview local settlers who might have known the way. Their packhorses, carrying food and ammunition, soon trailed behind and contact with them was lost. As the country grew steeper, the men were forced to dismount and lead their horses. Ahead of them a great jutting wall of sandstone marked the position of the Giant's Castle cliffs, but with no clear pathway upwards, they drifted steadily to their left. During the night they struck a valley which seemed to lead upwards through the cliffs, and Durnford doggedly led them along it. When dawn broke the next morning, a dense and shimmering sea of mist hung over the foothills below, blotting out any landmarks. Durnford's plan had called for them to be at the head of the Bushman's River Pass by this time, but instead the mountains still towered above them and the outcrops known as the Giant's Castle were nowhere in sight.

The men were cold, exhausted and lost, and the strain had begun to affect their faith not only in their mission, but in Durnford's ability to command. Several of the Carbineers had straggled on the trail, and some had already dropped out. Having not served in action under Durnford before, and unused to the demands of professional soldiering, several of the Carbineers now looked for leadership to their drill instructor, Sergeant William Clark, a former regular with a good deal of practical soldiering in southern Africa behind him. Clark seems to have taken a dislike to

Durnford, and even before the party reached the summit he had emerged as a catalyst for dissent. On his part, perhaps influenced by doubts sown during the coronation expedition, Durnford seemed uncertain how best to control his men, taking refuge in an abrupt and distant manner which further exacerbated the tension.

Then, about 10.30 that morning, disaster struck. Durnford was leading his horse, a white BaSotho pony named Chieftain, up a steep slope through loose rock and grass made slippery by the rain, when the horse lost its balance and slipped backwards, pulling Durnford after him. Durnford fell 'and went head over heels like a ball, bounding down for about fifty yards [46 metres]'.[5] The nearest men rushed to his aid and helped him sit up, but he was badly hurt – there was a deep gash across his head and his left shoulder had been pulled out of its socket. The force of the fall had been such that his sword – given to him by his father – had been tossed out of the scabbard and the scabbard bent almost double. The men reset Durnford's shoulder and bathed his cuts, and, with typical determination, he insisted the expedition continue, according to his biographer, his brother Edward, merely remarking, 'I'm alright now, we must push on'.[6] He was helped onto Chieftain again and the advance continued, this time up slopes so steep that the men often had to crawl forward on their hands and knees, pressed in by steep cliff-faces on one side of them and dizzying drops on the other. They were nowhere near the Giant's Castle Pass; instead, ahead of them wound a steep staircase of rock named the Hlatimba Pass. As a second night fell, they struggled on, but at about 9 p.m., perhaps 130 metres below the summit, Durnford fainted from pain and exhaustion. There was hardly level ground enough for him to lie down, but a young trooper named Robert Erskine – whose father was Natal's Colonial Secretary – tended him until he recovered consciousness.

The party rested here a while. The men were shattered by their ordeal, and several more stragglers had fallen out. There were now just thirty-six white troopers and fifteen Sotho left in the corps, and many of the Carbineers had lost all confidence in their commanding officer.

By 11 p.m. Durnford had recovered, and was determined to continue. He could scarcely walk, however, and it took him two hours to cover the final distance to the top of the pass, helped on by three men – a Carbineer and two Tlokoa – who threw a blanket round his back and dragged him up holding the corners.

At the top of the pass Durnford allowed the men to rest briefly again.

The ascent had been a dreadful experience, and Durnford had suffered grievous injuries, but it says much for his determination that he allowed neither his own pain nor the difficulties endured by his men to deflect him from his commitment to duty.

Ahead of them, in the clear, bitterly cold moonlit air, stretched the undulating summit of the uKhahlamba, the mighty 'Barrier of Spears', the greatest mountain range in southern Africa. They were 11 or 12 kilometres from the head of the Bushman's River Pass, and a day late for the rendezvous with Allison's party, and at about 2.30 a.m. Durnford ordered the men forward again, riding ahead with some of the Tlokoa. They arrived at the head of the Bushman's River Pass at about sunrise on the morning of 4 November, to find a herd of cattle grazing nearby. The herdsmen were astonished to be suddenly confronted by white men on horseback, and one of them took up a gun, but was quickly disarmed. Durnford thought they must be Sotho, and asked them if they knew anything of Langalibalele's people; 'we are they', they replied simply. Looking down the pass in the early morning light, back into Natal, Durnford saw long columns of cattle and people toiling up towards him.

He had successfully intercepted at least part of the amaHlubi's flight, but it was already clear that his party was unsupported – there was no sign of Allison's men. In fact, Allison had found that the Champagne Castle Pass marked on his map simply did not exist, and with no way up through the rock-face had abandoned his mission. Durnford and his men were alone on the mountain top.

Unknown to Durnford, the people he saw below were merely the amaHlubi cattle guard. The majority of Langalibalele's people had already crossed over safely into BaSotholand, Langalibalele among them.

Durnford now found himself in a dangerous position. He was himself in a good deal of pain, and his left arm was useless, and his men, struggling up behind him, were exhausted, outnumbered and already discouraged. To him alone now fell the responsibility of stopping the amaHlubi flight, and while the damage to Government prestige if he failed was obvious enough, so too was the danger for his command.

Yet to Durnford the demands of duty were not easily evaded. He decided to try to stop the amaHlubi with the men at his disposal, and as his men reached the summit he placed them in a line across the head of the pass. To lift their spirits he ordered that one of the cattle grazing nearby be killed, but he refused to allow a shot to be fired in case it provoked a confrontation, and the Tlokoa had to stab several beasts before one fell. There was however no means of cooking the meat, and the men had little choice but to suck on strips of it raw.

By this time large numbers of amaHlubi men were emerging from the pass. Their *izinduna* seemed well aware of the danger of the situation, and tried to keep them under control, pushing and shoving them to keep them away from the troopers. Many of them took up a position among rocks on a hillock overlooking Durnford's men, however, and made a show of taunting the troops, sharpening their spears ostentatiously and pointing their guns. Durnford and the interpreter, Elijah Nkambule, went forward to talk to the amaHlubi leaders, who included Langalibalele's senior *induna*, Mabuhle.

Up to this point it seems that Durnford had hoped that a resolute show of force might have been enough to discourage the amaHlubi, and to persuade them to go back down the pass. Now, however, it was probably too late for this, as the weakness of Durnford's position was starkly obvious and, with Langalibalele already in BaSotholand, there was in any case no reason for the amaHlubi to return. Mabuhle, who clearly saw Durnford's hesitancy to employ open force, simply refused to take the amaHlubi back.

Their position was critical and Durnford rode back to his men. Elijah Nkambule was convinced that the amaHlubi were about to open fire, and Sergeant Clark was heard to say that if they stayed where they were they would all be killed. Exasperated, Durnford cried out 'Will no one then stand by me?' Trooper Erskine stepped forward and said 'I will, Major', and he was joined by Troopers Bond, Potterill, Spiers and Raw.[7] The rest seemed undecided, however, undermined by Clark's evident doubts.

Durnford then noticed that groups of amaHlubi seemed to be moving along rising ground to one side to cut off their retreat. Seeing that nothing could be done, he gave the order to abandon the head of the pass and retreat the way they had come. It was a crushing moment, to have to admit defeat after enduring so much, and the Carbineers were just moving off when the tension suddenly snapped. A Hlubi named Jantje kaSilele fired a single shot from the rocks, and a ragged volley broke out. As the bullets struck among them, all semblance of order collapsed among the Carbineers, and they put their spurs to their horses.

They were not quick enough, and Durnford and the men who had stood by him bore the brunt of the amaHlubi's fury. Trooper Erskine, Durnford's loyal supporter throughout, was struck in the body by a second shot from Jantje and fell dead from his horse. Trooper Bond was shot through the head, and a Tlokoa named Katana fell into the bed of a nearby stream. Trooper Potterill's horse was shot under him and he struggled free and set off after the retreating Carbineers at a run. Three amaHlubi overtook him, and Potterill turned to face them, only to be shot by the man nearest him, Latyinga. As Latyinga rushed forward to stab Potterill on the ground, a Carbineer turned, saw him, and shot him – and Latyinga fell dead across Potterill. It was too late to save Potterill, however, as the other two amaHlubi quickly speared him to death.

Durnford himself was now cut off with Nkambule alongside him. Nkambule's horse fell, and Durnford turned to try to haul him up onto his own horse, but as he tried to mount Nkambule was shot dead. Two amaHlubi grabbed Chieftain's bridle but the horse was plunging uncontrollably and Durnford managed to shoot both dead with his revolver. One of them had managed to stab at him twice before he fell, however, the blade grazing Durnford's side and running clean through his left elbow. Chieftain broke free and galloped after the retreating Carbineers.

A few hundred metres further on Durnford called on the men to rally, but it seems they did not or would not hear him. Sergeant Clark was by now in the lead, and pointed out ground ahead where he said it would be safer to make a stand. The party were still under fire, and Jabez Molife and another Tlokoa begged carbines from some of the troopers to fire at their pursuers. There was, however, no attempt to rally, and the party rode on until it reached the top of Hlatimba Pass, the route they had come up. Most of the amaHlubi gave up the pursuit after a few kilometres and were content to return to herd their cattle into BaSotholand, but a few shadowed Durnford's men as far as the pass. Here Durnford, still bleeding from his injuries and in a fury of frustration, tried to collect the men together. Seeing they would not respond, he turned Chieftain about to return to the scene of the flight, but Hlubi intercepted him and would not let him go. In truth, there was nothing for it but to return down that dismal pass leaving their dead on the field and their mission in tatters.

The party picked their way down from the mountains in a collective misery of pain and despair. When at last they reached field headquarters, Durnford submitted to only cursory medical attention before, hearing that detachments sent out to support him were apparently lost, setting off in driving rain to look for them. He was exhausted and his wounds stiff and sore but, characteristically, he sought relief in action from the overwhelming emotional turmoil which assailed him.

The expedition had been a military, political and personal disaster. Durnford would never fully recover from the physical or emotional pain he had suffered. The spear-thrust through his already injured left arm had destroyed the nerve, and he would never recover the use of his hand; for the rest of his life he would wear it thrust, Napoleon-like, into the front of his tunic, a lasting reminder of the sourness of his first taste of battle.

In the first hours after the descent, Durnford was tormented by the thought that the expedition's failure was his fault. The fate of young Erskine, who had stood by him throughout, particularly troubled him, and he wrote a few days later to Colenso that 'it is useless now to talk; all that remains is to bury the dead and avenge him'.[8] It was a comment born of the self-loathing which then consumed him, but his savage tone did not escape Colenso's notice, and it brought in reply an admonition that 'I, and we all, look to you to check when it can reasonably be checked, the effusion of blood.'[9] Durnford was cut by the rebuke; he replied that of course he only sought revenge in the context of an open and fair fight in the field, but it is hard to avoid the conclusion that he was losing faith in the idea that Victorian warfare was a gallant and knightly affair in which victory fell to the most honourable.

A few days later Durnford took a detachment of troops back to the now-deserted amaHlubi location, and up the course of the Bushman's river to the pass at the top. The weather continued to mirror the prevailing mood, a heavy drizzle giving way on the summit to bouts of driving rain and sleet. Most of Durnford's party this time were regulars; the Carbineers had been reluctant to return to the spot, even to bury their dead, and only one had agreed to accompany him – Theophilus Shepstone's son George. On the summit they found the bodies of the fallen Tlokoa and Carbineers, stripped and disembowelled according to local custom, lying cold and pale in the sodden grass. Charlie Potterill's right hand had been cut off, no doubt as a potent source of war medicine. The remains were collected and buried close together, and from each of the fallen Carbineers Durnford took a lock of hair and directed George Shepstone to pass it on to their relatives. The burial service was read by an Anglican vicar, George Smith, from the village of Escort below the escarpment, and cairns of stones were piled over the graves.

Nearby, the soldiers also found the body of one of the amaHlubi Durnford had shot, placed carefully between rocks and covered with his shield.
In a gesture which strikes right to the heart of his deeply ambiguous feelings
about the affair, Durnford ordered that he, too, be covered with stones.

If Durnford hoped that by laying the dead to rest he might assuage his
troubled conscience, he was soon to be disabused; by the time the party
returned to the bottom of the mountains, a campaign of retribution against
the amaHlubi – and those who had given them succour – had begun in
earnest. The amaHlubi location had been surrounded, and troops swept
through it looking for those Langalibalele had left behind. Mostly these
were women, children and the elderly – those unable to make the long haul
up the pass – but here and there they found a few men under arms whom
they took into custody or, if they displayed any sign of resistance, simply
shot. When it became obvious that the amaHlubi's neighbours, the Phutile
(amaNgwe) people, had sheltered some of Langalibalele's cattle, they too
found themselves at the sharp end of the Government's wrath. The Phutile
*inkosi* Mbalo was arrested, together with many of his fighting men, and all
firearms found in his location were confiscated. The Phutile herds were
appropriated wholesale, and those who resisted this were shot. Settler
volunteers wrote elated letters to the press exulting in the 'rabbit shooting'
they had enjoyed.

Indeed, for the most part the settler community heartily approved of
the severity of the retribution. They saw it as a means of cowing the African
population in the colony as a whole, but they recognized, too, the
commercial advantages it afforded; after formally dissolving the amaHlubi
and Phutile locations, Lieutenant-Governor Pine's last act of punishment
was to offer their lands to the white farming community.

Bishop Colenso was appalled. The whole affair had stripped away the
veneer of paternalism with which Shepstone had cloaked his actions and
opened Colenso's eyes to the realities of colonial rule – his personal
relationship with Shepstone would never recover. Colenso embarked upon
a long and very public campaign to publicize the injustice and brutality of
the official response, a crusade which would further set him at odds with
settler opinion. Indeed, it was the aftermath of Langalibalele's 'rebellion'
which marked his true emergence as a major figure in the struggle for
African rights in Natal, a struggle which would consume much of his
remaining life, and which would earn him the African name *Sobantu* – the
father of the people.

Anthony Durnford was deeply troubled, too, by the turn events had taken. It struck to the core of the beliefs he held most dear – that soldiering was an honourable profession and the British Empire a just cause. He wrote to his mother, 'There have been sad sights – women and children butchered by our black allies, old men too ... Thank God no woman or child was killed by my command, no old men either, but others have committed these atrocities for which there is no defence in my mind ...'[10]

And *inkosi* Langalibalele himself? Freedom proved as illusory in the great upland plateau of BaSotholand as it had done in the uKhahlamba foothills. On 7 December 1873, scarcely a month after the skirmish at Bushman's River Pass, Langalibalele was betrayed to the Cape colonial forces by his nervous Sotho hosts. Sent back to Natal, he was led in chains through the streets of Pietermaritzburg, where crowds jeered and spat upon him and Charlie Potterill's father – who had taken to drink since his son's death – dashed out of the crowd to strike him. A few weeks later the old *inkosi* was subjected to a show trial on a charge of high treason conducted under 'native law' before Sir Benjamin Pine. Pine was hardly a disinterested party, of course – and he was assisted by Theophilus Shepstone himself, by George Barter – a Captain in the Natal Carbineer who had been present with Durnford at the pass – and Major Erskine, the Colonial Secretary whose son Robert had been killed in the conflict. Langalibalele was allowed no lawyer to assist his case, and judgement was passed before all the evidence was heard. He was sentenced to be exiled from Natal for life, and dispatched to Robben Island, off Cape Town – neither the first nor last of a long line of southern African political prisoners to be consigned there.

Anthony Durnford had returned from the mopping-up operations in the locations to find himself the subject of a good deal of anger among the settler community. It was widely rumoured that he was critical of the Carbineers' behaviour at the pass, and their cause had been taken up in high dudgeon by the leading Pietermaritzburg paper, the *Natal Witness*. Durnford found his judgement and leadership openly ridiculed, and colonists sniggered and called him 'Don't Fire Durnford' in stage whispers as he passed by. It was a bitter blow for someone who placed such reliance on personal honour, and who had behaved with extraordinary courage throughout the affair, but he bore the slights largely without complaint until the death of his dog Prince – apparently poisoned – led him to abandon his lodgings in town and retire to a marquee inside the perimeter of the town's Fort Napier garrison.

He sought solace from his misgivings by taking up the cause of the Phutile. He had found 400 of them housed in the Pietermaritzburg jail, brought there on the same day as Langalibalele, and largely abandoned to their fate by the authorities. In a gesture calculated to distance himself from the hysterias of public opinion and to reassert his battered sense of justice, Durnford took them into the care of the Colonial Engineer's department. At first he employed them on road-building projects about the city, ensuring that they were at least well fed and well treated but, tiring of the triumphalism so rampant in Pietermaritzburg, he then volunteered to take them back to the mountains to block the passes between Natal and the interior. It was a gesture designed in part to reassure the upland farmers, and Durnford must have known that it was largely futile – that refugees and rustlers would still find ways to cross – but it offered him a typically energetic, practical and physical outlet for his frustrations. The Government agreed, no doubt relieved to be rid of him for a while, and for two months, from late May 1874, Durnford, a small escort and his Phutile labourers, camped out in the biting winds of the uKhahlamba winter, hewing boulders from the cliff-face by hand – they had no explosives – until the passes were blocked.

It was hard and uncomfortable work but it served to restore Durnford's moral compass. Although he never compromised his duty by criticizing the authorities' policies publicly, he would continue, often in the face of official opposition, to champion the cause of the Phutile – insisting on fair treatment for prisoners, winkling out children sold off to white farmers as 'apprentices', and agitating for the relief of those left in the hills – for years until the growing threat of a greater conflict overtook him.

His stance naturally drew him closer to the Colenso family. In particular, it was at this time that Durnford became increasingly attached to one of the bishop's younger daughters, Frances. Frances Ellen Colenso (known as Nell) undoubtedly fell in love with Anthony Durnford, but if he was fond of her, he could not allow himself to become too deeply involved in return. He was damaged, and he knew it; he still had a wife in England, and a daughter, and he placed too great a price on honour to compromise hers – or lose his own. Indeed, by 1874 honour was one of the few things Anthony Durnford had left, and he clung to it all the more tenaciously. But in holding himself aloof, he merely increased his allure in Nell's eyes.

The attacks on Durnford's conduct at Bushman's River Pass continued until at last the senior British officer in Southern Africa, Lieutenant-General

Sir Arthur Cunynghame, agreed to hold a court of inquiry into the whole affair. It met in October 1874 and took evidence from many of those involved. Avoiding any controversial judgements, it praised Durnford's personal courage and tenacity, and absolved the Carbineers of any direct blame because of the difficult situation in which they had been placed. Several criticisms were implicit, however, and it was left to Cunynghame to sum them up on reviewing the judgement. It was self-evident that the mission had been compromised before it began by Pine's farcical 'don't shoot' order, and by poor organization and coordination among the troops. Greater thought, Cunynghame suggested, should have been given to the question of supplies – for which Durnford, in his eagerness, had been largely to blame – while the effectiveness of the Carbineers had been undermined because they had not worked with Durnford before, and seemed uncertain of the proper chain of command. Cunynghame was undecided, too, as to whether Durnford had understood the proper tactics to be employed under such difficult circumstances, but he was prepared to make allowances for the physical strain he had been working under at the time.

If the inquiry largely exonerated Durnford of any obvious misconduct, however, it left nagging doubts about his character. These remained unresolved – least of all for Durnford himself – and would resurface in a curiously similar situation when, a few years later, Anthony Durnford found himself once more commanding men at a pivotal moment of conflict.

Long before then, however, the Natal government was called to account for its heavy-handed response to the crisis. Colenso's vociferous criticism had caused some embarrassment in London and Sir Benjamin Pine had been recalled. In December 1874 Theophilus Shepstone was summoned to the Colonial Office to justify the administration's policies.

Durnford had come to believe that Shepstone had a good deal to answer for, but if he thought Shepstone's career was at stake he underestimated his political adroitness. A few months later Shepstone was back in Natal, his reputation untarnished, and charged with a breathtaking new imperial commission – and one that was destined to plunge Britain into a degree of bloodshed far greater than anything it had yet experienced in its already troubled tenure in southern Africa.

# 8

# 'Neither justice nor humanity'

## Intrigue and infidelity on the Mzinyathi border, 1878

When Theophilus Shepstone arrived in London in September 1874 he found the atmosphere at the Colonial Office rather different to what he had expected. The Secretary of State for the Colonies, Lord Carnarvon, had indeed been greatly concerned by Natal's handling of the Langalibalele affair and, following Bishop Colenso's frequent and loud protestations had decided that Sir Benjamin Pine had mishandled it and should be recalled. Ironically, though, throughout Pine's tenure of office it had been Shepstone who had managed African affairs, according to his usual policies, and the crisis had ultimately been of his making, yet Carnarvon was content to abandon Pine to his critics, and it was to Shepstone that he now turned for a solution as he fretted over 'these South African questions [that] are a terrible labyrinth of which it is hard to find a clue'.[1]

Shepstone, no doubt relieved that Carnarvon seemed to attach no particular blame to him, was only too happy to enlighten him. The tentative vision he had been groping towards in his policies for nearly thirty years had now very largely taken concrete shape in his mind, and he had a clear view of how British interests might be consolidated and expanded, not merely in Natal but across southern Africa as a whole. With the discovery of diamonds, those policies were no longer focused upon strategic control of the Cape alone, but were now a complex mesh of military, political and economic objectives on both a global and local stage. A 'terrible labyrinth' indeed, but one that might be resolved, Shepstone claimed, by abandoning Britain's historical reluctance to expand its territorial possessions in the region, and accept a greater degree of influence over independent neighbouring states – both those African kingdoms which had hitherto survived the great imperial progress unscathed and the Boer republics, which were at best uncooperative and at worst actively hostile. Shepstone's faith in his vision was unshakeable and his fabled insight into 'the native mind' unchallengeable, and Carnarvon melted before his arguments, not least because they offered a long-term solution to festering antagonisms which had already dragged the British military into a series of messy conflicts with Africans and Trekkers alike – not to mention a potential economic return to offset the decades of blood and coin which had already been expended.

Such an ideal would only be practicable, however, if the various antagonistic Boer and African states could be managed as a whole, and to Britain's advantage – if their political, ideological and cultural differences could be set aside, and a common administrative and financial infrastructure imposed over all of them. Such a policy had been tried with some success in Canada, and Shepstone assured Carnarvon it could work in Africa too.

In May 1875, largely as a result of his discussions with Shepstone, Carnarvon announced a major new political initiative, the first serious gear-shift in British policies in southern Africa since the occupation of the Cape seventy years before. The British Government, he declared, was to implement a 'confederation' of southern Africa, bringing the various groups there under British control. A new High Commissioner was to be appointed to the Cape to oversee the policy; in the meantime, Shepstone had already been sent back to Natal to prepare.

Yet, given their tangled and tortured histories, such a spirit of cooperation was unlikely to be readily forthcoming among such disparate peoples, many of whom had already come to recognize the British Empire as the greatest threat to their independence and the survival of their traditions. So Carnarvon's decision raised a number of very pertinent political and military questions, not least, what would happen to those who chose to resist?

*

Even as Shepstone was arguing the case for confederation in London, King Cetshwayo was reviewing the state of his kingdom from his private quarters at the top of the great circle of huts which constituted his new royal homestead at oNdini.

A more vigorous, less subtle man than his father, Cetshwayo had nonetheless grown up against the background of Mpande's patient struggle to rebuild the apparatus of central authority in the aftermath of conflict with the Voortrekker and the subsequent civil wars, and it had been clear from the attitude of the great northern barons at his coronation ceremony that that work was far from complete. Yet, with the power of the British in Natal to intervene in Zulu affairs increasing, the Utrecht Boers still encroaching upon Zululand's western boundary, European traders leaching the country of cattle resources, and missionaries at its very heart undermining Zulu belief, it seemed to the new king that a sense of national unity under a strong central government was a prerequisite to the continued cultural and political survival of the kingdom.

Central to the exercise of royal authority, of course, was the *amabutho* system, which placed the kingdom's young men under direct control of the king. During King Mpande's time, power had slipped away to the northern barons, and both Prince Hamu and the Mandlakazi had found reasons to hold their men back from the king's assemblies, Hamu going so far as to raise *amabutho* of his own. From the beginning of his reign Cetshwayo attempted to reverse this by reinvigorating allegiance to the national *amabutho*. Mpande had allowed a number of men to escape their obligations by granting various exemptions from service – notably those undergoing the training to become diviners – but Cetshwayo tightened up the number of acceptable excuses and endeavoured by his personal support of the younger *amabutho* to make service fashionable again. His success was reflected in the large size of the *amabutho* he was personally responsible for raising – notably the uKhandempemvu, iNgobamakhosi and uVe[2] – and for the most part the move was welcomed by a generation of young men like Mehlokazulu who felt themselves beleaguered by outside pressures and saw a solution in the ardent support of Zulu traditions.

Yet the revival of the *amabutho* was not without its consequences. The monopoly over control of the right to marry had always been a crucial part of the system, since marriage marked the point at which members of an *ibutho* ceased to be youths, *izinsizwa*, and became men in their own right. With wives, homesteads of their own and cattle, they assumed responsibilities which largely excluded them from service to the king, except when their *ibutho* was mustered for the harvest ceremonies, or, in time of national emergency, for active service. They were in effect lost as a direct resource to the king, and to limit this successive Zulu kings had taken to themselves the right to grant each *ibutho* as a group the right to marry. This had the effect of keeping the men in service as long as possible, and permission was usually not granted until the *ibutho* was past its most vigorous years. But such a delay brought with it inevitable social pressures.

By the time most *izinsizwa* had reached the age of thirty or so, they felt themselves more than ready to pass through the last gateway to adulthood, and increasingly resented their exclusion from marriage and property. Their fathers, too, were often beginning to tire of the burden of supporting them at home during the long periods when they were not attending the king, while the fathers of their girlfriends looked forward with increasing impatience to the exchange of cattle which was due upon arrangement of the marriage contract. This created a groundswell of opinion which could be brought to bear upon the king through the local *amakhosi* and *izinduna*. For that reason few kings had been able to delay marriage of their men much beyond the age of thirty-five, although the exact circumstances in which the award was given was still open to manipulation.

The continued importance of this right in the role of the king was made clear when, at the harvest ceremonies of 1875, Cetshwayo gave permission for the iNdlondlo *ibutho* – composed of men in their mid- to late thirties – to marry. Zulu girls were also enrolled in *amabutho* of their own; their function was largely ceremonial and they were not expected to assemble to serve the king, but on such occasions it was usual for the king to select a female *ibutho* from which the lucky men might seek their brides. Cetshwayo had directed that the iNdlondlo take their brides from among the iNgcugce guild, which, typically, consisted of younger girls – in this case in their early twenties. To his surprise, many of the girls refused to comply; they had already formed relationships with men in younger *amabutho* such as the uDloko, uMbonambi, or even the iNgobamakhosi, who were their own age, and they complained that there were in any case too few potential husbands among the iNdlondlo. As a concession the king allowed the uDloko *ibutho* to marry as well, but the girls were hardly placated, and when several of the regional *amakhosi* hinted that they supported their cause Cetshwayo realized that he faced a major challenge to his authority.

His reaction was measured but firm. He assembled companies of the uKhandempemvu and iNgobamakhosi *amabutho* and sent them into those areas where defiance had been highest. Many girls wisely bowed to pressure from their parents and accepted the attentions of their older suitors but some tried to slip away with their lovers towards the borders. Here and there they were caught and killed, together with their boyfriends, and their bodies left lying across the pathways as a warning to others.

The crisis had passed by the end of 1876. The exact number of girls killed during the marriage of the iNgcugce was never resolved – estimates varied between a dozen and several hundred – but for the most part ordinary Zulus sympathized with Cetshwayo and blamed the girls' fate on their own folly. Furthermore, the incident had been a salutary reminder to the *amakhosi* of the practical limits to their aspirations for freedom from central control.

Nevertheless the incident was to have serious and unexpected repercussions. In two respects, it had highlighted the degree to which the Zulu kingdom was no longer able to ignore European influence upon its internal affairs. For the mission community – many of whom were increasingly frustrated by their failure to win widespread converts – the killings served as proof of the hard-line nature of Cetshwayo's administration, and provided a propaganda stick with which to beat him in letters to the colonial authorities in Natal, in which they increasingly demanded British intervention against him. Moreover, many of those girls who had tried to escape had avoided the clearly defined southern borders and had struck out instead towards the north-west, hoping to slip through the disputed territory, which was difficult to police, and into areas claimed by the Utrecht Boers. At a time when the boundary issue had became in any case problematic, this hardened Cetshwayo's resolve; he became increasingly inflexible in his attitude towards the Boers, and determined to establish an enforceable border.

The killings had also created tensions within the *amabutho*. Rivalry between them was in any case endemic, as it so often is between young men with a strong sense of group identity, and to some extent the competition was fuelled and exploited by the kings themselves, since it was easy enough to harness rivalries into battlefield aggression. Brawls between *amabutho* were common when they were gathered together in the emotionally charged atmosphere of the great harvest festivals, but the marriage of the iNgcugce had added an extra bitter twist to the usual intergenerational tensions. Just how keenly resentments were held became clear when, to the astonishment of both the king and his military officers, they exploded with an uncharacteristic degree of violence in the harvest ceremonies of December 1877.

Two of the king's favourite *amabutho*, the married uThulwana, of which he was himself a member, and the younger iNgobamakhosi had been quartered in the principal royal homestead at oNdini. Under normal circumstances it was highly unusual for both groups to be assembled in large numbers at the same time, but for the harvest ceremonies they were needed in full force. The iNdlondlo *ibutho* – whose marriage to the iNgcugce girls eighteen months before had triggered the furore – had been incorporated into the uThulwana and were therefore also present, and like all married *amabutho* they enjoyed to the full their right to entertain their wives at the royal homestead. The younger iNgobamakhosi resented these displays of affection, the more so since some of the new wives padding softly through the great homestead to seek out their husbands had former lovers in their ranks. One morning, when the *amabutho* had formed up in the great central enclosure of the homestead ready to take part in the day's ceremonies, some of the leading companies of the iNgobamakhosi clashed with the rearguard of the older groups as they were leaving by the main gate. A fierce stick-fight broke out, and the sound of dancing sticks thumping on hide shields or cracking on heads, of hoarse and indignant shouts and men shoving and pushing, carried across the homestead. Spears were never carried at these musters in case of just such eventualities, but the commander of the uThulwana – Prince Hamu himself – was outraged that his men should be attacked by mere 'boys', and ordered the uThulwana to return to their huts to arm themselves. They returned carrying their stabbing spears and a vicious brawl ensued on the plain in front of oNdini. When Cetshwayo heard what was happening he indignantly sent his messengers to call a halt to it, but as the iNgobamakhosi attacked every man with a head-ring and the uThulwana every man without, they could make no headway. The iNgobamakhosi eventually scattered to the hills, only emerging after dark; inevitably, they had got the worst of it, leaving sixty or seventy bodies tumbled among the huts or spread in the grass across the plain.

Cetshwayo was furious. Public consensus was that the iNgobamakhosi were to blame for their presumption, and the king bowed to pressure and sent the commander of the iNgobamakhosi, his friend Sigcwelegcwele kaMhlekeleke, away to his home near the coast in disgrace. He also ordered that each of the iNgobamakhosi pay a cow to the royal herds as a fine. Privately, however, the king blamed the excessive bloodshed on Prince Hamu's reaction, and saw in it proof that this most problematic of the northern barons had grown too easy in the assumption of royal prerogatives. Yet the simple fact was that Prince Hamu was too powerful for even the king to censure openly, and the incident further soured the already strained relationship between them. Equally damaging, the clash gave rise to a festering resentment between the iNgobamakhosi and the uThulwana, which spilled over to the other *amabutho* and created tensions and rivalries among the Zulu officer corps.

And all of this, as it would turn out, occurred just as hostile elements were beginning to swirl around the kingdom's borders: the Zulu were about to face the greatest external threat in their kingdom's history.

*

The first piece in Lord Carnarvon's confederation jigsaw had been laid in place even before the new British High Commissioner arrived in southern Africa. The South African Republic – popularly known as the Transvaal – controlled a great swathe of the rolling grasslands in the north central area of southern Africa, to the west of the uKhahlamba mountains, and for many Afrikaners it had come to assume an ideological role as the most perfect expression they had yet achieved of their political ideals. Like many of the Trekker settlements it had been born in struggle, for the central highveld had been occupied by the amaNdebele kingdom of *inkosi* Mzilikazi kaMashobane Khumalo – himself a refugee from the coastal strip – and the Trekkers had wrested possession of it by force, establishing their capital Pretoria where Mzilikazi's royal homesteads had once stood. There had been a good deal of resistance from other African groups, too, and some fearsome splits between Trekker factions.

So highly valued was independence of spirit among the highveld burghers, however, that by the mid-1870s the Republic was verging on anarchy. Many Boers in remote rural areas refused both to support the directives of their government and, in particular, to pay taxes to facilitate them, and in 1876 the Republic had blundered into a disastrous war with one of its African neighbours, the Pedi kingdom of King Sekhukhune woaSekwati. When an attempt had been made to impose taxation on Sekhukhune – and with it implicit acknowledgement of European authority – Sekhukhune had firmly declined. A desultory campaign had spluttered on through the middle of 1876 but had ultimately collapsed in bitter recriminations between Boer leaders and their African allies. The Pedi remained secure in their mountain strongholds.

The campaign had been a political calamity for the Republican Government of President Thomas Burgers. Not only had it seriously damaged Boer prestige, chipping away at the foundations of the assumption of racial superiority that was an essential prop of both Boer and British rule in southern Africa, but it had strained the exchequer to breaking point. There seemed a very real possibility that Republican rule in the Transvaal was about to collapse, dragging a good deal of European supremacist ideology down with it. Or so at least argued Theophilus Shepstone, when he wrote to the Colonial Office in London:

> Nothing but annexation will or can save the state, and nothing else can save South Africa from the direst consequences. All the thinking and intelligent people know this, and will be thankful to be delivered from the thraldom of petty factions by which they are perpetually kept in a state of excitement and unrest because the government and everything connected with it is a thorough sham.[3]

The timing was perfect, of course. Just as the British Government had accepted the necessity of securing its long-term interests by expanding its frontiers, one of the most important obstacles in its path seemed suddenly ripe for intervention. Quite how serious the crisis actually was in the Transvaal is open to question but the Colonial Office accepted Shepstone's interpretation of events wholeheartedly. He was authorized to re-establish order and good government in the Transvaal by overthrowing the Government of the South African Republic and annexing the territory on Britain's behalf. In January 1877 he handed his portfolio as Secretary for Native Affairs in Natal over to his brother John, and rode to Pretoria with a small military escort. After a quick and highly selective poll of Boer opinion he announced that the burghers would support the advent of a strong British administration to restore confidence in the Government, and on 12 April 1877 Shepstone ran up the Union flag in Pretoria. The South African Republic had ceased to exist, and the Transvaal had become a British colony; Shepstone himself was confirmed by the Colonial Office as its first administrator.

That the annexation was not immediately opposed seemed to reinforce the faith London had placed in Shepstone's judgement. In fact, however, the move had caught many burghers by surprise, and it would be months before its full implications filtered through the outlying rural communities – and when it did it gave rise to a groundswell of resentment that would one day cost the British dear.

*

The new British High Commissioner, Sir Henry Bartle Edward Frere, had landed in Cape Town just a fortnight before the Transvaal's annexation. He had arrived trailing his wife and four daughters, and his immediate impression of his new post was decidedly mixed. After years in India he appreciated the Cape's more temperate climate, but found Cape Town 'sleepy and slipshod ... dirty and unwholesome', and the inhabitants 'as idle as Italians but far more good-natured'.[4]

It was a judgement that reflected the fact that he was used to rather better things. An imperial pro-consul of the first order, Frere had enjoyed a glittering diplomatic career, but was approaching his retirement. He had taken the job at the Cape as his last – one rather less challenging than many he had held in the past – and largely, if family sources are to be believed, because he needed the money.

Frere was born into a family of minor gentry in Llanelli, north Wales, in March 1815, and had been educated amid the Georgian splendour of Bath before entering Haileybury, the East India Company's training college, which specialized in turning out future administrators for the British Empire in India. In 1834 he had travelled overland – no small feat in itself – to take up a minor post in the Company's Bombay Presidency, and he was destined to spend the majority of his professional career, more than thirty years, in India.

Those thirty years had been deeply testing ones for British interests in India, and he had witnessed not only the consolidation and expansion of imperial borders, but also the Indian Mutiny of 1857 – the greatest challenge mounted to British rule in two centuries of imperial domination. Frere had spent the rising as an administrator in the province of Sind, and his level-headed, practical and determined actions had ensured that it remained largely free of disturbances during the crisis. Still only forty-five, his reward afterwards had been an appointment to the Viceroy's Council and then a succession of influential posts which allowed him to work painstakingly for the restoration of British authority on the subcontinent. A firm believer in the sort of muscular Christian values that were popular among the British elite during Queen Victoria's reign, he had applied his considerable energies, among other things, to improving sanitation in the city of Bombay, an enormous task which involved rebuilding much of the city. By the time he left India in 1874 his reputation both as an administrator and as a humanitarian was impeccable.

His next posting – as the head of a British mission at the court of the

Sultan of Zanzibar – revealed another significant character trait, his ability to trust in his own judgement and to act decisively without recourse to higher authority. The British Government had earlier persuaded the Sultan of Zanzibar to abandon his interests in the slave trade, but the trade was so lucrative and Zanzibar's position within it so pivotal that the Sultan had turned a blind eye to its continuation. Frere's attempts to persuade the Sultan to stick to his earlier agreements were met by effortless evasion until he ordered that British warships blockade Zanzibar until the Sultan changed his mind. It was a perfect demonstration of gun-boat diplomacy, but in London the Liberal administration of Prime Minister William Gladstone was horrified Frere had so far outreached his authority. He had not only brought Britain to the brink of war with the Sultan, but had risked international relations further by ignoring the presence of other foreign embassies in Zanzibar. Gladstone promptly repudiated Frere's action – until, two days later, the Sultan caved in to British demands. Slavery was outlawed in Zanzibar, Queen Victoria indicated her approval by raising Frere to the Privy Council – and Gladstone was left to fulminate in private. The incident was undoubtedly a great personal success for Frere – and it would have dramatic implications just a few years later for the Zulu people.

By rights, the confederation of southern Africa was unworthy of a man of such distinction but Frere approached it with typical energy. Photographs of him at the time tend to belie his true character; he appears generally smaller than his true height of 2 metres and often looks to the side, in the manner of formal Victorian photography, yet even through the faded sepia his eyes have a steely determination.

It soon became apparent to Frere that Carnarvon's assessment of southern Africa was largely correct – it was a mess, and badly in need of sorting out. There was very little unity among the British colonies – the old Cape Colony had rather resented being saddled with the fledgling Natal – and certainly no widespread support for confederation. It was also unclear how the annexation of the Transvaal would play out, and there was, moreover, a wave of unrest shuddering through the disparate African communities, a common reaction to decades of dispossession and marginalization, which seemed likely to burst into violence at any moment. All Frere's political and personal skills would be needed to persuade, bully and cajole the region's population, European and African alike, to accept a common front.

Frere brought with him, too, a sense of Britain's global mission; despite the recent opening of the Suez Canal, which rendered largely obsolete the old strategic obsession with the Cape sea routes, there was still a possibility that in any confrontation with a major world power the security of the Cape would be vulnerable. In 1877 Britain's relationship with Russia was strained over conflict in Afghanistan, and it was at least theoretically possible that Russian gun-boats might attack the Cape. Frere recognized that the Cape's security could not be guaranteed against outsiders while it was divided internally against itself.

It did not take Frere long to arrive at a conclusion which seems outlandish at a distance of 130 years – that British interests in all areas could best be served by the destruction of the independent Zulu kingdom. In this, of course, he was straying once more into that grey area he had exploited so expertly in Zanzibar. Frere had no brief to interfere in Zulu-land – the British Government officially enjoyed a good relationship with King Cetshwayo. Yet Frere was now the man on the spot, and a degree of coercion had always been implicit in the concept of confederation – how else could reluctant groups be brought on board? Frere had been aware of the high regard in which the Colonial Office held Shepstone before he had set out for Africa and, while he was not particularly impressed by Shepstone's highly personal style of government in the Transvaal, he was increasingly influenced by his view of events.

A key factor here was Shepstone's own progressively hostile attitude towards King Cetshwayo. Prior to the annexation of the Transvaal, Shep-stone had sought to manipulate both the Boers and the Zulu in a manner favourable to British and Natal settler interests. Often, he had chosen to support Zulu interests against those of the Boers, particularly in the matter of disputed territory; he fondly believed that his participation in the coronation expedition had given him a degree of influence over Cetshwayo, and he sought to use this to check the advance of Boer territorial ambitions across the path of Natal's mythical 'road to the interior'. Now that he was also in charge of the Transvaal's affairs, the contradictions of his position had suddenly become all too apparent.

In attempting to reconcile the very different positions he had adopted among the Zulu and the Boers, Shepstone met with an embarrassing personal defeat. On 17 October 1877 he held a meeting to discuss the disputed borders with a delegation of 300 important Zulu *izinduna*, led by Mnyamana Buthelezi – the king's most senior and trusted adviser – at a stony ridge on the Ncome river known later as Conference Hill. The

Zulu party had arrived expecting Shepstone to honour his previous expressions of support, but found instead that – hoping to placate the Boers – he offered them a compromise, and one which denied the Zulu claim to much of the territory. Shepstone had come to the meeting convinced that he could exploit his influence over Cetshwayo to persuade the Zulus to accept his new position – and was shocked to find they would have none of it. Instead, the Zulu delegation was indignant that he had apparently caved in to Boer interests and accused him of betraying them. The meeting broke up in disarray leaving Shepstone angry and humiliated, the realization that his influence had been exposed as a sham souring his attitude towards Cetshwayo.

Much the same point had struck the Zulus too, for the man who had hitherto posed as their friend and protector had been revealed as the agent of British interests he always truly was. Afterwards, many of the senior Zulus present would consider that meeting the first true step on the road to war.

From that moment, Shepstone began to work to persuade Frere that the security of the Transvaal could best be assured by reducing the influence of the Zulu kingdom, and that by so doing a strong salutary message might be sent to other African groups inclined to resist confederation. Frere, looking for an easy solution to the 'labyrinth', was easily convinced: 'I have seen enough to feel sure that Shepstone is quite right', he wrote to Carnarvon, 'as to the influence of any Kaffir disturbance, and still more of any Kaffir success, on the Kaffir population everywhere.'[5] For Shepstone, a grand solution was obvious enough:

> Nor do I think it would be very difficult to break up the Zulu power, and when that is done, you may calculate more certainly upon peace in South Africa. Cetshwayo is the secret hope of every ... independent chief, hundreds of miles from him, who feels a desire that his colour should prevail, and it will not be until this power is destroyed that they will make up their minds to submit to the rule of civilization.[6]

This was a view that suited Frere's agenda perfectly. A quick and successful war against the Zulu would involve flexing just the right amount of military muscle to demonstrate British determination without the far greater risk of an open conflict with the Boers. In December 1877, he wrote to Carnarvon that he expected a 'trial of strength' with King Cetshwayo, and that 'neither Justice nor Humanity will be served by postponing the trial – if we establish a good cause'.[7]

Therein, however, lay Frere's dilemma, for far away in London the British Government was by no means convinced that a war with the Zulus was at all necessary. Lord Carnarvon himself had always been realistic enough to accept that a threat of military action might at some stage be necessary, but by the middle of 1877, with tension brewing with Russia and conflict looming in Afghanistan, he had far more important issues on his mind. He had made his position clear to Frere: 'I hope this does not mean we will have great pressure put on us to annex Zululand. This must and ought to come eventually, but not just now. There are signs, however, to this tendency.'[8]

Before Frere could change Carnarvon's mind, however, politics intervened. In January 1878 Carnarvon unexpectedly resigned in protest at Disraeli's handling of the Balkans crisis. Troubled at first by the impact this might have upon confederation, Frere was delighted to find that the new Secretary of State for the Colonies, Sir Michael Hicks Beach, was ready to admit to no experience in southern African affairs, and was content to rely instead on Frere's judgement. Hicks Beach was, he admitted candidly, 'disposed (as I have already told you) to prefer your opinion to my own'.[9]

This was, perhaps, a realistic view from an imperial administrator who knew his limitations when based 9,000 kilometres from the scene of the action – but it also amounted to carte blanche approval for Frere to pursue whatever policies he thought fit. And, Frere had already decided that a bold stroke would be the quickest and most assured way to further British interests in southern Africa. All he needed was to establish a good cause.

In casting about for the justification he needed, Sir Bartle Frere considered a number of possibilities. Certainly, the Zululand missionary community was actively denouncing Cetshwayo's administration, citing recent disturbances as proof of its excesses, but while an overt attack on a white missionary might have provided a useful pretext to outrage British sensibilities and harness London's support, none had been forthcoming, and the murder of one or two Zulu converts, under ambiguous circumstances, was hardly in the same league.[10] Nor would the deaths following the marriage of the iNgcugce and its aftermath suffice, since they were undeniably purely internal affairs.

Instead Frere looked to the troubled boundary between Zululand and the newly annexed Transvaal. There had been a marked increase in tension over the disputed boundary in recent years, and not merely because it had become a popular exit route for political refugees seeking to escape

Zululand. In 1876, at the height of its troubles with King Sekhukhune's Pedi kingdom, the Transvaal Republic had levied extra taxes on its citizens in an effort to pay for the war, and in the Utrecht district this had resulted in Boer officials demanding tribute from Africans living on some of the disputed farms. Many of the Africans had protested, arguing that they were subjects of the Zulu king not the Boer *Volksraad* – parliament – but their objections had been met with floggings and on occasion the destruction of their homes, and Cetshwayo's name had been abused and insulted. The king had held back, but the anger and resentment of the Zulu border communities towards the Boers had been steadily rising.

Privately, Frere may have had his doubts about the justice of some of the Boer claims, but publicly he posed as a champion of the beleaguered frontier settlers, and his dispatches began to soften the Colonial Office towards the possibility that it might be necessary to deploy British troops to protect them. His reports were peppered with lurid descriptions of King Cetshwayo's supposedly despotic nature and of the dangers posed by the *amabutho*, whom Frere envisaged as an army of celibate bloodthirsty savages, yearning to sink their stabbing spears into quivering white flesh.

Just as his propaganda campaign was getting up steam, however, a new and formidable opponent emerged on Frere's own doorstep. Sir Henry Bulwer was the lieutenant-governor of Natal – its senior administrator – and, although a believer in confederation, had become increasingly concerned by the turn events were taking, and in particular Frere's apparent readiness to adopt a confrontational policy towards the Zulu kingdom. Bulwer's worry, it must be said, was not a fundamentally humanitarian one – he was not so much concerned for the well-being of the Zulu people as for the long-term management of Natal's African population, inextricably linked as they were by the ties of history to the Zulu kingdom. Recognizing that the border dispute was being manipulated to provoke an open rift, Bulwer intervened to offer Natal's services as an impartial intermediary between the Transvaal and the Zulu. In that he was not overly optimistic of success; he urged Frere and Shepstone not to 'rush into war so long as it can be avoided', but was soon forced to the realization that 'we are looking to different objects – I to the termination of this dispute by peaceful settlement, you to its termination by the overthrow of the Zulu kingdom.'[11] However, it was an offer that Frere could only decline at the risk of exposing his own agenda, and it no doubt occurred to him that if the Natal authorities' proposed investigation of the dispute found in the Transvaal's favour, his case would be immeasurably strengthened, and London's ability to object to action severely curtailed.

It was therefore agreed that Natal would set up a Boundary Commission to meet both the Utrecht burghers and Cetshwayo's representatives and sift through the complex evidence regarding the dispute. Both parties would be bound by the Commission's decision, and King Cetshwayo, recognizing a way out from an increasingly uncomfortable position, agreed with alacrity. The Commission was headed by the colony's Attorney-General, James Galway, and it included both the acting Secretary for Native Affairs, John Wesley Shepstone – the very man who had failed to capture the Sithole Matshana kaMondise twenty years before – and the Colonial Engineer, Anthony Durnford.

The Transvaal delegation also included a Shepstone – Theophilus's son, Henrique, representing his father's official interests as Administrator – together with a leading Utrecht burgher, Petrus Lefras Uys. Uys was a man with impeccable Voortrekker credentials, for he had lost his father and brother to Dingane's warriors in the battles of 1838. The Zulus were represented by *inkosi* Sihayo, in his capacity as official guardian of the border, Sintwagu – a confidential messenger of King Cetshwayo – and an elderly *induna*, Muwundula kaMamba, who knew the history of the dispute in detail from King Mpande's time.

The three parties met on 12 March 1878 at Jim Rorke's old farm on the Mzinyathi. Rorke himself had died a few years earlier and his widow Sarah had sold the property on. It had been briefly occupied by two settler families, the Stockills and the Surtees, but they had found the situation on the border too tense to stay long, and the property had recently passed into the hands of the Swedish Mission Society's first representative in southern Africa, Reverend Otto Witt. The choice of the site was of course a deliberate one, for Rorke's Drift represented one of the last fixed points on the border – above it, the disputed territory began.

At first the Zulus displayed little confidence in the proceedings – Matshana was still living close by, and his story was known the length of the frontier, and there were simply too many Shepstones involved in the affair for their liking – but in fact the Natal delegates went about their job with remarkable thoroughness. For several weeks they examined and cross-examined witnesses on both sides. It is probably true that they had entered the task with the assumption that the Zulu kings had a prior claim to the land, and that as a result they were intrinsically sceptical of the Boer claims, but even so they found little in the Boer arguments to change their minds.[12] By the time the meeting broke up on 14 April they had come to the categorical conclusion that 'that there has been no cession of land at all by the Zulu kings, past or present, or by the nation'.[13]

The commissioners presented their report to Frere on 20 June 1878 – and it was not what he wanted to hear. It flatly contradicted the impression that he had carefully cultivated in London that Cetshwayo's administration was a threat to British interests across the region as a whole, an implication which officials at the Colonial Office had been astute enough to spot for themselves:

> If the views of the Commission & of Sir Henry Bulwer are adopted there is no occasion to go to war with Cetywayo [sic]. It has been generally assumed that Cetywayo was in the wrong and would have to be repressed. Now he is pronounced to have been in the right, as indeed everyone always supposed he was until after the Transvaal had been annexed and Sir T. Shepstone took up a position adverse to his claims. But it appears to be a foregone conclusion in everybody's mind that there is to be war.[14]

A foregone conclusion indeed, but one Frere had no intention of abandoning so easily. While he pondered his next move, he suppressed the report, refusing to announce the Commission's findings on the pretext that they were under consideration by the Government in London.

This was a decision which cranked tension along the border almost to breaking point. Sihayo and the other Zulu delegates had left the conference delighted at the Commission's apparent even-handedness, and there was a widespread expectation that their findings would be acted upon immediately. Yet, as the weeks dragged by, it seemed that the British had no intention of implementing their own recommendations, and reports reached Cetshwayo that detachments of British troops had been dispatched to Utrecht, apparently to protect the burghers. The king began to suspect that the Commission had not met in good faith after all – and that he was being made a fool of. He wrote in frustration to Bulwer:

> I hear of troops arriving in Natal, that they are coming to attack the Zulus, and to seize me; in what have I done wrong that I should be seized like an 'Umtakata' [evil-doer], the English are my fathers, I do not wish to quarrel with them, but to live as I have always done, at peace with them. Cetshwayo says that he sees that His Excellency is

hiding from him the answer that has returned from across the sea, about the land boundary question with the Transvaal, and only making an excuse for taking time so as to surprise him.[15]

\*

By 1878 Mehlokazulu kaSihayo had already achieved a good deal of influence over the younger members of the amaQungebeni living on the western borders of Zululand. Now about twenty-five years old, he was already a man of distinction among the iNgobamakhosi *ibutho*. He probably commanded two or three companies of men his own age, and this had as much to do with his strong personality, initiative and personal charisma as it did his position as the son of one of the king's favourites. A few years later, in 1882, the traveller Bertram Mitford was certainly impressed, describing him as 'a fine, well-made man . . . with an intelligent face and a brisk, lively manner. A sub-chief among the Ngobamakosi regiment and a good shot, he is much looked up to by his younger compatriots as a spirited and daring warrior.'[16]

A daring warrior indeed. Mehlokazulu is remembered in his family today as a great hero. In later life he adopted the deliberate and distant aura of the legendary fighting men of old, like Shaka, and he ate his meals apart and in brooding silence. Even his family regarded him with awe – it was said that as a mature man 'they never knew his teeth', for he seldom smiled, and that when he was approached with even trivial queries about the daily running of his household he would fix a person with a steady, intimidating gaze.[17]

Many of these character traits were undoubtedly exaggerated by the bitter experiences that, in 1878, still lay in the future, but even in his youth Mehlokazulu was a man who believed in a direct approach to life's challenges. As a leading man in the iNgobamakhosi, and the heir apparent to the amaQungebeni, it is likely that he was fully involved in the king's efforts to prevent the girls of the iNgcugce fleeing across the western borders in 1876, and Frere, at least, believed he had been an instigator of the clash between the iNgobamakhosi and the uThulwana at the harvest ceremonies the following year. 'He believed', said his family simply, 'in fighting.'[18]

It was shortly after the Boundary Commission had packed up and returned to Pietermaritzburg from Rorke's Drift that *inkosi* Sihayo's unfaithful wives, Mehlokazulu's mother, MaMtshali, and MaMthethwa, took their fateful decision to abandon their husband in favour of their lovers across the river.

Their timing was surely deliberate. There had been hitherto almost no visible sign of white authority across the Mzinyathi border beyond the handful of African Border Police who monitored the crossing-points – nothing to reassure any would-be refugee that merely by picking their way through the treacherous river currents they could place themselves safely beyond the reach of Zulu law. Then, for over a month, Rorke's Drift had been at the very epicentre of the region's international affairs, and the meeting of the Boundary Commission stood as a tangible proof that the *abelungu* took their presence on the border seriously. The two women had gambled that in the autumn of 1878, with the focus of no less than three governments concentrated upon Rorke's Drift, their husband would not dare to risk an international incident merely to defend his honour. They trusted to the international fault line, so recently thrown into sharp relief, to protect them.

In many respects their judgement had been correct. Whatever the hurt to his personal dignity, *inkosi* Sihayo was far too experienced a frontier politician to risk his own position by compromising King Cetshwayo at such a delicate time. The Boundary Commission had unwittingly made MaMtshali and MaMthethwa untouchable. Or so they thought.

Yet they had, of course, seriously under-estimated the frustration felt by Zulu loyalists like Mehlokazulu along the length of the border. For Mehlokazulu their flight was not merely a betrayal of family honour which damaged the standing of the king's chosen local representatives, it was indicative of the degree to which the European presence was undermining the Zulu way of life. That his own mother, MaMtshali, had disgraced him in such a way was deeply insulting – and that she had chosen to hide behind the protection of the whites was an outrage he could scarcely tolerate.

His indignation was fuelled by the way in which the two women had not even troubled to move themselves a safe distance from the border – both had been content to lodge at the homestead of black policemen who watched over the Mzinyathi crossings. When, one day, a Zulu, returning across the river from a visit to friends on the Natal bank had spotted MaMtshali and confronted her, she had revelled in her defiance. She had taunted her son with his impotence and 'jeered and said "he was to tell Mehlokazulu to come and kill her"'.[19] It was a fatal error, for MaMtshali had misjudged her son's determination. He came.

Mehlokazulu had known, of course, that his father would not condone any direct move against his errant wives but this was easily circumvented. He waited until his father was called away to attend the king and then, galvanizing support among those family members left behind – his uncle and brothers – on 12 July 1878 they crossed the Mzinyathi, dragged MaMtshali back across the border, and killed her. A few days later the same fate befell MaMthethwa.

It is difficult to tell, at this distance, whether Mehlokazulu expected to be called to account for his actions. Certainly, the life of an unfaithful wife of an *inkosi* was forfeit under Zulu law, and 'hot pursuit' actions were well known along the length of the border and tolerated by both sides. In 1877 Mnyamana Buthelezi had become embroiled in a wrangle with the Utrecht Boers over a runaway girl from his household, while in January 1878 – just six months earlier – Cetshwayo had authorized the abaQulusi to arrest a man named Gwai who had been accused of conspiring to overthrow him, and who had taken refuge on one of the German-owned farms at Luneburg. But when news of the deaths of MaMtshali and MaMthethwa reached the royal court, '. . . the King was exceedingly surprised, and so was Sihayo shocked and surprised to hear of the evil doing of Mehlokazulu, and so were all the other *Indunas* who were present'.[20]

Mehlokazulu had undeniably over-reached himself; it was not the position of a wronged son to punish his errant mother himself, but merely to pass the crime to his seniors to judge. It was not just the young warrior's presumption that appalled the royal council, however, it was what the white men would make of it.

They were right to be concerned. When news of the killings reached Sir Bartle Frere, he knew he had found that incontrovertible and just cause for which he had been searching – the trigger that would allow him to convince London of the need to overthrow the entire Zulu kingdom.

# 9

# 'A very serious evil'

## Confrontation, December 1878

Mehlokazulu's attack upon his errant 'mothers' finally decided Frere upon the course he had been considering for some months – a British attack to destroy the power and influence of the Zulu kingdom. This was not without political risk. Frere knew at an early stage that he might have to embark upon an invasion without the wholehearted support of the Government in London. In his dispatches he had worked assiduously to convince Hicks Beach of the hostile nature of Cetshwayo's administration and to present any possible British intervention in a humanitarian light; nevertheless, the fact remained that any direct attack would be an act of aggression against a power with which the British Government officially maintained friendly relations. The Boundary Commission's report had undeniably been a disappointment since it had provided no evidence of Zulu expansionism directed against British interests; any charge of Zulu violation upon British territory must therefore rest largely on Mehlokazulu's actions. Just cause remained tenuous, however, and commitment to it was weakened by British entanglements elsewhere in the world – a new war in Afghanistan seemed highly probable.

In the final analysis Frere was prepared to take responsibility himself for starting a war. He gambled that it could be accomplished quickly, and that the apparently overwhelming British superiority in firepower would make for a comparatively bloodless victory. By the time London could object, the situation would already have moved on, and Frere would have tightened his control over southern Africa and established a secure basis for confederation. He might be subject to official rebuke, but British interests would have been greatly served by his actions.

Curiously, the one possibility that does not seem to have occurred either to Frere or to his advisers during the second half of 1878, as he began carefully laying the groundwork for his plans, was that a war in Zululand might be anything other than a walkover.

*

The man to whom the task of destroying the Zulu kingdom on the ground would fall was the senior British commander in southern Africa, Lieutenant-General Frederic Thesiger (soon to become Lord Chelmsford). The prospect was not one, on the eve of war, which gave Thesiger undue concern. Fred Thesiger was a career soldier, a typical product of the military elite of the mid-Victorian era, a representative of attitudes and of a system rooted in the military successes of an earlier age, which – like so much in British society at the time – were even then braced against onslaught from a younger, brasher generation agitating for reform.

Thesiger was nothing if not a gentleman, as photographs of him taken in late 1878 suggest. Invariably impeccably clothed in an undress blue uniform, his dark hair neatly parted and his beard trimmed, he poses erect, often fixing the camera directly with a gaze that is neither haughty nor familiar, a look by no means devoid of kindliness – but one which draws a proper degree of reserve over the inner workings of his mind. Above all, Thesiger's portraits suggest a comfortable air of authority, a sense of a man at ease with his own importance, assured of the correctness of his view of the world – and his own place within it.

The Thesiger family were German in origin; Frederic's great-grandfather, John Andrew Thesiger, was born in Dresden, Saxony, in 1722, and had emigrated to England where he had enjoyed a successful career as private secretary to Charles Watson-Wentworth, 2nd Marquess of Rockingham. The Thesigers inherited sugar estates in the Caribbean and moved effort-lessly among the Georgian establishment, taking their places in the middle ranks of the Army and Navy during the struggles against Revolutionary and Napoleonic France. Charles's third son (and Frederic's father), a midship-man present at the bombardment of Copenhagen, later turned to the law and Tory politics. Successful at both, he was appointed Solicitor-General in 1844 and was knighted, taking the title 1st Baron Chelmsford. In 1858 the family fortunes reached their pinnacle when Chelmsford was made Lord Chancellor under Lord Derby's administration. In 1822 he had married Anna Maria Tinling, and the couple had four sons and three daughters, of whom Frederic Augustus was the eldest.

Frederic Junior was born on 31 May 1827, and entered Eton at a time when the public school system was arguably at its most influential.[1] Public school ethics stressed the importance of patriotism, of a willingness to submit unselfishly to the dictates of duty, of modesty and stoicism, of sublimation of personal desires and ambition and, above all, a willingness to play the game even under the most desperate circumstances.[2] If it also gave its pupils a deep sense of national superiority – that the English were self-evidently the race most qualified to rule the world, a concept they found inescapable in the decades following Waterloo – it tempered it with an insistence that so great a privilege carried with it equally powerful responsibilities, of *noblesse oblige* and, increasingly as the nineteenth century wore on, of taking up 'the white man's burden'. And if those who emerged from the system did not end up psychotic sociopaths like Harry Flashman or insufferable little prigs like Tom Brown, they turned out much like Frederic Augustus Thesiger: deeply imbued with the ethics of Empire, unquestioning of England's role in the world, socially conservative, accustomed to exercising authority, quiet, modest, courteous in manner, and usually rather uncomfortable with the free expression of emotion.

On leaving Eton, Thesiger had entered the Army in December 1844 as a second lieutenant in the Rifle Brigade. Nevertheless, within a year he had been able to secure the transfer to the Guards, purchasing his new position, as was the established practice for officers in the British Army at the time.[3] Thesiger's early service had been typical of his time, soldiering on the distant frontiers of the expanding Empire. As aide-de-camp (ADC) to Lieutenant-General Markham in the Crimea he had witnessed at a senior level something of the logistical difficulties which made that campaign so gruelling, and he had watched from a distance the British attack on a Russian stronghold, the Redan. When the war ended he had returned to England, to be offered command of the 95th Regiment, which was then involved in the suppression of the Indian Mutiny. For Thesiger, this was to be the start of a long professional association with India – sixteen years altogether – which would greatly affect his approach to soldiering.

In 1868 an Anglo-Indian expedition had been dispatched to confront Emperor Tewodros in the highlands of Abyssinia, in the Horn of Africa, and Thesiger had been given a crucial staff post. A bizarre and largely forgotten incident now, the Abyssinian campaign was characterized more by the logistical difficulties of manoeuvring 13,000 British and Indian soldiers, 26,000 camp followers and 40,000 animals – including 44 elephants – into a position where they were able to confront Tewodros's followers

than by the fighting itself. As deputy adjutant-general it had fallen largely
to Thesiger to keep this force alive and on the move in one of the most
inhospitable landscapes on Earth. He had acquitted himself with distinction;
as his reward he had been made a Companion of the Bath and an ADC to
Queen Victoria. A spell commanding Shorncliffe Camp at Aldershot had
followed and then, in January 1878, his career took a sudden sideways
lurch, and he was offered command of British troops in southern Africa.

Thesiger's appointment was the result of a sudden flare-up among the
African population on the Cape frontier. It was the outbreak Frere had
expected since his arrival at the Cape and, ironically, it had almost engulfed
him personally. Frere had been touring the frontier on a fact-finding mission
in August 1877 when a clash between two rival African groups had exploded
into a full-scale rising among the Xhosa. It was to be the last rather sad
gesture of defiance among a people largely broken by no less than eight wars
over the previous century, and the violence had escalated quickly as Cape
colonial troops were sucked into the fighting. They were unable to contain
the rising, however, and Frere had been forced to authorize the deployment
of British regulars. Troops under General Sir Arthur Cunynghame had
methodically scoured the bush, drawing the Xhosa into two uncharacteris-
tically pitched engagements at Nyamaga on 13 January 1878 and Centane
on 7 February. In both battles the Xhosa had risked frontal attacks in the
open only to be mown down by the concentrated rifle fire of the redcoats.

Cunynghame's actions had restored order but had provoked a political
crisis between the High Commissioner and the Cape colonial Parliament.
Convinced that the Xhosa trouble was symptomatic of a much deeper
African threat, and scathing of the Cape's vacillating and ineffectual
response – and convinced the colonial administration in any case lacked the
resolve to pursue confederation – Frere had dismissed the Cape Government. It was a move which left him largely free to take control of the
colony's affairs but General Cunynghame had been a victim of the political
wrangling which followed. He had been recalled by the Commander-in-
Chief in London and, on the whole, Cunynghame had been happy enough
to go; a frontier war was a thankless task entirely devoid of all traces of
glory, and southern Africa was already proving something of a graveyard of
military reputations.

Thesiger, now fifty years old, had arrived at Cape Town towards the
end of February. Arguably at the height of his powers as a soldier, and with
a good deal of experience behind him and a record so far entirely successful,

his new post was nevertheless to be his first independent command. Before leaving the UK, he had, it seems, taken note of advice offered to him by an old friend, Sir John Michel, who had held a command during the fiercest of the earlier Cape Frontier Wars, in 1851:

> Do not hamper yourself with staff, they are all useless, as Colonels of the regiments do all the work . . . No plan or operation of yours can in any way circumvent the Caffre.[4] He is your master in everything. He goes where he likes, he does what he likes, he moves 3 miles [5 kilometres] whilst you move one, he carries no commissariat or only a day's supply. You possess only the ground you stand on. All you have got to do is take cattle, annoy him by burning his kraals, and eventually destroy his crops. You will scarcely believe that I who always commanded about half the Army, who was everywhere and saw everything, who nearly always commanded the whole patrol I was out with, never saw more than 30 Caffres together in my life . . . I am of the opinion that you cannot too carefully instil into comdg. officers and they their juniors, that in no case are they to move without their flanks fairly covered, unless where danger is not to be feared . . . The want of efficient Mounted Infantry will be a sad thorn in your side . . . I recommend you not to try night surprises. Ask Brownlee about my last, he was with me. It was most dangerous, and I ought to have suffered for it . . . Yours, my dear Thesiger, is a command of great danger to your reputation. The two best generals, Sir P. Maitland and Sir H. Smith, were dismissed, that is superseded, both most unjustly.
>
> . . . At present there are no mounted men of much value at the Cape. The Englishmen and Dutchmen are of little worth. I mean the Mounted Police, except in the open . . . The Burghers are in no way to be depended upon. British cavalry are utterly valueless.[5]

Thesiger had certainly not overburdened himself with staff. He was, in any case, an old school officer who believed in doing much of his work himself, and he was by nature reluctant to delegate. He arrived in southern Africa with just his Assistant Military Secretary – something of a misnomer, since he had no other military secretary – Lieutenant-Colonel John North Crealock, and two ADCs. Crealock had served with him at Aldershot, and Thesiger does not seem to have given much thought to his appointment, commenting 'I had never thought of him as my military secretary until he wrote and asked me to take him.'[6]

Thesiger arrived on the Cape frontier at the beginning of March 1878. He found that the Xhosa war was not yet over, and that a few remaining bands loyal to their *inkosi* Sandile had taken refuge in the traditional Xhosa stronghold of the amaThole mountains. Unencumbered by commissariat worries, the Xhosa could move across the steep valley sides and through shaded, tangled forests almost at will, seldom emerging on the open hilltops, and then only to strike at a careless enemy patrol. The white colonists dreaded the prospect of a war in the amaThole, and now that one seemed likely, it fell to Thesiger to reassure them.

His solution was to apply to the problem the same methodology he had used as deputy adjutant-general on the Abyssinian expedition. He broke up Cunynghame's ad hoc brigades and reorganized his forces, regulars and colonials alike, and painstakingly established a ring of positions around the hills. From these he began a series of sweeps, shelling the bush then driving through it like a buck-hunt. It was an effective tactic but it required a considerable degree of coordination to work properly, and that was not always forthcoming. Troops often failed to reach designated starting positions because of the difficult terrain or wet weather, advances stalled in the steep bush, and units sometimes became distracted by the prospect of looting Xhosa cattle, or were themselves attacked when they were at their most isolated and vulnerable. More often than not, when objectives were finally secured they were found to be abandoned; the Xhosa often defended positions from the bush in the daytime only to desert them after dark. It was deeply frustrating work, and several times Thesiger was required to call a halt to his operations to reorganize and begin all over again. Yet it was a war the Xhosa could not in the end hope to win. After a century of struggle against European encroachment, they lacked the manpower to resist indefinitely, their culture and their country already too far compromised by successive defeats and by the influx of white settlers. On 29 May 1878 *inkosi* Sandile was killed in a shoot-out in the densest part of the bush, and with him died the last hopes of the rebellion.

Although it had been hardly a glamorous one, Thesiger had by his patience and tenacity won an impressive victory, and it shaped his understanding of the nature of warfare in southern Africa. It had left him with a firm impression of the tactical risks and advantages of the landscape itself – of the relative safety of open areas and the dangers of the bush and broken country – and with a vague disdain for the unreliability of volunteer troops. It had reinforced his natural faith in his own men – the red-coated British regulars whose discipline and firepower he could depend upon – and most of all it had characterized in his mind the black south African as an enemy whose greatest strength lay in his elusiveness, in the ability to expose weaknesses, to hit and run, and to avoid being caught in an open battle which would inevitably mean his defeat. All of these views were profoundly to affect his thinking when Frere first raised the possibility of a campaign against the Zulu.

\*

Thesiger spent much of July 1878 as Frere's guest in the High Commissioner's residence in Cape Town, and together they pondered ways to improve southern Africa's woeful security. They toured the Cape batteries together and tutted at their lack of readiness against an imagined attack by a rival maritime power – but the sea defences could be repaired rather more easily than the region's bitter internal rivalries. In the aftermath of the Xhosa campaign, Frere had edged significantly closer to the open use of military force to implement confederation, and a Zulu war was already on his agenda. And if the findings of the Natal Boundary Commission had proved disappointing as a means to force London's hands, the news of Mehlokazulu's incursion – which arrived during Thesiger's stay – was ripe with interesting potential.

Lieutenant-General Sir Fred Thesiger did not think it appropriate to question Frere's interpretation of events. He was a soldier, and he saw his duty in straightforward terms – to act upon whatever policies his political masters believed would best further Britain's interests. Nor is there any suggestion that he doubted the view that the Zulu posed an active threat to the Transvaal and Natal. He had seen for himself how the Xhosa had been resistant to British authority on the Cape frontier, and it required no great leap of imagination to believe Shepstone's view that the Zulu were a bastion of African power and independence. From the first, he fully accepted that they were an enemy. 'The Zulu have been very kind to us in abstaining from any hostile movements during the time we have been so busily engaged in this colony', he wrote to Shepstone with unconscious irony as early as 8 July,

> If they will only wait until next month I shall hope to have the troops somewhat better prepared than they are at present – The state of uncertainty however as to whether it is to be peace or war is very much

against us – Zulus are ready; we are not, and cannot be so, until I have
permission to raise the requisite numbers of volunteers and native levies
– This cannot of course be done until a final decision has been come to
regarding the boundary question . . .[7]

In this Thesiger was to be frustrated by the reluctance of the British
Government to accept Frere's assurances that the invasion of Zululand was
necessary, and by the scepticism of Natal's administrator, Sir Henry Bulwer,
on the issue.

It was almost axiomatic that British commanders embarking upon
offensive operations in some far-flung corner of the globe would have to
do so with far too few resources for the job. In August Thesiger left the
Cape and travelled to Natal to assess the situation for himself. Faced with
the prospect of defending over 300 kilometres of open borders and
operating in terrain which was more challenging, if anything, than what
he had experienced on the Cape frontier, Thesiger was realistic enough to
recognize that he had too few regular troops to hand. In September he
wrote a long dispatch to London outlining his need for more men – and
received a very distinct snub in return:

> Her Majesty's Government are . . . not prepared to comply with the
> request for a reinforcement of troops. All the information that has
> hitherto reached them, with respect to the position of affairs in Zulu-
> land, appears to them to justify a confident hope that by the exercise of
> prudence, and by meeting the Zulus in a spirit of forbearance and
> reasonable compromise, it will be possible to avert the very serious evil
> of a war with Cetewayo . . .[8]

The War Office was prepared to authorize the dispatch of no more than
two infantry battalions and two companies of Royal Engineers to the Cape.
In effect the Government had called Frere's bluff; if the threat of a Zulu
invasion was as real of Frere claimed, such numbers were sufficient to
defend it. They were, however, quite insufficient to mount an invasion.

Nevertheless, mount an invasion Thesiger must. Faced with the prospect
of the long and completely unprotected Natal and Transvaal borders, and
of a highly mobile enemy in large numbers, Thesiger planned to use the
same principles of containment he had employed with success on the Cape
frontier. There were five traditional points of entry into Zululand – the old
Lower Drift across the Thukela, the Middle Drift upstream, Rorke's Drift,

by way of the 'hunters' road' from Utrecht, and through the Transvaal–Swazi borders in the far north – and Thesiger planned to attack along each of them. Aware of the political imperatives which underpinned Frere's policies, and of his own limited resources, Thesiger saw his greatest threat in any reluctance by the Zulu to be drawn into a decisive confrontation. He outlined his thinking to John Dunn – a transfrontiersman who had lived in Zululand and enjoyed an influential position in Cetshwayo's court – who

> advised Lord Chelmsford to divide his forces into two strong columns, so that either would be strong enough to cope with the whole of the Zulu army. Lord Chelmsford laughed at this idea, and said, 'The only thing I am afraid of is that I won't get Cetywayo to fight.' I said, 'Well, my lord, supposing you get to his kraal, and he won't fight, what will you do?' His answer was, 'I must drive him into a corner, and make him fight'.[9]

Thesiger intended his columns to converge on the complex of Zulu royal homesteads clustered around oNdini which constituted King Cetshwayo's capital. This offered him a viable strategic objective, and he was convinced the Zulus would be forced to make a stand before he reached oNdini.

He did not doubt for a moment that if he met the Zulus in open battle, he would be able to defeat them. 'Half measures do not answer with natives', he wrote to Shepstone. 'They must be thoroughly crushed to make them believe in our superiority; and if I am called upon to conduct operations against them I shall strive to be in a position to show them how hopelessly inferior to us they are in fighting power, altho' numerically stronger.'[10]

This confidence was not based by any means on ignorance of his enemy. Thesiger knew a good deal about the organization of the Zulu military, and he had taken the trouble to commission a Natal Border Agent, F.B. Fynney, who took an interest in such things, to compile a pamphlet on the way the Zulu army was raised, administered and fought. Although this document tried rather too hard to fit the *amabutho* system into the mould of a conventional European professional army, and many of the details about the ceremonial dress of specific *amabutho* were either incomplete or out of date, it was nonetheless a remarkable piece of intelligence work, and when it was issued to Thesiger's officers it meant that, for once, the British were incredibly well informed about those they were about to attack.

Despite this, neither Thesiger nor the professional soldiers under his command could quite bring themselves to accept the settler view that the Zulu posed very different challenges to the Xhosa. The British war artist Melton Prior had noted this during a meeting 'between General Thesiger and the different heads of the volunteer corps, well-known farmers, and Dutch and German Boers' in the closing stages of the Xhosa war:

> The conversation turned to the prospects of the Zulu War, as it was known that the nation was very disturbed.
>
> The Burghers and Boers, who had fought the Zulus in days gone by, assured General Thesiger that any army fighting the Zulus would have to *laager* at every halt made after crossing the border. General Thesiger said, 'Oh, British troops are all right; we do not need to *laager* – we have a different formation.'
>
> The Boers again and again assured him that it would be absolutely necessary, and that no column ought to halt for breakfast or dinner under any circumstances without *laagering*.
>
> Again General Thesiger smiled at the notion, but I was very much impressed at the earnest and serious way in which the Boers explained the risk, and the necessity for this action.[11]

In the years since, Thesiger has been much criticized for his failure to respond to settler advice, yet in fact his reservations were based largely upon a professional assessment of the capabilities of the two sides, and upon his recent experience. He was a full-time soldier who had seen a good deal of combat, and he knew what British troops armed with modern breech-loading weapons were capable of. He had recently won a difficult and messy campaign in southern Africa, while it had been forty years since settlers – British or Boers – had last fought the Zulu. The Voortrekkers had won a spectacular victory at Ncome River, yet their fortunes in the war of 1838 as a whole had been decidedly mixed. It is perhaps hardly surprising then that Thesiger was 'inclined to think that the first experience of the power of the Martini Henrys will be such a surprise to the Zulus that they will not be formidable after the first effort'.[12]

It merely remained for Sir Bartle Frere to engineer a war in which Thesiger could put his theories to the test.

*

Frere did not particularly expect either the Colonial Office or the Cabinet to accept the killings of MaMtshali and MaMthethwa as justification for an invasion, so he intended to circumvent their objections by a simple stratagem – he would only tell them of his plans when it was already too late for them to object. To that end he could exploit the delays in communicating with London; it took more than a month for a detailed dispatch to be shipped to London, and even the nearest telegraph station was situated on the Cape Verde islands, off the west coast of Africa – and any message had first to be sent there by steamer. Thus it took over a fortnight for the briefest of telegrams to reach London, and, allowing time for the Government to frame a reply and for the return journey, Frere knew he had a window of at least a month in which he could act without Colonial Office interference.

Although he seems to have decided on war soon after news of the deaths of Sihayo's wives reached him, Frere was content to let Thesiger set the pace for invasion. It would be easy enough to engineer a rift with King Cetshwayo – but less so for Thesiger's troops to be ready to exploit it. Transport had to be organized and lines of supply drawn up, troops marched to assembly points, and auxiliaries raised to offset the small number of available imperial troops. It was also important to choose a time of year best suited to the need of the invader; any invasion of Zululand would be heavily dependent upon transport animals – horses and oxen – which would have to be fed upon local grasses. In the middle of 1878 Natal and Zululand were in a period of drought which had already lasted several years, and there was little nourishment to be found in the brown swathes of rank grass cloaking the hillsides. The summer rains were due at the end of the year, in November or December, and while there was a chance they might again fail, it was problematic planning an invasion at any other time. Even so, there were risks, for the renewal of grazing stocks would be traded against rising water levels in the rivers, with all the difficulties that implied for wheeled transport. Nevertheless, Thesiger decided, the summer months were the most opportune, with the added advantage that with the onset of wet weather the Zulu might be distracted from resistance by the need to harvest their mealie crop.

Throughout the second half of 1878 Thesiger laid his plans. By November, he was approaching readiness, and Frere embarked on the last gambit in his campaign to outmanoeuvre both King Cetshwayo and the Government in London. At last he sent a message to King Cetshwayo announcing that he was ready to make public the detailed conclusions of the Boundary Commission and inviting Zulu representatives to receive them at a meeting to be held at the Lower Thukela Drift on 11 December. Although he sent an official notification of his intentions to Hicks Beach at the Colonial Office, it did not arrive there until 25 January 1879.

And by that time the state of affairs in southern Africa could hardly have been more different.

*

King Cetshwayo received the news that the Boundary Commission's award was finally to be presented to him with relief.

The preceding few months had undeniably been tense. Not long after Mehlokazulu's foray across the border, the king had received complaints about it from the Natal authorities. He was prepared to be apologetic, condemning Mehlokazulu and his brothers as 'rash boys' acting out of misplaced 'zeal for their father's welfare', and offering £50 by way of compensation for Natal's injured dignity.[13] Such incidents had usually been settled at local levels in the past, but on this occasion Cetshwayo had been troubled when Sir Henry Bulwer had replied that nothing less than the surrender of Mehlokazulu and his fellow ringleaders would suffice.

Against the background of the hanging Boundary Commission report, this had seemed indicative of a new, hostile attitude among British and colonial officials. The king had sent several conciliatory messages, all of which were firmly rebuffed, and a feeling of alarm had spread through Zululand as to what this might portend. Bowing to pressure from his council not to be bullied by the British, the king had assembled several of his younger *amabutho* in September and had organized a ceremonial hunt down almost the entire length of the border. While such hunts were not unusual, they usually took place in the country between the Mhlope and Mnyama Mfolozi rivers, far away from the more sensitive border regions, and the move was little more than a show of strength. If it had been intended to make the British think twice, however, it was a distinct failure – from Pietermaritzburg the image of thousands of Zulus under arms assembling just across the borders seemed to confirm Frere's impression of the king's truculence. And indeed Cetshwayo was becoming frustrated, deeply worried by the change in British attitudes yet unable quite to fathom their motives.

The *amabutho* had stood down towards the end of September, only to muster again briefly the following month when a rumour had spread that British troops building a small earthwork fort at Utrecht were the vanguard of an invasion force. They, too, had soon been dismissed – for one thing, there was not enough food until the rains came to feed them at the royal homesteads – but there was a prevailing feeling, even among ordinary Zulus, that the kingdom was sliding into a crisis which it could neither fully comprehend nor resolve.

These tensions had created a distinct split among the council of senior men who advised the king. Prince Hamu, still smarting over the insolence displayed at the harvest ceremonies towards his uThulwana *ibutho* by the young men of the iNgobamakhosi – Mehlokazulu among them – had declared flatly that if it came to war he would not fight the British, and had urged the king to give up Sihayo's sons. He had been supported by others who, while professing their loyalty, were nonetheless disturbed at the prospect of the damage the rift might do to their trading links with Natal. Some of the younger men on the council were indignant at the white men's presumption, and had stood by the Zulu right to defend themselves if necessary. *Inkosi* Mnyamana Buthelezi, the head of the council – who was by nature a thoughtful and considered political analyst – had urged caution, and Cetshwayo himself was naturally inclined to placate the British rather than fall into a full-scale confrontation. Yet the king had also been reluctant to give up Mehlokazulu, both because Sihayo was a personal favourite and because to do so would in any case risk an embarrassing public climbdown. In the end, Prince Hamu had left the council in irritation in November and returned to his home in the north, leaving the conflict among the council unresolved.

The summons to the meeting on the Lower Thukela had at least brought an end to the months of agonizing. Determined to appear reasonable, Cetshwayo responded by announcing his willingness to abide by the Boundary Commission's report, whatever its decisions might be. If he seriously hoped a gesture of goodwill would resolve the brewing crisis, however, he was destined to be bitterly disappointed.

\*

The Zulu delegation arrived at the river's edge on the morning of 11 December to find the Thukela in flood, a sheet of fast-flowing brown water 300 metres wide. To their consternation, they saw that the British had already fortified a knoll on the Natal bank, and had stretched a hawser

across the river – fixed with a ship's anchor in Zulu soil – to facilitate the
building of a pont.[14] There were fourteen Zulu representatives, together
with thirty or forty attendants, and they represented no great gathering of the important *amakhosi* of the nation but rather a diplomatic
mission of court functionaries. They were led by the *induna* Vumandaba
kaNthathi, a trusted attendant of the king who was the senior officer of the
uKhandempemvu *ibutho*.

Rather than risk their dignity to the swollen river, the delegates accepted
an offer to ferry them across in the pont. On the Natal bank they found
that a tarpaulin had been stretched across a clump of wild fig trees just a
few metres from the water's edge, and here they were invited to squat down
in the shade. The official Natal party was already there before them, headed
by the Acting Secretary for Native Affairs, Matshana's nemesis, John Wesley
Shepstone. Nearby, in a conspicuous display of imperial might, a Royal
Navy detachment from the warship HMS *Active* was drawn up on parade,
with a field-gun and a Gatling machine gun pointed ominously at the
Zulu party. As Shepstone began the proceedings, reading out the Boundary
Commission's judgement, a Durban photographer captured the historic
scene for posterity.

The award ran to several pages and it was past noon by the time
Shepstone had finished speaking. Now and then, as it became clear that the
Commission had largely vindicated the Zulu position, Vumandaba and his
colleagues muttered their approval. However, although the Commission
had largely discounted the Boer claims, Frere had insisted that those farmers
living on land now nominally returned to the Zulu should be allowed to
remain in residence – but if this struck the Zulus as a decidedly hollow
triumph they did not comment on it.[15]

The meeting now broke up for lunch; Shepstone had provided a cow to
feed the Zulu delegates, and as it was a hot day the *izinduna* were offered
water sweetened with sugar, which they quaffed enthusiastically. To their
surprise, however, the proceedings were not at an end – at 2.30 Shepstone
asked them to sit down again, and he began to read a supplement Frere
had tagged on to the award.

It was a long and complex document, and Shepstone read it carefully,
clause by clause, to be sure that the Zulus understood it. It was clear from
their reactions that they did, for they struggled at times to maintain their
diplomatic composure.

Frere had made the boundary award conditional. He reminded the

Zulus that Theophilus Shepstone had extracted promises of good government from Cetshwayo at the 'coronation' of 1873, and that in British eyes the king had failed to live up to these. This confused the Zulu delegates, for whom Shepstone's pompous declarations at the coronation had held no such binding significance – 'who has complained?' asked one of them sharply, 'the Zulu people?' Undeterred, Shepstone drew attention to the *amabutho* system, pointing out that as British possessions now bordered Zululand on two sides it was the British who were most likely to be at risk if the king opted to deploy his men in action. If the Zulu posed a threat to the British, he said, the British offered them no such threat in return. Gesturing towards the sailors still lined up, sweating in the sun, one of the Zulus said that if this was true then, 'what are these we see here?'[16]

Then came the crux. Shepstone listed a series of violations of British territory allegedly carried out by Zulu subjects. Prime among these was Mehlokazulu's killing of MaMtshali and MaMthethwa, but for good measure Frere also cited a raid carried out in the Transvaal by the Swazi prince, Mbilini. Mbilini had fled Swaziland after an unsuccessful succession dispute in the 1860s and had offered his allegiance to Cetshwayo; much as he had done with Matshana kaMondise, Cetshwayo had welcomed him and settled him near the German mission settlement at Luneburg on the Phongolo river in the far north. Mbilini was an expert marauder, however, and on several occasions had tried to rebuild his fortunes by raiding cattle both from the Swazi and from Transvaal border farms. Now that the Transvaal was British, Frere wanted him held to account. Frere also complained that two Natal surveyors from the Royal Engineer's department, examining the state of the crossing at the Middle Drift three months earlier, had been detained and jostled when they had trespassed onto the Zulu bank. Frere demanded that Mehlokazulu and his brothers be surrendered, together with Prince Mbilini, for trial by a British court within twenty days, and that Cetshwayo further pay a heavy fine in cattle.

Even that was not all, and the Zulu delegates were aghast as the full extent of the British demands was revealed. The king was to disband the *amabutho* system, and allow all Zulu men to marry at will. A British resident was to be appointed to the Zulu court to advise the king on his policies. The killing of Zulu subjects without trial was to cease. Missionaries were to be allowed to work freely in Zululand. An extra ten days was generously allowed for the fulfilment of these requirements.

Frere had not specified what would happen if the king did not comply, but the show of force implicit in the line of sailors did his talking for him. The boundary award had been converted into an ultimatum – an ultimatum which no independent sovereign, proud of his history and traditions, could reasonably be expected to accept. Had Cetshwayo done so, he would have handed the effective management of his kingdom to the British – and Frere would, thus, have secured his objective. But Frere had never seriously considered that the king would accept his ultimatum – it had been carefully drafted to give Cetshwayo little room to comply.

The Zulu delegates were stunned by the unexpected turn of events and by the brashness of the demands. 'You mean you are going to destroy Zululand for the sake of two foolish children?' one asked.[17]

That was exactly what Frere had in mind.

# 10

## 'An uncommonly rough road'

### Charlie Harford, the Natal Native Contingent, and Prince Sikhotha's shirt

It had been Thesiger's request to London for reinforcements in September 1878 which brought Charlie Harford and the first clutch of special service officers to Durban – a small consolation prize offered as a sop by an adroit War Office determined not to be bullied otherwise into a war it did not want to wage.

The *Edinburgh Castle* had arrived on 2 December, nine days before the formal presentation of Frere's ultimatum at the Lower Thukela. Even by that stage it was evident that Thesiger's claim that reinforcements were needed for purely defensive operations was a fiction. Both London and oNdini might still have been labouring under the illusion that a crisis could be averted, but Sir Fred Thesiger was already marshalling his troops, and the regulars who had recently suppressed the Xhosa rising were being moved up to Natal in batches. In Thesiger's headquarters obscure points on maps close to the border had been marked down as points of assembly.

Thesiger, indeed, was no longer Thesiger. On 5 October 1878 his father had died, and he had officially succeeded to the title of Lord Chelmsford. The change in his social standing seemed opportune – he was now fifty-one years old, fresh from a successful if rather minor campaign, and about to embark upon what must have seemed, even to him, the greatest challenge of his career so far. For the first time he was to be in charge of a campaign from its inception – whereas he had inherited the Xhosa entanglement from his predecessor, Cunynghame, the Zulu campaign was Chelmsford's to plan and execute from the very start.

The time available for him to do so was limited. Although it had been clear for at least six months that Frere was contemplating intervention in Zululand, Chelmsford was constrained by the pace of political developments, and in particular by the British Government's reluctance to sanction invasion. Only once the ultimatum was delivered would it be possible to prepare an offensive strategy openly and with an admissible sense of purpose. By then he would have just thirty days in which to position his troops and bring his command up to a state of war readiness.

Chelmsford's original plan called for five separate columns to advance towards oNdini from different positions along the border. Between them, these columns would cover the most obvious points of entry into the kingdom, and thereby restrict the ability of the Zulu to slip between them and launch a counter-strike in Natal. Since he was not at all convinced that the Zulu would stand and fight – a view largely shaped by his recent experience on the frontier – Chelmsford also hoped that these converging columns would ultimately leave the Zulu little room to manoeuvre, and that they would eventually be forced to engage with one or another of them. As each column would have to take its own baggage train to sustain it, Chelmsford was aware from the start that the pace of advance might be slow, limited by the speed of draft oxen and men walking on foot. There would, he knew, be little chance of any column advancing rapidly to support another, so he intended that each one be strong enough to resist the entire Zulu army on its own. London's refusal to supply fresh troops meant that he would have to accomplish this with the men already at his disposal in southern Africa – a total, in November 1878, of just nine infantry battalions, including the two en route from London, and only two Artillery batteries. At full strength an infantry battalion numbered 30 officers and 866 men, but those which had been in the field for any length of time were often woefully under strength, sapped by the natural wastage of time-expired men, or those lost through sickness and, some-times, battle casualties. It was not unknown for a battalion fighting unit to number little more than 600 men, and Chelmsford therefore faced the prospect of invading Zululand – whose army his own intelligence reports assessed at over 40,000 men[1] – with a backbone of redcoats numbering little more than 5,000.

Yet even this number of forces presented him with a huge logistical challenge. The Zulu army would be fighting on its home turf, in an environment to which its men were accustomed from birth – its men could cover greater distances than any the British might achieve, and, since the *amabutho* were seldom assembled in the field for more than a fortnight before the men dispersed again to their homes, it required only a minimum of logistical support. British troops, in contrast, could expect to be in the field for as long as the campaign lasted, and would have to carry with them everything they needed to stay alive and function as an army – food, tents, ammunition and equipment would all have to be transported over mountains and through rivers in a country which possessed only a handful of rudimentary tracks made over the years by traders' wagons. A single infantry battalion would require eighteen wagons to carry its tents, ammunition and equipment – and more to bring up regular supplies of food.

In a European theatre the British Army relied upon mule-drawn 'general service' wagons for its baggage requirements but there were too few of these available in southern Africa, and they had in any case proved unreliable in the veld because their narrow wheel-base made them prone to upsetting. Instead, Chelmsford instructed his officers to buy or hire civilian transport wagons – the great long, tough, heavy vehicles which were the mainstay of the colonial transport system. These required a minimum of sixteen oxen to pull them – more, often, when crossing rivers or hauling up rocky hillsides or through a difficult *donga*, or deep gully. Managing the oxen was an art in itself, for it was safe to yoke and work them for no more than four hours a day – in between they required long periods of rest and grazing if they were not to succumb to exhaustion or a frightening array of usually fatal diseases. For the most part the Army recognized its inexperience in this area and was content to hire civilian drivers and *voorloopers* – African lads who walked beside the team controlling the oxen with their long whips. While the rates of pay offered were certainly enough to tempt many volunteers – to the detriment, sometimes, of the Natal economy – few were used to working together in the long convoys the Army required, and the difficulties of managing large numbers of wagons on the road soon established itself as a characteristic of the campaign.

Chelmsford was well aware of the key role logistics would play in the invasion – it had caused him enormous problems on the Eastern Cape Frontier against the Xhosa – and he approached it now in his usual meticulous way. In a general order of November 1878 he specified that each column should include one transport officer in overall charge of the baggage train, assisted by a civilian head conductor, and by a sub-conductor for every ten wagons. Each wagon should have a driver and *voorlooper* and wagons were to move in sections of ten or columns of twenty. Each invading column was required to carry supplies for ten days, and should be ready to advance 16 kilometres a day.

The problem was, however, that there were neither enough wagons nor transport officers available on the eve of the invasion, even after Army agents had denuded the civilian economy in Natal by offering inflated prices for wagons and teams. Nor was there much in the way of trained logistical support – at the end of the battle against the Xhosa Chelmsford's Commissary General, Edward Strickland, had just nineteen officers and twenty-nine men available in the whole of southern Africa with whom to organize the transport for Chelmsford's entire Zulu campaign.

Reluctantly, Chelmsford bowed to the inevitable. He decided to concentrate his resources into three offensive columns, relegating the remaining two to a defensive role protecting exposed stretches of the border against possible Zulu counter-attack. The offensive columns would advance by way of the three best-established entry points into the Zulu kingdom, where there were at least tracks for them to follow. The first, designated the No. 1 or Right Flank Column, would cross at the Lower Thukela Drift; the next, the No. 3 or Centre Column, would cross at Rorke's Drift, while the third, the No. 4 or Left Flank Column, would advance from the direction of Utrecht and the Transvaal border. Of the defensive columns, one – No. 2 – would be positioned between numbers 1 and 3 on the high escarpment over the Thukela at Middle Drift to prevent a Zulu attack through the broken central border country into Msinga. The other, No. 5, would be placed at the northernmost point of the disputed territory. From here it could protect both the Transvaal and Swazi borders, and in the event that the inhabitants of either decided to enter the war on the wrong side prevent their intervention.

Each column was appointed its own commander and given specific objectives; from the first, however, it is clear that Chelmsford conceived his plan as a central thrust with flanking columns in support. To that end, he decided that he would personally accompany the Centre Column. This was the most likely, he had decided, to be in the thick of any fighting – and he intended to command the invasion very much from the front.

*

On their arrival, there proved to be more than enough positions left for the eager young men who had formed such easy friendships on the *Edinburgh Castle* on the way out to South Africa – and among them the unglamorous world of transport duties loomed large. The group had broken up when they landed, some heading straight off to report to Chelmsford's headquarters in Pietermaritzburg while others, like Harford, had lingered a day or two to make their final preparations for the coming campaign. While they would find themselves scattered among the assembling columns, several of the group were allotted similar duties, and the paths of some of them were destined to cross again.

For Lieutenants Cecil Williams and Horace Smith-Dorrien there were transport duties, Williams with No. 4 Column, then assembling at Utrecht,[2] and Smith-Dorrien with the Centre Column. If William Cochrane had hoped for something more exciting than his previous uninspiring service in southern Africa, he must have felt disappointed when he was ordered to report to No. 2 Column, which had been allocated a defensive position on the central Thukela. Lieutenant Courtnay, the cavalryman whom Harford had met while shopping in London, had better luck – he was appointed to the staff of the mounted troops of No. 1 Column.

Yet if the mundane reality of transport work came as something of a let-down after the high hopes of the journey out, scarcely likely to offer much hope of distinction or promotion, it at least afforded a taste of a healthy outdoor life in the exotic environment that was Africa, and the baby of the group, nineteen-year-old Horace Smith-Dorrien, soon developed a taste for it:

> It was a great experience for a boy. I found myself alone controlling the convoys, along a great stretch of road, supplying equipment, purchasing oxen, and generally keeping things going. The skilful handling of the teams of sixteen oxen made a great impression on me. The driver who wielded the whip was usually an Afrikander [sic]; the oxen were named and, when the pull became very heavy, were urged forward by name and pistol-like cracks of the whip. Such names as 'Dootchman', 'German' and 'Englischmann' [sic] were bestowed on them, and when a wretched animal possessed the last it seemed to me there was more emphasis in shouting it out, and more venom in the lash when applying it.[3]

Yet it was Charlie Harford's knowledge of isiZulu, he was convinced, that kept him on a winning streak – he was given the post of staff officer with a new African auxiliary unit, the 3rd Regiment, Natal Native Contingent. The regiment was assembling far out on the fringes of the colony, between Msinga and the Zulu border, and Harford was ordered to join it at the Sandspruit crossing, on the near side of the Biggarsberg heights on the road to Rorke's Drift:

I set to work to draw my pony and carbine, which the Government allowed and which, if still in existence at the end of the campaign, had to be returned. I visited the Pay Office to get some money, arranged for my baggage to be sent on as soon as it arrived at Durban, got a few items of saddlery from my old friend Williams, the saddler, and, as one pony would not suffice for my work, bought another, a sturdy little grey . . .

In a couple of days I was able to start. Riding one pony and leading the other, which carried all my requirements until the wagons arrived at Sand Spruit with the heavier baggage, which was a little over a month, I travelled to Greytown the first day, about forty-five miles [72 kilo-metres]. As there were several nasty crossings and *spruits* (streams), as well as an uncommonly rough road from there on to Sand Spruit, as well as the distance being a little greater, I stopped the next day at a little wattle-and-daub store . . . a little more than half way. This enabled me to get into camp the following day before it got dark.[4]

Even today the road from Greytown to the Biggarsberg is one of the most spectacular in KwaZulu-Natal, picking its way gingerly down steep rocky hillsides as it descends from Greytown into the hot, stony valley of the Mooi river, before climbing over the Msinga mountains, only to drop down dizzyingly again towards the formidable Thukela and, finally, Biggarsberg. At the end of it, for Charlie Harford, lay the Sandspruit, an undistinguished stream across the track, a spot that held no significance beyond that on a military map, an open swathe of waving grass, still dry and brittle before the rains. Yet there was at least activity here, signalled by a splash of white against the grass, and the bustle of men around them – the headquarters tents of his new regiment.

The 3rd Regiment of the Natal Native Contingent was assembling, and beside the tents lay a ramshackle sprawl of temporary grass shelters shrouded in a haze of dust and wood smoke. Groups of men were already making their way out of the hills to converge there, and more would follow on a daily basis – long straggling columns moving to the beat of deep, sonorous war-songs, the dark lines of men broken by blotches of white, black and brown from their great war shields, the sun glinting on the points of their spears, which they swung as they walked.

Charlie Harford was truly back in Africa again.

\*

The Natal Native Contingent was the result of Lord Chelmsford's efforts to bolster his regular troops by creating an auxiliary unit from among Natal's black African population. In this he had not been entirely unsuccessful – and nor had it been achieved without a struggle.

When he had first arrived in Pietermaritzburg in August 1878, Chelmsford had expected to find the colony already on a war footing, fully prepared for the daily prospect of the Zulu invasion which Frere and Shepstone had assured him was imminent. Instead he had been shocked to find that most colonists seemed detached from the prospect of a war; even Natal's senior administrator, Sir Henry Bulwer, remained determined, notwithstanding the Mehlokazulu affair, to head off a confrontation if at all possible. Apart from an old crumbling earthwork, Fort Williamson, built at the Lower Thukela during the scares of 1861, Chelmsford found the border with Zululand entirely unprotected, and only the haziest of plans existed among the civil authorities for the defence of the frontier farming communities.

The volunteer militia movement had a long history among the white settlers, pre-dating even the advent of British authority, and it had been given a boost by the scares which had accompanied the Langalibalele affair, but in 1878 Natal's military establishment still remained tiny. It consisted of just one full-time police unit, the Natal Mounted Police, and fifteen Volunteer Corps – 11 mounted, 3 infantry and 1 artillery. The colonial Government provided weapons and equipment for these while the men chose their own uniforms and elected their officers. The Volunteers were part-time soldiers whose only commitment, outside of an actual emergency, was to attend a training camp once a year. Most had very little military experience: while the police were regularly employed in civil law enforcement duties, only the Natal Carbineers – who had served under Durnford at Bushman's River Pass – had any experience of the rigours and scares of active service. Even so, Chelmsford recognized the value of the militia, for the men could ride and shoot and knew the peculiarities of the country well, and he was in any case desperately short of mounted troops for a campaign where good scouting would prove essential. Raised to defend the colony, however, the Volunteers were precluded by the terms of their enlistment from serving outside Natal's boundaries, and their numbers were in any case small – they totalled no more than a few hundred men, and most individual units were only forty or fifty strong. Their numbers might be bolstered by irregulars – full-time units raised locally for a limited period of service by the Army itself – but they still fell dramatically short of the numbers Chelmsford would require.

The colony's black population was an obvious alternative recruiting ground. Chelmsford estimated there were 65,000 African men within the colony capable of bearing arms. This was far in excess of his requirements – he needed, he anticipated, no more than 7,600 auxiliary troops – and, briefed upon the colony's history by Shepstone, Chelmsford was convinced that the historical animosity many African groups felt towards the Zulu kings could be exploited to his advantage

To get them – as well as the use of the Volunteer Corps – however, he needed Bulwer's support, since Bulwer's position as Supreme Chief meant that he was not only head of the colony's white troops but also supreme chief of the African population. Yet Bulwer was determined to give no encouragement to the war unless absolutely forced to it, and throughout September and October he had prevaricated as both Chelmsford and Frere put pressure on him. Finally, Bulwer was boxed into a corner, but he would not take it upon himself to overrule the Volunteers' terms of enlistment but instead agreed to ballot the members to see if they were prepared to place themselves under military control and serve in Zululand. The over-whelming majority had agreed – many of them persuaded by promises of land in a prospective post-war division of Zululand[5] – but even so Chelmsford had secured the services of no more than 370 men. He remained determined to mobilize black support for the invasion but not until the beginning of November did Bulwer cave in and the Natal Assembly agree to authorize the raising of Chelmsford's auxiliaries. By that time Frere had already drawn up his timetable for invasion – which meant the so-called Natal Native Contingent would have to be raised, trained, officered and equipped in a matter of just weeks.

The plan for raising the Contingent was given by Chelmsford to a man he considered most suitable for the job, an imperial officer who had, almost uniquely, served in action with black troops from Natal before, and understood something of both their strengths, and weaknesses – Anthony Durnford. If Durnford shared many of Bishop Colenso's reservations about the justice of Frere's policies, he was not prepared to let his private thoughts interfere with his duty, and he tackled the task with typical drive and determination. He came up with a plan to raise 5,000 infantry and 500 cavalry under white authority – 'patriarchal – the only kind suitable',[6] and to make up for any shortfall in regular Engineers he further proposed that 500 black Native Pioneers be raised as a trained labour gang.

Durnford's original plan had called for the contingent to be raised, organized and officered on essentially British lines, and to be issued with obsolete British uniforms and firearms to clearly distinguish it from the Zulu in the field. The Natal Assembly had baulked at supplying guns in any quantity, however, for the settler fear of an armed uprising among the colony's African majority ran deep. Nor, indeed, were there enough old uniforms in Government stores to go round, nor money to provide more, and in the end it was agreed that the men of the NNC would receive nothing more than a blanket and a red rag to twist around their heads or arm as a badge of their allegiance. One in ten of them – those selected to be non-commissioned officers (NCOs) – would be issued firearms, mostly old percussion models. The rest would be instructed to attend the muster with their traditional weapons.

The limitations this placed on the NNC were certainly obvious enough from the beginning, yet Lord Chelmsford never intended to deploy them tactically as shock troops. His principal need was for light troops who could match the Zulu for mobility, who could be employed as scouts, and who in action could be used to follow after a defeated enemy. For all this, despite obvious shortcomings, the NNC had a good deal to offer.

The men were to be raised according to the familiar *isibhalo* system, by which the Natal government had levied labour gangs in the past, and orders were sent out to white magistrates in the locations instructing them to raise a quota from each of the *amakhosi* in their district. The men were to gather locally first, then march to designated points for the enrolment of each regiment along the route of each column's march towards Zululand. Bulwer had hoped that Chelmsford might draw upon such vestiges of the *amabutho* system as still remained among the Natal chiefdoms, a system the men instinctively understood and which provided them with a continuity of group identity and considerable psychological support. Chelmsford, however, struggled to manage so great a break with British military tradition and in the end, while some attempt was made to keep men from the same chiefdoms together, they were forced instead into British-style formations. The contingent as a whole would be made up of three separate regiments, the first two comprising three battalions and the other, two. Each battalion was to consist of a headquarters section and ten companies. The commanding officers were all to be Europeans, as were the company officers – a captain, two lieutenants and six NCOs. There was, however, also to be an African officer in each company, together with ten black NCOs and ninety men.

By the end of 1878 it had already become problematic to raise an officer corps for the new contingent. Although Chelmsford could spare a few regular officers for senior posts, there were certainly not enough to go round, nor did he in any case intend to denude his own core of professional soldiers for the benefit of the auxiliaries. But as military preparations had intensified and rumours of war abounded, almost all whites in Natal prepared to serve with the Army in some capacity had either joined their Volunteer Corps units, enrolled as irregulars or signed on in the far more profitable – and less demanding – role of wagon-drivers. Chelmsford's solution was to look to the Eastern Cape for recruits, where many men who had recently served in the now-disbanded auxiliary or Irregular units there were still idling away their accumulated pay in frontier canteens. Among them were some who had already earned a good reputation as auxiliary commanders, men like Rupert LaTour Lonsdale, a short, wiry fresh-faced former officer of the 74th Highlanders and Frontier magistrate to whom Chelmsford now offered the command of the 3rd NNC. Lonsdale accepted, and his commitment had drawn a number of volunteers after him but Chelmsford was still forced to make up the numbers from those who remained. Some of these were the dregs of the disbanded Irregular units, men who had little understanding or sympathy for the Africans they were about to command, and who would not hesitate to use their fists to enforce their commands. Others were Europeans, mostly Germans or Scandinavians, descendants of retired British German Legion troops settled on the frontier a generation before, or itinerants who had come to work the diamond fields and drifted to the war instead. Many were decent enough men, but their linguistic skills were as limited as their military ones – almost none of them could speak isiZulu, and some of them struggled to understand English.

*

The strategic significance of the Sandspruit as the assembly point for the 3rd Regiment NNC reflected both the fact that it lay astride the road to Rorke's Drift and that it was on the boundary of the great Msinga location, from where the majority of its African soldiers would be drawn.

The choice of the Msinga chiefdoms as a recruiting ground had, of course, been because of Shepstone's belief that of all Natal's African groups those living in Msinga held the most intense antipathy towards the Zulu royal house. Their fortunes had been linked to the kingdom across the river since the rise of the Zulu half a century before, and Shepstone had assured Chelmsford that there were deep-seated animosities among them that could be easily mobilized to assist recruiting. Typically, Shepstone had a broader vision, too, and one quite audacious in its scope. By opening old sores within the African communities on both sides of the political divide, sores that harked back to the very conflicts which had created the Zulu kingdom, he hoped to pick away at the bonds that bound the kingdom together. He hoped to reduce the role of the Zulu monarchy, not only to destroy its political power but to undermine its significance as a fount of power and independence, and to reduce the *amakhosi* in both Natal and Zululand to a common position in which none acknowledged the ascendancy of another, and from which they would be powerless to unite against the imposition of a broader imperial authority. He hoped, no less, to turn the clock back to the time before King Shaka, before the Zulu had emerged as a focus for unity and strength. He was more than willing to exploit the resentments which still lingered among those in Natal who had remained outside the control of the Zulu kings, who remembered their bitter struggles of old, in order to achieve it. The violence of those days still echoed in the memories of those involved, and Shepstone intended to harness that lingering resentment and direct it against the people he believed had been responsible for it in the first place – the Zulu.

As a policy, this was almost the definition of 'divide and rule'. And the Msinga population in the late 1870s was undeniably ripe for it. Profoundly affected by John Shepstone's attack upon Matshana kaMondise in 1858, the balance of power within the location had shifted, since the ousting of the Sithole, in favour of the amaChunu people of *inkosi* Phakade kaMancingwana. The amaChunu certainly shared a tangled history with the Zulu kings – driven out of the Mzinyathi valley by Shaka, they had returned to Zululand years later, only to be harried and chased out again by Mpande. *Inkosi* Pakhade declared himself enthusiastically in favour of the proposed British invasion – he had little enough choice – but he was too old to take to the field himself, and sent his son and heir, Gabangaye, to represent him. Gabangaye was himself a middle-aged man – Harford thought him 'wizened-up' – but he was a noted orator and had a good command of the long and tangled history of his people's relationship with the Zulu. In all, more than 700 men of the amaChunu were to join the ranks of the 3rd Regiment, and they were to form the largest single group in its ranks.

Msinga was home, too, to many of those political refugees from Zululand who were opposed to King Cetshwayo. Many of these were iziGqoza, followers of the various rival princes who had fled Zululand in the aftermath of Cetshwayo's victory over Mbuyazi in 1856. Their numbers had been swollen over the years, most recently by men from the royal *amabutho* whose allegiance had been soured by the marriage of the iNgcugce. These, too, had been called upon to enlist, and altogether 300 of them complied – real Zulus all, as their officers never failed to note.

The iziGqoza were led by two men for whom Chelmsford entertained high hopes once the war was begun – two of Cetshwayo's own brothers, the Princes Mkhungo kaMpande and Sikhotha kaMpande. Both had lived in Natal for decades but they had maintained clandestine links with their supporters inside Zululand and Shepstone had continually advised Chelmsford that Cetshwayo's administration was deeply unpopular among ordinary Zulus. Chelmsford, indeed, had been so convinced that he had made provision for 'a large number of Cetewayo's subjects [who] may wish to avoid fighting, and may desire to come across our Border for protection . . . Every reliable account from that country', he wrote, 'shows conclusively that Cetewayo is most unpopular, and those who are best informed regarding the state of feelings in Zululand are of the opinion that an internal revolution is not only possible but probable . . .'[7]

Such a revolution seemed all the more possible if the British were in a position to enforce a legitimate regime change. Whatever the true strength of their claims, Mkhungo and Sikhotha were undeniably sons of Mpande, and would have more credibility in Zululand than any puppet king brought in from outside and propped up by British bayonets. Their willingness to support the invasion was, moreover, a considerable propaganda coup for Lord Chelmsford, and added apparent weight to Frere's claims that the invasion was not directed against the Zulu people but specifically against the man whom he had damned as a despot, King Cetshwayo.

Towards the end of 1878 the two princes had agreed to visit the muster at Sandspruit in a show of support for the invasion. Mkhungo, who was both the older and senior in rank, proved to be too portly to take to the field himself and was content to let his younger brother Sikhotha represent him. Sikhotha was fully prepared to cross the border and fight against his countrymen, and in recognition of his enthusiasm he was given an honorary position on Lonsdale's staff. Sikhotha was a handsome man in his early forties who looked a good deal like his father, King Mpande. His apparently soft physique belied his physical toughness and he had about him an air of authority, typical of the royal house, which impressed even those Europeans inclined to be dismissive of African airs and graces.

Sikhotha's presence legitimized the British invasion in the eyes of many in the ranks of the NNC, and as a conspicuous badge of their alliance Commandant Lonsdale offered him the gift of one of his shirts. Unfortunately Sikhotha was a large man and Lonsdale was not, and even the most generous of Lonsdale's shirts did not fit as well as it might. Undaunted, as if he realized it was emblematic of the role the British wanted him to play in Zululand, Sikhotha struggled to squeeze into it – and once it was on, he showed himself more than a little reluctant to take it off again. He wore it about the camp for several days afterwards.

*

Charlie Harford soon settled into his duties as Staff Officer to the 3rd NNC at Sandspruit. 'The work of organisation went on rapidly,' he noted, '. . . the European officers and NCOs had all arrived, and Lonsdale had already told them off to their Battalions. Commandant Hamilton Browne, "Maori", Browne, as he was called, had the 1st Battalion and Commandant Cooper the 2nd. All were adventurers – and the very best of fellows, ready to do anything and go anywhere.'[8] The very best of fellows? Perhaps. Privately Harford confessed to his mother that he had experienced 'a most awful time with these people, but I will say one thing the European officer and NCO are a thousand percent worse than the natives'.[9]

It was hardly surprising that Harford's new colleagues had about them more than a fair share of rough edges; most had been driven by misfortune, debt, failed romances or sheer wanderlust to drift rootlessly around the Empire, and in Natal had found themselves washed up, for a while at least, at the high-water mark of their adventurism. And of them all, the newly appointed commander of the 3rd Regiment's 2nd Battalion undoubtedly possessed a past which threatened to out-chequer them all. Born into a military family of Irish descent in Cheltenham in 1844, George Hamilton Browne[10] had shown a propensity for roistering at an early age. By his own account – which is by no means reliable – he had been:

. . . arrested, while a schoolboy from Cheltenham on his way to a shoot
at Wimbledon, on suspicion of being a Fenian; enlisted as a gunner;
blew up his father with a squib cigar; shot his man in a duel in
Germany; biked into the Lake of Geneva; went to New Zealand where
for twelve years he fought the Maoris; ate a child while starving, and
afterwards hunted bushrangers in Australia; took a schooner in search
of copper island, or anything else of value; next a Papal Zoave; under
Colonel Dodge in America he fought the Sioux . . .[11]

Quite how much of this is true it is difficult now to determine; certainly
Browne was universally known throughout his later career by the nickname 'Maori', and only after his death did it transpire that the New Zealand
government had no record of any service in his name prior to 1872, when
the last shots in the long cycle of wars there had all but spluttered out.
Hard-bitten, colourful, a practised storyteller, it seemed that George Hamilton Browne had few qualms about passing off, as his own, adventures
which had in fact befallen other men.[12] Nevertheless he had undeniably
knocked about the world and had recently fought with an Irregular unit,
Pulleine's Rangers on the Cape Frontier. In December 1878 Browne turned
thirty-four years old; he had boxed in his youth and was still lean and
tough, handsome with a heavy moustache and an intimidating look, a man
neither easily unsettled nor trifled with – and possessed of a full range of
contemporary prejudices which he did not shy away from expressing.

Like many of his colleagues, Hamilton Browne held the men under his
command in contempt, and he confessed himself disappointed to have
been attached to the NNC. 'I had been looking forward to having the
command of a troop of mounted scouts', he admitted.[13] Browne did not
hesitate to vent his frustration on his men, and despite the fact that
Chelmsford's headquarters had issued a booklet entitled *The General
Management of Natives* – which urged officers to refrain from abusive
language, to take note of African courtesies and forms of address, and
generally to look upon them as 'an intelligent child' – Browne habitually
referred to his own men as 'niggers', 'curs' and 'scum'.[14] It is perhaps
significant that Robert Baden-Powell – who met Browne years later in
Matabeleland, enjoyed his company and was realistic enough to acknowledge that it was by such men that empires grew – noted that Browne
enjoyed being photographed in swaggering poses, theatrically pointing guns
at cowering Africans.

If Harford found life among the contingent very different to the regular soldiering he was used to, there was, at least, an oddly touching personal reunion in store for him:

> The surroundings of my tent were looked upon as the *Indaba* [discussion] ground and all who had complaints to make, or who wished to ask questions, found their way there early in the morning and squatted patiently and silently in rows or semicircles until I made my appearance. . . . One morning I had a really wonderful, and at the same time very pleasant, surprise sprung on me. During the *indaba* a man suddenly stood up in the middle of the assembly and, putting his hand to his chin, exclaimed, 'Waugh! Ow! Wenu Charlie!!!' So I called him up and found that he had worked on our farm at Pinetown. . . . I took him on at once as my personal servant, and stuck to his old name of 'Jim' . . . [15]

There was another – unofficial – addition to the regiment's officer corps about this time too, when, shortly before Christmas, Charles Norris-Newman, the 'Special Correspondent for the *London Standard* and the *Cape Standard* and *Mail* arrived, accompanied by our medical officer, Dr Beresford'. While none of them knew of him, they 'made him very welcome, and he turned out to be an excellent and garrulous companion in our mess. Lonsdale at once named him "Noggs",[16] and by this name he was subsequently known throughout the 3rd Column.'[17]

The enigmatic Charles Norris-Newman – he is referred to by several who met him by the rank of captain, although no details of any military service, regular or colonial, have yet emerged – was shortly to find himself in that most envied of journalists' happenstance, the role of a rather minor reporter thrust unexpectedly into a scoop of world-class proportions.

The thirst for knowledge among the citizens of the British Empire was of course fed by a highly sophisticated and experienced newspaper industry operating from London, the hub of imperial power, and reporters and war artists – who produced sketches in the field which were worked up as woodblock engravings in an age before photographs could easily be reproduced – were constantly travelling the world in pursuit of dramatic events. Some of the best of the day – Melton Prior of the *Illustrated London News* and Charles Fripp of the *Graphic* – had been on hand to cover the closing stages of Chelmsford's conquest of the Cape frontier but so successful had Frere been at obfuscating his true intent in Zululand that they, along with a host of others in London, had abandoned Africa in favour of far more promising events in Afghanistan. It was left to local reporters to make what they could of what was expected to be no more than a little local difficulty. Norris-Newman, 'having been sometime previously residing in Natal',[18] saw his chance and took it.

Victorian war correspondents were every bit as 'embedded' as their modern counterparts, and few of them, like Noggs, had any qualms about approaching the war in a gung-ho style; many shared the same background and preoccupations as the Army's officer class, and few were ideologically equipped to make the great imaginative leap necessary to put themselves in the enemy's position and report Queen Victoria's wars in a truly unbiased manner. They knew, in any case, that in most situations their white skins would mark them out as being part of the British combatant forces – and they knew too that while the British public thrilled to the exploits of its thin red line of heroes, and relished tales of the dashing successes, or mindless folly, of its generals, the perspective of the average Maori warrior, Afghan hillman or Zulu sold few enough newspapers.

Norris-Newman had thus set forth fully intent on throwing himself into the thick of the unfolding drama. Guessing the Centre Column would play a prominent part in the action he had ridden down the same road as Charlie Harford a fortnight later. In Greytown, along the way, he had passed the camp of the 24th Regiment – 'I found both men and officers on the qui vive to hear the order given to march to the front'[19] – and fallen in with a civilian surgeon, Dr W.H. Beresford, who was one of a number employed by the Government and sent out to Natal to make up the deficiency in trained medical staff among the garrison there. Beresford was on his way to join the 3rd, and the two had followed the border road. Along the way the long overdue late summer rains had struck them, and with a fury stored up by years of drought, so that they were 'simply wet to the skin; and utterly heedless of the height and torrent of the swollen river, we plunged in harum-scarum, got through to the other side safely, and reached the accommodation-house on the other bank'.[20]

When they arrived at the Sandspruit camp Noggs had simply stuck with Beresford, 'and naturally thinking that, wherever there was any fighting, the native regiments would surely be in the van, I promised that I would go in with them ... This settled the matter. I sported the red puggree,[21] joined the senior mess, and in fact soon came to be looked upon as "one of them".'[22]

As the NNC shook themselves into an order of sorts, long lines of weathered, mostly bearded men in faded red coats began to march up the road and past the Sandspruit, heading towards the Biggarsberg heights, and the spot appointed for the assembly of the Centre Column. Norris-Newman's choice would prove more opportune than he knew.

# 11

# 'A Dreadful Sameness'

## The British Empire comes to Helpmekaar

Those lines of men the NNC had noticed marching past the camp at the Sandspruit were proof that, by the end of 1878, the pace of Chelmsford's preparations was accelerating. With the time allotted in Frere's ultimatum ticking away, and no decisive response from King Cetshwayo, Chelmsford was moving the regular elements of his invasion force to their assembly points.

Chelmsford had picked Helpmekaar, on the top of the Biggarsberg heights, as the assembly point for the Centre Column. In truth, Helpmekaar was scarcely a less bleak and empty spot than the Sandspruit. Although the Vermaak family continued to farm their scattered holdings across the ridge as they had done for forty years, Helpmekaar itself was no more than a junction on the road. There was no settlement to distinguish it, just a single store beside the wagon-track and, a kilometre or so away, a solitary church which catered for the spiritual well-being of the settler community. The main road still climbed up from Msinga through the old Voortrekker cutting that had given the place its name – Helpmekaar, help one another – and struck up across the open grass ridge-top on its way north to the hamlet of Dundee. At Helpmekaar, however, a side road branched off eastwards, dropping down off the ridge by way of the steep Knostrope Pass and trickling down into the valley, before meandering past Jim Rorke's lonely farmhouse and across the Mzinyathi and into Zululand.

Chelmsford, of course, had spotted the strategic advantages of Helpmekaar at once. Placed squarely astride the border road, it was directly linked to an established transport network which connected to the rear with a supply line running via Pietermaritzburg all the way to Durban; while ahead it afforded one of the few viable routes by which large numbers of men and – more to the point – heavily laden transport wagons might go directly into Zululand. Moreover, Helpmekaar would provide an easily defensive campsite on the open hill-top, with good views over the border a few kilometres away, and with the intense heat and possible wet weather of summer imminent, it was likely to be more healthy for the gathering of thousands of men and animals than the low-lying ground closer to the river.

Towards the end of November the grassy summit sprouted its first crop of white tents as the first elements allocated to the column began to arrive there. This increase in activity was not lost upon the Zulu community living on the other side of the border. While the king and his council were still undecided how best to react to Frere's ultimatum, one thing was clear enough to the amaQungebeni watching from their homesteads across the Mzinyathi from Rorke's Drift. The hollow promise of the Boundary Commission had been a sham, and instead of giving back Zulu lands, it seemed that the British were mustering to punish the Zulu for Mehloka-zulu's folly.

Matshana had been right all along: the British and their red soldiers were coming.

*

The disciplined core of the Centre Column were the regulars of two infantry battalions, the 1st and 2nd of the 24th Regiment, who began to arrive at Helpmekaar from the middle of December.

The infantry battalion – rather than the regiment – was the standard battlefield unit of the 1870s. Strategic theory dictated that, where a regiment consisted of more than one battalion, one battalion should always be kept on garrison duty at home in Britain while the other was overseas, but the simple truth was that the demands of the expanding Empire kept more battalions on active service than was strictly desirable. Even so, battalions from the same regiment might find themselves deployed at opposite ends of the globe, and it was highly unusual for two to be sent to the same theatre together. Nor was it anything more than coincidence on this occasion – the 1/24th had been stationed at the Cape for several years, while the 2/24th had only recently arrived to take part in the last of the mopping-up operations against the Xhosa. As luck would have it, both battalions had been deployed on the Cape frontier but while their paths had crossed in the field they had not fought side by side. The coming campaign in Zululand would be the first opportunity in their regimental history to do so, and both officers and men were delighted at the prospect.

To celebrate the fact, once the headquarters of both battalions had made the long trudge up to Helpmekaar, the officers of the 1st Battalion had invited the officers of the 2nd to dinner in their mess.

In truth, there was little of the glamour so beloved by modern film-makers about life in a regimental mess in the field in southern Africa in the 1870s – no regimental silver proudly displayed, no waiters in formal dress, and few enough arcane rituals or forced formality. Indeed, at least one officer noted ruefully that by comparison with the conditions apparently enjoyed by their counterparts then at war in Afghanistan they were positively disadvantaged:

> We ragged ones used to look with envy on the pictures in the *Illustrated London News* about the Afghan War. There the mess-tent of some regiment was shown, wherein was an officer digging into a plump ham; several servants handing round 'Simpkin' [champagne], and most striking of all, a tablecloth on the table. Why, there was not a mess in Zululand, unless it were the General's; our waiters were 'Tommy Atkins', simple and fairly pure; ham would have commanded the price of a dinner for six at the Club if it had put in an appearance . . .[1]

At Helpmekaar the officers of the 1st Battalion perhaps enjoyed the advantages of a marquee, and even the luxury of foldaway chairs and tables rather than furniture improvised from packing cases and biscuit boxes, as would become the norm later. They had husbanded a few bottles of wine from their time at the Cape, too, so the celebratory evening proved a great success, full of excitement and hope for the coming campaign.

It was a week or two short of a significant regimental anniversary, for thirty years before – on 13 January 1849 – the 24th, then a single-battalion regiment, had suffered the most disastrous engagement in its history. Engaged in a war to suppress rebellious Sikhs in the recently annexed Punjab on the western frontier of India, it had been ordered to assault a Sikh artillery battery well positioned on a rise above the swamps surrounding the village of Chillianwallah. It had succeeded and the battery had been captured – but the cost had been appalling. Two lieutenant-colonels had been killed – one commanding a brigade, the other the regiment – together with eleven other officers and nearly 300 men. The two officers carrying the Colours – those great symbols of regimental and national pride – had been cut down by grapeshot within a few metres of the muzzles of the Sikh guns. Both Colours had been rescued and the regimental Colour brought away safely, but the Queen's Colour had subsequently been lost; Private Martin Connolly, so the story goes, had wrapped it round his body for safety, and when he was later killed the Colour had been buried with him unnoticed.

For the officers of the 24th, Chillianwallah was a source of both intense pride – and regret. It was an example of how well a regiment might behave even in the midst of a grave blunder, and the significance of the anniversary on the eve of a new campaign was obvious enough. There was nothing gloomy in the memory of the slaughter that evening, however, for it seemed to cement the omen of the two battalions working together. In high spirits, two of the 1st Battalion officers, Captain William Degacher and Lieutenant Francis Porteous, proposed a toast, 'that we may not get into such a bloody mess, and have better luck this time!'[2]

Less than a month later, all the officers of the 1st Battalion who drank the toast, together with five officers of the 2nd, would be lying dead just a few kilometres away on the other side of the border, their bodies strewn among the whispering grass at the foot of iSandlwana hill.

*

Chillianwallah was merely one incident in a long and distinguished history which had seen the 24th involved in southern Africa at the very beginning of the British presence there.

The regiment had been raised under authority of King James II by Sir Edward Dering at the village of Pluckley in Kent in 1689. It had seen its fair share of action in the 190 years since, having fought in Ireland, in Marlborough's wars in Flanders, and in America. Its regimental titles had long since been established; in 1751 a royal warrant had regulated the Colours and uniforms of the regiments of horse and foot; formalizing the way in which regiments were distinguished by coloured facings – turned-back collars, lapels, cuffs and coat-tails – which contrasted with the red of their coats. The 24th had been authorized to wear 'willow-green' facings, and they wore them still in 1879 in the form of patches at the throat and pointed panels, edged in white braid, on their cuffs. In 1782 a further warrant sought to associate regiments with particular districts by establishing recruiting depots and allocating regimental titles – the 24th were designated the 2nd Warwickshires,[3] a title they were to enjoy for almost exactly a century. The location of the depot did not influence the demographics of recruiting, of course, for the drunken, the desperate and the adventurous continued to be seduced into the Army by the dubious promises of recruiting sergeants – who were paid a bounty for each man they brought in – from all over the country. Indeed, until the 1840s, when the potato famines and the wholesale emigration to the New World that followed had depopulated much of rural Ireland, the Irish remained the largest single group represented within the ranks of the British Army.

The 24th had been in Africa twice before. In 1802 it had taken part in the Alexandria campaign, Britain's attempt to oust Napoleon from Egypt, and its services had been recognized by the award of the Sphinx as its regimental badge. Then, in 1806 it had been part of the great amphibious expedition which had taken the Cape from the Dutch Batavian Republic; the 24th had suffered several casualties in the Battle of Blouberg – the first of a good deal of blood it was destined to shed in southern Africa. Then great struggles against Napoleon in the Peninsula had taken it back to Europe – the 24th was at Talavera and Salamanca – although the decades which followed Waterloo were something of an anticlimax, spent largely in dreary peacetime soldiering around the Empire. In 1846, however, it had been sent to India where the Punjab campaign and the Mutiny followed.

The Mutiny had deeply shocked the Victorian establishment, and in a wide-ranging review that followed, the Indian Army had been reorganized and the British Army increased to provide more troops against the risk of a similar challenge in the future. A second battalion was raised for each of the first twenty-five infantry regiments in the Queen's Army – including the 24th – effectively doubling their strength. Although the new battalions assumed the distinctions and traditions of their regiments, they remained separate administrative and battlefield units, and indeed it was never intended that they should fight alongside one another. As luck would have it, however, both battalions of the 24th were sent to the Cape, the 1st in 1875 and the 2nd three years later.

For the 1st Battalion, the Cape posting marked the end of nearly a decade of peacetime overseas postings. It had been sent from Ireland first to Malta in 1865 and then Gibraltar in 1872. As a result, the battalion had remained tight-knit, many of the men in the ranks being 'old salts' who had enlisted under the old system which required from them a minimum twelve years' service before they were awarded their Colours. There was always natural wastage, of course and just over half those who had left Ireland had moved on before the battalion had reached Helpme-kaar. They had been replaced by drafts in batches from home, but many of these had themselves already been in the ranks for several years by 1878, and even the most recent draft had joined the battalion in time to take part in some of the operations on the Eastern Cape. Both officers and men of the 1/24th were, in short, seasoned and experienced, used to the demands of overseas soldiering, accustomed to working together, and familiar with each other's strengths and eccentricities. When the battalion had arrived in Natal, the local press had commented that the colony had seldom been garrisoned by such an impressive set of men, many of them wearing two, three or even four 'long service and good conduct' chevrons above their right cuffs. Their NCOs, in particular, were mature men in their late twenties – the prime of a soldier's life – experienced in managing the men under their command in both the sudden excitement of battle and during the altogether more subtle pressures of peacetime duty. Many of the battalion's senior NCOs had enlisted in the middle 1860s, and had held their ranks for a number of years: Colour Sergeant George Ballard had attested in 1865 at the age of seventeen and Sergeant Thomas Cooper in 1866, and both had held their ranks since 1874; Frederick Wolfe had served even longer, enlisting in 1860 and being promoted Colour Sergeant in 1871.

It is a modern myth that the battalion was composed largely of 'little Welshmen from the valleys, singing Men of Harlech'. Its regimental depot, established at Brecon, south Wales, in 1873, was largely administrative, and while some recruits processed there were certainly drawn from the militia units raised along the Welsh borders, most came, as they always had, from the urban slums or depressed agricultural areas of England and Ireland.

The officers of the 1st Battalion were as close-knit and experienced as the NCOs. The commanding officer, Brevet Colonel Richard Glyn, had been born into a military family in Mirath, India, and had joined the 82nd Regiment as an ensign in 1850. He had served with them in the Indian Mutiny before transferring to the 24th in 1856. Promoted lieutenant-colonel in 1867, he had succeeded to the command of the battalion. Photographs of Glyn in old age suggest a rather overbearing manner, all furrowed brow and thrusting chin, but in middle-life, before his experiences in Zululand left their mark, he was affable in a rather reserved way, and one officer who served under him described him as 'as good a little man as ever breathed'.[4]

Glyn's adjutant, Lieutenant Teignmouth Melvill, the son of a distinguished civil servant in the East India Company, had been born in London in 1842, and was a Cambridge graduate. He had been gazetted as an ensign into the battalion in 1865 and been appointed adjutant in 1873. He was thirty-three years old at the end of 1878, married with two sons, and regarded as a thoroughly good and conscientious officer who had contributed a great deal to the efficient management of the battalion. Melvill seemed destined for higher things – he had passed his exams at the Cape to enter staff college – but before he could embark for England the Xhosa rising had broken out and Melvill had immediately applied to rejoin his regiment.

The 1/24th had enjoyed an adventurous time at the Cape which had left the men, by the end of 1878, fully acclimatized to its extraordinary landscapes and its extremes of temperature and weather. In 1875 three companies had been sent under Glyn to quell agitation among diamond diggers at Kimberley, although there had been no fighting, the nascent rebellion collapsing at the first sight of the redcoats.

In August 1877 the 1/24th had been replaced as the Cape garrison by the 88th Regiment, and had been moved forward to King William's Town on the frontier. They had only been there a month when the Xhosa trouble flared. At first the Cape administration had been determined to restore order using its own colonial police and volunteer troops and without involving the regular military, but by December it had become clear that the colonial forces could not contain the violence and Glyn was sent into the Transkei with 400 of his own men.

On 13 January 1878 he had been sweeping the country at the head of a small detachment when news reached him that an outpost camped a few kilometres away was under threat. Glyn had hurried to the scene to find a detachment of the 88th camped on open ground near the Nyumaga stream watching with some concern a force of perhaps a thousand Xhosa who had been gathering throughout the day on a nearby ridge. Fearing the Xhosa might disperse without being drawn into action, Glyn had resolved to attack them. He had formed his men into an extended line with light field-guns in the centre and mounted men on the flanks, and when the Xhosa retired behind the ridge at the sight of this, had advanced. Cresting the rise, he found the Xhosa drawn up on a succeeding ridge, and he had sent forward his auxiliaries to draw them on. The ploy worked and as Glyn had continued his steady advance, his men well spaced out, the Xhosa had streamed down to attack them. They had pressed their attack to within 40 metres but the steady drum-roll of Glyn's musketry had proved too much for them and they had at last given way, to be pursued mercilessly by Glyn's auxiliaries. After the battle Glyn's men had found fifty dead Xhosa in the bush – rather less than they had expected, but the victory had been achieved at the cost of just five British troops wounded.

A few days later, on 7 February, a much larger Xhosa concentration had attacked an outpost a few kilometres away on Centane hill. Here two companies of the 1/24th, under Captain Russell Upcher, together with a small Artillery and Volunteer detachment and supported by over 500 auxiliaries, had been awoken at dawn to find columns of Xhosa sweeping towards them. Upcher's position was well entrenched, his camp surrounded by a ditch and rampart, and in sporadic attacks the Xhosa dashed them-selves to pieces against the controlled fire of the 24th.

The Battle of Centane marked a turning point in the campaign, destroying the Xhosa ability to mount offensives and driving them into the bush. And both Nyumaga and Centane profoundly shaped the 24th's attitude to local warfare, giving them each a successful tactical blueprint for future conflicts and a confidence in their ability to face the challenges such warfare offered. They had certainly impressed their superiors – Bartle Frere described them as 'a ... seasoned battalion under an excellent, steady, sensible Commander, Colonel Glyn, and with very good young officers'.[5] General Cunynghame thought simply that 'there was no duty whatever which the 24th Regiment could not be found equal to.'[6]

Yet there was undoubtedly another element in their success, too. 'At no time', commented Cunynghame after Centane, 'had the power of the Martini-Henry rifle been more conspicuously shown; indeed, it was perhaps the first occasion when it had been fairly used by the soldiers of the British Army.'[7]

The adoption of the Martini-Henry rifle from 1871 as the standard small-arm for British infantry had marked a significant gear-shift in weapon technology. It was the first purpose-built breech-loader taken on by the British Army – the old Snider, which it replaced and which many auxiliary and volunteer units still carried in southern Africa, was a hybrid conversion of the earlier muzzle-loading Enfield – and was the result of a collaboration between a Swiss gunsmith, Frederich Martini, who designed the breech, and Alexander Henry, a Scot who designed the rifled barrel. Simple, robust and easy to use, the Martini-Henry was loaded by depressing a lever behind the trigger-guard, which caused the breech-block to drop downwards from the hinge, opening the breech at the top; the cartridge was installed, and the breech closed by raising the lever again. After firing, a repetition of the same simple manoeuvre opened the breech and out popped the expended cartridge. The weapon fired a .450 calibre unjacketed lead bullet weighing a bone-shattering 480 grains from a rolled brass Boxer-pattern cartridge which was stepped at the shoulder to contain the larger powder charge of the .577 calibre Snider.

The Martini-Henry was a much easier weapon than its predecessors to teach recruits how to use, and the rate of fire could be impressive – a modern marksman, under ideal conditions on the range with rounds laid out beside him, can achieve twelve rounds a minute or more. In fact, however, contemporary musketry manuals were very wary of rapid fire and encouraged instead a rate of no more than three or four rounds a minute – and then only in extreme circumstances, at the crisis of an attack. Rapid fire was not only very wasteful of ammunition, but also often ineffective since it encouraged men to blaze away without taking the care to steady their nerve and place aimed shots. Paradoxically, a high rate of fire was often counter-productive in breaking up an enemy attack because the comparatively few hits for the rounds expended created the impression among those on the receiving end that the fire was not destructive – a slow, measured, aimed rate of volley fire, when a designated group of men fired at the same time, was both more physically destructive and psychologically devastating. Moreover, the Boxer cartridge was loaded with a black powder propellant which burned with a thin cough of white smoke, and while the smoke from a single discharge soon dispersed in even a faint breeze, the repeated firing of a number of rifles produced great billows which hung heavily in the air and soon obscured the target. It was not unusual for troops to cease firing in the midst of a battle simply to allow the smoke to clear.

The long rifle version issued to British infantry was a metre (39 inches) long and weighed 3.9 kg. It was sighted for a range of up to about 1,400 metres, although only an extremely good marksman could hope to score a hit at such distances, and, while firing in battle was usually opened at around 730 metres, the Army considered the Martini-Henry to be most effective at ranges between 275 and 360 metres. At the higher ranges sighting was by means of a raised sliding backsight and, because of the weapon's steeply falling trajectory, the marksman was required to crane his neck at an uncomfortable angle to line up the backsight and high foresight; at 365 metres the backsight is folded down, however, allowing the marks-

'The secret hope of every independent chief': King Cetshwayo kaMpande, whom the British characterized as a bastion of African independence in the face of the steady European conquest of southern Africa. As a result, they resolved to destroy him.

'Eyes of the Zulu': Mehlokazulu kaSihayo, photographed under guard as a prisoner of war, September 1879.

A young and confident Zulu man in the 1870s, carrying his stabbing and throwing spears.

A Zulu man and his wife. Marriage marked an important rite of passage in Zulu society.

Sir Theophilus Shepstone – 'Somsewu' – the dominant voice in the management of Natal's African population for nearly half a century.

Theophilus' brother, John Wesley Shepstone – the man who tried to trap Matshana kaMondise.

An unusually expressive portrait of Sir Henry Bartle Frere, revealing a hint of the ruthless determination that lay behind his statesmanlike facade.

Lieutenant General Lord Chelmsford, looking relaxed and confident in Natal on the eve of the invasion of Zululand.

Confrontation: Durban photographer James Lloyd's historic photograph of the Zulu delegation at the Lower Thukela listening to Frere's ultimatum on 11 December 1878. Centre right is Vumandaba kaNtati, a senior commander of the uKhandempemvu *ibutho* who subsequently fought at iSandlwana.

John William Colenso,
Bishop of Natal – a stern
critic of Frere's policies
towards Zululand.

Anthony Durnford: a little known portrait,
taken shortly before the invasion of
Zululand, which suggests something
of the flint in his character.

Frances Ellen Colenso, Durnford's friend
Nell, who devoted the rest of her short life
to defending his in the aftermath of his
death at iSandlwana.

'Like the bottom of the sea with grass on it': Helpmekaar, the Centre Column's base of operations, with the small earthwork fort built after iSandlwana in the background.

The Mzinyathi border: Rorke's Drift, photographed from the Natal bank in 1879, with the ominous peak of iSandlwana looming on the skyline.

First comes the trader, then the missionary: Otto Witt, who had turned Jim Rorke's old store at Rorke's Drift into a mission station, only to see it destroyed by the fighting in 1879.

*Left*
The *amabutho*: a Zulu man in full ceremonial regalia. This particular costume and shield pattern is associated with the uKhandempemvu.

*Right*
Such regalia was too fragile and valuable to wear into battle; the men of the uKhandempemvu in fact looked much like this as they stormed the camp at iSandlwana.

Invasion: the ponts which carried part of the Centre Column across the Mzinyathi into Zululand on 11 January 1879, with the outline of Shiyane behind.

'Charlie Harford': Lieutenant Henry Charles Harford, photographed after his return to the 99th Regiment at the end of the war.

The life and soul of the party: William Cochrane in later life. He fought alongside Durnford at iSandlwana and survived.

A youthful Horace Smith-Dorrien, photographed at the very start of his long and adventurous military career.

Major Cornelius Clery, Colonel Glyn's staff officer: overshadowed by the presence of the Headquarters Staff with No. 3 Column, Clery was relegated to routine duties – among them choosing the site of the camp at iSandlwana.

'The military wasp': John North Crealock, Chelmsford's loyal but flippant, sarcastic and unpopular Assistant Military Secretary, pictured in 1869.

Colonel Henry Pulleine, 1/24th – the commander of the camp at iSandlwana.

man to fit the butt more snuggly into his shoulder and look easily down the barrel. It is no coincidence that time after time in the battles of the 1870s and 1880s once attacks reached this distance the destruction inflicted increased dramatically. The velocity of the bullet was such that when it struck a human target it tended to clip cleanly through unimpeded muscle and flesh but if it struck bone the lead flattened out, smashing its way through the body, splintering long bones or exploding the skull like a pumpkin.

The weapon had its limitations, of course, as all firearms do. When fired the sound of the discharge wraps around the marksman's head, like a stiff clap on the ears. The recoil produces a deep thump into the shoulder, not as sharp as the kick of modern high-velocity firearms but getting noticeably worse after ten or twenty rounds as the breech becomes steadily soiled with a thick greasy powder residue. It becomes difficult after a while not to flinch in anticipation, spoiling the aim. After ten rounds, too, the barrel – already uncomfortable after a day in the hot African sun – becomes too hot to touch, and veterans like the 24th soon learned to sew a length of cow-hide around the stock to save the tips of their fingers.

All weapons become stressed by repeated use, and the Martini-Henry was no exception, although most of the problems after heavy firing were due not so much to the rifle itself but rather to the thin brass of the Boxer cartridge. The spent cartridge was pulled out by retractors on either side of the breech; sometimes the retractors themselves broke, or, more commonly, after a hot breech had softened the brass, they simply tore the base off the cartridge, leaving the rest gummed into the barrel. Usually, however, it required no more than a cool head and the cleaning-rod with which each rifle was equipped to poke out the remains and get the gun working again.

Both battalions of the 24th were experienced in the use of the Martini-Henry in action, for the 2nd Battalion, too, had arrived in time to take part in the mopping-up operations on the Cape frontier. Sent from England as reinforcements in February 1878, the 2nd was, by and large, a younger set of men than the 1/24th, and many of them had enlisted only a year or two before under the controversial 'short service' system which had been introduced to make Army life more attractive to a better class of recruit.[8] Although the impetus of the Xhosa rising had been checked by the time the 2/24th reached the frontier in the middle of March 1878, there was more than enough work to keep it busy in Lord Chelmsford's sweeps through the bush, so that by the end of 1878 the 2nd Battalion, too, were no strangers to the 'whiz and rip of the assegais'. And they had learned the tricks of bush warfare quickly enough – on one occasion Chelmsford's Staff Officer, Crealock, had noticed a company of the 2/24th trying to cut off a Xhosa retreat and 'at a distance of 1300 yards were making good practice' with their Martini-Henrys.[9]

By the time they reached Helpmekaar both battalions looked very much the veterans they were. Most of the men had long since turned a deep mahogany brown, and they were heavily bearded. Their red coats had been dulled to an earthy terracotta by the effects of sun, rain and dust, and they had learned early that their issued white helmets, with their bright brass regimental plates on the front, made excellent targets for Xhosa snipers. The plates had been removed and the helmets smeared with dye made from tea leaves or coffee grounds or boiled mimosa bark until they had been rendered a less conspicuous khaki. Their white equipment belts were dyed, too, and their tunics and trousers – at the mercy of spiky aloe leaves or *wag-'n-bietje* thorn for months on end – heavily patched. Some men had lost their helmets altogether, and had replaced them with local wide-brimmed hats. Yet altogether what they had lost in soldierly smartness they more than made up in conspicuous business-like intent.

The headquarters and band of the 1st Battalion, together with four companies – three more were still on the road, and one was on detached duty in southern Natal – had reached Helpmekaar in time to spend Christmas there. Corporal H. Brown of the 2nd Battalion – which was still marching up from Greytown, and had spent Christmas 'wet through without anything to put under or over us' – was delighted at the reception accorded by the 1st Battalion when they marched at last into Helpmekaar, noting that they were, '. . . played into camp by the band of the 1/24th Regiment who were there before us. They had a nice bit of dinner ready for us, and did all our work for us when we got in; this was very good of them for doing it as we were all tired.'[10]

Nevertheless, there had been some odd omens on the road up. The Natal Carbineers had marched out of Pietermaritzburg alongside the 1st Battalion, and one of them, Trooper Fred Symons, had noticed that while the 24th's band was playing a song called 'Nancy Lee' they had been interrupted by the skittish behaviour of Trooper Fletcher's horse, which 'became restive at the sound of the drums and rearing up fell with him almost on top of the big drum. Thus our music came to an untimely end, a bad omen . . .'[11] A similar thing had happened at Helpmekaar when 'the 24th came marching in . . . a huge bull-frog, red and green, hopped up and stopped the band again, and the whole battalion swerved aside so as to avoid the bull-frog who sat placidly blinking at the men.'[12]

Symons did not consider himself particularly superstitious, but he thought two such incidents unlucky; a bad sign for the coming campaign.

*

Once in Helpmekaar, there were changes in the 1/24th's mess to prepare for the imminent invasion. In selecting the officers to command his columns Lord Chelmsford had been constrained by the limited number of men of an appropriate rank available, and for the most part he had in any case preferred to choose men with whom he had recently served on the Eastern Cape. He had worked well with Colonel Glyn and as the senior officer of the 24th Glyn was an obvious choice to command the Centre Column. It was an appointment which was incompatible with his battalion duties, however, and Glyn reluctantly gave up command of the 1/24th and moved out to establish a headquarters of his own. Since Glyn's second in command, Brevet Colonel Henry Pulleine, was then commanding the garrison at Fort Napier in Pietermaritzburg, command of the 1/24th fell to Captain William Degacher, with Captain George Wardell as his second. There was a happy regimental synchronicity in this, for Degacher's elder brother, Henry, was a lieutenant-colonel then commanding the 2nd Battalion – not only were the two battalions working together for the first time, they were now commanded by brothers.

Glyn's new role meant of course that he needed a staff to run the column. His senior staff officer was an eloquent Irishman, Major Francis Clery of the 32nd Regiment, a staff college graduate and a former Professor of Tactics at Sandhurst. Self-assured, observant, prone to gossipy judgements about his colleagues and a tad vain – in later life he would dye his greying whiskers and wear a corset under his tunic – Clery was a special service officer who had come to Natal in the hope of securing a plum appointment. Clery found Glyn to be 'a guileless, unsuspicious man, very upright and scrupulously truthful, yet of a slow, not to say lethargic temperament',[13] but his opinion was coloured by disappointment at his posting, for he had first been attached to Colonel Wood's column, then assembling at Utrecht. An old friend of Wood's, whose energetic style suited his own, Clery was looking forward to them serving together until, at the last moment, he had been transferred to Glyn's column and sent down to Helpmekaar.

Clery's frustration deepened when, at the beginning of January 1879, Chelmsford and his staff arrived at Helpmekaar. Chelmsford's presence put Glyn in a difficult position. Glyn remained in command of the column, of course, and etiquette dictated that Chelmsford should not interfere with its practical day-to-day administration – Chelmsford was in any case too much of a gentleman to do so – but inevitably his presence meant that the direction of the campaign was in his hands, the more so as his Cape Frontier Wars experience had exaggerated his natural tendency not to trust too much to his subordinates. 'Colonel Glyn and his staff are *allowed* to work the details,' commented Clery bitterly, 'posting the guards, etc, and all the interesting work of that kind.'[14]

To make matters worse, Clery took a hearty dislike to the man with whom he would have to liaise on Chelmsford's staff – Chelmsford's Assistant Military Secretary, Lieutenant-Colonel John Crealock. Crealock had a notoriously off-hand and acerbic manner – Bulwer had found him 'not very pleasant to deal with . . . a type of military wasp',[15] and General Sir Garnet Wolseley would later damn him as neither an officer nor a gentleman[16] – and Clery found him 'swaggering, feeble, self-sufficient and flippant'.[17] In return Crealock disdained the column staff; 'do not expect anything of Glyn,' he wrote, 'he is a purely regimental officer with no ideas beyond it.'[18] Their impotence seems to have had an adverse effect on Glyn, who became withdrawn and disinterested: Glyn 'was scarcely ever seen or heard of – the more so as he got anything but encouragement to interest himself in what was going on',[19] and leaving much of the routine running of the column's affairs to Clery.

Chelmsford himself, who found all such personality clashes distasteful, chose to ignore the air of tension which grew up at senior levels within the staff. As well as Crealock he had surrounded himself with three ADCs, Brevet Major E.H. Buller, Lieutenant-Colonel Matt Gossett and, as a courtesy to the Navy which had landed a detachment at the coast to support the invasion, Lieutenant Berkeley Milne of HMS *Active*. With Sir John Michel's parting advice no doubt ringing in his ears, he had not, however, troubled to appoint a chief of staff – and so a dangerous ambiguity prevailed at the heart of the command of No. 3 Column.

*

By the end of December the column was almost complete.

While the 3rd NNC had remained at the Sandspruit, snatching a few extra and desperately needed weeks of training, the last elements had passed them on the road to join the column headquarters at Helpmekaar. These included a single battery of Artillery, N/5 Battery and 5th Brigade Royal Artillery, who were also veterans of the Cape Frontier Wars campaign and had worked closely with the 24th on a number of occasions there. They were equipped with six 7-pdr rifled muzzle-loading guns (RML) – steel-barrelled guns mounted on wooden carriages – which had been originally designed as mountain guns and were arguably too light for the duties now required of them. They were all that was available, however, and the barrels had been mounted on the heavier 9-pdr RML carriage to make them more suited to the rough terrain, and as a result the limbers were drawn by six horses instead of the usual four. They were commanded by Brevet Colonel Arthur Harness, a reliable, conscientious and thorough officer who was nonetheless a rather fastidious man. Harness shared the prevailing pro-fessional soldier's wariness of the Cape Volunteers, and during the Cape campaign he had marked his refusal to let standards drop by refusing to grow – as most officers had – a beard. In that regard Zululand would in due course force him to succumb – and challenge him in other ways besides.

*

Sir Henry Bulwer's final collapse in the face of Frere and Chelmsford's dual offensive had seen a scramble, as 1878 skeetered to a close, to put Natal on a war footing. Most of the sons of the settler gentry who made up the ranks of the colony's small Volunteer Corps units had been delighted to vote for active service under military command across the border. The protection of settler interests was, after all, one of Frere's avowed reasons for confront-ing the Zulu kingdom in the first place, and the coming campaign offered an escape from the humdrum routine of farm life, the chance for adventure, and the possibility of land in Zululand once it was over.

Even so, the Government's call-up, when it finally came in late Novem-ber, had brought a sharp interruption to the flow of their civilian lives. Carbineer Fred Symons, who farmed near Pietermaritzburg, commented ruefully that 'the two thousand bags on [sic] mealies I expected to reap will be left to the pleasure of the kaffirs'.[20] The Carbineers, the oldest and most experienced of the Corps Volunteer units, had paraded through

Pietermaritzburg on 28 November. Looking smart in their dark-blue uniforms with white facings, they numbered three officers and fifty-seven NCOs and men, and in keeping with the standing they enjoyed in colonial society they were commanded by a representative of Natal's most influential family. Theophilus Shepstone Junior, known as 'Offy', was his father's third son and had been born in 1843, shortly before the family had moved from the Eastern Cape to Natal. 'Offy' Shepstone grew up speaking isiZulu fluently and had largely inherited both his father's attitudes towards African peoples and his sense of mission. He had entered the Natal civil service at an early age, and in 1865 had become secretary to the then lieutenant-governor, Colonel John Bisset, whose daughter Helen Offy would later marry. He had been a captain in the Carbineers and their commanding officer since 1872. Nor would Offy be the only one of Somsewu's sons to take to the field that summer in what proved to be a rather belligerent show of family loyalty in defence of the Natal settler interest.

Yet the gung-ho attitude of the younger Shepstones, in particular, was not necessarily shared by their fellow Volunteers Corps. Fred Symons would prove a dutiful member of the Carbineers, but he was a sceptic when it came to military pretensions and no admirer of Frere's forward policies:

> One day we halted on an eminence covered with soft green grass and as I lay there resting on the sward our Captain came up and said to me 'Well, Symons! Wouldn't you like to see this slope covered with dead Zulus?' I replied 'No, Sir, I wouldn't!' 'Why not?' said he. 'Because we have no quarrel with the Zulus and I consider this war an unjust one.' He turned and walked away without a word.[21]

Volunteer Corps units drawn from farming families along the Mzinyathi frontier had also answered the call. The Buffalo Border Guard (BBG), founded in 1873 just after the Langalibalele rebellion, numbered just twenty-nine men, although a handful had declined to take part in the invasion and would remain manning posts on the Natal side of the border. James Rorke had once served in its ranks as a lieutenant, and it was commanded now by his neighbour in the Mzinyathi valley, John Sutcliffe Robson. Robson was also the Border Agent along his stretch of the river, however, and the demands on his time were such that it was decided he should remain in Natal directing the local defence. He had two sons in the BBG, William and Tom, who would cross into Zululand, but command of the unit passed to the Smith family, who were influential settlers in the village of Dundee. Captain Tom Smith took command, seconded by his brother Lieutenant William Craighean Smith. The quartermaster was a thirty-eight-year-old Scot, Dugald Macphail. Fred Symons encountered the BBG after they had arrived at Helpmekaar – and he was no more impressed by their officers than he had been by his own:

> [There] was a long line of rocks ... and here men were placed [on piquet duty at night] singly at intervals of about fifty yards [46 metres] or more. It was bad enough to find your way about in the dark on this line, but much worse when an officer of the Buffalo Border Guard named S. was on duty. It might have been timidity on his part as be it what it might he was a perfect nuisance to the men on night guard. Relieved from guard we would have just settled down for a much needed sleep when clank, clank, clank, along would come the 'Man with the Knife' as we called him, on his visiting rounds. Of course he was not afraid to visit the line of sentries by himself, not at all! He only wanted to take the old guard along to shew [sic] him the way in case such a valuable officer got lost! ... He ... would leave one man with each sentry we came to and then pick them up on his return so that he was never alone. I am pleased to say that he disappeared from the scene shortly after and never troubled us any more – sent to buy horses or something of the kind.[22]

The final contingent of Volunteers Corps was supplied by the Newcastle Mounted Rifles, who drew their members from the surrounds of Newcastle, 40 kilometres north of Dundee. Raised as recently as 1875, they were hardly much stronger than the BBG, with just thirty members, and they were commanded by a darling of Newcastle society with a truly spectacular set of whiskers, Captain Robert Bradstreet. Bradstreet's second in command was Lieutenant Charles Jones, whose brother Samuel was a trooper in the ranks; a third brother, Ruben, had been turned down as too young, but had obtained work instead as a wagon-driver for the military. Lieutenant Jones was worried that his brother Sam was too adventurous to be allowed near the scene of any fighting, and had tried hard to keep him away. First, he had secured him a post as a commissariat officer with Wood's column at Utrecht; Sam would have none of it, however, and promptly begged to be allowed to rejoin his unit. Wood had agreed, but by the time Sam had returned to Newcastle he found that the Mounted Rifles had departed for the front, and that Charles,

. . . in order to put a further spoke in my wheel . . . had sold my horse, saddle and bridle. Horses were scarce and I was in an awful rage. The expense did not worry me, but the thing was to find someone with a horse to sell. In this unhappy frame of mind I took a walk up the street when I was hailed by an old friend, who was riding along on horse-back. Looking at me he asked what the trouble was. . . . In the end he agreed to sell his mount, saddle and bridle to me . . . A couple of hours later I set off after my troop. I rode the whole night through and caught up with them at Helpmekaar, over sixty miles [95 kilometres] away.[23]

At Helpmekaar the Volunteers Corps were in for an unpleasant surprise, however. Although they had voted to serve across the border, they remained sensitive to the extent to which they would be placed directly under military authority. Since they had volunteered under Natal statutes rather than Queen's Regulations, they were not bound by the Articles of War on active service, and could not be compelled or punished by conventional military law. Most had expected to be led by Major John Dartnell, an ex-regular who had served with the 88th Regiment in the Crimea, where he had been nominated for the Victoria Cross. Dartnell had retired to Natal and bought a farm at Mvoti in 1869 but his wife had found the life too lonely and he had secured instead an appointment to raise the Natal Mounted Police, the only professional full-time body maintained by the colonial authorities. Dartnell was a disciplinarian but his strong personality was widely admired throughout the colony and the Volunteers Corps in general held him in great regard. Dartnell had reported to Helpmekaar with a hundred of his police but to their disappointment the Volunteers Corps found they were not to serve under him but rather under a regular officer, Brevet Lieutenant-Colonel John Cecil Russell. Russell was a special service officer and a cavalryman – his regiment was the 12th Lancers – and Chelmsford hoped that he would bring a touch of professionalism to the part-time mounted troops. The Volunteers Corps had taken a dislike to Russell, however, although it is not entirely clear why – he may well have had too smart a manner about him for their liking, or he may simply have been sidelined by Offy Shepstone. Certainly it was Offy who orchestrated the Volunteers Corps' discontent:

Captain Shepstone spoke and said, as nearly as I can remember, – 'Men, you know under what conditions you signed your names and agreed to go into Zululand. One of those conditions was that Major Dartnell should have the command; by this order Major Dartnell is superceded in the command, and Captain Russell raised to the rank of brevet major, is placed in command over you. Now is your time to speak upon the subject; once you enter under the command of Captain Russell no murmuring or complaints of any kind must be heard or made. I ask you now, therefore – Do you accept Captain Russell as your commander or no?' The men, one and all, shouted most determinedly, 'No!' Captain Shepstone then asked, 'Are you willing to march tomorrow morning into Zululand, under the command of Major Dartnell?' One and all again shouted 'Yes, tonight if you like!' 'No, now at once' was shouted by some . . .[24]

It was a decision which must have revived Chelmsford's old concerns about the reliability of the colonial troops, but with the invasion imminent he could not afford to alienate the men who constituted the greater part of his cavalry arm. He offered a compromise, and the Volunteers Corps agreed; Russell retained his appointment but Dartnell was co-opted onto Chelmsford's staff.

*

By the end of December the 3rd NNC, too, were as ready as they ever would be to join the column, and on 2 January 1879 they marched up the road at last to Helpmekaar. By then, forward elements were already being sent down the road to Rorke's Drift, and the NNC were destined to join them. They did not camp at Helpmekaar, but Fred Symons remembered the excitement among the troops as they had marched past:

One day Ted Greene and I were standing and watching a regiment of the Native Contingent *gweering*[25] and capering and singing and shouting as they came along the road when I passed the remark that these men had better have been left behind. Why? Says Ted Greene; 'Because they will not fight and will get in the way of our troops', said I. 'Rot! Bloated rot!' said Ted. 'They are a splendid body of men!' Alright, said I, I bet they'll bolt at the first sign of the enemy, if I know the Natal kaffir. 'Rot!' says Ted. If noise and capering makes a good soldier then Ted ought to be right in his estimate . . .[26]

The journalist 'Noggs' Norris-Newman had availed himself of his privileges as a civilian and had returned to Pietermaritzburg for Christmas. By the time he was back at Helpmekaar on 5 January, he noticed a touch of self-

confidence emerging as the various component parts of the column were
becoming used to working together – a self-assurance boosted by the
conspicuous presence of Lord Chelmsford himself. 'The camp itself was
much larger in extent', he noted, 'and also slightly changed in aspect. The
Head-quarters-staff camp was pitched to the right of all the others, almost
in the centre. The Union Jack was flying in front of the tent of the General,
and his mule waggons were placed in position behind.'[27]

Yet as if to – quite literally – dampen the troops' sprits, the brewing
storms had finally broken over the exposed ridge-top at Helpmekaar. For
several years the rainfall had been below average, and the mealie crop had
withered on the stalks; the rains were late this year, too, but when they had
finally broken in the middle of December they did so with a vengeance.
The breathless heat of the afternoon gave way each evening to that sudden
flurry of wind which whips through the grass and sends fallen leaves
swirling in little funnels of dust, the harbinger of bright white thunder-
clouds which swell up suddenly on the horizon. Fierce electrical storms
broke over the heights, jabs of lightning striking the dolerite boulders and
splitting them into great jagged splinters. Then came the rain, drumming
down and flattening the grass, turning the dust into a thick red greasy
mud, and running in great streams down the hillside.

Crealock, who had served in India and experienced the monsoon,
thought these first summer rains at least comparable. 'The deluges of rain
are equal to the Western Ghats in India,' he wrote. 'I never got such a
ducking as my waterproof could not be got at until I was drenched. This is
the second 36 hours of rain in a week.'[28]

In a very short space of time the camp at Helpmekaar had become a sea
of mud. The road up the western slope of the Biggarsberg turned into a
greasy slide, and wagon transport ground to a halt. Streams and rivers
which had been dry for years filled and became impassable within hours.
Even the relative comforts of the NNC mess could not save Norris-Newman
from misery:

> The members of the mess had intended having a great feed that evening,
> having been successful in getting a buck and other little niceties; but
> just as the cook was preparing the savoury viands down came such a
> storm of wind, followed immediately by heavy rain, as not only to put
> the fires out, but even to blow over some tents, and quickly flood us all
> out. . . . after everything was wet through, and then, as our misery was

at its height, we made a journey through the camp to see how others had fared. . . .

One tent, in particular, had been erected over a pathway, and it was really a sight worth seeing to witness how – notwithstanding that the occupants had dug a deep trench around it – the stream, unchecked almost, poured through the tent and over its contents. A small stream, percolating through the sand, close by one side of the camp, soon became a roaring torrent, and not only carried away our only barrel (sunk to get decent water) but also upset the whole engineering scheme of one of the Captains, who had sunk several wells close to the stream in order to get water. These were now entirely filled up with soil, sand, and gravel. The last seen of the unfortunate barrel was a few of its staves floating down the stream some miles off . . .[29]

Dartnell's Natal Mounted Police, who had just joined the column, had been expecting a wagon-load of luxuries, including plum puddings, to brighten their Christmas on campaign, but their wagon had been swept away as it crossed the flooded Mooi River at Keate's Drift, and Quartermaster-Sergeant Hobson had nearly drowned. Most of the stores were later salvaged, apparently none the worse, but they did not reach Helpmekaar until 8 January. By then, however, there was more to worry about than a late Christmas dinner: Frere's ultimatum was about to expire, and the start of the war was just three days away.

# 12

# 'The shadow of the Great White Queen'

## Knowledge and ignorance on the Zulu border, January 1879

When he had taken his farewells of the friends he had made on the *Edinburgh Castle*, waving them off to their various postings among the columns preparing to invade Zululand, Lieutenant William Cochrane must have looked ruefully upon his own appointment with No. 2 Column which had already had its brief reduced from an offensive to a defensive one – there seemed little hope that either it, or Cochrane, could look forward to a very exciting war. The column had been placed above the Middle Drift on the central Thukela – between the eastern boundaries of the Msinga location and the Zulu border – and its main strategic purpose seemed to be to reassure the colony's border population, both black and white, by guarding against the possibility of a Zulu counter-attack.

From the start, it was obvious that the challenges the column would face would be practical as well as military. Although the Middle Drift had long been recognized as a major entry point into the Zulu kingdom, there were few roads in the vicinity and the approaches to it, even on the Natal side, were notoriously difficult. The column headquarters had been set up on a farm belonging to a settler named d'Almaine whose land stood squarely on top of a high bank of hills which framed the western bank of the Thukela, and from which the ground dropped away dizzingly to the river 300 metres below. On a clear day the heights command stunning views of the border, the Thukela glittering in broad sweeps as it snakes its way along the valley floor. On the opposite bank – the Zulu side – the approaches are less steep and intimidating but the ground rises up steadily to the twisted ridges and dark broken masses of the Nkandla forest beyond. The exact location of the drift was signposted for kilometres around by a solitary pillar of rock, known as Kranskop standing on the steep hill on the Natal bank, and a number of footpaths led from it down the rocky slopes to the river below. Ironically, except in time of high flood, the crossing itself was a good one, great sheets of rock offering a firm passage even for wagons, and shallows where men on foot could cross.

Hot, boulder-strewn, though awesomely beautiful, the valley floor had offered little to tempt Boer and British settlers into its depths – even today the contrast between the large, orderly commercial plantations on the heights and the subsistence farming in the densely populated and environmentally degraded valley is conspicuous – and as a result the African settlements there had been left largely unmolested. Most of these had simply been incorporated into the Msinga location, and by the end of 1878 many of the local *amakhosi* had been pressed to contribute their young men to the NNC. The people themselves were, however, tied to the communities on the Zulu bank by bonds no less complex than those upstream at Rorke's Drift. The difficulties this would pose for the coming campaign had already become apparent, not least in the apprehension of the two Natal surveyors some weeks earlier, whose seizure Frere had censured when giving his ultimatum to the Zulus.

Insignificant in itself, the incident had heightened awareness of the strategic significance of the drift on both sides, much to the concern of the Natal border population. The Ngcolosi people, who fronted the drift on the Natal side, were linked by marriage to the royal house of the Magwaza opposite. The Magwaza, ruled on behalf of his elderly father Maqondo by Qethuka, an age-mate and personal friend of King Cetshwayo, were, like Sihayo's amaQungebeni and Matshana's Sithole upstream, diligent followers of the royal house. With troops mustering behind them and the Magwaza steadfastly in front, the Ngcolosi must have felt themselves caught between the proverbial rock and a hard place. In the event, the continued benevolence of King Cetshwayo seemed to offer the more immediate advantage, and in the middle of September the inhabitants of forty-three Ngcolosi huts had slipped quietly across the river and placed themselves under Zulu protection – a fact which had done little to reassure the Natal authorities of the reliability of the border peoples.

When the column arrived at d'Almaine's on the high upland in late December, the first challenge to be faced therefore was to establish a route by which troops could be moved quickly from their posts on the heights above to the river below to secure the drift in the event of a Zulu attack. It was a task the freshly appointed column commander threw himself into with typical gusto. On 3 January he ordered his men to cut a path down to the drift for men on foot and horses. It hugged the steep hillsides precariously at times, but it was completed within three days, and with the date set for the invasion still five days off.

This was, after all, a minor task for the man who had once supervised the blocking of the uKhahlamba passes: the commander of No. 2 Column was Anthony Durnford.

*

It says something for Lord Chelmsford that he had not allowed himself to be swayed by the prevailing settler doubts about Durnford's capabilities when he began to plan for the invasion of Zululand. Unlike most of his other column commanders, Chelmsford had not served with Durnford in the Cape Frontier War, but the fact remained that Durnford was almost alone in possessing first-hand knowledge of campaigning in Natal.

Durnford's experience on the Boundary Commission had left him unconvinced of the justice of the Boer claims and he had expected that its findings would see the border issue resolved. There was, he believed, no legitimate reason for armed intervention in Zululand: 'There is a policy here to get up a Zulu row but it is not likely to succeed at present. I am not of course a negrophilist, and as a soldier I should delight in the war, but as a man I utterly condemn it.'[1]

Nevertheless, when Chelmsford appointed him to raise the NNC, his sense of duty had risen to the occasion, and the soldier in him triumphed over the man. Chelmsford had arrived in Natal not long after the Boundary Commission had submitted its findings and Durnford, when he met him, thought Chelmsford 'a pleasant man, a gentleman, and one can do a great deal for a man of that type'.[2] In return, Chelmsford seems to have been impressed by Durnford's drive and energy, and when he came to allocate the task of raising a black auxiliary force it was to Durnford that he had turned.

In the event, parsimony and the prevailing nervousness in settler society had prevented Chelmsford acting fully upon Durnford's plans but for all that Chelmsford had been impressed with Durnford's diligence and towards the end of 1878 had invited him onto his staff. It was Durnford who drew up the plans for the 'floating bridges' – the ponts – by which British troops were to cross onto Zulu soil, and who produced the maps from which the staff were to work. When the time to appoint column commanders came,

Chelmsford seems to have had no hesitation in offering Durnford command of No. 2.

The column was to be composed almost entirely of African troops, a regiment of infantry – the 1st NNC – supported by several troops of mounted auxiliaries. The blueprint called for the 1st Regiment to be composed of three battalions, each of 800 men, and from the first Durnford had confidently asserted his preference for the men he wanted under his command. He had asked for, and received, permission to call out men from the uKhahlamba foothills who were well known to him. First among these were the Phutile, whose cause he had championed for so long, together with a scattering of Langalibalele's followers who had been taken onto white farms. There were others, too, like the Phutile's neighbours, the amaNgwane, under their *inkosi* Ncwadi kaZikhali, who had suffered historically at the hands of the Zulu kings.[3] In the event there were only enough of these men to fill one of the 1st Regiment's three battalions, and the rest were made up from other groups – the amaThembu, amaBomvu, amaChunu and ama-Zondi, all residents of the Msinga location[4] – less well known to Durnford.

Ncwadi's men contributed troops, too, to the column's mounted contingent. The mounted troops were generally considered the best of the auxiliary forces, and they reflected the familiarity of the uplands people with the wiry BaSotho ponies of the interior. Nearly 160 amaNgwane had answered Durnford's call; mounted on their own horses, they were led by Nyanda, a junior son of the late *inkosi* Zikhali, and the British dubbed them Zikhali's Horse. The mounted troops received better pay than the foot-soldiers and were issued with jackets and trousers of hard-wearing yellow corduroy, and a red rag – the badge of the NNC – to wind around their hats. Every man was issued a Swinburne-Henry carbine and a bandolier of fifty rounds.[5]

Durnford's old friend Hlubi, who had stood beside him at Bushman's River Pass, answered the call, too, together with fifty of his Tlokoa. Indeed, so associated were the mounted troops with the hillmen that the British generally referred to them as 'Basutos', although only the Tlokoa were genuinely of Sotho origin. Hlubi himself was now in his mid-forties, still active but mature and dependable, and a firm ally of the colonial administration. Years later, he would say that he saw the invasion of Zululand as a philosophical struggle, a war between knowledge and ignorance in which the British Empire represented knowledge and the Zulu kingdom the timeless ignorance of Africa and its traditions. Hlubi saw that a new world was coming – and wanted to be on the winning side.

The Edendale mission community outside Pietermaritzburg saw the war in very similar terms. They were Christians of course, and few were of Zulu origin, but they had proved their Westernized credentials when Elijah Nkambule had fallen at the Bushman's River Pass. The community's response to the call to mobilize was significant. 'We have sat under the shadow of the Great White Queen for many years in security and peace', argued one of their leaders, Daniel Msimang,

> We have greatly prospered, and some have grown rich. We enjoyed great religious privileges, and have brought up our sons and daughters to honour God, and to walk in his ways. Our schools have provided a good education for our children, to fit them for a useful life in this land, and now their children are enjoying a like blessing. Under God and the Missionary Society we owe it all to the Government of the Great White Queen. We are her children, and in this time of great peril she sends to us to help her against our common foe. We all know the cruelty and the power of the Zulu King, and if he should subdue the Queen's soldiers and overrun this land he will wipe out all the native people who have dwelt so long in safety under the shadow of the Great White Queen. Shall we not gladly obey her, when she calls for the services of her dark children?
> They answered, we will.[6]

Sixty men volunteered to go – only fifty-four were accepted. They were led by one of the community elders, John Zulu Mtimkulu, but practical military command fell to a younger man, Simeon Nkambule – Elijah's son.

The Edendale men were keen to distinguish themselves from their traditionalist comrades. They were dismissive of the rations allocated to the auxiliaries, and asked to be given beef, bread, coffee and sugar like the regulars instead; when this was refused they determined to supply themselves. Where the amaNgwane and Tlokoa went barefoot, tucking their toes around the stirrups, the Edendale men reported in boots and spurs. Once in the field, they held regular prayer meetings, and their singing often put the regulars' church parades to shame.

Durnford was well aware that, whatever potential the men in the ranks possessed, much would depend upon the calibre of the white officers. The 1st Regiment alone would need 30 officers and 180 white NCOs, and further officers would be needed for each of the mounted troops. The rush to war had produced a number of applications from special service officers in England, and when they arrived in Natal Durnford was pleased to accept them onto his command, Cochrane among them. The rest would have to be recruited locally, from civilians or part-time Volunteer Corps soldiers, even the best of whom had only limited experience of active service. The pool of potential recruits was too small and there was considerable demand among the other auxiliary units too. Durnford's reputation did not always help him – when one member of the Natal Legislature heard that his son wanted to join the 1st NNC, he intervened to stop him: 'I knew that Colonel Durnford who was to command the native force was brave to rashness, and I therefore did not think my son should join it.'[7]

Nonetheless Durnford set to the task with typical determination, and several old friends rallied. Charlie Raw, who had served with the Carbineers in the Langalibalele expedition, volunteered and was given the rank of lieutenant in command of a troop of Zikhali's Horse. George Shepstone – who had stood by Durnford during the burial of the Bushman's River Pass dead – was appointed his political agent, effectively his senior staff post. It was not a post that reassured George's father, Theophilus: 'It is strange but true that when I heard he had been appointed to serve Colonel Durnford, I felt as if I had heard his death warrant. I had no confidence in Durnford's prudence or capacity to suit himself to the circumstances in which he might suddenly be placed.'[8]

Others were simply not up to the standard Durnford required of them. He interviewed one young applicant who had recently fought on the Cape frontier, and who offered the opinion that the only way to command black auxiliaries was to whip them into battle. Durnford responded that the man should make his will before the war started – and that if he found himself shot by his own troops, he had only himself to blame. His application was refused.

Durnford's column had assembled at Pietermaritzburg throughout December, and on Christmas Eve Durnford had ridden out to establish his headquarters at d'Almaine's. With the war now only a fortnight away, Durnford was keen to infuse his men with a sense of discipline and purpose and he adopted a strict regimen, alternating drill and parades so that the men recognized what was expected of them and learned to work with their officers. He often led mounted parades himself, and his personal manner with his officers was pleasant but firm; they soon came to realize that he was not a man to let them shirk their duties. One morning, when the commandant of the 1st Battalion of the 1st NNC, Captain A.N. Montgomery, was sick, his officers chanced their arm by parading without their horses. According to Captain Dymes, Durnford took the challenge in his stride:

> When day broke and Colonel Durnford rode down our line he stopped, and calling out our senior officer, asked him, 'Where is your horse, Captain Hay?' 'Well, Sir,' was the rather hesitating answer, 'the fact is, my horse is not well this morning.' 'Oh! Indeed' replied the Colonel, 'I am sorry to hear that; and are all the other officers' horses ill this morning?' 'Yes, Sir,' said our senior, reassured by his quiet manner, 'the fact is that they are all on the sick list.' 'Oh! Very good,' assented the Colonel, and said no more. We went through our usual morning drill, and the others thought it was alright, and that we should hear no more of our breach of discipline, which it certainly was, as the orders were distinctly that every officer should be mounted on parade. I, however, was not quite easy in my mind . . . I was not mistaken, for, after a while, he said in his quietest manner: 'Now gentlemen, I think we will do a little skirmishing.' Our faces fell, for we knew what that meant . . . He kept us at it for two hours, skirmishing over some very rough ground . . . All the drill was done at the double. I can honestly say that, what with the pace, and the encumbrance of my arms and accoutrements – not to mention the rough ground, and the tumbles into ant bear holes, etc – I felt thoroughly knocked up when the drill was over. At the end of it Colonel Durnford remarked to our senior Captain: 'I hope your horse will be fit for work tomorrow morning, Captain Hay.' I need scarcely say that we never again appeared on parade dismounted.[9]

The hard work, however, paid off. On 1 January 1879 Lord Chelmsford visited Durnford's column at d'Almaine's, and was impressed by what he saw. 'The officers speak very confidently about their men,' he wrote to Frere, 'and a very good feeling seemed already to have been established among them.'[10]

In truth, there was no doubt that Anthony Durnford was looking forward to going to war again. If he had no faith in the cause, he had, as usual, put his personal reservations aside and thrown himself into his duty. The fact was that he enjoyed the physical effort of campaigning, the busyness of assembling his own command, and in the mighty Zulu kingdom he discerned a more worthy foe than the reluctant amaHlubi. Now he would have a new chance to prove himself worthy as a soldier – and to wipe out the messy hurts of Bushman's River Pass.

He had been promoted, too. In December 1873, at the height of the wrangle over the Langalibalele affair, he had been made a lieutenant-colonel; ironically, on 11 December – the same day that Frere's ultimatum had been presented at the Lower Drift – he had received his brevet colonelcy.[11] And certainly he looked the part, writing home with a certain relish to inquire of his mother, 'I wonder whether you would admire my appearance in the field? Boots, spurs, dark corduroy breeches, serge patrol-jacket, broad belt over the shoulders, and one around the waist – to the former a revolver, and to the latter a hunting knife and ammunition pouch. A wide-awake soft felt hat with a wide brim, one side turned up, and a crimson turban wound around the hat – very like a stage brigand.'[12]

*

As December gave way to January, the first elements from the Centre Column began to push down the Knostrope Pass towards the crossing at Rorke's Drift.

By this time, even the most phlegmatic of the border farmers had largely abandoned their properties. Having failed to head off the crisis, Sir Henry Bulwer had little choice in the end but to put the colony on a defensive footing and Natal had been divided up into defensive districts, each with an officer appointed to look after its security. Places of refuge had been designated for the settler population – Natal's African citizens were expected to fend for themselves, since the authorities were still not entirely sure whose side they might join – and Border Agents put on a state of alert to watch the known crossing-points into Zululand. In addition to the NNC, Bulwer had been persuaded to authorize the raising of border levies from communities living along the Thukela and Mzinyathi, who were directed to provide men to watch the rivers, and to turn out in force in the event of an attack. Along the central Mzinyathi many of the farmers had already moved to Fort Pine, a purpose-built stone barracks completed only a few months before on the open heights between Helpmekaar and the village of Dundee further north. Others had packed their wagons ready to trek when war broke out; some, like the Vermaaks at Helpmekaar, had improvised defences on their own property.

Perhaps the most exposed of the Mzinyathi valley settlers that January was Otto Witt, the Swedish Lutheran pastor who had bought Jim Rorke's old property 'Shiyane' the year before. Despite high hopes initially that he had secured an 'open door to the Zulu country', Witt had struggled to make converts on either side of the border and, like many in the mission community, he blamed his failure on the hard-line traditionalist stance of King Cetshwayo. He was in favour of the imminent British intervention, justifying – as did many of his colleagues – the potential bloodshed as an evil necessary to overthrow a brutal heathen regime and open the country to salvation.

Witt's property was, of course, of considerable strategic interest to Lord Chelmsford. There were few permanent structures to shelter men and supplies on the border, and Rorke's buildings, with their good solid stone walls and thatched roofs, were ideally placed to house a garrison and serve as a commissariat depot. Chelmsford's agents had approached Witt and offered to lease his buildings for the duration of the war and, after a good deal of haggling over the price, Witt had agreed. Although Witt sent his wife and young daughters to the relative safety offered by a fellow missionary at Msinga, he stayed to watch that the troops did not do too much damage to his property. As things turned out, he would come to regret the bargain he had struck.

The Centre Column began to descend down the steep eastern slopes of the Biggarsberg from Helpmekaar on 1 January 1879. A detachment of the Natal Native Pioneers moved down to Rorke's Drift and began work preparing for the crossing. A hawser was thrown across to the Zulu bank, and construction of the ponts began. On the 2nd, the 3rd NNC passed through Helpmekaar and camped on the farm Knostrope, half-way down the escarpment – where Rorke's widow, Sarah, still lived – and then the regulars too began to move. By 9 January the column was assembled in a large sprawling camp close to the river on the Natal side – a total of 4,709 men, according to the official count, served by an accumulation of wheeled transport the like of which the Mzinyathi valley had never before seen – 302 ox-wagons and carts, 1,507 oxen and 116 horses and mules.

According to Norris-Newman, the descent from Helpmekaar to the border had been carefully watched by the Zulu on the opposite bank, and Offy Shepstone and his Carbineers had been provoked to intervene:

> Beacon-fires had been seen every night across the Border, and it had been noticed that whenever more troops came down the road towards

the Drift a signal was also made from a kraal on our side about two miles [3.2 kilometres] up the valley. So Captain Shepstone had caused it to be surrounded a few evenings before ... And captured the male inhabitants, sending them back to Helpmekaar as spies. They were the first prisoners taken in the war, and turned out to be some of Sirayo's [sic] people ...[13]

Spies perhaps they were, but the legal status of these men was questionable, for they found themselves prisoners in a war which had not yet officially begun.

The incident had heightened a growing sense of concern in the column regarding Zulu intentions. Throughout December border agents based along the river had reported an obvious level of agitation among the Zulu communities on the other side. Large numbers of men had been seen in the distance making their way towards Sihayo's kwaSogekle homestead, and on one or two occasions small bands of Zulus had crossed the river to loot livestock left unguarded on farms abandoned on the Natal bank. Then, on 8 January, the agents reported that the border seemed suddenly deserted. Most of the women and children had apparently gone into hiding, and the whereabouts of the fighting men could only be guessed at; the general assumption was that they had gone to join their *amabutho* mustering at oNdini.

Beyond that, Lord Chelmsford had little idea what to expect once he crossed the border. Months of propaganda by Shepstone and Frere had created in his mind the impression that *inkosi* Sihayo was one of Cetshwayo's most truculent and aggressive supporters, a man fiercely opposed to the whites who could be expected to resist the British incursion at all costs. Would Chelmsford find him waiting on the Zulu bank as he entered Zululand when the ultimatum expired?

The thought clearly troubled him, and on 8 January he wrote to Evelyn Wood, commanding the column to his left, suggesting that he mount a diversionary attack on Sihayo from the north. Two days later, however, Chelmsford was inclined to be bullish in his eve-of-invasion report to Frere: 'Report says that Sihayo is still at his kraal with a good following. I very much doubt his waiting for us to attack, as if he does, there is no means of escape for him when once our troops are in position.'[14]

The growing sense of anticipation was heightened on the 8th when a sentry reported mounted men riding down to the drift on the Zulu

side. 'It was impossible to distinguish who or what they were', claimed
Norris-Newman, so 'all turned out and hurried down to the Drift, where
the pont was working, and it was then discovered that the visitors were not
Zulus at all.' It fact it was two of Wood's officers who, with an escort of
troopers,

> ... had made a most adventurous ride from Colonel Wood's Column,
> which we learned had crossed the Blood River on the previous Monday
> morning, and were encamped a few miles in[to] Zululand. Captain
> Barton had been out exploring roads &c, and meeting with no oppo-
> sition had penetrated right through to our camp, a distance of over
> thirty miles [48 kilometres]. The Kafirs along the road had all been
> friendly, and gave them information and milk . . . [15]

If it struck anyone in the Centre Column as curious that the Zulu had
opted not to contest Wood's crossing into Zululand – despite Wood's
evident reluctance to wait upon the legal formality of the ultimatum – in
the light of the ferocious image of them which prevailed in Natal, they did
not comment on the fact.

By the 10th everything was ready for the invasion to begin, but at the
last minute tragedy almost befell the 3rd NNC. Early that morning Charlie
Harford had ridden across to the column headquarters to clarify orders
with the adjutant-general, Major Clery, to discover that the general was due
to inspect them that midday, but that the commandant had not passed this
on to the troops: 'Well, I rode off as hard as I could go, to camp. I found
Lonsdale sitting in his tent, looking over his Masonic orders and parapher-
nalia, and, on my breaking the news to him as quickly as I could, he said,
"Good God! I forgot all about it. Shout for my pony, like a good chap."'
Harford ordered fresh horses to be made ready, and men were sent
scurrying off to fetch in the companies. Harford and Lonsdale had no
sooner mounted up when,

> ... We had scarcely parted company when Lonsdale's pony shied at
> something and threw him off. I saw the fall. He appeared to have struck
> his head and then, rolling over on his back, lay quite still with one of
> his arms projecting in the air at right angles to his body. I got off at
> once and ran to his assistance, only to find that he was unconscious,
> and rigidly stiff. I shouted for the doctor, and as soon as he had come
> up with some natives and a stretcher, I galloped off again to collect the
> men. Eventually, after a real race for it, everybody was got in; but

Hamilton-Browne and Cooper were still getting their battalions
formed up on parade when the General and staff made their appearance.
. . . Through his interpreter [Chelmsford] expressed his pleasure at
what he had seen, and gave some sound advice on matters of discipline,
especially behaviour towards women and children and prisoners.[16]

For the men in the ranks of the 3rd NNC, Chelmsford's review had been
their first encounter with a style of military leadership very different from
their own. One man, Lugubu Mbata, recalled his impressions with a slight
trace of wonder, noting that Chelmsford 'had a very prominent nose, and
a rumbling, rasping voice. Whenever he passed, someone would shout
"Ten Shun" and soldiers and we had to stand and stiffen our bodies.'[17]
    Lonsdale's fall had been a serious one – still unconscious, he had been
taken to Helpmekaar hospital, where it was found that he had concussion
– and it would put him out of action for several days. The invasion would
have to take place without him; Major Wilsone Black of the 2/24th was
appointed to command the 3rd NNC until he recovered.

*

At the last minute, Chelmsford dithered regarding the role he had decided
for Durnford's column. As the deadline for the invasion drew near, he had
toyed with the idea of deploying it on the offensive after all, using Durnford
as a light flying column to support the advance of Colonel Pearson's No. 1
Column, on his right flank and down at the Thukela mouth. Then he
changed his mind, and ordered Durnford instead to move his men closer
to the Centre Column, to take up a position at the Sandspruit, where the
3rd NNC had assembled. This change of plan was apparently the result of
an appraisal Chelmsford had made after reaching Helpmekaar on 4 January.
He had made a hasty tour of the border defences, and had ridden as far as
d'Almaine's to discuss No. 2 Column's role with Durnford personally. He
confirmed his new requirements in writing on 8 January in terms which –
nonetheless, and significantly – suggested that offensive action on Durnford's part might not be ruled out entirely should the strategic situation
require it.
    Two days later Durnford began the move to the Sandspruit with the
bulk of the column, leaving only some of his infantry to guard the Middle
Drift and shore up the jittery border population. The order had come as a
great blow to his officers, most of whom saw it as confirmation of their

fears that they would sit out the war in a defensive role, on the wrong side of the border.

At Rorke's Drift, as the last hours of Frere's ultimatum ticked by, the Centre Column was gripped by a palpable sense of tension. Nervousness about what might lie across the border – the green hillsides apparently deserted now – was offset by excitement at the prospect of action, and a real fear that at the last minute their preparations might be frustrated by Cetshwayo caving in. But, as Captain H. Hallam Parr noted, with just a hint of satisfaction:

> The 10th of January was spent by No. 3 busily enough, in completing the loading of the provision waggons and in finishing the two ponts which were to take the infantry across the river. The day passed, and neither at the Lower Tugela, Rorke's Drift, nor at Bemba's Kop (the headquarters of the three columns) were any signs received of either Cetywayo's compliance with our demands or even of his willingness to treat.[18]

That evening Lord Chelmsford issued his orders to his officers in the column: the British invasion of Zululand would begin at dawn the following day.

# 13

# 'A big fuss over a small matter'

## Charlie Harford, still alive

At about 2 a.m. on Saturday, 11 January 1879, the stillness of the African night along the banks of the Mzinyathi river was shattered by the piercing cry of military bugles sounding the reveille.[1] The white tents, standing out clearly in the moonlight, suddenly bustled with troops taking up their weapons and accoutrements, then moving to their positions, and the camp came alive to the myriad sounds of an army assembling – of hoarse shouts of command, of booted footsteps on the hard stony ground, of the clanking of horse-harnesses, the creaking of wheels, and the lowing of reluctant oxen. Sir Bartle Frere's ultimatum had expired – and the British invasion of Zululand was about to begin.

Lord Chelmsford had circulated a general order the night before. The troops had been apportioned their crossing-places and they hurried, now, to take them up. The two ponts, anchored by hawsers stretching across the river in a deep pool just upstream of Jim Rorke's old crossing, were made ready to take the regular infantry across in workmanlike batches of a company at a time. The drift itself – a noisy and uninviting tea-brown torrent flowing chest-deep over the long jumble of rocks after the recent onset of the summer rains – looked too dangerous to trust to regulars on foot, and instead had been allotted to the colonial troops, the mounted men of the Volunteers and the 1st Battalion, 3rd NNC.

It was not at all clear, even at this eleventh hour, whether the Zulus would oppose the crossing. There had been no obvious activity on the far bank during the evening before, but as night fell it was impossible to tell if the enemy were massing quietly in the dark, the sound of their movements lost in the constant roar of the river. One of the Centre Column staff, Captain Henry Hallam Parr, had heard it said with conviction that King Cetshwayo had promised that 'we should be attacked before the water of the [river] had dried on our feet',[2] and while many had been dismissive of the exaggerated fear of the Zulu army which prevailed among the white colonists in Natal, their confidence suddenly seemed less assured. Off to the right, in an open space beside the road, Brevet Lieutenant-Colonel Harness's battery unlimbered, ready to provide a salvo in support should the dark smudges of bush which marked the far bank prove to contain Cetshwayo's army.

Then, just as the troops took up their positions, the mist began to rise off the river, thin and ethereal at first, then swamping the valley in a dense cotton wool which muffled and confused the sounds of war and reduced visibility to a few metres.

A tense silence fell over the army. The 1/24th had been ordered to cross first, and its leading companies filed into the ponts. As they pushed off into the gloom they were swallowed up by the mist, and as they reached the far bank, the men waiting their turn on the other side strained to hear the first sounds – a shout of alarm or command, a volley of shots, a war-cry – that might indicate that the Zulus were lying in wait. But nothing was heard beyond the creak of the hawsers on the near bank and the steady roar of the river.

Chelmsford had taken no chances and had ordered that the crossing take place over as wide a stretch of the river as was practical. A few hundred metres upstream a scatter of boulders breaking the surface of the water had suggested another potential drift, and the 2/3rd NNC had been ordered to try their luck. It was a moment Lieutenant Charlie Harford had waited for all his adult life; for the first time in a decade of military service, he was going to war:

> I was ordered to find a crossing for the 2/3rd Natal Native Contingent higher up the river. The fog was so dense one could barely see anything a yard in front, but at last, after hugging the bank very closely for about half a mile or more, we came to a spot that looked worth a trial. So I put my pony at it and got across alright, the bed of the river being nice and hard; but the water came up to the saddle-flaps, and there was a nasty bank to scramble up on the opposite side. However, it did not matter, it was good enough.
>
> Then followed a truly unforgettable scene . . . In order to scare away any crocodiles that might be lurking in the vicinity, the leading company formed a double chain right across the river, leaving a pathway between for the remainder to pass through. The men forming the chain clasped hands together, and the moment they entered the water

they started to hum a kind of war-chant, which was taken up by every company as they passed over. The sound that this produced was like a gigantic swarm of bees buzzing about us, and sufficient to scare crocodiles, or anything else, away. Altogether, it was both a curious and a grand sight.[3]

Downstream, at Rorke's true drift, the mounted men had pushed across too, but not without some drama. A horse ridden by one of the Mounted Infantry had slipped against the rocks midstream and the man had been in danger of being carried away by the current until Captain Hayes of the NNC jumped into the river and rescued him.

The troops were not to enjoy the honour of being the first onto enemy soil, however. The journalist Norris-Newman had been watching them make their preparations and at the last minute he saw his chance to write himself into history and spurred ahead of the Volunteers Corps already picking their way across. With some pride he was able to inform his readers that 'I was actually the first man in Zululand after the war was declared'.[4] It would prove to be the first of a number of scoops Norris-Newman would enjoy over the following fortnight.

After a while, when no deep sonorous Zulu war-cries reverberated through the chilling mist, the tension among the troops began to evaporate. Then, at last the deep gloom lifted with the rising sun, and, suddenly, they were afforded glimpses of the rolling green hills beyond. 'Then a very pretty sight presented itself', recalled Harford in pride and relief, 'as the troops were dotted about over the rolling hills in "Receive Cavalry" squares formation, their red coats showing up distinctly in the clear atmosphere.'[5]

The only Zulu in sight was a solitary herdsman, who watched in astonishment as a foreign army emerged from the fog; the Natal Volunteers Corps set off gleefully to rob him of his charges. The British Empire had come to Zululand, and the war had begun in fine style.

For Gabangaye of the amaChunu, it was an appropriate moment to remind his men in the ranks of the NNC why they were fighting and of the wrongs they had suffered at the hands of the Zulu royal house, and he

. . . asked permission to address the men. Never shall I forget his extraordinary elocutionary power, and the splendid oration he delivered. The old fellow got to the head of the Column then started off at a trot, going backwards and forwards at this pace for nearly an hour . . . Without stopping to take breath, he recounted the history of the Zulu nation, which was frequently applauded by a loud 'Gee!' and rattling of assegais on shields from the whole Contingent . . .⁶

As the temperature began to rise, George Hamilton Browne noticed a feeling of ennui with a sense of anti-climax – curious among an army on its first day on enemy soil – settle over the column:

> Now we were in Zululand, cold, wet through and shivering with our tempers short and crisp. The Colonial can grumble just as well as an old Tommy, and he has, as a rule, more command of language. However, it did not take me long to get my men into line, and we pushed on, up the rise, and took possession of the top of the ridge, which we lined.
>
> Just then the sun came up and away went the fog. For the first hour or so we enjoyed it. But when our clothes were dry we began to get dry ourselves and I may say we dried very quickly and began to scorch.
>
> There was no shade and as the sun increased in heat, there we lay on that bare ridge and roasted all that live-long day. Certainly we had plenty of water nearby as warm as ourselves, but that scorching sun would have been less intolerable had we been on the move.
>
> There was no enemy in sight, nothing to do, conversation died away, it was too hot to sleep, even the East London boatmen could not curse, and the only thing I could do was to stick four assegais into the ground, rest a shield on them, lie with my head in the shade of the latter and think of iced drinks.
>
> How we white men longed for the enemy or anything to break the monotony, but no enemy came . . .⁷

The whereabouts of the enemy was troubling Chelmsford, too, and he instructed Major Dartnell to take a mounted patrol ahead down the road to scout for any sign of Zulu movements. With most of the NNC strung out on pickets, there was little for Charlie Harford to do, and he was surprised and delighted when Dartnell asked him to accompany the patrol as his staff officer. The party rode out beyond the furthest outposts, following the road as it climbed gently out of the Mzinyathi valley then dipped down again into the Batshe beyond, before striking off to their left and following the course of the stream towards the site of the kwaSogekle homestead. The valley was pleasant and open, with large patches of green stalks – the amaQungebeni's still thriving late mealie crop. There was no one in sight, however, and the valley seemed eerily deserted until at last,

... we heard a war-song being sung, evidently by a large body of natives; but where they were, or what became of them, we were unable to find out. However, as this was the ground over which we were going to attack the next day, it looked as if it were certain that we should meet with some opposition. Other parties had also been sent out in various directions, and had captured a considerable number of cattle.[8]

The ease with which these first patrols were able to loot the amaQungebeni herds seemed encouraging to some observers in the column:

Crossing the river at this point, without any resistance, is a moral victory over the Zulus as important as if a battle had been fought and won. It is an established fact now that they are afraid, and afraid to meet our forces in a fair fight. It now becomes a question of what their tactics will be? Are they going to lead the forces into a battle-field of their own selection, or is it to be a guerrilla war, or are they going to fight at all?[9]

This was a fair assessment of the possibilities – and one that posed too many questions for Lord Chelmsford's comfort. The Zulu inactivity was puzzling – he had counted on a quick demonstration of imperial might to show that the British were in earnest. There were, moreover, important strategic and political imperatives requiring him to make early and decisive contact with the enemy. It was likely to take several days to ferry the column's supplies across the river and establish a secure depot on the Zulu bank, but once that was accomplished Chelmsford intended to continue his advance. If the amaQungebeni did not show their hand in the meantime, he risked a forward move leaving them unbeaten close to the very base of his lines of communication. Would they regroup – as the Xhosa had done on occasion on the Eastern Cape – after the main column had passed by, only to attack his outposts and convoys in the rear?

It was important, too, that he was able to reassure London of the aggressive intent of the Zulu border communities. Both the boundary dispute and the Mehlokazulu affair had formed a central plank of Frere's justification to the Colonial Office of the need to intervene in Zululand; if these same communities now proved themselves to be docile and compliant there was a real risk that Frere's carefully cultivated image of the terrible Zulu bogeyman might be exposed as a sham – and London might once again question the validity of the invasion.

In short, Lord Chelmsford needed a fight – and Dartnell's report that evening provided him with sufficient justification to orchestrate one.

Whatever the true meaning of the songs Charlie Harford had heard in the Batshe valley, they had certainly seemed like a gesture of defiance – and that was all Lord Chelmsford needed.

That night he circulated a fresh order that the column be ready to march out at dawn the following morning to attack the amaQungebeni.

*

It had taken most of the day to break up the old camp, to ferry the tents across the river and to erect it again on Zulu soil, but the work had been completed by the time the rain clouds threatened another downpour. It had been hot, tiring and frustrating work, but at last the night-time vedettes and pickets had been posted and the rest of the column retired to snatch what sleep they could. If the European troops faced the discomfort of sharing a dozen men to a tent, they were better off than the men of the NNC, for whom there was no shelter beyond what they could improvise from hastily cut brushwood and the cold comfort of a coarse woollen blanket on the damp ground.

As an officer, Hamilton Browne had a tent to himself, and he retired to it to enjoy '. . . a feed of bully beef and biscuit washed down by a pannikin of muddy coffee, the first food that day, [and] I had just finished my pipe and was rolling myself up in my blankets when the orderly officer arrived with an order that I was to parade eight companies of my men before daylight and join the party that was to attack Serhio's [Sihayo's] kraal next morning . . .'[10]

Out on the picket line, Captain Mainwaring of the 2/24th found the prospect of the forthcoming attack added to the discomfort of a night already made tense by anticipation of a Zulu response, and uncomfortable by the weather:

Soon after dusk the rain developed into a steady downpour. About 10 p.m. a fatigue party arrived with dixies full of hot coffee. This was most acceptable to all of us. But the rain continued all night in torrents. Some of the men tried to sleep, laying in pools of water but I kicked them up, telling them they would by the morning be crippled with rheumatism. So much to their disgust I forced them to keep awake as I did myself. We were thankful when daylight broke and the rain ceased.

At 6 a.m. Captain Harvey of my Regiment arrived with his company to meet me. Having obtained leave to withdraw my sentries I was away in the line carrying out this movement when some of the 1st Battalion sentries on my right commenced shouting 'There are four of the enemy on the right.' This soon became 'The enemy in force on the right'. My Colour Sergeant in charge of the support heard this and gave the alarm stating 'Mr Mainwaring says the enemy in force on the right.' This of course without my knowledge or permission. My Company had closed and was ready to march off, when we noticed the whole of the troops in the Camp swarming out onto the plain, 1st and 2nd Battalions 24th Regiment, Mounted Troops, Lord Chelmsford and all his Staff etc., etc. Just as I was about to move off Colonel Degacher, commanding the 2/24th Regiment rode up. He appeared very angry . . .[11]

Angry indeed. If the sentries had indeed seen Zulus they had disappeared by the time the sun was up; the incident looked suspiciously like a false alarm – and one played out right under the noses of Lord Chelmsford and the joint staffs.

Nevertheless, the column stood to smartly enough at first light that morning and those ordered to join the attack took up their positions with some enthusiasm. Chelmsford had drawn up the plan of battle himself, based upon the reports of the afternoon before, but had been courteous enough to give command of it to Colonel Glyn. Leaving the camp and their wagons, supplies and ammunition at the river, the troops would march along Jim Rorke's old wagon-track until they struck the Batshe valley, no more than 5 or 6 kilometres ahead. On the near side, the valley was framed by nothing more than an outline of low rocky ridges but on the far side, across the stream, it rose up towards a line of cliffs marking the ridges and spurs of the Ngedla hill. At the foot of these cliffs was a jumble of fallen boulders, and it was among these that Chelmsford and Dartnell had concluded that Sihayo's followers had been hiding the previous afternoon. Chelmsford's plan was simple enough – he intended to mount a frontal assault on the cliffs, supporting this with flanking parties either side. It was widely rumoured that kwaSogekle was heavily fortified, and after he had dispersed any enemy concentrations, Chelmsford intended to advance further up the valley and destroy it.

The troops marched quickly up the track, excited at the prospect of being in action. As they spilled into the lower end of the valley they struck off from the track to their left, forming up in a line facing towards the Batshe. Lord Chelmsford and his staff hung back on the high ground, to watch from a polite distance, while the mounted men, the police and Volunteer Corps units pressed on down the track, crossing the stream where the road went across the drift, before moving further south and looking for a way up onto the summit. The main assault would be spear-headed by the 1/3rd NNC in the centre, supported by the men of the 1/24th.

The exhortations of Gabangaye kaPhakade the day before had been timely; the men of the amaChunu and iziGqoza, it seemed, were to have their chance to settle old scores early. As they moved down the slope and began to pick a way through the stream – normally no more than a few inches deep, but swollen and angry after the recent rain – the first shots rang out from the far side, their sharp reports echoing among the rocks at the foot of the cliffs opposite.

The ball had begun.

*

According to British intelligence reports before the war, *inkosi* Sihayo commanded the allegiance of about 3,000 amaQungebeni men, but there were no more than 200 of them present in the Batshe valley that morning. A week earlier – once it had become obvious that the British were serious in their threat to cross the border – the king had summoned all the fighting men to oNdini to assemble his *amabutho*. Many of the border *amakhosi* had been instructed to leave some of their followers at home, however, to protect their homes and crops and scout out the movements of the British. Further downstream Sihayo's neighbour, *inkosi* Matshana, had taken to the Qhudeni bush with most of his followers, but Sihayo had made the decision to commit most of his men to the general muster. He had gone to oNdini himself, to take part in the final discussions of the royal council which would shape the Zulu response to the invasion – and then, if necessary, to fight.

Nor was his senior son, Mehlokazulu, at home. As his son was the leading man on the British 'most wanted' list, Sihayo had feared that the king might at the last minute cave in to British demands to surrender him, and had advised Mehlokazulu to go into hiding. Mehlokazulu was in contact with the exiled Swazi prince, the freebooter Mbilini, who had a refuge in the wild country along the Phongolo river in the far north of the disputed territory, and at the beginning of January he had left kwaSogekle to join him.

Instead, it was another of Sihayo's sons, Mkhumbikazulu, who had been left behind in charge of a small force guarding the amaQungebeni homesteads and herds. The previous afternoon Mkhumbikazulu had done what he could to secure their cattle in the face of the aggressive British patrolling. There was nowhere in the valley itself to hide them, nor on the open hilltops on either side, so instead they had driven them among the rocks in a place which had, in all probability, long been regarded as a safe spot. At the southern end of Ngedla hill the cliffs sweep inward, scalloped into a giant horseshoe, and along their foot here the boulders lay particularly thick. There were narrow passageways running between the rocks and up the steep slope to the foot of the cliffs behind, and here and there the cliff-face itself was pock-marked with caves, a great jumble of stone overgrown with a tangle of scrub and hanging creepers. Mkhumbikazulu had driven their cattle – and those women and children, too, who had not already fled before the British advance – into the gaps between the boulders, and at dawn that morning his men had prepared themselves for war, and joined them. They had taken up positions in the crevices and caves, blocking some of the clefts and fissures with thin barricades of fallen stones. Many of the men were carrying the old firearms Sihayo had accumulated over the years from passing traders, and making themselves as secure as they could, they had settled down to wait.

Yet Mkhumbikazulu must have known that his men were hopelessly outnumbered even before the long lines – the thin bright streak of the redcoats, and the darker masses of the NNC, their shields rippling as they advanced – formed up on the green slopes across the stream. It was to be the first clash of the war, and Lord Chelmsford had taken no unnecessary risks. He had brought almost half the column's fighting strength with him – the 1/24th, 1/3rd NNC and mounted men numbered 1,500, while four companies of the 2/24th, together with the 2/3rd NNC had been drawn up near the camp at Rorke's Drift ready to be sent forward as reserves. The 1/3rd NNC alone outnumbered Mkhumbikazulu's followers by five to one – the amaQungebeni were about to pay the price for the exaggerated reputation they had enjoyed across the border.

The Zulu's only hope was to make a stand among the rocks and inflict sufficient casualties to cause the British to flinch from a direct assault. And certainly they put on a brave face; a ritual challenge to the enemy was an integral part of Zulu warfare, and as the British came within earshot below Captain Hallam Parr noted that, 'They began to taunt us, making their voices sound through the still morning air in the curious way natives can: "What were we doing riding down there?" "We had better try to come up;" "Were we looking for a place to build our kraals?" etc., etc. This badinage, which was accompanied by a few shots by way of emphasis, did not last long . . .'[12]

In fact there was more to this than just the simple expression of defiance; Mkhumbikazulu's men were giving vent to a question which had troubled the border communities for months: just what exactly did the British want in Zululand?

One voice called out clearly – presumably in isiZulu – asking by whose orders the invaders had come. Norris-Newman thought there was no reply, but Hamilton Browne had a better story. 'My interpreter and right-hand man (Capt. R. Duncombe)', he claimed, 'answered "by the orders of the Great White Queen"' – which piece of imperial posturing was not entirely true, of course – and Hamilton Browne noted with unconscious irony that at this news 'the enemy, or those of them who had exposed themselves, at once ran back to cover'.[13]

Down in the valley, Charlie Harford was at the head of his men in the NNC, still moving into position opposite the cliffs, and he was scarcely able to contain his excitement. His baptism of fire was at hand, and his character was at last to be tested as the soldier he was:

> It was most unpleasant going, for above us, on our right, were hills with the usual cavernous rocks encircling them a little below their crests. It was evident that the warriors we had heard singing their war-chant the day before were ensconced in these caves, for the instant the troops got within range a continuous popping went on from these places. The crack, crack, crack of their guns and rifles echoed and re-echoed among the hills in the still morning air and made it impossible to detect exactly where the shots were coming from. Now and then a Zulu was seen in the open, and on one such occasion I saw the man taking deliberate aim at Colonel Glyn who was standing in an open patch above me. Shouting as loud as I could, I told him to get out of the way before the shot was fired.[14]

As the NNC advanced, Hamilton Browne passed Lord Chelmsford himself, who took the opportunity to offer a few words of advice:

> The General returned my salute and calling me over to him said, 'Commandant Browne, those krantzes are full of cattle; go down and

take them, but on no account are you to fire before you are fired at.'
He also said, 'I shall hold you responsible that no women or children
are killed.'

He then wished me luck in the most kind and courteous manner –
a manner that endeared him to all of us. No general that I ever served
under in South Africa, was liked and respected as he was, and certainly,
no Colonial officer ever said a word against him or blamed him for the
awful disaster that came later on . . .[15]

As the NNC entered the mouth of the horseshoe gorge, however, the
roughness of the ground began to break up their formations – their grasp
of British tactical formations had, in any case, been tenuous at best –
and they began to collapse. The battalion had thrown out a firing line
with supports behind but, as Harford noted wistfully, 'the firing line and
supports soon got mingled together'.[16] Hamilton Browne was, inevitably,
more scathing – 'a South African native cannot walk in a line, draw a line,
or form a line, and if placed in a line will soon mob himself into a circle'.[17]
There was worse to follow. As the first shots began to strike home, Harford
saw that 'one of our Natives, who was close by my side, got a bullet in the
thigh, breaking the bone'.[18] Hamilton Browne watched with some concern
the effect the first casualties had on his men:

> My men advanced leaping and jumping, singing war-songs, sharpening
> their assegais, and looking so bloodthirsty that I feared they would kill
> every woman and child we came across. But as we drew nearer the
> scene of the action, their zeal for fighting – like Bob Acre's courage –
> oozed out of them. Their war-songs dwindled away and they seemed
> indisposed to come on. In fact some of them suddenly remembering
> they had important business to transact towards the rear had to be
> encouraged with the butt of the rifle or the ready boot of my non-coms.
> As the native must be led, myself and all the officers were in front . . .[19]

Not all of them, according to Harford, who saw 'two NCOs sheltering
behind a rock instead of leading their men, [and] I went forward to drive
them on; and had just got them away when "ping" came a bullet and cut
away a bough just at the spot where my head was a second before. This
was luck!'[20]

Nevertheless, Hamilton Browne's men pressed on into the gorge, driving
through the bush and winkling out a number of Mkhumbikazulu's men
who had placed themselves behind the initial boulders. Many scrambled

back up the slope – some of them were shot as they ran – to join those hidden among the caves and rocks further back but, as Norris-Newman noted, with the cliffs behind them there was nowhere else for them to run, and they fought with an intensity born of desperation. A veritable hail of fire hit Hamilton Browne's leading men and his attack stalled. He tried to encourage them forward and set off at the head of a company of the iziGqoza – who were spared his usual contempt since he thought them 'real Zulus' and 'splendid fighting men' – in an attempt to rush the rocks:

> A ragged volley was fired at us by the enemy, but we charged on through it and up the rising ground to the mouth of the V which we found to be full of boulders. I had gained the mouth when I looked back. Ye gods of war, what a sight for a commandant! No. 8 Company, led by two of the best colonial officers I have ever met, were on my heels, but the rest. I saw their backs in a mad stampede while among them raged their furious officers and non-coms.[21]

The officers tried to stem the flow with blows and kicks, but the men would not advance – confronted for the first time by the men their fathers had dreaded for half a century, the exhortations of Gabangaye the day before were forgotten, and the call to avenge long-standing feuds collapsed in a sudden rush towards the safety of the rear.

It was an uncomfortable moment for Hamilton Browne, who found himself with the iziGqoza alone, and close enough to Mkhumbikazulu's men for the fighting to break out hand-to-hand:

> Shield clashed against shield, assegai met assegai and the hissing word 'Guzzie',[22] as the stab went home was answered by the grunt or yell of the wounded man. I had my hands full and had to use freely both my sword and my revolver. The enemy fought splendidly but my men would not be denied . . .
>
> My white officers and non-coms also fought like fiends and we drove them back over the rocks until at last they took refuge in rear of cattle jammed into the narrow end of the V. These had to be driven out before we could get at them again, and it was done; also a lot of women and children were brought out. Thank the Lord none of them were hurt, and they with the cattle were removed to the open. We now found that the enemy had retreated by a narrow path to the top of a cliff about 60 feet [18 metres] high and had blocked the path by rolling big boulders into it.[23]

Both Wilsone Black – commanding the NNC in the absence of Lonsdale – and Harford saw the danger Hamilton Browne was in. Black went forward to urge his men on, and stood in the open, waving his hat in one hand and his sword in the other, calling out encouragement in ringing tones. Trooper Symons of the Carbineers heard afterwards that a bullet had clipped Black's hat and torn it out of his hand; he had calmly bent down, picked it up, and gone on cheering his men. A few minutes later, according to Hamilton Browne, 'He was standing with his back turned to the rock and was waving his sword when the Zulus hearing him rolled over some stones; one struck the gallant Major on the – well, not the head – and he fell on his knees and poured forth a volume of Gaelic that filled my non-coms. with delight.[24] Harford:

> ... could hear Major Black's shrill voice in broad Scotch urging his men on, and, making my way up to him with supports, I found that he and Commandant Hamilton Browne were in a hot corner close to some caves, with hand-to-hand fighting going on. When I was within about twenty or thirty yards [18 to 27 metres] of the place, one of their men fell almost at my feet with a terrible assegai wound, which had nearly cut him in half, right down the back. The poor fellow was not yet dead, and although I could see it was only a matter of minutes my feelings almost led me to try and put him out of his misery with my revolver. But I abstained ...[25]

It was a shocking introduction to the realities of combat, but according to Hamilton Browne Harford was over it soon enough:

> Just then Lieutenant Harford of the 99th Regiment, who was acting as S.O. [Staff Officer] to Commandant Lonsdale, came up to me. He was a charming companion, one of the very best, but he was a crazy bug and beetle hunter, and would run about on the hottest day with a landing net to catch butterflies and other insects ... He had never been under fire before and had on two or three occasions talked to me about a man's feelings while undergoing his baptism of fire, and had expressed hopes he would be cool and good while undergoing his. Well we were in rather a hot corner and he was standing to my right rear when I heard an exclamation, and turning round saw him lying on the ground having dropped his sword and revolver. 'Good God, Harford,' I said, 'you are hit!' 'No, sir,' he replied, 'not hit but I have caught such a beauty.' And there the lunatic, in his first action, and under a heavy fire,

his qualms and nervousness all forgotten, had captured some infernal microbe or other, and was blowing its wings out, as unconscious of the bullets striking the rocks all round him as if he had been in his garden at home. He was just expatiating on his victory and reeling off Latin names – they might have been Hebrew for all I knew or cared – when I stopped him, and told him to get as quick as he could to the right flanking company and hurry them up. He looked at me with sorrow, put his prize into a tin box, and was off like a shot . . .[26]

Harford had noticed that most of the damage among the NNC was being inflicted by a group of Zulu marksmen hidden in a commanding cave. Some of the 2/24th had, by this time, been dispatched up the spurs to the left of the horseshoe, and they were trying to pick off the Zulu snipers, but with only limited success:

Confronting me over the bend was a large, open-mouthed cave, apparently capable of holding a good number of men, and hanging below it were several dead Zulus, caught in the monkey-rope creepers and bits of bush. They had evidently been shot and had either fallen out, or been thrown out, by their comrades when killed. Later on, I learned that a Company of the 24th Regiment had been firing at this particular cave for some time, and had been ordered to cease firing on it when our men came up. It was an uncommonly awkward place to get at, as it meant climbing over nothing but huge rocks and in many places having to work one's way like a crab, besides which a loss of foothold might have landed one in the valley below. However, there was not much time to think, and I determined to make an attempt, so, sending some men to work round below, I took a European NCO who was close at hand, and told him to follow me. Clambering at once over a big piece of rock, I got a rather rude shock on finding a Zulu sitting in a squatting position behind another rock, almost at my elbow. His head showed above the rock, and his wide-open eyes glared at me; but I soon discovered that he was dead.

Scarcely had I left this apparition behind than a live Zulu suddenly jumped up from his hiding-place and, putting the muzzle of his rifle within a couple of feet of my face, pulled the trigger. But the cap snapped, whereupon he dropped his rifle and made off over the rocks for the cave, as hard as he could go. Providence had again come to my aid, and away I went after him, emptying my revolver at him as we scrambled up. Out of my six shots, only one hit him, but not mortally.

I stopped for a second to reload, but finding the wretched thing stuck I threw it down into the valley below, at the same time turning round and shouting to the NCO, who I thought was following me, to let me have his revolver. But he remained behind, where I had left him at the start, and all he did was to call out, as loud as he could, 'Captain Harford is killed!' However, I soon put this right by shouting down, 'No, he is not, he is very much alive!'[27]

Nothing daunted, Harford looked back for the man he had been chasing, and saw him in the mouth of the cave. Calling to him in isiZulu, Harford urged him to surrender, promising him that he would not be harmed, and the man squatted down in submission. Harford asked him if there was anyone else in the cave, and being told there was not, gingerly edged into the opening:

Close to the entrance lay a wounded man with his feet towards me. Although unable to rise, he clutched hold of an assegai that was by his side, but I told him at once to drop it, that I was going to do him no harm, and questioned him as to who was in the cave. He stoutly denied that there were any others there. By this time I was getting accustomed to the darkness, and saw several likely-looking boltholes and kept on repeating that I knew there were others somewhere in hiding and that they were telling me lies. At the same time adding, in a tone loud enough to be heard by anyone near the place, that if they would come out I would promise on oath that no harm should be done to them and that I would accompany them myself to the General, who would see that they were well treated.

In a short time this had the desired effect, and presently a head appeared from a hole, and as the object crept out I kept careful watch for any sort of weapon that might emerge with it; another and then another crawled out from the same spot. All were unarmed, and squatted down close to me. I then wanted to know where the others were, but they swore that there was no-one else. As this seemed to be the case, I moved off with all my four prisoners, leaving the badly wounded man in the cave. We soon made our way down the valley ...[28]

In a private letter to his mother Harford admitted that two of his wounded prisoners died before he could get them down the slope.[29]

While the NNC had assaulted the Zulu positions on the cliffs, the mounted men had ridden round to the right, passing over the *nek*, or ridge,

at the southern end of the hills, and swinging up onto the heights in the
hope of catching the Zulus from behind. The grassy slopes seemed
to be deserted and the Mounted Police struck off to the left towards the
top of the cliffs. Colonel Russell ordered Offy Shepstone to send four of
the Carbineers to the right to look for any Zulu presence while the rest
of the men dismounted and horse-holders were picked out. Trooper
Symons was among those selected to go forward and they had not gone far
when they spotted a group of mounted Zulus ahead of them. On seeing the
Carbineers approaching, the Zulus turned away and disappeared behind a
heap of boulders and Symons and his companions tentatively set off after
them:

> What's going to happen now thought I but wasn't long in doubt when
> V-o-o-o-rr went a pot-leg or cumbrous missile over heads. At this we
> opened fire too along the whole line – a frightful waste of ammunition.
> On top (for we did not halt) we saw no sign of the enemy, and their
> horses were grazing quietly about half a mile to the right. Dan Scott,
> Sergeant Major C. Slatter and another beside myself went after them
> and when we had covered about half the distance we saw some Zulus
> charging down towards us. I shouted to the other Carbineers who were
> moving towards the left but they didn't hear, then Dan gave the order
> to fix bayonets (knives about nine inches long) on the carbines and
> kneel with presented arms while he shouted out 'Ulipi?' ['Which side
> are you on?'] once. 'Ulipi?' twice. 'Ulipi?' thrice, by this time the
> natives were about forty yards [36 metres] from us and I had one
> spotted fairly in the wind and was pressing the trigger when up went
> their hands and a shout of 'Nombulwan'. They were Contingent men
> who had pulled off the red badges from their heads through fear of the
> Zulus . . .[30]

In the valley below, Chelmsford had watched the scrimmage among the
rocks and had decided to order up his reserve from Rorke's Drift. These
had hurried up the road and as soon as they reached the valley Chelmsford
ordered them to work upstream, towards Sihayo's homestead, to support
the existing attack from the left.

Yet in truth the affair was already largely over. Mkhumbikazulu and
some of his men had managed to work up the cliff-face and onto the
heights, but here they found the British had beaten them to it. Two
companies of the 1/24th, flanking Hamilton Browne and the NNC's attack,

on the NNC left, had worked their way up some of the steep spurs running down from the gorge, arriving on the heights just as the mounted men were moving up in a leisurely fashion from the right. Caught between them, Mkhumbikazulu had rallied about sixty amaQungebeni who had made a rush towards the Volunteers. But Shepstone's Carbineers had seen them coming and the Zulus were met with a well-directed volley that knocked over nine or ten of them – and the rest had lost heart and turned to run away across the summit.

Down in the valley, Chelmsford's reserves, the 2/24th and 2/3rd NNC, swept through the amaQungebeni mealie fields for three or four kilometres until they were close under kwaSogekle. The homestead nestled on a low shoulder of land at the foot of another horseshoe of cliffs which commanded the approaches. The 2/24th expected the huts to be defended, and they deployed in extended order and advanced up the lower slopes cautiously – much to the amusement of some of the men of the sister battalion on the heights above, who could see that they were not, and who indulged 'in good-natured chaff at the energy displaced by their comrades of the 2nd Battalion'.[31] The huts were put to the torch and the sight of dense white clouds billowing up from the damp thatch served as a clear signal that the action was over.

Chelmsford gave the order to recall the men. The Volunteers had been roaming across the heights, and had examined a deserted homestead where they turned out several antiquated firearms, and marvelled at a new wagon they found there which they judged to be the property of Sihayo himself. There were a few short minutes to indulge that favourite sport of victorious armies across the ages, rooting out loot and souvenirs from the vanquished, and both the Volunteers and 24th brought away a few artefacts as trophies of their victory, though to the Volunteers' regret it proved impossible to move the wagon.

Once the last shots had been fired the NNC picked up its wounded and the whole force assembled in the valley. Hamilton Browne claimed scornfully that 'my beauties had bagged thirty-two of themselves',[32] but the official returns list just three of the NNC dead and Lieutenant Purvis, Corporal Mayer and fifteen unnamed men of the regiment wounded. Neither the 24th nor the mounted men had suffered a scratch.

The entire affair was over by lunchtime, and the troops began to return to Rorke's Drift in high spirits despite a sudden thunderstorm which burst overhead. They had captured over 400 cattle and some goats and sheep, much to the delight of the Volunteers, who expected to get a share of their worth when they were sold off by Government agents – a promise which, in the end, proved to be almost as illusory as the promise of farms in a conquered Zululand. A number of women and children had been captured – including apparently one of Sihayo's wives – and several firearms, '. . . many assegais, and much sour milk and other Kafir produce. None of the guns were modern, but consisted of old Tower muskets and carbines. A large quantity of ammunition was found, including several hundred rounds of Westley-Richards ammunition . . . The cartridges were brought away.'[33]

Two of the wounded Zulus were taken back to Rorke's Drift to be treated at the field hospital there, a sop to Lord Chelmsford's finer feelings; many more must surely have been left among the boulders to live or die without assistance or comfort of any kind. Estimates of the number of Zulu dead varied, but there were perhaps thirty Zulu bodies lying crumpled among the boulders along the cliff-face, or scattered over the grassy heights above. Among these someone claimed to recognize the remains of Mkhumbikazulu himself, lying sprawled where he had fallen at the head of the last charge of the day.

Lord Chelmsford was delighted; the action had achieved everything he hoped from it, and he wrote to Bartle Frere that evening in '. . . great hopes that the news of the storming of Sihayo's stronghold and the capture of so many cattle (about 500) may have a salutary effect in Zululand – Sihayo's men have I am told always been looked upon as the bravest in the country and certainly those who were killed today fought with great courage.'[34]

His Staff Officer, John Crealock, agreed: 'Our fight . . . showed the pluck of these Zulus. Of course, they had every advantage being in a most difficult position. If we are not attacked tonight it is thought we shall not meet a Zulu army for some time. On hearing of our having attacked his people, it is thought [Cetshwayo] will have taken instant action.'[35] Trooper Fred Symons, sceptical as ever, was unconvinced and thought it all 'a big fuss over a small matter'.[36]

Charlie Harford, however, had every reason to be pleased with his own performance. For years he had been troubled as to how he might react when the time finally came to test his courage in the crucible of battle, but in the event the first shots had carried him forward on a wave of excitement, and he had thrown himself into the skirmishing without pausing to think about his own safety. Afterwards, writing home to his mother, he allowed himself the luxury of a little self-satisfaction:

The Colonel and the Chief of his Staff who saw the whole proceeding complimented me very much on my success and the manner in which I got up to the cave so I hope it may do me good. My commandant specially mentioned me in his report to the General so I dare say I may have been mentioned in dispatches. I expect we shall have a rough time of it and the young boys of Cetewayo intend giving battle. They are determined to fight, it will be the best thing that possibly can happen to the Colony . . . we shall give him a tremendous thrashing he won't ever forget . . .[37]

Crealock was to be disappointed; that night no Zulu attack was made upon the camp at Rorke's Drift, and the column slept easily in a fug of self-satisfied content. Once again, it seemed, British troops had proved themselves the master of African enemies in the field. The evident courage and determination of the Zulu had only reinforced their prevailing sense of superiority. Whatever the Zulu chose to do next, Lord Chelmsford and his men felt themselves more than up to the challenge.

# 14

# 'Quite red with soldiers'

## Alarms and excursions, 12–20 January 1879

It is impossible to know, now, the exact moment when *inkosi* Sihayo, ensconced in the crisis meetings of the royal council 80 kilometres away at oNdini, first learned the grim news that his home had been destroyed, his son killed, his followers scattered and his herds looted. For a large country with no roads, characterized by wide rivers, soaring hills and patches of dense bush, information could be disseminated throughout Zululand remarkably quickly, however, and it is conceivable that the bare bones of the story reached him that same evening.

The news must have burst like a bombshell in the tense atmosphere of the Zulu court. For months – ever since the killing of MaMthethwa and MaMtshali back in July – the king had been locked in regular discussions with his most trusted advisers, trying to fathom the shift in British attitudes and to develop a strategy in response. In the early morning, a group of half-a-dozen councillors would meet in the great central enclosure, wrapped against the chill in the grey trade blankets which had inspired ordinary Zulus to name them *amanqe*, the vultures. From there they would proceed to the privacy of the king's personal quarters at the top of the homestead. They included some of the most powerful and influential members of the kingdom, including the king's senior *induna, inkosi* Mnyamana kaNgqengelele of the Buthelezi people and Ntshingwayo kaMahole of the Khoza, and their routine meeting was a sure sign to the inhabitants of the homestead that the times were troubled.

In November 1878, after successive placatory messages had failed to deflect British anger, Cetshwayo had summoned the full royal council, the *ibandla*, and the great men from across the Zulu kingdom had assembled to discuss the crisis. They included members of the royal family – the king's brothers Ziwedu, Ndabuko and Dabulamanzi – and powerful *amakhosi* from the northern districts, including Zibhebhu kaMaphitha of the Mandlakazi. Also present were many of the border *amakhosi*, including Sihayo of the amaQungebeni, Godide and his brother Mavumengwana of the Nthuli, and Qethuka of the Magwaza. Even Prince Hamu, who had refused to attend oNdini since the clash between the uThulwana and the iNgobamakhosi a year earlier, had made the long journey from the Ngotshe hills near the Phongolo river.

The meeting had proved a stormy one. Many of the councillors openly blamed Sihayo for bringing the wrath of the British down upon them and demanded not only that the king surrender Mehlokazulu – as the British demanded – but that Sihayo be punished for his inability to keep his family in check. This seems to have been coordinated by Prince Hamu, perhaps as a veiled attack – by means of his favourite – on the king himself. Tempers frayed, insults were exchanged, and Sihayo had been jostled and spat upon. In the end, however, the king had been compelled to stand his ground; while he was prepared to offer the British cattle as compensation for their injured dignity, he knew that he could abandon his favourites only at the risk of undermining his own authority within the kingdom.

It seemed a paltry sop to head off so much British indignation and in the end the great meeting had broken up with very little agreement, and all but the inner conclave had returned to their homes. Most had left resigned to the possibility of war; alone among them, Prince Hamu had returned to his kwaMfefe homestead to resume negotiations he had begun a few months before to defect to the British. For the rest, it merely remained to put their affairs in order, say goodbye to their families and gather their weapons.

Only the closest of the king's friends and advisers had been on hand, then, when the details of Frere's ultimatum reached them. It had taken several days to arrive at oNdini, for the Zulu delegation had been aware of the seriousness of their message, and had been nervous of the king's response, and by the time Cetshwayo had been able to discuss the British terms fully, time was already running out. His initial response had been to send a reply that he needed more time to consider the demands, but in truth Frere had left him little room for manoeuvre. Although the king finally agreed to consider the surrender of Mehlokazulu, the council could not accept that the *amabutho* be disbanded. Even the most conciliatory among them recognized that for what it was – a demand that the Zulu people acquiesce in their own subjugation.

As the days slid by, it had become increasingly clear that war could not be averted by negotiation and the council turned their discussion to how best the kingdom might be defended if it were attacked. In the first week of January – with Frere's deadline just a few days away – the king had accepted the inevitable and given the order for the *amabutho* to assemble.

The order had not been unexpected. The false alarms over the previous months had made the Zulu people all too aware of the unfolding crisis, but in any case summer was traditionally the time when the great gathering for the *uMkhosi* ceremonies that ushered in the new harvest was held. What made the order different in January 1879 was that the *amabutho* were ordered to leave their lavish ceremonial dancing-dress at home; this time they were mustering for war.

The *amabutho* could be summoned quickly enough; mechanisms for the rapid dissemination of news and information were a crucial part of the apparatus of state power. Runners – who could easily cover 40 or 50 kilometres a day – had set out at once from oNdini for the district *amakhanda*, the royal homesteads in the outlying areas which served as centres of local administration. For much of the year, when the *amabutho* were dispersed and the men living at home with their families, these homesteads were empty and eerily quiet, watched over only by the *izinduna* and caretakers appointed to look after them. Once the order to assemble reached them, however, they had been transformed into a hive of activity; fresh runners took up the word, carrying it to nearby *amakhosi* and dignitaries, while ordinary people had been called by the sound of the *impalimpala*, the signal-horn booming and reverberating through the valleys, or by shouts carried from hill-top to hill-top. By such means an order could be carried the length of the country in as little as twenty-four hours.

It is a measure of the seriousness of the threat facing the country that the king ordered all the *amabutho* to assemble – not just the *izinsizwa*, the young men who routinely served the king, but also the semi-retired assemblies of middle-aged and elderly married men. Only the border *amakhosi* were exempt – the amaChube in the Nkandla, the Ntuli and Magwaza at Middle Drift, Matshana's Sithole, the amaQungebeni, and further north the abaQulusi – all of whom had been directed to leave enough men behind to watch for the British.

For the rest, every man on hearing the order had gone to his hut, taken his spears down from the bundles suspended by woven grass strings from the thatch, sought out his gun and his meagre supply of powder and shot, and tied his sleeping mat into a bundle with the wooden headrest fastened under the string on the outside. As the word had been to assemble ready for war, most men left their ceremonial finery at home, although a few put on their cow-tail leg or arm ornaments or their headbands of otter or spotted-cat skin, and tucked into these a feather or two associated with their *ibutho*. They looked out, too, their necklaces of protective charms, and the small snuff-containers of carved wood or bone in which they kept the ground-up powders which stimulated their courage and made them immune to enemy weapons. Some of the older men also took with them the *igudu* smoking-horns they used to smoke cannabis, which was widely held not only to make them fierce in battle but to offset the effects of physical fatigue.

Then the long walk to the muster had begun. Boys too young yet to be enrolled in their own *amabutho* had gone with their fathers or brothers to carry their mats and supplies, a few roasted corn-cobs and hunks of raw meat wrapped in banana palms.[1] Often daughters and sisters had set out as well, carrying pumpkins or gourds of curdled milk for the journey; a few of the more adventurous would stay with their menfolk throughout the muster, even into the first day or two of the march to war itself, but the majority gave way on reaching the point of muster rather than face the boisterous assembled *amabutho*.

The men had first made their way from their family homes to their nearest royal homestead, where *izinduna* were waiting to sort them into companies according to their *ibutho*. If there was time, and their barracks not too far away, they had then gone to collect the war-shields of their *ibutho* from the stores in the raised huts – a noisy enough occasion as the men tried them for size, vying for the best ones, thumping them with sticks to test their soundness and clean off the dust. At each step of the journey the men shed a little of the skin of their everyday selves, encouraged by rituals designed to bind them together, by warriors' songs chanted in the heady company of so many of their age-mates, and by allusions to the past glories of their kings and their *ibutho*. They became no longer merely fathers, brothers or sons, pastoralists living by their cattle and their crops but assumed the role instead of *abaqawe*, heroes and warriors, their individuality submerged in the collective excitement which accompanied the prospect of imminent combat.

From the outlying centres they had walked to the royal capital, long lines of men rippling with dappled shields coursing down the hillsides, filing down ancient bush paths, and funnelling together at the well-known river drifts. 'Wherever the eye ranged across those hills,' wrote a missionary who witnessed such a muster, '. . . it met companies of those warriors, all converging on one focus – the king's place. Out of bushes, from behind rocks, out of gorges and the beds of rivers they came, and went singing their war-songs, and tramping, as only these people can tramp, formidable looking fellows enough, and formidable indeed if they chose to be your enemies.'[2] And in the summer of 1879, after years of tension and months of alarms, the chance to face the British openly as enemies at last came as something of a relief.

Cetshwayo had directed that the army assemble at his kwaNodwengu homestead on the Mahlabathini plain, within sight of his favourite oNdini homestead. A few kilometers away across the shimmering grasslands a great circle of fallen hut-frames and rotting palisades still marked what was left of the original homestead of kwaNodwengu. Cetshwayo had given his homestead the same name to honour his father's spirit, and something of the old king's transcendental power attached to it. It was here, rather than oNdini itself or any of the other great royal homesteads scattered across the hillsides nearby, that Cetshwayo preferred to stage many of the important national rituals of preparation, cleansing and healing. And, in January 1879, it was here that the *amabutho* gathered to undertake the last ceremonies necessary to prepare them for war.

As the men arrived – each new group singing and drubbing their spears and sticks rhythmically on their shields to announce their approach, and greeted by shrill whistles and chants from those already present – they had eagerly sought out their fellows and the *amabutho* had taken shape. There were perhaps 30,000 of them in all, a far greater number than even the concentration of royal homesteads on the plain could comfortably accommodate. Those who had been lucky enough to count one of the homesteads nearby as their barracks promptly occupied them, three or four men squeezed into each hut, but those whose headquarters lay far off in the outlying areas had had no option but to search out the nearest convenient patch of bush and cut down brushwood to make temporary shelters. The Mahlabathini plain, the same missionary had noted, appeared to be '. . . crammed to overflowing; indeed, temporary huts of green branches are being everywhere constructed to accommodate the host and all these the very flower of the country – magnificent men, few under six feet in height, and very models of form.'[3]

Now and then, when the *amabutho* passed each other, the overwrought atmosphere had led to scuffles, and blows were exchanged until the military *izinduna* restored order by striking shields or cracking heads with their sticks.

The assembly had been largely complete by 11 January – the very day Frere's ultimatum had expired. Even at that eleventh hour, the king had been prepared to demonstrate his willingness to negotiate, sending further messages to the British border posts asking for more time. It was too late. Late that same day, or at the latest the following morning, news arrived from the Mzinyathi border. The British had crossed into Zululand and attacked and destroyed kwaSogekle, and 'the country was quite red with soldiers' who had begun 'killing and laying waste far and wide'.[4]

*

News of the attack on kwaSogekle rippled down the length of the border, and high on the hills above the Middle Drift Durnford's command sensed a change in the mood of the Zulu communities opposite. Scanning the landscape through their field glasses from across the Thukela, British outposts found the countryside ominously deserted. Homesteads stood empty and abandoned, and women, children and old men had retired from the border, driving their cattle with them, to take what refuge they could among the steep hills or in the bush. For the most part there was no sign of the fighting men, but the British were afforded enough glimpses to know that some, at least, were still there – small patrols of them watching the drifts in their turn from the hill-tops, or in larger bodies breaking cover and emerging briefly into the open as they moved from one stronghold to another.

Then, on the morning of 13 January – two days after Lord Chelmsford's attack in the Batshe valley – Anthony Durnford received a convincing report that three *amabutho* had been spotted on the Zulu bank at Middle Drift, and were poised to strike into the colony.

The news seemed plausible enough. It had been sent by Bishop Hans Schreuder, the Norwegian Mission Society's leading representative whom Durnford had met three years before at Cetshwayo's coronation. During the difficult years of Mpande's power struggle with his ambitious sons, Schreuder had proved a useful ally to him and a touchstone of white opinion. He had remained on good terms with Cetshwayo after Mpande's death but in fact, like most Zululand missionaries, had played a double

game, betraying his relationship with his hosts by secretly lobbying for
Natal's intervention. When war seemed imminent Schreuder had moved
to another mission he had established on the Natal side of the border, at
kwaNtunjambili, near Kranskop. From here he had worked closely with the
local border agent, Eustace Fannin, gleaning from his spies, as war finally
arrived, something of the Zulu intentions. Now he had sent word that
several thousand Zulus were preparing to raid across the Thukela as a
reprisal for the attack on Sihayo.

Durnford could hardly afford to ignore the warning. He knew and
respected Schreuder's deep knowledge of Zulu affairs; moreover, the Zulu
timing seemed apposite since Durnford's recent movements had left the
drift only thinly defended. In response to Chelmsford's orders of a few days
before, Durnford had marched the bulk of his command towards the
Sandspruit, only to turn around again when Chelmsford had changed his
mind. That morning, most of No. 2 Column was scattered across a wide
swathe of country between the Sandspruit and their old headquarters on
d'Almaine's farm.

Durnford reacted to Schreuder's intelligence with typical resolve. After
sending orders to hurry his command back to the border, he took a cool
look at the drift and weighed up the risks of a Zulu attack. There had been
heavy sporadic rain over the previous few days, but from his position on
the high ground far above the Thukela Durnford could not judge the state
of the river and whether the drift was fordable. He decided to act in any
case; he scribbled a hasty dispatch to Lord Chelmsford telling him of his
intentions, then ordered his men to parade at 2 a.m. the following day to
move down the escarpment towards the drift.

Given the information at his disposal, and the flexibility with which
Chelmsford himself had regarded the column's role, this was perhaps a
legitimate response; underpinning the decision was something else, however. After a few tantalizing weeks in which it had seemed unlikely that
Anthony Durnford would have the chance, after all, to restore his tarnished
reputation by a glorious feat of arms, fate had handed him an opportunity
that was too good to miss. A ripple of excitement passed through his
column – their war had begun, and it seemed they were to get their chance
to invade Zululand after all.

Then the situation changed dramatically again. The troops were at their
posts before dawn on the morning of the 14th, and were preparing to
start the long descent down into the Thukela valley when a dispatch rider

galloped in with orders. Durnford was surrounded by his staff when he received them, and Captain Dymes was close enough to spot his reaction: 'I saw a change in his face at once. Suddenly he gave the word to retrace our way to camp and I well remember the look of disgust that crossed his countenance as he read the order.'[5]

Chelmsford had firmly countermanded Durnford's proposed action. Having no intelligence himself of any threat to the central border, his response was unusually tart:

Dear Durnford,

Unless you carry out the instructions I give you, it will be my unpleasant duty to remove you from your command and to substitute another officer for the command of No 2 Column. When a column is acting separately in an enemy's country I am quite right to give its commander every latitude, and would certainly expect him to disobey any orders he might receive from me if information which he obtained, showed that it would be injurious to the interests of the column under his command – Your neglecting to obey my instructions in this present instance has no excuse, you have simply received information in a letter from Bishop Schroeder, which may or may not be true and which you have no way of verifying. If movements ordered are to be delayed because reports hint at a chance of an invasion of Natal, it will be impossible for me to carry out my plan of campaign. I trust you will understand this plain speaking and not give me any further occasion to write in a style which is distasteful to me.[6]

It was a response which let slip something of the frustration Chelmsford had felt on the Cape frontier, when carefully coordinated sweeps through the bush had often fallen apart because colonial detachments had failed to follow his strict orders. Durnford was stung by the rebuke, but his composure quickly returned – he was long used to suppressing his true emotions.

As it turned out, however, the circumstances in which Chelmsford *would* allow a column commander to act independently had clearly been noted by Durnford. The incident seems finally to have decided Chelmsford on the role he wanted Durnford's column to play. The following day, the 15th, Chelmsford ordered Durnford to move to Rorke's Drift with his headquarters, mounted troops, rocket battery and his strongest battalion of the 1st NNC – the remaining two NNC battalions were to stay at Kranskop to guard the border as before. The situation at Rorke's Drift was changing, the Centre Column was preparing to advance, and Chelmsford needed Durnford close at hand for support.

The move seems to have offset Durnford's disappointment at being held in check. Whatever it portended, it seemed to offer a greater chance of involvement in the campaign – a chance to prove useful – than garrison duty at Middle Drift, and Durnford hurried his men to accomplish the move with typical energy. Once they had left d'Almaine's he kept them on the march well after dark, and with the intense physical activity his senses, once again, fizzed with suppressed excitement; 'you would have been pleased', he wrote home to his mother,

> . . . at seeing us in the night, marching, dark night, 'watercourse' roads, self leading, with an orderly and a lantern, then cavalry, each man leading his own horse, rocket battery next, then infantry, the wagon train straggling over some five miles [8 kilometres] of road. Crossing rivers in large boats in the night, horses swimming, then cattle killing, cooking on the red embers, horses feeding, men eating and sleeping etc. All the sights and sounds of camp life which I love.[7]

By the 18th Durnford had reached the Sandspruit, and the following day he pushed on to establish his headquarters at Vermaak's farm on top of the Helpmekaar ridge. It was a doleful spot, for the weather had closed in again, grey clouds hung over the heights, and a biting wind lashed his men periodically with cold downpours. Yet Durnford's clipped elation was infectious and his command – even the ordinary soldiers of the NNC, who had to improvise their own shelters each night – shared his excitement at the prospect of action to come.

*

A few miles further down the road, the miserable weather had added to the frustration of the Centre Column, still camped on the Zulu bank at Rorke's Drift. In the aftermath of the attack on kwaSogekle, Chelmsford had been keen to retain the initiative, but he found himself bogged down with supply troubles, and not yet in a position to advance. During the foray into the Batshe valley, he had noted the condition of the road, observing with some exasperation in a dispatch to Frere that 'the country is in a terrible state from the rain, and I do not know how we shall manage to get our wagons across the valley near Sihayo's Kraal.'[8] 'The rains and storms are simply the devil,' grumbled Crealock, 'it would save us any amount of trouble if the Zulus would come down and attack us, fail, and sue for peace.'[9]

Now that the army was ready to make a concerted push into Zulu territory, it was essential that a viable chain of supply be maintained. Convoys of supplies were being ferried up the road from Greytown and Chelmsford intended to establish large stockpiles at Helpmekaar and Rorke's Drift, from whence they could easily be sent forward as the column advanced. Yet, despite the weeks of preparation, he was forced to admit:

> I do not see a chance of moving forward in under a week, our supplies are not yet sufficient to warrant a forward movement and we have not yet put our road in working order. I am sending in an application for some colonial men skilled in pont work. We are at present working our pont and raft with handy men taken from amongst the Europeans of the Natal Native Contingent – these men however ought to go forward with the column as their services cannot be spared.[10]

A company of Royal Engineers – No. 2 Field Company, part of the reinforcements grudgingly sent out by London at the last minute – had arrived at Durban the week before and was on its way to join the column, but had been delayed on the road by the wet weather. Chelmsford sent an instruction asking for a detachment – an officer and half-a-dozen men – to be sent ahead. It had taken several days to ferry the column's transport wagons across, but to compound the problem the supplies needed to support the advance had failed to arrive at the depot at Rorke's Drift and were still on the road up. For most of the troops, there was nothing to do but sit and wait, to endure the changeable weather as best they could – and ponder among themselves how the Zulu were reacting to the news of the sacking of kwaSogekle.

The need to repair the road at least kept the NNC busy. Jim Rorke's old track climbed gently out of the Mzinyathi valley before sweeping in a curve to the right and dropping down towards the Batshe. In fine weather the stony drift across the stream was adequate, but after the heavy deluges the grassy approaches on both sides had become waterlogged and spongy, and there was little hope of getting the wagons through.

It was a dangerous spot, several kilometres ahead of the security afforded by the main camp, and close to the cliffs where the corpses of Sihayo's men still lay unburied among the boulders. To protect the work parties, Chelmsford ordered that a fortified post be built on the far side of the stream to be guarded by four companies of the 2/24th under Major William Dunbar. Dunbar did his best to hack down a swathe of bush on the scrubby slopes below the cliffs but his visibility and field of fire remained limited. At night particularly the position seemed exposed and vulnerable, and Dunbar was obliged to post a heavy screen of pickets from among men who were tired from working on the road all day.

Dunbar's concerns do not seem to have troubled Chelmsford, however, who was chafing at the bit to continue the advance. On the 15th he sent a strong patrol of mounted men under Colonel Russell far down the road to Siphezi mountain, 30 kilometres away. Russell returned to report that the countryside seemed largely deserted – there had been no sign of any Zulu concentrations and the homesteads along the road were empty – but that the road was unlikely to be passable without considerable work. Nevertheless, Chelmsford was encouraged enough by the news to outline his thinking to Evelyn Wood, whose No. 4 Column – 40 kilometres off to Chelmsford's left flank – was now actively harassing Zulus living on the middle reaches of the Ncome. With no signs of an imminent confrontation with the main Zulu army, Chelmsford intended to advance in stages, neutralizing the local *amakhosi* as he did so:

> Our first move must therefore be to the Isanblana hill where there is wood and water – I shall from there clear the Equideni forest or receive the submission of the chiefs and headmen residing in the district. Having settled that part I shall move on to ground between the Isepezi and Umhlabumakosi ... From Isepezi I should first work towards the mission station close to the little Itala, where I shall hope to establish Durnford's column ...[11]

There it is, then, that first mention in his dispatches of that fateful name. *Isanblana, Isandula, Isandhlwana*[12] – iSandlwana, the hill of death, destroyer of lives by the thousand, ruination of reputations. And kingdoms. But in that second week of January no more than a spot on the map, of no more significance or evil impute than Siphezi or Qhudeni, or any other of the exotically named Zulu hills about.

On 16 January, Chelmsford – always a man who preferred to see things for himself where he could – rode out from Rorke's Drift with his staff and a light escort. He stopped to inspect Dunbar's camp in the Batshe, and Dunbar took the opportunity to raise his concerns about its location. Dunbar was a big man with an impressive record who had fought in both the Crimea and the Indian Mutiny, and had been the senior captain in the 1/24th until promoted and transferred into the 2nd Battalion in 1874. He enjoyed a reputation throughout the regiment as a man not easily spooked, but he was clearly uncomfortable about the position of the camp, and asked that it be moved back across the Batshe to a spot where the ground was more open. Chelmsford listened politely enough, but as he discussed the situation with his staff Crealock said audibly, 'if Major Dunbar was afraid to stay there, we could send someone who was not'. Dunbar stiffened, turned and walked away; later that day he wrote to Chelmsford resigning his command.[13]

Crealock was notoriously acerbic, and the comment probably reflected the growing frustration at the column's inability to advance. Nevertheless, Chelmsford – who disliked any personal unpleasantness – was no doubt embarrassed by it, and it would take all his tact to smooth the matter over, for the story spread quickly among the officers of the 24th, and exacerbated the growing awkwardness between his own headquarters staff and Glyn's column command. Only after Chelmsford's personal intervention was Dunbar persuaded to retract his resignation.

Leaving Dunbar's ruffled feathers in their wake, Chelmsford and his staff rode on towards iSandlwana. They had not gone far when, to their surprise, they ran across a herd of cattle in the road being driven by a handful of herdsmen towards the camp at Rorke's Drift. The herdsmen claimed they belonged to Gamdana kaXongo, Sihayo's younger brother, who lived in the broken country below Hlazakazi, a few kilometres ahead. On the Cape frontier it had been a common Xhosa practice to bait ambushes with cattle but if Chelmsford had any doubts no one mentioned it, and indeed he seems to have taken the affair – the first encounter with the Zulu since the action on the 12th – at face value, as proof that the Zulu border communities were already beginning to crumble in their support of the king. Chelmsford had no desire to burden his patrol with cattle, and the herdsmen were told to return to instruct Gamdana to surrender in person. The party then started off again towards iSandlwana.

Even then the stark beauty of that rocky outcrop impressed the patrol. 'After two hours and three quarters slow riding', wrote one, 'we reached a peculiarly-shaped hill called Sandhlwana, where a short halt was made for breakfast.'[14] It was a clear day and the road, a thin ribbon of two overgrown wagon-ruts almost swallowed up by the waving sea of grass, was visible for kilometres ahead, stretching out towards Silutshana and Magogo and the whale-like bulk of Siphezi beyond. Further off, the spurs of Babanango shimmered enticingly in the haze.

There was no sign of life. Then, suddenly, someone spotted more cattle at the foot of the Malakatha mountain just a few kilometres to their right front. With the same breezy lack of concern which had characterized the earlier encounter, Chelmsford decided to investigate. It took forty-five minutes of careful riding over broken ground to reach them, and when the staff arrived they found 'a large number of men, women and children and cattle all ready to move somewhere'.[15] Chelmsford ordered them to hand over their weapons – 'twenty guns, of every make and kind . . . as well as a large number of assegais'[16] – and then began to interrogate them. They were followers of Gamdana, they said, and pointed out his homestead, a small collection of huts nearby, neatly framed, from that angle, by the peak of iSandlwana in the distance. Gamdana himself then arrived, and explained rather nervously that he had already been in touch with the Border Agent at Msinga, Henry Francis Fynn Junior, offering to surrender. Chelmsford was rather indignant to discover that important political negotiations had taken place behind his back – 'feeling very strongly that grave complications may arise if a Natal magistrate is in correspondence with a chief whom I may possibly find it necessary to attack,' he wrote afterwards, 'I have sent a summons to Mr [Fynn] to join me here at once . . .'[17] – but nevertheless offered his personal assurance that if Gamdana were to come to the camp at Rorke's Drift his safety would be assured, the more so if he were prepared to give up any cattle he might be tending on the king's behalf.

In Gamdana's acquiescence, Chelmsford saw a confirmation of his view that the apparently monolithic Zulu state would fall apart if pressure were applied to its constituent parts. And in one sense, of course, he was right, for it is difficult to avoid the feeling that Gamdana was taking advantage of the British presence to step out from the overweening shadow of his elder brother Sihayo, and perhaps to stake his own claim to a role in a post-war, British-dominated Zululand. Yet there was probably more to it than that. In fact, it is quite likely that Gamdana had been hedging his bets and, having made tentative gestures of compliance with the British, was about to slip away with the bulk of his followers into the rugged country below Malakatha when Chelmsford intercepted him. Whatever his loyalty to his brother and to the king, the British were to hand and they were not; nor indeed were most of the amaQungebeni fighting men, who had dispersed into the nearby hills after the defeat on the 12th. And if Chelmsford's staff noted Gamdana's obvious military weakness, they did not stop to ponder why.

By late afternoon, Chelmsford and his party were back at Rorke's Drift. It had proved a very relaxed reconnaissance with something of the air of an afternoon picnic about it – and certainly none of the tension which might be expected when the general commanding an invading army rode out, almost unprotected, far ahead of his men into enemy territory. There had been no sign of any response brewing to the attack on kwaSogekle – no large concentrations of men under arms had been seen, no one had mounted any resistance, no shots had been fired, and the only Zulus they had encountered seemed keen to avoid the war. The much-vaunted Zulu army seemed more like a bogeyman conjured up by the fevered imaginations of a jumpy settler society in Natal, and the war seemed set to resume the dreary and familiar pattern with which Chelmsford was familiar from his experiences on the Cape frontier. It was all rather disappointing.

The only sour note of the day came upon their return to Rorke's Drift, when the staff learned that the column had suffered its first European fatality. During the day a party of the Newcastle Mounted Rifles had gone for a bathe in the river and one of them – a Trooper Arthur Dixon, who could not swim – had been dragged into a hole by the current and drowned. Despite a desperate search by his comrades, his body had yet to be recovered.

There was nothing to be done for poor Dixon, and Lord Chelmsford returned to the more pressing work of hurrying along the column's supplies.

\*

Early on the morning of Sunday, 19 January 1879, George Hamilton Browne learned that, despite the apparent inactivity over the preceding days, there had been an interesting strategic development:

> On that morning I was visited by the General and his staff. He informed me that news had been received that the Zulu army was about to leave Ulundi that morning to attack us, and ordered, in case he was attacked, I was to move down and attack the right flank of the enemy. I suggested that as I lay in their road, they would eat me up long before they reached him. He thought not, but I requested the chief of the staff to

allow me to take my men off work and *laager* my camp. This he
refused . . .[18]

It is not entirely clear when, or how, Chelmsford had received this
information, whether by the usual – unreliable – system of spies maintained
by the Border Agents, or perhaps as a result of his communication with
Gamdana and his followers. Under the circumstances, he probably did not
consider it dependable, and he was, if Hamilton Browne is to be believed,
untroubled by it. If anything it offered the hope that the war might still,
after all, be brought to a speedy conclusion.

Later that day, however, Hamilton Browne reported some interesting
movements among the border population downstream of the Mzinyathi:

> That afternoon I received a note from Captain Duncombe who was in
> command of the picket on top of the hill, informing me that there was
> a large number of cattle in the valleys on his right, and requesting me
> to come up at once. This I did, taking with me two companies of my
> Zulus, the other one being on picket with him. On joining him on the
> top of the pass we moved carefully to the edge of some very rough
> ground consisting of deep valleys, and on looking into these we saw a
> large number of cattle herded by a few unarmed Zulus, who called to
> us to come down, as they wished to surrender themselves and the cattle.
> This was a temptation, a very nice bait indeed, but I saw through it. I
> had matriculated in ambush work in New Zealand, had had more than
> my share of it and with all my faults I have never been deemed a greedy
> or covetous man, so directed Captain Duncombe to shout to them
> ordering them to come up and surrender on the top, but this they
> refused to do.[19]

The men with Hamilton Browne were the iziGqoza companies of the NNC,
émigré Zulus who knew the country well, and Browne called over their
*induna* Mvubi for an opinion. 'That is a trap,' Mvumbi said firmly, 'those
bushes are full of Zulus. If we descend they will kill every one of us, but we
shall have a good fight first. I and my brothers are ready to descend with
the chief.'[20]

As reassuring a demonstration of fighting spirit as this undoubtedly was,
Hamilton Browne opted instead to send a runner back to Chelmsford's HQ
and,

as it was approaching sunset, [I] retired to my camp, leaving Captain Duncombe with a few good men (well hidden) to keep watch for any moves they (the Zulus) might carry on. The Zulus, seeing I had retired, came out of their ambush, some 1500 strong, and started towards a large military kraal which we knew to be several miles down the river ... Seeing they left the cattle behind, Duncombe and his men, as soon as they lost sight of the enemy, descended into the valley, captured some 150 head of them and brought them into my camp.[21]

Hamilton Browne's report arrived at Chelmsford's headquarters at about the same time as two newcomers to the column that afternoon. George Shepstone had been sent ahead by Durnford to inform Chelmsford that No. 2 Column was on the march to Rorke's Drift. Stopping off at the Msinga magistracy en route to see his old school friend, the magistrate Henry Francis Fynn, he had been there when the messenger arrived from Lord Chelmsford ordering Fynn to report to Centre Column headquarters. Fynn, known to the Zulu as Gwalagwala from the feather of the purple-crested lourie he habitually wore in his hat, had been longing for a chance to join the great military adventure, and was not in the slightest bit abashed by any implication of censure over the Gamdana affair implicit in Chelmsford's order. He had passed over care of his wife and children at the magistracy to his dashing colleague William Beaumont, the resident magistrate of Newcastle, and together he and Shepstone had hurried up to Rorke's Drift.

His arrival there was timely, for Chelmsford was anxious for Fynn's opinion on the Zulu movements in the bush towards Qhudeni, reported by Hamilton Browne. Fynn thought the Zulus they had seen were Sithole, followers of *inkosi* Matshana whose principal homestead, Nsingabantu, lay further down the Mzinyathi, but he admitted ruefully that his advice was received with some scepticism in the light of recent events. 'Sirayo's people having fled, I was twitted upon that result, I had sometime previously affirmed that the Zulus would fight, and pour themselves over fixed bayonets, breaking into a square of defence. "Impossible" was the reply...'[22]

Nevertheless, Fynn had already formed a clear impression of a viable Zulu strategy – that an army coming from oNdini might skirt behind the Hlazakazi heights, slip into the Mangeni valley and follow it down to the Mzinyathi: 'I pointed out the Zulu plan to descend the Mange valley of

the Mhlazakazi Mountain, there shelter in the Qudine forests until the
column had moved forward sufficiently to enable the Zulu army to creep
round from the Mange Valley up the Buffalo River, and so cut off the
column in the rear and close in upon them.'[23]

Much, it seemed, would depend upon the veracity of Lord Chelmsford's
reports from oNdini – and upon the intentions of *inkosi* Matshana himself.
Unknown to him, for the second time in his life Matshana was the subject
of considerable interest among his European enemies.

That evening, rumours of Hamilton Browne's encounter soon passed
around among the column; 'we are to have a night attack made upon us
by a large Zulu *Impi* [armed force] under Usirajo', Norris-Newman
informed his readers, adding sceptically that 'for my own part, judging
from what I have seen while out with patrols, I do not think there is any
large force of Zulus at present nearer than fifteen miles [24 kilometres],
though what number may be marching on here it is impossible to say.'[24]

That night, in their advance camp on the Batshe, Hamilton Browne
noticed a distinct uneasiness among his men. Yet the night passed without
incident, and morning brought a fresh distraction. The road through the
Batshe valley had been repaired as best it could, and over thirty wagon-
loads of supplies had at last arrived at Rorke's Drift.

It was Monday, 20 January 1879 – and No. 3 Column was finally ready
to abandon Rorke's Drift, and push forward into Zululand.

# 15

# 'Give the matter to us!'

## The road to iSandlwana

The attack on Siyaho's homestead had seen the last vestige of King Cetshwayo's hope of reaching any settlement with the British disappear, and as the days passed, his forces now prepared for all-out war. The *amabutho* had begun to arrive in strength on the oNdini plain on 8 January and by the 11th – the day the British ultimatum had expired – the army was largely complete. Despite the absence of those men left in the border districts to watch the British movements, this was to prove the greatest muster of men under arms in Zulu history. There were between 25,000 and 30,000 of them in all, and they had come from the far ends of the country: from the Phongolo river in the north-west, where many spoke SiSwati rather than isiZulu, but still considered themselves subjects of the Zulu king; from among the Mpungose, who lived in the great flats bordering the St Lucia wetlands on the north coast; from the Mandlakazi along the foothills of the Lebombo, from the Buthelezi and the Zungu on the Mfolozi Mnyama, from Biyela country in the misty hills on the middle reaches of the Mhlatuze, and from the Chube in the primordial Nkandla forests. The great royal homesteads scattered across the Mahlabathini plain – oNdini itself, kwaNodwengu, emLambongwenya, where Shepstone had crowned Cetshwayo six years before, kwaQikazi and kwaBulawayo, even kwaKhandempemvu a few kilometres further off at the foot of the twin-peaked amaBedlana hills – which between them contained more than 5,000 huts had quickly filled with men. Many more were camped out in sprawling bivouacs in the hills nearby.

Undoubtedly the man who most influenced the Zulu strategy in response to the British invasion was *inkosi* Mnyamana kaNgqengelele of the Buthelezi people. The *amakhosi* of the Buthelezi had played a prominent role in the forging of the new order which had been central to the rise of the Zulu kingdom; Shaka himself had raised Mnyamana's father to rule over the Buthelezi, disrupting the existing lineage, and Mnyamana himself had been a member of King Mpande's *ibandla*, his council. He was intimately acquainted with the ways of the *amabutho* and Mpande had given him command of the uThulwana during the 1850s when that *ibutho* contained many royal princes jockeying for influence, including Cetshwayo himself. It was at that time that Cetshwayo had first come to trust in Mnyamana, and over the years he had learned to rely on his thoughtful advice. When Cetshwayo had become king, it was Mnyamana whom he had appointed as the head of the council, and thus Mnyamana had slipped easily into the position of commander-in-chief of the Zulu army. A tall, spare, wiry man in his seventies with piercing eyes, a neatly trimmed and greying beard and moustache and a measured manner, Mnyamana was a great traditionalist who was deeply suspicious of Europeans and their ways.

Cetshwayo's local intelligence system was much more efficient than that of Lord Chelmsford, keeping him well supplied with information about the British build-up on the Zululand borders. Scouts in the border communities brought him regular updates on the movements in the hills opposite, while spies were able to slip almost with impunity into Natal to gather more detailed information. Nonetheless, it remained difficult for the council to assess exactly where the British would strike – rather as Chelmsford had hoped – for in addition to the five obvious columns, British warships had been seen steaming up the coast, raising the possibility of another strike by sea, or even from the Portuguese-held territory in Mozambique. One possible course of action was to mount a counter-strike into British territory at some point where the border crossings were weakly protected. This had the advantage that it might throw the British into confusion and, by attacking undefended civilian targets in Natal, put political pressure on Frere and Chelmsford to suspend the invasion. It would, furthermore, shift the impact of operations from Zulu civilians to those in Natal, since the passage of the warring armies was likely to wreak destruction on their lands and cause major disruption of their everyday life.

Yet Cetshwayo himself was firmly opposed to such a strategy. He considered himself the victim of British aggression, and he had both a realistic appreciation of his situation and was well aware of the advantage that the moral high ground might play in any subsequent peace negotiations, as he explained afterwards:

... he wished to be able to say, should things go against him, that he acted entirely on the defensive ... Cetshwayo hoped to be able to crush the English columns, drive them out of the country, defend his border, then arrange a peace. He knew the English in Natal could not bring a very large force into the field; but he had often been told by white men (traders in his country) that they had a very large army beyond the sea. He knew that if the English persevered in the war, he would get the worst of it in the end.[1]

There was one Zulu strategy, however, which Lord Chelmsford particularly feared. By retiring to natural strongholds in the hills – as the Swazi had done in the past in the face of numerically superior Zulu raids – it was possible that the Zulu might deny the British the opportunity to win a decisive victory in the field, and prolong the war beyond the limits of British logistical resources and political will. Ironically, however, the council never seriously considered this option – and the young men gathering in their thousands in the countryside around them were the reason why. Since King Shaka's time the army had been wedded to an essentially aggressive approach – to attack the enemy in force where they found them, and destroy them as quickly as possible – and there were also very real limits as to how long the army could be sustained in the field. Historically, it was unusual for the army to remain assembled for more than two or three weeks at a time, even in the most testing campaigns, because the *amabutho*'s aggressive spirit tended to wane with the lack of immediate tangible objectives, and because it was difficult to provide even a basic level of provision for any longer.

If the army was to operate at its most efficient then, even when fighting on its own turf, it would need to find and attack the British as soon as possible. It merely remained to decide which of the many threatening columns appeared to be the most dangerous.

*

While Cetshwayo and his council deliberated, the army gathered about him underwent the crucial rituals necessary to prepare it for war.

With so much at stake, it was imperative that the army be cleansed of any spiritual impurities and be bound together, inured as well as possible by supernatural means against harm in the coming fight. Overseeing the process were specialist *izinyanga* who had prepared large quantities of potent medicines, the exact ingredients of which were a closely guarded secret.

First came the cleansing. The doctors had carefully selected a spot by the Ntukwini stream, close to its junction with the Mfolozi Mhlope, and here they had dug deep, narrow pits in the ground, each about 0.5 metres across and 2 metres deep. Here the army was marched and the *amabutho* ordered to squat on the surrounding hillsides. Each *ibutho* was called out in turn and the men came forward in groups to the pits. The *izinyanga* proffered pots of medicine, and each man took a stiff gulp. The effects were immediate, according to a teenager in the uVe *ibutho*, one Mpashana kaSodondo, a violent retching which cast out their spiritual impurities together with the contents of their stomachs into the holes:

> Two, three or four may go up to this hole at one time. There is naturally a desire to finish quickly, and have done with the vomiting, but the doctors will not allow crowding. These, two of them, stand on either side of the hole and see that everyone conforms to his instructions. Here and there the stick may be used on men who have merely pretended to drink the medicated water and therefore are unable to vomit into the hole as required. And so the vomiting goes on practically all day long.[2]

Their part in the ceremony over, the men returned to their comrades on the hillsides until the entire army had been purified, and bound together by the shared experience. When the vomiting was complete, the *izinyanga* carefully dipped twists of grass into each hole, soaking them in the liquid essence of the assembled army, and these twists were then taken to be bound into the national *inkatha yesizwe*, the sacred grass coil which embodied the unity of the Zulu people. The holes were then carefully filled in and the location disguised to prevent any enemy from using the contents for evil purposes.

Once the vomiting ceremony was under way, a young *ibutho* who had already completed it was picked out and marched to the royal homestead at kwaNodwengo. The next part of the ceremony was a rite of passage which each *ibutho* would perform in turn. A young black bull had been selected from the king's herds – the symbol of masculine strength and vitality, untamed and fierce – and the men of the youngest *ibutho* were required to wrestle it to the ground and kill it with their bare hands.[3]

The carcass was taken to an open wood fire where the presiding *izinyanga* stripped off the hide, then cut the flesh into long strips and roasted them. The strips were then smeared with powdered medicines and taken into the centre of the great cattle pen, where the rest of the *amabutho* were assembling after the vomiting ceremony. The *amabutho* were formed into a great circle, an *umkhumbi*, and the *izinyanga* walked among them, tossing the meat-strips into the air. Each man was supposed to grab a strip as it flew past him and quickly chew the end, sucking in the juices and the full worth of protective medicines, before tossing it back into the air for others to take their turn. If the meat fell to the ground at any point it was considered to lose its potency immediately, and they were on no account supposed to swallow any.

The excitement was intense, the men, who had eaten only erratically since the muster began, for 'one day we hungered, and another day we feasted, just as the king happened to give us beer or beef', jostling one another, and the dust rising from the trampled soil and cattle dung underfoot on a dry day into a choking fog that stung the eyes and caught in the throat. Mpashana kaSodondo found the whole event trying:

> ... many of the troops are extremely hungry and even emaciated [and] they sometimes swallowed the piece bitten off, although it is quite contrary to custom and requirement to do so ... it not infrequently happened that forbidden [i.e. dropped] meat was picked up and consumed during the excitement going on round about ... During the eating of the meat-strips ceremony, several of the half-starving and weak men may be seen to fall forward, fainting on account of the exertion and heat caused through being in the midst of so large a concourse violently contending for the meat-strips. These will perhaps pitch forward, shield and assegais falling clatteringly from them, and thereafter be helped by their friends or relations to some place where they can recover.[4]

The ritual of the meat-strips concluded the first day's ceremonies, and the *amabutho* returned to their overnight bivouacs. The following day the king sent for the *amabutho* in pairs, picking out those who were close in age or who often mustered together and were thereby considered linked. The rivalry between such *amabutho* was intense, so much so that they were forbidden to bring their spears, and attended only with dancing sticks, for this part of the ceremony, the *ukuxoxa* or 'challenge', was designed to direct their competition to good effect on the battlefield. That day Cetshwayo

called out the iNgobamakhosi – Mehlokazulu's *ibutho*, confident young
men in their mid-twenties – and their rivals the uKhandempemvu, who
were a few years older:

> A man of the Ngobamakosi lot got up and shouted 'I shall surpass you,
> son of So-and-so. If you stab a whiteman before mine has fallen, you
> may take the kraal of our people at such-and-such a place . . . you may
> take my sister, so-and-so.' Having said this he will then start leaping
> about (*giya*'ing) with his small dancing shield and a stick (for assegais
> are not carried on such occasion in the presence of the king, for it is
> feared that troops may stab one another with them). The other who has
> been addressed may now get up and say 'Well, if you can do better than
> I do, you will take our kraal . . . and my sister . . .' He will then *giya*.
> Whilst the *giya*'ing goes on, he is praised by those of his regiment, and
> if a man happens to be known to the king and be trusted by the king,
> the king will hold out his arm towards him, pointing the first or first
> two fingers at him, and shaking them and that hand approvingly.[5]

It was a time for those who aspired to the unique prestige accorded the
*abaqawe*, the heroes, to step forward and stake their claim to future glory.
After the fight, while no one seriously expected the wagers made in the heat
of the moment to be honoured, the king would inquire from his commanders whether those who had proclaimed themselves *abaqawe* had lived up to
their boasts, and any failure to have done so could lead to a very public
embarrassment. One young man of the iNgobamakhosi, Ntobolongwane
kaBheje, who had earned the reputation among the missionaries at the
St Paul's mission in central Zululand as 'cock-of-the-walk', danced out
before his comrades that morning and 'boasted that . . . he would go ahead
of the army and be the first to kill one of the enemy'.[6] In the days to come
he would live up to his boast – but at a cost which would leave him
scarred for life. A few days later, two more *amabutho*, the uNokhenke
and uMbonambi, were called out to challenge one another, leaving these
four *amabutho* in particular burning with a desire to prove themselves in
front of each other and the rest of the army in the crucible of battle.

The challenges complete, there remained just one further ritual to
perform. The entire army was brought into the central enclosure at
kwaNodwengu and formed into an *umkhumbi* – a circle – several rows
deep. The *izinyanga* had prepared more medicines for them which were
bubbling in a pot over a fire in the centre. Each *ibutho* was called out in

turn, and the men ran past the doctors who used cow-tails to spatter them with medicines from the pots, great arcs of liquid raining down on the men's shields, faces and bodies. Mpashana, preparing for war for the first time in his life, was reluctant to look too closely into the pots. 'I have noticed', he recalled years later, 'the stuff burnt in the circle of men smelling like flesh, without thinking what flesh it could be.'[7] His squeamishness is understandable, for body parts taken from a fallen enemy – a strip of skin from the forehead or right arm, the penis and anus, flayed beard or moustache, all of them potent symbols of masculine power – were universally acknowledged to provide the best ingredients for war medicine.

With the ceremonies complete, the men in the *amabutho* had entered a new spiritual state, cut off from everyday life, their transformation to warriors complete. They could no longer mix with their families, and were prohibited from making love to their girlfriends and wives lest they contaminate them or, worse still, destroy the purity of their war-like being. They were bound together as one, the manhood of the nation entire, immune to the dark forces they might unleash through bloodshed, and impervious to enemy arms. Caught up in the excitement of coming combat, they lived in a universe of war, more ready to fight with every step they took on the road towards the enemy. It merely remained for the king and his generals to instruct them – and unleash them in battle.

*

The attack on Sihayo's homestead on 12 January had brought the British strategy into focus, giving an indication at last of where the greatest threat lay and enabling King Cetshwayo to decide his strategy. Chelmsford had certainly intended the assault on the homestead to send a clear message to the king, yet it was not merely the obvious aggressive intent which led the council to conclude that the Centre Column was by far the most dangerous. The British left flank column, No. 4 – Wood's command – had also been energetic from the start, crossing into the disputed territory even before the ultimatum expired, and not only raiding energetically for cattle but working to detach local *amakhosi* from their allegiance to the king. Yet the northern theatre was far away from oNdini, and Cetshwayo was rightly confident that the abaQulusi, who hovered menacingly on Wood's flank, could be relied upon to contest the British advance there at every stage. On the other side of the country, in the coastal sector, the British advance seemed less dangerous to the national cause, if only because the coastal sector had already been exposed to decades of white penetration. Parts of it had also been depopulated by the recent defection of the frontiersman John Dunn, who, having enjoyed a privileged position at Cetshwayo's court, had been warned to leave as the situation grew hotter and, with his Zulu followers, had crossed the border back into Natal in December 1878.

What made the Centre Column so dangerous was the fact that, just a day into the war, it seemed to be deliberately seeking out and targeting significant supporters, not merely of the royal house, but of Cetshwayo's personal administration. If the council had struggled to understand British antipathy towards Sihayo in the run-up to the war, the attack made their purpose all too clear – throughout the crisis the British had targeted him as a cornerstone of the king's personal authority, and it was suddenly obvious that their true target had nothing whatever to do with the contested border.

It was clear, too, that of all the British columns, the one marching from Rorke's Drift most represented those old conflicts which had echoed up and down the length of the coastal strip since Shaka's day, including as it did a sinister alliance of old enemies. The king's intelligence service was certainly sophisticated enough to know who these were: the amaChunu under *inkosi* Phakade's heir Gabangaye and the amaNgwane under Nyanda kaZikhali, a grandson of the famous Matiwane, whom King Dingane had consigned to the hill of execution. Worst of all, the invasion had realized Cetshwayo's worst nightmare – his long-standing fear that rivals within his own family, his brothers who had escaped the bloodletting of 1856, might one day return and try to overturn his succession. For with the Centre Column too were hundreds of iziGqoza, those émigré Zulus who had fled to Natal rather than live under his authority, and at their head one of his own brothers, Prince Sikhotha kaMpande, young, fit, active, and entirely legitimate, the perfect figurehead for a British-sponsored change of regime. Viewed from oNdini, Lord Chelmsford's Centre Column had a disturbing whiff of nemesis about it. But if the Centre Column represented the head and chest of the British threat, the council could hardly afford to ignore its wings.

In the end, the Zulu strategy was simple: enough troops would be consigned to check the British flanks, but the main response was to be directed against the centre. In the north, the abaQulusi and Prince Mbilini's marauders would form the basis of the defence against Wood's column. In the south, towards the coast, Pearson's Right Flank Column might be delayed by those elements which had remained near the border to watch the British advance, reinforced by a contingent from the troops gathered noisily at oNdini.

In the event, the council's final strategy was a compromise which walked a precarious line between maximizing its resources to oppose threats on several fronts and overstretching them. A sizeable detachment of royal troops – some 5,000 men – would be sent to reinforce the coastal districts. After careful deliberation, the council appointed *inkosi* Godide kaNdlela of the Nthuli people, son of King Dingane's leading general, to command them.

With their flanks secured as best they could, it merely remained to direct the main response against the Centre Column. There was no question of the king commanding his army in person. Shaka had done so, but none of his successors – it was far too dangerous for kings to risk themselves, and the spiritual well-being of the kingdom as a whole, once they had assumed the throne. Cetshwayo confined himself to offering advice to his appointed commanders before they set off to the front – and to awaiting anxiously the reports of his army's progress, which reached oNdini several times a day.

As commander-in-chief it was *inkosi* Mnyamana's prerogative to lead the army, but he too preferred to remain at oNdini, controlling the war effort across all fronts from the nation's administrative hub. Instead, he deferred to his friend *inkosi* Ntshingwayo kaMahole, whom the council appointed its senior general. To assist Ntshingwayo, the king himself selected Mavumengwana kaNdlela Nthuli, a much younger man in his mid-forties, an age-mate and personal friend of the king who had served with him in the uThulwana *ibutho*. It is difficult to avoid the impression that his appointment was a political one which allowed Cetshwayo a representative, his 'eyes and ears', at the heart of his field command. Nevertheless, Mavumengwana was a member of the established Zulu elite – he was the younger brother of *inkosi* Godide, who had been given the coastal command. As the king himself later explained, his generals 'had orders to drive back the columns, and were not hampered with any particular instructions, but were left to act independently as they saw fit.' There was, however, one important proviso: 'I told Tyingwayo who was at the head of these troops, not to go to the English at once [to attack them], but to have a conference and then send some chiefs to the English to ask why they were laying the country waste and killing Zulus . . .'[8]

It would be absurd to suppose that Cetshwayo seriously believed that once the two armies were in close proximity an all-out war could still be averted by last-minute negotiations, yet there was undoubtedly a very real political purpose behind the order. The king wished it to be clearly understood that it was the British who were the aggressors, not the Zulu – and that even when defending his own country, he would only fight once they had made a confrontation inevitable. It was a knowing instruction designed to protect Cetshwayo's air of injured innocence – and no doubt both Cetshwayo and *inkosi* Ntshingwayo understood its limitations. Everything would depend upon Ntshingwayo's judgement, and in the end it required no more of him than to manoeuvre the Zulu army to a point where the British could not fail to attack him so that his response would be justified.

Only the mood of the army – which saw their duty in far simpler terms, to seek out the enemy and destroy them where they found them – would remain problematic, and it remained to be seen whether their enthusiasm could be contained until the right moment.

Ironically, then, Ntshingwayo found himself in a similar predicament to Durnford's during the Langalibalele affair – both were ordered to achieve crucial military objectives while being denied political control over the initiative. Six years after Bushman's River Pass, however, the stakes were infinitely higher.

*

In the last days of the doctoring ceremonies, a good deal of attention was given to the firearms carried by the *amabutho*. Once it had become clear, over the previous months, that a confrontation with the British was a real possibility, Cetshwayo had attempted to address the disparity in weapons. It was well known that the British had guns, and good ones, too – far better than anything the Zulu could hope to deploy. But while it is unlikely that either the king or his advisers ever seriously hoped to match their enemy weapon for weapon, there was a real belief that quantity might, in the heat of battle, prove at least equal to quality. Yet even in this regard, first impressions had proved depressing. Towards the end of 1878 the king had reviewed his youngest *amabutho* – who were conspicuously short of guns, since the gun-trade naturally favoured mature men who had accumulated enough resources to buy them – and, as Mpashana of the uVe recalled, had been disappointed in what he saw. '"Lift up your guns." We did so. "So are there no guns? Each man with a beast from his place must bring it up next day and buy guns of Dunn."'[9]

It had been one of John Dunn's functions, over the years, to procure firearms on Cetshwayo's behalf, and with the tacit support of the Natal authorities he had imported thousands into Zululand over the years; even at the last minute, with war hanging in the balance, it seems he was still able to secure them by the wagon-load. Between 1872 and 1877, 60,000 guns had been legally imported into Natal, 40,000 of which had been re-exported, and 20,000 of these shipped to Mozambique – the main point of entry for firearms into Zululand. One report of 1878 estimated that there were as many as 20,000 stands of arms in Zululand, of which 500 were modern breech-loaders, 2,500 recent percussion models, 5,000 older percussion models and the rest obsolete flintlock muskets. The availability of supply had been reflected in the price – a good double-barrelled muzzle-loader, when first introduced into the country by John Dunn, had cost the princely sum of four head of cattle. By 1878 it could be bought for just one cow, while the Enfield percussion rifle – which had been standard issue among the British Army a generation before – could be had for just a sheep.

Not only were most guns owned by the Zulu old, but few had been stored in ideal conditions, and the trade in spare parts was virtually non-existent. Termites had often taken their toll of the wooden stocks and butt, springs were broken, and moving parts rusty. A few Zulus knew very well how to shoot – some important individuals, like Prince Dabulamanzi, had benefited from a close acquaintance with John Dunn or other traders, and had been well taught, while professional hunting parties from Natal, who obtained concessions in King Mpande's time to slaughter the wildlife, had often trained local Zulus to assist them. The majority, however, had only the haziest idea how to use firearms properly; the need to raise the rear sight when firing at long ranges had been observed among hunters, and from that most Zulus had concluded that raising the sight added power and distance. And if the means of firing did little to enhance accuracy, neither did the ammunition available, for traders often sold a weapon with just a handful of rounds, and once these had been expended the owner was left to improvise his own, hammering lead – or anything else – roughly into a shape to fit the barrel.

The supply of powder had, indeed, been another problem the king had sought to address, and he had procured the services of a Sotho *inyanga* from beyond the uKhahlamba mountains. The Sotho were regarded with envy by many of their African neighbours as they had been producing their own powder since the 1850s, and Cetshwayo's early efforts had led to the manufacture of hundreds of kilograms of coarse black powder before the start of hostilities. The quality was inevitably poor, however, and it often burned unevenly, producing a great volume of smoke and giving the gun a fearsome recoil – many Zulu further sacrificed accuracy by holding the butt away from their shoulders to avoid the bruising thump.

It was perhaps to address these shortcomings that during the great preparatory rituals the Sotho *inyanga* burned medicines on a potsherd in front of the assembled *amabutho*, then called out the men with guns, directing them to file past with the muzzles of their weapons pointed down over the fire, so that the smoke drifted up the barrel, imparting the magical ability to make them fire straight and true.

*

Altogether, the ceremonies designed to strengthen, purify and inspire the *amabutho* took nine days. At last, it remained only for the king to address his forces, and to instruct them on their objectives. Early on the morning of 17 January, the *amabutho* crowded into the central space at kwaNodwengo once more, drawn up in order of precedence in a great circle, and here, from the centre, standing with his commanders, the king addressed them.

First the *ibutho* destined to be sent to the coast was called out – the uMxapho – and then for the rest there was a simple enough directive. 'He told us', recalled Mhlahlana Ngune of the uKhandempemvu 'that he wanted certain regiments to go and eat up the white men at Isandhlwana. The first one he pulled out was the Unokenke, the next was the Ukandempemvu, then came the Indhluyengwe, who were followed by the Umbonambi, the Ingobamakosi, the Uve and the Udhloko.'[10] To these men he said simply, 'I am sending you out against the whites who have invaded Zululand and driven away our cattle. You are to go against the column at Rorke's Drift and drive it back into Natal ... You will attack by daylight as there are enough of you to eat it up, and you will march slowly so as not to tire yourselves.'[11]

It was no more than a statement of intent, but to the *amabutho*, unsettled by months of speculation and foreboding, wound up to a pitch of excitement by days of ritual, it amounted to the confirmation they had longed for. 'I have not gone over the seas to look for the white man,' declared the king, 'yet they have come into my country and I would not be surprised if they took away our wives and cattle and crops and land. What shall I do? I have nothing against the white man and cannot tell why they come to me. What shall I do?'[12] It was a rhetorical question, and there was only one possible answer; ' "Give the matter to us," we replied, "we will go and eat up the white man and finish them off. They are not going to take you while we are here. They must take us first!" '[13]

It was to be war, at last – and the men of Zululand were exuberant, shouting out their approval in terms which reaffirmed the king's defiance:

> . . . we, the chosen ones, sang loudly, saying 'Cetewayo, Zulu, Ndabezita, Gumede, you are the little mealie cob that puts out the fire started by Mantshonga and Ngelebana. You are the bow-legged one who, on account of his legs, can baffle the police. You are the stalk that grows by itself at Nhlungwana, while other stems grow in large clusters. You are the one who turns his back on the Ulundi and the Drakensberg mountains. Bayete!'[14]

Then the great army turned, and the *amabutho* began to file out of the gate of the royal homestead, forming up on the open ground beyond. As they went each chanted its own war-songs, and the air was full of shouts and cries and shrill whistles, the excitement so intense that at times men could not contain themselves within the ranks, and danced out to *giya*.

The king himself had appointed the order of march, for the honour of leading the way – of 'drinking the dew', of being first to walk out each morning through the long wet grass – was jealously guarded and given as a mark of favour to one of the younger *amabutho*. At last, after much shuffling, the army moved off across the Mahlabathini plain, heading towards the nearby drift across the Mfolozi Mhlope with the uNokhenke in the lead. Each *ibutho* was marked by its distinctive shields, which the men carried beside them, sweeping them over the top of the grass, so that from a distance they looked for all the world like cavalrymen, or swinging them up shoulder-high and moving them to the rhythm of their songs. Many older men carried the great full-length 1.25-metre shield favoured in Shaka's time, the *isihlangu*, while most of the younger men favoured the smaller *umbhumbhulozu*, no more than a metre long.

Ironically, even in that great *impi* going to war to defend its traditions and lands against the effect of the white man, the economic impact of European penetration could be seen. In Shaka's time, when armies were smaller and the country rich in cattle captured in war, the colours of the shields of the entire *amabutho* had been precise and uniform. Now, half a century after his death, the king's inability to raise vast herds of cattle was reflected in the varied hides used for the shields carried, particularly by the younger *amabutho*. While the status of the senior men was still obvious in their great white – or predominantly white – shields, it had not been possible for big *amabutho* like the uKhandempemvu to choose a pattern which could be supplied in large enough numbers to equip the entire assembly. Cetshwayo had been forced to allocate different patterns to particular companies within it, so that the uKhandempemvu carried white shields with great broad patches across the centre, or dark brown shields with large white patches to one side, or black shields with small patches at the edge. And for the iNgobamakhosi and the uVe, the youngest men in the army – and among the largest of the *amabutho* – there were only the commonest colours of all, plain black or brown.

Even so, they were such an extraordinary sight that summer evening, throwing up great clouds of dust as they walked down to the river, that Gumpeka Qwabe's heart ached at the recollection of them more than fifty years later, for it looked as if there were 'so many men in them that they seemed to stretch from there right to the sea'.[15] And scattered among them, alongside the generals appointed by the king, were representatives of almost all the great lineages of the kingdom. Several of the royal princes were there, including Cetshwayo's full brother, Ndabuko, his favourite younger brother Dabulamanzi, and Prince Magwendu. Zibhebhu of the Mandlakazi was present, and so too – despite the resentment of some of his colleagues – was Sihayo. There were other important *amakhosi* too, like Mkhosana kaMvundlana of the Biyela, Ntizwa kaNhlaka, brother of the Mdlalose *inkosi* and Muwundula kaMamba of the eMgazini. Mnyamana Buthelezi had sent several of his sons to represent him, and many of the king's favourites were present, like Sigcwelegcwele kaMhlekeleke, who commanded the iNgobamakhosi, and Vumandaba kaNthathi, who had headed the deputation which received Frere's ultimatum, and was now commanding the uKhandempemvu.

It was an army of national unity, deeply indignant at British presumption, and determined to drive the foreign invaders off Zulu soil. And like soldiers going to war the world over, they were convinced of their own invulnerability, and that the struggle would be a short one. The fighting, thought Mshapi kaNoradu of the uKhandempemvu, 'would take a single day'.[16]

*

In the British camp at Rorke's Drift the reveille was sounded as usual before dawn on 20 January. It was the day of the Centre Column's advance, and a great noisy bustle began as equipment was hurriedly packed away, tents were struck, rolled up and loaded onto wagons, oxen marshalled into their traces and men fell in, all of it to the accompaniment of shrill bugle calls, shouted orders, the lowing and groaning of the oxen, the cracking of the long *voorloopers'* whips, cries of encouragement and hoarse curses, and the clatter and clank of horse-drawn transport.

To men who had endured a long week of boredom at the mercy of the sun and rain, it was an exciting moment. Trooper Fred Symons of the Carbineers allowed himself an uncharacteristic moment of elation at the sight of the column as it shook itself into order and

> ... slowly wound its way up the grassy slopes overlooking the river, which were then covered with a carpet of green; then down thro the thorns in the Ibatshe valley; up under the frowning rocks of Sirayo's stronghold, then turning abruptly to the right and ascending a steep incline and came in view of a curiously shaped hill called by the natives 'Isandhlwana'.
>
> Several companies of the 24th had preceded us for the purpose of making a road and also the Natal Native Contingent whose camp was on the banks of the Ibatshe stream. They fell into their places as the Column advanced.
>
> The vanguard made a short halt in its debouchment from the valley till the wagons had got over their difficulties on the muddy road where they could only travel in single file.
>
> The Mounted Infantry under Colonel Russell formed the advance guard followed by their wagons. Natal Police supported, Carbineers bringing up the rear. Then came the 1/24th Regiment, with band playing merrily, succeeded by the long dark lines of Native Allies, the 2/24th Regiment forming the rearguard. No. [5] Battery R.A. was also with the column.
>
> Resuming its march the army passed through an open piece of country flanked on the left by a long stony ridge, and falling on the right towards the Buffalo; and entered another valley bestrewn with mimosas, aloes and rocks.
>
> During our march along the clear country the band broke off suddenly, in the middle of a verse of 'Don't you love me Mollie Darling' ...[17]

It was the third time, Symons noted ominously, that the band had been interrupted on its way to the front.

As the head of the column passed Hamilton Browne's NNC outpost, Lord Chelmsford took the opportunity to inquire further about the encounter of the day before:

> On the General reaching us, he questioned myself and Duncombe as to what we had seen and we reported fully. This interview being over, I was ordered by the C.S.O. [Column Staff Officer] to move my men on and clear the road, a rough wagon-track over the pass, of any boulders and stones that might be lying on it and was to be supported by a party of the second 24th, under Lieutenant Pope.[18]

Satisfied that there was nothing in Hamilton Browne's report to trouble him, Chelmsford let the advance continue.

On the final approach to iSandlwana the column ran into difficulties again as it entered Symons' valley 'bestrewn with mimosas'. The track meandered at the foot of rising ground on its left before descending an open rocky slope towards the bed of the Manzimnyama stream – the 'black water', so called because the water flows here and there across beds of black shale. But the drift across the Manzimnyama was steep and narrow and several badly positioned boulders made the crossing particularly difficult. According to Charlie Harford,

> Large working parties both from the 24th and ourselves [were] sent forward to render the road passable for the wagons. If it hadn't been for the services of two of our officers, Captain Krohn and Lieutenant Vane, who were expert wagon-drivers and did nearly the whole of the driving themselves at the bad places, many would have broken down and the Column would have been delayed for weeks.[19]

With a final effort, the head of the column dragged itself out of the stream-bed and pushed up the slope on the far side before spilling at last over the *nek* below iSandlwana hill.

It is difficult, now, to judge the men's first impressions of this extraordinary spot, for most of their accounts – noted afterwards – were heavily coloured by hindsight. Yet there seems little doubt that the stark solemn rock, rising up suddenly from the undulating sea of green, made an impact on all but the most unimaginative among them. Several officers of the 24th noted the similarity between the profile of the hill – 'queer shaped', according to Hamilton Browne, 'like a sphinx lying down'[20] – and their regimental badge. The mountain was promptly dubbed 'the Little Sphinx' – although not all of them thought this was a good omen. Trooper Symons thought iSandlwana a 'grim sentinel of a myriad years'.[21]

Today there remains something achingly evocative about the silent weathered face of iSandlwana. Left stranded millennia ago through some geological quirk, an isolated island peak in the undulating grass, it stands apart from the stony iNyoni ridges less than a kilometre above. Somehow it draws the eye from far away, peeking out beneath the altogether more ordinary skyline, and seeming from some angles to hang suspended, hunkered down low on the horizon, between the earth and the sky.

There was no time to stand and marvel, however, for the hill marked the end of the day's march and a new camp needed to be marked out. Henry Francis Fynn, enjoying the freedom that being attached to Chelmsford's staff gave him to speak out, '. . . pointed out the open flat two miles [3.2 kilometres] farther as good camping ground. Some said it was too sandy, they not knowing otherwise, when it was observed that Colonel Cleary, Col. Glynn's Chief of Staff, had already begun marking off the encampment on the southwards of Sanhlwana slope; and so that matter rested.'[22]

And so it seems, then, that the exact site of the camp was chosen almost by accident, Glyn and his staff having little to do but attend to such routine duties. Certainly, it was Clery who directed Hamilton Browne, as he arrived, to '. . . move to my left so as to be ready to encamp, he riding with me, and pointing out the ground on which my camp was to be pitched, which would be on the extreme left of the line'.[23]

Was the position a good one? Certainly its strengths and weaknesses have been debated exhaustively for more than a century since, but in truth Zululand is not easy country – perfect defensive positions by the roadside were thin on the ground, and Chelmsford had few better options within range of the day's march. From a defence perspective, visibility around the site was good; the view from the foot of the mountain is shut in by the iNyoni ridge, just a kilometre or two away to the north – to the British left – but pickets placed on the edge of the escarpment would have a view across 8 or 9 kilometres of undulating country extending towards the eastern spurs of the Ngedla range to the north-west and the low curve of Mabaso further to its east. Directly to the front, the view eastwards was blissfully open for almost 20 kilometres, as far as Silutshana and Magogo; only to the right did the rugged bulk of Malakatha and the Hlazakazi ridge block out the broken country downstream on the Mzinyathi. And provided a pickets was placed to the rear of the mountain, it should have been easy enough to secure the line of communication back down the road to Rorke's Drift. The spot advocated by Fynn, beyond the Nyogane stream, would have offered a clearer view of the close approach to the camp, perhaps – an uninterrupted field of fire across a crucial 500 or 600 metres on all sides – but done nothing to offset the limitations of the broader topography.

And there were other considerations besides defence. A column of nearly 4,000 men and 1,600 animals could not remain anywhere for long without a plentiful supply of water, and the Manzimnyama behind iSandlwana was unusually full after the recent rains, and there was more water running in the Nyogane. The column needed wood, too, not merely to make cooking fires, but to build shelters for the men of the NNC, and the steep boulder-strewn slopes behind iSandlwana were covered in a scrub not easily found on the plain further on.

All in all, iSandlwana seemed as good a place as any to camp; after all, Lord Chelmsford did not intend to stay there long.

*

After crossing the Mfolozi Mhlope on the 17th, the great Zulu army had entered the *emaKhosini* valley, the traditional heartland of the Zulu people. Here the Zulu *amakhosi* had lived and died in the time before Shaka. Their graves, still recognized by clumps of *uhlalankosi* bush, were among the most sacred places in the kingdom, and royal homesteads, many of them bearing ancient names, dotted the hillsides. It was essential that the spirits of the royal ancestors give their blessing to the coming campaign, and the *amabutho* paraded from one grave to another, chanting the sacred songs of the nation of Shaka's day – Durnford's 'song without words':

> O ye, iye he yiya! Ha! O hu yiyi!
> Ha! O ho hu. Oye iye! Iya! Ha O,
> Hi I ya! Ihi.

At each grave *inkosi* Ntshingwayo stepped out to call out resoundingly the praises of the man concerned. The ceremony complete, the army bivouacked that night along the banks of the Mkhumbane stream before starting out at first light the next morning on the long haul up the Mthonjaneni heights. Many of the senior *izinduna* – those like Sihayo or Zibhebhu of the Mandlakazi, who had long enjoyed trading links with the whites – were on horseback, but Ntshingwayo himself preferred to walk, keeping pace with his men, and sharing their hardships. More than that, Ntshingwayo was a traditionalist, and the Zulu army was going to war in the time-honoured way.

*

At iSandlwana Clery had selected an obvious spot for the camp – a broad swathe of green grass which extends along the base of the hill, and which, away from the steeper, broken ground at the foot of the outcrop, falls gently away towards the east. As their wagons came up the road, the various units took up the places allocated to them and began unpacking their baggage.

The camp was spread out in a line, with the 1/24th at the southern end, to the right of the track, and across from them the mounted troops, then the Royal Artillery. Next to them, in the middle and squarely in front of the mountain, were the 2/24th, with Chelmsford's headquarters' tents behind them. The NNC – the 1st Battalion and then the 2nd – completed the camp to the left. The whole frontage was about 750 metres, and the tents were laid out according to regulation, the infantry camps in square blocks, officers at the top, and the empty transport wagons behind. The mounted men's tents were arranged on three sides of a square, open to the front, with the horse line – ropes tied to poles set in the ground to which the horses were tethered at night – protectively in the centre. Some of the NNC had been delayed on the road, their men pressed into service as labour gangs on the Manzimnyama drift, so that, according to Charlie Harford,

> ... we got in just in time to get the tents pitched during the afternoon. Our camp was on the extreme left, close to the main road and just below Isandhlwana hill itself, with our wagons parked at the base of it immediately in our rear. Plenty of wood being close at hand behind the hill, the natives soon set to work to run up shelters for themselves on the other side of the road, clear of our camp. A queer-looking place they made of it, being packed in like sardines, the space allotted to them being limited.[24]

Trooper Symons grumbled that, 'The ground upon which the Carbineers set up their patrol tents was very swampy, and it was necessary to dig deep trenches round the tents which was soon done and Jack and I packed away our things in expectation of a lengthy stay.'²⁵ The column had camped in much the same way at the earlier halt at Rorke's Drift – although Hamilton Browne thought it 'much more extended'.²⁶

No attempt had been made to fortify the Rorke's Drift camp, and none was made at iSandlwana either. In his *Regulations for Field Forces in South Africa, 1878* – published in November – Chelmsford had specified how permanent camps were to be protected: 'By day the camp should be guarded against surprise by vedettes thrown out at a distance on all surrounding points of observation. Horses and oxen when out grazing should have mounted guards. The former will be knee-haltered. By night horses should be picketed and oxen placed in a wagon-*laager*. The camp should be partially entrenched on all sides . . .'²⁷

Yet these directives were by no means as definitive as they seem to be in retrospect. On the Cape frontier it had been the usual practice to fortify only those camps that were intended for use as long-term bases for offensive operations, rather than halts on the march, and Chelmsford had undoubtedly come into Zululand with the same intention in mind. True, the 1/24th had fortified the camp at Centane – but only when they knew it was likely to be attacked. It was not until February 1879 that a revised edition of the Chelmsford's *Regulations for Field Forces in South Africa* specified that camps in the field should be fortified, or at least protected by screens of thorn-bush cobbled with broken glass, and that wagons should be *laagered* 'when halting, though but for a few hours'. But by February circumstances were very different indeed.

It is clear that some officers felt the lack of any sort of physical barrier at iSandlwana. Glyn himself suggested some protection was required, but received a curt reply which can only have reminded him of the impotence of his role as column commander: 'It is not worthwhile, it will take too much time, and besides the wagons are most of them going back at once to Rorke's Drift.'²⁸ There was some truth to this, for although every column was supposed to employ an experienced *laager*-master, Glyn had approached several likely individuals but they had all refused, and the post had not been filled. The supply wagons, moreover, would indeed need to return to Rorke's Drift as soon as they had been unloaded. No fortifications were started because the men were too tired on the evening of the 20th, and on the 21st half of them would be away from the camp and the other half unloading the wagons or repairing the road. Nor was the ground ideal – it was too hard and rocky, even after the recent rain – and to have dug a trench around a perimeter stretching a thousand metres on the front alone would have been a huge undertaking.

Yet there were other options available. In his camp at Fort Thinta on the Ncome, 50 kilometres to the north, Evelyn Wood had built a number of small stone sangars at key points to anchor his defences in the event of an attack – and there was nothing at iSandlwana if not rocks. The real reason that Chelmsford did not insist upon the camp being fortified was that he did not for a moment believe that the Zulus had the capacity to attack it – and he was keen in any case to press on with the invasion as quickly as possible.

Not everyone shared this view; Hamilton Browne wrote:

> As soon as the tents were pitched, and we had some food, I was joined by Commandant Lonsdale, who had that day come out of hospital. I was talking to some of my best officers when he joined us and his first words to me were, 'My God, Maori, what do you think of this camp?' I replied, 'Someone is mad.' The Colonial officers were loud and long in complaint, and Duncombe said, 'Do the staff think we are going to meet an army of school-girls? Why in the name of all that is holy do we not *laager*?'
>
> In the evening I strolled over to the 24th lines to have a chat with the officers, all of whom I knew well. Whilst there, I had a yarn with Colonel Glyn who was acting as Brigadier-General, and would have had command of the column had not the General and staff decided to join us at the last moment. He was a very old friend of my family's and had served as a Lieutenant under my father. He did not seem to be in good spirits, but said nothing about the camp and on my remarking it looked very pretty though rather extended, he looked hard at me, shook his head and said 'Very'.[29]

Indeed, according to the regimental history,

> A field-officer of the 2nd Battalion 24th, being on duty with the picquets [sic] on 21st January, expressed his strong misgivings to a staff-officer whose duty it was to point out the ground to be occupied, and remarked that the broken ground was no protection, and that there was not even a picquet in rear. 'Well, sir,' was the answer, 'if you are nervous, we will put a piquet of pioneers there' ... The same day ... Lieutenant and Adjutant Melvill, 1st Battalion 24th, remarked to the field officer above mentioned who was looking out to front: 'I know what you are thinking

of by your face, sir; you are abusing this camp, and you are quite right! These Zulus will charge home, and with our small numbers we ought to be in *laager*, or, at any rate, be prepared to stand shoulder to shoulder.'[30]

The staff officer was apparently Clery, and the field officer Dunbar; a second imputation of nervousness can hardly have improved the latter's temper – or reassured the officers of the 24th. Nonetheless, it is interesting to note that from the moment of their arrival the 24th's officers had clearly been assessing the lie of the ground.

Nor was the ordinary precaution of scouting a new campsite neglected. Trooper Symons was among a patrol of Carbineers sent out 'During the afternoon to the left front of the camp at about ten miles [16 kilometres] distance, but the only Native man we saw was a deformed one with a head like a baboon. He knew, he said, nothing of the movements of the Zulu Army; and we were very tired and glad to get back to our mess and rest.'[31]

With still no sign of his enemy, Lord Chelmsford decided to leave his men setting up the camp, and to ride out again with his staff to view the country ahead. The landscape, he knew, was about to become more demanding – and the intentions of those who lived there would prove to be of the greatest importance.

# 16

# 'We laughed and parted'

## 20–21 January 1879

By the time Lord Chelmsford moved forward to iSandlwana on 20 January, the Zulu population had largely abandoned the Mzinyathi valley opposite Rorke's Drift. Most, of course, had been sensible enough to leave before the invasion began, but the attack on kwaSogekle on the 12th had made it clear to those still hiding there that even established places of refuge were not safe so close to the advancing British Army. The amaQungebeni fighting men who had taken part in the skirmish had scattered at first, moving further north towards the Nquthu hills, or south towards the Malakatha range. Here, after a few days, some of them had tried to regroup but the advance of the entire British Centre Column to iSandlwana had left them largely powerless to resist, and they found themselves facing the same stark choice as their leaders – should they prepare to bow down to the invaders, as Gamdana had done, or should they hold out, trusting to the king to send an army from oNdini to support them?

Muziwento kaZibana, a young boy of the amaQungebeni, who was perhaps eleven or twelve years old at the time of the war, has left a vivid impression not only of the moral challenges the war posed to the civilian population, but of the extent of ground it was necessary to cover to elude Lord Chelmsford's increasingly far-ranging patrols in those first weeks of the invasion:

> The white men reached the Buffalo river. It was said that they had come to fight with the Zulus. Soon they fought with the people of Sihayo who were few in number. These were all killed [i.e. defeated]; some however survived. They for their part killed a few white men and [black] men too. O! We scampered away, [we young ones]. We went to Malagata. It was then said that the white men were coming to Malagata. Some said 'it is good that homage be paid to the white men.' Said our father,

'Whosoever desires to do homage, it is good that he be off, and go and do homage [to them].' Our father went away with his men [to resist]. Others deserted him and did homage. We pushed on . . .[1]

By 20 January a great swathe of country around iSandlwana lay empty, the homesteads of the amaQungebeni deserted and forlorn. Here and there a few armed bands hid out in the hills, avoiding any direct contact with the British patrols and watching and waiting. Others moved down the Mzinyathi valley towards the Qhudeni bush, to join up with Matshana's Sithole, who were still hiding there in large numbers.

The only real hope for the border peoples, however, lay with the king, and the great army assembled at oNdini. And whether Cetshwayo would send it to support them – and if so, when it would arrive – was a subject about which they were scarcely better informed than the British invaders.

*

The emptiness of the landscape troubled Lord Chelmsford. When he had crossed the border nine days earlier, he had been confident that *inkosi* Sihayo was a determined enemy against whom a strong demonstration of force was necessary, but ahead, further up the road beyond iSandlwana, the political map appeared more complex.

It was a crucial part of Chelmsford's carrot-and-stick strategy that he try to detach local *amakhosi* from their allegiance to the king, and while he had been encouraged by Gamdana's apparent willingness to defect, he found it rather more difficult to determine the attitude of the *amakhosi* whose territory now lay across his line of advance. Off to his left front, around the Siphezi mountain, lay the territory of the Mchunu *inkosi*, Matshana kaSitshakuza, about whom Chelmsford had decidedly conflicting intelligence. An officer in the iNdabakawombe *ibutho*, this Matshana was said to command the allegiance of about 800 fighting men – more than enough to make him a formidable opponent if he so decided. On the other hand, it had been suggested that his personal relationship with the king was poor, and that he was 'favourable to the English; being very rich and the King having ill-treated him', despite the fact that his son, Mizo, was married to one of Cetshwayo's sisters.[2]

Yet if Matshana kaSitshakuza's loyalties were difficult to judge, those of his namesake, Matshana kaMondise, were even more so. Matshana's Sithole lay to Chelmsford's right front, their territory in the corrugated country towards Qhudeni large largely blocked from his view by the line of the the Malakatha mountain and Hlazakazi hills. Although Chelmsford struggled to distinguish between the two men – he tended to lump them together as 'the two Matyanas' – he was well aware of Matshana kaMondise's tangled history with the Natal authorities and with the Shepstone family. Much would depend now on Matshana's attitude towards those past conflicts: was Matshana the diehard enemy of European interests that the Shepstones painted him? Or, after more than twenty years living again under the authority of the Zulu kings, would Matshana welcome the chance to escape the yoke of Zulu tyranny and return to the more enlightened administration offered by the British?

It says much for the self-delusion of British military and colonial officials in southern Africa that Chelmsford seriously considered that the second option might be a viable one.

Under the circumstances, the meaning of the Zulu movements spotted by Hamilton Browne in the direction of Matshana's homestead at Nsinga-bantu was crucial. Were these simply local men making their way to the safety of the Qhudeni bush? Or were they part of some coordinated movement of the main Zulu army from oNdini? Either way, they suggested that Henry Francis Fynn's interpretation of the Zulu strategy – that the big army might approach by way of Qhudeni, masking its approach behind the Malakatha and Hlazakazi heights, and then sweep round towards Chelms-ford's rear – might have some truth to it.

Viewed from the foot of iSandlwana on the 20th, as the column struggled to unpack its baggage wagons and mark out its camping ground, the fresh green summer landscape ahead, empty in the midday sunshine, offered few answers, and Chelmsford decided to ride out to scout the outlying features himself. It was a task that might have been performed equally well by a reconnaissance party, but Chelmsford liked to form his own impressions before acting on them. He decided to take with him his usual staff – Crealock, and his ADCs, Captain Matt Gosset, Captain E.H. Buller and Lieutenant Archibald Berkeley Milne of HMS *Active* – and Major Dartnell as well as Lieutenant Melvill, the adjutant of the 1/24th, and Henry Francis Fynn. Colonel Glyn went with him – so too did Glyn's orderly officer, a young and ambitious lieutenant in the 1/24th, Nevill Coghill. Dublin-born Coghill, whose twenty-seventh birthday was just a few days away,[3] had spent three years at the Cape, most of it serving as an ADC, first to General Cunynghame and then to Bartle Frere, but had asked for

for permission to return to regimental duties and had hurried up from
Pietermaritzburg to join the column just in time for the invasion.

The party struck south-east from iSandlwana late in the morning of the
20th, passing the high shelf of the Malakatha and then making for the foot
of the Hlazakazi heights. Here they turned to follow the Ndaweni stream
up onto the high ground, then rode eastwards along the grassy ridge-tops
towards the Mangeni valley. Off to their right, the country dropped steeply
down to the twisted ridges which lay between the heights and the lower
reaches of the Mzinyathi – it was here, sixty years before, that Jobe Sithole
had first met King Shaka.

There was still little sign of the Zulus. 'We saw a few women running
away with bundles on their heads', Chelmsford said afterwards, 'but
otherwise the country was deserted. Some natives say the inhabitants have
gone to the king, others they are in the [Qhudeni] bush.'[4]

It was certainly a landscape rich in hiding places. From the heights
Chelmsford could look down into the tumbled splendour of the Mangeni
as it slashed its way past the eastern and southern sides of Hlazakazi and
carved deep twisting valleys on its way to join the Mzinyathi. Far off to the
left lay the great grey bulk of Qhudeni while beyond the Mzinyathi river
the hills rose in blue folds towards the distant peaks of Msinga. Somewhere
down there lay Nsingabantu, Matshana's homestead; somewhere down
there lay the fighting men Hamilton Browne had spotted. Yet the hot air
hung listlessly in the dry valleys, and nothing moved.

The party made its way across the summit until Hlazakazi came to an
abrupt end at the remarkable Mangeni gorge, a dramatic and narrow
crevice, where now a thin stream of water tips suddenly over a sheer drop,
falling a hundred metres into a deep green pool before winding on between
steep high banks, hugging the foot of the ridge. Chelmsford and his staff
halted here and searched the countryside below through their glasses,
though Major Crealock had time to make a watercolour sketch of the
panorama downstream. Down below, in clear patches between the bush,
cattle could be seen grazing, so far away that they 'looked like ants'. There
was no sign of the men Hamilton Browne had seen the day before, but
'that the Zulus were there there were no doubts expressed however'.[5]

At that moment it must have seemed to Chelmsford that Fynn's analysis
of the Zulu movements was all too possible. Somewhere eastwards, across
the hills, lay oNdini – and perhaps a Zulu army already on the march. If
that army skirted to Chelmsford's left and crossed the Mangeni high up, it

would advance squarely down the open plain towards iSandlwana. But why would it? It had only to shift a little to Chelmsford's right to be able to move down into the country he saw below, sweep round the foot of Hlazakazi and Malakatha, and, as Fynn predicted, strike at Rorke's Drift behind him. And any attempt by Lord Chelmsford to intercept it there would make his sweeps through the Xhosa strongholds in the Eastern Cape look like a walk in the park.

Matshana, Chelmsford decided, was already down there somewhere, and under arms; Coghill thought, 'The position is naturally immensely strong and tho' by no means impregnable might necessitate much loss of life and time before it could be cleared so it is to be hoped that they have evacuated the position . . .'[6]

After pondering his options for an hour or two, Chelmsford ordered the party to remount and descend from the heights, taking an easy route down towards the Mangeni above the falls, and head for the foot of a distinctive conical hill called Mdutshana. The flats above the waterfall would be a good spot, Chelmsford decided, for his next camp, one from which he could command the road to Qhudeni, and isolate any hostile concentrations downstream in the Mangeni valley.[7] Satisfied with the results of the day's outing, he then returned to iSandlwana.

For the second time in a few days Chelmsford had left his command to ride out deep into potentially hostile country virtually unprotected, and for the second time he had experienced nothing to make him reassess the Zulu threat. They had seen no one all day – and no one had offered them the slightest challenge. There was to be one mishap on the way back, however; according to Fynn, '. . . the party proceeded westward for Sandhlwana camp for some two miles [3.2 kilometres]. When passing a deserted Zulu kraal Coghill, Melville and Milne chased a fowl. Coghill fell, dislocating his kneecap. It was soon replaced and he was remounted, suffering much pain . . .'[8]

'I put my knee out,' grumbled Coghill, whose diaries and letters reveal a propensity for strains, sprains and rheumatism unusual in a healthy and active young man.[9] Perhaps he was just accident prone, for he had injured the same leg the year before when he was struck by a spear during a sporting contest in one of the field camps. It hurt so much that Coghill retired, on his return to iSandlwana, to the tent that he shared with Captain Hallam Parr, convinced that he would have to lie up for several days to recover.

Back in camp, Chelmsford formulated a plan of action, based on the day's impressions. He had decided that the whole Malakatha and Hlazakazi range needed scouting 'more thoroughly than I was able to do',[10] not only to clear away the men Hamilton Browne had seen on the 19th, but also to probe for signs of any approaching army. It would be a difficult job for the regulars, but it was ideally suited to the colonials who not only understood the country well but also were the most mobile element in the column. Some detachments of both the mounted troops and the NNC would have to be left at the camp to provide pickets, but Chelmsford decided to send the rest on a long sweep around and across the hills. The whole force, he decided, would be commanded by Major Dartnell of the Mounted Police, who had not only been privy to his thoughts throughout the day but enjoyed the respect of the colonial troops. The force would start out at dawn the following morning – the 21st – and return by nightfall. Clery noted sourly that

> ... He gave orders to the commandant of the natives to take his two battalions out at daybreak the following morning to work through some ravines about ten miles [16 kilometres] off, and he also gave orders to the commandant of the volunteers to go in the same direction and co-operate. The instructions to both these commandants were given personally by the general himself, and this was absolutely necessary in this case as neither Colonel Glyn nor myself knew in the least where they were being sent to, or what they were being sent for.[11]

That evening, according to Charlie Harford,

> ... Lonsdale was sent for by the General. I was sitting in Pope's tent, (one of the young fellows of the 24th Regiment) at the time, looking at some sketches of his and he at mine, and presently he came to tell me that the 3rd NNC were to start at daybreak the next morning and reconnoitre the ground over the Malakatha Hills, together with some mounted Police under Major Dartnell, who were to work round on our left. Two companies of the Contingent from each battalion were to be left in camp to furnish outposts and a camp guard, and food taken out for the day. Very stupidly, however, very few of us took out anything but a few biscuits, thinking that we should be back in camp again before nightfall, but our experience on this occasion taught us a lesson that I don't suppose any of us have forgotten, as it was some fifty-six hours, or a little over two days, before we got any more food of any sort, though there was splendid water to drink everywhere. As soon as

Lonsdale had given me his instructions, the necessary orders were issued and I went off to see the officers of the four companies detailed to remain in camp, as all for outpost duty would have to parade at once and accompany me to their positions.

One or two of them were terribly disappointed at the thought of being left behind in camp and lose the chance of a fight, and begged hard to be allowed to find substitutes, and as these were forthcoming, matters were satisfactorily arranged. Little did any of us conjecture what a momentous difference these exchanges were going to make in the course of some twenty-four hours . . .[12]

In the Carbineers camp, recalled Fred Symons afterwards, 'that evening the members of tent no. 3 whose names were Sergt. Methley, and Troopers Davis, Green, Macleroy, Slatter, Sibthorpe and myself sat down in cheerful mood to a good dinner provided by our genial Qmr. London, little dreaming that we should never all mess together again.'[13] For Norris-Newman, the news confirmed the wisdom of his decision to attach himself to the NNC, and he went to bed that night dreaming of further scoops. He was destined not to be not be disappointed; indeed, 'from this time', he noted simply, 'our troubles began'.[14]

*

For Charlie Harford, the prospect of imminent combat added an extra intensity to the iSandlwana dawn that Tuesday, 21 January 1879:

Overhanging Isandhlwana and the camps was a long, tortuous, more or less low-lying dark cloud, based on the horizon, much in the same form as a trail of smoke from the funnel of a steamer and ending immediately above Isandhlwana hill, which as the sun got higher was tinted almost blood red, then passing into ashy-brown with broad golden edges, assumed a marvellous variety of tints with the rise of the sun. And there it hung for the best part of the morning, frowning, as it were, over the fated camp. I have never forgotten it.[15]

In truth the camp had had little sleep that night. At about midnight Dartnell had paraded the mounted men and, sensitive as ever to the limitations of their service, had told them, according to Trooper Sam Jones of the Newcastle Mounted Rifles:

. . . that a certain percentage of us were wanted to go and intercept the enemy. Volunteers were told to step two paces forward. It is hardly necessary to say that nearly every one of us did so, with the result that so many men were picked from each troop. My brother, thinking he had a good excuse, seeing my horse was lame, told me to get back into the ranks. But even then I was not beaten. The first thing I did was to make my way direct to Captain Bradstreet's tent to ask him whether I could have the old horse I had sold them for carrying packs. My brother then arrived on the scene and a few strong words passed between us, but in the end I had my way and was allowed to go.[16]

Among the Carbineers, Fred Symons noted they were issued a single day's rations in accordance with the intention to be back that evening, 'four biscuits for each man and a tin of salmon between two men. The men with the soundest horses were selected; the rest under Lieut. Scott to the number of twenty-nine were left in camp for vidette duties.'[17]

For the regulars, it was disappointing news that only the NNC and mounted troops were to go. Dining that night with the NNC officers, Lieutenant Pope of the 2/24th had loudly decried his bad luck; 'Poor Charlie Pope! ... many of us recollect even now how sorry he was at not being able to join our party in the morning, and how eagerly he looked forward (like others) to the first real fight with the enemy ...'[18]

Even so, there seems to have been a sense of foreboding hanging over the camp. Perhaps it is not to be wondered at – it was common knowledge by this time, after all, that a Zulu army was thought to be approaching. As the NNC prepared to move out, Hamilton Browne spotted an old friend from the Cape Frontier Wars, Henry Pulleine of the 1/24th, who had recently joined the column, 'and he chaffed me, saying "A lot of you nigger leaders will be knocked-over today." I answered, "If that is so, when I return to camp I shall not find one of you alive." We laughed and parted ...'[19]

Leaving behind those designated for picket duty, the rest of the NNC battalions set off in high spirits from iSandlwana.

*

After Dartnell's force had departed, the camp at iSandlwana fell into its daily routine. The men of the 24th had paraded in front of their tents before dawn but stood down once Dartnell's force had disappeared from view. Pickets were placed and the oxen turned out to graze. There was no sign of any Zulu presence nearby, and the most excitement the men could look forward to was unpacking some thirty wagons loaded with food supplies which were due to return to Rorke's Drift where a fresh stockpile awaited them.

At about 9 a.m., after breakfast, Chelmsford decided to ride out to see Gamdana again. He was anxious to confirm his surrender, and curious to see how the reconnaissance was progressing. Glyn accompanied him, and the two staffs set off guided by Fynn, who led them down the conspicuous track in the grass made earlier that day by the NNC. Gamdana's homestead lay on a spur at the foot of the Malakatha, close to the Ndaweni stream; some of the NNC had passed that way that morning, and Chelmsford was not surprised to find the homestead deserted when he arrived; 'Gamdana', declared Fynn pithily, 'was in hiding on the Buffalo River, fearing Zulus as well as European forces.'[20] Chelmsford and his party off-saddled, and Crealock took the opportunity to draw a pen-and-ink sketch of the scene looking back towards iSandlwana. The NNC had passed down the Ndaweni only about four hours before, but try as they might the staff could spot no sign of them. The landscape seemed to have simply swallowed them up.

The staff were still in the region of the deserted huts when a solitary horseman rode up. It was George Shepstone, Durnford's political officer. Shepstone had had a tiring few days; after arriving at iSandlwana on the 19th, Chelmsford had sent him back to Durnford to check the progress of No. 2 Column's advance, and he had just returned to iSandlwana that morning with the news that Durnford's column was still at Msinga. With the pace of the invasion hotting up, Chelmsford promptly ordered him to return to Durnford again with instructions to hurry his men to Rorke's Drift as quickly as possible.

Chelmsford was disappointed at Gamdana's absence, and the staffs returned to iSandlwana, arriving about lunchtime. He was preparing to ride out again, this time onto the iNyoni ridge to the north of the camp, when Gamdana came hurrying in. He was apologetic; he had been hiding, he explained, because he understood that Cetshwayo 'had sent an *impi* to eat him up, for giving up his arms to the English; he had expected the *impi* that morning (21st) but it had not arrived'.[21] If this news struck Chelmsford or any of his staff as significant, they did not record the fact. The conversation with Gamdana then developed into a wrangle about the number of guns he was to surrender, and ended with his being sent away with orders to return the following day with his weapons.

Chelmsford did not allow the interview to interrupt his plans, but set out for the iNyoni escarpment. 'On reaching the summit of the highest hill', Milne reported afterwards,

> . . . I counted 14 horsemen watching us at the distance of about four miles [6.4 kilometres]; they ultimately disappeared over a slight rise. Two vedettes were stationed at the spot from which I saw the horsemen; they said they had seen these several times during the day, and had reported the fact. From this point the ground was very nearly level; there were slight rises, however, every now and again, which would prevent our seeing any men who did not wish it.[22]

It was now late afternoon, and Chelmsford had been observing the undulating heights for a while when his ADCs, Major Matt Gossett and Captain E.H. Buller, hailed him. Chelmsford had sent them out that morning with Dartnell to report on the reconnaissance, and they returned now with some interesting news. About 20 kilometres away, among the hills close to the headwaters of the Mangeni, Dartnell and his men had run into Zulus in significant numbers, and 'Major Dartnell [had] sent in for instructions as to what he was to do'.[23]

*

After spending the night of 17 January in the emaKhosini valley, the great Zulu army had travelled the short distance up the Mpembeni stream and had camped the following night near the esiPhezi royal homestead, on the slopes of the Mthonjaneni heights. The commanders had been anxious that the men should not tire themselves before reaching the front, and even the king had urged them to travel slowly and save their strength for the trial that lay ahead. That day the detachment under Godide kaNdlela, who had been deputed to reinforce the men defending the coastal districts, had separated off and struck out towards the south-east. On the 19th the main army had crested the heights, moving out towards Babanango mountain in the west.[24]

For those first few days a cloud of girls and young boys had hung on the flanks, carrying food – raw meat, pumpkins, roasted mealies, gourds full of curdled milk – for fathers and brothers in the army. At night, the girls had had to sleep away from the men for fear their presence might destroy the potency of the pre-battle protective rituals, and after a day or two, their supplies consumed, most had abandoned the army and begun to return home. Most of the boys had remained, however, carrying mats, rolled shields and headrests, eager to find any excuse to stay and be a part of the excitement to come. Once the army came within striking distance of the enemy, there was a very real risk that they might be caught up in the fighting, and their presence was tolerated on the understanding that they must remain in the rear when a battle began. Even so, many hoped that the campaign might offer them a first taste of real warfare, and had no intention of remaining behind – an enthusiasm which was sometimes connived at by their relatives in the ranks.

Within two or three days the supplies they carried had been eaten, and provisioning the army became problematic. The king had provided a number of cattle to be slaughtered along the road, but it was hardly enough to feed over 25,000 men who, in their civilian lives, ate twice a day, mid-morning and evening. The traditional solution was that the army foraged from the civilian population it passed on the way, rounding up any cattle and goats that had not been concealed carefully enough, and raiding the grain-pits of abandoned homesteads.

The passage of an army, then, could be a difficult time for Zulu non-combatants – even those who acknowledged the *amabutho* as liberators come to protect them from the worse ravages of the invading whites – so, 'As we went the people hid their food and fled with their cattle, into the most inaccessible places. Nevertheless, we managed to get at them, and fed. Our path was known by the cattle bones which strewed it, by the remains of dishes and corn, and here and there by a body. What people were they, say you? Why, our own – the Zulus.'25

On the 19th the army had split into two columns, which continued to advance on a parallel course a few kilometres apart. *Inkosi* Ntshingwayo commanded the left column, the uNokhenke, uKhandempemvu, uDududu, iSangqu and iMbube *amabutho*, while Mavumengwana commanded the iNgobamakhosi, uVe, uMbonambi, uThulwana, iNdluyengwe, iNdlondlo and uDloko on the right. This was standard practice on nearing enemy territory, to prevent the entire army being surprised on the march, and it reflected the fact that, although the Centre Column was still at Rorke's Drift at that point – a good 60 kilometres away – the Zulu generals were not prepared to risk discovery at the hands of distant British patrols.

It had probably been then, too, that men were picked out of the *amabutho* to serve as scouts. Certainly, a man named Zimema of the uMxapho later recalled that, among those *amabutho* detached to march to the coast, he had been picked out as a scout that same day; '. . . all the regiments of the *impi* were called together. Then Mahatu, Mgewu and I were told to stand out of the ranks . . . we three were told to go and spy the movements and position of the white man.'[26]

Scouts were selected not only for their ability to observe and report, but for their initiative, courage and stamina. They would be sent out many kilometres in front of the army as it advanced to watch for any signs of enemy presence. But watching was only part of their brief; if they encountered enemy scouts, they were expected to attack them, to screen their own troops from discovery and to try to deny the enemy any intelligence he may have gathered. Often, when operating on Zulu soil, men were selected who lived locally, and who knew the terrain intimately. It seems that Zibhebhu kaMaphitha, the dynamic and influential head of the Mandlakazi lineage of the royal house, was appointed as overall intelligence commander during the iSandlwana campaign, assisted at various points by the *amakhosi* whose territory the army passed through on its way to the front.

As the army advanced, its numbers fluctuated on an almost daily basis. Some men who had been late at the muster hurried in to join their *amabutho*, as did parties of men living locally who had stayed at home at the behest of their *amakhosi* to guard cattle and crops, but who now rallied to the *impi* as it passed. Others dropped out along the way, either for a day or two – taking advantage of the advance to visit nearby family – or, in the case of a few sick or elderly men whose initial enthusiasm had outstripped their stamina, permanently.

Among those who joined the army en route was Mehlokazulu. He had remained in his discreet exile, at the homestead of the Swazi pretender Prince Mbilini on the Phongolo river during the first few days of the war – 'I was away with Umbelini's division when the English crossed the Buffalo River and attacked my father's stronghold', he admitted coyly, 'but when the men were assembling at Ulundi, Ketchwayo sent a messenger to tell me to join my regiment, the "Ngobamakosi", at once. When I arrived I found that the army had left . . .'[27]

Cetshwayo treated Mehlokazulu like a naughty schoolboy whose misdeeds were forgiven when his talents were needed on the sports field; he had caught up with the army on the march, and the iNgobamakhosi had been delighted to see him – for the younger generation, he was a symbol of their pride in their institutions and their independence, and of their indignation at the presumption of the whites. And, more than that, he was a courageous and charismatic young man whose skills as a leader could scarcely be more needed.

The night of the 19th the army had bivouacked on the uplands east of Babanango, and the following morning pressed on towards Siphezi mountain. Each night the commanders selected as a camping ground the banks of a sheltered river or stream, for if the men could get by without regular food, they could not survive without water. A sudden wave of wet weather was passing over them as they moved westwards, miserable enough as they walked in the daytime but wretched indeed at night as they huddled, all but naked, into the wet grass to snatch what sleep they could.

*

Dartnell's command had struck out on the morning of the 21st, heading almost due south towards Gamdana's homestead at the western end of Hlazakazi. The mounted men had inevitably drawn ahead and before they reached the hills they turned away from the route the NNC were following. While the NNC continued to head towards the great stony rampart of Malakatha, the mounted men turned further east, following the foot of the northern Hlazakazi heights and heading towards the Mangeni waterfall.

Dartnell had about 120 mounted troops under his command, some 46 Mounted Police under Inspector Mansell, 27 Carbineers under Offy Shepstone, 20 Newcastle Mounted Rifles and 16 Buffalo Border Guards. Fred Symons was with the Carbineers – so were his brother Jack and his friend Ted Greene. A kilometre or so further on, the party divided again, Dartnell continuing along the same route at the head of the Mounted Police while the Volunteers Corps turned to their right, working up the slopes of the ridge – steep enough in places for them to have to lead their horses – then driving across the summit, sweeping eastwards again.

The NNC, meanwhile, had continued south until they reached the edge of Malakatha, near the course of the Ndaweni stream. Here the two battalions separated, Lonsdale ordering the 1st Battalion under Hamilton Browne to follow the stream onto the summit while he led the 2nd in a great sweep round the western end of the mountain. Lonsdale's course would take him around the southern foot of Malakatha, turning eastwards towards the lower reaches of the Mangeni, then following the river upstream and into the gorge below the waterfall. Between them, all four elements in Dartnell's reconnaissance would thoroughly scout the range on both sides and across the top; their orders were to rendezvous near the waterfall at the far end that afternoon, and return to iSandlwana before nightfall.

The view over the 'great Thorn Valley of the Malakata'[28] on the southern side of the mountain struck both Harford and the journalist Norris-Newman – preoccupied though they must have been. Both banks of the Ndaweni, noted Norris-Newman, 'are magnificently covered with foliage, dotted with Zulu kraals and mealie fields',[29] while Harford thought it '. . . a beautiful spot where a stream that ran through the valley above us dropped over a precipice in a most picturesque waterfall, and on getting up into the valley' there was 'a dense mass of mimosa bush with precipitous krantzes and kloofs on either side, and Zulu kraals and mealie fields dotted about below . . .'[30]

It was not easy country to sweep, however. On a summer's day in January the temperature regularly soars above 40°C, the hot air hangs limpid in the hollows, and a heavy torpor settles over the landscape. Sound carries for miles on such days, but there is little enough noise from the distant hills, just a constant background whirr of insects and the occasional piercing, rhythmic cry of a bird, which grates increasingly on the nerves. On the summit, Fred Symons noticed the quiet. 'The country might have been a desert, for the only sound was the howling of a dog in the distance and one sign of humanity a wreath of smoke rising in a vertical column beneath the hills on the left. No living things were visible when the sun rose, not even the NNC. In our rear the tents gleamed white and peaceful.'[31]

For Europeans not used to it, the sun can turn skin lobster-coloured in an afternoon, scorching and peeling the tops of the ears. Sweat gathers in your hatband, dribbling now and then to collect in droplets on your eyelids. You need water; for as you walk your boots knock heavily against the boulders, and spiky aloes clutch at your clothes, drawing red weals across carelessly exposed skin.

The going was particularly heavy for Lonsdale's men. The European officers and NCOs were mostly acclimatized to the worst weather southern Africa could throw at them, but even so by midday the march was taking its toll. 'In going round,' said Norris-Newman, 'we had some very difficult ground to get over, which seemed to try the powers of our non-coms – who were not mounted – very considerably. In fact, it is not to be disputed for one moment that white men cannot keep up with [Africans] in a day's march over stony and hilly country.'[32] The whites on foot, Harford admitted, 'were very nearly dead beat'. There was, moreover, almost nothing to show for their efforts, for 'all the kraals that we came across were empty, and no Zulus were seen by anyone'.[33]

On the summit Hamilton Browne's battalion had more luck. The top of Malakatha is an undulating plateau and although he reported that 'the valleys became hot as furnaces' the going was much easier. Gamdana's followers had driven a large quantity of cattle up there, and there were still a few civilians in the huts who had hoped to avoid the soldiers' attention. In that they were unlucky, and Hamilton Browne set to questioning them with his usual gusto:

> We captured some hundreds of head of cattle, though all the kraals we passed contained only old men, women and children.
>
> To a girl, I returned some goats which one of my men had taken from her, and through Duncombe, questioned her as to the movements of all of the men. She replied 'That they had all been ordered to join the King's big army.' We again asked, 'where was that?' She pointed with her chin over to the N.E., at the same time saying, 'They would attack us in two days' time.' This bore out the opinion I had formed, after hearing the news on the 19th that the army had left Ulundi.
>
> In our next drive I captured two young men and questioned them. They had no goats to be given back to them, but there are more ways than one of extracting information.
>
> They were led apart and well questioned. War is war and you can't play at savage war with kid gloves on. The information amounted to this. They had both left the big army and had come over to see their mother. We inquired, 'Where is the big army?' They pointed in the same direction as the girl had done. 'When was the attack to take place?' They did not know, but the moon would be right in two days' time.[34]

It is difficult to know what to make of this incident. Hamilton Browne's memoirs display a distinct tendency to wisdom after the event, but if it occurred as he described the implications were ominous.

Not that anyone else had seen any Zulus. On Hlazakazi the Volunteers had pushed on right across the top until they had reached the far end, where it dropped suddenly into the Mangeni gorge. They had encountered no one on the way, and had then stopped to rest. 'Even numbers off saddled, odd numbers stood to their horses and videttes were posted around. While we lay resting here munching biscuit and fish "whoo-aa" came the report of a gun from the direction the Police had gone. The day was warm and bright and not another sound broke the stillness, not even the distant lowing of cattle, or the chirp of a bird.'[35]

After a while, Offy Shepstone ordered the men to saddle up and led them along the top of the gorge, leaving vedettes on each high point as they passed. Symons was unimpressed with Shepstone's apparent indifference towards the meaning of the distant shot, for the Volunteers 'marched away from the person who had fired the shot[,] in fact travelling with the sound instead of against it to see where it originated. I never heard what the Police thought of these tactics.'[36] Finally pausing at a particularly impressive viewpoint – possibly the same one where Chelmsford and his staff had halted the day before – the Carbineers looked down into the narrow valley below and at last saw far below 'the white shields of the NNC glittering in the sunlight'.[37]

Lonsdale's battalion had swept right round the southern foot of Malakatha, and had followed the Mangeni upstream into the gorge. 'On perceiving us,' said Symons, 'Capt. Lonsdale brought up the NNC'[38] – a disarmingly simple phrase which concealed a good deal of sweat on the part of Lonsdale's men. There is no easy way up from the bottom of the Mangeni gorge near the waterfall, and the NNC had to pick their way up a steep cattle track which clung precariously to the eastern end of Hlazakazi. Suddenly there was the sound of more shots, an urgent flurry this time, 'but it was only Drummond galloping after a Steinbok and shooting at it with his revolver'.[39]

By this time Hamilton Browne and the 1st Battalion had arrived at the rendezvous point of the waterfall, and

> I at once suggested we should return to camp and inform the General of what we had learned. This was decided on and as we were then seven miles [11 kilometres] from camp Captain O. Murray was immediately dispatched, with two companies, to drive the captured cattle there. The remainder of us rested; as the white non-coms, most of whom were on foot, were very tired after their rough day's work in the stony, rugged valleys. Poor Murray! I never saw him again . . .[40]

It was now perhaps 4 p.m., and the NNC and Volunteer Corps were spread over the western end of Hlazakazi. There had been no sign of Dartnell and the Mounted Police since the mysterious shot an hour earlier, but they suddenly came into view now on the flats below Hlazakazi above the waterfall. They had been scouting the hills a few kilometres beyond, and one of them told Fred Symons they had seen 700–800 Zulus a little way to the north. Norris-Newman was later told that the Mounted Police '. . . accompanied by Major Gossett, ADC, had come across a large body of the enemy (considerably over 1,500) on the nek of the Upindo hill, due east of us, where they held a very strong position in a krantz, taunting our few mounted men, who, of course, without infantry could do nothing.'[41] 'Things now began to liven up,' said Symons,

> The videttes were called in, and marching back with the Police to a little stream at the apex of Matyana's fortress we off-saddled again – strange proceedings I thought – and those who had billies prepared to make tea. The Police were much better provided for than the Carbs. They were wise enough to bring their camp kettles upon packs; and there was their Sergt. Major, a man of renowned energy in his shirt sleeves fetching wood and urging the men to make speed.[42]

A small isolated conical hill, Mdutshana, stands just above the waterfall to the north, no more than half a kilometre from the foot of Hlazakazi. The thinnest of wagon tracks snaked over the *nek* between Hlazakazi and Mdutshana, winding closely above the waterfall, then drifting off towards iSandlwana to the west and Qhudeni to the east. Behind Mdutshana is a circle of bigger hills which form the watershed of the Mangeni – Magogo, and just to the north of it Silutshana, which between them form the eastern end of the iSandlwana plain. A little to the north-east is another isolated stony outcrop, surrounded by broken cliffs and caves, known as Phindo, and further off in the same direction the greater bulk of Siphezi.

The NNC had remained on the top of Hlazakazi, watching the Volunteers resting below. Major Dartnell himself rode around Mdutshana to see if he could spot any signs of the Zulus his men had seen earlier. It was now early evening, and the reconnaissance party should have been on its way back to the camp but the report of an enemy presence had left the men buzzing with excitement, and there was a distinct feeling that to break contact now, before the intelligence they had gathered had been properly verified, would cancel out all the day's hard work. Suddenly a messenger from Dartnell rode up to the Volunteers calling, 'Saddle up immediately and follow the Major!' Symons was disappointed; his billy had not yet boiled and 'we cared more for a rest and some tea than all the Zulu armies just then'.[43] Nevertheless, they mounted up and rode over the *nek* below Mdutshana, turning north a little way into the hills beyond. In the tension a young Mounted Police trooper, Parsons, tried to load his revolver on horseback and accidentally fired a shot – his horse bucked and threw him, much to the amusement of his comrades. Irritated by the distraction, Dartnell ordered him back to the camp at iSandlwana; 'I felt very sorry for him', recalled Symons, 'and considered that under the circumstances the Major was too severe with him for a trifling offence done under nervous excitement, one word of encouragement to the boy just then from the commander would have made a hero out of him.'[44] As it turned out, Dartnell's punishment would prove to be severe indeed.

The Volunteers rode gingerly into one of the small valleys that sculpt the southern slopes of Magogo, immediately north of the Mdutshana knoll – it is difficult to be precise about the spot today – where Dartnell had apparently seen the party of Zulus on the ridge-top less than an hour before. Symons again:

> We halted about half a mile [0.8 kilometres] from the hill upon which the Zulus lay (of whom not one was visible) and six men, Jack amongst the number under Lieut. Royston, were sent out to reconnoitre. We anxiously watched the small party disappear over the brow of the hill and when we saw them riding down the rocky hill side at a much more rapid pace than when they went up we knew something was after them and our surmise was correct for, from one end of the ridge to the other, as if by magic, rose a long line of black warriors advancing at the double in short intervals of skirmish order. It was a magnificent spectacle and no British regiments could excel in keeping their distances in skirmishing at the double. They uttered no sound and on reaching the brow of the hill their centre halted while the flanks came on thus forming the noted 'horns' of the Zulu *impi*s.
>
> We all thought we were to be attacked but a shout came from the hill top answered by one from the right horn. The *impi* then halted, another shout and the Zulus slowly retired till only three or four [were] visible on the ridge. Some of us considered it was a ruse to entice us to attack but the Major was not quite as easily beguiled but waited for the reinforcing NNC to join us. These, however, did not come so after waiting a considerable time and as the sun was sinking behind the western hills we faced about under the impression we were to return to camp . . .[45]

From his elevated position with the NNC on top of Hlazakazi, Charlie Harford had watched the entire encounter:

> ... the natives, with their sharp eyes, at once spotted a lot of Zulus on the opposite hill, across a very steep and rugged valley about 800 or 900 yards [732 or 823 metres] off in a straight line. The men were ordered to keep well out of sight below the hill, and from behind some rocks Hamilton-Browne, Cooper and I watched the Zulus stealthily moving about, their outline being well defined against the clear evening sky ... [Major Dartnell] had seen the enemy and had found them to be occupying a very strong position, and as it was still daylight he called for volunteers to go over and try to draw the Zulus out in order to see what sort of force confronted us.
>
> Instantly a number of men jumped on their horses and were off, with orders on no account to engage the enemy but simply draw him out and gallop back. The manoeuvre was most successful; scarcely had our men crossed the valley and got up to within 800 yards of their position than a regular swarm of Zulus, which we estimated at over 1000 men, swept down upon them in their horn formation and tried to surround them. Our men got back as hard as they could; no shots were fired and the Zulus returned back over the hill again ...[46]

Norris-Newman, with the journalist's instinct for the dramatic, thought the Zulus closer to 2,000 men. In either case, the encounter was undoubtedly serious.

It was now about 5 p.m. and the sun was sinking fast. According to his original orders, Dartnell should have been on his way back to iSandlwana by now to report on the day's findings. He could still have done so – but to retire with the night coming on and a Zulu force in the rear afforded obvious risks, particularly to potentially nervous troops like the NNC.

The encounter had taken place at the worst possible time, moreover – after a day of learning nothing, just as tangible proof of a Zulu presence had been discovered, it seemed that nightfall would allow them to slip away, confounding what little intelligence advantage Dartnell had gained. It was a genuine dilemma, and after discussing the situation with the NNC officers, Dartnell decided the entire force should find a secure spot on the eastern edge of Hlazakazi for a bivouac and stay there for the night.

It was nonetheless crucial that Lord Chelmsford be informed of the situation, and the two ADCs, Gossett and Buller, were sent back to iSandlwana to ask for further instructions. After they had gone, Dartnell and his command settled down to take what rest they could after their exhausting day.

As the gloom settled over the hills, Zulu campfires sprung up somewhere on the slopes behind Mdutshana.

# 17

# 'Did you hear that?'

## The Hlazakazi Ridge, 21–22 January 1879

The arrival of Gossett and Buller brought Chelmsford and his staff down from their viewpoint on the edge of the iNyoni escarpment. Chelmsford had not been unduly troubled by the distant glimpse of Zulu scouts on the uplands. It was only natural that the Zulu should be watching his movements, but the summit seemed for the most part open and empty, and he merely remarked that the heights would need to be thoroughly scouted the following day.

The news brought by his ADCs was far more interesting. Gossett and Buller had covered the 20 kilometres from Mangeni back to iSandlwana in the dusk without incident, and while the exact details of their conversation with Chelmsford are not reported, it seems likely that they were able to give him a thorough appraisal of the unfolding situation. Chelmsford's decision to send his own ADCs out with Dartnell in the first place suggests that he expected at some point to hear the details of the reconnaissance from men whose judgement he trusted. Gossett and Buller had been present during Dartnell's encounter with the Zulus, and could give Chelmsford a first-hand account of it; they knew, too, the ground Dartnell intended to occupy overnight. They had been in a position to urge against Dartnell staying out overnight if they felt Chelmsford might seriously disapprove of this, and the fact they did not do so suggests they concurred with his decision.

There was nothing, in other words, in their reports seriously to alarm Chelmsford, and his response to the news was relaxed and unhurried. He gave orders that a detachment of Mounted Infantry under Lieutenant Walsh be sent out to Dartnell, taking with them packhorses with extra rations and orders that Dartnell was to attack the Zulus 'when he thought fit'.[1] Nevertheless, Major Clery – Glyn's staff officer – was keen to put on record his reservations about the decision after the event:

I had felt from the first very much averse to this movement of sending
irregulars, under command of irregular officers, amounting to half the
force, on a roving commission of this kind, and now when word came
in that they were going to bivouac out I could not help speaking
strongly to Colonel Glyn on the possibility of this sort of thing dragging
the rest of the force into any sort of compromising enterprise these
people may get messed up in.[2]

Walsh's men set off not long after dark, and that evening the tattoo was
sounded at iSandlwana at 8 p.m. and all the lights in the camp extinguished.
It had been the custom of the 24th's bands to play the tattoo in turn; which
one played on the night of the 21st is unrecorded, but, given what was to
come, it is particularly poignant if it was the 1st Battalion. Before playing
'God Save the Queen', the band struck up 'Home Sweet Home'. In the
Mounted Police camp, Trooper Hayes – one of those left behind for vedette
duties – found the tune unsettling, and disturbed his tent-mate Trooper
Dorehill by warning that disaster was imminent. Hayes slept fretfully,
calling out several times in the night that the Zulus were coming. Curiously,
both Hayes and Dorehill would survive the next twenty-four hours – but
Hayes would be dead within two months from fever, so perhaps his
presentiment of coming evil owed something to its early grip.[3]

Otherwise a heavy silence settled over the camp at iSandlwana with the
night, broken only by the occasional muffled snore, by the shuffling of
animals in their picket lines, and by the regular calls of the sentries
sounding off as they paced their posts.

*

After the departure of Gossett and Buller, Dartnell had organized his men
for the night. The mounted troops had retired to the summit to join the
NNC – 'I don't believe they ever intended joining us in the valley so near
the foe', grumbled Symons – Dartnell's entire force prepared to bivouac on
a suitable spot near a stream at the eastern end of Hlazakazi, above the
Mangeni gorge. 'By this time we were all pretty well famished,' admitted
Symons,

and much was there of grumbling and dissatisfaction at having to sleep
out there without blankets or food, nevertheless it was a great relief to
get rid of the heavy rifle and cartridges which had been on our shoulders
since 4 a.m. On the other side of the stream were some Zulu kraals and

where manure is there, at this time of year, the black-jack and pig-weed will be found growing; so as soon as we off-saddled I suggested gathering some and Jack, Methley, Green and I walked over and collected as much spinach as our helmets would hold, rinsed it in the brook and returned to cook our frugal meal. Our great difficulty was finding firewood and the mess seemed to us hungry fellows to take such a dreadful time to cook. The NNC were not troubled with our scruples and pulled down the kraals for fuel, we had not yet reached that hardened state and I never shall . . .[4]

Symons, it should be noted, was not in the least concerned for the hardship inflicted on the absent Zulu owners of these ruined homes, but because of the number of saplings the construction of each hut required, 'and I know what it was to get the young trees planted out at Claridge and Kingsbury. The man who burns a hut down even in warfare ought to be condemned.'[5]

Dartnell arranged his men in a square, with the NNC on three sides and the mounted men on the fourth – 'we were on the side furthest from the enemy', noted Symons, 'whether by accident or design I cannot say' – and the horses brought into the centre and tied together. Vedettes were pushed out beyond each side of the square. According to Lieutenant John Maxwell of the NNC, an uncomfortable night lay ahead for those who had already had such an exhausting day sweeping the thorn valleys of the Malakatha. 'We then made ourselves as comfortable as we could. Officers had the best of it. They had their saddles for pillows but no cloak or blanket, and laid down in the rear of their respective companies as also did their non coms who were all whitemen . . . But they were not mounted, and in consequence had no pillows. I remember the night was fine but quite dark . . .'[6]

As staff officer to the regiment, Charlie Harford didn't expect to get much sleep at all:

I should have to be constantly on the move all night while Lonsdale was superintending the formation of the bivouac. I went off to post the outposts. It was now getting dark, and a rare business it was. The Natives showed unmistakable signs of being in a mortal funk, and all wanted to clump together in one spot. At last, however, we strung them out like a thread of beads, each man squatting and touching his neighbour, and behind each section a European NCO and a superior native were ordered to keep up a continual patrol to see that they kept awake and didn't stir from their position . . . In this manner more than a mile of outposts was strung out, almost encircling the bivouac. By this time the Zulus had lighted fires all along their position and kept them going throughout the night, and from this fact we felt pretty certain that we would be attacked in the morning. There was very little fear of a real attack during the night, as night fighting was not the Zulu method.

Having satisfied myself that the outposts were working, and after taking special note of different features, such as bushes, rocks etc. to guide me on my visits during the night, I got back to the bivouac. Then, hitching my pony to the others, went to report to Lonsdale whom I found sitting chatting with some of the officers and Newman Noggs. I think the subject of this conversation was food, everyone was hungry and from my holster I produced a solitary biscuit that had been husbanded all day, which we all shared, each of us getting a piece about the size of a shilling which was better than nothing.[7]

Hamilton Browne was not at all impressed with the situation in which they found themselves:

> Here we were at least eleven miles [17.7 kilometres] from camp, no food, no spare ammunition, well knowing that a huge army of Zulus must be in our close vicinity. Well I was not in command, but begged Lonsdale even at that hour to return to camp. I said, 'We know the camp is going to be attacked, every cock fights best in his own yard. When the General hears our news he will order the camp to be *laagered* and we can put up a fight there against the whole Zulu nation, whilst out here we shall be stamped flat in a minute.' But no, Lonsdale would not grasp the situation . . .[8]

Two of Hamilton Browne's officers, however, Lieutenants Avery and Holcroft, slipped away without orders and returned to iSandlwana.

As darkness came on, the site of the bivouac was clearly visible against the black hillside, marked out by the NNC's campfires. At first a buzz of voices hung over the spot as the men clustered around their fires for warmth and human comfort, but at last the hubbub gradually subsided and even the horses, Symons noted, were 'too tired to move about'. It was not long after the camp had settled down, however, that Walsh's party arrived from iSandlwana, the rumble of hooves and shouted challenges bringing the bivouac to life again. 'George Macfarlane, Harry Stirton and I were on first relief camp-guard', said Symons, 'and during our watch some mounted infantry arrived with packs carrying provisions and provisions for the Carbs and Police.'[9]

It was now quite dark, but Walsh had ridden across the plain safely, although one of his men told Maxwell that some shots had been fired at them about halfway from the camp. If so, this was a worrying development since it suggested an increase in Zulu activity on the plain after Gossett and Buller had ridden across it without incident a few hours earlier. The supplies Walsh's men brought were very welcome, especially among the Carbineers, but their news less so. During the day, they said, a patrol of their men led by Lieutenant Edward Browne had scouted out from iSandlwana along the northern side of the plain, and somewhere on the far side of Silutshana had run into small parties of Zulus. Shots had been exchanged, and as the Zulus had shown every inclination to attack, Browne had withdrawn.[10] It was not a report likely to lighten the mood that night on Hlazakazi – any more than the orders Walsh brought to Dartnell that his command was to stay where it was.

Symons had been relieved of first guard, and, 'I lay there between sleep and waking when a shot was fired away in front, i.e. in the direction of the Zulu army. I was all there in two winks you may be sure! The[re] followed more shots in quick succession. Mac! Did you hear that? "Yes" he replied. Waking Stirton and grasping our carbines we rushed to our posts . . .'[11]

Hamilton Browne, despite his misgivings, had just dozed off:

> I had loosened my revolver belt for a minute, meaning to buckle it again, but went to sleep without having done so. I do not know how long I slept when I felt myself rushed over and trampled on. I tried to get to my feet, but was knocked down again. I then tried to find my revolver, but was unable to do so. I never let go of my horse's bridle which I was holding in my hand, and at last staggered to my feet. The square was broken, natives rushing all ways mixed up with plunging horses, while the night was made horrible with yells, shouts and imprecations. 'My God,' I thought, 'why am I not assegaid?' as half-mad natives rushed by me jostling me with their shields . . .[12]

Norris-Newman had been lying near Lonsdale in the centre of the square when,

> . . . the first thing I remember was being trampled upon by horses, and a hoarse shout arose, and several dusky forms, naked and with brandished weapons, ran over me, at which, waxing wrath, and very naturally

imagining the Zulus had come, I 'up with' my rifle and clubbed one man down, and then went to try and find my horse, which I did not for some time. I was coming back with revolver in hand prepared for anything, when I recognized the red strip on some of the men's heads, and then knew they belonged to the Contingent . . .[13]

Charlie Harford, too, had been jolted awake by the sudden shots from the darkness:

. . . and in a second the whole square rose up. Hearing the noise the men were making, rattling their shields and fumbling about for things, I rushed up and speaking to them in their own language ordered them to keep quiet and lie down. Their own company officers, too, did all they could to establish calm, but it was of no avail. The whole lot made a clean bolt of it and came bounding over us like frightened animals, making their way down the hillside behind us. In this terrific stampede of some 4000 men the wretched ponies were swept along in a solid mass, kicking and struggling, with several Europeans hanging on to try and stop them. As these passed me, on looking round I caught a glimpse of both Lonsdale and Noggs turning a somersault as a lot of natives bounded over them. Poor Noggs, who highly resented such treatment, spent the rest of the night with the Mounted Police, having, as he afterwards told me, 'had enough of the Contingent'.[14]

In the Volunteer Corps lines, Symons heard the Sergeant-Major of the Mounted Police calling out above the din, for his men not to fire. 'I liked that man's voice,' admitted Symons, 'it inspired confidence, and courage.' Instead, the Volunteers protected their horses from the fleeing mob with their rifle butts. Above the confusion, 'a roar like Howick Falls in flood',[15] Symons heard an NNC officer trying to rally his men – probably Hamilton Browne, who cheerfully admitted that he snatched a stick from a man running past and began to lay about him, and with his white officers 'backing me up splendidly we soon quelled the uproar and thrashed the cowardly brutes back into their places'.[16]

Someone had managed to find Harford's pony for him, and, seeing some sort of order restored at the bivouac, he set off to see if he could find those who had already disappeared into the night. He was afraid they might already be halfway on the road back to iSandlwana, but in fact found them 'almost at the foot of the hill, squatting in various-sized clumps, and addressing them in anything but Parliamentary language, hounded them back to the bivouac. In the darkness of the night it was impossible to say whether everyone had been rounded up, but there was no time for further search as I had to get to the outpost line as quickly as I could . . .'[17]

Harford was afraid that there was no one now screening the bivouac from the Zulus should they attack. Riding out to where he had placed the line just a few hours earlier:

> Not a soul was to be seen, but only a very short distance from me a dark mass of something that I had no recollection of having seen when posting the men loomed up largely to my front. 'Zulus!' I said to myself, and rather a shiver went down my back. Everything was dead silence, and I sat on my pony for some minutes, watching it, but as no movement took place, and feeling certain that I was mistaken, rode up to it and found that it was nothing but a mass of rock cropping out of the ground, which had not caught my eye in the daylight but in the darkness showed up considerably. The company, however, had vanished.
>
> Further on, I was more successful and found Lieutenant Thompson with his company intact, and as we met I asked him what on earth had happened at the outpost, and told him all that had taken place at the bivouac. He solved the problem by telling me that an NCO of one of his sections, who should have been patrolling in company with a Native, had sat down and fallen asleep, then suddenly waking up and seeing, as he thought, a Zulu coming towards him, fired at him. He said, 'It's no use your going any further, as directly the shot was fired the remainder of the outpost went. There is no-one now on my front.'
>
> However I thought it best to go and see for myself, but only found that he was quite right. Everyone but his company had vanished. A nice state of things, had we been really attacked![18]

The incident certainly soured the temper of the white troops in the bivouac. For Trooper Symons, it confirmed the caustic judgement he had first formed of the NNC when they marched into Helpmekaar. 'What did Ted Greene think now of this splendid body of men?' he asked with heavy sarcasm, 'Where the "bloated rot" so glibly spoken of?'[19] Hamilton Browne simply dismissed his own men as 'curs'.[20]

Yet there was more in the incident than just the undermining of mutual confidence between officers and men. Dartnell was clearly beginning to wonder whether his command would hold together – and he was right to be concerned. It is difficult to judge at what time the scare took place, but it was probably no later than nine or ten o'clock. Several hours of darkness still lay ahead, and while the majority of the NNC were already unnerved, the Zulu campfires still twinkled menacingly in the darkness a few kilometres away on Magogo. But if staying where he was – with every possibility of a Zulu attack at dawn – was an uncomfortable prospect, an orderly retreat to iSandlwana, already a fragile hope in the twilight earlier, must now have seemed an impossible undertaking. Instead, Dartnell opted for the only other choice available to him. According to Hamilton Browne, 'As soon as I met Lonsdale again I urged him to return to camp, even at this hour, and perhaps he might have done so when Major Dartnell came over to us and informed us that he had sent an orderly back to camp to request the General to reinforce us.'[21]

Hamilton Browne was not impressed. Such a decision, he grumbled, would just make the situation 'worse and worse'. He directed his spleen against his unfortunate men, promising that 'the next man who moved would at once be shot', and to unleash the iziGqoza upon any company that wavered.[22]

Sometime in the early hours, a dense mist rose out of the Mangeni valley, settling over the hills and smothering the anxiety of Dartnell's men in a cold damp blanket. And so the 'weary night dragged on, no chance of sleep, no chance of rest, as we had to watch our wretched [men], and I was very pleased to see the east lighten and grow pale'.[23]

*

Ironically, the same question which teased Lord Chelmsford also preoccupied those of the Zulu border population who had opted to linger in the bush close to their homes as the British advanced – just where was the king's main army?

It is highly likely, of course, that news of its approach had filtered through the civilian population at least twenty-four hours before it had reached Lord Chelmsford's ears. As Hamilton Browne had noted, its arrival seemed to be common knowledge among the women, children and old men the NNC had interrogated – only the timing was open to question.

The approach of the *amabutho* undoubtedly galvanized the local Zulu, sending the faint-hearted, like Gamdana, scurrying to secure the protection of the invaders for fear of reprisals, but putting courage into the hearts of those determined to resist. According to the careful intelligence report compiled at Lord Chelmsford's order before the war began, *inkosi* Matshana kaMondise commanded the services of about 700 of the Sithole. If that assessment is correct, then they must have been significantly reinforced if Hamilton Browne's description of the men he saw lying in wait in the valleys running down to the Qhudeni bush – 'some 1500 strong'[24] – on the afternoon of the 19th is to be believed. Most of the newcomers were probably indignant amaQungebeni, regrouping after the attack on kwa-Sogekle on the 12th; buoyed up by the prospect of royal support, Hamilton Browne's NNC must have seemed to them that afternoon a tempting target from which to exact revenge for the destruction of their homes and the loss of their cattle.

Lord Chelmsford had, of course, entertained hopes that Matshana might follow Gandana's example and defect, and it is possible that Matshana, living out in a cave somewhere at the foot of Qhudeni, or in a temporary shelter of grass and brushwood away from the comforts of his Nsingabantu homestead, may have weighed up the possibility. Chelmsford's stick-and-carrot strategy towards the local *amakhosi* – coaxing in waverers like Gamdana and falling rigorously on those, like Sihayo, who remained loyal to the king – was hardly subtle, after all, and surrender would at least have removed the risk of an immediate attack upon himself and his followers.

Yet Matshana had been very aware that he was regarded as a fugitive from justice by the Natal authorities, and the easy promises of protection made so blithely by Chelmsford must have seemed distinctly hollow when compared to the long memories and longer reach of Theophilus Shepstone and his family. In Natal he had been betrayed and attacked, his followers broken up and his cattle confiscated, and he had been forced to flee like a common criminal. In Zululand, in contrast, under the king's protection, his ruffled dignity had been restored. He had taken two of Cetshwayo's sisters in marriage, his authority had been returned to him, and the Sithole people had begun to restore their fortunes in the very lands where their ancestors lay buried.

So all in all it had not been so much of a choice at all. Matshana had remained in the bush, his men ready to harass the British where they could – and awaited the royal instructions which would surely come with the arrival of the main army.

That call had come late on the evening of the 20th or early the following morning. Even as Lord Chelmsford had been scouring the country from the top of the cliff above the Mangeni gorge, the big *impi* had arrived on the fringes of Matshana's territory, 16 or 17 kilometres away to the west, and unseen messengers had hurried through the landscape stretched out so torpidly at Chelmsford's feet. The king's generals had sent instructions for Matshana and his men to join the royal *amabutho* at their bivouacs before they contested the advance of the invaders.

The bulk of the Sithole fighting men had made their way to the rendezvous on the 21st, although Matshana himself planned to follow them the next day. They had pushed westwards in groups from the Qhudeni bush, keeping in the broken country on the flanks of the rising escarpments, and had emerged from the Mangeni valley somewhere on its eastern side even as Dartnell's men were beginning their sweep across Malakatha and Hlazakazi. By late afternoon Matshana's men were somewhere in the vicinity of the rocky outcrop known as Phindo, and it was here that Dartnell, at the head of the Mounted Police and accompanied by Chelmsford's ADCs, had first spotted them. Though Dartnell had broken off contact and retreated towards the head of the Mangeni, where he knew the rest of his command was to gather, his small numbers – just fifty men – had been enough to tempt Matshana's followers to pursuit. They had moved onto the southern flanks of Magogo, heading west, where they had encountered Dartnell again – and this time it was the Zulus who had refused to engage, retiring back over the skyline and into the dusk.[25]

Had they been, as some of the Volunteers suspected, trying to draw Dartnell into a trap? Quite possibly; they knew, after all, what Dartnell did not – that somewhere in the hills behind them lay the long awaited main Zulu army. That night Matshana's followers lit campfires on the slopes of Mangeni, intending the next morning not only to continue the march to the rendezvous point, but if possible to draw the British after them.

*

Dartnell's second message to Chelmsford was taken through the night by Lieutenant Walsh and three of his Mounted Infantry. They had ridden the 20 kilometres from iSandlwana once already that night and Charlie Harford was impressed when they attempted the feat for a second time: 'Walsh's was a very perilous journey with a fifteen-mile ride in the dark, over very stiff country, hills, valleys, bush, krantzes, dongas etc., all quite unknown to him, an occasional kaffir path, perhaps, leading to goodness knows where, and with every chance of being attacked by a lurking body of Zulus.'[26]

Nonetheless, Walsh accomplished the journey safely, arriving back in the camp at about 1 a.m., and reporting to the headquarters tent of the column staff. According to Clery,

> About 1.30 that night a message written in pencil was brought to my tent from the commander of the force bivouacking out, to say that the enemy had shown in increased force and that it would not be prudent to attack them in the morning without some white troops. I took this at once to Colonel Glyn who simply said I must take it to the general. The general's tent was close by, so I roused him up. Lying on my face and hands close by his camp-bed I can still remember how I read from that crumpled piece of notebook written across in pencil, word after word what I had previously had such difficulty in deciphering in my own tent.[27]

It was a development which probably did not surprise Chelmsford after the report brought by Gossett and Buller that afternoon; certainly Clery gives no hint that it did. Many times in his career Chelmsford must have been alerted by a new piece of intelligence to a change in the strategic situation and been required to make a decision on the spur of the moment for an appropriate response – it is, after all, the essence of command. The hour made no difference. Yet it is tempting to conjure him at that moment, about to give an order which probably seemed ordinary enough at the time – but which would shape not only the course of the next twenty-four hours but impact upon the destiny of thousands of men, and upon the fate of a nation. Trooper Symons had noted how cold it was on the exposed ridge-top at Hlazakazi at that hour, and dark, for it was almost time for the new moon; no doubt Chelmsford was wearing the nightshirt and nightcap he habitually slept in, and Clery had no more than a lantern or candle to read Dartnell's message by. If Chelmsford was still sleepy, however, he showed no sign of it, but reacted to the news with a typically firm decision:

> The general did not hesitate much. He said, 'Order the 2nd Battalion 24th Regiment, four guns and all the mounted troops to get ready to start at day-break.' He also added, 'Order up Colonel Durnford with the troops he had to reinforce the camp' ... This was overheard by Crealock in the next tent, so he joined in by asking (very properly I think), 'Is Major Clery to issue the orders to Colonel Durnford?' – for Durnford's was an independent command hitherto. So the general said, 'No, let you do it.'[28]

It was a decision Chelmsford would be called to justify many times in the years that lay ahead, yet made in the darkness of that hour it is not difficult to comprehend his thinking. Certainly the Zulu movements fitted the conclusion he had reached since he had arrived at iSandlwana of the risk to his right flank posed by the broken course of the Mangeni. Now his probes had encountered an enemy concentration of undetermined strength in the direction of oNdini lying at the head of the Mangeni gorge – were they about to slip past him, and strike into Natal across the Mzinyathi downstream of Rorke's Drift, as Henry Francis Fynn had argued they might? If they were, what were his options? He had seen the nature of the ground there for himself, and knew from his experiences on the Cape frontier how difficult it could be for a European force to bring an African enemy to battle in it. He could draw in his forces at iSandlwana – as many of his colonial officers claimed afterwards they had urged him to do – but he was not at all confident that the Zulu would choose to attack him if his position seemed too strong. He was not trying to avoid a battle – he sought one, preferably at a time and on ground over which he had some choice and which was at least moderately favourable to him, as he was convinced he would win it. If he were to advance the entire column, by the time he had waited until daylight and packed up the tents, then moved forward only at the lumbering pace of the ox-wagons, the enemy would be sure to have moved position again. And it was a worst-case scenario that the Zulu should move down the course of the Mangeni.

His best hope then, or so it seemed, was to split his force, sending out a portion of the column that could move quickly enough to reach the Mangeni before the Zulu dispersed, and that was nonetheless strong enough to deal with any possible threat it found there. There was nothing unusual in such a plan in itself; it had been commonplace for troops to leave their camps to make sweeps through the bush on the Eastern Cape frontier. Even at that moment Colonel Evelyn Wood, commanding the Left Flank Column 50 kilometres away to the north, was marching across country to attack abaQulusi concentrations around the Zungwini and Hlobane mountains, leaving considerably fewer men to guard his camp at Fort Thinta than Chelmsford would leave at iSandlwana.

Chelmsford would keep a strong force at iSandlwana – certainly enough to protect it in the highly unlikely event of a Zulu attack – but his earlier instinct to move Durnford closer to hand had proved correct; Durnford could now be brought forward in support. It is interesting to note that whatever Chelmsford had in mind for Durnford once he arrived, Clery was under the impression he was to 'reinforce the camp'.

Glyn and his staff would accompany the advance, and the troops selected for the foray certainly reveal Chelmsford's aggressive intent. The five companies of the 1/24th would remain as camp guard, but six companies of the 2/24th would go out – only G Company under Lieutenants Pope and Godwin-Austen, who were on picket duty, together with a number of men on other duties or on the sick list, were to remain behind. Each man carried his usual 70 rounds of ammunition, but the battalion reserve supply – a further 200 rounds per man – was left with Quartermaster Edward Bloomfield who had orders to make it ready to be sent forward should Chelmsford ask for it. Lieutenant-Colonel Henry Degacher, commanding the battalion, decided to leave the 2/24th's Colours in the camp, and the reasons for his decision reflect the understanding the infantry had of the role they were about to play, '. . . for not only was the battalion short of officers, but experience gained in the Kaffir war had proved how impossible it was to take the colours out bush-fighting or scaling krantzes, and on some such expedition the column was supposed to be bound.'[29]

Most of the 2/24th bandsmen also accompanied the force – it was their duty to act as stretcher-bearers during an engagement – together with two ambulances. Two sections of Arthur Harness's N/5 Battery – four guns in all – were to accompany the force, leaving one section behind at the camp under the command of Lieutenant Curling. So too were most of the Mounted Infantry under Colonel Russell.

Chelmsford was anxious that the men should start before dawn, without alerting any Zulus who were watching unseen out in the darkness, so the camp was awoken without bugle calls, the only sound being the low hum of muted orders. To his chagrin, it fell to Clery again to organize this:

> As I did not want to give any warning to the enemy or disturb the camp I went direct to each of the commanders and gave the general's orders. This took some time and the general was soon dressed and impatient to be starting. The troops too turned out well. The general had given no orders about the camp, except that Colonel Durnford was to move troops up there; but in trying to gather my wits together after giving out the different orders for the march personally myself, as to what further should be cared for before marching off, it occurred to me that some instructions should be left to the officer left in command of the

camp. It was too late to refer to Colonel Glyn, who of course would only have referred me to the general, so I ventured on the responsibility of issuing them myself. So I wrote to poor Colonel Pulleine who commanded the 1st Battalion 24th Regiment, officially as follows: 'You will be in command of the camp in the absence of Colonel Glyn. Draw in your line of defence while the force with the general is out of the camp. Draw in your infantry outpost line in conformity. Keep your cavalry vedettes still well to the front. Act strictly on the defensive. Keep a wagon loaded with ammunition ready to start at once, should the general's force be in need of it. Colonel Durnford has been ordered up from Rorke's Drift to reinforce the camp.'

I sent this to Colonel Pulleine by my own servant and, just before leaving camp, I went myself to his tent to ensure that he had got it. I saw him again and verbally repeated what he had already received in writing, laying stress on the point that his mission was simply to hold and keep the camp. I must add that at that moment nobody from the general downwards had the least suspicion that there was a chance of the camp being attacked. I merely took these precautions myself to leave nothing to chance.[30]

Chelmsford, it seems, was already preoccupied with the imminent attack; thinking ahead, he had given little attention to what he was leaving behind. Later, when Clery reminded him that orders had been left for Pulleine to 'act strictly on the defensive', Chelmsford said 'I cannot tell you what a relief it is to me to hear this.'[31]

A buzz of excitement passed through the camp as the force prepared to depart. Chelmsford had no intention of burdening his men with heavy baggage, and they set out in light marching order, with just a day's rations, leaving their tents still standing and all their equipment and personal possessions still in them. Nevill Coghill, still suffering from his dislocated kneecap, was not fit for a long ride, and the officers of the staff left their servants behind them to look after their kit. Chelmsford's French cook, Monsieur Laparra, remained in the camp, and so did Crealock's servant, Colour Sergeant M.C. Keane of the General Staff, and Lieutenant Milne's sailor batman, Signaller First Class W.H. Aynsley. According to Captain Hallam Parr, most of them shared the 1/24th's disappointment at being left behind:

On looking back to that Wednesday morning, how every little detail seems to stand out in relief! The hurried and careless farewell to Nevill

Coghill, who shared my tent, and whose name will not be forgotten while the Zulu War is remembered; my servant, who was to leave for Natal that morning, saying when he brought my horse, 'I shall be here, sir, when you come back; the wagons are not going to start today, now that this force is going out'; the half-laughing condolences to the 1-24th as they watched the troops move out of camp; the men not for duty turning out for the routine work of the camp; the position of the tents and wagons – many trifles fixed in the mind serve to make stronger the contrast between the departure and return to that ill-fated camp.[32]

Others seized the opportunity to be in on the adventure. Lieutenant Nathaniel Newnham-Davis of the Mounted Infantry found that he was among those

Told off to stop in camp on outlying piquet duty, and thinking that I was to be left in camp all day I went to Lord Chelmsford and requested leave to go out with the main force. My request was acceded to on the condition that I found somebody who would exchange duties with me. Well, I discovered a rather fat and elderly captain who was glad to have a quiet day about camp, so away I went . . .[33]

It was about 3 a.m. when Chelmsford rode out of iSandlwana. Those staying behind watched the column pick its way slowly down the track, across the difficult *dongas* in front of the camp, until they were swallowed up by the mist and the darkness.

# 18

# 'The valour of ignorance'

## A picnic at Magogo, dawn, 22 January 1879

On 8 January, hurrying up from Greytown to join the column headquarters before the war began, Nevill Coghill had passed two transport officers struggling to manage supply convoys at the difficult crossing of the Mooi river at Keate's Drift. Looking forward himself to the prospect of action, Coghill had not envied their situation; 'here I found Huntly and Smith-Dorrien' he wrote, 'superintending the Transport Duties, and very arduous work it was and a more abominable locality than the "Thorns" to live in I cannot imagine.'[1]

Coghill had ridden on to join the invasion but it had taken Smith-Dorrien another week to reach the border. Of all the hopeful young officers who had landed together on the *Edinburgh Castle* a month before, Smith-Dorrien had so far had perhaps the dullest war, entirely preoccupied with the passage of supplies up the line of communication – those same supplies whose delay in reaching the front had so hampered Lord Chelmsford's plans to advance. Yet Smith-Dorrien was not in the least daunted; it was his first overseas posting and his appointment allowed him a degree of freedom and independence granted to few young lieutenants on regimental duties, and he drank in the experience, revelling in the people he found himself among, the landscape and weather – rain and all.

With the supplies finally accumulating at Rorke's Drift, Smith-Dorrien was at last close to the scene of the action. As the column advanced, it would fall to him to ensure the smooth passage of convoys of loaded wagons up the line to the forward camps, and then, empty, back down again to the rear supply depots to refill. He would soon surely cross into Zululand – and the prospect delighted him.

The order to do so came on the afternoon of 21 January. The supply wagons which had accompanied Chelmsford's move from Rorke's Drift to iSandlwana the day before had been unloaded, and an officer was needed to oversee them on their return to Rorke's Drift, where a new stockpile of supplies was waiting. Smith-Dorrien was ordered to ride forward to iSandlwana, but by the time he arrived it was late afternoon, and there was no possibility of ushering the wagons safely back to the drift before nightfall. He bedded down at the camp, expecting to make the journey at first light the next morning, but instead he was awoken in the small hours by a staff officer[2] and told that because of recent developments – Lord Chelmsford's decision to march out to Dartnell at Mangeni – the wagons would not be starting for the time being. There was, however, a more exciting duty to hand – Smith-Dorrien was to leave right away for Rorke's Drift carrying Chelmsford's new orders for Durnford.

It was a mission not without its risks. It was a dark night, and misty along the river-beds; Smith-Dorrien hardly knew the track, and most of the landmarks were in any case lost in the gloom. Although there had been no incidents on the road since the column had marched up it on the 20th, he would have to pass through the Batshe valley, and a lone dispatch rider would be an easy target for any of Sihayo's disgruntled followers who might be lingering there. All in all, it was to be a great adventure:

> It ought to have been a very jumpy ride, for I was entirely alone and the country was wild and new to me, and the road little better than a track; but pride at being selected to carry such an important dispatch and the valour of ignorance (for I only realised next day that the country was infested with hostile Zulus) carried me along without a thought of danger.[3]

He reached the drift safely at about 6.30 a.m. It was light by then, and he found Durnford's column easily enough – Durnford had finally reached Rorke's Drift and had crossed the river and was camped close to the ground Chelmsford had recently vacated. When he reported to the headquarters tents, however, Smith-Dorrien found that Durnford was absent – he had set off earlier that morning to visit the Biggarsberg farmers to try to persuade them to give up their wagons to the invasion. A little disappointed, Smith-Dorrien passed over the orders to George Shepstone instead. He would have to return to iSandlwana later that morning.

*

Young Muziwento kaZibana and his band of amaQungebeni refugees had continued to flee before the British advance. While they were hiding out at

Malakatha, Muziwento's father, Zibane, had taken most of the fighting men off to look for signs of the approaching royal army, and the band now largely consisted of women and children. They had lingered at Malakatha for a few days but 'having seen some soldiers in our neighbourhood'[4] – Dartnell's reconnaissance on the 21st – abandoned the area. They drifted westwards, through the disturbed countryside towards Siphezi and the headwaters of the Mhlatuze river, only to find that they were now straying into the path of the Zulu army, and that the landscape was suddenly alive with groups of armed men seeking to join the *amabutho*. As Muziwento noted, some of these were already suffering from the rigours of just a few days' campaigning in the unpredictable weather:

> In the afternoon there appeared through the fog the Bongoza regiment.[5] They saw the many sheep belonging to our father and other people. Up came the 'horned' Usutus[6] and said, 'A bit of food for us, this, master!' They stabbed some of the sheep; they drained our calabashes; they took the [dead] sheep away with them. Suddenly one of the warriors espied an exceedingly fine kid. He seized it. Our father [uncle] seized it, and the warrior seized it too. The next moment up came the *induna* and scolded the regiment. The men ran off and continued their march. We went on. We came to a kraal and stayed there. We happened upon five warriors. They were just starting off in the early morning, it being very cold indeed. One of them was chilled with the cold; he had no longer any power to get along quickly. [When] he arrived at the kraal he was exceedingly cold. He warmed himself at the fire. The others derided him. They said, 'It is not a young man of any worth. It is just cold for no reason at all' . . .[7]

*

The royal army had approached Siphezi from the direction of Babanango, two great columns screened by scouts, on the 20th, and had spent that night camped alongside the stream-beds on the western slopes of the mountain.[8] While messengers fanned out through the countryside carrying news of the army's arrival to the *amakhosi*, *inkosi* Ntshingwayo pondered the political landscape. It seems unlikely, given the extent to which Zulu scouts had watched British movements, that he was unaware that Chelmsford had now moved forward to iSandlwana. It was customary, when operating in friendly territory, to involve local *amakhosi* in the process of making strategic decisions, but while Sihayo was present with the army, his territory – which lay to the army's right front – had already been ravaged and pacified by the British. A flanking move to the south of iSandlwana – the very thing Chelmsford feared – was still an option, for the army could simply shift to its left, screened from iSandlwana by the line of the Silutshana and Magogo hills, and enter the Mangeni valley high up. But such a move would depend to some extent on the willingness and ability of Matshana kaMondise to cooperate – and here Ntshingwayo found himself troubled by the same question which had perplexed Lord Chelmsford: exactly whose side was Matshana on?

The conundrum lay in Matshana's history, for the very factors which had made his allegiance so politically useful to Cetshwayo when he had first entered Zululand more than twenty years before had earned him the suspicion of the Zulu establishment. Matshana had straddled the great divide, the huge ideological gulf which separated colonial and traditional forms of government; he represented an old and respected lineage which had once grown great under the protection of the Zulu kings, and while living under colonial rule he had risen up to embrace that legacy, thrown off colonial authority and returned to the Zulu fold. He had added considerably to Cetshwayo's prestige at the time in so doing. Yet to the men who constituted the inner circle of the Zulu kingdom, the highest born councillors and military commanders, men whose families had been at the centre of affairs since Shaka's time and who had lived all their lives in Zululand, Matshana remained an outsider. He had not been born free in Zululand, and for some he would always remain a *khafula*, one of those 'spat out' by the Zulu kings. To them he was less a hero of the struggle against white dominance than one tainted by his association with them – he had changed his allegiance once, and he might do so again; could his loyalty be relied upon now?

It was a question that was all the more pressing when, on the morning of the 21st, his scouts brought Ntshingwayo reports of an increase in British activity in Matshana's territory. Matshana knew the country intimately, and his intelligence value to the high command, if he could be relied upon, was immense – but if he could not? Could Ntshingwayo risk moving the army through countryside where the people's loyalty might already have been compromised?

The decision he took next would have a crucial impact on the course of the campaign, and sadly there is not enough surviving evidence to explore it in detail, but it seems that the suspicion felt by the high command towards Matshana was a telling factor. Certainly, Fynn believed that 'the great leaders mistrusted him',[9] while according to uGuku, a soldier in the ranks of the uKhandempemvu, 'it was intended that Matshana kaMondisa was to be the chief in command, but having been a Natal Kaffir the other three were jealous of him, and did not like him to be put over them; they had therefore devised a plan of getting him out of the way on the day of the battle.'[10]

And it was a simple enough plan, and one which reflected the develop-ing threat on the Zulu left front. Ntshingwayo had sent for Matshana, ordering him to bring his forces to meet the main army. Matshana had concurred willingly enough, and on the evening of the 21st, the first of the Sithole armed men had begun to emerge from the Mangeni valley, moving towards Siphezi, where the army had been camped the night before. When they arrived, however, they found the army gone: Ntshingwayo had already ordered the *amabutho* forward, leading them on a course which avoided the British forays to his left – and took them instead much closer to iSandlwana.

*

Perhaps an hour after Horace Smith-Dorrien arrived at Rorke's Drift on the morning of the 22nd, Chelmsford reached the foot of Hlazakazi close to Dartnell's bivouac.

Trooper Symons – and he was by no means alone – had wondered throughout the night whether he would live to see the dawn rising that morning, and he had been greatly relieved when the first grey streaks appeared over the hills in the east.[11] Dartnell had roused the command early, and while the NNC waited nervously on the heights he had ordered the Volunteers to saddle up and lead their horses down the northern slopes of the ridge in the hope of meeting any reinforcements coming along the track. The mist was still lying heavily in the plain and visibility was severely limited, and there was no sign of movement until the sudden sound of horses alerted them to a small group of horsemen riding out of the dark fog.

It was Chelmsford and his staff. The track from iSandlwana had proved difficult to negotiate at night, and the column straggled behind them, scattered across several kilometres. The guns and ambulances, in particular, had had a difficult journey, and had stuck fast several times in the *dongas*, so that it had been necessary to haul them through with ropes, and they now trailed behind, lost from sight in the mist.

Charlie Harford had spent the last weary hours since the panic trying to restore some order to his outposts, and was on his way back when he stumbled across the staff picking their way up onto Hlazakazi:

> The morning of the 22nd was just dawning, as I was nearing the bivouac, and on rounding a ridge of the hill came upon Lord Chelmsford and Hallam-Parr, the others of his staff being some way down the hill. He plied me with a number of questions and after having pointed out the position the Zulus had occupied during the night – and carefully said nothing of our little escapade – took him up to the bivouac and found Lonsdale and Major Dartnell, who commanded the Police, with whom he wanted to confer, and went on my way.[12]

*

As the sun broke clear of the horizon and the mist began to rise, relief passed through the men of the NNC at the sight of the red smudge of soldiers on the road from iSandlwana. Almost immediately, their spirits began to recover, but Lieutenant Maxwell at least was well aware of how dangerous their predicament had been. 'We had quite recovered by this time', he said, '. . . and a stranger coming upon us would never have thought from our appearance that we had had such an experience a short time before. If the Zulus had attacked we must have been cut to pieces, as our fellows during this scare would have been easy prey . . .'[13]

It is interesting to wonder whether anyone revealed to Chelmsford the true extent of the NNC's nervousness during the night – and whether it would have altered his assessment of the situation at all if they had.

What undoubtedly troubled Chelmsford rather more was the apparent disappearance of the Zulus. Even with the mist still trailing across the summits of Magogo and Silutshana, it was obvious that the force seen by Dartnell the night before had vanished. Chelmsford had accomplished his night march with some determination and was clearly frustrated that it appeared to have been for nothing. 'The general', noted Clery, 'was from the first much disappointed and annoyed at what was taking place';[14] the situation must have reminded Chelmsford of many similar failed sweeps on the Cape frontier, and can hardly have confirmed his faith in the judgement of his colonial officers.

But if the Zulus had gone from the flanks of Magogo, it was all the more pressing to find out where they were now. The 24th and Harness's guns were still struggling along the track, but Chelmsford brought the NNC down from the hills and directed them to form up in a line facing east towards Magogo. The Volunteers and Mounted Police were placed on their right, near the track running along the foot of Hlazakazi and facing towards Mdutshana. As the regulars at last began to arrive, Chelmsford had them fall in to the left of the NNC, towards the foot of Silutshana. When the 2/24th companies came up, Hamilton Browne was accorded another opportunity to voice his misgivings:

> Colonel Glyn rode over to me and drawing me aside said, 'In God's name Maori, what are you doing here?' I answered him with a question, 'In God's name sir, what are you doing here?'
>
> He shook his head and replied, 'I am not in command.' And fine old soldier as he was, I could see he was much disturbed.[15]

It was now about 8 a.m., and Chelmsford gave the order for the whole line to advance.

*

If the mist still lying on the hills had added to Chelmsford's frustration, it had also led *inkosi* Matshana into a deadly and quite unexpected danger as he had emerged from the Mangeni valley that morning. Many of his men had passed through the evening before, heading towards a rendezvous with the king's generals, but their movement had been interrupted by the sudden encounter with Dartnell's patrol. Matshana's followers had seemed inclined to drive Dartnell off, but had probably thought better of it when they realized the mounted troops were not alone. Later, it suited the British to think that the Zulu movements were part of a deliberate ploy to lure Chelmsford away from the camp – it was easier to accept defeat at the hands of an enemy possessed of such a rare degree of cunning – but there is no evidence to suggest that this was the case, and indeed it is extremely unlikely. For one thing, it would have required the main Zulu commanders to improvise a very complex plan at short notice, and to coordinate disparate Zulu movements over a distance of many kilometres; for another, the Zulus had no way of knowing Chelmsford would react to Dartnell's encounter by splitting his force.

Instead, the men on the hill-tops that night had deliberately marked their position in the darkness by lighting fires, hoping to hold Dartnell in position; then, before sunrise, the Zulus had continued their journey towards Siphezi, hoping, no doubt, that Dartnell would follow them – and be delivered into the hands of the king's *amabutho*.

In any case, all this had passed Matshana by. There had been very little shooting during the encounter the previous evening, and Matshana, who probably spent the night deep in the Mangeni gorge, was almost certainly unaware that it had taken place. He was accompanied by the remainder of his armed men, some of whom had been hand-picked for their courage to serve as his bodyguard. They emerged from the gorge before the mist had fully cleared, and Matshana had no idea of the extent to which the British had come to dominate the hills lying above. When his followers pointed out that there were men with shields on the summit of Magogo, Matshana naturally assumed they were the king's soldiers – and he set off towards them. He was in for a shock:

> Matshana, when he went with his force towards the General [i.e. Chelmsford], had not the least idea that they were enemies; but, seeing some of the natives attached to the General's force, he thought it was the Zulu Army, for the Zulu *Indunas* had ordered him to come and join them at the rendezvous near the place where the Whitemen were. So he went on, not knowing that the enemy was there, and on foot, a little ahead of his men, his horse being led by the bridle. As they drew near, they heard the sound of the enemies' firearms. His people tried to make him go back, and they too fired, so that Matshana might have an opportunity of escaping. So he mounted and rode off, but all his force died, only Noju and another were left.[16]

Trooper Symons was among the first to see Matshana and his men emerge into the basin above the waterfall. As the Carbineers moved forward along the track towards Qhudeni, Symons had seen the NNC off to his left 'advancing up the mountain side' but soon lost sight of them as the mounted men passed along the southern foot of Mdutshana. The Volunteers were moving down into the basin above the Mangeni waterfall when someone suddenly spotted a party of Zulus off to the right. After the tension of the night, Major Dartnell gave way to a sudden burst of exuberance, and according to Fred Symons

> ... mounted his steed and before we were ready started off shouting 'Come on boys!' and we followed at a gallop, best horses first. The

Zulus (about eighty) drew in line on a low ridge, shields to the front, as though meditating resistance but changed their minds and made for a high hill one side of which was precipitous and the other a grassy slope but steep. We echeloned to the left to prevent them from reaching the rocky heights but only managed to turn them onto the grassy side. Jack and I dismounted and opened fire on several who had turned half way up the mountain and were making for the caves. Each fired in turn so as to see where the bullets struck in order to get the range. My last shot got the range and Jack's next sent him rolling over the krantz.[17]

At that moment Captain Offy Shepstone rode up and upbraided the brothers for dismounting, and ordered them to join the others who were firing at the same group further off. One Zulu in particular had caught their attention – he was walking calmly up the hillside, studiously ignoring the bullets which struck the rocks all around him, and turning now and then to fire with his old percussion rifle:

It seemed cruel to fire at him, but no-one appeared to hit him. There was one boulder on the hill-side and he took cover behind this and aimed several times at us but his gun missed fire for we could hear the cap snap. He had a nice little rest and then stood up and walked away quietly over the brow of the hill amidst a shower of dust sent up by bullets. Whilst some of our fellows stood below firing[,] the Major and a few others rode up the mountain to try and intercept the enemy, but only succeeded in capturing one old man . . .[18]

The Zulus now took refuge among the crevices which lay between the boulders lying at the foot of a broken shelf of rock on the hillside. Like so many places in the iSandlwana saga, it is difficult now to be certain exactly where this was, but the south-western foot of Phindo hill remains the most likely, not least because this spot would have been clearly visible to the NNC advancing in a line across the summit of Magogo a few kilometres further west. The NNC had encountered no one on their move up the hill – 'a hard pull up, and no success in "finding ebony"', as Norris-Newman put it[19] – but Charlie Harford had noticed the abandoned campfires they had seen from a distance the night before, and had the uncomfortable feeling that that 'the few men that we had seen exposing themselves and moving about had only been left there to make us imagine that the place was occupied by a large force'.[20] There was no time to dwell on this, however, for suddenly Lieutenant Maxwell, on the right of the 2/3rd NNC line,

> ... heard firing in that direction, and saw about a mile off some natives, I should say about 400 or 500, coming over a *kopje*. They were running in all directions followed by the Carbineers, who appeared to be in skirmishing order. The enemy made for a kranz – or in other words a precipice in which there were caves. I passed the word down the line of skirmishers that the enemy was on my right and waited for orders. Commandant Lonsdale came galloping up and told me to intercept them in their rush for the caves. We endeavoured to do so but the enemy got to earth with few exceptions.[21]

As the 2nd Battalion was ordered to move rapidly down from Magogo to join the skirmishing at the foot of Phindo, the 1st Battalion was ordered to continue its sweep across the summit. According to Harford, the British positions were now widely scattered among the hills, and were beginning to lose touch with each other; he had already lost sight of both Lonsdale and Hamilton Browne, both of whom had apparently ridden off in pursuit of Zulu stragglers.

Nevertheless, Harford led the 2nd Battalion towards the caves and soon 'met with rather a strong reception, bullets began to rain down on us from all directions, and a few men were hit'.[22] The battalion's officers marshalled the men into a sheltered spot, then gave orders for different companies to work their way up to specified sectors in the jumble of rocks. Some of these proved to be very dangerous, with the Zulus well ensconced and commanding good fields of fire; in one place thirteen men of the NNC were shot one after another by Zulus hiding unseen in a large cleft between the boulders, roofed over with slabs of strata. Harford thought his men behaved remarkably well, it 'being day instead of night'.[23] Captain Davis and Lieutenant Maxwell managed to make their way among the boulders at the entrance to the cave and exchanged futile shots with those hiding in the darkness inside. Some of the NNC ventured onto the rocks above, but 'there were a few fissures on top which the enemy took advantage of by firing through'.[24] Maxwell then saw Harford come up, accompanied by Norris-Newman, 'a smart fellow but wary',[25] and clamber round onto the rocks above the cave:

> ... the correspondent standing out of harm's way a little distance off, begged of Captain Harford to come away or otherwise he would be shot. We had two or three pistol shots through these fissures, but I am

unable to say whether any damage was done. For a couple of hours we were employed in trying one way or another to induce those inside to come out. What success others may have had I cannot say, but those in the cave I and some of the Native Contingent were engaged at, took in a lot of promises. At last one ventured out and informed us there were six inside who were afraid to come out thinking they would be killed. I told him to return and tell the others to come and surrender and that they should be well treated. This native went in again with the message and there remained. Shortly after a NNC native venturing too far in the entrance of the cave was shot through the heart . . .[26]

Harford decided the place was too dangerous, and ordered the men to leave it and move on. Later someone brought up some brushwood in the hope of smoking the Zulus out, 'but this was put a stop to'. There were, in any case, other difficult positions to clear, and for the second time in a fortnight Harford found himself scrabbling among the rocks:

> At another place where several of us were being held up by snipers, I spotted a man at the entrance hole of a mass of large rock some twenty or thirty yards [18 or 27 metres] off taking a deliberate aim at me, and I quickly shot at him. I then went after him, and, crawling on all fours, found him badly wounded, with a dead Zulu lying close to him. It was a curious little den, quite lighted up through the aperture in the rocks, with space enough for four or five men, and on one side a natural shelf of flat rock much like a bunk on board ship, broad enough for a man to lie on.[27]

Norris-Newman also saw this second incident – no doubt again from a safe distance – and was suitably impressed, remarking that 'this officer did the same thing at Usirajo's strongholds, and would seem to have a charmed life. May he long keep it.'[28]

It had not taken long for *inkosi* Matshana to realize the true nature of the force he had blundered into. While his men had struck off towards the cover of Phindo, jeering and taunting the mounted men so as to distract them, Matshana himself had hurriedly mounted his horse and tried to gallop off towards a low rise to the east of Phindo which masked a steep drop on the far side. The sight of a solitary Zulu on horseback had attracted the attention of Offy Shepstone, who claimed to recognize him – it is hard to avoid the impression he was on the look-out for Matshana – and had set off in pursuit. It would, of course, have wiped out a long-standing family sore if Offy had done what his uncle John had failed to do twenty years before and captured him – but Matshana knew the country too well, and had lost little of the agility which had served him so well under similar circumstances in his youth in Natal. Dropping over the ridge, he had slipped out of his saddle, and scrambled off down the slope on foot. It had been impossible to follow him on horseback, and Shepstone had reined in, fuming, at the top before abandoning the chase and turning back to join his men.

Fred Symons' brother Jack had the honour of rounding up Matshana's black horse and bringing it back in triumph.

The Volunteers had had a few adventures of their own in the meantime:

> One Zulu ran down onto the flat across which we had ridden from Matshana's whither he was now making for, but Trooper Hayhow … rode after him and after a mile or two chase captured him and brought him back. Harry Pennefather also had an adventure while he was peering over the rocks. He heard a Zulu loading his gun preparatory to having a shot at Harry and the latter just saw it in time to get first shot and laid him low.[29]

With the NNC now trying to ferret the Zulus out of the Phindo caves, the Volunteers had been recalled and had stood down nearby. A Zulu prisoner taken in the caves had been passed into their care, and several of the men were feeling thirsty after the morning's excitement:

> Close to us was a tiny rill and feeling thirsty, Ted Greene and I and one or two others left the prisoner with some other Carbs and went down for a drink. An exclamation from the man who got there first of 'Hullo here's a shield' brought us to him and we noticed the water under the rock was muddy. So we knew a Zulu must be concealed beneath. We shouted to him to come out but he refused to come out until I told him the Natal Natives were approaching and from whom he would receive no quarter. This news had a magical effect on him and an immediate resurrection took place. Asked if any more were in hiding he pointed a little lower down and we told him to call them. On hearing his voice they came out at once and reached us just in time, for an NNC ran up and before we knew what he was about struck one of them a heavy blow in the back. I gave him a thump in the ribs with my carbine and told him if he touched my prisoner again I should put a bullet in him. He didn't appear to understand my behaviour and stood

with assegai poised about to stab the prisoner, but he soon saw we were
in earnest and moved off. I think Ted Greene's opinion of this splendid
body of men is on the back track . . .[30]

The Carbineers returned from the stream to find that the haul of prisoners
numbered nine men. One was an old man with a head-ring and a
demeanour Symons considered 'vicious' who carried an Enfield carbine
and a table knife, which were promptly removed from him. Another, by
contrast a 'fine looking' married man, was bleeding from a gunshot wound
in the leg, received during the skirmishing. The third was a 'cheeky' youth,
clothed incongruously in a fur coat, who refused to give up his weapons
but laughed at the idea – 'at first'.[31]

The prisoners were interrogated, but had nothing useful to tell. They
knew nothing of the whereabouts of the Zulu army, but said they 'had
heard the English were coming, and were on their way to see if it was
true'.[32]

*

After he had set the line to advance, Lord Chelmsford and his staff, with
Glyn and his officers trailing behind, had spent the morning riding north-
eastwards up the narrow valley which separates Magogo hill to the south
from Silutshana to the north. If Dartnell was to be believed, last night's
Zulus had gone in this direction, and Chelmsford was hoping that he might
catch sight of them ahead if they broke cover to flee the NNC sweeping
across Magogo on his right. Chelmsford was accompanied by the Mounted
Infantry, and two companies of the 24th and Brevet Lieutenant-Colonel
Harness's guns had been ordered to follow him. As soon as these left the
relative comfort of the track, however, they found the going heavy, and
the guns in particular lagged behind.

At the far end, the valley rises to a narrow *nek* between the two hills,
and here, at the top, Chelmsford ordered a halt. In front of him the country
opened up, dropping away below the *nek* in a grassy swathe, then rising
again towards Phindo, slightly to Chelmsford's right front 3 or 4 kilometres
away. From his vantage point Chelmsford could clearly see the NNC
advance to engage the Zulus hidden in the Phindo caves. Further off, to his
left front and about 10 kilometres away, lay the isolated bulk of Siphezi
mountain. Parties of Zulus could be seen hurrying across the plain towards
Siphezi, but they soon disappeared into folds in the ground.

It was now mid-morning, and despite his troops scouring a wide area, Chelmsford still had no very clear impression of Zulu intentions, or even their numbers. As he watched through his field glasses, he could see some emerging onto the foot of Siphezi, and apparently rallying there. Was the skirmishing at Phindo a rearguard action? Were these men the forerunners of the main army he was expecting, or simply locals, fleeing before his advance? In order to find out, Chelmsford dispatched his Mounted Infantry escort down into the valley below.

The Mounted Infantry were commanded by Lieutenant-Colonel John Russell, whom Chelmsford had kept close to him after Russell's spat with the Natal Volunteer Corps at the start of the campaign. They had already learned a proper degree of respect for their enemy after the incident the day before when Lieutenant Browne's patrol had been fired upon in the more open country to the north of Silutshana, and Russell was clearly wary of being lured too far away from Chelmsford's supports. He led his men down the slope ahead, turning left along the foot of Silutshana and into the plain beyond. Here they turned out several parties of Zulus who promptly broke cover and made off at a run towards Siphezi. Russell turned to give chase, but after a kilometre or two began to feel concerned that his men might be in danger of falling into a trap:

> This hill was covered with the enemy in very large numbers and we saw the spoor in the valley where their masses had come down from the hills where they had been in front of the General that morning. This valley is about four miles [6.4 kilometres] long and terminated in a high neck [sic] from which there is a rapid slope to a very broken country in which we could not recognise any tracks or landmarks. Instead of entering an unknown bit of country, therefore, and allowing my retreat to be cut off – I retired down the [Siphezi] valley again, and decided to try and rejoin the General. A good many of the natives came down from the hill, and commenced firing at us, but a long way off.[33]

When Russell reached the foot of Silutshana again, far away from any Zulu threat, he allowed his men to halt for an hour to rest. The sun was now high overhead, and it was getting very hot.

Having watched Russell start off on his ride, Chelmsford had then decided to break for breakfast. This was a far cry from the luxurious picnic of cinematic myth – Monsieur Laparra had been left in the camp at iSandlwana, and there were no wagons on hand with fine porcelain and silver cutlery – and Chelmsford and Glyn and their staffs had to make do with whatever provisions and foldaway camping utensils they had brought with them in their saddlebags. Chelmsford used the time to mull over his strategy. It seemed clear now that the danger Dartnell had discerned in the dusk the night before had been overestimated; there were no obvious signs of any Zulu concentration in the sort of strength Chelmsford expected from King Cetshwayo's main army. Yet the scenario envisaged by Fynn did not seem entirely spurious, for there was no doubt that the local *amakhosi* were gathering on the Mangeni–Qhudeni line, and that if he continued to follow his original line of advance – from iSandlwana to Siphezi and then Babanango – he would be leaving a hostile force on his flank. Chelmsford had already considered diverting his advance to the right, veering south-west towards Qhudeni to ensure that 'the two Matyanas' – Matshana kaSitshakuza and Matshana kaMondise – were properly suppressed, and the morning's actions seemed to confirm the wisdom of the idea. There was little point now in ordering the force all the way back to iSandlwana, only to pack up camp and return to the same spot; instead, he decided that after breakfast he would concentrate his scattered forces in the Mangeni basin, above the head of the gorge, and send word back for the camp garrison to pack up the baggage and advance to join him. Given the difficulties of the road and the fact that it was already past noon it was unlikely the wagons would reach him before nightfall, and the troops would have to be prepared to bivouac in the open. As more than half the force had already left the camp, however, and there might be a shortage of the hard labour necessary to pack up the tents and equipment at iSandlwana quickly, Chelmsford decided to order the 1st Battalion of the NNC back to camp immediately.

These had spent much of the morning searching Magogo, and had just descended to join the 2nd Battalion in the skirmishing at the foot of Phindo when Chelmsford's order reached them. The change of plan did nothing to assuage Hamilton Browne's prevailing mood of exasperation:

> I was just going to try and kick a charge out of my beauties, when a mounted orderly rode up with orders for me, which were that I was at once to report myself with my battalion to the General, and that he was to guide me to the place where the General was waiting for me.
>
> Getting my men together and advising Lonsdale of my orders, I

requested him to take over my skirmish, and on his relieving me with the 2nd Battalion I moved down a valley and found the General and staff quietly at breakfast.

Never shall I forget the sight of that peaceful picnic. Here were the staff quietly breakfasting and the whole command scattered over the country. Over there the guns unlimbered, over the hills parties of Mounted Infantry and volunteers looting the scattered kraals for grain for their horses, a company of the 24th one place, and another far away . . .

As soon as I halted my men, the General rose and kindly greeted me asking if I had had any breakfast. I replied, 'No, nor had any of my men had any.' I might have added 'and no dinner or supper the night before'. Of course he understood that, as commandant, I could not eat in the fasting presence of my men.

I said 'Are you aware, sir, I was engaged when I received your order?' He said 'No', then turning to the CSO [Commander's Staff Officer] said 'Crealock, Browne tells me he was engaged when he received the order to come here.' Colonel Crealock came to me and said 'Commandant Browne, I want you to return at once to camp and assist Colonel Pulleine to strike camp and come on here.' I nearly fell off my horse . . . However I was only a poor devil of a Colonial Commandant and as a simple irregular not supposed to criticise full-blown staff officers, so I saluted and said, 'If I come across the enemy?' 'Oh', he said, 'just brush them aside and go on,' and with that he went on with his breakfast . . .[34]

It had been a remark couched in Crealock's usual flippant manner, yet it reflected a general assumption prevailing among the staff: after the passage backwards and forwards of so many troops across the plain towards iSandlwana during the previous twenty-four hours, there seemed no risk of there being any major Zulu presence behind them.

Hamilton Browne had just returned to his men to prepare them for the eturn march when a solitary dispatch rider cantered up the valley from the direction of iSandlwana. He had a message from the camp which he handed to Captain Hallam Parr; Hallam Parr scribbled the time of receipt upon it – 9.30 a.m. – then handed it to Clery. Clery should, of course, have taken it to Glyn, as column commander, but he was clearly getting tired of following protocol, and took it directly to Chelmsford himself. The contents of the note were nothing if not enigmatic: 'Staff Officer. Report just come in that the Zulus are advancing in Force from the left front of the Camp. 8.5 a.m. H.B. Pulleine, Lt. Col.'[35]

According to Clery, Chelmsford received this report with a calm bordering on indifference:

> He returned it to me without a word. I said, 'What is to be done on this report?' He said, 'There is nothing to be done on that.' So I took myself off and only then showed it to Colonel Glyn ... I said nothing more; but the fact is that, whether from overwork or other causes, the general has got rather irritable since we knew him and particularly touchy about suggestions being made to him. So the general gave some directions about following up the people we had been engaged with and turned his glass on the camp which we could plainly see, though 12 miles [19 kilometres] off.[36]

When the rider had delivered his dispatch, however, he returned past A and C Companies of the 2/24th, which had been moving up the valley in Chelmsford's wake and had taken advantage of the general's halt to take a rest themselves. Whatever he said to them gave the impression that something distinctly more exciting was happening at iSandlwana:

> About 9 a.m. a mounted police orderly rode up to where the general stood and delivered a despatch; having done which and answered a few questions, he rode off to where the two companies 2nd Battalion 24th were resting, and began talking to the men. Colonel Degacher noticing that the news he communicated to them caused great excitement, asked the cause, and was told: 'He says "sir, that the camp is being surrounded and attacked!"' This was startling intelligence; but as there was no stir among the staff or sign of anything unusual, the men were told not to let the police orderly chaff them, as, if true, 'We should all be marching back as fast as we could.' The men, however, were much impressed, believing that the orderly on his way had seen much more than was reported in the despatch ...[37]

Yet perhaps, after his experiences that morning, Chelmsford can be forgiven for not over-reacting to further reports of mysterious Zulu movements. Clery had, after all, said, 'Nobody from the general downwards had the least suspicion that there was a chance of the camp being attacked.'[38] And an entire battalion of NNC was, after all, about to start back across the plain.

From their position in the valley between Magogo and Silutshana, moreover, the staff could see iSandlwana in the distance. The hill itself can be curiously obscure from that angle, its distinctive outline sunk below the Biggarsberg horizon beyond and the contours blurred by the heat haze coming off the plain. A white smudge suggested that the tents were still in place, but to be certain Chelmsford ordered his Naval ADC, Lieutenant Milne, to scramble up the side of Magogo and try to get a better look with a powerful Navy telescope.

At twenty-three years old, Milne had curiously 1920s film star good looks – a rather smouldering manner in his portraits, and a dashing centre parting – which no doubt helped early on to shape his enjoyment of high-born female company. He had a number of influential contacts in royal circles, which would lead to his appointment in the 1890s as commander of the royal yacht *Osborne*, and to the friendship of Edward VII and Queen Alexandra who called him 'Arky-Barky'.

Bounding and keen in 1879,[39] Milne picked his way up the steep shoulder of Magogo as quickly as he could, and found a comfortable spot on which to perch – if local legend is to be believed, a large sloping rock shaded from the sun by a solitary kiepersol tree.[40] It was a spot which gave him a good view both backwards and forwards, up and down the valley, towards iSandlwana in the west and Siphezi in the east. Yet he was by no means on open ground; he was below the summit of Magogo, and the mass of Silutshana blocked his view to the north entirely. Indeed, although he could see iSandlwana clearly enough, the flanks of Silutshana blocked out the iNyoni escarpment. It was the best view he could find, however, and he had to make of it what he could, and his report suggests that he was rather more interested in what was going on in front than in the rear:

On reaching the summit [sic] I could see the camp; all the cattle had been driven in close around the tents, I could see nothing of the enemy on the left. The main body of the enemy who had been on our front all morning, were now assembled at the foot of the [Siphezi] hill, watching the movements of the Mounted Infantry, who were scouring the plain some short distance off, but on their approach they all retreated to the table-land on top of the [Siphezi] mountain.

I also saw small clusters of the enemy on every hilltop around us, observing our movements. Distinct firing was heard at small intervals in the direction of the Mounted Police.[41]

It is difficult to say exactly when Milne began to observe the camp at iSandlwana, and for how long. If he set off after Chelmsford received Pulleine's note, he must have arrived at his vantage point at about 10 a.m., and may have stayed for an hour. As the heat began slowly building the morning became 'intensely hot',[42] the grassland at the foot of the hill rippling in the rising haze. The white streak of the tents stood out clearly enough; for the rest, there was nothing more than a series of dark smudges which Milne took to be cattle. Later, he would be troubled by whether he had misinterpreted the significance of those smudges, yet in fact he could not have concluded more than he did, for whatever was happening then at iSandlwana, it was occurring on the ridges to the north, beyond his line of vision – and it was but a curtain-raiser, for the main event had yet to begin.

Even so, Milne's report was to have a significant impact on the day's events. As Clery had suggested, Pulleine's note had included nothing to challenge the staff's underlying assumption that the camp had been left secure; with its vague description of Zulu movements nearby, it had conveyed no sense of urgency, and certainly not of menace or vulnerability. Chelmsford had sent Milne up his hill seeking signs of normality to re-assure himself that everything was indeed as he left it – and in that snapshot of the tents standing peacefully in their rows, Milne had given him just that.

Curiously, at about this time – between 11 and 11.30 a.m. – a similar report reached Colonel Russell and his Mounted Infantry. After retiring from the direction of Siphezi, Russell had halted at the northern foot of Silutshana to allow his men and horses to rest and – as Milne had observed – to forage. While they were there a solitary European NCO from the NNC had appeared. Not knowing exactly where Chelmsford had gone, this man seems to have struck out along the old intended route of advance, heading directly east – and Russell's party were the first he encountered. He asked if Russell knew where Lord Chelmsford was; he had been sent, he explained, to tell the general that the camp was under attack. Russell seems to have taken his report in his stride, and if he asked for details of who sent this man or for a further explanation, his report doesn't mention it. Probably, as the man was not a fellow Regular, he did not take it too seriously. He pointed the messenger towards the *nek* between Silutshana and Magogo where he had last seen Lord Chelmsford, and the man rode off. Russell later admitted that he had thought him too frightened to go alone, and that he had probably given up his quest – and he may have been right.

It was now late morning, and Russell had received no further instructions from Lord Chelmsford. Not at all clear what was expected of him, he ordered his men to move 'quietly along the outside of the hills', round the northern edge of Silutshana, heading west, while he rode off to try and find Chelmsford. In that he had no luck, and when he returned to his squadron several of his men told him that they had heard the sound of distant cannon fire. Shortly after this another messenger arrived from the camp, carrying much the same message as the earlier one. Now rather concerned, Russell sent off Lieutenants Walsh and Davey, each with a small escort, to try and find Chelmsford 'and give him the information which we had received'.[43]

Where had Chelmsford gone? Soon after Milne had returned from Magogo, and realizing that it would be some hours before Hamilton Browne's NNC got back to camp on foot, he decided to send Captain Alan Gardner, a special service officer from the 14th Hussars attached to Glyn as a staff officer, back to iSandlwana with, according to Gardner, an order addressed to Pulleine 'that the camp ... was to be struck and sent on immediately, also rations and forage for about seven days'.[44] Second Lieutenant Thomas Griffith of the 2/24th, who was 'doing duty as a commissariat officer', was also ordered to return 'to make the necessary arrangements' and it occurred to Lieutenant and Adjutant Henry Dyer, 2/24th, that since

> ... the men had been called up at 1.30 a.m. on an intensely dark night, and as no lights were allowed to be struck, all their small belongings, of such comfort to a soldier campaigning, were of necessity scattered about the tents. They had brought with them only their ball-bags, haversacks and water-bottles; and to collect and pack all the articles left behind in the camp – the equipment of a battalion – there were only one company on piquet and a few stray men. Whilst discussing how the order was to be carried out with as little confusion and loss to the men as possible, Lieutenant and Adjutant Dyer ... remarked that he had perhaps better ride back with Lieutenant Griffith and help the quartermaster.[45]

Griffith, 'a young officer, thoughtful beyond his years', was no doubt glad of Dyer's company, for something in the atmosphere, and in Pulleine's dispatch to Chelmsford, had given him a sense of foreboding, and he 'took a gloomy view of matters' as they set off.[46] It is not clear whether the two 24th officers left with Gardner, or caught up with him along the road, but by the time they arrived at iSandlwana they had been joined by two more officers, both of whom had decided to return to attend to the affairs of their own units. Lieutenant Francis MacDowel of No. 7 Company Royal Engineers was the senior Royal Engineer with the Centre Column, and the news that the camp was to be brought forward made it necessary for him to return, not merely to pack up the Royal Engineers' equipment but to supervise anticipated work on the road in front of the camp, and to see whether the detachments from No. 5 Company, which Chelmsford had asked to be sent forward from Greytown, had arrived yet. A few kilometres along the road, as the party passed some of the guns from N/5 Battery, still struggling through the *dongas* at the foot of Hlazakazi, Major Stuart Smith decided to join them, as the battery equipment and reserve ammunition were also in the camp.

It was now approaching noon, and Chelmsford's force was very scattered indeed. After he had left his breakfast spot, the general had ridden east over the shoulders of Magogo to descend towards Siphezi on the far side, where the 2/3rd NNC were still engaged in desultory skirmishing on the slopes of Phindo. The two companies of the 2/24th, A and C, followed him on foot, but arrived too late to take part, much to their disgust. Two more infantry companies – D and E – were still struggling up the valley, while another two, F and H, were still on the road, escorting Harness's struggling guns. At least 8 kilometres separated Chelmsford's mounted detachments – the Mounted Infantry, resting at the foot of Silutshana to the north, and the Volunteers off-saddled below Phindo in the south, while Hamilton Browne's battalion was already on the road back to iSandlwana.

If nothing else, this suggests that Chelmsford had abandoned by this point any real hope of fighting a major engagement against the main Zulu army in the Mangeni hills – if he had, even he must have realized that he was in the greatest danger of being destroyed piecemeal. It was hardly a satisfactory morning's work – the Volunteers had claimed about sixty Zulu casualties between them, together with a handful of prisoners, but an unknown number of NNC had been killed, and it was difficult to see what military objective had been achieved. And while Offy Shepstone was adamant that he had chased *inkosi* Matshana himself, all the Carbineers had to show for it was a captured horse.

At about 1 p.m. Chelmsford accepted the inevitable and ordered that his command assemble in the basin above the Mangeni falls, where he intended to establish the new camp.

Below Phindo, Fred Symons was relieved at the chance the apparent lull in the skirmishing afforded for the mounted men to rest and breakfast:

> We had off-saddled near the stream and those who had tea made it and shared it with those who had none, and so it should be with comrades ... All I had to eat that day was part of the contents of a 1lb tin of salmon and I thought I should never care to taste the fish again. Tinned fish on an empty stomach is not good. It must have been about 12 or one o'clock when I went out to relieve the first guard and had not been long before the low boom of a canon [sic] reached my ear, a second and a third followed. I drew my mate's (Harry Stirton) attention to the sounds. Those three interruptions to the guard kept running in my mind and I had a presentiment that something was going to happen either to us or those at the tents and I chafed inwardly as I walked to and fro listening to the guns at Isandhlwana ... .[47]

At about the same time, Lieutenant-Colonel Russell, still trying to find Chelmsford, came upon Harness's guns and two companies of the 24th. Harness had managed to get his teams back on the road and was heading towards Mangeni, but Russell found that he had just received an extraordinary report from a messenger sent by Hamilton Browne. According to Harness, this stated that 'the camp was surrounded by Zulus and, unless it had assistance, must be taken'[48] – and its tone was urgent enough that Harness suggested returning to iSandlwana.

# 19

# 'We commence work in earnest'

## iSandlwana, dawn, 22 January 1879

Anthony Durnford had arrived at Rorke's Drift at the head of his column on the afternoon of the 20th. He had, typically enough, pushed his men hard on the march, but that evening the water in the Mzinyathi was low enough to cross without incident, and there was no point in remaining on the Natal bank so he decided to cross immediately – it was impossible to say when the river might rise again, and there was nothing to be gained by being trapped on the wrong side should he be needed by Chelmsford in a hurry. Nevertheless, it was dark before the last of his wagons had been brought over and his camp established on the Zulu bank.

Now that they were on Zulu territory, a sense of excitement and tension pervaded his command. Wyatt Vause, 25-year-old son of the Mayor of Durban and commander of No. 3 troop of the amaNgwane Horse, wrote to a friend that night that 'we . . . commence work in earnest now'.[1] Walter Stafford, a transport rider who had been lured into the 1st NNC by George Shepstone's promise of fifteen shillings a day and a farm in Zululand once the war was over, remembered that night vividly:

> I was ordered to place a picket, and after having done so was summoned to the Colonel's tent. Colonel Durnford, and Shepstone, and Tom, the Colonel's cook, were present, and I was surprised to see Lieut. 'Wally' Erskine, who was on picket duty, in the tent.
>
> Col. Durnford informed me that the Native picket in Lieut. Erskine's charge had refused to remain at their post. Although this news was disagreeable, it was not altogether a surprise to one who had been brought up among the Natal natives. The names of Chaka and Cetewayo were terrifying to the poor devils, for as far as they could remember, the Native women had used these names to frighten their children when they became unruly, and they had never been allowed to forget the mighty deeds performed by the Zulu armies . . .

After placing Lieut. Andrews in charge of a fresh picket, the rest of the evening was spent over a game of cards. The popular games in those days were 'twenty-five' and 'all fours'. A chap by the name of Lieut. Black, who had not long been out in this country, was one of the losers, and I remember this officer staking his 'farm in Zululand' against his opponent's prospective piece of ground. I jokingly told him that the only plot of ground he would ever get in Zululand would be one measuring six feet by three . . .[2]

The column stood to at 3 a.m. the following day, 'armed to the teeth', according to Vause, 'waiting for the Zulus to attack us',[3] but the dawn of the 21st offered no prospect of imminent excitement, and instead the camp fell in to its routine duties.

Energetic and impatient, Durnford took the opportunity at first light on the 22nd to ride up the road to Helpmekaar. He intended to visit the local farming community in the hope of persuading them to release more of their wagons to increase the supply of military transport. It is unclear why he needed new wagons – perhaps some were showing the strain of the recent hard march – but in any case it was likely to be a forlorn mission, for most of the Biggarsberg settlers had already parted with those wagons they were willing to risk in Zululand, even at exorbitant rates of hire, and guarded jealously those that remained.

As it happened, Durnford's powers of persuasion would not be put to the test as Smith-Dorrien arrived in the camp a few hours later and delivered his dispatch to George Shepstone. Shepstone read it, and sent a rider on to locate Durnford. Whether he drew an inference of urgency from the orders, or whether he simply knew that Durnford would want to act on them immediately, Shepstone ordered the column to pack up the tents and be ready to move forward as soon as the colonel rejoined them.

William Cochrane was close to Durnford when the dispatch caught up with him. Cochrane did not see the contents, but since the exact wording was to prove controversial later, it is worth noting – and how Durnford seemed to interpret the dispatch when he first read it. The note had been written by Crealock at Chelmsford's behest:

22nd, Wednesday, 2 a.m.
    You are to march to this camp at once with all the force you have with you of No. 2 Column.

> Major Bengough's battalion is to move to Rorke's Drift as ordered
> yesterday. 2/24th, Artillery and mounted men with the General and
> Colonel Glyn move off at once to attack a Zulu force about 10 miles
> [16 kilometres] distant.
>     J.N.C.
>     If Bengough's battalion has crossed the River at Eland's Kraal it is to
> move up here (Nangwane Valley).[4]

It is significant that the order made no reference whatever to Durnford's
intended role once he reached iSandlwana, and yet was entirely consistent
with Chelmsford's recent suggestion that his column was to be deployed to
support the action against Matshana. The postscript, too, is worthy of note:
the 2nd Battalion 1st NNC, commanded by Major Harcourt Bengough,
had been trailing in Durnford's wake, and had got no further than the
Sandspruit. Chelmsford was aware of this – George Shepstone had kept
him informed – and had recently ordered it to strike across country
towards the Mzinyathi at Eland's Kraal, a route which would have brought
the battalion into Zululand at the confluence of the Mzinyathi with the
Mangeni. Such a move would have supported Dartnell's reconnaissance on
the 21st nicely, but in fact Bengough did not receive the order in time, and
did not reach the river until the morning of the 22nd, too late, too, for
Chelmsford's latest countermand to reach him.

Cochrane was at pains later to point out that he did not read Chelmsford's order himself, but noted Durnford's reaction to it: 'I was with
Colonel Durnford, and he remarked to me, "Just what I thought, we are to
proceed at once to Isandhlwana. There is an *impi* about eight miles from
the camp, which the General moves out to attack at daybreak." He returned
to Rorke's Drift camp at once . . .'[5]

Certainly, the restless energy with which Durnford applied himself now
to moving his column forward suggests a relief that the uncertainties of the
previous fortnight appeared to be resolved. His column was in fact a highly
mobile one, for apart from two companies escorting the rocket battery, he
was missing most of his NNC infantry and was left with the rocket battery
and his mounted men, all of whom soon saddled up and were on the road
by about 8 a.m., leaving their wagons, loaded with tents, ammunition and
supplies, still at the drift.

The routine work of seeing them safely to iSandlwana should have fallen
to Cochrane, but it was the first time in his career that he stood a chance

of seeing any action, and he was anxious to get to the front, and Durnford had taken pity on him; 'My orders were to see all the wagons in spanned, start them all off, and hand them over to Conductor McCarthy, and then join Colonel Durnford . . .'[6]

Durnford had made good progress along the road, and had almost reached iSandlwana before Cochrane caught up with him. The horsemen had just crossed the Manzimnyama stream and were winding up the slope on the far side when a solitary officer came riding in the opposite direction. He was a fellow Royal Engineer, Lieutenant John Chard, and he had an interesting story to tell.

Chard was the officer who had been sent ahead of his company, No. 5 Field Company, which was still labouring on the road from Greytown, in response to Chelmsford's request that trained personnel be sent forward as quickly as possible to work the ponts at Rorke's Drift. He had arrived with a Royal Engineers' light wagon full of equipment at the head of a detachment of five sappers on the 19th.[7] They had pitched their tents close to the drift, and had spent the intervening days repairing the over-worked pont. That morning, however, Chard had received an order that his sappers were required at the camp; not sure whether his own presence was needed or not, he had loaded his men into the wagon and set off on horseback with them to iSandlwana. The wagon had made slow progress, and Chard had ridden ahead. On reporting to the headquarters tent, he was told that only his men were needed – presumably to begin work on the difficult crossing in front of the camp which had delayed Chelmsford's departure during the night – and that he was to remain at the drift.[8]

Just as he was about to set off, however, a report came in that there was a Zulu presence on the iNyoni heights to the north of the camp. Chard borrowed a field glass from an NCO of the 24th – it was, he admitted, better than his own – and could plainly see large numbers of Zulus on the hills. They seemed to be moving round to the left, above iSandlwana, and it occurred to Chard that they might be 'going to make a dash at the ponts'.[9] This set him hurrying on his way, but he had not gone far when he met Durnford coming the other way. Chard told him what he had seen, then rode on, telling Durnford's men too as he passed them about the Zulus, at Durnford's request.

A little further on he came to his own men riding in their wagon, and he ordered them to get out, and follow Durnford's men into the camp on foot while he returned with the equipment and Driver Robson to Rorke's Drift.

*

After he had delivered his dispatches to George Shepstone at dawn on the 22nd, Horace Smith-Dorrien had crossed the river and busied himself with routine transport duties but soon found himself at a loose end. His empty wagons were still at iSandlwana, and would not arrive that day; he was not privy to the grand decisions of Chelmsford's strategy, but the general's early morning departure clearly portended something, as did the speed with which Durnford had broken up his camp on the Zulu bank and set off down the road. And if something exciting was brewing, it was far more likely to occur at iSandlwana than on the wrong side of the border at Rorke's Drift. He made up his mind to return to iSandlwana.

Before he left, however, he went up to the mission station, where a solitary company of white troops – B Company, 2/24th – and one of the NNC had been posted to guard the stores his wagons were due to collect. Worried, perhaps, after his night ride that he might be vulnerable on the road riding alone, Smith-Dorrien went to the company commander, Lieutenant Gonville 'Gunny' Bromhead,[10] and asked him if there was a supply of Government-issue revolver ammunition at the post. It seems not, for the best Bromhead could offer him was eleven loose rounds from his own stock. Smith-Dorrien took it gladly, and set off across the river again. He passed Durnford's wagons on the road, and got into the camp without incident just after Durnford and his column of mounted men had arrived.

*

After the advance column under Chelmsford's command had left, the garrison at the camp at iSandlwana had prepared for a day of routine duties. The departure had highlighted problems with the road ahead, as the guns struggled to cross the Nyogane *donga* in the dark. Once it was first light, Quartermaster Edward Bloomfield of the 2/24th, tasked with loading the battalion's reserve ammunition, ready to be dispatched should Chelmsford send for it, went down to look at the road, and was concerned by what he found, although Nevill Coghill did not take his reservations too seriously. In a note scribbled that morning to Clery, Coghill wrote:

Dear Major

Bloomfield QrMaster came to me just now with his finger in his mouth saying the light spring waggon would not hold the 2,000 rations [ammunition?] so I have requisitioned a larger one from the M.I. There was no escort so I sent down to the 1/24th to know if they could provide one. I was waiting for an answer when Pugh came and told me you had sent an order to the same effect.

I do not think any waggon can cross the last donga near the Kraal. Perhaps waggon and escort could take advantage of the stone cattle kraal, pulling down the huts and wait til the NNC come for their rations.

Yours,

Nevill J.A. Coghill[11]

As things turned out, this was probably the last note Coghill wrote. A fatigue party of the 1/24th under Lieutenant Edgar Anstey was sent out to improve the road.

The camp had been left under the command of forty-year-old Lieutenant-Colonel Henry Burmester Pulleine of the 1/24th. Although he is a pivotal figure in the events that followed, Pulleine remains a shadowy one whose personality evoked little comment among his contemporaries – perhaps because, despite more than twenty years with the 24th, he had spent most of his recent service on detached duties. A Yorkshireman, the son of a parson and grandson of a colonel in the Scots Greys, Pulleine had passed through Sandhurst and in 1855 had been gazetted into the 30th Regiment. Three years later he had joined the 2/24th – just then being raised – and had served with it in Mauritius, Burma and India before purchasing his rank as major in the 1st Battalion in 1871. He had done service with it in Malta, Gibraltar and at the Cape, where he had been given his brevet lieutenant-colonelcy in 1877. During that time he had earned a high reputation as an efficient administrator, but his career had coincided with a particularly bloodless period in the 24th's history, and it was only with the outbreak of the Cape Frontier Wars in 1877 that he had seen active service. Even then, he had not exercised command in a major engagement, but instead been detached from regimental duties to help raise two Irregular corps. One of these, raised with Lieutenant Fred Carrington of his battalion, was the Frontier Light Horse, which was to earn an enviable reputation both at the Cape and later in Zululand; the other was an infantry unit known as Pulleine's Rangers. The Rangers were recruited from the dross of settler society and proved almost as much trouble as they were worth; Hamilton Browne had served with them for a while – during which time they had mostly been employed building roads – and nick-named them with heavy sarcasm 'Pulleine's Lambs'. While it is perfectly possible that Pulleine had, during his time on the frontier, heard the odd shot fired in anger, he had certainly not exercised command in a major engagement, nor had he been present during his own battalion's extensive operations there. With the end of hostilities, the 1/24th were sent to Natal, where Pulleine occupied a series of important administrative posts. On the outbreak of war on 11 January 1879, however, he had begged Chelmsford to be allowed to rejoin his regiment on active service, and when this was granted had rejoined the 1st Battalion.

Pulleine's personality remains elusive – which is a pity, since it would be useful to know more of what he thought. In the best known of his portraits he seems to epitomize the ideal of the self-made Victorian man, staring confidently off to one side and sporting a pair of well-groomed mutton-chop whiskers. It comes as something of a surprise, then, to see him in group photos where he appears rather below average height, and in at least one sports a forage-cap at a buoyantly jaunty angle. Zealous, thorough, energetic – all adjectives applied at times to Pulleine by his superiors – yet his fellow officers in the battalion left few impressions of his character and manner. One exception is an odd remark by Mrs Glyn, after his death; she must have known him well in the regimental family, and after iSandlwana suggested he might have willingly escaped the bloodletting, and 'would be found behind a wagon-wheel or a large stone'.[12] There could be no more serious imputation against the reputation of any Victorian Army officer, and why she said it remains a mystery – certainly nothing has emerged to justify it. Perhaps to Mrs Glyn, Pulleine's administrative posts made him pall in contrast with his more glamorous front line fellow officers.

With Glyn out of camp with Chelmsford, Pulleine had assumed com-mand at iSandlwana as the senior officer. The core of his command was, inevitably, his own 1/24th Battalion, but it was by no means at full strength. The battalion had marched to Zululand by companies, and two (D and G) had only recently reached Helpmekaar, while another – B – had been left to garrison southern Natal. Captain Mostyn's F Company had finally caught up with the column on the 20th as it advanced from Rorke's Drift. It had not been possible to bring all the wagons into the camp that day, however, and they had been left overnight by the Manzimnyama drift while Mostyn's company bivouacked with the rearguard. It had only marched into iSandlwana on the 21st. The men were in high spirits – 'Thank goodness', Mostyn said, 'here we are at last.'[13]

Even with Mostyn's F Company, the battalion only numbered its headquarters and five companies – less than 450 officers and men. Apart from Pulleine, the officers were William Degacher (acting Major); Lieutenant and Adjutant Melvill; Captain Mostyn and Lieutenants Anstey and Daly (all F Company); Captain Cavaye and Second Lieutenant Dyson (E Company); Captain Wardell and Lieutenant Atkinson (H Company); Captain Younghusband and Lieutenant Hodson (C Company); Lieutenant Porteous (A Company); Paymaster (Honorary Major) White and Quartermaster Pullen. Nevill Coghill, Glyn's orderly officer, had also of course been left behind, but it should be noted that all the battalion's companies were significantly below full strength.

Also in camp was G Company, 2/24th, under Lieutenants Pope and Godwin-Austen. G Company had been on picket duty overnight, and was due to be relieved at first light by H Company, but H had marched out with Chelmsford. There were also a large number of unattached men of the 2/24th in the camp, also under Pope's command, giving him 173 in his charge in all.

In addition to the infantry, Pulleine had Lieutenant Curling's section of two 7-pdr guns from Harness's N/5 Battery. There were about seventy gunners in the camp, considerably more than just the crews of Curling's guns; the duties of the rest reflected the wide range of rear echelon personnel necessary to support a battery in the field – farriers, shoeing smiths, collar-makers and wheelers. To provide mounted outposts, thirty men of No. 1 Squadron Mounted Infantry had been left in the camp, together with just over one hundred Volunteers and Mounted Police. These fell under the command of the senior Volunteer officer, Captain Robert Bradstreet of the Newcastle Mounted Rifles.

Four companies of the 3rd NNC had also been left in the camp to provide pickets – two from each battalion, Nos. 6 and 9 from the 1st and Nos. 4 and 5 from the 2nd. The 2nd Battalion companies were both amaChunu, Pakhade's men, and Pakhade's heir and representative, Gabangaye, had remained in camp with them. No. 6 Company were amaBhele, but No. 9 were all Zulus, iziGqoza, and, despite the fact that the remaining iziGqoza were out with Chelmsford, their leader, Prince Sikhotha, had also remained in the camp. Altogether Pulleine had about 1,200 black and white troops to guard the camp – more than enough, it was felt, for anything the Zulus might throw at it.

One of the first duties of the day was to rotate the pickets and outposts. Since the column had been established at iSandlwana, an efficient system of pickets and outposts had been developed. By day mounted men patrolled an arc about 5 kilometres in front of the camp, while a screen of sentries on foot was established closer, about 2.5 kilometres from the camp.[14] At night the mounted vedettes were withdrawn, and the infantry pickets moved closer to the camp, about a kilometre away. These sentries were also posted in the Manzimnyama valley, behind iSandlwana, and each unit was responsible for a specified sector. The NNC covered the rear and northern approaches, swinging round to the front of the camp where they were replaced by the 2/24th, and ending with the 1/24th who extended as far as the foot of the Mahlabamkhosi ridge to the south. Extra outposts were placed on obvious vantage points; during daylight an NNC picket occupied the amaTutshane 'conical hill', although it was withdrawn closer to the camp at night. To the north, an old foot track extended from iSandlwana up onto a spur of the iNyoni ridge, and as this was considered a vulnerable spot – the easiest line of approach from the north – a picket was placed both day and night on Mkwene hill, a high point on the escarpment a few hundred metres beyond which overlooked it.

The departure of Chelmsford's column had to some extent disrupted the routine that morning. The 24th pickets were recalled into the camp shortly after first light but no reliefs were sent out to replace the NNC companies. Captain James Lonsdale's No. 9 Company, 1/3rd, had only been on duty overnight, and was stationed on a rocky rise between the Mpofana and Nyogane *dongas*, directly in front of the camp, but Captain Barry's No. 5 Company, 2/3rd, had occupied the Mkwene post since the column had arrived at iSandlwana thirty-six hours before. It was due to be relieved by Captain Krohn's No. 6 Company, 2/3rd, but while Krohn's men fell in early in front of the NNC bivouacs, they seemed in no hurry to go out onto the hills.

Nevertheless, at about 4 a.m. mounted detachments were sent out to provide a forward screen as usual, and it fell to the Natal Carbineers to post vedettes in pairs along the iNyoni ridge. Troopers Barker and Hawkins rode out and stationed themselves on iThusi, a high knoll on the edge of the escarpment about 4 kilometres from the camp. Their position was a commanding one, and gave them a good view across the undulating heights, along the edge of the escarpment as it began to curl away northwards, and across the plain to their right. Further west, on a slight knoll on the lip of the ridge, midway between the Mkwene and iThusi high-points, were stationed Trooper Whitelaw and another man. Lieutenant Durrant Scott had taken up a position somewhere to their rear, between them and the camp, possibly on the amaTutshane 'conical hill'.

Some time around 7 a.m. these outposts had been surprised to see parties of Zulus moving openly on the heights to the north.[15] No one seemed to form a very clear impression of where they came from – they simply appeared out of folds in the ground – or what their intentions were, as they made no direct attempt to attack the outpost. It seems that Barry's NNC noticed them first; Lieutenant Walter Higginson of Krohn's company was in the camp, and had just allowed his men to take their breakfasts when he saw Lieutenant Vereker of Barry's company ride in.[16] The news he brought clearly surprised Higginson, who was told that there were 'Zulus in sight in the plain close to [Barry] who had come close enough to speak to his men'.[17] Vereker went out again to rejoin his company, and as nothing could be seen from the low ground at the foot of iSandlwana an officer of Krohn's company, Lieutenant Gert Adendorff, was sent out to get a detailed report from Barry.

In the meantime, the Carbineer pickets further east had also seen them. On iThusi, Troopers Barker and Hawkins had not been in their positions for long when they noticed a party of horsemen in front of them. These came steadily closer until it was possible to recognize them as Zulus; Barker thought they were trying to surround them, and after signalling their presence to the camp they abandoned their position and fell back to Lieutenant Scott. After hearing their report, Scott had just decided to ride up to the lip of the escarpment himself when Trooper Whitelaw and his companion rode in. They reported that 'thousands' of Zulus had appeared and had come so close that they had been obliged to retire. Sure enough, as Scott and his party looked up towards the skyline, two Zulu parties suddenly appeared, one on iThusi, and the other in the centre of the iNyoni ridge; as they watched, a third party appeared and filled the gap between them. Curiously, the Zulus made no attempt to rush the pickets and did not open fire upon them. Scott sent Trooper Whitelaw back to the camp to report their presence; after a while he returned with orders that Scott should 'watch the enemy carefully and report their movements'.[18]

The appearance of the Zulus at the eastern end of the ridge would have been clear enough to Pulleine and the other officers in the camp, but when Lieutenant Adendorff returned from Barry's picket he was able to give no very clear description of the Zulu movements. Adendorff was a German – his father had been a surgeon sailing to the East Indies who had decided to stay when his ship touched land at Cape Town – and it is possible that he struggled to make himself understood. Lieutenant Higginson decided to ride up to the outpost himself to see what was happening, taking along his sergeant-major, Williams. 'We found Captain Barry and Lieutenant Vereker watching some Zulus about half a mile from them in the plain before stated, we also saw large bodies of natives off to the left front of the 2nd Batt. NNC [i.e. on the escarpment above Lonsdale's company – where Whitelaw reported them]. I remained there about half an hour watching the Zulus, and then we returned . . .'[19]

Even the notoriously jittery NNC pickets did not seem unduly alarmed, so whatever the Zulus were doing they did not appear to be offering any immediate threat. Nevertheless, Pulleine reacted sensibly enough. The 'Fall In' was sounded, and the 24th companies lined up in front of the 2/24th tents, facing eastwards. Krohn's NNC company was ordered to remain in the camp rather than march out to relieve Barry's outpost. Lonsdale's NNC company, still occupying the same rise between the *dongas* where it had spent the night, was told by its officers that the Zulus were in sight, and ordered to return to the camp. It had no sooner arrived, however, than it was ordered out again to re-occupy its old position.[20]

Clearly there was no alarm in the camp at this stage. Lieutenant Curling, the senior Artillery officer left in camp, who was still 'congratulating myself on having an independent command' after Harness's departure, heard about the Zulu presence but 'did not think anything of it', as 'we none of us had the least idea that the Zulus contemplated attacking the camp, and having in the last war often seen equally large bodies of the enemy never dreamed they would come on.'[21]

It was about this time that John Chard of No. 5 Field Company, Royal Engineers, borrowed the field glass from an NCO of the 24th, and decided in the light of what he saw to head back to Rorke's Drift.

Despite the lack of immediate concern, according to the column interpreter James Brickhill, Pulleine took proper precautions for the safety of the camp. Brickhill was a civilian; he was in his early forties and had worked as an interpreter for the Natal government since the 1860s, and he had been living with his wife and brother at Knox's Store in Msinga, not far from Henry Francis Fynn, when the war broke out. He had volunteered his services and been taken on as No. 3 Column's interpreter and he knew many of the local settlers who were serving with the column. Since Smith-Dorrien's empty supply wagons were still parked on the *nek* below iSandlwana, Pulleine now sent for Brickhill and ordered him to tell the wagon-drivers to collect up the cattle, which were wandering about among the camps, and 'might impede the action of the troops'.[22] The wagon-drivers were ordered to tie the oxen in their yokes, but not inspan them. While he was on the *nek*, Brickhill noted the vedettes behind iSandlwana signalling that two bodies of troops were approaching up the road from Rorke's Drift. Brickhill hurried off to the headquarters tents to report this to Pulleine, and on the way back he met several of the Volunteers he knew, Captain Robert Bradstreet of the Newcastle Mounted Rifles, Quartermaster Willie London, Sergeant Bullock and Trooper Moodie of the Carbineers. The group had been listening to the distant sounds of gunfire,

> ... what we thought was the General engaged with the enemy. We could almost have sworn that we heard rapid artillery firing, then volleys of small arms, then single shots, and afterwards the firing seemed to come from a more northerly direction than the General could possibly have been in, so that we concluded that Colonel Wood's column had come up and was engaging another portion of the enemy. This illusion (for such it afterwards proved to be) was caused by the echoes and reverberations from the surrounding hills of a lot of small arms discharged by the NNC and Volunteers at a number of small flying parties of the enemy . . .[23]

Even today, the acoustic peculiarities of the countryside around iSandlwana remain not the least of its mysteries. Sudden sounds bounce off the hills, returning a split second later from unexpected directions, amplified and distorted. During the occasional re-enactments that have taken place on the battlefield, the ragged crack of the rifle volleys snap backwards and forwards, giving almost no clue as to their point of origin, yet still oddly muffled from some directions, as if lost in acoustic shadows.

If Brickhill or anyone else in the camp that day – or indeed elsewhere – hoped the sounds of gunfire from the unfolding conflict would give them a clue as to what was going on, they were to be sadly disappointed.

At about this time a party of eight Zulus appeared near the road carrying an improvised white flag and Brickhill was called away to interview them. Despite the mysterious gathering of the Zulu on the hills, they were allowed into the camp under guard, although Brickhill took the precaution of leading them to the column office by a route that led behind the tents, so that they could see little of the troops still stood to in front. The party proved to be *inkosi* Gamdana and his advisers, who had come in as they had told Chelmsford the day before that they would. They brought with them eleven antiquated guns, which were promptly taken from them. They were disappointed, however, to find that Chelmsford was no longer in the camp and, perhaps worried by the Zulu movements nearby, they asked if they might be allowed to leave again, as their cattle were grazing unprotected on the plain near Hlazakazi.[24]

Pulleine was pondering his response to this when the decision was taken out of his hands. Sometime after 10 a.m. Durnford rode over the *nek* and into the camp at iSandlwana at the head of his men. Or at least at the head of his mounted troops – the less mobile elements under his command, his transport wagons, infantry and the rocket battery, trailed behind him on the road. If his conversation with Chard had influenced him at all, it seems to have hurried him to the camp to discover the truth of the reported Zulu sightings; he clearly did not share Chard's concern for the vulnerability of the road to Rorke's Drift – or the unprotected baggage train he had left moving up it.

Durnford halted his command close to Glyn's headquarters tent, and allowed his men to off-saddle in a gap in the tents between the NNC and 2/24th camps. The 24th companies were still lined up a short distance to the front, a thin splash of red facing the rippling green of the open plain, but there was now no sign of any Zulu presence on the iNyoni skyline to the left.

Durnford sought out Pulleine. It is possible the two men had met before, but if so it can only have been briefly for their paths had seldom crossed despite their service in Natal, and they had certainly not worked together in the field before. Nonetheless, there should have been no awkwardness between them, as their respective positions were perfectly clear. As a brevet colonel Durnford outranked Pulleine, who was a brevet lieutenant-colonel: although Durnford held an independent command, he was now the senior officer at iSandlwana, and the protocol would have been well known to both men: while he was present in the camp, Durnford was deemed to have taken command of it. Cochrane leaves little room for doubt on this point:

> I entered the Isandula camp with Colonel Durnford about 10 a.m., and remained with him as acting staff officer. On arrival he took over command from Colonel Pulleine, 24th Regiment. Colonel Pulleine gave over to Durnford a verbal state of the troops in the camp at the time, and stated the orders he had received, viz., to defend the camp; these words were reported two or three times in the conversation.[25]

Pulleine was keen to stress the orders Chelmsford had left him because he remained bound by them, despite an obvious uncertainty now as to Durnford's role. Durnford had no doubt expected to find fresh orders from Chelmsford awaiting him in the camp, yet there were none. Chelmsford's previous messages had strongly implied that he intended to maintain the independence of Durnford's column, and use him to support the advance against Matshana. He had given good grounds for Durnford to suppose that he was being brought forward to support Chelmsford, Glyn and the forward party, rather than merely reinforce the camp garrison, yet there was nothing now that he had arrived at iSandlwana to confirm this. In fact, it is unlikely that Chelmsford had finally decided on Durnford's role; he had merely wanted him closer at hand in order to exercise a tighter control over him, and to be free to deploy him as the situation unfolded. Wrapped up as he was in the unfolding disappointment of the pointless skirmishing at Mangeni, 20 kilometres away, Chelmsford had probably given Durnford very little further thought that morning.

Yet it was obvious to Durnford that the situation at iSandlwana had changed since the general had left before dawn. Chelmsford suspected nothing of a Zulu presence on the heights, and while Pulleine was able to give a good account of the Zulu movements once they had appeared on the skyline, he had only a hazy understanding of what might be unfolding beyond. Indeed, as Pulleine and Durnford stood discussing the situation, Walter Higginson rode in from Captain Barry's picket on the Mkwene high-point. Despite having watched the Zulus for some time, Higginson could add little beyond the fact that several parties were moving about on the uplands.

Durnford greeted the news with a flicker of impatience: 'I made my report to the Colonel and he then ordered me to send some men to the top of Isandhlwana to watch the hills, the men had been up about half an hour without sending down any news, so I sent another native up with orders to come down with news at once, he returned very soon and brought news that the natives were retiring.'[26]

In fact, the silence of the men on top of iSandlwana owed a good deal to the fact that their vantage point was not as commanding as it seemed from the foot of the hill. The summit is lower than the iNyoni escarpment, and the men posted there could have gained an impression of the Zulu movements that was only a little better than those below. Pressed to answer Durnford's demands, they could only add to the confusion. According to Cochrane, 'Constant reports came in from the scouts on the hills to the left, but never anything from the men on top of Isandhlwana hill, that I heard. Some of the reports were: "The enemy are in force behind the hills on the left", "The enemy are in three columns", "The enemy are retiring in every direction", "The columns are separating, one moving to the left rear, and one towards the General." '[27]

'And one towards the General . . .' – a small shining nugget of significance, almost lost now in the jumble of contradiction, but one that struck Durnford immediately. When they appeared on the skyline, the Zulus had shown no inclination to attack the camp – and what if that was never their plan? What if, instead, they intended to seize the opportunity to isolate Chelmsford, to cut the British command in two by moving between the Mangeni detachments and iSandlwana? The camp, with its hefty garrison – 1,700 men now that Durnford had arrived – might be safe enough, but what of Chelmsford and his men, scattered in small pockets all over the countryside, and with only minimal food and ammunition supplies? The threat certainly seemed real enough, and it made Durnford's mind up for him. 'Upon this latter report', said Cochrane, 'Colonel Durnford said he would go out and prevent the one column from joining the *impi*, which was supposed at that time to be engaged with the troops under the General.'[28]

As a column commander himself, this was Durnford's prerogative; whether it was in accordance with Chelmsford's thinking remained to be seen – but Durnford would no doubt justify himself on the grounds of the changing local situation.

Durnford's conversation with Pulleine had been a curiously public one. They seem to have remained outside throughout, no doubt pointing out and discussing the relative positions of the Zulus and Lord Chelmsford's detachment. Cochrane, as Durnford's acting staff officer, was there, as was

George Shepstone, and several of Pulleine's officers from the 24th, including Lieutenant and Adjutant Melvill. At one point Brickhill joined them, escorting Gamdana and his attendants, who had come in to surrender their guns – Durnford had met Brickhill before, and seemed pleased to see him and, after weighing up his advice, decided to let the Zulus leave the camp again freely. Other individuals came and went, following the routine business of the camp, including Smith-Dorrien, who had just got back from Rorke's Drift, and James Hamer, a civilian attached to Durnford's commissariat staff.

Several witnesses were aware, then, of the direction the conversation took after Durnford had decided to follow up the Zulu movements. According to Smith-Dorrien, 'As far as I could make out, the gist of Colonels Durnford and Pulleine's discussion was that the former wished to go out and attack the Zulus, whilst the latter argued that his orders were to defend the camp, and that he could not allow his infantry to move out.'[29]

According to Cochrane – who certainly believed that he had been the closest witness – Durnford asked Pulleine to give him two of the 24th companies from the camp garrison. Pulleine had clearly been uneasy at the request, pointing out that it was hardly compatible with his orders to 'defend the camp'. After a few minutes' discussion among the officers of the 24th, Lieutenant Melvill approached Durnford and said, 'Colonel, I really do not think Colonel Pulleine would be doing right to send any men out of the camp when his orders are "to defend the camp".' Durnford did not force the point, replying, 'Very well, it does not much matter. We will not take them.' Cochrane thought Durnford's manner was 'persuasive' throughout rather than 'peremptory', and that 'there were no high words'. Nevertheless, Durnford went on to comment pointedly, 'Well, my idea is, that wherever Zulus appear, we ought to attack. I will go alone, but, remember, if I get into difficulties, I shall rely on you to support me.'[30]

This is a deeply revealing conversation. It is clear that, despite the veneer of professional courtesy, Durnford's request had been so startling that officers of considerably junior rank had been moved to object. That Durnford was trying to intervene in a clearly established chain of command says much about his own determination to act decisively – and the demons that drove him. The laxness in Chelmsford's orders had created an ambiguity which he did not hesitate to exploit – and the mysterious Zulu movements on the heights presented an opportunity to restore his tarnished record in action. His attitude can hardly have impressed the officers of the 24th – and whatever assurance of support he had gained from Pulleine would in any case be limited by the practical constraints imposed by the order to defend the camp.

Durnford asked Pulleine if he could spare Higginson – 'Certainly', Pulleine replied[31] – and returned to his men. About this time, Pulleine decided to send a company of the 24th up onto the ridge. Although Durnford is usually supposed to have instigated this move, there are several reasons why it might have been Pulleine's alone. The recent reports from the picket on Mkwene had suggested that some of the Zulus had moved off westwards above the camp, possibly threatening the rear approaches. The NNC picket was too far way to command the valleys that drop round behind iSandlwana from the north, and it would have been a perfectly sound decision by Pulleine to cover these with regular infantry. If the imperative was to guard a weak spot on the camp perimeter, the move was entirely in keeping with Pulleine's orders, and the company could offer little support to Durnford in any case. The company sent out was E Company, 1/24th, under Lieutenant Cavaye, and the men followed the foot-track to the spur until they crested the ridge west of Mkwene. Here they disappeared out of sight from the camp, moving down into the valley beyond the skyline, and taking up a position which allowed them to watch for any Zulu movements towards the Manzimnyama upstream of iSandlwana.

Durnford's men, meanwhile, had been resting between the NNC camp and 2/24th tents and, according to Lieutenant Davies of the Edendale troop, the officers had been given a good account of the morning's excitement by Quatermaster Bullock and a group of Carbineers who had strolled past, probably the same men Brickhill had listened to the sounds of distant gunfire with earlier. Durnford ordered his men to mount up, then to move forward beyond the tents – 'fours right, left wheel!' – where they formed up in the open in troops and he gave them their orders.[32]

It was now about 11.15 a.m., and the rocket battery and its NNC infantry escort had just arrived in camp. They were tired after the march from Rorke's Drift but Durnford ordered them to follow him as soon as they could. The baggage wagons were still not in the camp, and Durnford ordered Lieutenant Wyatt Vause and No. 3 Troop, Zikhali Horse, together with a company of the 1st NNC, to go back and bring them in. The two remaining troops of the Zikhali Horse, under Lieutenants Raw and Roberts, he ordered up the spur onto the northern edge of the escarpment, and then to drive across the summit, pushing any Zulu they found there in front of them. Raw's troop was to keep to the left, close to the escarpment, while Roberts' troop was to 'skirmish the valley beyond'.[33] According to Lieuenant Davies of the Edendale troop, Durnford '. . . told Raw before leaving that there was a company of Native Infantry on piquet duty on the ridge; he was to take this piquet with him to support it if it became necessary.'[34]

George Shepstone was to accompany Raw's troop, and Captain William Barton Roberts's. Durnford himself would take the remaining two troops – Hlubi's Tlokoa and the Edendale men – eastwards across the plain, following the foot of the iNyoni escarpment, turning northwards after it passed the iThusi high-point. The rocket battery would follow Durnford as soon as it was ready. The two detachments would therefore converge on an unspecified point somewhere to the north-east, roughly where the Zulus had been seen in the far distance that morning; the movement would simultaneously drive the Zulus away from the camp and from any position where they might attempt to threaten Chelmsford's left rear. Durnford simply told his men that the enemy were retiring, and that he intended to follow them up.

The two troops heading up the spur set off first, while Durnford led his detachment away from the camp about fifteen minutes later. It was now about 11.30 a.m., and the sun was high in the sky on a hot, breathless day.

Durnford set out eastwards, riding at a canter. They crossed the two *dongas* that bisect the plain close in front of the camp – the Mpofana and the Nyogane – and after passing the amaTutshane 'conical hill' they passed round the base of the iThusi spur, and angled northwards up the valley of the Nxibongo stream. They soon left the rocket battery trailing in their wake. The rockets were mounted on mules, and could not keep up with the pace set by the horses, and they were escorted by Captain Cracroft Nourse's D Company, 1/1st NNC, which was on foot. 'They went too fast', Nourse admitted somewhat testily, 'and left us some two miles [3.2 kilometres] in the rear.'[35]

The men watching Durnford from iSandlwana soon lost sight of him, as he vanished into the shimmering haze as his course took him beyond iThusi. Cochrane thought they cantered 8 or 10 kilometres from the camp,[36] while Lieutenant Davies noted that they had 'proceeded round the pointed hill on the left front of the camp, and were about two miles beyond the ridge on the left point of the camp (we could not see the camp)' before seeing the Zulus.[37] There were small scattered groups retiring in front of them as fast as they could. Durnford remarked to Jabez Molife, 'If they are going towards the General we must stop them at all hazards.'[38]

They had not gone much further, however, when they were overtaken by two Carbineers galloping up behind them. They had been sent by Lieutenant Scott, who was back on his post on top of amaTutshane, and who had some startling information. The situation had changed drastically on top of the iNyoni heights – and Durnford was suddenly in grave danger of being cut off. The news seemed absurd, and there is a tone of frustration, anger even, in Durnford's response; for a split second his emotions, usually so carefully controlled, seem to have risen jaggedly to the surface. Jabez Molife, of the Edendale troop, heard him snap 'What are those scouts I sent out about all this time?'[39] According to Davies:

> Colonel Durnford remarked, 'the enemy can't surround us and if they do we will cut our way through them.' He asked me where the rocket battery was, I told him a very long way behind. He then told the two Carbineers to return and tell Lieut. Scott to support him with his piquet – the N.C. [Natal Carbineers] replied that Lieut Scott would not leave his position on any account whatever, as he had strict instructions from Col. Pulleine not to leave his post on any pretence whatever. Col. Durnford replied 'I am Col. Pulleine's senior, you will please tell Lieut. Scott to do as I tell him.' It was during this conversation that our scouts reported the enemy in sight. We looked up the ridge on our front and could see the enemy in great numbers about 1500 yards steadily advancing . . .[40]

# 20

# 'The king's day!'

## iSandlwana, noon, 22 January

On the evening of 21 January, William Beaumont had received an interesting report from the commander of one of the parties of auxiliary troops watching the crossing-points on the Mzinyathi river.

The young and rather dashing Beaumont – he had been a darling of Pietermaritzburg society before being posted to the sticks – had been Resident Magistrate in Newcastle, a small coal-mining town situated at the very northern tip of Natal, but on the outbreak of war had been appointed commandant in charge of civil defence of the northern border. With Henry Francis Fynn's departure to join Chelmsford's staff he had moved to Fynn's magistracy at Msinga to be closer to the scene of his responsibilities. Under his charge were the Border Guard – a levy raised from local chiefdoms and placed under white officers – which was posted to watch the minor drifts where no imperial troops could be stationed. The Border Guard inevitably produced a stream of reports daily, every minor irregularity on the other side of the river being the subject of a good deal of speculation which was passed back down the line to Beaumont. Sandhurst-trained, Beaumont responded to these with the usual degree of scepticism.

This particular report, however, had troubled him. It had been sent back by an Edward Woodroffe, a civilian Levy Leader whose post lay near the junction of the iSibindi stream and the Mzinyathi, 8 or 9 kilometres below Rorke's Drift, and opposite the lower reaches of the Mangeni valley. Like many young settlers living on the very fringes of the colony, Woodroffe had married a number of Zulu wives – in this case from among Matshana's Sithole people, most of whom had remained on the Zulu side of the border when the war broke out, and who had now taken to the Qhudeni bush. Through them Woodroffe had received a disturbing message: that the main Zulu army would be passing through Matshana's territory the following

day, and that Matshana's men were preparing themselves to act in concert
with it.

When this report reached Beaumont, he had dispatched a messenger to
Rorke's Drift to try to find Lord Chelmsford, and given orders for the levy
in his district to mass on the hills above Woodroffe's crossing. Beaumont
himself had ridden out to command them, and had spent an uncomfortable
night on the hills, waiting for a Zulu attack which never materialized.

At first light the following morning – the 22nd – however, Beaumont
had been delighted to see a large force of auxiliary troops winding their
way down to the crossings. This was the 2nd Battalion, 1st NNC, commanded by an able regular officer, Major Harcourt Bengough. Bengough's
battalion were the infantry troops who had lagged behind on Durnford's
energetic march to Rorke's Drift, and who had been left behind at the
Sandspruit, below the Biggarsberg hills. When Chelmsford had been framing his attack on 'the two Matyanas' two days before, he had intended to
exploit Bengough's presence at the Sandspruit to do exactly what he was
now doing – to strike north-east towards the Mzinyathi downstream of
Rorke's Drift. By crossing near iSibindi, Bengough would effectively seal
the Mangeni at its confluence with the Mzinyathi – blocking the escape of
any Zulus attempting to flee Dartnell's reconnaissance through the hills. It
was a move typical of Chelmsford's Cape Frontier Wars tactics, but in fact
Bengough had only received the order on the 21st, and was too late to be
of any use to Dartnell's operations. In any case, when Chelmsford had
decided to march to Dartnell's support early on the 22nd he had changed
his mind and directed Bengough to move up to Rorke's Drift instead. That
order, sent via Durnford, had also come too late, for Bengough had already
set off towards iSibindi. Bengough arrived at the river determined to cross
into Zululand as per his original instructions, and he asked Beaumont to
assist him. 'The river was high', commented Beaumont, 'but the regiment
was safely piloted over.'[1]

Bengough's battalion was delighted to be on enemy soil for the first
time. While the officers sat down to a midday meal, the men prepared
themselves for imminent combat. They were 'proportionately excited and
pleased with themselves,' observed Bengough, 'eating medicines, and sprin-
kling themselves after their fashion'.[2]

While this was going on, the flat sound of distant artillery fire could be
heard from somewhere over the high hills in front of them. Bengough
wondered what it meant, and Beaumont 'thought this was from the

reconnaissance that the General had told me would be made, and I told [him] so'.[3]

After a while, the firing ceased. Bengough had expected to receive fresh orders during the day, but nothing was forthcoming, and his men sat on the hillside, taking what cover they could from the scorching afternoon sun. As nothing was happening, Beaumont decided to cross the river again and, after seeing his Border Guard safely back to their posts, he set off again for Msinga.

It was late in the afternoon when one of Bengough's officers brought him a startling report. The gunfire they had heard earlier had not been the sound of skirmishing in the Mangeni hills, but something infinitely more sinister:

> Towards evening Kinsman, my interpreter, came to me and said that a Zulu had just come in with the report of the English '*impi*' having been destroyed (lit. 'eaten up'), at a place called Isandhlwana, and the English 'boss' killed . . . He added that a Zulu *impi* was on its way to 'eat us up'.
>
> The matter was, in any case, serious and urgent, and I had to decide, without delay, on what should be done. Had our position been defensible, I should have been inclined to hold it, as the men were, as I have said, in great fettle at being on Zulu ground, and the rocks on which we were, surrounded by the river, seemed to offer at first sight reasonable means of defence; but the river was fordable almost anywhere, and the rocks would offer but little real defence to the active Zulu, so I decided on evacuating our position and on taking up a post on the high ground on the Natal side of the river.[4]

In the meantime, Beaumont had arrived back at the Msinga magistracy and had gone to Fynn's house, where he was staying, late in the afternoon. It had been a long and tiring day, and he was exhausted by the time he got home, but his rest was interrupted by a sudden and terrible surprise:

> I had barely reached the huts and laid down when I saw a man – a Mr Brickfield [sic; Brickhill], who has a house on the Umsinga Mountains – sitting on his horse and talking in an earnest manner to Mrs Fynn and her sister. Guessing that something had happened, I went out. Beckoning him to me, I asked him what was the matter. He told me he was in the camp as an interpreter and was riding with only a sjambok in his hand watching the fighting when all of a sudden the Zulus surrounded the camp and everyone in it was being slaughtered. Being

mounted and knowing the country and every path in it he made his escape and had come to warn Mrs Fynn.[5]

Brickhill was shocked and exhausted, and overwhelmed by the horror of the events he had just survived, and it is doubtful if he gave Beaumont a very clear picture of what had happened. Beaumont was in any case stunned – the news seemed incomprehensible. Then, as it sank in, it occurred suddenly to him that there was now no force of any consequence between the Zulu army and the Natal border – and iSandlwana was hardly more than 25 kilometres away.

*

From Siphezi the great Zulu army had struck north-west on the 21st, moving away from the developing danger posed by Chelmsford's reconnaissances on its left front. The movement would be masked by the iNyoni upland from the camp at iSandlwana during the final approach, but even so it was a very dangerous march, passing as it did through the open, undulating country north of Siphezi, and within easy range of British patrols. To minimize the risk the *amabutho* broke up into clusters of companies, moving along the folds in the ground, so as not to be visible as a dense mass, and scouts were sent out to protect the left flank. Nevertheless, they were very nearly discovered, for it was at this point that Lieutenant Browne's Mounted Infantry patrol had nearly stumbled across them. Nevill Coghill, who presumably heard the story from Browne himself, counted the incident a British success, but in fact the Zulu scouts had successfully prevented Browne from learning anything of the army's movements. 'According to Usibebu', the magistrate J.Y. Gibson noted after the war:

> ... who superintended the scouting, he encountered and drove in a patrol which would otherwise soon have come in view of the army ... Undabuko, Cetshwayo's brother, informed the author that some of the scouts from what he believed to be the force that was reconnoitring in Matshana's country actually saw the army, or a portion of it, but did not apparently realise the importance of the discovery they had made. The army advanced in day time across open country, and ought, with proper vigilance, to have been discovered.[6]

It is a criticism that cannot easily be refuted more than 130 years after the event; in the long chain of incidents that culminated in the battle itself, perhaps the greatest Zulu masterstroke was to move some 25,000 men undetected to within 8 kilometres of the British camp – and the greatest British shortcoming their failure, despite extensive patrolling, to intercept them.

That afternoon – the 21st – the Zulu army had slipped into the valley of the Ngwebeni stream.[7] Undoubtedly this had been Ntshingwayo's objective from the moment that he had decided on his line of advance, and it reflected the growing influence of Sihayo in the command council. The army was now moving on his turf, and Sihayo's intimate knowledge of the terrain was an inestimable asset to the high command. And he had picked his spot perfectly – there are certainly few other spots within striking distance of the camp at iSandlwana which so large a force could have hoped to occupy overnight and remain unseen.

Late afternoon, as the weary men settled into their bivouacs along the banks of the stream, Zibhebhu and his scouts had ridden out again, searching for any sign that the British at iSandlwana might be aware of their presence. And in the distance, a few kilometres away across the undulating heights, on the lip of the escarpment, they had seen Lord Chelmsford and his staff – looking back at them.

The question was, what now? Having brought his army so close to the enemy, Ntshingwayo had been perfectly placed to deliver a surprise attack at first light the following day. That evening he had called together the commanders of the *amabutho* for a command conference.[8] Yet, far from deciding a plan of attack, they had remained troubled by the king's admonition given to the generals 'not to go and attack the English at once, but to have a conference and then send some chiefs and ask the English why they were laying the country waste and killing Zulus'.[9] There can be little doubt that they understood the true significance of this order – under the circumstances, with so many men under arms and psychologically committed to battle, it would have been absurd to try to open fresh negotiations at that late stage, with the two armies close enough to blunder into each other at any time. What the king wanted, of course, was for battle to take place in circumstances which clearly showed the British as the aggressors; he wanted after the war was over to be able to demonstrate that his policy was reactive and in defence, and that he had fought only when forced to it. It was a requirement which, just as Pine's order had hampered Durnford at the Bushman's River Pass six years before, effectively deprived Ntshingwayo of the initiative – until, that is, he decided the moment was right to exercise his independent judgement and overrule the king's request.

That night, however, no plans had been laid to attack the camp on the 22nd, and no arrangements were made for the final crucial rituals, the last application of war medicines, which would be vital to top up the spiritual potency of the ceremonies the men had passed through at oNdini, and which were so important to protect the men from harm as they went into battle. The *izinduna* had broken up the meeting, with instructions to reconvene in the morning.

The night passed, the *amabutho* snatching what sleep they could among the boulders along the floor of the Ngwebeni valley. It was then that Mehlokazulu, travelling down from the Phongolo in response to the king's summons, had rejoined the iNgobamakhosi.[10] Some of the men had lit campfires, but their *izinduna* told them to put them out; 'orders were given to hide ourselves', said Nzuzi Mandla, a young man in the ranks of the uVe, 'so that the English would not know how many we were';[11] there was no hope of a hot meal that night.

In the morning, the Zulus woke to find themselves enveloped in a dense mist. The first of them began to rise and go down to the river to drink, the dark patches of their shields looming eerily in the mist, as if dancing with a life of their own; for generations the Ngwebeni would be known as *Mahaweni* – the place of the war-shields.

Most of the men knew, of course, that the English were close at hand, as it would have been impossible to prevent stories spreading of the skirmishes between parties of scouts the day before. 'On our way there,' said Nzuzi Mandla, 'we saw about ten mounted men who were the advance party of the English, and we know that they saw us, too.'[12] Despite the tiring march and the debilitating weather, despite the increasing shortage of food, a fierce enthusiasm to attack the invaders pervaded the army, stoked by the pre-battle rituals, by the excitement of being part of so large an army on the cusp of battle, and by a genuine indignation and anger at the British invasion. From the moment the *amabutho* entered the Ngwe-beni, there was a very serious risk that their commanders would not be able to control them, and that any crack in their fragile discipline would produce a rush to the front which it would be difficult to restrain.

Yet one religious belief kept them in check. According to Gibson, 'The 22nd of January was the day of the new moon. She was to begin her new life at eight minutes before two o'clock in the afternoon, and her "dark day" was considered by the Zulus as unfitting for an engagement in battle.'[13] There can be no doubting the strength of this belief, or that it was generally accepted. L.H. Samuelson, a missionary's daughter who grew up in Zululand during Cetshwayo's reign, noted that 'It would be thought likely that the Zulus in times of war or other serious trouble, should be on the look out for changes in the sky which are supposed to foretell success or failure, as it is generally to the spirits of their ancestors that their attention is directed at such times.'[14]

The day of the 'dead moon' was a time of *umnyama*, 'blackness', when dark spiritual forces lurked close to the fragile membrane which separated them from the world of the living, and when they might break free at any point to wreak havoc in the affairs of men. To embark on a battle on such a day – especially one in which the fate of the kingdom hung upon the outcome – risked a disaster of apocalyptic proportions. '*Umnyama* is what affects an *impi* as a whole', explained Mpashana kaSodondo,

> [it] brings darkness onto them whilst it is light on the side of their assailants. And this word 'darkness' is used also in a metaphorical sense, for it means anything that may overtake or come on the enemy, either physical darkness, paralysis of action inspired by fear, oversleeping themselves, futility or stupidity of plan when engaging their assailants, being overtaken by a mist whilst it is clear for their foes, etc . . . Moon dying. Attack not to be that very day. It is a time of *umnyama* . . .'[15]

'No orders were given to attack on the 22nd,' said Mehlokazulu afterwards, 'it was not our day. Our day was the following day; it being the new moon we did not intend to fight.'[16] 'At first we had not intended attacking the camp that day', an unknown man of the uMbonambi told the traveller Bertram Mitford after the war, 'as the moon was wrong.'[17]

In the circumstances, the timing was undoubtedly fortunate; it gave Ntshingwayo a further twenty-four hours to weigh up his options. He was perfectly placed, after all, to take advantage of events as they unravelled; as Nsuzi Mandla put it with an unusual degree of perception, 'We were lying without any intention of fighting, although we were ready to engage with them if they started. We lay right under their noses to put temptation in their way and make them start fighting . . .'[18]

But if the *amabutho* were to be frustrated in their hopes of an early attack, the work of scouts screening for the enemy and the feeding of the army went on as usual. At first light, scouts were dispatched again to watch the British camp, while foragers were sent out from each *ibutho* to plunder the deserted homesteads and mealie fields nearby, and to search out cattle hidden away by the civilian population. These foragers were not the herd boys of cinematic myth, but grown men, picked out of the ranks for their physical stamina and their courage since foraging could be a dangerous business, especially so close to the enemy.[19] Indeed, as they spread out in small bands in all directions, they had no choice but to emerge from the Ngwebeni valley, passing beyond the Mabaso hill which hid it from view from the south. Some of them followed the Ngwebeni upstream where they found abandoned mealie fields which they began to loot enthusiastically, or drifted across the open country looking for deserted homesteads along the foot of the hills to the west. In so doing, they would have broken cover, and they must have been visible to the NNC outposts on Mkwene hill, several kilometres to the south.

An air of mystery undoubtedly pervades the Zulu movements that morning, but Zibhebhu's scouts were probably trying to drive back the British pickets on the iNyoni ridge, to prevent them seeing too much of the foragers' activities nearer the bivouac. Almost certainly, these were the men who menaced Troopers Barker and Hawkins of the Carbineers, driving them off the top of iThusi. With the high-points along the eastern end of the iNyoni heights securely in Zulu hands, the Zulu scouts had an uninterrupted view of the camp at iSandlwana and any British movements on the plain.[20]

Yet the Zulus learnt little from so closely observing the camp at iSandlwana, and nothing much that hinted at British intentions. Mehlokazulu was among those sent out that morning, and he and three companions, all *izinduna*, watched the camp from a high-point for some time. The tents stood out plainly against the grass at the foot of the mountain, and wagons were drawn up in lines behind them. Another group of wagons was parked on the *nek*; oxen could be seen moving in the camp. Now and then bodies of men – both redcoats and African troops – could be seen forming up and marching about. 'We could see the English outposts (mounted men) quite close to us', said Mehlokazulu, '. . . and could also see the position of their camp. The outposts evidently saw us, for they commenced to move about, and there seemed to be a bustle in the camp, and some were in spanning the wagons and others were getting in the oxen.'[21]

Is it possible that the Zulus had entirely missed Chelmsford's departure during the night? Certainly Mehlokazulu thought so – 'we . . . did not know that the army had been divided, as we did not send spies into their camp'.[22] This lapse is perhaps not quite as surprising as it seems; Chelmsford had, after all, intended the move to be secretive, and the soldiers had not given themselves away with loud bugle calls. They had left in the last hours of darkness, and had then been submerged on the road in the pre-dawn mist; by the time the sun rose and the mist lifted they were 16 or 17 kilometres away, near the Mangeni. Even if Zulu scouts had stayed to observe them through the night – and it is likely they did not – there had been no moonlight and it would have been impossible to observe the British movements by the stars alone. On such nights even the keenest eyes can do little more than pick out the dark silhouette of iSandlwana against the faint luminescence of the sky, while the ground below it, and everything on it, is swallowed up in a uniform blackness.

Mehlokazulu returned to report his observations to Ntshingwayo, and the general's reaction explains, more than any other surviving eyewitness comment, the apparent unresponsiveness of the high command that morning. 'All right,' he said, 'we will see what they are going to do.'[23] Ntshingwayo was still content to play the waiting game; he had turned away and given orders for the commanding officers of the amabutho to attend him, to continue their deliberations from the night before.

An hour or two after sunrise, however, a faint crackle of distant gunfire drifted across the men still waiting in the Ngwebeni valley. This was the same shooting that Brickhill heard from the camp, and the Zulus, too, struggled to distinguish the direction from which it was coming. In the ranks of the iNgobamakhosi, lying midway along the course of the river, Mhlahlana Nguni heard it, but was unimpressed; to his comrades in the iNgobamakhosi, the interruption did not seem worth the sacrifice of a much-anticipated breakfast. 'Just as the sun was beginning to light up the tops of the hills we heard firing. We listened for a while and then said to ourselves "There is going to be no fighting today ... because there is no moon." Being hungry we took no more notice of the firing, but started to collect the mealies we had been cooking over our fires ...'[24]

Yet among the amabutho camped further west, upstream along the valley, the sound of shooting had an electrifying effect. It seemed to be coming from somewhere to their left, and the general assumption was that it originated with the iNgobamakhosi. Many of the amabutho were jealous of the royal favour enjoyed by the iNgobamakhosi, and in particular their rivals, the uKhandempemvu,[25] who had exchanged challenges with them at oNdini only a week before, were alarmed by the impression that the iNgobamakhosi might already be gaining glory by fighting with the whites. One of the uKhandempemvu, uGuku, heard the gunfire and thought that 'the iNgobamakhosi were engaged, [and] we went up from the valley to the top of the Ingqutu, which was between us and the camp'.[26] The sight of the uKhandempemvu running up the slopes away from the bivouac and towards the enemy was too much for another of the *amabutho* who had been engaged in the challenging ceremonies; 'we were sitting resting', said a member of the uNokhenke, lying further up the valley and closer to iSandlwana, 'and we armed and ran forward in the direction of the sound'.[27]

Perhaps these are just rationalizations by ordinary soldiers of more complex tactical decisions by their officers that they were not privy to; perhaps these early movements in fact foreshadowed the tactics Ntshing-wayo intended to employ if and when he committed the entire army to an attack. Yet no evidence of this has survived, and it is significant that neither *ibutho* had been sprinkled with the last application of ritual medi-cines, or been addressed by their commanders, as they surely would have been if the move had been a planned one. Sometimes events are just what they seem – and it would not be the last time in the war that the Zulu abandoned all discipline in their desire to attack the enemy wherever they found him.[28]

The uNokhenke and uKhandempemvu pushed across the heights, but were surprised to find that no obvious battle had begun, and that 'the Ngobamakosi were not engaged, but were quietly camped lower down the valley'.[29] Between them, the uNokhenke and uKhandempemvu *amabutho* were a large force – more than 4,000 men altogether – and certainly enough to constitute the 'thousands' of men that so alarmed Trooper Whitelaw of the Carbineers. Some moved across the heights towards the NNC outpost on Mkwene, coming close enough to call across to them, while the majority followed Zibhebhu's scouts onto the summit of iThusi.

From here they could plainly see the British camp – and the inescapable fact that no fighting had started at all. The rest of the Zulu army had not come up to join them, they were unsupported, and their own commanders were absent, still discussing the situation with Ntshingwayo. And the mystery of the gunfire was soon explained: 'we were soon told', said the soldier of the uNokhenke with more than a tinge of regret, 'that it was the white troops fighting with Matyana's people some ten miles [16 kilometres] away to our left front, and returned to our original position'.[30]

They drifted back towards the bivouac in large masses. As they disappeared again over the skyline, Trooper Barker and some of his companions followed them up, riding back up to the top of the ridge to see where they were going. Across the heights, they saw a number of the uKhandempemvu lingering on a hill – probably Mabaso – 'a large army sitting down'.[31]

Some of these bands were reluctant to return to the bivouac, and indeed the foragers had continued their activities across the heights, rounding up a few head of cattle. By about 11 a.m., however, most of the men were back in their places in the bivouac. Ntshingwayo was still discussing the situation with his commanders – it is difficult to believe that by this stage they had not discussed plans for an attack on the camp at first light on the morning of the 23rd – while Mhlahlana was smugly congratulating himself on his decision to remain with his breakfast. He would not have long to enjoy it, however. 'It was decreed though that we were not to enjoy eating them because while we were gathering them one of our *induna* arrived and told us to arm ourselves and get ready for the fight. While we were doing so, the white men were already fighting with the Ukandempemvu.'[32]

Ntshingwayo's council meeting was also rudely interrupted. 'When the day dawned my chiefs were again consulting about sending to the English before fighting,' explained Cetshwayo himself, '. . . but suddenly they heard the roar of guns and saw the dust and smoke rising up to heaven, and our foragers rushing back to camp, and saying "that the cavalry was near". Then the chiefs, knowing that the work of death was being executed, broke up the meeting and went to their different regiments . . .'[33]

The battle of iSandlwana had begun.[34]

*

Raw's and Roberts' troops had ridden out of the northern end of the camp, following the narrow footpath up onto the spur. Cavaye's company were probably in place off to their left as they did so, although as they were extended in open order they would have appeared no more than a scatter of red dots among the boulders. When they reached Barry's NNC picket on Mkwene they paused to pass on Durnford's order that he should follow them in support, and the whole party then pushed on, Raw keeping to rising ground on the right while Roberts' troop moved off to the left, down towards the shallow valley formed by the headwaters of the Ngwebeni. Despite the undulating terrain, the two troops were clearly in sight of each other, less than a kilometre apart, small splotches of yellow corduroy and dark horseflesh against the backdrop of green, their courses trailed with dust. They had, of course, lost all contact with Durnford, who was somewhere on the plain below the escarpment to their right.

Ahead of them, small parties of Zulus could clearly be seen – foragers and stragglers from the earlier movement who had not yet made it back to the hidden bivouac. Men could be seen moving about in mealie fields further down the valley, but the Ngwebeni stream curved out of sight behind the rocky hump of Mabaso hill, which hid whatever might lie beyond. 'We saw a handful of Zulus, not many', said Raw's African officer, Zikhali's son Nyanda, 'who kept running from us.' 'The enemy', said Raw, were 'in small clumps retiring before us for some time, drawing us on four or five miles [6.4 to 8 kilometres] from the camp'.[35]

The terrain seemed to be channelling the Zulus down the course of the Ngwebeni, and Raw's men spotted a group trying to hurry away some cattle. They gave chase, veering away from their original course to the left, converging towards Roberts' men already in the valley. Unable to reach the easy route down the course of the river, the Zulus scurried over a rocky spur at the western foot of Mabaso and dropped out of sight.

What happened next came as a surprise to everyone present. 'We tried to capture some cattle', recalled James Hamer, who had ridden out with Raw in company with his friend George Shepstone; 'They disappeared over a ridge, and coming up we saw the Zulus like ants in front of us, in perfect order as quiet as mice and stretched across in a long line.'[36] 'All of a sudden', said Nyanda, 'just as Mr Shepstone joined me on the crest of a ridge, the Army of Zulus sprung up, 15000 men.'[37]

Walter Higginson was a few hundred metres away when the encounter happened; he had been sent up after George Shepstone with orders from Durnford, but by the time he had reached the top of the escarpment, in the company again of Sergeant Major Williams, Zikhali's men had been several kilometres ahead of him. He had ridden after them, and had caught up with Barry and his company, straggling 300–400 metres in their wake. Just as he reached Barry, he saw 'A large number of Zulus coming from the rocks at the foot of the hill facing us. The mounted contingent at once opened fire on them, and gradually retired, trying to prevent themselves from being outflanked.'[38]

'They turned and fell upon us,' reported Raw laconically, 'the whole army showing itself from behind the hill in front where they had evidently been waiting.'[39]

*

The return of the uNokhenke and the uKhandempemvu had had an unsettling effect on the *amabutho* still waiting along the banks of the Ngwebeni. 'Dead moon' or no, that distant firing in the morning, and the unsupported forward movement of so many young men, had created a buzz of excitement among the rest, an anxiety that, however events should unfold, their *ibutho* should not be the one to miss out. With the senior commanders still at their meeting, it was left to their lieutenants to try to calm the men, but 'there had been much agitation in the camp ... and restraint was becoming difficult'.[40]

The uNokhenke and uKhandempemvu had hardly returned to their places, however, when the foragers came running in, calling out that they were being pursued, and almost immediately Raw's men appeared on the high ground above them:

> Just after we sat down, a small herd of cattle came past our line from our right, being driven by some of our scouts, and just when they were opposite the umCijo [uKhandempemvu] regiment, a body of mounted men on the hill to the west, galloping evidently trying to cut them off. When several hundred yards off they perceived the umCijo and, dismounting, fired one volley and then retired. The umCijo at once jumped up and charged, an example which was taken up by the uNokhenke and Nodwengo on their right, and the inGobamakhosi and uMbonambi on their left.[41]

*

It was immediately obvious to those who saw them that there could be no more waiting on propitious omens now. The sound of Raw's volley rippled through the Zulu bivouac like a shock wave, snapping the days of accumulated tension, interrupting breakfasts and ablutions by the riverside and sending men scurrying back to the rocks where they had left their weapons. According to Mehlokazulu:

> The Zulu regiments were all lying in the valley ... but the Umcityu [uKhandempemvu] made their appearance under the Nqutu range, and

were seen by the mounted men of the English forces, who made at the Umcityu, not seeing the main body of the army. They fired, and all at once the main body of the Zulu army arose in every direction, on hearing the fighting. The attention of the English mounted troops was drawn to the few men who had exposed themselves under the range, and before these mounted men knew where they were the main body of the Zulus got up and swarmed in every direction. On their seeing we were so numerous they retired, and the Ukhandempemvu regiment fired . . .[42]

'The whole *impi* became very excited and sprang up',[43] said a man of the uMbonambi, while in the ranks of the iNgobamakhosi a brother of Mhlahlana 'was very excited, and shouted out with a loud voice to make us strong, "This is the king's day!" '.[44] With their commanding officers still in conference with Ntshingwayo and Mavumengwana, there were few present among them with enough authority to stem the flow. Muziwento heard the story from his father, Zibana, who had now successfully joined the main army, and his words echo the relief that most felt now that the waiting was over:

> At once [Raw's men] found themselves in the close embrace of the Kandempemvu even as tobacco [is mixed] with aloes. The Zulu generals forbad [an attack], seeking to help the white men. But the regimental officers simply mutinied. They marched forward; they went into battle. They [Raw and the Zulus] were rolled along together towards Isandhlwana . . .[45]

\*

Reverend A.W. Lee, a missionary who worked in the iSandlwana district a generation later, often heard tales of the battle from those who took part, and the impressions he gathered echo the exuberance of that first rush. 'We sped on at the lope like a pack of wolves, spurning the dust with our feet as we passed. Men leaped aloft like spring-bok in their eagerness to get forward to their first view of the enemy. So, running, leaping we swept up to the crest of the ridge . . .'[46]

The uKhandempemvu and uNokhenke, already unsettled and lying nearest Raw's incursion, were the first to emerge from the valley, dragging the uDududu, iMbube and iSanqu on their right after them. Downstream, the uMbonambi, iNgobamakhosi and uVe were lying beneath the centre of

Mabaso, and faced a steep climb up the rocky hillside ahead of them. There was no time now for the last-minute rituals before battle, and most of the *amabutho* went forward unprotected. In the heady rush of contact they had left themselves dangerously vulnerable, and Ntshingwayo and his senior officers hurried to stem the flow of men into battle; they were, however, only able to restrain those *amabutho* furthest upstream, to the east, away from the encounter – the senior men of the uThulwana, iNdlondlo, iNdluyengwe and uDloko. These *amabutho* 'formed a circle and remained where they were. With the latter were the two commanding officers, Mavumengwana and Tshingwayo, and several of the king's brothers.'[47] The commanders forced these men into order, and Ntshingwayo strode about in the centre of the circle, inspiring them in the manner of commanders the world over with an appeal to their heroic traditions and their honour as warriors:

> Ntshingwayo kaMahole at [iSandlwana] declaimed the praises of Sen-zangakhona and Shaka, and holding up his shield said, 'This is the love charm of our people.' As he said this he shook his shield and said, 'You are always asking why this person is loved so much. It is caused by the love-charm of our people. There is no going back home.'[48]

No turning back, boys, remember who you are, death or glory; stirring words, yet it was galling, even for the mature men, married men with families at home, to remain behind now while others rushed forward. For some, it was too much, and one *induna* of the uThulwana, the fiery heir to the Magwaza chieftainship, Qethuka kaMaqondo, broke away, taking several companies of his men with him and streaming round to join the left horn.

Although they spilled out of the valley in confusion, however, the Zulu officers tried to deploy them in some kind of order once they reached the more open country beyond. 'We heard firing on top of the rise,' said Mhlahlana of the iNgobamakhosi, 'and as soon as we got on the top we saw the Ukandempemvu and the white men at grips with each other. We were then brought round to get into line with the Ukandempemvu . . .'[49]

The original marching order had probably reflected the planned battle dispositions of the *amabutho* – those in the right column on the right, and those in the left on the left – but in the rush, as the uNokhenke eyewitness explained, 'the original Zulu left became their extreme right, while their right became their centre, and the centre the left'.[50] Even so, improvised as it was, this disposition was a remarkable triumph on the part of middle-ranking officers, and probably reflects the re-establishment of discipline when the commanders of the individual *amabutho*, fresh from discussing plans for the assault on the camp, finally caught up with their men.[51] Now the uDududu, isaNgqu and iMbube *amabutho* formed the right horn, hurrying up the open upper reaches of the Ngwebeni towards the high point of Mkwene across the heights, while the uNokhenke, uKhandempemvu, uMbonambi and a few companies of the uMxapho formed the chest, and the iNgobamakhosi, uVe and Qethuka's uThulwana the left horn, the extreme flank of which emerged from the valley to the east of Mabaso.

Now was the time for men who had brought their own protective medicines to apply them, chewing roots or snorting the coarse ground powders into their nostrils.[52] As the formation took shape, so each *ibutho* shook out its skirmishers, some of the fittest and most courageous men in the army, who set off at a run in extended order to screen the main advance and to drive back the British outposts.

The rest set off at a steady jog, great dark lines streaking across the summer grass, their shields held up so as not to trip them, the white patches on them catching the sun. Here and there knots of men on horseback, mounted *izinduna*, directed them with hoarse shouts and whistles, and now and then their excitement broke out in spontaneous chants and songs.

The moment had finally come to throw back the tide of decades of insidious white influence, to bring an end to those long years which had seen their lands stolen from under them, their traditions eroded by missionaries, their cattle appropriated by traders, and the king's authority and prestige curtailed by the nagging demands of his white neighbours.

It was time to drive out the invaders.

It was the king's day.

Squarely in the centre of them, their position marked by splutters of shot and clouds of gunsmoke, Raw and Roberts had drawn together for support, and were falling back before the attacking Zulu. Barry's NNC infantry, appalled by the enormity of the force unfolding around them, promptly fled, abandoning their officers. George Shepstone turned to Raw's *induna*, Nyanda, and told him – rather superfluously – 'you must retire fighting and draw them towards the camp'.[53] Raw and Roberts managed to put a few hundred metres between their men and the nearest lines of the uKhandempemvu, enough to allow them to dismount, fire a volley, then mount up and retire again before repeating the procedure. The Zulus fired back.

One of Raw's men was knocked out of the saddle by a Zulu bullet. UGuku saw him fall, and thought he was dead – the first of the invaders to die – but according to Nyanda he was only wounded, and the amaNgwane managed to heave him onto his saddle and bring him in.[54] Whether he would survive the day remained to be seen.

# 21

# 'The lightning of heaven'

## iSandlwana, 1 p.m., 22 January 1879

When the first messengers arrived to report to Cetshwayo, 100 kilometres away at oNdini, that a battle had begun at iSandlwana, the king retired immediately to the private hut of the *inkatha yesizwe*, the sacred coil of the nation.[1] It was crucial that the awesome power of long-dead members of the royal house, including Shaka himself, and of the disparate groups which had been bound together to form the kingdom – represented by the myriad of scrapings twisted together into the grass rope – be channelled to support and protect the army in its moment of trial, and the king himself was the conduit: '. . . he took his seat on the *inkatha*, holding the crescent-shaped *inhlendla* – the ceremonial spear with its barbed blade – in his hand. He did this to ensure that his warriors would fight with unity of purpose, that they would not waver, and that victory would be theirs. It was generally believed that if the king was sitting on the *inkatha* the influence of his personality would reach out to his people ensuring the unity of the nation.'[2]

So powerful was the ability of the *inkatha* to bind and protect that it transcended the practical constraints of time and space, functioning on a supernatural plane that recognized no time-lag between the sending and receipt of reports, and took no account of the fact that the battle was undoubtedly over by the time the king was told it had begun. Yet there were dangers, nonetheless, for if the king left the *inkatha* for any reason before he heard the outcome of the battle, the circle of psychic unity would be broken and, as his mothers – Mpande's widows – warned him, 'if he did, the battle could not possibly end in his favour'.[3]

Cetshwayo attended the duty gravely, but after several hours he found it difficult to ignore completely the demands of nature and of his court; 'Fleet-footed messengers kept coming in with hurried reports about the progress of the battle. When the king heard that his regiments were heading towards victory, he began to leave his seat on the *inkatha* every now and

Rupert Lonsdale, Commandant of the 3rd Regiment NNC, who rode into the camp at iSandlwana on the afternoon of 22 January only to find it in the possession of the Zulus.

A man of ruthless action, fierce prejudices, and questionable background – George 'Maori' Browne, the scourge of the 3rd NNC.

Major John Dartnell of the Natal Mounted Police, who commanded Chelmsford's reconnaissance on 21 January 1879.

Theophilus Shepstone's son George, Durnford's political officer, who was killed at iSandlwana.

*Above* The Red Soldiers – the ill-fated band of the 1/24th, photographed on the Eastern Cape shortly before their departure for Zululand.

*Opposite top* Auxiliaries: men of an unidentified unit of the Mounted Native Contingent, who fought for the British in 1879.

*Below* The men who defended iSandlwana – H Co., 1/24th, photographed just three months before the battle. Their officers are (sitting front, left to right) Lt. Charles Cavaye, Lt. Charles Atkinson and Captain George Wardell, all of whom were killed with their men.

Men of Major Bengough's battalion of the 1st NNC. Some of these men crossed into Zululand downstream from Rorke's Drift on the morning of 22 January.

This is widely held to be one of only two photographs to have been taken of Ntshingwayo kaMahole, the senior Zulu commander at the battle of iSandlwana.

Zibhebhu kaMaphitha, the young, ambitious and daring head of the Mandlakazi lineage of the Zulu Royal House, who led the Zulu scouts during the iSandlwana campaign.

*Left*
Sigcewelegcwele kaMhlekeleke, who commanded the iNgobamakhosi at iSandlwana.

*Right*
The iziGqoza: Prince Sikhotha kaMpande, a brother and rival to King Cetshwayo, who fought at iSandlwana with the NNC.

Prince Dabulamanzi kaMpande, the king's younger, self-confident brother who commanded the attack on Rorke's Drift, photographed in 1873. Dabulamanzi was a friend of Cetshwayo's white adviser John Dunn (on the right here), and through him learned to appreciate both horses and guns.

Perhaps the most accurate contemporary sketch of Zulus advancing into battle in 1879, drawn by Charles Fripp who witnessed the sight at Ulundi – an *ibutho* deploying into line by companies with supports coming up behind as the first British shells burst overhead. They are young men, led by an older *induna*, and carry a typical mix of traditional weapons and firearms.

'Fix bayonets and die like British soldiers do!' How *The Graphic* portrayed the last desperate stages of the battle of iSandlwana to its readers.

Melton Prior's stark portrayal of the horrors of iSandlwana – bodies sketched on the battlefield during the burial expedition of 21 May 1879. When this picture was published in the *Illustrated London News,* the remains were discreetly censored, and the original image is published for the first time here.

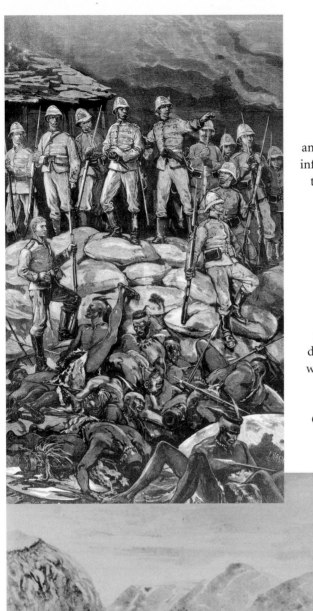

*Left* Aftermath: Lts. Chard and Bromhead survey the carnage inflicted on the uThulwana during the hours of desperate fighting at Rorke's Drift.

*Below* The grisly reality of iSandlwana – of stripped and disembowelled bodies mixed up with the carcasses of slaughtered animals – is evident in this eye-witness sketch of Lord Chelmsford's withdrawal from the stricken field at first light on the morning of the 23rd.

then.'[4] The royal mothers scolded him; he would see, they said, the consequences of his inattention when the army returned.

*

Captain Gardner and the other officers sent back by Lord Chelmsford with orders to pack up the camp had arrived at iSandlwana about noon. They had ridden across the plain without seeing any sign of the Zulus, but not long after arriving, Gardner had been making his way to the headquarters tent when the sound of firing drifted across the tents from somewhere beyond the escarpment. The gunfire aroused little more than mild curiosity, the men scouring the skyline of the iNyoni for clues as to its source. But nothing could be seen; Barry's picket was no longer on Mkwene, and Cavaye's company had moved forward out of sight. From the foot of iSandlwana nothing was visible beyond a few puffs of dust marking the movements of the Carbineer vedettes 8 kilometres away on iThusi. Pulleine did not trouble to emerge from his tent.

Then, suddenly, there had been a commotion on the spur, and Brickhill looked up to see three horsemen galloping down

> . . . at full speed. Captain G. Shepstone, who was one of them, rode into the 1/24th camp and asked for the officer in command. I was taking him to Colonel Pulleine's tent when one of our officers shouting the Colonel's name came out, but before Captain S. could sufficiently recover his breath to speak to him Captain Gardner of the General's staff rode up with a letter from the General which the Colonel read aloud, only four of us being present. It was an order to strike the camps and come with all speed leaving a sufficient guard behind to protect such as could not be moved without delay. Captain Shepstone then said 'I'm not an alarmist, Sir, but the Zulus are in such black masses over there, such long black lines that you have to give us all the assistance you can. They are fast driving our men this way.' As he spoke the Basutos (Durnford's Horse) came retiring over the hill . . . keeping up a steady fire as they retreated before the advancing Zulus. Captain Gardner then said to Colonel Pulleine, who seemed thoroughly perplexed as to what he ought to do, 'Under the circumstances I should advise your disobeying the General's order for the present at any rate. The General knows nothing of this, he is only thinking of the cowardly way in which the Zulus are running before our troops over yonder.'[5]

Pulleine can be allowed his moment of confusion. Just an hour or two earlier the sound of firing at Mangeni had confirmed in the minds of almost everyone in the camp at iSandlwana that Lord Chelmsford was engaged in a significant action 20 kilometres away. The recent Zulu movements on the heights had been mysterious, but hardly threatening; now the news brought by Shepstone seemed to turn their understanding of the situation on its head. Shepstone was agitated after his ride, breathless and clearly excited by what he had seen, a fact which probably exaggerated the scepticism among the 24th's officers which had prevailed towards Durnford's command after his extravagant requests earlier that morning. And the terrain offered Pulleine no clues – apart from a few of the amaNgwane, who had rallied on the skyline near Mkwene and were firing at targets out of sight of the camp, nothing of the heights could be seen from the foot of iSandlwana.

It was a crucial moment of decision for Pulleine, and in effect his first under major combat conditions. He took Gardner's advice, and scribbled a brief note in reply to Chelmsford's order, reporting the firing to the left, and that he could not move camp *at present*. It was a report that conveyed little sense of urgency, largely because at that stage Pulleine felt none. Even so, Gardner afterwards thought it needed some amplification, and sent a note of his own: 'Heavy firing near left of camp. Shepstone has come in for reinforcements and reports the Basutos falling back the whole force turned out and firing about 1 mile [1.6 kilometres] to left flank. Alan Gardner, Captain.'[6] This report would not reach Clery until 3 p.m.

Brickhill then saw Pulleine walk away with Gardner, and any comments Pulleine may have made, any expansion on his decision or orders he may have given to his adjutant or the 24th Battalion officers are lost to history. Nevertheless, bugles sounded and troops fell in, and Brickhill, who was carrying only a sjambok – a tough hide whip used as a riding crop – went off to see if he could find a gun. Shepstone and Hamer, having presumably received some reassurance of support, mounted their horses and rode out again to rejoin their men on the ridge.

The 24th companies fell in in columns in front of their tents. The threat seemed to be coming from one specific direction – the north – and Pulleine reacted accordingly, husbanding his troops until the situation became clearer. The 24th officers had been assessing the camp's defensive potential since the column had arrived at iSandlwana two days before, and Pulleine's initial deployments reflect a good understanding of the ground. Any Zulu threat developing from the iNyoni heights would have to descend the escarpment facing the left side of the camp. At the foot of the slope are a network of *dongas* which drain the high ground, meander directly east for a few hundred metres, along the foot of the ridge, then curve lazily south, feeding into the deeper Nyogane complex. On the far side of these *dongas* the ground rises again towards the flats on which the camp was built, and the contour where the ground levels out is marked by scatterings of large boulders.

Viewed from the tents, the hollows created by the *dongas* would be dead ground – ground that could not be reached by rifle fire – which could serve to shelter the Zulu advance once it reached the foot of the escarpment close to the left of the camp. If the British troops pushed further out, however, positioning themselves somewhere on the near slope, looking across the *dongas* to the foot of the escarpment, they would dominate the depressions and turn the *dongas* to defensive advantage, into a barrier that might break the momentum of the Zulu attack.

Before the war, Chelmsford had issued standing orders to his column commanders on his preferred fighting formations. Although primarily intended for defending moving columns, rather than fixed points like camps, these were based on the successful expedients of the Cape Frontier Wars campaign, where it had not been necessary for infantry to fight in close-order formations. Instead, Chelmsford had recommended anchoring lines upon a fixed and strong centre – field-guns – and deploying infantry in extended formations to the sides. On the frontier this had provided a wide enough defensive front without any apparent dilution of firepower. Mounted troops or auxiliaries were to be placed on the wings to provide a mobile counter-attack to any enemy attempt to envelope the flanks. Both Durnford and Glyn had been issued with copies of these orders, and indeed, by a strange combination of circumstances, both copies were later found on the battlefield. It is extremely unlikely that Glyn had not discussed their tactical implications with the officers of the 1/24th long before the column crossed into Zululand.[7]

Pulleine's initial dispositions reflect Chelmsford's instructions. With the crackling of gunfire still going on beyond the skyline, Pulleine sent his Artillery component – Curling's two 7-pdr guns – out to a point about 400 metres to the left front of the camp. Lieutenant Curling was congratulating himself at the prospect of his first independent command in action, but he was to be disappointed; just as the guns were being limbered up in

the camp, Major Smith, who had ridden back from Chelmsford that
morning to supervise the packing up of the battery equipment, arrived to
take command. Later, Curling would find some relief in this, as it 'of course
relieves me of all responsibility as to the movements of the guns'.[8] The
gun-carriages made across the open flat in front of the camp and halted
on the edge of the falling ground, looking across the *dongas* and towards
the escarpment beyond. When the guns had been unlimbered they were
unsupported, but shortly afterwards one of the 1/24th companies was sent
out from the camp. They took up a position in two lines behind the guns,
the men kneeling down to await further orders.

In the meantime, the sound of firing on the hills had increased, coming
from further to the left now, where a haze of smoke began to rise up from
the area where Lieutenant Cavaye's company had been posted earlier. With
no sign of a Zulu threat anywhere else along the skyline, Pulleine dispatched
a second 24th company to support it. Captain Mostyn's F Company had
only arrived in the camp the day before from the long march up country:
they were in luck it seemed – they had arrived in time to join the fun.

Captain Edward Essex of the 75th (Stirlingshire) Regiment was a special
service officer attached to the column as Glyn's Director of Transport (a
post which made him Horace Smith-Dorrien's boss). Essex had watched
the earlier alarms that morning, but had retired to his tent when the Zulus
had withdrawn and was busy writing letters home when he was interrupted
by news of the unfolding drama:

> About noon a sergeant came to my tent and told me that firing was to
> be heard behind the hill where the company of the 1st Battalion 24th
> had been sent. I had my glasses over my shoulder and thought I might
> as well take my revolver: but did not trouble to put on my sword, as I
> thought nothing of the matter and expected to be back in half an hour
> to complete my letters. I got on my horse and galloped up the hill,
> passing a company of the 24th on its way to the front . . .[9]

As Essex rode past, Mostyn – who was on foot – asked him to take a
message to Cavaye, telling him to look out for his right flank, as Mostyn
intended to take up a position on his left. This is an interesting remark,
since it implies such a disposition had been planned in advance – probably
in response to the difficult terrain extending around the back of iSandlwana
to the north-west.

As he rode up the track leading up the ridge, Essex could see something of the amaNgwane falling back at the top, near Mkwene, but nothing of Cavaye's company until he crested the skyline. He was now on a rocky spur which framed iSandlwana to the north, and the ground fell away in front of him towards a stream that drained westwards towards the Manzimyama. Ahead of him, across the stream, the ground rose up again, an open slope heavily strewn with boulders, but to his right the high-point of Mkwene blocked out the country beyond. Below him, on the near slope, Cavaye's company were spread out in extended order, thin pin-pricks of red dotted among the brown boulders and green grass. Off to his left, Essex could see that Cavaye had detached a section under Second Lieutenant Dyson to a high-point about 500 metres away in an attempt to protect his flank. From their position Dyson's men could cover the lower sweep of the stream as it began to curl round steeply into the Manzimnyama valley.

Essex was surprised to see them firing at an impressive Zulu formation on the slope opposite. The Zulus were about 700 metres away, and were advancing from somewhere behind Mkwene hill; they were not coming straight at Cavaye's men, however, but were moving to their right, across Cavaye's front, the men stooping as they ran, and ducking behind boulders. The impression they made on Essex suggested a chilling possibility: 'Their line was about 1000 yards [914 metres] in extent, but arranged like a horn – that is, very thin and extended on their right, but gradually thickening towards ours. They did not advance, but moved steadily towards our left, each man running from rock to rock, for the ground here was covered with large boulders, with the evident intention of outflanking us.'[10] Essex could see nothing of their supports behind Mkwene, though he noted with professional respect that 'they skirmished very beautifully, and I saw that very few, considering we now had about 3000 opposed to us, were hit'.[11]

As Mostyn's men came up, they formed up in the gap between Cavaye and Dyson. Essex was well known to the men of the 24th, and he now assumed the duties of a company officer, cheering the men on, directing their fire and encouraging them not to waste ammunition. He noticed that the Zulus began returning their fire, but that it was badly directed, and most of their shots fell short or whistled over the men's heads. After a while he became aware that there was an NNC company on his right, but admitted that he 'did not notice the latter much; except that they blazed away at an absurd rate'.[12]

*

At the far eastern end of the high ground, 10 kilometres away, the uVe and Qethuka's uThulwana had spilled out of the Ngwebeni to the east of Mabaso hill, and were sweeping rapidly along the eastern edge of the iNyoni uplands towards the valley of the Nxibongo stream. The uVe were young men, boys no more than nineteen or twenty, and the name was a wry comment on their enthusiasm – uVe is the isiZulu name for the flycatcher, a bird that darts rapidly hither and thither in pursuit of its prey. And the uVe would need their energy, for circumstances had placed them furthest of the attacking *amabutho* from the British camp, with the greatest distance to cover if they were to sweep round as the encircling left horn.

They had not gone far, however, when they streamed off the undulating high ground and down towards the source of the Nxibongo – only to find Durnford at the head of his men moving towards them from the opposite direction. For William Cochrane this was the first time in his military career that he witnessed an attack launched against British troops in anger – and he, too, was impressed. 'They were in skirmishing order, but ten or twelve deep, with supports close behind. They opened fire at us at about 800 yards [732 metres], and advanced very rapidly. We retired some little way . . .'[13]

According to Lieutenant Davies, commanding the Edendale troop, Durnford reacted coolly enough to the threat as it developed. 'Let the enemy come a little closer', he ordered, 'then fire and retire; keep the enemy at a distance of about 200 yards [183 metres]';[14] 'Durnford gave the order for us to extend our men, and wait for the enemy to come within 400 yards [366 metres] of us, then Henderson and my troop to retire and fire alternately towards the camp. We did as we were ordered, my troop being on the left was of course nearest the camp, and also the ridge . . .'[15]

According to Jabez Molife, 'After this we remounted and retreated 20 yards [18 metres], always in a long thin line, then dismounted and fired, up again for another ten yards, dismounted and fired again, and so on ten yards at a time, firing always, slowly back towards the camp. We were not very many, but because of the way we were handled by our leader we were enough to stop the Zulus on that side for a long time.'[16]

Just 10 or 20 metres each time; a very short distance indeed. It was, of course, far more reliable to dismount and fire, for firing even a carbine on horseback was a difficult process which did little for accuracy, even for experienced cavalrymen, and made the horses difficult to control. Even so, with the inevitable time it took to perform the operation each time, the

Zulus must have very soon reduced the gap between the two forces, making it an increasingly dangerous move, and it says much for Durnford's powers of command that his men stuck to his orders – although perhaps the risks made the distances seem shorter to Jabez than they actually were. Even so, Durnford's command numbered scarcely a hundred men, and with no impression of the events unfolding on the rest of the field, they must have felt acutely aware of just how outnumbered they were – the uVe alone numbered over 3,000 men.

Durnford was undaunted, however. He had, it seemed, already recovered from his earlier momentary flicker of irritation; with the fighting begun, his personal demons evaporated in the controlled excitement of command. He was in battle again, in a fair and open fight, unconstrained this time by uncomfortable and inconvenient orders. It was the moment Durnford had waited for all his professional career; iSandlwana, it seemed, offered him both validation and vindication.

On the receiving end of Durnford's fire, uNzuzi Mandla of the uVe recalled how the Zulus soon came to realize what halting and dismounting among their enemy foretold, and how they ducked down into the grass in anticipation of the volleys: 'As long as they fired we kept still, but as soon as their shooting ceased, and they retired to their camp on their horses, we followed, making the *impi* into the shape of horns.'[17] Yet the bullets still fell among them, and the uVe began to suffer their first casualties of the day.

According to Davies, this fighting retreat continued for about 4 kilometres down the Nxibongo, until Durnford's command passed the ama-Tutshane 'conical hill' and began to swing in a more westerly direction, back towards the camp. They had not gone far when they came across the remnants of the rocket battery.

*

The rocket battery had set out not long after Durnford's horsemen, but from the first it had lagged behind. The battery consisted of three troughs firing 9-pdr rockets, and both the apparatus and ammunition were carried on mules. The rockets themselves were ingenious contraptions reflecting the engineering and mechanical optimism of the Victorian age; they were launched from steel troughs with a flat V-shaped profile, each of which was fitted with collapsible legs which unfolded and extended to form a supporting tripod. The Hales-pattern rockets were simple cylindrical shells with no fins or sticks to stabilize them in flight; they were filled with a rapid-burning propellant which burned unpredictably but with a great rush of sparks and smoke. There were three vents at the base of each rocket, and they were fired by attaching a friction tube and lanyard to one of the vents then yanking hard to ignite the propellant – the vents were screened by angled flanges which were supposed to direct the burning jets, giving the rocket a spinning motion. Their accuracy and range was unpredictable at the best of times, however, and they were acutely susceptible to any imperfections in the launch or to encounters with obstacles in flight. If the rocket was set up on uneven ground it might spin off in an unexpected direction; the lanyard-man was supposed to lay the cord under his foot and give it a sharp pull with his other hand – a process with an inherent degree of rough handling inimical to precision. A cross-wind in flight might divert the rocket, and if it hit a bush or boulder it was highly likely to bounce back towards the crew. If the rockets had been badly stored, the propellant burned unevenly, giving a distorted spin, and sometimes causing them to break up in a spray of flames in flight; in the Cape Frontier Wars one rocket had exploded as it left the trough, and a piece of it had flown back and cut off the lanyard-man's ear. Even if they did strike their targets, the results were unpredictable – they had no detonating war-head, and while they sometimes burst in a shower of burning propellant, they were equally liable to writhe around in a spray of smoke and sparks until they fizzled out.

Nonetheless, although their limitations were well known, they had their advantages; they were portable in a way that heavier artillery was not, and they could be a highly effective incendiary weapon. There was also a pre-vailing view that they were exactly the sort of white man's magic guaranteed to overawe unsophisticated enemies.

The rockets were under the command of Major Francis Broadfoot Russell of the Royal Artillery, who was assisted by Bombardier Gough and by nine men seconded from the ever-dependable 1/24th. They were escorted by one of Durnford's NNC companies, D Company 1/1st NNC, commanded by Captain Cracroft Nourse. The NNC were on foot, and the ground covered by Durnford had been rough, seamed by *dongas* and broken by stones which slowed the mules. It had not been long before Durnford's men had disappeared from sight, leaving the rocket battery moving alone across the plain. They too, could see nothing of the events on the high ground above the escarpment to their left, but they had heard the shots from Raw's encounter clearly enough, and after a while firing from somewhere beyond iThusi and amaTutshane. They had no idea what it meant, of course, and Russell had continued his advance.

When they were about 2.5 kilometres from the camp, they met Troopers Barker and Hawkins of the Carbineers coming towards them. Barker and Hawkins had gone up onto the high ground after the earlier Zulu withdrawal, and from there they had seen the attack spilling out from the Ngwebeni in the distance, then 'advancing slowly' as they took up battle formation. While Barker and Hawkins had ridden down to warn Lieutenant Scott, another of their colleagues had set off after Durnford. Scott had sent Barker and Hawkins back to the camp to report, and '. . . we met the rocket battery, who enquired the enemy's whereabouts. We advised the officer to proceed to where Lieut. Scott was stationed, but he asked if he could get up a hill to his left. We informed him that the Zulus were advancing towards that hill, and most probably would be seen on it within half an hour. The officer decided to proceed up this hill . . .'[18] According to Nourse, '. . . a vedette rode down to us from the hill and said – I quote his words – "If you want any fun come to the top of the hill. They are thick up there." We decided to go . . .'[19]

Several of Russell's crew claimed that one of the Carbineers offered to lead them to a short cut by which they could join Shepstone's men. Russell's position at the bottom of the slope was certainly a vulnerable one with limited visibility, and it made sense for him to try for higher ground where he could see what was happening and get a clear view of possible targets. He gave the order for the battery to head up the escarpment, aiming for a notch on the skyline just to the west of iThusi.

Their route took them through more difficult country as they struggled in the searing midday heat to pull the mules up through the *dongas* which scoured the lower slopes of the escarpment. Russell himself was mounted, and pressed on ahead, cresting the summit; he only stayed there a few moments, however, before turning his horse and galloping down the slope, shouting out 'Action front!'

The mules had reached a slight spur jutting out from the escarpment about halfway down. The skyline was a few hundred metres in front of them; off to their left a *donga* cut into the slope, but the top of the knoll was relatively flat and large enough to set up the rocket troughs.

Beyond the skyline, the iNgobamakhosi were moving rapidly towards them. They had kept to the high ground, leaving the valley of the Nxibongo,

and with it the uVe and Qethuka's uThulwana, on their left, and they had
thrown out a cloud of skirmishers before them. The sight which greeted
Russell as he crested the rise must have been an awesome one, for the
iNgobamakhosi skirmishers cannot have been far off, coming straight at
him, with their main body perhaps a kilometre behind, and the other
*amabutho* ranging off to his left.

With little idea of what was about to descend on them, the crew
unpacked the rockets and set up the troughs as quickly as they could. They
were nearly ready to fire when the first Zulus appeared over the crest in
front of them. Russell gave the order to fire, and one rocket screeched off,
showering out fat yellow sparks and stiff white smoke; a few years later, the
traveller Bertram Mitford met a Zulu who had been under it as it passed
overhead, and who had been showered with burning propellant – he was
'marked about the chest and shoulders as if he had been tattooed with
Chinese white'.[20] The Zulus displayed no obvious signs of superstitious
terror, but even so they were struck by the weapon's strangeness. Years
later, Mehlokazulu told the missionary Reverend A.W. Lee that a man of
the iNgobamakhosi named Manzi kaShodo who was a praise-singer suddenly called out

> Mbane, mbane wezulu, kuyacwazimula,
> Langa, langa amaZulu, liyashisha konke!

'Lightning, lightning of heaven', he called, 'it glitters and it shines; the sun,
the sun of the Zulus, it consumes all!' It was a quick-witted retort, seizing
on the apparent harmlessness of the British 'lightning', and contrasting it
to the all-consuming 'sun of the Zulus', and the iNgobamakhosi 'caught up
the song, and quickly three thousand throats were yelling it as we moved
forward down the ridge'.[21]

The Zulu skirmishers quite sensibly veered off towards the *donga* to one
side of the battery's position. Here they disappeared for a few seconds,
dropping down among some rocks about 200 metres away from where they
fired a volley – and Russell's command immediately fell apart. According
to Captain Nourse:

> The Zulus were lying not a hundred paces off in the tall grass, and with
> that buzzing Usutu of theirs they were on us. It electrified the donkeys,
> which hee-hawed down the hill with the speed of race-horses, in spite
> of their packs. My men disappeared as if by magic, and though a bit

slow on the take-off, I myself reached the hill in respectable time. Major Russell, who was mounted, was with me. As the Zulus were not pressing their success with undue haste, we halted to survey the scene. Just then a shot struck Major Russell and caused him to drop from his horse. I lifted him onto his horse and thought he could manage to get clear . . .[22]

Nourse lost sight of Russell in the scrimmage, but Private Johnson of the 24th saw him, and tried to help him away, but Russell was an obvious target and they had only gone a few paces when he was hit again and fell dead from his horse.[23]

In fact Nourse's men had managed to fire a few shots before their courage deserted them. Private Trainer of the 24th noted that 'a number of them were unable to extract the empty cartridges after firing, and I offered to do so for some of them but they refused to give me their rifles'.[24] Nevertheless, at the bottom of the slope five men stood by Nourse, and he directed them to a clump of rocks nearby where they made something of a stand.

The iNgobamakhosi made no effort to drive them out, and the two sides shot at each other in a desultory manner for a while, several of Nourse's men being killed. The Zulus were in no hurry; it was the job of skirmishers to clear the way for the advance of the main body, and they knew what Nourse did not – that the main army was rolling its way steadily across the heights, and would be with them soon enough. Nevertheless, the respite was enough to allow the survivors from the rocket battery, including Bombardier Gough and Privates Johnson and Trainer of the 24th, to make their way back towards the camp.

The skirmishing was still going on when Durnford reappeared around the southern edge of amaTutshane. 'Just as we got round the pointed hill', said Davies:

I came upon Captain Nourse who was fighting hard, he had only four of his men standing by him out of 120. He remarked on our meeting that the Rocket Battery was done for, mules bolted; he then returned with us. I saw a little to our left a mule with two boxes of rockets. I sent one of my men to get it; he had to go pretty close to the enemy to do so as the mule was between us and the enemy. He brought the mule and we sent it off to camp; we also saw here some boxes of ammunition or rockets. We made some of our men carry them, but they abandoned them after a while, the enemy being so close . . .[25]

A little further on, they came across the survivors of the rocket crew, and Durnford himself asked Private Johnson where the battery was; Johnson was unimpressed and clearly thought the Zulus more intimidating than Durnford. 'I told him that the battery was cut up and the Captain shot, when he said you had better go back and get him. I then pointed out that the enemy had already nearly surrounded us . . .'[26]

*

Durnford's baggage wagons had finally arrived in the camp at iSandlwana about noon, escorted by Lieutenant Wyatt Vause's No. 3 Troop, Zikhali Horse, and by men of D Company, 1/1st NNC, commanded by Lieutenant Walter Stafford. Vause and Stafford had been sent back by Durnford just under an hour earlier, and they had found the wagons and brought them in without incident. The situation they found on their return had been very different, however.

Durnford had not troubled to appoint a camping ground, so it is difficult to know where his wagons were left, and whether they were outspanned. The wagons, however, were the least of their problems, for Vause and Stafford found that heavy firing was going on just out of sight, above the spur to the north about 2 kilometres away from the left boundary of the camp. There was no sign of Durnford, but the sound of more distant firing could also be heard, probably from the direction of amaTutshane.

On the heights above, still out of sight from the camp, the Zulu attack was now developing. Those *amabutho* who had bivouacked furthest upstream on the Ngwebeni, towards iSandlwana – the iSangqu, uDududu and iMbube, all associated with the kwaNodwengo royal homestead – formed the right horn passing close under the Nquthu hills to the west, and it was probably these whom Essex had noted running so determinedly across Cavaye's front. They had disappeared somewhere in the direction of the Manzimnyama valley, behind iSandlwana. On their left were the uNokhenke and uKhandempemvu, whose skirmishers, entangled in the fight with Raw and Roberts, had drawn ahead of their main bodies. Further east, next to the uKhandempemvu and largely uncommitted, were the uMbonambi and a few companies of the uMxapho. On the far left, the iNgobamakhosi, uVe and elements of the uThulwana had already become engaged with the rocket battery and Durnford's men.

A serious tussle now developed for the high ground around Mkwene, and the ridge which sloped off it to the west, where Cavaye and Mostyn were posted. This ground commanded the Zulu right, and if the Zulus could drive the British off the ridge-tops they could use the ground to mask their deployments without interference. The right horn had successfully passed across the front of the British positions, but if the British continued to occupy the Mkwene area they would effectively drive a wedge between the right horn and the chest of the Zulu army. As the vanguard of the uNokhenke came up, it made a determined effort to drive off Raw and Roberts, throwing out a horn of its own which threatened to surround them to the west, until it ran squarely into the face of Mostyn and Cavaye's companies.

Raw had turned his troop to his left, to avoid the danger of being outflanked, but then found that his right flank and even his rear was threatened by the uKhandempemvu coming up rapidly behind Mkwene. It was now becoming obvious that, despite their mobility – being on horseback – Raw and Roberts could not hope to stem the tide of the Zulu advance in that sector alone, and they began to retreat down the spur towards the camp. Seeing them go, the skirmishers of the uNokhenke rushed forward to follow them up.

Before Raw and Roberts reached the bottom, however, they met Vause's troop who, with Stafford's men on foot trailing behind, had been sent out to support them. According to Vause, 'I got back with the wagons and hearing firing about two miles [3.2 kilometres] to the front of the camp, I at once gave the order to trot and started off to find Colonel Durnford. I soon came across Captain Shepstone and he asked me to stop with him. I dismounted the men and we extended them in skirmishing order.'[27]

All three troops then advanced back up the hill, and Vause found his men 'Soon under a hot fire, but [we] continued to advance tho' very slowly as the Zulus were under good cover and we had to expose ourselves every time we advanced.'[28]

The sudden increase in fire from the amaNgwane caught the uNokhenke just as they crested the skyline, causing heavy casualties and driving them back over the ridge in some disorder, many of the Zulus dropping their shields and spears as they ran. The amaNgwane then pressed forward to re-occupy the ridge.

It was about this time that Lieutenant Walter Stafford and his fifty NNC infantry arrived on the heights. Years later, Stafford struggled to remember the exact dispositions he found as he crested the skyline – 'but we were all in a line on the first ridge of Isandhlwana'[29] – but he seems to

have been placed in the gap which still remained between Mostyn's
company and Dyson's flank-guard to the left of the 24th line. Stafford
remembered Captain Essex was there, and 'next to him was Wyatt Vause'.[30]
Even at this stage, fighting their own battle on an isolated sector of the
battlefield, the troops had taken up a position reminiscent of Chelmsford's
standing orders, with the regulars in the centre and auxiliaries on the
flanks. There may well have been other NNC in the area too, the remains
of Barry's picket who had started the morning on Mkwene but had buckled
under the pressure of Raw's encounter near the Ngwebeni. Certainly a few
of their white officers and NCOs had rallied once they were close enough
to the 24th for support.

More to the point, Stafford noticed that a large body of Zulu were
directly opposite him across the valley. Stafford lived to be an old man, and
told the story of the battle many times, differing in minor details as the
years went by. In some accounts he pictured the Zulus 'advancing steadily',
and in others 'sitting down', but there was no doubt how threatening they
seemed. Probably these were the skirmishers of the uNokhenke, regrouping
after their checked rush down the spur, and waiting for the main body to
come up. 'When I arrived on the ridge,' recalled Stafford, 'I halted and my
*induna* Ntini came to me and asked me to show him how to regulate the
sight of his rifle. There were a large number of Zulus sitting down about
800 yards [732 metres] away from us. I put my sight up to 700 yards and
fired into them. The bullets struck short and I put my sight up to 800 yards
and that bullet struck home.'[31]

As the battle for the ridge intensified, so a sense of isolation enveloped
those engaged in it. Strung out in the shallow valleys west of Mkwene, the
troops could not see the camp, 2 kilometres behind them, nor could the
men in the camp see them; they were assaulted by the din of battle, by
the drum-roll of the infantry volleys and by the constant popping of the
amaNgwane's carbines, by the excited buzz of the Zulus opposite and their
sudden sonorous war-cries. There was no relief on the exposed rocky slopes
that hot Wednesday afternoon from the full force of the summer sun, and
a haze of white powder-smoke hung in the breathless air. Most soldiers
experience a degree of tunnel vision in combat, preoccupied with events
going on directly to their front, their senses heightened and distorted by
the effect of adrenaline, by the heady mixture of exhilaration and downright
fear, and the men on the ridge certainly had little sense of anything
occurring elsewhere around them.

Yet they were by no means alone. Essex had been helping to supervise the fire of Mostyn's company for a while – he thought it 'five minutes' but it was probably longer – when 'I was informed by Lieutenant Melville, Adjutant of the 1st Battalion 24th Regiment, that a fresh body of the enemy was appearing in force in our rear, and he requested me to direct the left of the line formed . . . to fall slowly back, keeping up the fire . . .'[32]

In the camp, Pulleine and his officers had at last been granted their first glimpse of the Zulu attack – and they could see what Essex and the men on the ridge could not, that a large body of men, the main body of the uKhandempemvu and uMbonambi, were beginning to crest the skyline along the length of the iNyoni ridge, east of Mkwene. If these men pressed down the slope – and there was very little to stop them – they would pass to the right and rear of the men battling for the ridge, who were now in grave danger of being cut off.

Within minutes of their appearance on the ridge, the forward positions of the British around Mkwene became untenable – and the battle for the ridge was lost. Melvill had presumably passed on the same order to fall back to George Shepstone, since Vause suddenly became aware that '. . . the enemy in overwhelming numbers were coming up from behind, and fearing our ammunition would be expended before we could regain the camp, Captain Shepstone gave the orders to retire back to our horses.'[33]

Essex did as Melvill instructed him, riding out to deliver the order to Dyson's detachment on the far left. He then turned back towards the centre of the line to find that it had already withdrawn, both the 24th and the amaNgwane funnelling down the narrow track of the spur. According to Wyatt Vause:

> Fortunately the Zulus were shooting very badly and as yet very few casualties had occurred on our side. As soon as the Zulus perceived we were in retreat, they came on with a shout and were rapidly gaining on us when we regained our horses. As soon as the men were mounted, we retired slowly on the camp, dismounting at every few yards and firing a volley but without holding the enemy in check as they did not seem to mind our fire at all . . .[34]

'We retreated to the bottom of the hill,' admitted Raw's *induna*, Nyanda, ruefully, 'mixed up with the company of redcoats that had advanced with us.'[35] The uNokhenke rushed forward to occupy the ridge-top, and Essex was forced to turn away and find his way down alone – 'I therefore followed in the same direction, but being mounted had great difficulty in descending the hill, the ground being very rocky and precipitous.'[36]

The battle on the ridge had been conducted entirely at rifle range, and Essex agreed that 'the enemy's fire had hitherto been very wild and ineffective', while Nyanda thought 'up to this time no soldiers had fallen'.[37] The point is significant because after the battle there were persistent rumours that Mostyn and Cavaye's companies had been cut off and destroyed on the ridge, and recently a new myth has emerged to the effect that Dyson's detachment was overrun and wiped out before it could rejoin Cavaye's company. This seems to be based on the fact that a grave – apparently since disappeared – once lay on the slopes of the spur. In the 1960s an official in the then Natal Monuments Council was commissioned to repair many of the outlying graves, and indicated that at least one grave on the ridge contained 'buttons, boot protectors and bones'; he was adamant, however, that 'this is not, of course, evidence that the casualties at these positions were very heavy'.[38]. Essex makes no mention of undue casualties among Dyson's men, merely remarking that the Zulus 'rushed forward as soon as our men disappeared below the crest'.[39] It is also significant that there are no surviving traditions among the Zulu – who were intensely jealous of the honour of being the first to 'stab' the enemy – to suggest that either the right horn or the uNokhenke were engaged in close-quarter fighting on the hills.

When he reached the bottom of the spur, Essex was relieved to discover that Pulleine had deployed his reserves to cover the retreat, and that Mostyn and Cavaye's men had already taken up a new position. 'On arriving at the foot of the slope I found the two companies of 1st Battalion 24th Regiment drawn up at about 400 yards [366 metres] distant in extended order, and Captain Younghusband's company in similar formation in echelon on the left.'[40]

*

As the sound of rifle fire from the heights had increased to a steady drum-roll, Pulleine had deployed the remainder of the camp's garrison in accordance with Chelmsford's instructions to 'defend the camp'. The full extent of the Zulu attack was not at all clear, but Pulleine had clearly decided to defend the rising ground on the near side of the *dongas* which ran across the foot of the escarpment.

The two guns from N/5 battery remained key to this line. A company of the 1/24th had been sent to support them early on, and after a while a second company arrived. They deployed each side of Smith's guns, Lieutenant Porteous's A Company to the left and Captain Wardell's H Company to the right.

The companies deployed, as Essex noted, in extended order. The 1870s were on the cusp of great changes in tactical doctrine as the British Army strove to adapt its fighting formations to the increased range and effectiveness of breech-loading weapons, moving away from the solid formations of the Napoleonic Wars – when battles fought at close range amid great clouds of smoke required that the men be kept under tight control – to more fluid and adaptable ones. The instruction books of the day laid great emphasis on the rapid deployment from column of march to open skirmishing formations, and although regular infantry were equally trained to fight in tight lines, shoulder to shoulder, the experience of the Cape Frontier Wars had seemed to confirm the necessity to keep lines open when fighting in such difficult terrain. A company extended in a single line – officers to the rear, directing the fire – was recommended to allow 76 centimetres between each man. At iSandlwana, it may well have been more; reviewing the 2/24th at Pietermaritzburg before the war, Chelmsford had ordered the intervals to be doubled, and one of his staff officers – it sounds suspiciously like Crealock – remarked, 'Do you not think, General, that single rank extended would be sufficient for this scum?'[41] On that basis, with an average of 1.5 metres between each man and taking a company at field strength to be about eighty men, a company would take up a frontage of over 120 metres – a very thin red line indeed. If the company were deployed in double ranks – the men behind in the spaces between those in front – the frontage would be much smaller, but the difficulties in covering a wide perimeter all the greater.

With Porteous, Smith and Wardell's companies at the centre of his line, a long way from camp and seemingly dwarfed by the escarpment beyond them, Pulleine filled in the gaps on either side. Captain James Lonsdale's No. 9 Company, 3rd NNC, recalled during the earlier scare, had marched out again to occupy its overnight position on the rocky rise between the *dongas*, and now found itself a few hundred metres to the right of Wardell, facing the open plain to the east, as it had before. Pulleine sent out Lieutenant Charlie Pope's G Company of the 2/24th – which had also been on picket duty overnight – to fill the gap between them. Pope's company seems to have been swollen to almost double its normal size through the

addition of the men left in the camp after the departure of the battalion
with Lord Chelmsford, and Pulleine presumably intended it to serve as a
strong anchor to his right flank. The entire line, Gardner noted, was 'facing
the hill on our left';[42] there was still no sign of Durnford out across the
plain.

The line on the flats was initially roughly aligned with the deployment
on the ridge, but considerably to its rear. By this time Pulleine had
presumably begun to consider the possibility of withdrawing from the
ridge, and if that occurred the units fighting there would fall in at the
bottom of the slope to the left of Porteous. To cover their retreat, Pulleine
sent Captain Younghusband's C Company, 1/24th, to deploy on the far
left, and it formed up a little to the north of the tail-end of iSandlwana,
deployed in echelon, angled to the left so as to command the hollows at
the foot of the spur which fell away towards the Manzimnyama.

Pulleine also had a small detachment of mounted men at his disposal,
a handful of Mounted Infantry, Newcastle Mounted Rifles and Buffalo
Border Guard under the command of Captain Bradstreet. These too were
lined up at the bottom of the escarpment, and at one point moved forward,
presumably to cover the retreat of the men on the ridge. In the camp,
Captain Krohn's company of the NNC had been moved down and lined
up in front of the NNC camp to act as a reserve.

In truth, there was still little enough for the regulars stretched out on
the plain to see, for the battle so far was taking place beyond their line of
sight. A few on the right might have seen the sudden flash and streak of
fizzing smoke that marked the overrunning of the rocket battery far out at
the foot of iThusi, but otherwise all that was visible was the overspill of the
fight for the spur – the retreat and advance again of the amaNgwane horse,
and the sudden appearance of the uNokhenke vanguard, exposed briefly on
the ridge-top before it ducked behind it again. The infantry were probably
kneeling rather than standing, almost lost in the grass which grew waist
high in places – a small relief as they waited in the heat of the day, although
the stony ground must have been hard on their knees – and anticipated the
coming encounter with a confidence born of their successes on the Cape
frontier.

Only Stuart Smith's guns had targets to shoot at. When the uNokhenke
first appeared, Smith opened fire, the first shots screaming over the heads
of the amaNgwane to burst over the Zulus beyond. The guns were firing
shrapnel shells at this stage, which were designed to burst in the air over

the target, showering the enemy with lead balls, but the guns were firing at close to their maximum range – about 3 kilometres – and after the war there was a fierce debate among artillery theorists as to whether the 7-pdr shell had sufficient bursting charge to be effective. And while it was the Artillery officer's job to estimate ranges properly, the fuses were sometimes unpredictable, the shells bursting before they reached their target, or passing over it without inflicting damage. It is unlikely, then, that those early shots caused many casualties among the Zulus, and the risks in firing in close support of friendly units became apparent when the men on the ridge abandoned their positions. The guns kept up their fire to discourage Zulu pursuit, but according to Stafford one shell burst over the head of Roberts's amaNgwane troop as it descended; 'Lieutenant Roberts of Pinetown ... had managed to get his men into a cattle kraal on the ledge of the ridge. I heard subsequently that this officer and his men had been shelled by our artillery, and that Roberts had met his death as a result of this blunder. Our artillery fire was erratic...'[43]

As the men on the ridge fell back in a jumble, and tried to sort themselves out on the line, the men on the plain caught their first sight of the Zulu chest as it spilled over the crest along the entire length of the iNyoni. The iNgobamakhosi probably appeared first, long lines streaming down the notch in the hillside where Russell's command had come to grief. Then, at the opposite end, the uKhandempemvu, just to the right of the Mkwene high-point, and in between them the uMbonambi. They came screened by the usual rush of skirmishers – they 'appeared to grow almost out of the earth. From rock and bush on the heights above started scores of men; some with rifles, others with shields and assegais'[44] – and then, as these rushed down the slope, picking their way between steep rocky patches and running from cover to cover, up came the main body.

By this time most of the men still left in camp – officers' servants, grooms, cooks, artillery artificers, medical, commissariat and transport staff, civilian wagon-drivers and black *voorloopers* – had emerged from among the tents to see the battle unfold. Horace Smith-Dorrien was one of them, and despite a long and eventful career ahead of him, he would remember vividly that first sight of the 'chest': '[They] showed in large numbers, coming down into the plain with great boldness ... It was a marvellous sight, line upon line of men in slightly extended order, one behind the other, firing as they came along...'[45]

Here and there the Zulus bunched together, constricted by impassable tracts of ground, and the hillside rippled with the movement of their shields. Smith-Dorrien noted the sound – 'a curious, humming-buzzing noise'[46] – they made; 'They were giving vent to no loud warcries, but to a low, musical murmuring noise, which gave the impression of a gigantic swarm of bees, getting nearer and nearer.'[47]

That the advance of the Zulu centre had produced a new and serious challenge was obvious. Pulleine had remained in the camp to this point; Walter Higginson had abandoned his position on the ridge earlier – leaving there his sergeant-major, Williams – to make his way back with Barry's officers. He had been intending to rejoin his company when he saw Pulleine and went to report on the state of things on the ridge; he had just finished doing so when the Zulu chest appeared, and Higginson heard Pulleine say 'March all the men out of camp who can carry arms.'[48]

The extent of the attack seems to have surprised Pulleine, for it had only been in the past ten or fifteen minutes that the strength of the Zulu threat from the north had been revealed – and their false assumptions about the whereabouts and intent of the main Zulu army laid bare. At this point Pulleine should have ordered the tents to be struck, to clear the field in the event that the fighting closed in upon the camp – yet he did not. Perhaps at that stage he was still confident that the Zulus could be contained further out, at the foot of the escarpment; perhaps, with the situation changing so rapidly, he simply forgot.

As the uKhandempemvu and uMbonambi filtered down the escarpment, Smith changed target, firing now at the men dangerously exposed on the forward slope directly in front of him. The escarpment was beyond effective rifle range, however, and it was not until the Zulus began to regroup at the bottom, on the far side of the *dongas*, that the infantry began to open fire.

Essex noted, 'Affairs now looked rather serious as our little body appeared altogether insignificant compared to the enormous masses opposed to us. The 24th men, however, were cheery as possible, making remarks to one another about their shooting, and the enemy opposed to them made little progress; but they now pressed within 500 yards [457 metres] of our line.'[49]

It was probably at this point that Curling noticed that the 24th companies on either side of the guns advanced 'about 30 yards'.[50] By moving down the gentle slope ahead of them into the low ground above the *dongas*, the 24th were giving themselves a better field of fire. Quite how far they went is open to debate – they may briefly have lined the edge of the *donga* to exploit its defensive potential; certainly, in 2000, an exploratory archaeological excavation found a scatter of spent Martini-Henry cartridge cases on the slope, while there are a number of intriguing hints from contemporary accounts that they may have gone further and occupied the *donga* itself.[51] While the move may have increased their fire control over the ground at the foot of the escarpment facing them, it was bought at the price of an awareness of what might be taking place elsewhere on the field. From the low ground, the hills shut in the view, and visibility is limited in front to the iNyoni, curving round to amaTutshane off to the right; there is, in particular, no clear sight of what might be taking place far out across the plain, in the direction Durnford had taken.

By this time the men who had retreated from the ridge had formed up at the foot of the slope, some of them apparently using the *dongas* there for cover. It is, once again, difficult to be certain about the exact dispositions, but Younghusband's company was on the left, and next to it a cluster of the NNC. Then there were the three troops of the amaNgwane – Raw, Vause and Roberts's leaderless men – then Bradstreet's mounted men, then Mostyn and Cavaye's 24th companies, which had fallen in close to Porteous's men. The amaNgwane certainly seem to have used the *dongas* as cover – 'we got to the sluit to the left of the camp'[52] said Nyanda – dismounting again, and leaving their horses sheltered in the gulleys.

The interpreter Brickhill had tried to find a spare rifle in the camp 'in the hopes of . . . joining in the fight', but rifles were suddenly in demand and he was unsuccessful. Instead he 'betook myself to a fairly commanding position in front of the column office', and had been watching these deployments on the left, and congratulating himself that the amaNgwane were '. . . keeping up a steady galling fire which, with that of the mounted white force on the right, checked what at first was a very determined advance in the direction of the camp'.[53]

Then, looking up, he noticed something far more sinister. 'Durnford's Horse now appeared to the right of the Conical Hill, keeping up a steady fire and retiring parallel to the road to the Mangeni valley. A much larger force now confronted them than we had yet seen, showing that the enemy had had a large accession to his strength from the hidden end of the [iNyoni] behind Conical Hill . . .'[54]

*

On the Zulu left, the iNgobamakhosi had kept to the high ground, on the eastern end of the iNyoni ridge, while the uVe had driven Durnford up the course of the iNxobongo beside them.

Mehlokazulu had discharged his scouting duties when he had watched the British camp at first light, and on his return to the bivouac he had made his way back to his *ibutho*. Now, as the iNgobamakhosi surged across the heights, he was leading a company of his men. As the company came off the escarpment, a little to the west of amaTutshane, picking up its skirmishers, who had overrun the rocket battery, along the way, it drew close to the uVe, who were sweeping round on the extreme left, on the other side of the conical hill. Durnford's men, falling back before the uVe, had passed amaTutshane before the iNgobamakhosi had been able to intercept them, although Mehlokazulu saw them go, and remembered how they had brushed aside the last of Lieutenant Scott's Carbineer vedettes:

> There is a little red hill which overlooks Isandhlwana, within sight of the camp, and thence the Ngobamakosi, to which I belong, came in contact with two companies of mounted men. This was on the left . . . we were on the height looking down. Some of these mounted men had white stripes up their trousers (Carbineers); there were also men dressed in black, but none of the Native Contingent on the brow of this hill. The Ngobamakosi and uVe regiments attacked on this side. The English force kept turning and firing, but we kept on; they could not stop us . . . [55]

Far away, in the camp, Captain Gardner was among those who, like Brickhill, saw the advance of the left horn. Although Pulleine's left and centre were protected by the *dongas* at the foot of the escarpment, the British right now seemed vulnerable. Here the ground was less helpful, for the *dongas* turned southwards, feeding into the Nyogane complex, and the British right hung uneasily among a line of jagged boulders which marked the contour above it. It was this rocky outcrop which Pope had sensibly occupied – echeloned, it seems, to the right – and a little way beyond him stood Lonsdale's company of the NNC, facing out across the plain. Both positions might have been adequate against an attack launched from the iNyoni alone, but the sweep of the left horn was far greater than anyone in the British camp had anticipated, and although the iNgobamakhosi and uVe were still a long way off, there was a very real danger that – unless

Durnford made more of an effort to stop them – they would simply continue their swing and effortlessly outflank Pulleine's line.

The Hussar Alan Gardner rounded up '30 or 40' mounted men and went to Pulleine to ask permission to take them out to the right. These were Bradstreet's volunteers and Mounted Infantry, who had hitherto been supporting the amaNgwane on the left, but Gardner had spotted an ideal cavalry opportunity on the right: '. . . had there been a regiment or even two squadrons of cavalry, the disaster . . . would not have occurred. The enemy's advance across our front which was requisite in order to turn our right, was in extremely loose order, the ground was an open plain and could easily have been cleared by a determined charge . . .'[56]

But there were no regular cavalry, just Bradstreet and his hotch-potch of left-behind part-time Volunteers, and Gardner was wise not to attempt the charge. Instead, he led them at a canter across the open ground past Pope and Lonsdale's companies to the drift where the track to Mangeni crossed the Nyogane nearly 2 kilometres away. The Nyogane is 12 to 15 metres wide at this point, and the banks 2 to 3 three metres deep, and after the recent heavy rains water was flowing through it ankle-deep. The Volunteers dismounted, leaving their horses in the middle of the stream, and nestled down against the far bank. Ahead of them, to the left, the ground sloped unevenly up towards amaTutshane; somewhere between them and the hill, Durnford and his men were falling back towards them with several thousand Zulus in pursuit.

In fact, Durnford also had with him Lieutenant Scott and the Carbineer vedettes whom he had collected shortly after he met the survivors from the rocket battery. Trooper Barker – who had ridden back to the camp after passing the rocket battery earlier, to replenish his supply of ammunition – had just ridden back out again when he saw Durnford, 'followed by some mounted natives', who called out 'Carbineers, hurry up and follow me' before leading his men into the Nyogane just above Bradstreet's position. Here they 'dismounted, Hawkins, myself and others giving our horses to one of Durnford's natives to hold, promising to tip him when the fight was over. However, he left our horses after a time and rejoined his troop . . .'[57]

That anonymous trooper can hardly be blamed, for within a few minutes it became clear that Durnford now had a determined fight on his hands. One of the Carbineers, Trooper Wheatland Edwards, remembered that:

... This donga was a very deep one – like a great hollow basin – and we managed to get all our horses into it with ease. The natives were now in full view, and we opened fire on them without delay. Nearly every one of us was a good shot, and we were able to knock our men over at 500 or 600 yards [457 or 549 metres] with fair certainty. At this stage each of us was quite cool, although the appalling danger the camp was in was not lost on any of us.[58]

The men directly facing them were the young lads of the uVe, who had pursued Durnford down the valley of the Nxibongo. Coming up behind them, the iNgobamakhosi were streaming off the iNyoni escarpment close to amaTutshane. 'On the side of this little hill', said Mehlokazulu, 'there is a donga, into which the mounted men got, and stopped our onward move there; we could not advance against their fire any longer. They had drawn their horses into this donga, and all we could see were the helmets.'[59]

The gentle slope towards the stream, covered with mealie patches today but then swathed in long grass, was a perfect killing ground, entirely exposed to the British fire at a range of 100 metres or less. Few of the young men facing Durnford had been under fire before that day, and certainly none of them had experienced anything to rival the ferocious intensity as bullets rained down upon them, raking through the grass, clipping through hide shields and tearing them from men's grasps, sending them spinning away. The uVe had suffered a stream of casualties during the pursuit of Durnford's men, but now they were falling heavily, dropping down suddenly or sent tumbling backwards by the impact of the bullets, limbs shattered or heads blown open like pumpkins. Half a century later *inkosi* Zimema could still remember the terrible shock of his first exposure to the full fury of British fire: 'Some of our men had their arms torn right off ... The battle was so fierce that we had to wipe the blood and the brains of the killed and wounded from our heads, faces, arms, legs and shields after the fighting ...'[60]

The youngsters of the uVe withstood the fire as long as they could, but its effects were too discouraging. 'We started to creep towards the enemy on our hands and knees', recalled Mhlahlana Ngune, 'but they shot at us so badly that we came back to get our hearts again.'[61] They fell back to regroup, then began to extend to their left, trying to work their way downstream, looking for a way past Durnford's right flank.

As they did so, the iNgobamakhosi came up behind them, groups of men rushing forward in short bursts, throwing themselves down in the long grass to try and avoid the volleys. They fared little better; Mehlokazulu later told the missionary Reverend A.W. Lee that he tried to advance with twenty men of his company but the fire caught them and all but him fell dead or wounded.[62] Somewhere near Mehlokazulu in the ranks of the iNgobamakhosi, Mlamula Matebula also experienced the destructiveness of the British fire across the final approach to the banks of the Nyogane:

I fought at the Isandhlwana battle and received four bullet wounds on my body, the one on my left leg below the knee dropped me down but I soon got up, the three others were flesh wounds ... We fell down by hundreds, but we still advanced, although we were dying by hundreds we could not retreat because we had encircled them.

I, with many others, adopted the style of crouching as we advanced in order to avoid the bullets as our shields could not stop them. While crouching I received a wound on my back, the bullet entered over the shoulder blade and came out lower down, it only made a flesh wound. All four wounds are still visible. The soldiers were entrenched [i.e. protected by the *donga*], it was a fight in the open . . .[63]

Watching from far off behind the tents, Brickhill was shocked by the losses endured by the Zulu left:

They did not come on in lines but evenly distributed. Nowhere could you catch three men walking together and rarely two, so that in some places their front was three-quarters of a mile [1.2 kilometres] in advance of their rear. This gulley they, the mounted force, held most tenaciously, every shot appearing to take effect, so much so that ... a thousand Zulus must have lain between the Conical Hill and the gully. They lay just like pepper-corns upon the plain. The leading Zulus, finding they were being mown down so terribly, threw themselves flat on the ground to wait for others to come up, when they jumped up and came on again . . .[64]

With so many men lying down in the grass, Brickhill's estimate of the dead was probably an overstatement, but there is no denying the fury of the fire. The iNgobamakhosi could make no headway against it, admitted Mehlokazulu, and 'when the firing became heavy – too hot – we retired towards the left wing'.[65]

So long as Durnford could hold the Nyogane, it seemed, the Zulu attack might be checked.

*

Most of Pulleine's forces were now engaged. On the left, the 24th companies were still deployed forward, and Brickhill admitted he 'could see nothing of the details of the infantry fighting because of the low-lying ground'.[66] A heavy pall of smoke now hung over the firing line, and the constant splutter of musketry was punctuated by the regular thuds of the Artillery. The Zulus were returning the fire, but much of theirs was poorly directed, either falling short or passing over the heads of its target to fall, whining and spitting and kicking up puffs of dust, on the open flat closer to the camp. Now and then a few shots struck among Krohn's company of the NNC, still waiting nervously in reserve, or among the tents. One hit Quartermaster Willie London of the Natal Carbineers, although he was not seriously wounded.

Even so, the first British wounded began to arrive back in the camp from the forward positions. Essex saw that 'a few casualties began to occur in our line'[67] and injured men were brought back by stretcher-bearers to the hospital tent at the rear. Private Wilson of the 1/24th band, who was acting as a stretcher-bearer, remembered that when the first alarms had taken place that morning the stretcher-bearers had fallen in with the companies on their parade grounds, following them out as they fell in to their firing positions.[68]

The stretcher-bearers fell under the command of Surgeon Peter Shepherd, No. 3 Column's senior medical officer. Chelmsford's force was, of course, short of trained medical personnel – like everything else – but even so considerable efforts had been made to ensure that each of the invading columns had a mobile field hospital attached to the headquarters and a base hospital in the rear; Shepherd's base hospital had been established at the mission station at Rorke's Drift. Shepherd was in his late thirties, a Scot from Aberdeenshire who enjoyed a good reputation as a pioneer of first aid treatment to the injured. He had held the rank of surgeon-major in the Army Medical Department since 1876, and had joined the St John's Ambulance Association as an instructor shortly after its formation in 1877; he had been preparing a series of notes on primary treatment for the injured when interrupted by the call to serve in southern Africa. Shepherd was an early advocate of the modern concept of first aid, and his sensible advice stressed the importance of staunching bleeding by applying pressure, pads and bandages, and of keeping wounds clean.[69]

Those early injuries suffered by British soldiers in the battle at iSandlwana were caused by gunshots – 'wash, stop bleeding, fix parts in natural position without delay'[70] – and they reflected the poor quality of the weapons in Zulu hands. Most Zulu guns lacked the power to kill outright at longer ranges, the irregular or home-made bullets seldom penetrating deeply, but often twisting through the body on odd courses, tearing muscle and lacerating flesh. The sheer impact of the ball might break bones, although sometimes even a direct hit failed to pierce the skin, causing massive bruising and a later atrophy of tissue instead.

As the intensity of the Zulu attack increased, so too did the number of men brought in from the front, jolted painfully about between the stretcher-bearers who were themselves at risk from the stray fire falling on the flats. After a while, recalled Wilson, Shepherd ordered the stretcher-bearers to remain close to the hospital tents. Presumably he needed them to assist with the growing number of wounded; the companies at the front would have to bring in their own men as best they could.

There was another inevitable consequence of the prolonged fire-fight, too: Essex noted that by the time Mostyn and Cavaye's companies had retired to the foot of the escarpment they were 'getting short of ammunition'.[71]

'Getting short' is, of course, an ambiguous phrase, and any company officer worth his salt would have addressed the question of resupply long before his men actually ran out of ammuntion. Even so, since this issue has become part of the mythology of the battle, it is worth considering the evidence carefully. In fact, the expenditure of rounds by front line companies in battles of the Victorian era is often surprisingly low. During the Battle of Khambula, three months later, Evelyn Wood noted that the imperial infantry 'expended in four hours an average of 33 rounds a man'.[72] The fighting at Khambula was no less intense than that at iSandlwana, although arguably individual companies were in action for longer periods of sustained firing at the latter. Nevertheless, the tactical doctrine of the day placed great emphasis on a slow and steady rate of fire, and there were good practical reasons for this. The excitement of battle inevitably encouraged a feeling that the best way to halt an enemy attack was to produce as much fire as quickly as possible, but in fact this was more likely to be ineffective, since men 'blazed away' without taking careful aim, and the target soon became obscured by dense clouds of smoke. A slow and steady rate of fire was much more conducive to accuracy, not only because the men had time to choose their targets, but because officers could direct their fire according to the movements of the targets. Similarly, volley fire tended to be more effective than independent fire in the climax of an attack, not merely because the rate of fire could be carefully controlled, but because the psychological effect to the enemy on the receiving end was as discouraging as the casualties it actually inflicted. Despite the extravagant rates of fire which modern target-shooters can achieve with these weapons under ideal conditions on the range, with rounds laid out next to them beforehand, the training manuals of the day advocated that only when desperately pressed should musketry officers authorize their men to fire at a rate of four rounds a minute. And, inevitably, in any battle there were long pauses when some companies did not fire at all, either to allow the smoke to clear, or because they had no targets, the enemy having changed position or gone to ground.

Certainly, Mostyn and Cavaye's companies had by this point been in action for some time, perhaps half an hour, or more. There is no record of how many rounds they had expended, but they were not profligate; Essex himself had helped to direct the fire, and most of the 24th were experienced men who had been in battle before, and were 'old steady shots'.[73] They had started the battle with seventy rounds apiece – forty in packets in the buff leather pouches either side of their waist buckle, and thirty loose rounds in the 'expense pouch' or 'ball bag' worn suspended from the waist-belt over their right hip. Even allowing for the tendency of the 'ball-bag' to spill a few loose rounds when the men were scrambling across the veld, their rate of fire would have to have been unusually wasteful for them to be running seriously low by this stage of the battle.

Nevertheless, with the Zulu attack still developing, Essex thought it wise to ride into 'the camp and bring up a fresh supply. I got such men as were not engaged, bandsmen, cooks etc, to assist me, and sent them to the line under an officer'.[74] That officer was Essex's junior in the Transport Department, Lieutenant Horace Smith-Dorrien. In his memoirs Smith-Dorrien gives a vivid description of his attempts to organize a resupply, which has been much quoted – and even more misunderstood:

> I will mention a story which speaks for the coolness and discipline of
> the regiment. I, having no particular duty to perform in camp, when I

saw the whole Zulu army advancing, had collected camp stragglers, such as artillerymen in charge of spare horses, officers' servants, sick etc, and had taken them to the ammunition-boxes, where we broke them open as fast as we could, and kept sending the packets to the firing-line ... When I had been engaged at this for some time, and the 1/24th had fallen back to where we were, with the Zulus following closely, Bloomfield, the quartermaster of the 2/24th, said to me 'For heaven's sake, don't take that, man, for it belongs to our battalion.' And I replied, 'hang it all, you don't want a requisition now, do you?'[75]

Upon this anecdote has been built the myth of over-zealous quartermasters refusing to issue rounds to unauthorized companies, sticking to the letter of their orders at the expense of their duty. Yet this was not the tenor of Smith-Dorrien's anecdote – which was rather to stress the regiment's professionalism under fire – and there is in any case more to this story than meets the eye. Smith-Dorrien was a young officer not attached to the rifle companies and he had brought the men assembled by Essex to the closest ammunition wagon to the line. With the 1/24th's camp further away, below the road, they had found the 2nd Battalion's supply first, the ammunition wagon clearly marked, according to Chelmsford's standing orders, by a small red flag. Yet Bloomfield's response, as he came upon them breaking open the first boxes, was in fact a perfectly reasonable one; this was the reserve supply Chelmsford had left strict instructions to be kept ready for rapid dispatch if necessary to the battalion out at the Mangeni. To allow it to be plundered without senior authorization would have made Bloomfield guilty of serious dereliction of duty – the more so because the true nature of the threat to Lord Chelmsford was not at all clear. If Bloomfield had given up his supply to the first young lieutenant who asked for it, the consequences if Lord Chelmsford was suddenly in need of the ammunition might have been very severe indeed.

In fact, Essex arrived about this time, and persuaded Bloomfield of the need to over-rule Chelmsford's instructions. Having dispatched Smith-Dorrien to the firing line – in a letter written to his father the day after the battle Smith-Dorrien confirmed that he 'was out with the front companies of the 24th handing them spare ammunition'[76] – Essex 'followed with more ammunition in a mule cart. In loading the latter I helped the Quartermaster of the 2nd Battalion to place the boxes in a cart, and while doing so the poor fellow was shot dead. The enemy's fire was now increasing and I could hear the whiz of bullets all over the place.'[77]

Haphazard as it seems, Essex's impromptu line of supply was not out of keeping with contemporary practice. There were no official regulations detailing how ammunition was to be distributed within individual regiments, and the exact means was left to the discretion of commanding officers. It was common to round up men not employed in other duties and to press them into service as ammunition runners when the need arose.

How many boxes Essex sent out, of course, can only be guessed at. The regulation ammunition carts could accommodate thirty boxes – each box contained six hundred rounds – but there were no such carts available in Natal. Instead, the Army had bought up a number of locally made mule-drawn 'Scotch carts' instead. A 'Scotch cart' could easily carry thirty boxes, although with each full box weighing around 36 kilograms the load may have been testing to the mules; under the circumstances, it is unlikely Essex loaded so many, but there is no reason not to suppose that thousands of rounds reached the front companies successfully.

Nor would there have been any difficulty in accessing them. Rounds were transported in stout wooden boxes – officially the Mark V or VI ball ammunition box – made from mahogany or teak to a basic pattern which pre-dated the issue of the Martini-Henry and which was designed to protect the rounds from rough handling in transit. The sides were dovetailed together and the base secured with copper screws, and the whole box further held together with two copper retaining bands. Access to the contents was by means of a wedge-shaped sliding panel in the top which was held in place by a single brass screw. When rounds were issued in normal circumstances this screw was removed with a screwdriver; in an emergency, however, a sharp blow to the edge of the sliding panel would bend the screw and split the washer-housing away from the wood. It is absurd to suppose a battalion as experienced in field service as the 1/24th could not open its own ammunition boxes, and the most serviceable tool for knocking the edge of the lid was probably a tent peg mallet, of which there were hundreds in the camp at iSandlwana.[78] The box was lined with tin to protect the contents against damp, and this was fitted with a wire handle which could be pulled back, rather like a modern ring-pull, once the wooden panel had been removed.[79] Interestingly, the 2000 exploratory archaeological survey uncovered a number of discarded lining handles along the firing positions to the north of the camp, confirming that some of Essex's boxes had been opened there.

Yet the 24th were not the only units in the firing line; both the NNC and the amaNgwane had by this time been engaged for some time. Private Johnson noted that when the rocket battery was overrun early in the battle, the NNC's unfamiliarity with firearms had been problematic in the stresses of combat, and they had fired off their rounds quickly, to the extent sometimes of damaging their weapons; Essex also noted the 'absurd rate' at which the NNC had 'blazed away' on the ridge.[80] Out towards the right of Pulleine's line, Malindi, one of Prince Mkhungo's supporters in James Lonsdale's company, noted that after firing at the Zulus at a range of 600 or 700 metres for a while – 'our fire checked those opposite to us but those who were a little out of our line of fire still kept on' – their ammunition failed. Despite the notoriously fragile infrastructure of the NNC, however, Malindi recalled that 'we got more from the camp'.[81]

The situation among Durnford's men was more problematic. They had started the battle with fifty rounds apiece, and their rate of expenditure is likely to have been higher than that of the regulars; Raw noted that after all the skirmishing up and down the ridge, by the time his men finally retreated to the bottom they were almost out of rounds.[82]

After dispatching his wagon full of ammunition, Essex rode back to the line. He was surprised to find that the 24th companies had fallen back a little, and were now closer to the camp.[83] They had abandoned the vicinity of the *donga*, and moved back out of the low-lying ground, onto the crest behind it. This had brought them level with the guns again, and had allowed Wardell's company to their right to occupy the broken ground which marked the higher contour. It had improved their line of vision, too, opening up the view to the right, and giving them an uninterrupted vista down the course of the Nyogane and across to the slopes of amaTutshane beyond. What they saw there, however, was hardly reassuring, for the repositioning had been prompted by fresh Zulu movements which threatened to destroy the integrity of the British line altogether.

*

In the bed of the Nyogane, Durnford had given himself up to the exhilaration of battle. According to Jabez Molife of the Edendale contingent:

> Here we made a long stand, firing incessantly. The Colonel rode up and down our line continually, encouraging us all; he was very calm and

cheerful, talking and even laughing with us. 'Fire! my boys', 'well done, my boys,' he cried. Some of us did not like his exposing himself so much to the enemy, and wanted him to keep behind us, but he laughed at us and said 'All right! Nonsense!' Sometimes as he passed amongst us one of the men brought him his gun with the old cartridge sticking and he dismounted and taking the gun between his knees, because of having only one hand with strength in it, he pulled the cartridge out and gave back the gun. There were not very many of us, but because of the way in which we were handled by our leader we were enough to stop the Zulus on that side for a long time. We could have carried him off with us safely enough at this time, only we knew him too well to try. But we now say, 'If we had known what would happen, we would have seized him and bound him, no matter if he had fought us for doing so, as he certainly would; no matter if he had killed some of us, we would have saved his life, for he was our master.' Now we say that we shall always remember him by his commanding voice, and by the way in which he gave us all some of his own spirit, as he went along our line that day, and those amongst us who had not served under him before, as I have, say, 'Why did we not know him sooner?'[84]

Durnford's men were clearly inspired by his leadership at this critical moment, yet not everyone in the stream-bed reacted to him now as Molife did. Alfred Henderson, commanding the Edendale troop, saw in Durnford's mood a streak of hysteria, and wrote afterwards that 'If I had known what sort of man Durnford was I don't think I would have gone with him. He was close to me during most of the fight and he lost his head altogether, in fact I don't think he knew what to do . . .'[85]

Nevertheless, Durnford's men – and Bradstreet's beside them – held the Nyogane for perhaps twenty minutes or half an hour. During that time the Zulu left, the iNgobamakhosi and the uVe, could make no headway against them, and began to shift to their left, hoping to cut past Durnford downstream. This was ominous enough, since there was nothing to the right of Durnford to prevent them making for the camp thereafter, but after a while a new and more pressing threat developed which would soon make Durnford's position untenable.

The uMbonambi were perhaps the last of the main *amabutho* to crest the iNyoni heights. They had been moved into position to the left of the uKhandempemvu during the advance to form the left of the Zulu centre, the chest, with the iNgobamakhosi and uVe on their left. In the rush across the heights they had been outstripped by the uKhandempemvu and the uNokhenke, who were moving fast in the hope of intercepting the retreating amaNgwane horse. The left, too, had run ahead, in the tradition of the encircling horns, and by the time the uMbonambi descended onto the plain the other two *amabutho* were already engaged. The uMbonambi moved down the ridge a little to the west of the notch, spilling onto the plain close by the amaTutshane 'conical hill'. Here they struck the upper reaches of the iNyogane, and found themselves directly opposite the most vulnerable sector of the British line – the gap of 800 to 900 metres which lay between Lonsdale's NNC, on Pulleine's right, and Durnford's stand further downstream.

In the bed of the Nyogane, where he had been directing the deployment of the Edendale men, William Cochrane saw the danger, and drew attention to it. The uMbonambi were massing in a homestead on the western foot of amaTutshane, and Cochrane asked if he might send an orderly to request the Artillery to shell the huts and disperse them. Durnford replied, 'No, they may not attend to him, you had better go yourself.'[86] Cochrane set off across the exposed flats towards the guns to deliver the message; afterwards, he considered that that chance order had saved his life, for he never saw Durnford alive again.

When he received Durnford's request, Major Smith ordered one of the 7-pdrs to be limbered up, and took it off to the right. Brickhill saw the effects of its first shelling among the uMbonambi: '[The Zulus] sought to keep together under cover of a kraal in front of the conical hill. A well-placed shot from one of the field pieces caused considerable havoc and scattered them from there.'[87] Several shots were also fired at the iNgobamakhosi, and in the Nyogane, Harry Davies thought that 'shells were being fired over our heads; it was shrapnel shell they were firing, I could see them bursting'.[88] Even so, Brickhill thought the Artillery fire erratic, but recognized that when it was accurate the effect of the air bursts on the Zulus could be devastating. 'The Artillery threw about 25 shots from different parts of the field during the battle. Four of these were very effective, each tearing up what appeared to be an acre of ground in the enemy's masses. One of the guns however always appeared to shoot high, whilst one shot burst half way, nearly over our foot native contingent.'[89]

There was a terrible novelty for the Zulus in the experience of that shellfire. Most of them, young men, had never fought a European army, and only the oldest had experienced the devastation of the Boer musketry at the Battle of Ncome forty years before – and even that paled in comparison with the steady execution caused by so many modern breech-loading rifles. The sound alone was overwhelming, unlike anything they had ever heard, the great rolls of gunfire reverberating backwards and forwards around the hills; in his dotage, one Zulu who took part could tell his family nothing of the battle except that 'it was loud'.[90] And punctuating the sound of the volleys was the ominous crack of the guns, followed a few seconds later by the sound of a bursting shell.

Mangwanana Mchunu was a teenager in the ranks of the uVe at the time, and more than fifty years later he remembered the mysterious and awesome sound: 'The "bye-and-bye" fired at the uKhandempemvu and uMbonambi only when they were approaching. The "bye-and-bye" were in front of the wagons [limbers], about fifty feet [15 metres] in front, and they kept growling ZU-ZU-ZU-ZU-ZU; I should say they fired about sixty times but I was so excited I could not say for certain – but over thirty times anyway.'[91]

Yet the Artillery could not keep the uMbanambi back indefinitely, and indeed the pressure from the uKhandempemvu further to the left meant that Smith had to return his gun to its original position. With almost no reserves available – beyond Krohn's NNC company, still standing in front of the NNC camp and apparently forgotten – the only alternative was for Pulleine to extend the right of his line. Pope's company rose up from their position next to Wardell, and moved behind Lonsdale's NNC to a new position on the right. 'At this point', noted one of the column's African intelligence staff, 'a company of the 24th moved away and joining some of our native outposts on the ridge across the watercourse from the camp, in the same direction taken by the Basutos and Edendale men, came into action.'[92]

This move has often been interpreted as an attempt by Pulleine to honour his commitment to support Durnford in his 'difficulties' – but perhaps it was not. Even in their new position, Pope's men were a long way beyond the effective rifle range necessary to cover Durnford's flank – and given his priority to 'defend the camp' Pulleine's practical support could amount to little more. So long as he remained so far beyond Pulleine's field of fire, Durnford was on his own; in effect, the separation of their forces meant that the British had no choice but to fight two distinctly separate battles at iSandlwana.

Pope's new position did at least offer him the chance to command the middle reaches of the Nyogane, however, and the rocky ground provided him with a natural bastion of sorts upon which to anchor Pulleine's right flank. The company's firepower was considerable because of the 2/24th men it had absorbed into its ranks.[93] An unknown man in the ranks of the uMbonambi remembered how Pope's move deprived them of their chance to push through unopposed to the front of the camp:

> Here, where we are standing (my informant's kraal was situated close to the rocket hill before mentioned), there were parties of soldiers in red coats who kept up a heavy fire upon us as we came over. My regiment was here and lost a lot of men; they kept tumbling over one upon another. (The narrator became quite excited, and indulged in much gesticulation, illustrating the volleys by cracking his fingers like pistol-shots.) The Ngobamakosi regiment, which formed the left horn of the *impi*, extended and swept round on the south of the rocket hill so as to outflank the soldiers, who, seeing this, fell back and took cover in that donga (pointing to a donga which intersects the field about a mile from the camp), and fired upon us from there. By that time the Ngobamakosi had got among the 'paraffin' (rockets) and killed the horses, and were circling round so as to shut in the camp on the side of the river, but we could not advance, the fire from the donga was too heavy . . .[94]

Smith-Dorrien, still handing out ammunition to the 24th's firing positions, noted a shift in the tempo of the battle, as if the Zulu attacks were beginning to run out of steam. The 24th, he noted with admiration, were 'no boy recruits, but war-worn men, and fresh from the old colony where they had carried everything before them. Possessed of a splendid discipline and sure of success, they lay on their position making every round tell.'[95]

They did not literally make 'every round tell' of course – in battle conditions, with nerves stretched taut with excitement, the battlefield obscured by smoke, and the enemy trying their best not to be hit, it took a remarkably high number of rounds to kill or incapacitate a single enemy – an average of forty or fifty was normal at the time. But there can be little doubt that the men of the 1st Battalion were above average shots – they had been in action before, and their officers prided themselves on their musketry instruction.

And to be on the receiving end of British fire was indeed an awesome experience – so much so that at this point the Zulu attack seemed in danger of stalling along its centre and left flank. On the right of the chest, the

uNokhenke had abandoned their advance down the spur after the punishment they received at the hands of the men posted on the ridge, and had
retired to safety beyond the skyline, moving to the right, in the wake of the
right horn, and down towards the valley of the Manzimnyama. This had
left the uKhandempemvu to face the full fury of the British centre alone.
When the forward companies of the 24th retired to the top of the slope
behind them, they had offered the uKhandempemvu a few moments'
respite, and the men had rushed forward to seize the *dongas*, bunching
behind the cover afforded by the banks as the 24th's bullets spattered the
rocks around them.

The soldiers were now only 300–400 metres ahead of them, but to
reach them they needed to abandon their cover and run up a gentle slope
squarely into the face of fire. They could not do it, and their attack faltered.
As uGuku succinctly put it, 'We then shouted "Izulu!" again, and got up
out of the dongas. The soldiers opened fire on us again, and we laid
down.'[96] 'The soldiers who lay on the flat the ground in front of the camp',
said a man named uMhoti of the uKhandempemvu, 'poured volley after
volley into the *impi*; we crouched down and dare not advance.'[97] 'A lot of
our men had been shot down by the enemy', confirmed Kumpega Qwabe
sadly, 'as we were crawling through the grass.'[98] Curling thought that the
'huge mass of the enemy' to the Artillery's front, 'remained almost station-
ary',[99] and the guns played heavily upon them. Driver Elias Tucker of the
Artillery thought the 24th's fire was 'cutting roads through them',[100] while
Higginson, far away in the camp, thought it 'simply swept them away'.[101]
Afterwards, a man of the uNokhenke assessed the damage caused by British
firepower at iSandlwana: 'The Umcityu [uKhandempemvu] suffered very
severely, both from artillery and musketry fire; the Nokenke from musketry
fire alone; while the Nodwengo [i.e. the right] suffered least.'[102]

Even above the din of the battle, isiZulu speakers in the camp could
hear the Zulu *izinduna* trying to steady the men. Lieutenant Wally Erskine
of the NNC heard shouts of '*inqaka amatshe phezulu!*' – 'Catch the hailstones!' – rising out from the ranks of the uKhandempemvu.[103] It had been
a boast before the war that the uKhandempemvu would treat the enemy's
bullets with contempt, catching them on their shields as if they were
nothing more than hailstones – and the memory of their words served to
put heart back into them. Erskine noticed too that the Zulus learned to
recognize when the guns were about to fire by the way the gunners stood
clear of the guns to pull the lanyard, as the movement was greeted by

shouts of 'uMoya!' – 'the wind!' The Zulus would then throw themselves down flat to avoid the rush of the shells.[104]

As Smith-Dorrien noticed, an easy confidence still prevailed among the men of the 24th, despite the Zulu attack developing around them. Little is known of the way the officers of the 24th handled their men in the course of the battle, but there are suggestions that when the forward companies fell back from the *dongas* they abandoned their overextended formations in favour of a more conventional open order. Furthermore, the drill instructions of the day allowed for infantry to exploit cover provided it did not interfere with the momentum of an attack, and the 24th now was in good ground, particularly to the right where Wardell and Pope's men nestled in among the boulders, kneeling or even lying down, aiming their shots carefully at targets which were now comfortably within the Martini-Henry's most effective killing range.

In 2000, archaeologists surveying this part of the battlefield found a poignant reminder of the fight; in between two large boulders, perfectly placed to provide an improvised sangar, they found, just below the surface, a cluster of five spent Martini-Henry rounds. It is impossible to know who fired them, of course, but their placing, one on top of another, strongly suggests that the rounds were fired in a calm and unhurried manner. Whoever he was, this unknown private or NCO of the 24th, he probably shared the prevailing self-confidence described by Smith-Dorrien. Perhaps he was one of those whom Essex thought as 'cheery as possible, making remarks to one another about their shooting'.[105] No doubt he thought, as he snatched glimpses of his targets through the drifting smoke as they bobbed up briefly from the grass or dodged between the boulders, that the Zulus were enduring a dreadful punishment, and that a British victory remained the most likely outcome. But if he did, he was wrong, for the situation was poised to change dramatically. Very soon he, and everyone else in the front line companies, would be dead.

\*

Far off in the bed of the Nyogane stream, Lieutenant Harry Davies of the Edendale troop noted with some concern that the uMbonambi were massing in the hollows further up to his left, and that some of them were risking cross-fire to try to press between Durnford's left and Pope's company. Davies tried to stop them, but the extended firing was beginning to take its toll on his men:

On our seeing the enemy in front of us lying down I directed my men
to fire on the flank of the other portion of the enemy who were then
very near the camp, coming down the left ridge and were in great
numbers. They seemed more numerous on the left ridge than elsewhere.
After firing one or two volleys on the flank of the enemy on our left,
my men called out they were short of ammunition. I took 15 with me
to get ammunition.[106]

Unfortunately, due to his impatience to advance that morning before his
baggage train had arrived in the camp, no one in the force directly under
Durnford's command knew where his ammunition wagons had been
parked. The best Davies could do, therefore, was secure 'some 200 rounds
from the Carbineers camp out of a box I found opened in one of the
tents'.[107]

Davies' absence had left Durnford curiously short of white officers.
Cochrane had not yet returned from his errand to the Artillery, while
Henderson had also become separated from his men, also in pursuit of
ammunition, according to Jabez Molife, as '. . . at last our cartridges were
nearly done. The Colonel had sent a messenger back to the camp for more,
but none came. Then he sent Mr Henderson and another.'[108] Afterwards,
Simeon Nkambule, who took command of the Edendale troop in Davies'
absence, commented archly that 'they lost their English Officers, how and
where they could not tell'.[109]

According to Davies, he was on his way back with the ammunition
when he saw that the situation had deteriorated. Small groups of the
uMbonambi had penetrated between Durnford and Pope's positions and
were fast approaching the tents; 'A lot of Zulus, about 40 here, got into the
camp by driving a lot of our oxen that had run out of the camp before
them. We shot some of them . . .'[110] It was too late. As Davies watched,
Durnford's men suddenly emerged from the bed of the Nyogane, and
began riding back towards the camp.

In truth Durnford's position was no longer viable. With his ammunition
largely expended, he could no longer prevent the uMbonambi from
outflanking him on his left, while the iNgobamakhosi and uVe were making
a serious move towards his right. It had become impossible to hold his
ground any longer – and his men knew it. According to Trooper Edwards:

Men began to realise the hopeless position in which we were landed.
Suddenly one of them shouted hoarsely, 'The Zulus are in the camp!'

And they were, with a vengeance. Then came the order, whipped out grimly, 'stand to your horses; retire to camp.' We all dashed for our horses, but mine had disappeared. I looked round with growing despair, when a quiet voice behind me said 'Here is a horse; is it yours?' Colonel Durnford was holding it and walking close behind me. Without more ado we went back to the camp . . .[111]

But Durnford's collapse would have desperate consequences for Pulleine's line; Pulleine's right flank, Pope's company, was now isolated, and already small groups of uMbonambi, encouraged by Durnford's retreat, were beginning to push towards the camp, effectively outflanking the infantry on their right and to the rear. Further off, there was nothing but open ground now between the iNgobamakhosi and the uVe and the tents.

Both Essex and Gardner immediately recognized the danger, and rode out to confront Durnford. Gardner met Bradstreet and the Volunteers first; 'observing the mounted men retiring, I went back to them, and, in reply to my question as to why they were retiring, was told they were ordered by Colonel Durnford to retire, as the position taken up was too extended. This same remark was made to me by Colonel Durnford himself immediately afterwards.'[112]

Durnford himself rode towards the infantry line, and Essex intercepted him along the way. 'He had, I think, already observed the state of affairs, and was looking very serious. He asked me if I could bring some men to keep the enemy in check in our rear.'[113] Essex could not; there were none to spare.

# 22

# 'Kill me in the shadows'

## iSandlwana, afternoon, 22 January 1879

Far out on the plain, George Hamilton Browne had spotted Durnford's retreat. Hamilton Browne's NNC battalion, the 1/3rd, had been dispatched earlier that morning to return in order to assist in the packing up of the camp. After their uncomfortable night on the Hlazakazi heights the men had been tired, and Hamilton Browne was in his usual irascible mood:

> We marched very slowly on, the day was intensely hot, and my white non-coms who were on foot very fagged. They had had a very hard day the day before. They had had no sleep and no food, and somehow over the whole command there seemed to hover a black cloud.
>
> However, push on was the word, and at 10 o'clock myself and Adjutant-Lieutenant Campbell, who were riding some distance in front, flushed two Zulus. They bolted and we rode them down. Campbell shot his one, but I captured mine and on Duncombe coming up we questioned him.
>
> He was only a boy and frightened out of his life so that when asked where he came from, he pointed to the line of hills on the left flank of the camp, saying 'he had come from the King's big army.' 'What are you doing here?' we asked, to which he replied that 'he and his mate had been sent by their *induna* to see if any white men were among the hills' we had just left, 'but as they were sitting resting under the shade of a rock they did not hear the white men and were caught.' 'What was the size of the army?' he was asked. 'There were twelve full regiments.'[1]

Hamilton Browne had scoured the countryside with his field glasses, but there were no Zulus in sight; in the distance the tents still stood at the foot of iSandlwana. Nonetheless, he had ordered a Lieutenant Pohl to take a hurried note to Lord Chelmsford:[2] '10. a.m. I have just captured a Zulu scout who informs me the Zulu army is behind a range of hills on the left flank of the camp. Will push on as fast as possible. The ground here is good for the rapid advance of mounted men and guns.'[3]

The battalion had resumed its progress towards the camp, but a little further on – he thought it was about 11 a.m., but it was perhaps an hour later – Hamilton Browne had spotted a puff of smoke on the ridge above the camp, then another. Looking through his glasses, he saw 'A huge black shadow that lay on the hills. Presently another puff and in a moment I knew they were bursting shells. Not a cloud was in the sky, and I knew that the black shadow resting on the hills must be a Zulu army moving down to attack the camp.'[4]

He had sent a further message to Chelmsford – 'The Zulu army is attacking left of camp. The guns have opened on them. The ground here still suitable for guns and mounted men. Will push on to act as support to them' – this time by a Sergeant Turner, but 'neither himself or Mr Pohl could find him but reported these facts to Officers they met on the road'.[5]

Hamilton Browne had again ordered his men to advance, but they too had seen the Zulus and it took some muscular persuasion on the part of the NCOs to get them moving. When they were about 6 kilometres from the camp, descending into the shallow valley of the Nxibongo stream, Hamilton Browne had again ridden ahead and looked through his glasses. 'I saw a cloud of Zulus thrown out from their left and from the left horn of the army. These men swept round and attacked the front of the camp, and I saw two right companies of the 24th and one gun thrown back to resist them. There was also plenty of independent firing going on within the camp, as if all the wagon men, servants, and in fact everyone who could use a rifle was firing away to save his life.'[6]

By now it was sometime after midday. Hamilton Browne had dispatched yet another message to Lord Chelmsford, but the road back to Mangeni shimmered in the heat haze, and no troops came hurrying along it in support.

The battalion's presence seems to have gone entirely unnoticed by the Zulus, preoccupied as they were with the attack on the camp. Yet the track by which the battalion had left the camp was now cut off by the *amabutho* sweeping across its front, and so Hamilton Browne gingerly shifted his march to the left, hoping to get round the tip of the horn. They crossed the Nxibongo, and Hamilton Browne then rode up out of the valley to take another look at the camp. It was now about 1.30 p.m.:

Good God! What a sight it was. By the road that runs between the hill
and the *kopje*, came a huge mob of maddened cattle, followed by a
dense swarm of Zulus. These poured into the undefended right and rear
of the camp, and at the same time the left horn of the enemy and the
chest of the army rushed in. Nothing could stand against this combined
attack. All formation was broken in a minute, and the camp became a
seething pandemonium of men and cattle struggling in dense clouds of
dust and smoke.[7]

The position of Hamilton Browne's battalion had deteriorated dramatically
in just a few minutes. He had expected to join up with the troops in the
camp – now he was suddenly isolated, in open country, and close to an
overwhelming and hostile force. His one hope was to fall back to more
secure ground – a long stony ridge lay to the south of the track about
2 kilometres to his rear – and hope that the Zulus did not spot him. He
ordered his officers '. . . to form their companies into rings, after the Zulu
fashion, and retire, dismounting themselves and hiding all the white men
among the natives. This we did, and although there were large parties of
the enemy close to us, they took no notice of us.'[8]

It was time for a final message, and this time Hamilton Browne did not
mince his words. He sent Captain Develing – 'a fine horseman and a finer
fellow' – to tell Lord Chelmsford 'For God's sake come back, the camp is
surrounded and things I fear are going badly.' Then he led his men up on
to the ridge, 'and determined to await the course of events'.[9]

*

At iSandlwana, several things had happened in such quick succession that
it is impossible, after the passage of so much time, to be sure of the
sequence of events.

After restraining and doctoring the oNdine *amabutho* back in the
Ngwebeni valley, and dispatching them to cut the road to Rorke's Drift,
the *amakhosi* Ntshingwayo and Mavumengwana and their staff had
hurried across the heights in the wake of their attacking army. By the time
they had reached the escarpment the battle was already under way. They
arrived at the edge at a point just east of the Mkwene knoll and took up a
position at the top of a sheer cliff-face, the iNyoni rocks.

The view from there is a striking one, and the features of the battlefield
could be seen spread out below, the tail of iSandlwana straight ahead and

the amaTutshane 'conical hill' at the foot of the escarpment to the left. To the right lie the folds and undulations of the spur, which had been so bitterly contested just a short time before and were now strewn with Zulu dead.

Looking down, the positions draped in thick white smoke, the battle was unfolding at Ntshingwayo's feet. Directly below the Zulu generals lay the uKhandempemvu, bunched together in a long line, the men still pressed closely into the cover afforded by the banks of the *dongas* as the British soldiers rained shot and shell upon them. Ntshingwayo and Mavumeng-wana must have plainly seen, further off, the uMbonambi pushing tenta-tively round the crumbling British right, providing an opportunity which needed to be rigorously exploited. Yet, just at that moment, it was the uKhandempemvu who were in the position to do so, and if the Zulus did not continue their advance there was every chance 'they would get the whole *impi* beaten'.[10] Ntshingwayo turned to one of his *izinduna*, the *inkosi* of the Biyela people, Mkhosana kaMvundlana, who commanded a wing of the uKhandempemvu, and told him to run down the slope and urge his young men on.

Mkhosana was far from being the old man of tourist myth; he had been enrolled in the iNdlondlo *ibutho*, and he was in his early forties and had left one of his wives pregnant at home. According to family tradition, he was magnificently dressed that day, wearing the full regalia of an *inkosi* – leopardskin collar, long crane feathers tucked into his otter skin head-band and bunches of lourie feathers over his ears – and carrying the white shield of his *ibutho*. Picking his way quickly down the steep slope of the escarpment and striding across the flats at its foot, oblivious to the bullets striking around him, he pushed through the huddled men until he could clamber up onto the bank beyond. There he strutted in front of them, haranguing them, apparently invincible as the British bullets spattered on boulders and kicked up spurts of dust around him, calling out fiercely that famous phrase from the king's praises which they knew so well, the phrase that harked back to Cetshwayo's defiance of the whites at the Battle of Ndondakusuka twenty years before: '*Uhlamvana ubul'mlilo ubaswe uMantshonga no uNgqelebana kashongo njalo!*', 'The Little Branch of Leaves', he cried, 'that extinguished the great fire kindled by [the white men known as] Mantshonga and Ngqelebana gave no such order as this!'[11]

It was a stinging rebuke, a tart recall to their duty, and a reminder of the shame that awaited them when they returned home if they failed to honour the name of their *ibutho*. Their response was immediate – rising up from the cover of the *dongas*, suddenly unaware of the British fire, 'they all shouted "Usutu!", and waving their shields charged the soldiers with great fury'.[12]

Mkhosana would not live to enjoy his triumph. Even as he turned towards the enemy, 'he was shot clean through the forehead' by a bullet that took away the back of his head.[13] As he fell dead, the uKhandempemvu streamed forward across his body.

*

On the Zulu left, Mehlokazulu noted that Major Smith's artillery fire did not trouble the iNgobamakhosi too much:

> It only killed four men in our regiment, the shot went over us. When we saw the smoke at the cannon's mouth, in a direct line for us, we opened out, and the ball passed and lodged behind. Occasionally a man would run, thinking to avoid it, and the shell would burst and he would be struck. We lay down flat on the ground when we knew a cannon ball was coming, and then rose again after it had passed. When we saw the smoke at the cannon's mouth, it was an indication to us that the ball was coming, when we heard the report the ball was already with us. There are two reports, that from the cannon's mouth, and that when the shell bursts.[14]

Mehlokazulu saw the retreat from the Nyogane, and thought Durnford's men had left it in some disarray:

> We retired towards the left wing . . . and they withdrew . . . they retired on the camp fearing lest we should enter the camp before they could get into it, and that the camp would not be protected . . . When they were rising out of the donga and retreating on the camp we shot two Carbineers . . . They mounted their horses which they had drawn into the donga with them. The Carbineers were still fighting when the Edendale men got into the camp . . .[15]

The moment was not lost on an *induna* named Ndlaka, who, according to Muziwento, had taken up a commanding position on the slopes of 'Amatutshane hill and cried, "Never did his Majesty the King give you this command, to wit, 'Lie Down upon the ground!' His words were; 'Go! and toss them into Maritzburg!'"'[16]

This was premature, particularly for the uMbonambi, for Pope's company was still laying down heavy fire along the middle reaches of the Nyogane, and 'up started the warriors, but again they lay down, being endangered by the bullets. The soldiers hoped and said, "Perhaps we have now killed them all" . . .'[17]

It was just moments later, however, that *inkosi* Mkhosana arrived among the uKhandempemvu, and at the sight of the *ibutho* abandoning the *dongas* and running forward to attack the remaining British positions a ripple of excitement passed down the length of the Zulu line. It was a particularly galling moment for the iNgobamakhosi, who only a few days before had exchanged boasts with the uKhandempemvu before the king that they would be the first among the enemy. They were a long way out, now, far off to the left, with none of the enemy directly in front of them, but one of their *izinduna*, Sikizane kaNomageje, stood up among them and called out, 'Why are you lying down? What was it you said to the uKhandempemvu? There are the uKhandempemvu going into the tents . . . Stop firing. Go in hand to hand!'[18] 'With that', Nzuzi Mandla of the uVe remembered fifty years later, 'the whole lot of us rushed the camp.'[19]

A few years later, the traveller Bertram Mitford received a demonstration of just how quick that final charge could be. 'They would rush forward about fifty yards [46 metres], and imitating the sound of a volley, drop flat amid the grass; then when the firing was supposed to have slackened, up they sprung, and assegai and shield in hand charged like lightning upon the imaginary foe, shouting "Usutu!"'[20]

Many of the Zulus fired one last shot before leaving their guns on the ground and joining the charge. The cumbersome process of reloading muzzle-loaders, in particular, was too slow in the excitement of the moment and, said Gumpeka Qwabe, 'we found that after firing one shot we had no time to load again so we just had to use our spears'.[21]

From his vantage point behind the tents, James Brickhill saw them coming. 'A simultaneous forward movement was now made by all the Zulus',[22] he said simply, while James Hamer, who had 'joined some soldiers in front of the camp', thought 'the Zulus came on us like ants on all sides'.[23]

The men of the amaBele in Captain Krohn's NNC company saw them too. Oddly, this company was still lined up in front of the NNC camp, despite the fact that if ever there was a moment for Pulleine to commit his reserves, this was it. The regulars, of course, had a tendency to overlook the

potential of the NNC, and it is difficult to avoid the suspicion that Pulleine
had simply forgotten about them; if, on the other hand, he had judged
them to be inadequate as a means of shoring up the folding line, he was
probably right. According to Walter Higginson, the sight of the Zulu surge
was too much for Krohn's men:

> It was with great difficulty we kept our men in their places, for the
> bullets were dropping amongst us, and every one that came near made
> them all jump up, and try to run away . . . the Zulus extended all round
> the front of the camp, and as they got on the right flank they made a
> rush for the camp, and drove back the few men that opposed them,
> when my company saw them coming nothing could stop them, they all
> jumped up and ran, and though I knocked one man down with my rifle
> it was no use. I then saw the men of the 2nd Batt NNC running and
> looking for the 24th men, I saw that they were retreating also, but very
> slowly . . .[24]

The 24th companies were retiring in response to their orders. Quite what
those orders were will never be known; throughout the battle Pulleine's
presence remains shadowy, and his decisions a matter for conjecture.
Beyond eyewitness statements that he was near his tent when the battle
began, there is no direct contemporary evidence detailing his movements.
Perhaps he remained there throughout, hoping to control the battle from
a position that, like Brickhill's, gave him an overview of sorts of the
battlefield. Perhaps he recognized the shortcomings of that position and
rode out to the rifle companies to see for himself, only to find that visibility
there, swathed in smoke and pressed in by the ridge, was worse. Either
way, none of those with whom he discussed the management of the battle
or who held front line commands under him survived to pick over his
decisions afterwards.

Yet the truth was that Durnford and the Zulus between them had
removed almost all his options. There can have been little more than a few
minutes between Durnford's withdrawal from the *donga* and the start of
the fresh Zulu assault, and those few moments would have dramatically
confirmed to Pulleine what he must surely have suspected since the Zulu
chest appeared in large numbers on the iNyoni skyline – that his firing line
was too far forward and too extended to contain an attack of such intensity.
With nothing now to stop the *amabutho* on the plain from sweeping round
Pope's company and entering the camp from his right, Pulleine's only

option was to try to withdraw as quickly as possible and take up a new position closer to the tents. And he had to do it, moreover, before the Zulus beat him to it.

The bugles sounded the 'Cease Fire' and then 'Retire', the sound being passed from one company to another down the line. Among the ranks of the uKhandempemvu, even over the din of battle, the Zulu uMhoti heard the calls; 'Then, at the sound of a bugle, the firing ceased at a breath, and the whole British force rose from the ground and retired on the tents. Like a flame the whole Zulu force sprang to its feet and darted upon them . . .'[25]

And at that moment the extent to which the 24th had been the rock that had sustained the nerve of the auxiliary units still scattered among them, whose nervousness had increased with the Zulu threat, became apparent. Suddenly the auxiliaries were exposed, stripped of their protectors – and the Zulus were coming. Captain Essex saw what happened next:

> I noticed a number of native infantry retreating in haste towards the camp, their officers endeavouring to prevent them, but without effect. On looking round to that portion of the field to our right and rear I saw that the enemy was surrounding us. I rode up to Lieutenant-Colonel Durnford, who was near the right, and pointed this out to him. He requested me to take men to that part of the field and endeavour to hold the enemy in check; but while he was speaking, those men of the Native Contingent who had remained in action rushed passed us in the utmost disorder, thus laying open the right and rear of the companies of the 1st Battalion 24th Regiment on the left, and the enemy dashing forward in the most rapid manner poured in at this part of the line . . .[26]

These men were the iziGqoza, the émigré followers of King Cetshwayo's rivals who made up James Lonsdale's No. 9 Company, 1/3rd NNC, which had been holding its position on the rocky rise between the two *dongas*, sandwiched lately between Captain Wardell's H Company, 1/24th, and Pope's G Company, 2/24th. Despite the paucity of firearms among them – scarcely twenty in the entire company, including the white officers and NCOs – they had stood their ground well, but according to Malindi, who was among them, they now also began their retreat in good order:

> [We] remained firing until the Zulus were within 100 yards [91 metres]. We were then ordered to retire as we were also threatened on our rear by the advancing left of the Zulus, and fall back on the camp, which we did, crossing the watercourse opposite the camp of the Lt. General. The

Company of soldiers was with us and on nearing the tents knelt down
and commenced firing at the enemy. Below them, some distance to the
west, was another company or more of soldiers, also kneeling and
firing.[27]

Falling back towards the tents with his men was the pretender to the Zulu
throne, Prince Sikhotha himself. Sikhotha was mounted on horseback, and
as he reached the tents he met Gabangaye kaPhakade of the amaChunu.
Sikhotha had already noted the way the battle was turning, and he urged
Gabangaye to save himself; but the amaChunu's resentments against the
Zulu kings were deep-seated, and even at this stage Gabangaye still placed
hopes in the men of his Mbungulu *ibutho*, who were serving in the NNC
ranks, to restore the honour of his people. Muziwento, the young Zulu lad,
heard the story of what passed between them from his father, who knew
Sikhotha after the war:

> There was present too Usikota [Sikhotha], brother of Cetshwayo; he
> saw the Zulu army coming up and cried, 'O! Not for me! I'm off!
> I know those fellows over there. It is just "Coming, come" [i.e. no
> stopping] with them. They are not to be turned aside by any man, and
> here we are sitting still for all the world like a lot of turkeys!' Then he
> called to his brother, 'Away! Let's away Ungabangaye, let's make a run
> for it.' Said Ungabangaye, 'Oh stop a moment just till I see them tackled
> by the white men!' 'O!' cried Usikota, 'A pleasant stay to you!' He seized
> his horse and bolted . . .[28]

In fact the amaChunu had been drifting from the field for some time.
Barry's company had been so disheartened by the sight of the Zulu army
spilling out from the Ngwebeni that most of them had refused to rally,
even when they reached the camp. Captain Erskine's No. 4 Company had
remained in the line on the left, but like the iziGqoza the sight of the
redcoats in apparent retreat was too much for them. Lieutenant Erskine of
the 1st NNC saw them go:

> I saw no white officer with Pakadi's men; no commander at all. They
> were acting entirely on their own account. They kept up a fire against
> the Zulus until the latter were within 300 yards [274 metres] of them;
> when, being out of control, they bolted. Some of the *indunas* called out
> 'mani buya', meaning 'return to the fight'; but a panic had evidently

seized them, and they would not obey the *induna*; that is, if they heard him.[29]

It is interesting to speculate whether that *induna* was Gabangaye himself. If it was, his last minutes would reveal to him a desperate truth, that the struggle between the amaChunu and the Zulu kings had always been an unequal one, for, in Muziwento's words, 'up came the Zulu army and made an end of Ungabangaye'.[30] Where he fell and the exact circumstances of his death are not known, but until quite recently his descendants used to swear 'by the death of Gabangaye at iSandlwana'.[31]

There was shame, too, for some of the white officers of the fleeing NNC. Although he was also mounted, Captain James Lonsdale could not bring himself to follow Prince Sikhotha's example. According to Malindi, 'Our Captain now got off his horse and gave it to me, telling me to take it to the ammunition wagons, and, turning back . . . he joined the red soldiers who were firing and I never saw him again.'[32]

For the Artillery, too, the 24th's sudden withdrawal led to an uncomfortable moment. As the uKhandempemvu started up out of the *dongas* towards the British line, the guns had switched to firing case-shot – canisters packed with lead balls which were designed to break up on leaving the muzzle, spraying the enemy like a giant shotgun. The effect on naked bodies at close range could be horrific but, according to Curling, it was not enough to stop the Zulus:

> The Zulus still continued to advance and we began to fire case but the order was given to retire after firing a round or two.
>
> At this time out of my small detachment one man had been killed, shot through the head, another wounded shot through the side and another through the wrist. Maj. Smith was also shot through the arm but was able to do his duty. Of course no wounded man was attended to, there was no time or men to spare. When we got the order to retire we limbered up at once but were hardly in time as the Zulus were on us at once and one man was killed (stabbed) as he was mounting in a seat on the gun carriage. Most of the gunners were on foot as there was not time to mount them on the guns.
>
> We trotted off to the camp thinking to take up another position there . . .[33]

By this time, too, the amaNgwane horse were in full retreat. Raw had noted that even as his men took up a position at the bottom of the ridge, beside

Younghusband's company, his men were running low of ammunition, and with the withdrawal of the regulars the amaNgwane position became hopeless. According to Nyanda, Raw's *induna*, 'We then looked round and saw the guns retreating. We were then chased into the course of the camp.'[34]

Wyatt Vause tried to organize a supply of fresh ammunition for his men, but no one had been left at Durnford's wagons to deal with the distribution. 'After regaining the camp to our dismay it was found that the ammunition boxes had not been opened and the Zulus being so close on our heels we had no time to look for screwdrivers. Fortunately one of my Kafirs came across a box with a few in which I distributed amongst mine [i.e. my men] . . .'[35]

Ntabeni and Hlohlwane, of the column's Intelligence department, saw the British positions dissolve before their eyes:

> At this moment the guns passed along the front of the camp towards the road at a gallop, and we never saw them again. Sikali's mounted men had already passed, going in the same direction, followed by the NNC. The Zulus were by this time quite close to the soldiers, who were kneeling or lying down firing very rapidly and inflicting heavy loss. Then the Zulu closed in hand to hand and we ran away . . .[36]

*

From his position behind the camp, Brickhill could see that the battle was about to roll up and engulf the tents and the rear echelon personnel there. 'Troops of all description were now streaming through the various camps towards Rorke's Drift',[37] but even those who had tried to retire in good order found themselves losing whatever formation they had managed to retain as they blundered through the tangled web of tents and guy-ropes. The camp was also full of animals – the wagons on the *nek*, whose return to Rorke's Drift had been postponed, had teams of oxen tied to them, but not inspanned, while large numbers of draught and slaughter animals, horses and mules, had been driven closer to the camp by the commotion of battle. James Hamer had ridden into the camp when the line collapsed, and found the scenes at the top, near the *nek*, 'baffled description, oxen yoked to wagons, mules, sheep, horses and men in the greatest confusion, all wildly trying to escape'.[38]

And soon there were Zulus, too. To Cracroft Nourse 'it seemed that the

24th were keeping their front clear, but the enemy rushed their camp from the rear and the tents went down like a pack of cards'.[39] While the 24th was still trying to hold the uKhandempemvu back to the north, some of the uMbonambi had braved the fire from Pope's company and dashed across the flats trying to intercept those in retreat. As the gun-carriages clattered and jangled their way across the front of the camp, Curling noted with horror that they had already been overtaken by Zulus rushing in from their left, and that the camp 'was in possession of the enemy who were killing the men as they ran out of their tents. We went right through them and out the other side, losing nearly all our gunners in doing so and one or two of the sergeants'.[40]

In fact, many of the non-combatants in the camp, the wagon-drivers, *voorloopers* and civilian contractors, had already abandoned it before the line collapsed, and a steady trickle of them had made off down the road to Rorke's Drift long before the first Zulus reached the tents from the front. Yet there, on the winding track through the Manzimnyama, a fresh horror awaited them, for they discovered the truth Essex had first been groping towards an hour or so earlier – that those first Zulus, streaming off the ridges, had made no attempt to attack to their front, but 'arranged like a horn' had moved towards the British flank. Preoccupied with the Zulu centre and left, the British had given no thought to the movements of the Zulu right. The *amabutho* from the kwaNodwengo royal homestead, the iMbube, uDududu and iSanqu, had descended off the hills into the valley of the Mamzimnyama, and had already cut off the road to Rorke's Drift. The uNokhenke, driven back in their attacks down the spur, had followed them, keeping tight in beneath the steep and rocky western face of iSandlwana.

It was an integral part of the 'chest and horns' formation that one horn should go forward surreptitiously, making careful use of the ground and remaining hidden until it had encircled the enemy, then wait until the centre and the other horn drove the enemy towards it. That point, according to a man of the uNokhenke, had now been reached:

> While the Kandampemvu were driving back the horsemen over the hill north of the camp, we worked round behind Isandhlwana under cover of the long grass and dongas, intending to join the Ngobamakosi on the 'neck', and sweep in upon the camp. Then we saw the white men beginning to run away along the road to 'kwaJim'; many of these were

cut off and killed, down in the stream which flows through the bottom of the valley. More and more came over, some mounted and some on foot. When they saw that the valley was full of our warriors, they turned to the left and ran along the side of the hill towards Umzinyati (the Buffalo); those who had not got horses were soon overtaken. The Nodwengu pursued the mounted men, numbers of whom were killed among the thorns and dongas, but I heard that some escaped. Our regiment went over into the camp. The ground is high and full of dongas and stones, and the soldiers did not see us until we were right upon them . . .[41]

Trooper Barker of the Carbineers had returned to the camp after Durnford had abandoned the *donga*, and had tied his horse to the horse-lines in the Carbineers' camp, 'intending to change saddles later on'. He emerged from the tents to see the uMbonambi rushing into the front of the camp, and,

I then went down the hill to our immediate front, about a hundred yards from our lines, and joined some Carbineers, Hawkins, Swift, two Tarbotons, and Edwards, and commenced firing. The Zulus were then advancing from the *donga* we had just left. After firing about a dozen shots I noticed, or rather heard, a rush from behind, and on looking round I saw the soldiers who were left in camp literally surrounded by Zulus, who had evidently come in from our rear, and as the soldiers and natives repassed us in confusion we retired back to our Carbineer lines . . .[42]

*

To the north of the camp the 24th companies had remained in good order as the line folded around them. They had retreated steadily towards the tents, stopping every few metres and 'firing at us all the time',[43] laying down such burst of intense fire at close range that the Zulus were now unable to close to their front. It is not clear what the intentions of Pulleine or his company officers were at this stage, but they appear to have been trying to withdraw to the *nek*, perhaps in the hope of forming in a line behind the tents, with iSandlwana hill protecting their left flank and the Mahlabamkosi *kopje* the right.

If so, they never made it. As soon as they abandoned their positions, both the NNC and amaNgwane horse fled, leaving large gaps between the 24th companies that they struggled to close. One company on the far left –

presumably Captain Younghusband's C Company, 1/24th – retired down the narrow and claustrophobic corridor between the rear of the camp and the foot of the hill, a route which at least severely restricted the approach of the Zulus trying to attack them.

Out on the flats, the remaining four companies of the 1st Battalion – Mostyn's, Cavaye's, Porteous's and Wardell's – had no similar advantages in the terrain to exploit, but were fully exposed to the rush of the uKhandempemvu before them. Colour Sergeant Wolfe of Wardell's company seems to have tried to screen the retreat with a rearguard action, holding a spot on the rocky ridge above a Zulu homestead, but he stood no chance and he and the twenty men with him were overwhelmed.

Nevertheless, the companies managed to form 'receive cavalry squares', the standard infantry tactic of the day when threatened at close quarters by overwhelming numbers, the men rallying round the officers in the centre, forming two ranks shoulder-to-shoulder – a small clump of redcoats with a frontage, at field strength, of no more than ten or twelve men. It is not at all clear whether the companies managed to draw together; uGuku of the uKhandempemvu thought that they did:

> ... the whole of my regiment charged the infantry, who formed into two separate parties – one standing four deep with their backs towards Sandhlwana, the other standing about fifty yards [46 metres] from the camp in like formation. We were checked by the fire of the soldiers standing near Sandhlwana, but charged on towards those standing in front of the camp, in spite of a very heavy fire on our right flank from those by Sandlwana. As we got near we saw the soldiers beginning to fall from the effects of our fire ... As we rushed on the soldiers retired on the camp, fighting all the way, and as they got into the camp we were intermingled with them.[44]

Out on the right, further east, Pope's company, which had extended its position just a few minutes before the collapse, was now cut off from the 1/24th companies, and began to retreat slowly towards the camp; the scouts Ntabeni and Hlolwane saw them making a stand on the banks of the Mpofana *donga*.

As the 24th entered the camp, the tents disrupted its formations. Even if, as Nourse thought, many of the tents had collapsed by this stage under the weight of struggling figures passing through, the tangle of canvas, poles and ropes was enough to slow the infantry down and prevent them from

forming together, allowing knots of Zulus to press between them. Much of
the fighting was now hand-to-hand, Zulus braving the fire to run up close
and fling their spears, or take advantage of the time it took to reload
between volleys to run in close and drag down stragglers or wounded men.
Essex saw the 24th officers struggling to keep their men under control; 'the
men became unsteady. A few fixed bayonets, and I heard the officers calling
on their men to keep together and be steady.'[45] That they did so under
such impossible circumstances is an extraordinary tribute to their courage
and discipline. Lieutenant Stafford of the 1st NNC heard one officer calling
on his men to 'Fix bayonets!' and 'The only orders that I heard given out
in the camp were by a young Imperial officer of the 2nd 24th Regiment,
who was endeavouring to rally the remnants of his men, and actually got
them into some sort of formation.'[46]

According to Zofikasho Zungu of the iNgobamakhosi, the fighting had
now become desperately confused:

> I suddenly noticed I was fired at by some soldiers who were trying to
> get back to Isandhlwana. I would have liked to have attacked them but
> could not get to them. I saw a line of soldiers near the tents who were
> in a line shoulder to shoulder and I was afraid to go and attack them
> as they had chucked away their guns which were broken using them as
> clubs, and were standing with those small spears that they carried at
> their sides. I saw them like a fence holding hands against the attackers,
> and they were soon all killed by the Mkandempemvu and Mbonambi
> regiments.[47]

A general panic had by now swept through the men still in the camp.
When he saw Durnford retreat, James Brickhill had gone down to the
camp of the 1/24th where he met Louis Dubois, one of three brothers who
farmed near Brickhill's home in Msinga, and who had taken a job with the
Army as a wagon conductor:

> I saw Mr Du Bois who asked me in Zulu how it looked. I replied 'ugly',
> he said 'yes, the enemy have scattered us this day'. Above the 1.24th
> camp I met my poor tent companion, Quartermaster Pullen, who
> shouted to the running soldiery 'Come on men – rally here – follow me
> – let's not be running away like a parcel of old women – let's try and
> turn their flank.' Turning to me he said, 'Mr Brickhill, do go to Colonel
> Pulleine and ask him to send us help as they are outflanking us here on

the right.' He went away towards the front of Stoney Kopjie, followed by several of the soldiers.

I went round the Volunteer camps into that of the 2/24th. Men were running everywhere but I could see no officer . . .[48]

Out on the Zulu left, the iNgobamakhosi and uVe had hurried forward as they saw the uMbonambi and uKhandempemvu entering the tents, but they arrived to find a terrible scene of confusion. Fifty-six years later, it was that terrible chaos which most remained in the mind of Sofikasho Zungu, a member of the iNgobamakhosi. 'When I got in sight of [iSandlwana] the whole place was a twisting mass of soldiers and natives fighting – the Mkandempemvu and Umbonambi were all killing, and then we attacked . . . One can remember little and saw less except for the twisting mass of men . . .'[49]

*

There are odd glimpses of Durnford at this time, moving through the maelstrom, and as he watched the British position fall apart about him, so all his dreams of redemption disintegrated in bloodshed and horror.

After parting from Gardner and Essex on the flats, he seems to have ridden to the camp, perhaps to seek out Pulleine. There he encountered Captain Nourse, and pressed him for further details of the rocket battery's demise; according to Nourse, Durnford was again struggling to contain a mass of conflicting emotions:

> I was in the camp with four of my men. It was then that Colonel Durnford, who had been forced back, rode up to me and asked where Major Russell and the rocket battery were. I told him of the fate of the battery and Major Russell. The Colonel appeared very distressed and spoke about surviving the disgrace. I concluded that the disgrace lay in exceeding his orders, which were to defend the camp. He had made an attack, which had failed, and he feared being made a scapegoat of.[50]

Raw's *induna*, Nyanda, saw Durnford about that time near the centre of the camp; perhaps he could not find Pulleine there, for shortly afterwards Harry Davies caught his last glimpse of his commanding officer that day. Durnford was out near the firing line, an isolated and deeply forlorn figure, and 'his mounted orderly was standing before him with a drawn sword and the Zulus all around'.[51]

And then, in an apocalyptic touch entirely in keeping with the dark grandeur of the iSandlwana story, and as if to mirror Durnford's inner turmoil, the sky suddenly turned dark above him.

*

In a small pocket notebook William Cochrane had taken with him into the field, a printed entry for Wednesday 22 January 1879 noted that a solar eclipse would take place that day, visible to the southern hemisphere, including southern Africa. In the eastern coastal strip the moon obscured the sun to no more than 65 per cent. It began about 1 p.m. local time, and was at its height shortly after 2 p.m., the moon having entirely passed by 3.30.[52]

The eclipse coincided with the peak of the battle at iSandlwana; in a stunning piece of natural symbolism, on the bloodiest day in the history of the Victorian Empire, the sun darkened. As one African folk story has it, in that moment God closed his eyes, for he could not bear to look upon the horror that Man was inflicting upon himself.

There was no dramatic reduction in the light levels, but far out at Mangeni Trooper Symons noticed a heavy stillness settle over the atmosphere. In the camp at iSandlwana, the eclipse frayed nerves already overstretched by the adrenaline rush of blood-lust and terror amid the smoke and dust. 'Our eyes were dark,' said uNzuzi Mandla of the uVe, 'and we stabbed everything we came across.'[53] The worlds of the living and of the ancestors were entwined in a terrible embrace, and the sky seemed rent by some terrible form of *umnyama*; 'the sun turned black in the middle of the battle', a man of the uNokhenke told Bertram Mitford in 1882. 'We could still see it over us, or we should have thought we had been fighting til evening. Then we got into the camp, and there was a great deal of smoke and firing. Afterwards the sun came out bright again.'[54]

And for hundreds of men, that hellish vortex of human rage and violence swirling in the unnatural gloom would be their last vision of the living world.

*

When the right horn entered the camp from the rear, Trooper Barker and the other Carbineers who had been firing from in front of the Volunteer camp scattered. According to one of them, they had stopped to cover the retreat of Durnford's men until, the Zulu pressure became severe [when] about half-a-dozen of us fell back covering the retreat of some of our mounted men towards the little hill, when, half way up the track, Bradstreet shouted 'God, they're in behind us,' and we could see many of the Zulus coming over the road from Rorke's Drift. A few minutes later we realized that all was up. I had no pistol, and the extractor of my rifle had jammed, so I was defenceless. I realized that a horrible sauve qui peut had commenced.[55]

Barker had gone back to the horse-lines in the Volunteer tents to retrieve his horse – 'I found one of my horses shot in the side and kicking on the ground. Luckily it was the one not saddled'[56] – lost sight of his companions, and ridden back towards the *nek*, convinced they might make a stand there.

He was wrong. In fact a group of them had rallied around Captain Bradstreet close to the rear of the Volunteer camp, on the road between it and the 1/24th's tents. Trooper Edwards heard Lieutenant Scott calling out 'Carbineers, come to the front!', and 'we all endeavoured to fight our way to him'.[57] There were more than thirty of them altogether, a dozen Volunteers – mostly Carbineers – and twenty or so Mounted Police. The road was the one clear passage through the tents, and it afforded an opportunity of sorts to hold back the Zulus, though it is uncertain whether that was Bradstreet's main concern – many of the men were now without their horses, and their one chance of survival lay in sticking together, and close to their reserve ammunition.

Trooper Edwards never reached them, pushed back by a Zulu rush:

I was with a fellow named Whitelaw, and the two of us had become isolated. Back to back, we fought like furies with our short rifles and small dagger-like bayonets in a great effort to get back to our companions. We were cut off entirely from the ammunition tent, although we could still hear the little piccanin shouting 'M'nition baas! M'nition, baas!' in a high pitched voice. As brave a little fellow as one could hope to find. And all the time he handed out cartridges to those who could get near the tent. He must have gone on doing so until he was killed with the others. We had filled our tunics and belts with bullets, but they did not last long, and we were soon reduced to using the butts of our rifles. Every here and there I could see small groups of men selling their lives dearly, using their fists, rifle butts and daggers to terrible purpose.[58]

As the 24th companies had been broken up among the tents, a number of them had made their way to join Bradstreet and Scott, and here Durnford had found them. After seeing for himself that there was nothing he could do for the infantry, he had returned to the tents. What he was looking for there will never be known – the remnants of his command? The means of making a tactical stand? Or simply a moment in which to redeem his honour? It must have been clear to him that the battle was beyond salvation, and there could be no question of an officer of his rank and responsibility surviving such a debacle. It is doubtful if the idea even crossed his mind. It was expected of a British officer that he should share the fate of his men – and there could be only one acceptable course of action now.

It is not the least of the brutal ironies of the iSandlwana saga that the men fate now contrived to place in Durford's way included so many Carbineers – the same unit he believed had let him down at Bushman's River Pass. Perhaps there is an echo of his experience in that earlier battle in the words he uttered as he joined them. 'Now, my men, let us see what you can do' someone heard him say – who did not stay himself.[59]

It was Mehlokazulu who saw the end:

> When the Carbineers reached the camp they jumped off their horses and never succeeded in getting on them again. When they got into the camp, they dismounted, made a stand, and prevented our entering the camp, but things were then getting very mixed and confused – what with the smoke, dust, and intermingling of mounted men, footmen, Zulus and natives, it was difficult to tell who was mounted and who was not. It was a long time before they were overcome – before we finished them. When we did get to them, they died all in one place, altogether. They threw down their guns when their ammunition was done, and then commenced with their pistols, which they used as long as their ammunition lasted; and then they formed a line, shoulder to shoulder and back to back, and fought with their knives.[60]

'I repeatedly heard the word "Fire!" given by someone', he said, 'but we proved too many for them, and killed them all where they stood. When it was all over I had a look at these men, and saw a dead officer, with his arm in a sling and a big moustache, surrounded by dead Carbineers, soldiers, and other men I did not know.'[61]

*

As the fighting reached the outskirts of the camp, a wave of exultation swept through the *amabutho*. James Brickhill heard it, and knew that it spelt the end:

> The Zulus for the last 300 yards [274 metres] did not fire 25 shots, but came on with the steady determination of walking down the camp by force of numbers. I consider they were 30 to 1 of us. At 150 yards [137 metres] they roused a shout of 'Usutu!' . . . The cry then was '*Luminyile Elsutu*' (the Usutu has swallowed up or overwhelmed). They now came on with an overwhelming rush. I went back to the head of the 1/24th camp to see if I could see anything of my companion [Quartermaster Pullen] but could not, so seeing that the Zulus were already stabbing in this camp as well as the others I joined the fugitives retreating over the neck . . .'[62]

In the Volunteer camp Trooper George Sparks of the Mounted Police heard the Zulus running through the tents, and members of the izinGulube *ibutho* exhorting one another to 'Stab the white men!' He turned to his friend Trooper Pearce and said 'Things look black!' 'My oath they do!' replied Pearce. 'Come on man,' said Sparks, 'let's ride off. We shall be killed.' Pearce hesitated – 'What a choking off I'll get if the Sergeant-Major sees me riding with a snaffle instead of the regulation bit', he replied, and turned back. Sparks never saw him again.[63]

When the NNC had fallen back towards the tents, Walter Stafford had gone with his *induna* Ntini to find ammunition. He was returning with a box when he noticed that the 24th was falling back, and that his men had fled. Charlie Raw came past and said, ' "Stafford, where is your horse?" I replied that I had left it tied to the wagon. He said "You had better get hold of it as it is all up with us." There appeared to be no-one in command.'[64]

Stafford ran to get his horse and suddenly the tents were full of Zulus. Thrown spears 'came down like hailstones'. One struck Ntini and he fell, while 'My horse received one assegai behind the crupper staple and a second one down his nose which cut the skin, and I received a cut through the skin of the knuckle of my foot.'[65] Somehow Stafford managed to turn his horse away, and headed towards the *nek*.

Cracroft Nourse had lost his horse when the rocket battery was overrun, and:

Being alone on foot with an empty revolver, my chances of escape appeared most remote, but just as I was thinking of making for a donga my native servant rode up, handed me my horse and shot away without my being able to question him. Hope had revived, and I now had a loaded revolver.

The thought then occurred to me that if I could get into the thousands of animals that were rushing through the nek, bellowing, braying and bleating, with a cloud of dust hanging over them, I might get through. It reminded me forcibly of the Biblical description of the defeat of the Babylonians. I joined the maddened beasts and got through.[66]

Troopers Edwards and Whitelaw finally abandoned their attempts to join their fellow Carbineers. 'A few of us had managed to work our way to the picket lines', said Edwards, 'where we undid our horses with feverish haste. Every now and then a mounted man rushed past, followed by a hail of flying assegais. One poor fellow got an assegai right in his spine; he rose in his saddle for a moment and then pitched forward, stone dead ... We made a great effort to get out before it was too late. . .'[67]

At about this time, as he too turned to flee, a civilian wagon conductor named Martin Foley saw 'the Union Jack in front of the General's tent . . . pulled down and torn to pieces';[68] he thought the time about one o'clock – if he was right, it was no more than an hour after Raw had first blundered into the Zulu army at the Ngwebeni.

*

Most of Durnford's men had stuck together in their troops, which afforded them the best chance of survival; Brickhill saw some of them passing over the *nek* near Chelmsford's tent, shouting to one another, rallying for a while at the foot of iSandlwana, and firing at men of the uNokhenke hurrying to cut them off. Without their white officer, the Edendale men had followed their sergeant, Simeon Nkambule, who told them that if it was God's will they would reach Natal if they stuck together. Very few of Durnford's men had ammunition left, however, and Nkambule saw one of the 24th's wagons behind the tents, and that

... the Zulus were too busy in the tents to bother about the wagon yet. He rode up with his men and found no-one there but a little drummer boy, who sat on top of the wagon and said he was in charge. Simeon asked him to give him and his men a packet of cartridges each, just to help them defend themselves. But the little boy informed them this ammunition belonged to the 24th Regiment; and as long as he was in charge, no one else should have any of it. Simeon felt the boy was obeying orders, and respected him. Then he saw there was a lot of loose cartridges lying on the grass around the wagons. Men who had come in for cartridges were in such haste to fill their belts that they dropped many on the ground. So, Simeon and his men each picked up a few and put them in their belts.

Simeon's heart went out to the boy who was sticking to his post of duty. He told the boy the battle was lost, the camp was in the hands of the enemy, the fighting all over, and, indeed his was the only body of men holding together. He begged the boy to leave the wagon and he would take him in front of his saddle and as long as he had life, he would defend him. The boy was surprised and hurt to think anyone could think he would desert his post. His officer had placed him there and no one should move him out of it while he still had life in him. With a very sad heart Simeon had to leave him there . . .[69]

Walter Higginson had stayed for a few minutes after his company had bolted, until he saw '. . . all the mounted men riding past as fast as they could, and I then thought it was time to go too, so, firing one more shot, I mounted my horse, Sergt. Major Williams holding my rifle while I did so, and rode off. As I came amongst the 24th tents, I found myself beside Lieut. Cochrane, 32nd Regiment, and rode on with him . . .'[70]

Most were not so lucky. Lieutenant the Hon. Standish Vereker of the 3rd NNC had made his way back to the camp from the ridge, and, having lost his horse earlier, had managed to find another. He had just mounted it, however, when one of the auxiliaries ran up and claimed the horse was his. It may well have been – and Vereker dismounted and let him have it. It was a gentlemanly gesture that would cost him his life.

When the 24th companies had begun to retire towards the camp, Horace Smith-Dorrien had returned to the tents, probably searching out fresh ammunition. Here he met Louis Dubois, apparently searching for a horse. '"The game is up," said Dubois, "If I had a good horse I would ride straight for Maritzburg." I never saw him again. I then saw Surgeon-Major Shepherd, busy in a depression, treating wounded. This was also the last time I saw him.'[71]

'Before we knew where we were they came right into the camp, assegaing everybody right and left', Smith-Dorrien confided afterwards in a letter to his father, 'everybody then who had a horse turned to fly.'[72] Smith-Dorrien's horse was by no means a good one, a 'knock-kneed pony' he had borrowed which had had little rest over the previous thirty-six hours, but he jumped on it and set off towards the *nek*.

As Harry Davies crested the *nek*, however, a terrifying sight greeted him on the other side. 'I saw from here a great many wagon drivers, leaders, and many others leaving the camp[,] they were making direct for the river. I saw from here the Zulus running down in great numbers at the back of the Isandhlwana hill thereby cutting off our retreat, this was evidently their right arm.'[73] As he watched, Davies saw a covered wagon drawn by twelve mules start off down the road towards Rorke's Drift. It was one of Surgeon Shepherd's ambulance wagons, marked by a large red cross painted on the canvas, a desperate attempt to evacuate some of the wounded before it was too late. But the road was closed – and there was no way out of the camp now to wheeled traffic; 'They had got about 100 yards [92 metres] from the hill when all the mules were stabbed and the occupants of the wagon. I saw the Zulus jumping into the wagon . . .'[74]

There was no way through, either, for the guns. Any hopes Smith and Curling may have had of rallying on the *nek* were dispelled by the slaughter of their gunners as they passed through the camp. 'The road to Rorke's Drift that we hoped to retreat by was full of the enemy', said Curling, 'so no way being open we followed a crowd of natives and camp followers who were running down a ravine.'[75] The gun-carriages were forced off the road to their left, descending at an angle down the slope of Mahlabamkhosi towards the bed of the Manzimnyama stream. For the first 300–400 metres the going was good, the ground stony and swathed in long grass, but flat; beyond that, however, it crumpled and split into a network of *dongas* draining towards the stream. Here the horses struggled to get down a low bank a metre or two high, and the Zulus caught them:

> The ravine got steeper and steeper and finally the guns stuck and could get no further. In a moment the Zulus closed in and the drivers who now alone remained were pulled off their horses and killed. I did not see Major Smith at this moment but was with him a minute before. The guns could not be spiked there was no time to think of anything and we hoped to save the guns up to the last moment. As soon as the guns were taken I galloped off and made off with the crowd . . .[76]

Like most Victorian soldiers, Curling did not dwell on the horror of that scene – on the sight of the horses, pumped up by their gallop, spraying out blood as they were stabbed until they fell, the dying dragging down the living still linked in their harnesses, the screeching of horses and men, the triumphant shouts of '*uSuthu!*' and the '*Ji!*' of exultation. Yet echoes of their terror still haunt iSandlwana. In 2000 archaeologists investigating the battlefield excavated a cairn in the side of the bank where lengths of bone had become exposed. After careful study it proved to be the burial pit for some of the limber horses, full of the long bones and skull fragments of six horses. A few centimetres below the topsoil on the slope beyond were found metal remains of the traces, studs and buckles, some with fragments of rotting leather still attached. And at the very bottom of the pit, their significance missed by the burial details who collected the remains many months after the battle, were two human limb bones – the remains of Curling's drivers.[77]

*

There was, of course, no opportunity for those on foot to escape. While the men of the 1st and 3rd NNC, who had made off when the firing line collapsed, before the Zulu horns had completed the encirclement, could move through the countryside just as easily as the Zulus there was by this point no hope that the whites left could do the same. Whether they were infantry of the 24th, or Volunteers without their horses, their only hope of survival lay in sticking together and fighting so hard that the Zulus would leave them alone in favour of easier targets. And so a grim truth underpins those legends of the 'last stand' at iSandlwana, so heroic and melancholy as it seems from a distance of 130 years – the infantry stood and fought because the only alternative available to them was to scatter and be killed.

Nevertheless, the discipline of the 24th served them well at the end, and the companies remained together as they retired through the camp. The tents – whether standing or flattened – disrupted what remained of their formations, the ropes tangling and tripping the unwary, and the Zulus followed them as closely as they dared. 'As we rushed on the soldiers retired on the tents', said uGuku of the uKhandempemvu, 'fighting all the way, and as they got into the tents we were intermingled with them.' Clearly, they were trying to join together, but the pressure from the Zulus was too great:

One party of soldiers came out from among the tents and formed up a little above the ammunition wagons. They held their ground there until their ammunition failed them, when they were nearly all assegaid. Those that were not killed at this place formed up again in a solid square in the neck of Sandhlwana. They were completely surrounded on all sides, and stood back to back, and surrounding some men who were in the centre. Their ammunition was now done, except that they had some revolvers which they fired at us at close quarters. We were quite unable to break their square until we had killed a great many of them, by throwing our assegais at short distances. We eventually overcame them in this way.[78]

One party – probably Porteous's and Wardell's companies – made a stand in the 1/24th camp area – and afterwards, the bodies of Wardell and Lieutenant Dyer, the adjutant of the 2/24th, were found among a clump of sixty bodies.

Pope's company, originally on the right of Pulleine's line, had made a stand briefly on the banks of the Mpofana *donga* but, pressed in by the uMbonambi to the front and outflanked by the uKhandempemvu to its left, it had withdrawn steadily up the slope until surrounded in the vicinity of the 1/24th camp. After the war, an unnamed Zulu *induna* told Norris-Newman that:

> . . . when they were surrounding the troops at the camp, on the neck of the plain, two officers with pieces of glass in their eyes came forward shooting at him with their revolvers. One fell dead from a gun shot, and the other kept firing his revolver at the *induna*, a bullet grazing the right side of his neck, another grazing his left side, and another entering his leg. The *induna* flung an assegai, which entered the officer's breast. The officer, with supreme effort, almost succeeded in pulling out the weapon (here the Zulu writhed his body in pantomime of the efforts of the officer), but the *induna* fell on him and instantly finished his dreadful work with another assegai. This minute account of the deaths of two officers, there can be little doubt, relates to Lieuts. Austin and Pope, of the 2/24th, who were the only two officers of that regiment who constantly wore eye-glasses.[79]

Many of the 24th who survived the fight through the camp rallied on the *nek* below the southern peak of iSandlwana, disrupting, according to Mehlokazulu, the meeting of the Zulu horns:

When the Zulus closed in, the English kept up a strong fire towards the Buffalo. They were concentrated near the rear of the camp, and the fire was so heavy as to enable them to make an opening, and thus a great many of the mounted men escaped through this opening. The attention of the Zulus was directed to the killing of men in the rear, and so they did not attend to the closing up of this opening, and thus let the mounted men out ... The resistance was stout where the old Dutch road used to go across; it took a long time to drive back the English forces there; they killed us and we killed them, and the fight was kept up for a long time. The British troops became helpless, because they had no ammunition, and the Zulus killed them ...[80]

Younghusband's company fared better than most. It managed to retreat behind the camp and retire up onto a prominent shoulder of iSandlwana above the *nek*. It is impossible to be certain of the route it took, but given the overwhelming evidence of the speed with which the Zulus penetrated the camp, it is unlikely that Younghusband's men could have climbed up the southern slopes of the hill with their backs to the enemy and the Zulus among them. Given a scattering of graves there, it is far more likely that the men retired up the line of a shallow incline which rises from the northern foot of iSandlwana and ends in a knoll below the cliffs. An unknown man of the uVe described them as retiring 'slowly, and always fighting, up the slopes of Isandhlwana'. Here, among great isolated slabs of rock, the company held its ground. It was a commanding position in many respects, a difficult one for the Zulus to attack, and the soldiers could shoot downwards to cover the men struggling below. Yet their ammunition could not last forever, and once it was spent there was nowhere for them to go, and it became more difficult to prevent knots of Zulus clambering up the slopes to attack them hand-to-hand. 'Gradually', said the same Zulu, 'the English on the koppie got fewer and fewer.'[81]

Below them, on the *nek*, the big stand was still going on, and Younghusband must have decided to chance his luck and lead the survivors down to join them. According to a man of the uNokhenke:

They fought well – a lot of them got up on the steep slope under the cliff of the camp, and the Zulus could not get at them at all; they were shot or bayoneted as fast as they came up. At last the soldiers gave a shout and charged down upon us. There was an *induna* in front of them with a long flashing sword, which he whirled around his head as he ran – it must have been made of fire. Wheugh! (Here the speaker made an expressive gesture of shading the eyes.) They killed themselves by running down, for our people got above and quite surrounded them; these, and a group of white men on the neck, were the last to fall.[82]

Some of them, at least, made it down, for the bodies of Younghusband and his subaltern, George Hodson, were found among the dead at the foot of the mountain. Of the fate of other officers only fragments of information remain. One of the last sights of the battle Captain Nourse glimpsed as he was riding away was 'about half a company of the 24th, with their Colonel in their midst, assegaid, just out of reach of their bayonets'.[83] It is possible that this may have been Henry Pulleine's fate, for others later claimed to have recognized his body among the dead of the stand at the foot of the hill. Lieutenant Pat Daly of F Company was seen waving his hand and shouting to the mounted men as they rode past, before turning back to his men, while the body of Paymaster White was found in the 2/24th camp. Lieutenant Macdowel of the Royal Engineers, who had only arrived back in camp as the battle began, was last seen carrying ammunition forward from Chelmsford's tent to the firing line, when a Zulu fired at him at close range and shot him dead.[84]

The novelist Rider Haggard was told how another – unknown – officer died:

Shortly after the disaster, one of the survivors told the present writer of a duel which he witnessed between a Zulu and an officer of the 24th regiment. The officer, having emptied his revolver, set his back against the wheel of a wagon and drew his sword. Then the Zulu came at him with his shield up, turning and springing from side to side as he advanced. Presently he lowered the shield, exposing his head, and the white man, falling into the trap, aimed a fierce blow at it. As it fell the shield was raised again, and the sword sank deep into its edge, remaining fixed in the tough ox-hide. It was that that the Zulu desired; with a twist of his strong arm he wrenched the sword from his opponent's hand, and in another instant the unfortunate officer was down with an assegai through his breast.[85]

Milne's servant, Signalman Aynsley, also stood his ground among the wagons, with his back to a wheel. Here he defended himself with his cutlass, cursing the Zulus and challenging them, beckoning them forward one at a time to fight him, cutting each one down in turn – until one of their comrades crawled under the wagon and stabbed him through the spokes.

George Shepstone had returned to the camp when the amaNgwane line collapsed early in the battle, and had ridden off looking for Durnford. Whether he found him or not will never be known, but it is tempting to think that he did – for while Durnford was making his stand to hold back the Zulus left along the road, George Shepstone made one of his own, high up on a jagged spur close under the south-western foot of iSandlwana. This may have been the rocky spot where Brickhill saw Durnford's men rally briefly, and it is quite likely that the men who fought here were NNC. Whether they were Erskine or Barry's amaChunu or Lonsdale's iziGqoza, Krohn's Bele or Stafford or Nourse's amaNgwane, they fought desperately among the boulders, holding back, for a while, some of the uNokhenke, and playing their part in allowing the mounted men to escape. Unlike the 24th or the Volunteers, no details have survived of the struggle, and there would be no grand Victorian paintings commemorating their stand – but they fought and died nonetheless. Shepstone himself was killed by a brother of Muziwento, as he reported: 'We were told that there was present a son of Somseu. He fought very bravely. He killed our people. The others feared to approach him. Suddenly there dashed in our brother Umtweni before he could load, and killed him.'[86]

Once the last great concentration of the 24th was broken up on the *nek*, the survivors, Lieutenant Anstey among them, were pushed over into the valley of the Manzimnyama. Pressed in by the right horn, and trying to avoid the left, they veered off the track and down a slope scoured with *dongas* and strewn with boulders. By now the infantrymen must have been out of ammunition, fighting with bayonet alone. Many were no doubt wounded, all of them exhausted, traumatized, and moving slowly through the broken ground, backs now and then pressed against each other, every stumble over a rock, each snag on the spiky leaves of an aloe, risking a tumble that might send them sprawling at the mercy of the Zulus pursuing them.

As they descended into the valley, the hills closed in, robbing them of easy landmarks, leaving them to follow in the wake of the mounted men, or cling to the memory of the direction of Rorke's Drift. Finally, nearly a kilometre from the *nek*, they struck the banks of the Manzimnyama, and they could go no further. The valley was full of Zulus killing stragglers, and the banks were so steep there was no hope that they could scramble down them in any kind of order. Here they were overrun and died, all forty of them together in a clump, with Anstey in their midst – the true 'last stand of the 24th'.[87]

There was, in truth, little that is romantic about this desperate fighting in the last stages of the battle, not much of the stalwart sergeant, upright and unbowed, or the calm and doe-eyed drummer boy that the Victorians – and many since – found so appealing. Once the ammunition was gone, the killing was carried out at close quarters with an almost medieval visceral savagery, with sharp weapons that skewered bodies, tore jagged flesh wounds, pierced or caved in skulls – close enough to see the expression in a man's eyes as he was struck down, to hear his shrieks or curses and to be sprayed by his blood. Many men on both sides must have been injured time and again before they finally fell, only to be run through on the ground by a British bayonet, or repeatedly stabbed with Zulu spears.

Mehlokazulu left a vivid insight into the mechanics of killing:

> Some Zulus threw assegais at them, others shot at them; but they did not get close – they avoided the bayonet; for any man who went up to stab a soldier was fixed through the throat or stomach, and at once fell. Occasionally when a soldier was engaged with a Zulu in front with an assegai, another Zulu killed him from behind. There was a tall man who came out of a wagon and made a stout defence, holding out for some time when we thought all the white people had been driven out of camp. He fired in every direction, and so quickly as to drive the Zulus some one way, some another. At first some of the Zulus took no notice; but at last he commanded our attention by the plucky way in which he fought, and because he had killed so many. He was at last shot. All those who tried to stab him were knocked over at once, or bayoneted; he kept his ground for a very long time.[88]

Individual details from the slaughter remained in the minds of those who had participated in it for decades afterwards. Kumpega Qwabe recalled how he came across one man, a Volunteer perhaps or an officer of the NNC, who was defending himself with a pistol: 'Dum! Dum! went his revolver as he was firing from right to left, and I came along beside him and stuck my assegai under his right arm, pushing it through his body until it came out between his ribs on the left side. As soon as he fell I pulled the assegai out and slit his stomach so I knew he would not shoot any more of my people . . .'[89]

Vumandaba kaNthathi, the commander of the uKhandempemvu who had been part of the deputation that had received Frere's ultimatum six weeks before, explained that the Zulus had not been impressed by British revolvers – 'For every man they killed,' he said, 'they fired a great many shots without hitting anybody.'[90]

uMhoti of the uKhandempemvu had followed the retreating 24th companies into the camp and

> Just as I reached the tents a bald-headed man, unarmed, rushed out of one and tried to dodge around it, but was assegaid. I then attacked a soldier whose bayonet pierced my shield and while he was trying to extract it I stabbed him in the shoulder. He dropped his rifle and seized me round the neck and threw me on the ground under him, my eyes felt as if they were bursting and I almost choked when I succeeded in grasping the spear which was still sticking in his shoulder and forced it into his vitals and he rolled over, lifeless.[91]

Nearly forty years later, Mangwanana Mchunu of the uVe remembered intimately the details of the man he had killed. 'This man', he said, 'had a red coat and black trousers with a red line up the trousers; he had a brown hat on. He turned to shoot one of my friends of the uVe armed with an *umkhonto* [spear]. He raised his right arm which had a revolver (*volovol*) in it and as he was about to fire I stabbed him in the armpit. I pushed it in, I did not hear him cry out, I pushed and pushed it in until he died.'[92]

Mlamula Matebula of the iNgobamakhosi, who had been hit three times during the rush on the camp, was injured again in the fighting:

> I killed three on that day, the third one was a native, one of the Basutho, who was on the soldiers' side, [he] was armed with a gun and a sheath of short stabbing spears on his back, his ammunition was finished, he and many others were then using these short spears. I approached him, he struck first with the spear, I lifted my shield to guard, but unfortunately too high and it caught me on my forearm. I jumped upon him, banged him with my shield on his face and speared him. He fell down dead and I praised myself in the name of my regiment.
>
> There was one soldier who had alone killed very many of our men. There were heaps of dead bodies in front of him, he was taking shelter behind two aloe trees which were growing together, when spears were thrown at him he dodged behind one of these aloe trees. We were a lot of us attacking this man, [but] when they saw others dropped down by

the firing of this soldier they hesitated, and the onward rush checked. I pushed them aside, flew at him and stabbed him at close-quarters, praising myself, and killed him. He was wearing a red jacket and a cap with a tuft of wool on it.[93]

A man named Maqedindaba kaNtshingwayo Mdlalose described how, during the rush through the tents, he

Saw a little white house standing by itself and I sprang into its opening, looking for the White man's drink. At a table there was seated an officer, who when he saw me appear plucked out a little gun and shot me through the cheek. I staggered, but found myself still alive. So I sprang upon him and finished him with my spear. That is why I am called Maqedindaba [lit. He Who Finishes the Matter], because I killed the chief *induna* of the army. And here is the scar of the wound he gave me.[94]

This story has often been taken as testimony of the last moments of Pulleine, but Maqedindaba obviously had no idea of the identity of the man he had killed, beyond that he was an officer.

According to Muziwento, the last stages of the battle were raw and brutal, an intense frenzy of killing:

Some seized their rifles and smashing them upon the rocks hurled them. They helped one another too; they stabbed those with the bayonet who sought to kill their comrades. Some covered their faces with their hands, not wishing to see death. Some ran away. Some entered into the tents. Others were indignant; although badly wounded they died where they stood, at their post.[95]

Later, the traveller Bertram Mitford was told by astonished Zulu veterans that when their ammunition was gone many soldiers fought on with just their pocket knives, or with their fists. 'Ah', one of them was supposed to have said, 'those red soldiers at Isandhlwana! How few they were, and how they fought! They fell like stones, each man in his place.'[96]

Not everyone who fought on the Zulu side was impressed; Mgelija Ngema admitted that 'My feeling towards the soldiers was very angry for them coming with their guns to kill us, but I thought they fought like cowards; they shot at us when we were far away but they wanted to run away when we arrived.'[97]

In the last stages of the battle, the transformation among the Zulus from herdsmen to warriors became complete. Many were consumed by an emotional state they characterized as 'seeing nothing but red', a fierce anger towards the enemy, a deep instinctive urge to kill. 'There was just one big shout of "Usutu" as we fell upon the white men,' recalled uNzuzi Mandla, '... many of whom said to us in our own tongue, "Have mercy on us. Spare our lives. What wrong have we done Cetewayo?" "How can we give you mercy," we replied, "when you have come to us and want to take away our country and eat us up? How can we give you mercy? Usutu!"'[98]

Swept along in the surge of excitement, many young Zulus struck out at anything that moved in the gloomy confusion of smoke and dust and dwindling sunlight. 'I also killed a horse and a donkey,' Mbongozo Mbonambi admitted ruefully, 'and some oxen that were in yokes.' 'During the first phase of the battle our eyes were dark', agreed Nzuzi Mandla, 'and we stabbed everything we came across. But when we got light into our eyes again we spared what stock was left.'[99] Some young Zulus who had never seen a white man before stabbed into the coarse sacks of grains piled up among the tents as they ran past.

A few white men – soldiers, Volunteers or civilians, it is not clear – tried to escape by climbing the top of iSandlwana hill, or hiding among the boulders and caves scattered around the base of the cliffs. There is a path, now, which leads to the top, by way of a scramble up through the rocks on the western edge, and onto the small grassy back of the hill. It might perhaps have been a good defensive spot, for a while at least, for half a dozen men with guns, but for panic-stricken men it offered no refuge. 'The uKhandempemvu climbed up the hill at Isandlwana', recalled Sofikasho Zungu, 'and killed a few white men up at the very top of the hill, and threw them down off the top of the rock.'[100] 'I remember one incident I heard a lot of talk of that occurred at Isandhlwana', said Mangwanana Mchunu:

Near where the highest point is, one of the soldiers was chased up the rocks by a member of the Nokenke regiment, who was transferred to our regiment as an *induna*, called Muti Ntshangase. This soldier could speak Zulu and appealed to Muti, saying 'Do not kill me in the sun, kill me in the shadows.' I imagine he wanted to get into a place to hide. Muti stabbed him to death. It was a funny thing that we all talked about that Muti went mad soon after. Cetewayo was told of this incident.

Muti was taken down from Isandhlwana to Ulundi under control and
Cetewayo, who thought a lot of him, sent for some Shangaan doctors to
make him right again, and they succeeded . . .[101]

One of the 24th, a survivor of Younghusband's company, had not joined
the last rush onto the *nek* below with his captain, but had instead retreated
to the foot of the cliffs below the high peak. Here there is a small cave, no
more than 2 or 3 metres high, extending back about the same distance into
the hillside. The entrance is screened by several large fallen boulders, and
the last few metres of the approach are steep. This the soldier defended,
shooting or bayoneting every Zulu who came near, until at last they grew
tired of him, and several Zulus with rifles fired a volley into the cave – and
killed him.[102]

When this story became known it attracted the attention of the Dublin
painter R.T. Moynan, who produced a large canvas based on the scene; the
soldier stands courageously above the boulders, his left hand raised, a
mystical look in his eye as the shot strikes him, while the awestruck Zulus
draw back at his feet, like Roman soldiers at the crucifixion. It is a
wonderfully evocative painting, full of the self-confident martyrdom inherent in a good deal of late nineteenth-century imperial ideology – the white
man's sacrificing his life in the cause of civilized progress. A visit to the
cave suggests an altogether more ghastly and tragic truth.

Inside the cave at the back, easily overlooked by visitors today and in
the gloom of the shadows, is a small chamber. Largely filled by loose sand
and rock hyrax dung, it is no more than 0.5 metres high, and perhaps
2 metres deep. It is just big enough for a desperate man to wriggle into,
and to move his arms and work a rifle. From here he could easily shoot
any Zulus who exposed themselves over the boulders at the entrance a
metre away – and he would be almost impossible to hit in return.

It is said that this anonymous survivor held his ground until 'the
shadows were long on the ground'[103] – that is, several hours at least after
all his comrades were dead at the foot of the hill below, and the Zulus were
in complete possession of the field. Several hours pressed in by solid rock
on all sides, becoming stiff and sore, and assailed by the smell of animal
urine; several hours in the cool, claustrophobic shade, staring out across
the stones and through the wider entrance at the sky, listening to the
sounds of the triumphant Zulus below, and firing whenever something
moved fleetingly across his view, his hearing paralysed each time by the

report of his own shots echoing fiercely in the confined space. Perhaps he hoped Lord Chelmsford might return before it was too late; probably he feared what would happen when his ammunition finally ran out. Perhaps, towards the end, he was hardly able to think at all.

# 23

# 'Do you hear that?'

## iSandlwana and Mangeni, 22 January 1879

After leaving iSandlwana at about ten o'clock that morning, Lieutenant John Chard had seen nothing on the road back to Rorke's Drift to justify his earlier worries that the Zulus might cut round behind the column and 'make a dash for the Drift'. Apart from a few individuals making their way to and from the camp on routine duties, the track had been deserted, and after the recent activity the landscape had seemed quiet and peaceful in the morning sunshine.

Chard brought his wagon across by the pont and parked it close to his tent near the drift. During his absence he found that Brevet Major Henry Spalding, 104th Regiment, the deputy assistant adjutant and quartermaster-general attached to the headquarters staff, who was temporarily in charge of the lines of communication from Helpmekaar forward, had issued fresh 'morning orders' for the protection of the ponts, now that Durnford's column was no longer securing the Zulu bank. A guard of one NCO and six privates had been posted by the river from Gunny Bromhead's company of the 2/24th, stationed up at the mission buildings, supported by fifty African privates from a detachment of the 3rd NNC commanded by Captain Stevenson. This duty was a temporary one, for Captain Rainforth's G Company, 1/24th, which had been delayed on the road by the wet weather and was due from Helpmekaar, had been ordered to build an entrenched post to protect the ponts. Rainforth had been at Helpmekaar for several days, and should already have arrived, but his had been the only garrison protecting the stockpile of supplies there until another company of the 1/24th, Russell Upcher's D Company, arrived on 21 January to relieve him.

By mid-morning, when Chard had returned to the drift, there had still been no sign of Rainforth, and Chard had reported the developments at iSandlwana to Spalding:

[He] Pointed out to him that in the event of an attack on the Ponts, it would be impossible with 7 men (not counting the natives) to make an effective defence ... Major Spalding told me he was going over to Helpmekaar, and would see about getting it down at once. Just as he was about to ride away he said to me

'Which of you is senior, you or Bromhead?'

I said, 'I don't know.'

He went back into his tent and looked at an Army list, and coming back said,

'I see you are senior, so you will be in charge, although of course, nothing will happen, and I shall be back again this evening early.'[1]

With that Spalding had ridden off. It was now late morning, and in the absence of his sappers, Chard had had little to do. He had returned to his tent by the river, 'had some lunch comfortably', and begun writing a letter home.[2]

\*

At iSandlwana, the sight of the ambulance wagon being overrun and the men inside dragged out and stabbed had caused Harry Davies of the Edendale troop to pause for a moment on the *nek*. 'I looked round for my men', he said, 'but they had gone with the crowd. I here saw Henderson and asked him what was the best thing to do, he did not reply. I said I think it is a case of run and take pot luck. The soldiers were fighting hand to hand and the enemy were all over the camp. I then made up my mind to make a dash through the enemy who were all round . . .'[3]

Brickhill too saw that the right horn was passing rapidly down the course of the Manzimnyama, and that the uVe, who had at last completed their move up from the Nyogane stream, were beginning to appear over the crest of the Mahlabamkhosi ridge to the left:

I found all communication by the road we had come along cut off by several lines of Zulus running across. These were evidently those Zulus who had been compelled to go over the neck by the well-sustained crest fire of the Basuto. They had come along behind Isandhlwana and thus intercepted our retreat. The Zulus' left horn had now come over the ridge south of the stony Kopje. They could have completed their circle, but I think preferred leaving this gap so that they might attack us in our rear to bring us to bay when each man would have done his best. The

Isandhlwana horn edged us away more and more to the left and these
two kept up a constant cross-fire upon us.[4]

Walter Stafford was surprised to see as they passed over the *nek* that the
road was already littered with the corpses of men who had left the camp
early, and 'we passed many killed who could not possibly have taken part
in the fighting'.[5] Brickhill noted that by the time he left the camp the way
was already marked by debris left by men in flight, much of it cast aside by
the NNC. 'Our flight I shall never forget', he said,

> No path, no track, boulders everywhere – on we went, borne now into
> some dry torrent bed, now weaving our way amongst the trees of
> stunted growth, so that unless you made the best use of your eyes you
> were in constant danger of colliding against some tree or finding
> yourself unhorsed at the bottom of some ravine. Our way was already
> strewn with shields, assegais, blankets, hats, clothing of all description,
> guns, ammunition belts, saddles (which horses had managed to kick
> off), revolvers and belts and I don't know what, whilst our stampede
> was composed of mules with and without pack saddles, oxen, horses in
> all stages of equipment and flying men all strangely intermingled – man
> and beast apparently all infected with the danger which surrounded us.
> One riderless horse that ran up alongside me I caught and gave to a
> poor soldier who was struggling on foot, but he had scarcely mounted
> before he was knocked off by a Zulu bullet.[6]

A few hundred metres beyond the broken ground where the guns came to
grief, a *donga* rises high on the slope of the southern end of the Mahlabamkhosi ridge, shallow at first as it cuts through thin, hard bands of
ancient sediment, then plunging through dark layers of softer shale and
sand so that in places lower down it is 10 metres deep and 6 metres wide.
Normally there is no more than a greasy slick of moisture in the bottom,
but in the wet summer of 1879 the water was flowing freely, falling here
and there along the way over sudden rocky steps in miniature waterfalls
before emptying into the Manzimnyama at the bottom of the valley below.
The vegetation along the hillside was thinner then than it is now, but the
middle and lower reaches of the course were masked by a tangled mat of
thorn-bush and aloes which obscured the full extent of the *donga* until the
last moment, so that the long straggling chain of fleeing men struck it
unawares. 'Whilst going down into a deep dry torrent bed', said Brickhill,

I saw Lieutenants Melvill and Coghill and Conductor Foley about 200 yards [183 metres] ahead only more to our right. A stream of Zulus running on their right was fast pressing them down towards the course we were on. Scrambling over this rocky bed as best we could we came up the hill on this side fully exposed to the enemy's rear and cross fire. We here came to an abrupt halt by reason of a huge chasm or gully which opened to view in front of our horses. There was nothing for it but to turn sharply round and follow the course of this gully down in the hope of finding a crossing somewhere. The constant pinging of the Zulu bullets made one's ears tingle again and one of us, a mounted infantryman, impatient of our Indian file type of following one another, put his horse at the gully. It was a noble grey, but the horse fell far short and the rider lay crushed beneath his horse about twelve feet [3.7 metres] below. I have little doubt that both horse and rider had found their grave. We found a crossing to the gully, but so steep that on coming out on this side I laced my arms round my horse's neck and threw my head as far forward as possible and even then it will remain a puzzle how our horses got out of this without falling backwards . . .[7]

'We had very bad country to get over,' agreed James Hamer,

. . . large rough boulders and stones. Some distance from the camp is a small ravine which was hid by bushes, the greatest part of the fugitives fortunately went above it, but several (with myself) went too low down. I met it at the centre, we could not go above as the Zulus were too near, and we had to go to the end of it before we could cross. The Zulus saw this and large numbers tried to cut us off, I and four others were the last to get round, and we had to use our revolvers very freely, for the Zulus followed us up quickly, this ground being very bad for horses, and footmen had not the ghost of a chance. Several men were stabbed on their horses. My horse (Dick) had had a great deal of work that day and with making over stones he got completely done and would not move a step further. I was in a jolly predicament when (thank God) a man of the rocket battery galloped up with a led horse and let me have it. I had just taken the saddle off poor Dick when a bullet struck him dead and the poor fellow who gave me the horse had only ridden ten yards [9.1 metres] when I saw him fall killed from his horse . . .[8]

'Here', said Trooper Barker of the Carbineers, 'I heard for the first and only time the awful scream of a terrified or mad horse. He was a black horse with the saddle turned round, and he passed us and went crash against the mounted man in front of us, rolling over the krantz . . .'[9] While James Brickhill came up with

> . . . poor Band Sergeant Gamble tottering and stumbling about amongst the stones. He said, 'for God's sake give us a lift.' I said 'My dear fellow it's a case of life and death with me,' and closing my eyes I put spurs to my horse and bounded ahead. That was the last I saw of him. The next I came up with, also a soldier, said 'well I'm pumped, I'm done – the Zulus can just come up and stab me if they like', and just sat himself quietly on a stone to await his death.[10]

Brickhill's instincts were probably correct – it is unlikely he or Gamble would have survived if his horse had tried to carry both of them, but Gamble was killed just a few metres on, and Brickhill's decision was to trouble his conscience for years to come.[11]

Harry Davies and Walter Henderson had separated after their meeting on the *nek*, and Davies had a lucky escape as he struck off after the mob of fleeing men and animals:

> When I had got about 400 yards [366 metres] from the camp my horse was stabbed[,] luckily in a fleshy part of the leg; . . . In the ditch about 600 yards [549 metres] to the right rear of the camp I saw two soldiers stabbed, both the Zulus were shot directly after, a Carbineer and myself shooting one each. When about 900 yards [823 metres] from the camp I had to pull up and walk, the country being so bad, I was afraid of my horse knocking up as he was bleeding very much from the wound he had received. Two Zulus then ran towards me, one fellow got hold of my bridle, I tried to stab him with my bayonet (I had fixed it on leaving the camp). He got hold of the rifle and pulled it out of my hand as if I had been a child; my horse reared and shied which saved me; an assegai was thrown at me by the other fellow. I here used my revolver to advantage . . .[12]

Walter Stafford was approaching the *dongas* when he came across a wounded man on the ground:

> After several attempts to get his foot into the stirrup of my saddle I eventually pulled him up behind me. He had an assegai wound under his arm and was already so weak from loss of blood that I could hardly feel his grip on me. All went well for a few hundred yards during which

time he managed to tell me that his name was Young of Lonsdale's [company]. We were now approaching a wide donga about twelve feet [3.7 metres] in width and in taking the jump my horse's hind feet could not have gained a firm footing on the other side. During the horse's recovery poor Young lost his seat and fell back. By this time the pursuers were right on us and Harry Davies came alongside and made a splendid revolver shot, putting a bullet through the head of the nearest Zulu. I was carrying a Martini-Henry carbine on my thigh and using it at every available opportunity, but I had only seven rounds of ammunition left.

Shortly after that we came across Lieut. Erskine, who was lying against a rock with an assegai wound through the calf of his leg, quite exhausted and unable to proceed further, opportunely I was able to get Erskine up behind me just in the nick of time. The scene now baffles description. It was perfect pandemonium. The mules and pack horses and oxen, some with ghastly gashes, were galloping over the veld at will, some with saddles and others only with blinkers. How sad to think what these noble animals are called upon to suffer in their masters' wars. Fortune favoured us now as a large white horse with a rein around his neck came alongside us, evidently instinct prompted him to seek protection, and we were able to catch the charger. The rein was twisted around the lower jaw, as all youngsters who are brought up on a farm learn to do, and Erskine was placed on his brave back.[13]

After separating from Harry Davies, Alfred Henderson had fallen in with his own troop, Durnford's Tlokoa, who were still holding together under Hlubi Molife. They had been joined by a number of other fugitives, including Lieutenant Gert Adendorff of Krohn's company, who had resorted to desperate measures to escape – his horse had been killed as he left iSandlwana, and he had commandeered another from a passing mounted auxiliary at gunpoint. The Tlokoa was one of only two groups who tried to get away in any kind of order, and it forced its way through the right horn by shooting a volley at a point where the Zulu horns were thinnest. The horn soon closed up behind it; these were the last men to escape by the Rorke's Drift road.[14]

Yet, according to the missionary Reverend A.W. Lee, Hlubi had been luckier than he knew:

At one period of the fight Mehlokazulu caught sight of the leader of the Basutho levies, Hlubi kaMbunda, and set out to kill him. I remember overhearing a conversation between the two which took place at a time when old animosities were but dying embers. 'You, son of Mabunda,' said the Zulu to the Mosutho, 'you had a narrow escape on that day. I saw you riding away, and I caught and mounted a loose horse of the English soldiers to overtake and kill you. But your *idhlosi* (your ancestral snake) was over-watching you on that day, for while your horse was swift mine put its feet down where it had lifted them up, and I could not catch you.'

'Not so', replied Hlubi, taking a huge pinch of snuff and speaking his bad Zulu through his nose, 'it was your good fortune not to catch me, for I had a gun and you had none, and I should not have died on that day.'[15]

Mehlokazulu had pursued them a little way down the road, then given up the chase and returned to the camp to join in the killing of the last men fighting.

The Edendale men, too, had kept together, but were pushed down the Manzimnyama by the right horn, and went the way of most of the survivors, striking off towards the Mzinyathi downstream of Rorke's Drift, following Simeon Nkambule who seemed to know the way. Cochrane had left with Walter Higginson of the NNC, and put his escape down to 'a good horse, hard riding, and good luck'. In later years he was wont to tell anyone who asked that he had survived by 'damn all but my horse's ears'.[16]

Surgeon Shepherd must at last have recognized that tending to the wounded in the camp was hopeless, for Trooper Muirhead saw him just beyond the big gully. Muirhead had set off with a friend, Trooper George Macleroy, known to his fellow Carbineers as 'Kelly', when

> Kelly staggered in the saddle, evidently hit with an assegai. I stopped my horse to see what was the matter, and tried to support him, but could not, and had to lift him off onto the ground. At that moment Dr Shepherd came galloping past. I called out to him, and he dismounted to examine poor Kelly. After carefully examining him he said, 'Ah, the poor fellow! Too late, too late!' I had just mounted my horse and Dr Shepherd was in the act of putting his foot into the stirrup, when he was struck fatally with an assegai.[17]

Horace Smith-Dorrien, too, had left the road and struck off across country:

I could see the Zulus running in to complete their circle from both flanks, and their leading men had already reached the line of retreat long before I had got there. When I reached the point I came on the two guns, which must have been sent out of camp before the Zulus charged home. They appeared to me to be upset in a donga and to be surrounded by Zulus.

Again I rode through unheeded, and was passed by Lieutenant Coghill (24th) wearing a blue patrol jacket and cord breeches and riding a red roan horse. We had just exchanged remarks about the terrible disaster and he passed on towards Rorke's Drift. A little further on I caught up with Lt. Curling RA and spoke to him, pointing out to him that the Zulus were all round and urging him to push on, which he did.[18]

Smith-Dorrien also noticed a curious fact about the pursuit – that all the imperial officers who got away were wearing dark blue patrol jackets – 'I heard afterwards that they had been told by their King Cetywayo that black coats were civilians and not worth killing'[19] – and it is noticeable that very few men in red coats got away. Certainly British troops were widely known in Zululand as '*amasoja ebomvu*', red soldiers, but many troops in the camp – Artillerymen, Volunteers, even civilians – were killed regardless of their uniforms. Perhaps more to the point, those in red coats were more conspicuous during the flight in the bush – and were on foot. The simple fact is that many of those who wore dark uniforms were mounted – officers, Artillerymen and Volunteers – and that the real route to survival lay on a horse. Another of Smith-Dorrien's comments is equally intriguing, since it hints at those layers of conflict of which the white men were generally unaware. 'The Zulus throughout my escape', he wrote, 'seemed to be set on killing natives who had sided with us, either as fighting levies or transport drivers.'[20]

The reference to Coghill is also interesting. Nothing is known of Coghill's movements after Chelmsford left the camp that morning until this point; it is possible that as a member of the column staff he acted as an ADC to Pulleine throughout the battle, although it is equally likely that his knee injury prevented him from taking an active part. There is a glimpse of him in the chaos of the closing moments when he rode up to Private Williams, Colonel Glyn's groom, and asked him to pack up the colonel's tent. In the event there was no time to save Glyn's things, and Williams later saw 'Lieutenant Melvill leaving camp with the Queen's Colour and

Lieutenant Coghill close behind him: the latter told me to come on or I should get killed'.[21] Another survivor, Private Bickley, started off across country on foot, but managed to catch a riderless horse. He had ridden a little way when he came across Lieutenant Melvill, and 'Mr Coghill afterwards joined us and reported to the Adjutant that Colonel Pulleine had been shot'.[22]

Lieutenant Teignmouth Melvill had taken the Queen's Colour of the 1st Battalion in the dying moments of the camp. The Colour represented the allegiance of every British battalion to queen and country, but more than that, it embodied the tradition and past glories of the regimental family for which successive generations of its members had fought and died; it was in effect the manifestation of a battalion's soul. To lose it in action was a great disgrace, and it is usually assumed that Pulleine entrusted them to Melvill once it became clear that the battle was lost, with orders to carry it to a place of safety. A rumour to this effect first appeared in the Natal press shortly afterwards, possibly spread by Glyn himself – yet in fact there is no survivors' evidence on the point one way or the other. None of those who got away mentioned any such incident, although several of them – Essex, who was in the firing line with the 24th, Gardner who acted as a staff officer, even Williams, Glyn's groom – might have been in a position to witness it, and the story was worth repeating if it was true, as it would have been much to the battalion's credit.

In fact it is quite likely that, as the rifle companies began their withdrawal, Melvill either took it upon himself, or was ordered, to fetch the Colour from the guard tent where it was usually stored. As adjutant the safety of the Colour fell within his remit, but its primary function on the battlefield in the 1870s was to serve as a rallying point when a battalion was hard pressed. Certainly by the time the 24th had been pushed back through the tents the time had come to unfurl the Colour, to serve not only as a physical marker, a bright splash of red white and blue in the billows of smoke and dust, where the troops could reform, but also to stiffen them with the resolve not to betray nearly 200 years of distinguished service.[23] Given the speed with which the Zulus overran the camp, it may be that Melvill decided it was already not possible to fight his way through to the stands on the *nek*, and that saving the Colour was the only viable option.

Certainly, the Colour was never unfurled. It was wrapped for protection on the march in a heavy black leather sheath with a brass top known as a case, and it was still in its case when Melvill set off, a considerable weight and an almost impossible burden for a man riding – which speaks volumes for both Melvill's horsemanship, especially over such rough ground, and his determination.

At any rate, Melvill left the camp at about the same time as Coghill, but not in company with him. Curling makes no mention of seeing Melvill when he passed Coghill, while Smith-Dorrien first saw Melvill only much later. Brickhill had seen the two close together at the top of the great *donga*, but shortly afterwards passed Melvill on his own, carrying the Colour. Melvill turned to Brickhill and asked him, 'Mr Brickhill, have you seen anything of my sword back there?' He must have just lost it, for Brickhill glanced 'back on our path for his satisfaction' but admitted he had not.[24]

Brickhill then saw both Melvill and Coghill again on the banks of the Manzimnyama. Those fugitives who had been lucky enough to strike round the top of the great *donga* had mostly followed the far bank closely on their way down, keeping the steep gully on their right as an obstacle to the pursuit, although the Zulus chasing them had pulled a number off their horses and killed knots of men on foot on the way down. At the bottom of the valley, however, where the *donga* joined the Manzimnyama, the ground was particularly broken up, seamed with run-offs, and the banks of the Manzimnyama itself were 2 metres high. As Brickhill explained, it was impossible to go through it while mounted:

> Going down into the Manzimnyama Blackwater we had some very bad country, so bad that we all got off and led our horses. Here we were compelled to take one narrow pass. The flying party all converged there, there was a great crush. Seeing the danger of Melvill's position, for there was a steep precipice on his immediate left, I backed my horse and kept all others back as well as I could, as a collision there might have sent him and his horse rolling down for several yards. It was then that I became aware that Mr Coghill was just behind, as he shouted 'get on your horse there Mr B——, this is no time to be leading a horse, get on your horses you fellows in front there.' Someone near him said 'you get off yours, this is no place to be riding one.' I did not know then that he suffered from an injured knee and could not walk. As we shot down (now riding) into the bed of the Manzimnyama we had to slither down a steep bank of 8 or 9 feet [2.4 or 2.7 metres]. The impetus of Mr Melvill's horse had carried him under a tree, a large branch of which caught his right shoulder and nearly unhorsed him.

The impetus of my horse had just brought me up in time to receive the
return swing of this same branch on my left shoulder and it tore my
coat well down. Rising on this side we were again exposed to the full
fire of the enemy still in hot pursuit . . .[25]

Although most of the mounted men managed to scramble out on the far
side of the stream, it was to prove the end for any white man on foot.
Mgelija Ngema of the uVe noticed the unusually high level of the stream,
which made the black shale under foot impossibly slippery. 'There was so
much water sweeping down the Manzimnyama river that the [Zulus] could
not keep their footing to stand and stab soldiers in the river.'[26] It would
be close to here, later, that Anstey's infantry would at last be brought
to bay, while the river bed and *dongas* were alive with Zulus searching
out the exhausted and terrified stragglers. 'I saw a white man hiding in
the long grass in the water's edge', remembered Sofikasho Zungu of the
iNgobamakhosi, 'and I crept up to him and stabbed him in the neck. Other
[Zulus] were annoyed and stabbed at me, saying "Why put your assegai
into our meat?" '[27]

A few, perhaps, crossed the stream, then foundered on the slopes on the
far side, or followed the winding course of the Manzimnyama downstream,
only to be overtaken somewhere on its twists and turns, their bodies never
found. 'I saw a man on a white horse who was hiding behind Isandhlwana
and the Manzimnyama', remembered Mangwanana Mchunu:

> . . . he was surrounded and I could see he had no escape. He dismounted
> and I saw him do something to a wallet on his horse, I thought he was
> sending a message for help and he hit his horse hard and it ran through
> in the direction of Vant's Drift. This white man had no gun only a stick,
> and he was soon killed. I saw no-one get across the Manzimnyama, I
> saw many stabbed and many sank in the water. I turned back . . .[28]

The main thread of the survivors struggled up the steep rocky sides of a
hill known as Mpethe, still heading for the Mzinyathi, and in the direction
of Rorke's Drift upstream, 9 kilometres away as the crow flies but longer,
of course, if you follow the river. Behind them the Zulu pursuit stalled in
the Manzimnyama valley, where they took time to flush out the last
survivors and finish off any remaining stubborn knots of resistance, and
this allowed the mounted men some respite. Struggling up onto the summit
of Mpethe they could see the bulk of Malakatha mountain coming into

view on their left, and then the hills rising above the Natal bank of the Mzinyathi, although the river itself was still lost in the deep gorge below. Several rills rise on the summit of Mpethe, and here some of the horses floundered and the survivors scattered, 'each seeking his own way out'. Brickhill's '... horse got bogged, he heaved and reared and my spectacles fell off. So serious was the loss that for a few seconds I peered down into the green mass to try and catch some reflection of them, but the whiz of a Zulu bullet not far off reminded me that time was precious, so on I sped.'[29]

For perhaps half a kilometre the route continued across the top of Mpethe. Most followed the same track, still clearly marked by grass trampled by the first fleeing NNC, but now and then a man would strike off on his own, hoping to find a short cut down into the Mzinyathi valley, and sometimes falling to the handful of Zulus who had doggedly pursued them all the way from the camp. There was still no sign of the river from the crest, but the dull roar of the water steadily grew more noticeable until, as the terrain began to slope below them and the survivors began the descent, it came into view on their left front, a thick ribbon of tea-brown water. Across it lay Natal, British territory, and up ahead, through the press of hills, the distinctive outline of Shiyane came into view again for the first time since they had turned off the road behind iSandlwana – and with it the hope of a friendly garrison, and salvation.

Yet as they gazed down the steep hillside into the valley below, a new horror greeted them. The river was full of a mass of struggling men and horses, all being carried rapidly downstream by the surging current, while those who were still gathered on the near bank were under attack from Zulus who had swept down a valley to their right to intercept them. The Zulus had cut the line of retreat; there was no way through to Rorke's Drift from this bank, and their only hope lay in that terrifying passage across the raging waters.

*

Hamilton Browne's third messenger, Captain Develing, had ridden hard down the road towards Mangeni, encountering Brevet Lieutenant-Colonel Harness and the four guns of N/5 Battery en route. Harness had turned away from the difficult march towards Lord Chelmsford's breakfast spot, between the Magogo and Silutshana hills, and had regained the track at the eastern foot of Hlazakazi. With the troops in the Mangeni hills scattered over such a wide area, it had not been entirely clear where Chelmsford

wanted him to go, however, and Harness had halted the guns on a slight
rise while Major Black of the 2/24th, who was with him, rode off to find
Chelmsford to ask for more specific instructions. While they waited, F and
H Companies of the 2/24th, under the commands of Captains Church
and Harvey respectively, which had also been sent back to join the road,
together with a party of Native Pioneers, had come up to them and halted
to rest.

Black had not been gone long when Harness heard the report of guns
from the direction of iSandlwana; Church judged them to be about 13
kilometres away:

> We did not know what to make of this, and were puzzled how to act,
> when about one o'clock a body of about 1000 natives suddenly appeared
> on the plain below and between us and the camp. Our Native Sappers
> pronounced them to be Zulus; and as it was advisable to ascertain for
> certain, I suggested to Colonel Harness that, if he would let me have
> one of his artillery horses, I would go and find out. He at once gave me
> a horse and sent a mounted sergeant RA with me. I galloped towards
> them, and when I was getting near, a European rode out to meet me,
> and said 'The troops behind me are Commandant Browne's contingent
> and I am to give you this message – Come in every man, for God's
> sake; the camp is surrounded and will be taken unless helped at once.[30]

Church immediately rode back to Harness, where he found Major Black
had returned with Chelmsford's ADC, Major Gossett. Gossett was not
impressed; 'It's all bosh', someone heard him say, 'I do not hear big guns.
You had better continue your march as ordered.'[31] He offered to bet a
hundred pounds that the camp was safe. Harness and Black were not so
sure; Captain Develing was a credible messenger, and they pointed out that
Chelmsford – who was by now somewhere near Phindo – could not
possibly know of the changed circumstances at iSandlwana from his present
position. Harness decided to return to the camp and Church and Harvey
agreed to go with him. He sent a lieutenant, Parsons, to accompany Gossett
to Lord Chelmsford to explain the decision.

It took a while to turn the limbers on the broken ground and Harness
had only gone 3 kilometres when Gossett returned with Chelmsford's
response: the Artillery was to turn about and head for the new campsite
and Mangeni, as originally ordered. If it is hard to believe Chelmsford's
apparent complacency, Clery provides something of an explanation. 'Curi-

ous reports arrived during the day, first of all of the camp being attacked, next of the camp being taken; but these were generally treated lightly, for it was presumed the general had any correct information that arrived ... even I who thought we had been acting imprudently, could not still realize that any such calamity hung over us as the loss of the camp.'[32]

Chelmsford had by this time ridden down to the Mangeni, to the point upstream where Dartnell and the Volunteers had rested during the NNC's skirmish at the foot of Phindo. A number of officers were standing on the *nek* below Mdutshane, a little way off. From here the camp could be seen far off across the plain, almost lost in the haze; someone claimed to have seen Zulus – they may have been Hamilton Browne's men – and several men took out their glasses to look. Suddenly there was the faint sound of shells bursting against the iNyoni ridge. Some Zulus captured in the skirmish were being questioned nearby, and one said 'Do you hear that? There is fighting going on in the camp.'[33] A messenger was sent down to Chelmsford, who immediately rode up with his staff, and 'Every field glass was levelled at the camp. The sun was shining brightly on the white tents, which were plainly visible, but all seemed quiet. No signs of firing, or of an engagement could be seen.'[34] Reassured, Chelmsford returned to set up the new camp site.

While this had been going on, Lieutenant-Colonel Russell and his Mounted Infantry had completed their sweep around the northern edge of Silutshana, and had halted on the plain, wondering where to go to find Chelmsford. From his position on the ridge closer to iSandlwana, Hamilton Browne had seen them; thinking they had been sent in response to his messages, he had been stunned by their activity, and he sent Captain Hayes to apprise them of the situation. Russell had acknowledged the message but did not advance; he too was confused. After a while, he had ordered his men to mount up and ride towards Mangeni. Here, on the road, he met Harness just as he was turning the guns back to the new camp site and, increasingly unsettled, Russell decided to look for Chelmsford himself, and he set off guided by Gossett.[35]

Russell's further report from Hamilton Browne seems to have finally persuaded Chelmsford that something was amiss at iSandlwana. Quite what he did not know, and it is highly likely that he did not for a moment believe the reports that the camp was in danger. They had, after all, originated from colonial officers – and he had left more than enough men to guard the camp. Nevertheless, he decided to return to the camp with his staff, and he sent orders to Dartnell to provide an escort. The Volunteers and Mounted Police saddled up and set off after him. After a few kilometres they passed Harness's guns and the companies under Church and Harvey, now marching east again towards Mangeni.

Major Black was so astonished by proceedings that when he arrived at the new campsite with Harness he sought out Colonel Degacher of the 2/24th, and said 'Colonel, have you heard the news? They say the camp is attacked and hard pressed; we were on our way back to help them, but they have brought us back here!'[36]

As Chelmsford and his escort rode down the road, Dartnell ordered Inspector Mansell of the Mounted Police to ride ahead to reconnoitre:

> We came to rising ground from where we could see the camp. I should say that we were about six miles [9.6 kilometres] distant from it. Of course all the men were eager, having heard the rumours, and eagerly looked out for the camp. There certainly were some tents standing, but they seemed very few, and away to the left front of the camp there was some smoke, though not much, and it was high up, just as if there had been musketry fire, and the smoke had floated away; but there was certainly no musketry fire going on then. A few seconds afterwards a sergeant of the police said, 'There go the guns, sir.' I could see the smoke, but we could hear nothing. In a few seconds we distinctly saw the guns fired again, one after the other, sharp. This was done several times. A pause, and then a sharp flash-flash. The sun was shining on the camp at the time, and then the camp looked dark, just as if a shadow was passing over it. The guns did not fire after that, and in a few minutes all the tents had disappeared. The sergeant said, 'It's all over now, sir.' I said, 'Yes, and I hope it is the right way.' We could see there was fighting going on, but of course did not know which way it had gone. The men all thought the Zulus had retired; but I felt doubtful in my own mind, but had no idea really of the catastrophe that had taken place.[37]

*

Once the last stands had been broken up on the *nek*, and the last struggling bands of the 24th forced down into the valley of the Manzimnyama beyond, the Zulus suddenly found that they were in possession of the British camp – and the battle was over. Here and there a few men still held out where they had managed to find some cover among the wagons or behind boulders, but the firing died to a few spluttering shots, and the great hubbub of conflict, the roar of gunfire, war-cries and commands faded to the terrible aftermath, with the groaning and sudden sharp shrieks of the hundreds of wounded. The cry went up, a man of the uMbonambi told Mitford, that 'all the white men had been killed, and then we began to plunder the camp'.[38]

'When it was over,' recalled uNzuzi Mandla of the uVe:

> We went into the tents and took what clothes and blankets we could find, and also collected as many rifles as we could. The tents were cut into strips and we left them lying there. We did not touch any of the food because we thought it might have been poisoned, so we cut open the bags and smashed the boxes, throwing the contents all over the veld. The oxen and mules that were left we took, but we killed all the horses because they were the feet of the white men and we had not been ordered to take those back to the king.[39]

After the terrible exertions of the battle, many Zulus were desperately thirsty, and they searched the camp for drink. They were particularly keen to find alcohol, which they knew by the English word 'canteen'. 'I found a bottle', remembered Mbongoza uMbonambi, 'and I was so hungry for it that I did not wait to take out its stopper. I just broke the neck off and drank.'[40] Yet there was danger in this, for the camp was full of bottles, and not all the contents were safe to drink. 'We found twala [beer] in the camp', a man of the uMbonambi later told Bertram Mitford, 'and some of our men got very drunk. We were so hot and thirsty that we drank everything liquid we found, without waiting to see what it was. Some of them found some black stuff in bottles (probably ink); it did not look good, so they did not drink it; but one or two who drank some paraffin oil, thinking it was 'twala', were poisoned.'[41] As late as the 1940s the author H.V. Morton found an echo of the terrible surprise caused by the white man's 'canteen'. He met a man, a son of Prince Sitheku kaMpande, who was born shortly after the battle, and who had been named by his father in honour of that shocking disillusion Nkantini.[42]

Everything in the camp was now available to those who could find and carry it. There was a rush for rifles, particularly the Martini-Henrys which had caused such devastation such a short time before, but there were probably no more than 1,000 modern rifles in the camp, far too few for all the Zulus who wanted one. Mlamula Matebula had quickly snatched the one dropped by the soldier of the 24th he had killed between the aloe-trees,[43] but Sofikasho Zungu was disappointed to see that many of those lying among the bodies appeared to be useless, either jammed or broken in the hand-to-hand fighting.[44]

If rifles were in short supply, however, there was plenty of ammunition. First, the Zulus searched the bodies of the dead soldiers but, said Mehloka-zulu, many had fired off their last round, and although in their ammunition pouches 'Some had a few cartridges, most of them had none at all; there were very few found. Some had cartouche boxes, others cartridge belts; the belts were empty but a few cartridges were found in the cartouche boxes. Each man helped himself . . .'[45] There were, however, thousands of rounds packed away in the reserve supply of the two 24th battalions, and more in the camps of each of the other units.

The ammunition boxes presented rather more trouble to the Zulus than they had to the 24th, and some Zulus tried to prize off the copper retaining bands with spears or captured bayonets. But in the end, said Mehlokazulu, 'the cases of guns and ammunition were smashed open, and broken, with stones'.[46] For those who had to be content with the old percussion and flint-lock muzzle-loaders with which they had begun the battle, the car-tridges at least offered a ready supply of good quality powder and lead bullets to recycle, and they either took the cartridges away with them to deal with later, or pulled out the bullets with their teeth, broke open the cartridge, and took away the powder. Even books and letters could be pressed into service, the paper torn out to be used as wadding.

Other of the white men's weapons were in demand too, but largely as trophies. Few Zulus had been impressed with revolvers, but they took them anyway, together with swords, bayonets and clasp knives and, indeed, whatever took their fancy. A wonderful cornucopia of exotic European delights had fallen to them by right of conquest, and according to Mehlokazulu, 'each Zulu helped himself to watches and such property as they could lay hands on and carry away'.[47] 'We smashed up the whole camp,' agreed Sofikasho Zungu, 'ripping up the tents, and the harness and poles of the oxen. We drove off the oxen but we left the mules. We had never seen a strange animal like a mule before and so we left them as we did not know what to do with them . . . I took a good red coat and a braided hat, these were lying on the ground. I knew of a man who got 20 golden sovereigns, but I didn't know what money was . . .'[48]

Of more practical use to Mgelija Ngema, like many others, was a good Army greatcoat. A number of the *amakhosi*, including Sihayo, who already owned horses, instructed their men to collect saddles and horse-kit. Some took away strips of the canvas from the ruined tents to serve as blankets, while others dragged off foldaway chairs and officers' camp-beds, trunks and boxes, china teapots, tin cups and plates, useful leather *reims*, tent mallets, rugs, top-boots, brass candlesticks, lanterns, 'soldiers' valises, a gunner's oil-bottle; a pair of ammunition boots; a pearl-handled knife, a cake of soap and a sponge'.[49] As late as 1991, Mehlokazulu's son, uMnandi Ngobese, then in his nineties, could still remember growing up as a child in his father's homestead among items pillaged from the battlefield.[50] Even spent cartridge cases and brass foul-weather muzzle-covers from the Martini-Henrys had their uses, though there were plenty to spare and only the best taken – revolver cartridge cases in particular made excellent snuff containers and fitted neatly into pierced ear-lobes.

When everything of worth had been taken, the battlefield was left strewn with the broken, the useless and the incomprehensible – and lying on it everywhere were the freshly dead. They were scattered thickly throughout the ruined camp, mixed up with the wreckage of the fallen tents, tossed in among the wagons, and sprawled across each other in great clumps on the *nek*, lying twisted and tangled where the maelstrom had overtaken them, black and white together. Among them, particularly above the tents and on the *nek*, were the carcasses of hundreds of animals, struck down in the fury of the struggle, sometimes in whole teams where they had been tied together just a few hours earlier by their *voorloopers* ready to inspan. Violent death is seldom a clean business, less so in a conflict carried out at close quarters with stabbing weapons, and men and animals alike had often been struck many times before dying. The bodies bore terrible rips, gashes, and close-range exit wounds. 'The green grass was red with running blood,' said uNzuzi Mandla, '. . . and the veldt was slippery, for it was covered with the entrails and brains of the slain.'[51] A heavy, cloying smell from ruptured bodies and burnt powder hung in the air.

The horror was exacerbated by the Zulu treatment of the dead. Many of the British bodies had been repeatedly stabbed after death by men following behind. This was a testimony to the fierceness of the enemy's resistance, and the honour that accrued in overcoming them. It was a custom known as *ukuhlomula* and it originated in the hunt, as Mpashana kaSodondo of the uVe explained:

Those *hlomula*'ing became more numerous by reason of the fact that they had been fighting such formidable opponents, who were like lions – for it is the custom among us in lion-hunting that the one who *hlomula*'s first, i.e. after the first to stab, gets a leg, the second gets a foreleg, whilst the last gets the head. This custom was observed with regard to Isandhlwana because it was recognized that fighting against such a foe and killing some of them was of the same high grade as lion-hunting . . . anyone *hlomula*'ing first, second or third . . . was looked on as responsible in some way for its death.[52]

If the ritual preparations they had undergone before setting off to war had placed the men of the *amabutho* outside the bounds of ordinary society, had cocooned them in a protective psychic state designed to shield them from the powerful streams of *umnyama* their own acts of bloodshed had unleashed, the treatment of the enemy dead was a first step in the journey away from the dangerous and contaminated state of the warrior on the return to civilian normality, the beginning of a slow correcting of the universe which would see them mix freely again with their loved ones without taint or contamination. When a man killed an enemy, he was required to *qaqa* the body, to cut the abdomen, to remove and wear some part of his victim's clothing until he had undergone important cleansing rituals, and to refrain from cleaning his own bloody weapons. Before undergoing the cleansing he was in a state of limbo, a hero, marked by the captured dress as a successful warrior, yet at the same time possessing an aura of powerful spiritual threat. Such men, still wearing the clothes of the enemy dead and carrying their spears encrusted with dried gore, were known as *izinxweleha* and said with awe to be 'wet with yesterday's blood'.

The stomach cut was accomplished to allow the spirit of the dead man to pass safely to the afterlife. 'After killing them', said Kumpega Qwabe, 'we used to split them up the stomach so that their bodies would not swell.'[53] In the sight of a body bloating as the gasses produced by decomposition expanded quickly in the hot sun, Zulu traditional belief recognized the frustration of a spirit unable to leave its earthly form. If the killer did not cut the stomach, the spirit's wrath would attach to him and he would suffer all manner of misfortunes, his own body might swell like a corpse, and he would be driven mad. Trooper Stevens of the Mounted Police saw it done, and was haunted by it; he had paused on his way out of the camp to look back, and 'Saw one of the most horrid sights that I ever wish to see. The

Zulus were in the camp ripping our men up, and also the tents and everything else they came across, with their assegais. They were not content with killing, but were ripping the men up afterwards . . .'[54]

Often, it was carried out in the aftermath, as the Zulus passed over the field, *hlomula*'ing the dead and removing their weapons and clothes. 'All the dead bodies were cut open,' said Mehlokazulu, 'because if that had not been done the Zulus would have become swollen like the dead bodies . . . As a rule we took off the upper garments, but left the trowsers, but if we saw blood upon the garments we did not bother.'[55] 'We took off the Europeans' things at Isandlwana', agreed Mpashana. 'They were all stripped. This was done to *zila* with. The things of the deceased are put on, for the warrior does not want his things smeared with blood and things of harmful influence.'[56]

Other mutilations were undoubtedly carried out as well. The impressive beards sported by some of the British dead aroused particular attention, it seems, and overcome by the glut of butchery 'some of our bad men cut away the lower jaws of those white men who had beards and decorated their heads with them'. Other Zulus were disgusted by this, however and, according to Kumpega Qwabe, 'One of our big *indunas* told those men who had cut off the bearded chins of the English to throw the trophies away. He told them the mighty Zulus did not get their strength by cutting up dead bodies and carrying bits around with them.'[57]

In fact, the remains of men who fell fighting bravely in battle were a potent form of war medicine. Body parts associated with male vigour – a strip of skin from the breastbone, the right forearm, the forehead, the penis, or even facial hair, including beards – could be used by specialist *izinyanga* to prepare the *amabutho* in future campaigns, giving them a supernatural ascendancy over the British when they met them in battle again, and there is no doubt that a number of such items were taken from the dead at iSandlwana.

As they moved over the ground that afternoon, the Zulus turned up a few individuals who had been hiding or feigning death. UMhoti of the uKhandempemvu was enjoying some sugar he had found among the tents when he was startled by a shot from the slopes of Mahlabamkhosi; 'A soldier had been lying there and seeing a Zulu approach, fired at, and killed him, and then made a run for it; but was soon overtaken and speared.'[58]

Their own dead and wounded, too, needed attention, hundreds of them, not just in the camp where the fighting had been hand-to-hand, but spread in a great arc across many kilometres of the approach to iSandlwana. 'Zulus died all round Isandlwana',[59] admitted Mehlokazulu mournfully. The Zulu army included no organized medical or burial details, and it simply fell to friends and relatives who noticed their comrades were missing to go over the field and seek them out. Many who fell a long way off, whether dead or injured, were simply missed in the long grass or among the boulders. There was no hope of removing bodies to their own homesteads for the conventional funeral ceremonies, and indeed the pre-battle rituals had to some extent prepared their spirits for a passage to the afterlife. It was merely necessary to give the bodies a token burial, and scores were dragged into the deserted homesteads around the battlefield and tipped into the underground grain pits beneath the cattle byre or bundled into the *dongas*. When, later, the army began to retire back the way it had come, towards the Ngwebeni, many of the dead were left in the *dongas* at the foot of the iNyoni escarpment, where the uKhandempemvu had sheltered during the battle, and fragments of their bones have continued to wash out into recent times. For the rest, it was merely necessary to cover them over with their great war-shields in a symbolic burial.

A number of important men had been killed during the assault, and their relatives did their best to find their bodies. *Inkosi* Mkhosana ka-Mvundlana, who had been shot dead encouraging the uKhamdempemvu to advance at that critical stage of the battle, was lying near the *dongas* where his men had sheltered, and his brother Mthiyaqhwa found him and placed a shield over him. One of *inkosi* Mnyamana Buthelezi's sons, Mntumengana, had died too, and he was buried by his brother Mkhandumba. Other important men 'left behind' on the battlefield included Sigodi kaMasiphula, whose father had been *inkosi* of the eMgazini people and the senior councillor to King Mpande, and Mzi kaManyosi, whose father had been an *iqawe* and a great favourite of King Shaka. Sigodi's brother, Maphoko, was badly wounded, and so too were two sons of Ntshingwayo. Manzi kaTshodo, the man who, at the beginning of the fight, had struck up the chant 'Lightning of Heaven' among the iNgobamakhosi, had been killed in the storming of the camp.

The wounded could expect little more than the rough first aid carried out by their comrades. For men like Mlambula Matebula, wounded four times during the rush on the camp, there was no pain relief, and little more could be done than stop the bullet wounds with moss, and stem the bleeding by binding up the injuries with grass. If the men were mobile, there then began the long agonizing journey home, when their survival would largely depend on whether they had friends and relatives enough to support them. Most, of course, were fit healthy young men, used to an outdoor lifestyle, and inured in their daily lives to a degree of pain which would have incapacitated their white counterparts. If they could make it to their homes before shock or an infection killed them, there was a chance for them, for the Zulu herbalists were experienced at treating cuts and broken bones. Wounds were regularly washed, torn flesh sewn up with sutures of sinew, fractures bound with improvised splints, and compresses applied with herbs known to combat infection.

Yet the range of injuries inflicted by British firepower was horrific, and much of it beyond the skill of even the most experienced *inyanga* – limb bones splintered by Martini-Henry bullets, shattered joints, fractured skulls, arms and legs blown off by shellfire. Many wounded passed out on the battlefield, and lay undiscovered or mistaken for the dead, to die from shock and loss of blood when no care was forthcoming. Others recovered consciousness hours or days later, and with raw and open wounds dragged themselves on their bellies many kilometres across the veld; a few were found and helped by civilians nearby, but many died in excruciating pain, alone and forgotten.

By late afternoon the orgy of destruction at iSandlwana was complete, and the exhausted *amabutho* began to withdraw across the iNyoni heights towards the Ngwebeni and their bivouac of the night before, carrying their loot and their wounded with them. And a terrible stillness settled over iSandlwana.

For others, however, the day's excitement had not yet begun.

# 24

# 'Get on man!'

## Afternoon and evening, 22 January 1879

Still out on his ridge a few kilometres to the east across the plain from the stricken camp, Hamilton Browne had been waiting in growing frustration for the return of Lord Chelmsford's command. Instead his messenger, Captain Develing, came riding up the track from Mangeni alone.

'Well,' said I, 'who did you see?' 'I first saw Major Black with the second 24th and repeated your message – he at once turned back. Then I saw Colonel Harness with the guns – he at once turned back. Then I saw the mounted men, and they turned back.' 'Well,' said I, 'where are they?' 'Why, sir,' he replied, 'as we were marching back we met the staff and the troops were ordered to go back again, so I came on alone.'[1]

The long afternoon passed. All firing had long since stopped at iSandlwana, and dark smudges on the slopes of the iNyoni escarpment suggested that the Zulus were now retiring. 'Towards evening', said Browne,

I saw a small body of horsemen riding towards us. On using my glasses I discovered that it was the General and his staff and I at once mounted and rode to meet him.

He looked very surprised when he saw me and said, 'What are you doing here, Commandant Browne? You ought to have been in the camp hours ago.' I replied, 'The camp has been taken, sir.'

He flashed out at once, 'How dare you tell me such a falsehood? Get your men into line at once and advance.' I did so, and led my 700 miserables supported by the staff against the victorious Zulu army.

We moved on about two and a half miles [4 kilometres] until we had opened out a good view of the camp, when he called to me and said, in a kindly manner, 'On your honour, Commandant Browne, is the camp taken?' I answered, 'The camp was taken at about 1.30 in the afternoon, and the Zulus are now burning some of the tents.'

He said, 'That may be the Quartermaster's fatigue, burning the debris of the camp.' I replied, 'Q.M.'s fatigue do not burn tents, sir,' and I offered him my glasses. He refused them, but said 'Halt your men at once,' and despatched an officer to bring up the remainder of the column.

I had just halted my men and placed them in the best position I could, when to my utter astonishment I saw a man on foot leading a pony, coming from the direction of the camp, and recognized him as Commandant Lonsdale.

He came up to me and said, 'By Jove Maori, this is fun; the camp is taken.' 'Don't see the humour,' I said, 'but go and tell the staff; they won't believe me.'[2]

Lonsdale's story was an extraordinary one – and devastating. After hearing it, Lord Chelmsford could have no more doubts that something had gone terribly wrong at iSandlwana.

Lonsdale was still suffering the after-effects of his concussion from a fortnight before, and the early start that morning and hard riding took its toll, so when he had been 'within a few miles of the camp', he had asked Chelmsford if he

might ride on ahead, get back to the camp and get a rest. This was granted, and I rode on my way ... I approached the camp we had so lately left, but being three-quarters asleep did not notice that anything was amiss until I was well inside it. The first thing that woke me up and put me on the *qui vive* was a Zulu coming at me with a stabbing assegai, already red with blood, in his hand. I was wide awake enough then, and on the alert in a moment. I glanced around me and became instantly fully alive to what had taken place, and that the camp had been captured by the Zulus. I saw in a flash dead bodies of both Zulus and soldiers all over the place, tents rent in fragments, bags of flour cut open and the contents strewn about, boxes of ammunition broken open, every hinging, in fact, smashed and done for. Last but not least, Zulus with assegais still reeking with blood sitting and wandering about in all this incredible chaos. I saw it all in a flash, turned and fled. My horse was as tired as I was. Many Zulus, becoming alive to the fact that an enemy and a white man was among them, rushed after me yelling and firing at me. It was the most deadly, awful moment I have ever had in my life, and you know we've had some pretty tight fits together. I could only screw a very moderate canter out of my poor gee, and as you know, old man,

Kafirs are uncommonly fleet of foot. It was two or three minutes before
I was clear of these howling devils. It seemed to me like two or three
hours. At length they all gave up the chase, and I went on my way to
rejoin the column. . . . When I rode up to the General and reported
what I had seen I believe he thought I was mad . . .[3]

It is possible Lonsdale's tale may have grown in the telling, for Norris-
Newman, who heard him, was under the impression that he was still several
hundred metres from the NNC camp when the truth dawned on him. Even
so, there was no denying the devastating nature of the news – and the looks
of 'amazement, grief and horror'[4] which passed between those who heard
it. 'I can't understand it,' someone heard Lord Chelmsford say, 'I left a
thousand men to guard the camp.'[5]

*

Earlier that afternoon, the Zulu reserve had streamed out of the Ngwebeni
valley following a course that would see them swing wide of the right horn,
descending the iNyoni escarpment into the Manzimnyama valley a little to
the west of the main attack, and perhaps half an hour behind it. They had
been among the last to arrive at the bivouac, and had found themselves
camped furthest down the river, and they had been the last to leave – and
the only ones to receive the proper last-minute doctoring rituals.

These were the senior men, the *amabandla emhlope*, 'white assemblies'
of married men mostly in their thirties and forties, carrying predominantly
white shields, whose barracks were at oNdini itself. They consisted of the
uThulwana, Cetshwayo's own *ibutho*, two *amabutho* who had been attached
to it, the iNdlondlo and the iNdluyengwe, and another of slightly younger
age, the uDloko.[6] The appointed commanders of the uThulwana included
some of the most senior men in Zululand, including Prince Hamu and
*inkosi* Mnyamana Buthelezi, but none of them were present now, and their
most senior officer, Qethuka kaMaqondo, had joined in the rush for the
camp, taking several companies of the uThulwana with him. Instead, the
reserve was commanded now by Prince Zibhebhu kaMaphitha.

A member of the uMxapho *ibutho* himself, Zibhebhu was an officer
in the uDloko and a few years younger than his men, but as the head of
a collateral branch of the royal house, the Mandlakazi, his prestige was
immense, and he was already earning an impressive reputation as a dynamic
and resourceful leader, an *iqawe* of note. It was he who had commanded

the scouts on the final approach to the Ngwebeni and driven off Lieutenant Browne's Mounted Infantry patrol the day before, and he was probably given command of the reserve simply because he was the most senior officer who had not joined in the general rush towards the camp.

A number of other important men were with the reserve, mostly in the ranks of their own *amabutho*, the most significant of whom was Prince Dabulamanzi kaMpande of the uDloko, the king's self-confident and handsome younger brother. A royal favourite, he was a great friend of the white *inkosi* John Dunn, and from him had learned to be a good horsemen and an excellent shot.

It is impossible to be sure of the timing, but the reserve probably reached the Rorke's Drift road at about the time that the uNokhenke rushed into the camp from the rear. The first stream of British non-combatants had already left the camp, and the right horn was at work among them. The reserve kept to the high ground on the west bank of the Manzimnyama, but once it became clear that a number of fugitives were escaping between the points of the encircling horns, it divided. The uThulwana, iNdlondlo and uDloko struck off across country, heading for the Mzinyathi downstream of Rorke's Drift, intending to seal off the minor drifts and any possible line of retreat by way of the Zulu bank. As they went, they meticulously searched the countryside along the way '... and "drove" every mealie garden, firing heavily all the while, killing many Europeans and natives who were trying to escape from Isandhlwana'.[7]

In the meantime, the iNdluyengwe, Zibhebhu encouraging them from horseback, had struck off along the higher ground above the Manzinyama, aiming to intercept the fugitives at the point where they hit the border. As they crested the summit of Mpethe, they struck the tail of the stream of survivors just as they began their descent into the Mzinyathi valley.

It is quite likely that the first of these, having slipped round the tip of the right horn and crossed Mpethe, had hoped to follow the Zulu bank upstream towards the beacon of Shiyane in the distance, but the geography had thwarted them. On the other side of Mpethe, as it sloped down steeply towards the river, another stream, the iSikhubuthu, fed into the Mzinyathi through a scalloped valley on their right, cutting across their front, and the hills then rose up steeply again on the far side. The iSikhubuthu flowed into the main river at a crossing-point of sorts, a jumble of rocks scattered across the Mzinyathi which could only be forded when the water was at its lowest, dignified on some colonial maps with the name Sothondose's Drift, after the *inkosi* of the Nxumalo people who had once lived there. The Natal bank opposite was white-owned farmland, but a few Nxumalo had been allowed to remain, working as labourers in lieu of rent, and although Sothondose now lived in the Msinga location, a number of his people had been pressed into the border levies.

But the water was not low that day. After the recent heavy rain, it was a thick mud-brown torrent 100 metres wide in places, flooding the mud flats beyond its banks, tearing up bushes that had survived previous floods, submerging great boulders 2 metres high or more – a tumbling, swirling deluge that lay squarely between the fugitives and the sanctuary of Natal beyond. And now – a crushing sight after the slacker pursuit across Mpethe – they found the Zulus were there ahead of them.

Not at first the king's *amabutho*, for the iSikhubuthu valley provided a short cut to the amaQungebeni settlements along the Batshe, and Sihayo's followers, and numbers too of Gamdana's, who had been living in the hillsides close to their homes, had hurried down it to exact their revenge for the destruction of kwaSogekle. There had not been many of them – one or two hundred – but they were enough to close the Zulu bank, forcing the survivors, most of whom were utterly drained by the sights they had seen and by their flight over rough ground in the desiccating heat, into the river. 'My natives tell me that the Zulus who were left in the kraals as loyal men did more harm at the river', said Harry Davies, 'than the men we were fighting with. It seems they let all the armed men pass and stabbed all the men without arms. I know some Zulus came out of huts and chased us.'[8]

Even before they reached the river, Simeon Nkambule and the Edendale men 'heard the yells of men, the neighing of horses, and the bellowing of cattle. When they arrived upon the banks above the drift they found it choked with men and beasts. On every rock stood two or three Zulus stabbing every man they could reach . . .'[9]

By the time Walter Stafford arrived at the foot of Mpethe, 'A strange sight greeted us as we got to the edge. The various uniforms presented all the colours of the rainbow. Half a dozen bodies were washed ashore on the bank at the end of the river on our side. This confirmed my opinion that these non-combatants left the camp when the first danger was noticed.'[10] Stafford noticed that a number of survivors had collected in one spot higher up, on the edge of a wide pool that lay above the worst of the rapids. Most had long since cast away any weapons they had, but here the ground offered them some shelter against the Zulus, though the river remained a daunting prospect:

> The bank of the river that we came to was very steep, rugged and bushy and to the best of my recollection there was a narrow flat on this side running into a krantz higher up. The remnant of our men were gathered there. I noticed the late Joseph Lister amongst them. He was an old Pondoland trader from my part of the world, and he and I were well acquainted. Old Lister was very excited and could not swim. I advised him to go up where the current was not so strong and that directly my horse got into the water I would slip off it's [sic] back and catch hold of it's tail, and be towed to the other side and advised him to do the same. By this method all those who could not swim were safely brought across the river. I think there were thirty-three in all.[11]

It seems that it was here too that the Edendale men got across, still in a body, for according to Nkambule he 'Rode down to the drift, calling to the fugitives to cling to any animal or the stirrups of his men. He drove that mob of men, cattle and horses before his troop and brought into safety every man, wounded or unwounded.'[12]

Stafford recognized Captain Essex among those who got across here. Trooper Dorehill of the Mounted Police had an extraordinary escape. He was working his way upstream along the bank, looking for a calmer spot in the water to cross, when he saw three Zulus running to intercept him. Two were young *izinsizwa* and the third an older man with a head-ring. As he

> turned upstream looking for deep water to jump into, he heard a double report and feeling no effect thought that they had missed him. However, on glancing round he saw the *kehla* [married man] with a gun smoking and the two young Zulus lying dead. His friend shouted in English 'Jump into the river' which he did, but dropped his carbine into the water. He got to the other side by hanging on to his horse's tail, and while looking for a path out of the river gorge he heard a voice which he recognized as that of his half-section Hayes, calling for help. He was stuck in the mud in the reeds of the river bank. With the assistance of Sergeant Costello of the artillery, and Gascoigne, of the M.I. [Mounted Infantry] who had arrived, they released Hayes but had some trouble with a Native fugitive who had collared his horse and was making off with it when Gascoigne went after him and knocked him off and brought the horse back. While this was going on 20 or 30 Zulus

appeared on the opposite bank and opened fire on the party, but the only damage they did was to Costello's great coat, which was rolled on his saddle.[13]

In fact, Sergeant Costello escaped on a charger of Major Smith's named Black Eagle, and it was Smith's foul-weather cloak that bore the brunt of the Zulu fire; it still exists, the great rents and rips testifying to just how close Costello came to death.[14] Some months later Trooper Dorehill found out the identity of his unknown saviour – he was one of Fynn's *izinduna* at Msinga, a well-known Government employee named Jacob, who had been given his double-barrelled shotgun as a present by a grateful judge whom he used to accompany on hunting expeditions. He had thrown off the badges which distinguished him as a member of the NNC and had escaped by passing himself off as a Zulu. All the more remarkably, Jacob noticed that Dorehill lost his carbine in the river, and days later, when the river had subsided, he returned and recovered it, and it eventually found its way back to Dorehill.[15]

Trumpeter Stevens of the Mounted Police also lost his horse in the river, and found on reaching the Natal bank that an African was making off with it 'and it was only by threatening him with his revolver that he regained his mount'. Later Stevens noticed that the chamber had fallen out midstream, and that his revolver was useless – 'it was fortunate that the native did not notice'.[16]

Smith-Dorrien was among the last of the fugitives to reach the river. He was still on top of Mpethe, approaching the descent into the valley, when

> ... at least half a mile behind Coghill, Lieutenant Melvill (24th), in a red coat and with a cased Colour across the front of his saddle, passed me going to the drift. I reported afterwards that the Colour was broken; but as the pole was found eventually whole, I think the casing must have been half off and hanging down. It will thus be seen that Coghill (who was orderly officer to Colonel Glyn) and Melvill (who was adjutant) did not escape together with the Colour ... [17]

And at that moment, Zibhebhu's iNdluyengwe struck them, appearing suddenly over the hill from their right, and forcing the last survivors away from the trodden path and hard off to their left. The hillside dropped steeply down to the river here, and there was no viable route down, just a helter-skelter descent over sudden drops and across huge boulders, all of it tangled with bush. Smith-Dorrien came across:

A man in a red coat badly assegaid in the arm, unable to move. He was, I believe, a mounted infantryman of the 24th named Macdonald, but of his name I cannot be sure. I managed to make a tourniquet with a handkerchief to stop the bleeding, and got him half-way down, when a shout from behind said 'Get on man; the Zulus are on top of you.' I turned round and saw Major Smith, RA, who was commanding the section of guns, as white as a sheet and bleeding profusely; and in a second we were surrounded, and assegais accounted for poor Smith, my wounded MI friend, and my horse.

With the help of my revolver and a wild jump down the rocks, I found myself in the Buffalo River, which was in flood and eighty yards [73 metres] broad . . .[18]

Lieutenant Curling was somewhere nearby: 'We had to climb down the face of the cliff and not more than half those who started from the top got to the bottom. Many fell right down, among others Major Smith, and the Zulus caught us here and shot us as we climbed down. I got down safely and came to the river which was very deep and swift.'[19] For years afterwards, the site of this desperate scramble was marked by the scrape marks of horseshoes on the boulders and by the bones of the horses.

The appearance of the iNdluyengwe led to a mad panic among the last survivors to get into the river. 'No time for choosing the best crossing then,' admitted Brickhill,

There were the Zulus in running lines making for the stiller water higher up. My horse plunged in, swimming at once, but had scarcely gone six yards [5.5 metres] before he stumbled over something large and nearly fell into the rushing stream beyond. I clutched his mane and guided his rein with care, and yet four times I thought that all was lost, not ten yards [9 metres] below me was a waterfall in the seething pool of which three riderless horses were swishing round and round.[20]

Curling's horse 'fortunately swam straight across though I had three or four men hanging on his tail and stirrup leathers etc'.[21] Wally Erskine found himself in a similar predicament; after he arrived at the river he:

Could not get my horse into it on account of his being nearly exhausted. I made for Captain Cochrane, whose horse mine then followed. When I got into the middle of the stream, out of the horse's depth, four or five men caught hold of his tail, so that he could not move. While they were still holding on the Zulus came up and assegaid some, while others let go and were carried away by the stream, only to be murdered further down.[22]

Two or three Mounted Infantry reached the bank together. Twenty-one-year-old Private Samuel Wassall of the 80th Regiment:

> ... drove my horse into the torrent, thankful even to be in that, and was urging him to the other side, when I heard a cry for help, and saw that a man of my own regiment, a private named Westwood, was being carried away. He was struggling desperately, and drowning.
>
> The Zulus were sweeping down to the river-bank which I had just left, and there was a terrible temptation to go ahead and just save oneself. But I turned my horse round to the Zulu bank, got him there, dismounted, tied him up to a tree – and I never tied him more swiftly. Then I struggled out to Westwood, got hold of him, and struggled back to the horse with him. I scrambled up again into the saddle, pulled Westwood after me, and plunged into the torrent again, and as I did so the Zulus rushed up to the bank and let drive with their firearms and their spears. But most mercifully I escaped them all, and, with a thankful heart, urged my gallant horse up the steep bank on the Natal side ...[23]

Smith-Dorrien was being swept away midstream when a riderless horse came past:

> And I got hold of his tail and he landed me safely on the other bank; but I was too tired to stick to him and get on his back. I got up again and rushed on, and was several times knocked over by our mounted niggers, who would not get out of my way, then up a tremendous hill with my wet clothes and boots full of water. About twenty Zulus got over the water and followed us up the hill, but I am thankful to say they had not their firearms. Crossing the river, however, the Zulus on the opposite side kept firing at us as we went up the hill and killed several of the niggers around me. I was the only white man to be seen until I came to one who had been kicked by his horse and could not mount. I put him on his horse and lent him my knife. He said he would catch me a horse. Directly he was up he went clean away ...[24]

Later Smith-Dorrien identified the man as James Hamer; not surprisingly, perhaps, Hamer does not mention the incident in his own account. Faced with a long walk on foot, Smith-Dorrien lay down on his back, put his feet in the air, and let the water drain out of his boots.

Simeon Nkambule had managed to get the Edendale men across safely, probably at the deeper pool upstream where Stafford had seen so many swim their horses. Once on the other side he kept them together, and they stopped to fire a few volleys across the river to drive the Zulus back. Trooper Barker of the Carbineers was among those who recognized that many of the survivors owed their lives to this: 'Had it not been for these Basutos I doubt if a single white man would have escaped by Fugitives' Drift, as they kept the Zulus in check while the few escaped. As we ascended the hill on the Natal side the firing of the Zulus was very good, and I saw a contingent native drop in front of us, and shortly after we passed another who had been shot. The Zulus would then be about nine hundred yards [823 metres] off.'[25]

The wagon conductor, Louis Dubois, whom both Smith-Dorrien and Brickhill had seen in the camp, had managed to find himself 'a good horse', and had reached the river safely; as he climbed out on the other side, however, he was shot dead. Wally Erskine was luckier:

> On getting out on this side the Edendale men told me to lay flat on my horse's neck, which I did, thinking the Zulus were going to fire at me, but was surprised to hear our own men firing over my head; they killed about a dozen Zulus. While watching this little skirmish I saw one of our kafirs brought to bay by a Zulu. After some preliminary guarding on the part of both, the Zulu stabbed our kafir in the shoulder; thereupon our kafir jumped up into the air and stuck his assegai into the Zulu's heart. Both of them then rolled into the river . . .[26]

Brickhill had managed to get out safely but looked back to see Melvill in the water and in difficulties. 'Our impulse was to go to his assistance, but his horse gave a plunge and I thought was climbing out. My guides were scudding away and I hastened out . . .'[27]

Walter Higginson had stuck with Cochrane all the way from the camp:

> As we got to the river I met Lieuts. Melville and Coghill, the former officer carrying the Queen's Colour in a case, as I overtook them, they were agreeing to stand by each other, if either were hurt; we got down to the bank at last and a frightful scene it was, men and horses all struggling together in the river. I put my horse in behind Mr Cochrane's, but he made a bad attempt at swimming and getting on a big stone in

the middle of the river, he turned over and threw me off. I sank at
once, as I had my rifle and ammunition with me, but on dropping
them managed better; the current carried me downstream a good
distance, but I, fortunately, came on a large rock which I held on to; . . .
I then saw Melvill coming downstream towards me, he having also been
thrown by his horse, he asked me to catch hold of the Colour. I did so,
and the force he was going pulled me off the rock into still water;
Coghill who had got out alright then rode his horse down to Melville to
help him, but as he rode into the water the Zulus who were on the bank
we had just left opened fire on us, and one of the first shots killed
Coghill's horse; we were thus all three in the water, and also I think the
last three to cross the river. We got out alright . . .[28]

Indeed they did; but as they left the rock, floundering again towards the
Natal bank, the current finally tore the Colour out of Melvill's exhausted
fingers, and it disappeared beneath the surface.[29]

All those who reached the Natal bank were utterly spent. Quartermaster
Macphail of the Buffalo Border Guard found himself afflicted with that
terrible thirst which strikes so many in the physical and emotional exertion
of combat. He noticed a small stream flowing into the river on the Natal
side, just below where he had crossed, and 'had a good drink. Somebody
said, "You're damned cool," just those words, I said "I'm damned hot."'[30]
Wyatt Vause, who lost his horse in the river, reached the opposite bank
'thoroughly exhausted [and] had to sit down and rest and had it not been
for a little Kafir boy giving me a seat behind him on his horse I am quite
sure the Zulus would have been upon me before I had gone many yards
further'.[31]

It is clear from most of the survivors' accounts that they felt much safer
once they had reached the Natal bank. It is unlikely that many Zulus
crossed at the drift; the Zulu did not have a culture of swimming, and
indeed most dangerous fords in the country had a local guide living nearby
whose duty it was to assist travellers across a river safely. For the most part,
it was the custom to cross particularly dangerous rivers en masse, as Charlie
Harford had seen the NNC do at Rorke's Drift, but there was no possibility
of a group of men surviving the crossing at Sothondose on foot that day.
Private Wassall noticed a few Zulus in the water, and that 'they had a
curious way of using their elbows which made them able to get across',[32]
while Smith-Dorrien claimed to have seen about twenty on the Natal bank,

but without their rifles – indeed, it is difficult to see how any could have got across still holding their weapons. It is possible these were ama-Qungebeni rather than the king's men, simply because, living locally, they were more likely to have known the easiest ways across; even so, both Smith-Dorrien and Brickhill noted that large numbers of Zulus ran away from the drift along the banks looking for better places to cross.

Yet Cetshwayo had specifically instructed his men not to cross the border and carry the war into Natal, and those who were tempted to do so earned a stiff rebuke from their commanders. The other bank was now completely overrun by the Zulus, who searched among the *dongas*, in the bush and in caves between boulders on the water's edge, flushing out survivors. The iNdluyengwe had moved upstream, but groups of men from the battlefield, who had been delayed by the fighting in the Manzimnyama, were still coming up, and some of them, mostly iNgobamakhosi, seemed intent on crossing over. Prince Sikhotha, the Zulu pretender, had just reached the Natal bank in the company of four wagon-drivers, when he heard:

> A Zulu *induna* on horseback on the other side 'shout . . . in a loud voice' to his men who were about to cross into Natal, 'Has he said you were to cross? He is not invading! He is only defending the land of the Zulus! Come back!' This *induna*, it appears, was Vumandaba . . . Sikota . . . and the four men with him, and also some white men who had got across, first began to draw breath after hearing the words of the *induna*. 'We were saved by that alone; for, if they had come across, we should have been killed, being utterly exhausted . . .'[33]

One of King Cetshwayo's brothers, Prince Ndubako reached the river with some men of his own uMbonambi *ibutho* and, in the heat of the moment, urged them to cross over with him, but they refused, discouraged no doubt by the presence of the commander of the uKhandempemvu, Vumandaba, and excusing themselves on the grounds that their wounded needed attention.[34]

Yet there were still dangers for the British survivors. The hills rise steeply on the Natal side, the rocky slopes covered with tall grass and scattered with boulders. Melvill, Coghill and Higginson had made their way off the flats and worked their way up the slopes, a remarkable feat of endurance given all they had been through, the heat of the day, and

Coghill's bad knee. They were not far from the top of the rise when, according to Higginson:

> Coghill called out, 'here they come', I turned round and saw only two men close to us, and turning to Melvill said 'For God's sake fire, you both have revolvers', they did so, and I saw both the Zulus drop; Melville then said 'I am done up, I can't go any further': Coghill said the same, I ran on, passed them and got to the top of the hill, where a few Basutos on horseback had stopped, seeing me coming, when I got to them I caught hold of a horse's tail and ran on; I could see nothing of the two poor fellows behind me, so I guessed that they had been overtaken.[35]

The deaths of Melvill and Coghill, although they have become central to the imperial mythology of the battle, remain mysterious. Perhaps they were killed by the handful of Zulus Smith-Dorrien had seen on the Natal bank – they were certainly easy enough targets. Yet there is another intriguing possibility. In 1919 a Zulu named uMbulwane Mdine who fought in the battle, and was then living at Qhudeni, described how he had been incapacitated early in the fight by a shot through his knee fired accidentally by 'one of my own side who did not know much about the workings of his old [Snider] gun'. Because of this, uMbulwane did not see anything of the pursuit, but he was told by some of his friends who were 'Of the regiment that followed the fugitives to the Buffalo River. They told me they killed quite a number of soldiers along the path between Isandlwana and the Buffalo river. When my friends got to the Buffalo river they shouted to some Natal natives who were on the Natal side of the river and warned them not to allow the soldiers to get away – "if you don't kill them, we'll kill you".'[36]

This may have been the case. The noise and commotion of the approaching rout was surely enough to arouse the curiosity of the Nxumalo living on the white farms in the area. If they had turned out to watch, they could have been left with few illusions of the invincibility of white troops. While if they had decided to side with the Zulu – confirming every settler's worst nightmare – they could have expected severe retribution from the colonial authorities, this might have seemed a more distant and distinctly preferable evil than the very real threat of the victorious Zulu army poised on the facing bank. Alternatively, while many survivors noted the courageous way individual members of the NNC came to their rescue, in the chaos of the crossing it is also possible that some thought it safer to be on the winning side.

Whatever the truth, no white survivor saw Melvill's and Coghill's end. According to the regimental records, Melvill's watch stopped at 2.10 p.m., 'probably at the time he was washed off his horse',[37] and while a stopped watch is proof of nothing – it may have stopped the night before, or run down days afterwards – it seems unlikely that many men got across the river alive much after this; Melvill and Coghill may have been among the last to die on the riverside.

Trooper Barker of the Carbineers saw Higginson shortly afterwards. Barker had halted at the top of the hill on the Natal bank with his friend Trooper Tarboton,

> To see if we could find any of our fellows, and as I fancied I saw a man who I thought was Hawkins some way down the hill, I rode back, but it turned out to be Lieut. Higginson, so he informed me, of the native contingent, and had got hurt in the river where his horse had washed away. As my horse was too tired to carry two, I assisted him to mount, and he rode away leaving me to follow him on foot. Tarboton, Henderson, and Raw, recognizing him on my horse, took the horse from him and came to meet me with it, of which I was right glad, as I had run for about three miles [4.8 kilometres]. Higginson told them he could not have walked any further, and he knew I was fresh, and that he was sending the horse back for me. Raw obtained a horse for him by dismounting one of his Basutos . . .[38]

It was the third time that day that Higginson had found an excuse to leave men behind him.

Just after he had had his drink, Quartermaster Macphail noticed that Captain Essex was nearby. Essex, Gardner and Cochrane had met up on the Natal bank, and stopped for a moment to confer. Essex was in favour of making some kind of stand, but it was too late and the men too exhausted. Macphail heard him say, ' "We had better get into some order and go to Helpmekaar", but there was no order at all. Nobody took any notice, but a lot did go to Helpmekaar.'[39]

Essex gathered those who were willing, including Stafford, and Gardner paused long enough to send a note with a Mounted Infantryman to warn the garrison at Rorke's Drift. Then they all set off together towards the Biggarsberg ridge, which loomed above them on the western skyline.

Smith-Dorrien missed them in the confusion, and he had no horse; dolefully, he set off on foot, in his sodden uniform and heavy riding boots. He had begun his day's adventures before dawn, riding with Chelmsford's dispatch to Durnford at Rorke's Drift before returning to iSandlwana and the battle. Now, Helpmekaar was 30 kilometres away, much of it uphill, but despite everything he had already been through, he had little choice.

Scarcely a hundred white survivors had made it through the crossing and Essex, Cochrane, Gardner, Curling and Smith-Dorrien were the only imperial officers among them. Of 67 officers and 1,707 men who had been in the camp at the start of the battle, not a single officer of the 24th had escaped, including Pulleine. In addition Durnford, George Shepstone, Majors Russell and Smith, Captain Bradstreet and Lieutenant Scott – all were dead, although Raw, Vause, Davies and Henderson survived. According to official estimates – which were probably understated, particularly with regard to the auxiliaries – the survivors left at the foot of iSandlwana or on the long stony road to the river the bodies of 727 of their white and 471 of their African comrades.

And the Zulu dead? According to an *induna*, Cajana kaMathendeka, they were 'not to be counted, there are so many'.[40] Soon the whole Zulu kingdom would be 'mourning and weeping' – for the day's toll was not yet over.

*

Out at Mangeni, Chelmsford had ordered his men to disengage from their fruitless skirmishing, and to assemble on the flats above the gorge, where the new camp was to be. They were still doing so as Chelmsford and his staff had started back to iSandlwana, overtaking Hamilton Browne and his NNC.

Most of the NNC had not eaten since the day before, and their officers took advantage of the wait to allow them to fall out to forage. Charlie Harford was amused to see that, 'After warning them not to get out of reach of bugle call, they were told to fall out, and in less than five minutes there was not a vestige to be seen of something like 4000 men; being hungry they bounded off like a herd of scared deer in all directions in search of kraals and mealie fields, and were soon out of sight.'[41] Passing some homesteads where six elderly Zulus were taken prisoner – 'we saw a few women and children also, but these were not interfered with' – Lieutenant Maxwell of the NNC managed to catch a chicken.[42] He had just managed to pluck and clean his bird, and started to make a fire when, about 2 p.m., the general assembly sounded:

> Needless to say how disappointed I was at being compelled to leave the bird behind. We fell in and I found myself with the rearguard on the road marching back to Isandhlwana. I imagined something was wrong – but was struck almost speechless when our Commandant, having waited on the road for me, told me that the camp had been destroyed by the enemy during the morning and everybody slaughtered and that we were marching back to retake the camp – He said no more, except requested me not to mention this to anyone.[43]

The news, however, soon became common knowledge. According to Harford it took some time to get the men together again, and as he arrived at the rendezvous on the *nek* below Mdutshana hill where Chelmsford had ordered the men to assemble, he came across:

> Major Black, 2nd Battalion, 24th Regiment, who, like other officers, was scanning the ground towards Isandhlwana with his field glasses and was evidently in a great state of anxiety. I said to him, 'What's happening, Major?' and he replied, 'The camp has been attacked and something very serious has occurred', adding, as he turned away, in his particularly delightful Scotch accent, 'Eh, Harford, keep your d ... d black fellows well out of the way!'[44]

Captain Hallam Parr was with the regulars nearby marching to the new camp site when the news broke:

> Some one said 'Hallo! there's a man in a hurry. He ought to have a horse behind every hill at that rate.' 'Who's that man?' said another. 'I can't see; have you your glasses?' said the first speaker. 'By Jove! It's Gossett. I hope nothing has gone wrong.' Interest in the rider being awakened, we watched him gallop up the hill towards us, his horse evidently blown and weary. 'Well, Gosset, what is it? You seem in a great hurry.' 'The General's orders are that you are to saddle up and march towards Isandhlwana at once,' said Gosset; 'the Zulus have got into our camp.' 'The Zulus have! You're not joking?' 'I wish I was. Lonsdale met the General about five miles [8 kilometres] from the camp; he had ridden close to the camp, and had seen the enemy in amongst the tents. The General is waiting for you, with the mounted men.'[45]

There was no languor in Chelmsford's order – 'march at once' – although he was later criticized for it. The truth was that with his command so scattered it took time for it to reassemble and get back on the road. Waiting with the General and Hamilton Browne's NNC, Trooper Symons of the Carbineers found the delay unbearable:

> We stood for about three hours watching the sacking of the camp. My head, and my heart, ached, too with the thought of how the survivors must be willing us to their help, for survivors there must have been when first we came to our present position, and how they must have cursed us for the delay. 'When will the infantry come up?' was the universal groan. No-one stopped to think that it was not the infantry's fault, but the General's for leaving them behind and ignoring all reports about the enemy.[46]

The men were also weary, of course. Dartnell's command had had little sleep the night before, while the 24th had been up since 3 a.m., and all of them had covered great swathes of difficult country in the stifling heat. Small wonder that the road back to iSandlwana seemed far longer than it had on the way out. It was evening by the time the infantry caught up with Chelmsford's men, halted on the banks of the Nxibongo. The soldiers fell out briefly to fill their water bottles at the stream. It was nearing the end of a beautiful summer's day, the sun steadily sinking behind iSandlwana. The hollows filled with shadows, and a deep gloom spread out from the foot of the hill, hiding the horrors that lay there. Far off to the right, however, large black masses could be seen on the iNyoni escarpment, and there was no mistaking them now for cattle: they were the victorious Zulu army, retiring from the camp.

Chelmsford addressed the men. He was not by nature a great orator – he was not enough of an extrovert – but his words, while not in the league of a Colonel Tim Collins or even Ntshingwayo, certainly made their point. 'Whilst we were skirmishing in front', he said, '. . . the Zulus have taken our camp. There are ten thousand Zulus in our rear, and twenty thousand in our front; we must win back our camp tonight, and cut our way back to Rorke's Drift tomorrow.'[47]

It was hardly reassuring, but several men managed to respond with 'All right, sir: we'll do it.' Trooper Symons noted that Chelmsford added, 'No man must retire'. 'As there was no place to retire to, this last order was superfluous, but we cheered most heartily.'[48] Henry Francis Fynn wasn't so sure; he thought the 2/24th refused to cheer.[49]

The men were formed up, Harness's guns in the centre, on the track, with the 24th in fours on either side. To the right were the 2/3rd NNC in line of column, and beyond them the Mounted Infantry and Police in troops. To the left were the 1/3rd NNC, flanked by the Carbineers, Buffalo Border Guard and Newcastle Mounted Rifles. The 24th marched well, keeping up a steady pace, with the NNC trotting silently beside them – 'there was no *gwia*-ing or capering now. The only sound from them ... was the rattling of their sticks or assegai handles as they clicked against one another.'[50]

There were some strange encounters on the road. According to Fynn, a white man, one J. Raymond, 'rode up from a donga south-eastwards of Sandlwana, and reported his escape from the Zulu forces in Sandlwana camp that morning'.[51] A little further on a man holding a shield and spears suddenly stood up in the grass, and Symons noticed that '... an active little Mounted Infantryman scouting in front no sooner saw him than he sprang from his horse and fired several times, missing each time though, before he could be told to stop. The native was a deserter from the NNC who had yearned for home earlier in the day but found his way blocked so waited there until we came up. Several more got up as we advanced.'[52]

Darkness was now falling, and,

> ... we had to regulate our movements by the rumbling of the gun and cart wheels for that and the clicking of sticks and the swish, swish of the men's and horses' feet was all the sound we heard. Fires sprang up in the camp and hope began to revive in us that perhaps our men had held it after all or retaken it. Before darkness set in we had seen the Nqutu mountain so covered with Zulus that it looked like it would be in winter time when the grass had been burnt off freshly. I never saw such a crowd in my life.[53]

As the column neared the Nyogane, passing over the ground swept across by the left horn, the mounted men, to the left of the road, began to notice their horses 'move aside for something peculiar that we could not discern in the dim light; these objects were dead Zulus lying face downwards and their shields over their backs'.[54]

A little further on the Volunteers dismounted in skirmishing order – 'odd numbers led the horses' – ready to take the camp, and Chelmsford

gave the order for Harness's guns to unlimber and fire some shells into the
tents to drive out any Zulus who might be waiting there. It was now quite
dark, and Symons thought there was an odd beauty in the guns' practice:

> At the first discharge of the cannon the fires which were lighted about
> the camp with one sweep were extinguished, the Zulus being wiser in
> that respect than our NNC ... It was a pretty sight to see the bright
> flash of the gun and the graceful curve of the shell as it passed like a
> meteor through the air, to fall and rebound over the nek. Sometimes
> the shell would strike Isandlwana and bring down rocks with a crash.
> Some went into the valley beyond.[55]

There was no response from the camp, and being a moonless night there
was nothing to be guided by but the faint light of the emerging stars. The
24th fixed bayonets, and the long line advanced again, strung out right
across the front of the camp. Trooper Symons noticed his first dead man
in a red coat, and that the horses were shying with increasing regularity.
Lieutenant Newnham-Davis had one of those strange fateful experiences
which sometimes happen in war: 'As I began to traverse the path which led
up the slope to the hill my horse perceived a dead body and shied at it. I
looked down and saw a face. It was the face of the old captain who had
exchanged places with me ...'[56]

Lieutenant Maxwell of the NNC, out on the flank, followed his skirmishers into one of the *dongas* running across the camp. His horse
stumbled in the darkness, and suddenly he found himself flat on his back
on the ground with his reins in his hand and the horse standing next to
him. Though shaken, he managed to remount and, calling to his men,
found they were nearby. Having got into the *donga*, however, they could
not find a way out, and had to follow the *donga* upstream until they
eventually struck a path.[57]

On the other flank, Offy Shepstone's African servant, who was leading
his packhorse, came to a sudden stop. The packs had slipped, and in the
gloom the man was frightened of being left alone, thinking that each man
that passed him was the last, and begged them to stay with him. He was
weeping with terror but stuck to his charge, and Symons and several others
waited with him while he righted the packs, until Shepstone came up and
said 'Get on man, get on. What are you waiting for?' Symons pressed on,
'so I presume he stayed to see the Native off'.[58]

A little way on they halted again. They were now approaching the 1/24th camp, and Major Black was ordered to take the left half-battalion of the 2/24th and seize the commanding summit of Mahlabamkhosi. At the head of his men Black marched off into the darkness, and for a few tense minutes the remainder of the column listened for the sound of an attack. None came, and instead a cheer rolled out of the night as Black's men announced their success. 'Such cheering I never heard,' said Symons, 'and with lighter hearts we advanced towards the nek.'[59] Just below the 1/24th camp Chelmsford halted them for the last time – they would spend the night there. The troops were brought together and formed into a hollow square astride the road.

By now, even though it was too dark to make out more than the vague shapes of the men in the line on either side, evidence of the battle was thick on the ground. Out on the right, Harford noticed that:

> . . . the undulating ground over which we advanced had been trampled quite flat and smooth by the Zulu army, but no dead were left lying about, so without doubt they must have carried off their own casualties. On the left, towards the 'nek' where the 24th and others of our men made their stand, the dead lay thick, and it was a ghastly sight. Had it not been for the seriousness of the situation, the manner in which my lot of NNC had to be driven along would have been amusing. A two-deep line formation was not at all to their liking, all were in a most awful funk, nothing on earth could make those who were armed with rifles keep their place in the front rank, and all the curses showered on them by their officers could not prevent them from closing in and mixing up in clumps. I had an awful time of it, too. Directly it got dusk, doing nothing but ride from one end of the line to the other, hustling them on to prevent lagging . . .[60]

Fynn noticed that the amaChunu were particularly restless, 'for they were excited about the absence of Gabangaye (left in Sanhlwana that morning) their presumptive chief, son of the hereditary Chief Pakade Mcunu'.[61]

Lieutenant Maxwell had emerged from the *donga* to find himself close to the camp '. . . at which we made a rush and got in among some wagons. On a buck wagon we came across some of the enemy drunk, about eight or ten. Some of the 24th being close by then, I shouted to them. They mounted the wagons and put the bayonet through them.'[62] This was the first of a number of reprisal killings that Lord Chelmsford and his officers would make no effort to stop over the next twenty-four hours.

The accounts of those who spent that night on the fresh battlefield at iSandlwana have a surreal quality about them, the horror of the situation bearing down on nerves already stretched taut by hunger and exhaustion, by concern for the fate of comrades they had left behind that morning, and by fear at their own predicament. And of course by the overwhelming presence of the dead, all the more terrible because they could not be seen, but lay just an arm's length away in the inky blackness, their stiff and cold limbs ready to snag and trip the unwary. A heavy stillness hung in the air, and with it a smell that would haunt Sam Jones of the Newcastle Mounted Rifles for more than half a century. 'And the stench! It was awful. I can still smell it at times. Some things remind me of it, as for instance a sweet potato that has been cooked when it is just beginning to go bad. And when I smell such things I become quite ill.' The experience also haunted a young trooper of the Mounted Police, James Walker, who after the war would be invalided home to spend his days in a London mental institution.[63]

Odd noises broke the still of the night. Trooper Cunningham of the Newcastle Mounted Rifles swore he heard jackals in the distance, screaming at the smell of blood,[64] while Symons thought that the squeals of injured mules sounded unnervingly like children crying. Somewhere at the foot of the mountain a badly wounded man was groaning, and now and then a drunken Zulu would call out. Symons was placed on horse duty while his comrades dozed fitfully; the Volunteers were bivouacked close to Durnford's stand, near their old tents, and Symons stumbled across the bodies of three men he knew – Troopers Swift and Jackson of the Carbineers, and Trooper Gutteridge of the Buffalo Border Guard. A Mounted Infantryman told him later that '. . . he had been looking for a drink of water and coming across a man lying down said, nudging him, "Got a drink in your water bottle, mate?" No reply, so he felt for the bottle and his hand came in contact with the man's disembowelled body.'[65]

Sam Jones noticed in the morning that several men's mackintoshes were caked in the bloody mud in which they had unknowingly lain down to sleep.[66] Several men asked permission to go over the ground and search for friends or relatives, and Dan Scott of the Carbineers sneaked away to look for signs of his brother, the lieutenant, only to be called back. Sam Jones stumbled across the carcass of a horse, and noticed it had a red bandage wound round its leg – it was his own, and he realized that his eagerness to get to the battle the day before had in fact saved his life. Fynn found himself close to the veterinary surgeon's wagon, which had been thoroughly looted. Bottles of medicines and chemicals had been smashed, and the wagon gave off a nauseating smell. Nearby he found a Zulu, still alive, who was paying the price for his indiscriminate choice of 'canteen'; 'Many had drunk of these chemicals as war charms and eaten carbolic soap as biltong and died; one elderly Zulu on the ground, a Thulwana, becoming conscious thus explained to me the particulars, and died an hour or so later beside me.'[67]

John Maxwell would have a worse memory to live with. He had lain down behind his men, using his saddle as a pillow, and dozed off. An hour or two later, he was woken in the dark by someone who claimed that Chelmsford had asked for him by name. The staff were close by, recognizable in the light of the lantern Clery was carrying:

The General asked me to accompany him and show him where the sentries were placed. It struck me it would be easier to do this than to find the officer who was in charge. The sentries I was asked to point out were the sentries of the 2nd Battalion NNC and all I knew was that the first one was placed on the right of the neck on the western side of the mountain. But having found this one I could learn where the next one was, and so on. We started, I leading, the others following, over as rough a ground as any person would care about walking on [in] broad daylight. As I expected, I found the first in his place and then things were easy, with the exception of the ground, which as we proceeded became more precipitous. I now only required to visit the last one, but to my surprise and after search I failed to find [him]. I waited now for what the General would say, and it was not long before he remarked 'You are a pretty fellow, not to know where your sentries are.' In self defence I was compelled to state the truth, so answered 'they are not my sentries General.' This satisfied him, and he replied 'I beg your pardon, I was informed you were the officer on duty and I am sorry you were disturbed, do you know where your staff officer and officer on duty are?' On my answering 'I thought I could find them', he told me to return and tell them to join him there as soon as they could. I turned from them and started on my way back, this time without any light, and had only proceeded a few paces when I tripped and fell down the mountain some ten or twelve paces. Naturally I had my hands in front in the position I can remember of one about to take a dive, and a dive it was, for I found myself with my hands in the inside of what turned out to be the body of a 24th man, and my heels uphill. The

Major having heard the fall turned the lanthorn and discovered me in the above predicament. Luckily I was not hurt, but my hands and wrists were in a nice mess.[68]

While some men never managed to sleep all night, others were so exhausted they fell asleep immediately, and not even the issue of the tins of bully beef and biscuits they had with them could rouse them. Hallam Parr was given the task of distributing the rations, and after the regulars and Volunteers had been given theirs passed them to the white officers and NCOs of the NNC:

> One officer – I could not see his face and have no notion who he was – asked leave to draw for six or seven of his comrades, and as he had forgotten to bring his haversack, and could not carry six or seven rations of loose biscuit and tinned meat in his hands, I told him he had better hold out his hat for the biscuit. 'Sir,' said he stiffly, 'I must object to your suggestion. I should prefer to go without my rations than carry them in my hat.' As it then seemed highly probable that before long there would not be many of us with either a head to put a hat on or a mouth to put a biscuit into, and as there was not any time to waste, I sent this gentleman away in a hurry to fetch someone else to draw rations . . .[69]

Charlie Harford managed to sneak off for a few moments to visit the site of his tent under the pretext of visiting his outposts. When he returned he was amazed to find that a large number of the NNC had moved down the slopes of the Manzimnyama valley, presumably looking for a more secure spot to pass the night. He rounded them up and 'literally drove them back to the square'. Several times he blundered into moving figures who did not give way to him – afterwards, it occurred to him that they were probably Zulus. When he reported the incident to Lord Chelmsford, Chelmsford sent two men of the 24th to watch over the NNC with fixed bayonets and orders to stab the first man who left his position – and 'after this there was no further trouble'. The visit to Harford's tent had in any case

> . . . proved a blank, everything had gone, and the same with Lonsdale's tent, which was next to it. But between our tents lay the bodies of two artillery men, disembowelled and terribly mutilated.
>     Within a few yards of where our wagon had been drawn up I found the dead bodies of our two drivers, with their faces blackened, and it

struck me at the time that they must have done this themselves in the hope of being able to escape.[70]

Near a hospital wagon Harford saw a body lying face downwards, stabbed in the neck; he thought it was Surgeon Shepherd, whom he had known several years before, although other accounts suggest he got further. Several times during the night Major Clery came over, and he and Harford were walking on the *nek* when

> We came across a large tarpaulin rolled up, and being a comfortable-looking seat both of us at once sat down but silently rose up again somewhat horrified on feeling that we had sat on something soft, and undoubtedly a dead body. Why we neither of us thought of unrolling the tarpaulin to ascertain whose body it was I don't know, except that under the circumstances of the moment, with dead all round one, we had no stomach for curiosity.[71]

Colonel Glyn and some of his officers searched about for the bodies of their comrades, and Glyn thought that he recognized both Pulleine and Lieutenant Hodson. Newnham-Davis was given permission to go with a party of Mounted Infantry to search out more provisions in the wagons behind the ruined tents. Here they found the body of Lieutenant Milne's servant, Signalman Aynsley of HMS *Active*. Aynsley's pockets had been rifled, and several photographs were strewn about him. Newnham-Davis collected the photographs and passed them over to Milne, but took Aynsley's cutlass and kept it as a souvenir.[72] He also found an undamaged tin of bully beef and later, much to Harford's disgust, 'As we tramped in together to Rorke's Drift the following morning [he] demolished the lot, never offering me or anyone else a mouthful. I don't think another officer, NCO or Private in the whole column would have been guilty of such selfish gluttony.'[73]

The night was broken by several false alarms. The regulars of course blamed the NNC – Hallam Parr noted that the regulars 'were quite steady – the 24th not firing a shot, but merely rising to the knee'[74] – but Maxwell commented archly that 'there were two or three alarms during the night, and they were not caused on this occasion by the Contingent'.[75] Certainly Offy Shepstone seems to have been demoralized, wondering, perhaps, about the fate of his brother George – according to Symons 'he and a few others began shaking hands and saying goodbye to each other, "For we shall never see the sun rise again". From that moment I lost faith in the Captain.' In contrast, Symons heard Major Black call out several times on the summit of Mahlabamkhosi to steady his men, 'Don't shoot boys – cold steel is our motto.' Symons was impressed – 'Major Black's the man for me ... no going around saying goodbye about him.'[76]

Inevitably, in such a fraught atmosphere, tales of the awful horrors lying half-glimpsed in the darkness beyond the square began to circulate, finding a ready audience among men made overwrought by fear and grief. Trooper Sam Jones thought he saw 'One sight, a most gruesome one, [which] I shall never forget. Two lads, presumably little drummer boys of the 24th Regiment, had been hung by butcher's hooks, which had been jabbed under their chins, and then disembowelled; all the circumstances pointing to the fact that they had been subjected to this inhuman treatment while still alive.'[77]

'Even the little drummer boys that we had in the band' wrote one man of the 2/24th, 'they were hung up on hooks, and opened like sheep. It was a pitiful sight.'[78] A month later, revisiting the battlefield, Trooper Symons would see the bodies lying not far from the butchers' poles, and the tale of the little drummer boys, hung up and gutted like sheep, soon became part of the contemporary mythology of the battle, a 'babies tossed on bayonets' tale used to frighten recruits and stiffen resolve.

Yet it is difficult to know exactly what to make of such stories. There were, for sure, horrors enough in the camp, yet all the witnesses stressed the darkness of that moonless night. A light drizzle came on in the early hours, the cloud blotting out even the starlight,[79] men struggled to see their own hands in front of their faces or to recognize those to whom they were speaking, while John Maxwell had been unable to see his own hands deep in the entrails of a dead man until Major Clery's lantern revealed this to him. Only a handful of men, mostly officers, were allowed to go over the field with lights; true, there were a few low fires burning in the camp, mostly the smouldering remains of tents set alight by the Zulus, but the flickering pools of firelight served only to distort visibility further, so exacerbating the dread of what lay in the darkness beyond. Under the circumstances atrocity stories were inevitable, but Captain Penn Symons of the 24th – who was there that night and later contributed to the regimental records – stated categorically that 'no single case of torture was proved against [the Zulus]. The wild stories current at the time, and repeated in the English papers, were untrue.'[80] One of Bertram Mitford's informants, a member of the uMbonambi, was emphatic that 'All were killed on the field, and at once; no white men were tortured: it is the Zulu custom to kill everyone on the spot; prisoners are never taken.'[81]

The story of the drummer boys also implies a degree of deliberation which seems untypical of the frenzied last moments of the camp. That the Zulus would have killed and disembowelled boys as well as men in such circumstances, of course, need not be doubted; it was the Zulu habit in battle to 'sweep everything clear', to kill not only enemy soldiers but the non-combatants who supported them, and if boys there were, they were part of the invading force – they had taken the Queen's shilling, and took with it their chances with the rest. Yet a study of the rolls of the 24th reveals that there were no boys in either the band or the service battalions who could readily be described as 'little'. It is true that 'Boy' was then a rank in the British Army, attributed to under-age lads taken onto the regimental strength, usually the sons of serving soldiers. Altogether there were five in the camp that morning with the rank of Boy: Thomas Harrington[82] and Robert Richards of the 1/24th, and Daniel Gordon, James Gurney and Joseph McEwen of the 2/24th. Although the records are incomplete, Joseph McEwen appears to have been the youngest of them at sixteen – officially – on 22 January. At a time when the state in Britain considered a boy of thirteen fully educated and old enough to earn his own living, this is hardly the callow youth of popular myth. None of the boys were drummers, which was an appointment only open to adult soldiers and most of whom were mature men.

Although sometimes called upon to play the drums on parade, the main duty of the drummers by 1879 was to play the bugle calls by which orders were transmitted on the battlefield – they were also, incidentally, responsible for the decidedly adult duty of inflicting punishment by flogging. Of the twelve 1/24th drummers killed at iSandlwana the two youngest were eighteen and the oldest was in his late thirties. It is possible that one or more of the Boys was in the band, since the band of the 1/24th had been present in the camp, and its members had been employed as stretcher-bearers. Perhaps it was one of them whom Simeon Nkambule encountered at the 1/24th's ammunition wagons; it is certain that all of them were killed.

Of course, there were probably other boys in the camp too, the sons of civilian wagon-drivers, perhaps, and certainly some of the African servants and *voorloopers* leading the ox-teams were young lads. But if it need not be doubted that Sam Jones and others had many terrible glancing sights that night by the dim starlight, what they thought they saw and what they actually saw cannot now be distinguished with any degree of certainty. Indeed, it remains a possibility that the slim pale carcasses stretched out and ripped open on the scaffold were no more than the butcher's ration of fresh meat, prepared that morning and overtaken by events.

Let the last word go to Lieutenant Maxwell, who was certainly unimpressed by these 'terrible stories about mutilated bodies. These were invented for the occasion, as it was impossible for those who told these yarns to have distinguished anything in the night, it being exceptionally dark.'[83]

But if the night hid the horrors close at hand, it revealed others further off. Hamilton Browne had just finished eating his rations – and sharing with Major Black a bottle of port his servant had salvaged from the wreckage – when

> I looked across the Buffalo Valley. By the road it was a long way, but as the crow flies quite a short distance, and in the direction I knew Rourke's Drift to lie I noticed a lot of tiny flashes. I called Black's attention to them, saying 'those flashes must be musketry.' He looked in the direction indicated and said, 'Yes.' I told Duncombe to call Umvubie [Mvubi of the iziGqoza] and ask him. Umvubie at once said, 'Yes, the Zulus are attacking the white man's camp by the river.' I said to Black, 'Do you know if the store camp was *laagered*?' He talked in Gaelic for a few minutes. He might have been praying but it did not sound like prayers, and just then all along the Natal bank of the Buffalo huge fires broke out, and Duncombe exclaimed, 'By God, the Zulus are in Natal. Lord help the women and children!' There could be no doubt about it. The fires we saw were the friendly kraals and farmhouses burning, and all we could do was to echo Duncombe's prayer, 'God help the women and children.' In a few minutes we saw a great flare over Rourke's Drift, and thought that the base hospital, the store camps and supplies, were in the hands of the enemy . . .[84]

Major Clery had noticed Chelmsford's expression a few hours earlier, in the last of the daylight. 'The general's countenance is always an expressive one,' he said, 'and the look of gloom and pain . . . told only too plainly what was going on within. But he was all there – never apparently flunked.'[85] Whatever expression Chelmsford wore now, it was mercifully hidden by the darkness, for the pain and gloom had multiplied. His men were exhausted and tense, with only those rations they had managed to scavenge to sustain them, and whatever ammunition remained in their pouches after a day's fitful skirmishing. That something had gone dreadfully wrong at iSandlwana was obvious enough, but the extent of the disaster remained as yet unknown. And all Chelmsford knew of the whereabouts and intentions of his victorious enemy was that some of them, at least, now lay between his command and the Natal border – their only route to salvation.

# 25

# 'We stood up face to face, white men and black ...'

## Rorke's Drift, 22–23 January 1879

At noon on the 22nd an air of languor had settled over the post at Rorke's Drift. After the departure of Durnford's column early that morning, the Mzinyathi valley above Shiyane hill had seemed suddenly deserted again. For nearly three weeks the open green riverside had sprouted a crop of white tents, first on one side, then the other, a glaring intrusion of modernity into a timeless African landscape, and the natural soundscape of the grasslands had been overdubbed by the discordant noises of an army on the move. Even at night, when the column slept, its presence had dominated the ambient sounds of the valley, the constant thrum of the river and the rhythmic whine of frogs on damp nights, with the white noise of snoring, the grunting and snuffling of hundreds of animals, and sentries sounding off.

Now it was all gone, the old camp sites no more than a smear of flattened grass and mud on the slopes on either side of the drift, the military presence confined to John Chard's solitary camp, just two tents beside the deep pool where the pont was moored, and a clutch of white tents a kilometre or so away at the foot of Shiyane, behind Jim Rorke's old storehouse. The sun was high in the sky, it was a hot, hot day, and the natural sounds of the veld, the whirr and click of insects and the monotonous bird-calls, had relentlessly reasserted themselves. Down by the river Lieutenant Chard took his lunch alone and sat writing letters home; at the mission station, Lieutenant Gunny Bromhead and Assistant Commissary Walter Dunne, in charge of the supplies stockpiled at the post, dined together in the shade of an awning they had improvised by stretching a tarpaulin over two tent-poles.[1] Until the convoy of empty supply wagons arrived from the column at iSandlwana to collect the supplies, there was precious little for the garrison at Rorke's Drift to do, and it seemed suddenly left behind.

It had become obvious as soon as Durnford's men had broken camp that morning, even to the private soldiers stationed there, that something had been afoot. Major Spalding's departure to chivvy along the companies still at Helpmekaar had confirmed it, and so too had Smith-Dorrien's determination to return to iSandlwana, armed with the revolver ammunition he had begged from Lieutenant Bromhead. What these movements meant to those not privy to the discussions among Lord Chelmsford's staff was of course obscure, but it was clear that if some sort of action were imminent, the garrison at Rorke's Drift would not be a part of it. The war was moving on, the garrison was on the wrong side of the river, and unless the arrival of the companies from Helpmekaar freed some of them to go forward to join the column, the men at Rorke's Drift could look forward to whiling away an uneventful war on the safe side of the border, carrying out routine garrison duties on the lines of communication, which was undeniably strategically vital work – but dull.

Since Otto Witt had leased his property to the military in December, the mission had been converted into a staging-post where supplies were accumulated before being sent forward to the column, and the sick and injured could receive treatment en route the other way. The buildings had hardly changed structurally since Jim Rorke's time, apart from some internal modifications to the house when it was occupied briefly after Rorke's death by two settler families, the Stockils and Surtees, who had shared the living space and blocked up some of the internal doors to provide more privacy.[2] The house was now in use as the Centre Column's base hospital, and about thirty sick – one or two suffering from injuries inflicted in the attack on Sihayo's homestead, the rest from ailments typical of life on campaign in Africa, from fever to diarrhoea and blisters – were being tended by a small medical detachment commanded by Surgeon James Reynolds of the Army Medical Department. The men lay crammed into the small, stuffy rooms on beds made by the simple expedient of laying straw mattresses on rows of planks raised a few inches off the floor on bricks. Although Otto Witt had sent his family to Msinga for safety on the outbreak of war he had remained to keep an eye on his property. He had moved out of the house into a tent nearby which he shared with a young Swedish friend, August Hammar, who, with impeccable timing, had arrived to visit him just a few days before.

Witt had used Rorke's barn-like store as a church, but the military returned it to its original purpose, and it was packed to the rafters with the supplies that Smith-Dorrien's convoy was supposed to have collected that morning. These were mostly sacks of corn, each one weighing about 90 kilograms, a general-purpose ration intended primarily to feed the auxiliaries and horses, and heavy wooden boxes, each about 70 centimetres square, containing coarse biscuits or tinned meat rations. There were so many that the storehouse could not contain the provisions, and two great pyramids of sacks stood neatly piled in front of the veranda, and the whole lot was under the care of a detachment of Commissaries led by Walter Dunne.

Until Captain Rainforth's company arrived from Helpmekaar to garrison the entrenchments Chard had been ordered to build above the pont, the guard consisted of one company of regulars and one of auxiliaries, both based at the mission buildings. Lieutenant Bromhead's company, B Company of the 2/24th, was mostly young short-service men in their early twenties, but it had already proved itself efficient and steady when the battalion had taken part in the mopping-up operation at the end of the Cape Frontier Wars campaign, although it was short of officers. During one of the sweeps through the bush, the company commander, Captain A.G. Godwin-Austen, had been wounded when the man behind him had accidentally discharged his rifle and had been invalided home, and command had passed to his subaltern, Gunny Bromhead. Both Godwin-Austen and Bromhead had brothers serving with the battalion, a testimony to just how tightly knit the regimental family could be in the 1870s; Bromhead's older brother, C.J., was on leave at the beginning of the campaign, but Godwin-Austen's younger brother, Fred, had been with Pope's company at iSandlwana that morning.

Lieutenant Gonville 'Gunny' Bromhead was thirty-three years old and came from a titled Lincolnshire family with a distinguished military record – his great-grandfather, Boardman Bromhead, had served as an ensign under General Wolfe at Quebec, his grandfather was a lieutenant-general who had fought in America's Revolutionary Wars, and both his father and uncle had fought against Napoleon.[3] Relaxed and confident in the officers' mess, he was awkward and reserved outside it, perhaps because of a hearing complaint which was getting steadily worse, but which, contrary to popular myth, seems to have affected neither his career nor the duties allocated to B Company.[4] In the absence of another subaltern, Bromhead was effectively seconded by the company's senior NCO, Colour Sergeant Frank Bourne. Only 1.6 metres tall and not yet twenty-five years old, Bourne had held his rank since the previous April; he was still known to his men as 'the kid', and admitted that he had been nervous when first promoted, but after nine months felt that he was 'getting along quite well'.[5]

The company was a little under strength, as usual in the field, and contained the normal mixed demographic; Bourne himself had been born in Sussex, and his men ranged from former farm labourers from Gloucestershire, Leicestershire and Devon to men from the slums of London, Liverpool, Manchester and Birmingham as well as the inevitable smattering of Irishmen. Since the battalion had arrived in the Cape, following garrison duty in Britain it had received a regular supply of recruits, some of whom reflected the notional association with Wales which followed the establishment of the headquarters depot at Brecon in 1873. The 2/24th had a marginally higher proportion of Welshmen in the ranks than was usual in the British Army, and there were five men named Jones in B Company and four named Williams – none of them related to each other – but while several hailed from Monmouthshire (a border county then officially neither English nor Welsh) the origins of the rest were more mixed.

Rather less is known for certain about the auxiliaries, a company of the 2nd Battalion, 3rd NNC. They were probably abaThembu who had arrived at the muster late, and had been on their way to join the rest of the regiment when they had been told to wait at Rorke's Drift instead. The company was commanded by a Captain Stevenson – or Stephenson, even the spelling is in doubt – and seemed to be short of both officers and white NCOs, and it is unlikely they had received much military training. The regulars took little notice of them, and reports of their strength vary from 100 – which was about right for a company – to 300. They had provided a daily guard over the ponts, but no one mentions where they were camped.

Shortly after noon the first sounds of distant musketry from the direction of iSandlwana floated across the valley, although Chard, perhaps because of his position on the low ground by the river, appears not to have heard them. They caused a flurry of excitement among the troops up at the mission, however, and Bourne and several of his sergeants went up onto a shoulder of Shiyane to see if they could see what was going on. They were unsuccessful as the bulk of Shiyane blocks out the view from the buildings entirely, and Bourne had no opportunity to climb all the way to the top for a better look.[6]

Others did, however. It was a quiet day in the hospital, and Surgeon
Reynolds and Otto Witt decided to climb to the top of the hill. They were
joined by George Smith, the Anglican vicar of Estcourt in the uKhahlamba
foothills, the man who, in 1873, had buried Durnford's dead at Bushman's
River Pass. Smith had volunteered to serve as chaplain to the Natal
Volunteer Corps and was on his way to join the Centre Column, but had
got no further than Rorke's Drift.

There was no path to the summit of Shiyane, and it is a deceptive climb,
particularly on a hot summer's day. It is easy enough to pick a way through
the line of broken sandstone, pitted with nooks and crevices, that stretches
for about 300 metres from the rear of the buildings, but beyond that the
hill rises steeply, a long pull up through the boulders, before sloping off
again, and only at the very far end, at the highest point of the hill, does the
view open up. From here the vista is spectacular, however, an almost 360-
degree panorama of the Mzinyathi valley, which sweeps round from the
Biggarsberg ridge behind, across the drift to the left, past the Batshe valley
directly ahead and the cliffs where Sihayo's followers had made their stand,
to the rear face of iSandlwana a little to the right, framed by Siphezi way
off on the skyline beyond, and round to Malakatha and the broken country
where the river disappears into the gorges downstream. Only the plain east
of iSandlwana is hidden from view, blocked out by the hill itself, while the
high ground above Sothondose's Drift crowds in to hide the river squeezed
below.

It must by then have been about 1 p.m., and Reynolds, Smith and Witt
settled down comfortably at the top to see what they could see.

*

Once the last survivors had been flushed out and killed on the Zulu bank
at Sothondose's Drift, the *amabutho* who had followed the fugitives from
the camp began to drift back towards iSandlwana, singing a great victory
song from King Dingane's day. Many of them took advantage of the
shallows to slake the terrible thirst that consumed them, or drank from the
waters of the Manzimnyama as they stopped to pick over the British dead,
carrying away their weapons and disembowelling and stripping any corpses
that had been missed in the fighting. To most of them, Vumandaba's
scornful reminder that their duty to the king ended at the border had come
as a relief; as J.Y. Gibson, who interviewed many Zulu participants after the
war, put it, 'They had fought their fight and would do no more that day.

They were, indeed, too tired for further effort. Most of them had left their bivouac without having eaten; they had covered a great distance over very rough country, and their method of fighting had imposed great physical strain.'[7]

Yet the reserve *amabutho*, whose role in the great victory had been confined to killing men running away, were neither spent nor satisfied. They had missed out not merely on the glory of taking the camp, but also on the share of the loot that had fallen to those who did – and while their bitter rivals, the young men of the iNgobamakhosi, would return home to brag to their mothers and girlfriends about the part they had played in the battle, displaying the white men's trinkets they had won as a prize, the uThulwana, in whose ranks so many princes of the royal house had been enrolled, would have nothing to show for the day's adventure.

The iNdluyengwe had swept down the steep riverside slope of Mpethe hill, killing Major Smith and the last British stragglers, and driving Curling and Smith-Dorrien into the water. Even as the last survivors were being flushed out, Smith-Dorrien and Brickhill had noticed the Zulus moving restlessly in a body upstream. They had been lost to sight in the narrowest part of the gorge, a kilometre or two above Sothondose's Drift, but sometime later had re-emerged onto the heights on the Natal bank. Quite how they got across is something of a mystery, although a local tradition has it that they crossed where the Mzinyathi is channelled through a narrow cleft in a hard shelf of strata. The fissure is 3 or 4 metres wide, a long jump when the water is thumping through under intense pressure half a metre below, but perhaps they used uprooted trees on the river banks to form some sort of bridge across.

Their commander, Zibhebhu kaMaphitha, was with them, it seems – although he may well have had to leave his horse on the Zulu bank – but once in British territory he clearly considered he had discharged his responsibility to the king. They were no longer acting under royal authority, and while it was obvious to the lowest of them that the whole of the central Natal border was open to them, with no white troops to protect black and white homesteads alike along 12 kilometres of the Mzinyathi valley, they were very much on their own. While some opted to stay together under junior officers, others were more than willing to break away in groups to see what they could forage. As they emerged onto the heights they squatted down to rest, and to snort the protective powders they carried with them as snuff. Then, while the main body began to move in a leisurely manner up-river towards Shiyane hill and Jim Rorke's old storehouse, smaller groups broke away, some moving downstream and others pushing towards the foot of the Biggarsberg heights, searching out and pillaging a solitary abandoned white farm and a score of deserted African homesteads.

Most of the civilian population had run away once it became clear that the Zulus had reached the river, but some were not quick enough. As late as the 1960s, an elderly lady known simply as Gogo ('grandmother') Nxumalo, whose family lived between Sothondose's and Rorke's Drifts, recalled as a child being bundled by her parents into an underground grain store, and listening in the dark to the sounds of the Zulus ransacking the huts above her. According to a careful colonial report, no less than twenty women and four young boys were killed by the Zulus on the Natal bank on 22 January, and four women and three boys were captured and taken back to Zululand.[8]

Zibhebhu himself struck off on his own. He had undeniably played a distinguished part in the iSandlwana campaign, but his later career would reveal an ambitious, self-serving and acquisitive streak and he was certainly not prepared to let the opportunity that now presented itself go to waste, though, as he told Gibson, the consequences of his adventures were to prove unexpectedly dangerous:

> He had pursued the fugitives into Natal, and seized a number of cattle within the border of the colony ... Occupied till late in the evening with his efforts to get the booty through the river, he had been unable to reach Isandhlwana till darkness had set in. There was no moonlight, and he was not aware of the presence of the British troops until he found himself amongst them. Being unacquainted with the ground his escape was rendered extremely difficult. But, stumbling over boulders and falling into water-courses, he picked his way to, and eventually joined, his comrades with no worse an injury than a broken finger. The mark of that injury he was to retain for life ...[9]

With Zibhebhu retired from the field, the main body of the iNdluyengwe moved away from the Mzinyathi gorge, and found that the rest of the reserve – the uThulwana, iNdlondlo and uDloko – had also crossed the river in the more open country upstream.

Their progress had been watched from the top of Shiyane although, even with the aid of field glasses, Witt, Reynolds and Smith had struggled to make any sense of the events in the Manzimnyama valley, wreathed as they were in smoke. After the war, Witt was to arouse the ire of the settler population in Natal with some caustic comments on their racial attitudes, and as a result scorn was poured on the veracity of his account of the day's actions. In fact, however, his description of what they saw from the top of Shiyane has a ring of authenticity about it. 'The Zulus descend and draw themselves in long lines between the camp and river. From where I stood I could see the English forces advancing to the attack; but I could not see any hand-to-hand fighting. I observed that the Zulus were fighting heavily, and presently I saw that the English were surrounded in a kraal some distance from the camp.'[10]

The three men were troubled by those 'long lines'. For a while, they hoped they might be the NNC, making their way back towards Rorke's Drift, but as the lines reached the river there could no longer be any doubt:

They crossed the Buffalo River about four miles [6.4 kilometres] below Rorke's Drift, just below where the river makes a bend, almost at right angles between precipitous rocky sides, firing repeatedly into every cave, bush and crevice that might have afforded shelter for refugees. Being satisfied with the result so far, they came onto a small green hill, sat down – and took snuff all round.

Companies 2 and 3 then followed the example of No 1, keeping some distance apart. They also advanced in open order – after going through various exercises, dividing off (apparently) into hundreds, then into tens, wheeling and quickly reforming; they crossed the river just above the bend, repeatedly firing amongst the bushes and rocks on both sides. They remained a long time in the river, forming a line across it, either for bathing or to assist one another in fording the stream.

By the time they had gained the rising ground upon this side, and had sat down to take snuff, up started ten men of No. 1, and ran in advance up the valley which lies between the high land at Helpmekaar and the hills at the back of Rorke's Drift.

In the meantime another party of Zulus, who must have crossed the river some miles lower down, had set a European house and kafir kraal on fire, about four or five miles [6.4 or 8 kilometres] away at the back of Rorke's Drift.

No. 1 Company followed their advance guard at an easy pace. No. 2 started off, bearing away to their left, apparently to support No. 1.

No. 3 Company started off two men straight for Rorke's Drift, who ran as fast as they could, followed by ten others who took it more easily,

then came on the rest, headed and led by two very corpulent chiefs on
horseback.[11]

These *amabutho* too were without their appointed commanders but Prince
Dabulamanzi had already emerged as their natural leader, not merely
because of his innate authority, but because he was more than willing to
give the men what they wanted – a chance to plunder in Natal. He knew –
they all did – that they were flying in the face of the king's orders, but
Dabulamanzi trusted in his good personal relationship with Cetshwayo to
protect himself and his men from the repercussions. Asked after the war
what his intentions were, he admitted frankly that he 'wanted to wash the
spears of his boys'.[12] A few years after the war Walter Stafford, who had
bought a share in a store in northern Zululand, hearing that Dabulamanzi
was visiting the district, took the opportunity to seek him out and swap
stories of iSandlwana:

> I asked him if it had been his intention to invade Natal. He said 'no',
> that Cetywayo told him that the flooded rivers were a bigger king than
> he was. I then said, 'Then why did your men shout out, both at
> Isandhlwana and Rorke's Drift, "Nina manga" – which means you are
> kidding yourselves – "tomorrow night we will sleep with your wives
> and sisters in Umgungundlovu (Maritzburg)"'? He said that was only
> bravado . . .[13]

Certainly, the *impi* did not behave as if it were intent on invading Natal.
With no British troops in a position to intercept him, Dabulamanzi might
easily have slipped round the southern spurs of the Biggarsberg and struck
at the unprotected African locations in Msinga, and the tiny garrisons at
Helpmekaar and Rorke's Drift could have done little to stop him. Yet it
would have been impossible for so small a force to have achieved anything
of strategic consequence beyond an extended raid, and even granting its
mobility its lines of communication to the border would have been acutely
vulnerable. Moreover, the late afternoon of a day when his men had already
tired themselves running across country and crossing a major river in flood
was not ideal timing to begin an invasion, all the more so when the main
army was spent and in no position to support it.

By crossing the river Prince Dabulamanzi had, however, aroused the
deep-seated fears of the settler community. 'If that [the invasion] had
happened', said Walter Stafford with a shudder, 'all the Natal natives and

the Cape natives would have joined him as a matter of policy to save their skins. It is too awful to contemplate what the result would have been.'[14] Such a view ignores the complex political divisions within the African communities in Natal, and their willingness to fight in pursuit of their old quarrels with the Zulu royal house – but in any case a deep strike by the Zulu into Natal was not a practical possibility that day.

Instead, falling into place behind the iNdluyengwe, the uThulwana, iNdlondlo and uDloko continued their advance up the valley towards Rorke's Drift. It is impossible to know how many of them there were; by F.B. Fynney's careful account on the eve of war, these *amabutho* numbered about 6,000 men at full strength, but an unknown number had failed to attend the muster for one reason or another, while some had remained with their *amakhosi* to protect their home districts. Furthermore, several companies of the uThulwana had followed Qethuka in the attack on the camp at iSandlwana, so it seems likely that not many more than 4,000 crossed into Natal. Of these, numbers of the uThulwana, too, broke away from the main body to look for plunder, so perhaps no more than 3,500 moved on towards Rorke's Drift. The fighting men among them may have numbered less, for it seems that some of the uThulwana were still attended by their sons, who had been carrying their mats for them on the long march from oNdini.

They knew the store at Rorke's Drift was there, of course; it had been a feature of frontier life for a generation. If it had not been for the king's prohibition on crossing the border, it might have been perceived as a legitimate military target, the anchor of the British invasion; as it was, it was exactly the sort of small but potentially profitable target the reserve had hoped to encounter. After the destruction of the camp at iSandlwana that morning, the chances of victory seemed overwhelming, and the uThulwana went forward eagerly. 'O!' they said simply, 'let us go and have a fight at Jim's!'[15]

High on the top of Shiyane, Surgeon Reynolds noticed the Zulu advance was preceded by a number of white men galloping wildly on horseback; he hurried down the hill, Witt and Smith trailing in his wake, to see what it all meant.

\*

It was Lieutenant Gert Adendorff of Captain Krohn's NNC company who interrupted Chard's reverie at the drift.

Adendorff had stuck with Hlubi's troop all the way from iSandlwana. They had picked up a few other survivors, too, as they had forced a way through the right horn, including their own officer, Lieutenant Henderson, a civilian meat contractor who had been in the camp named Bob Hall, and a Natal Carbineer, Trooper Sibthorpe. Keeping together, husbanding their few remaining rounds of ammunition to fire a volley now and then at any groups of Zulus who came too close, they had reached a point several kilometres upstream from the Zulu reserve, clear of any pursuit. Somewhere along the way a crowd of non-combatants had joined them for protection, driving their cattle, either camp followers or Gamdana's people, and up at the mission station Dunne and Bromhead saw them on the road, wondering at their significance.[16] When they reached the river, probably at the old wagon drift, Hlubi allowed his men to dismount to let their horses drink and rest, while Adendorff and the Carbineer rode half a kilometre upstream to where Chard was sitting outside his tent above the moored pont:

> . . . my attention was called to two horsemen galloping towards us from the direction of Isandhlwana. From their gesticulations, and their shouts, when they were near enough to be heard, we saw that something was the matter, and on taking them over the river, one of them, Lieut. Adendorff of Lonsdale's Regiment Native Contingent, asking if I was an officer, jumped off his horse, took me on one side, and told me, the camp was in the hands of the Zulus, and the army destroyed; that scarcely a man had got away to tell the tale, and that probably Lord Chelmsford and the rest of the column had shared the same fate. His companion, a Carbineer, confirmed his story. He was naturally very excited, and I am afraid I did not, at first, quite believe him, and intimated that he probably had not remained to see what did occur. I had the saddle put on my horse, and while I was talking to Lieutenant Adendorff, a messenger arrived from Lieut. Bromhead, who was with his Company at his little camp by the stores, to ask me to come up at once.[17]

Chard ordered his solitary remaining sapper, Driver Robson, to pack up his camp and equipment and load it in the wagon to await his orders. A Sergeant Williams and six men of B Company had been stationed at the pont in response to Spalding's orders, and Chard posted them among a rocky outcrop on the slopes of the knoll rising above the banks.[18] He then set off towards the mission station at a gallop; Adendorff went with him, but the Carbineer rode on.

Bromhead and Dunne had been watching Hlubi's horsemen approach the drift, and had been about to go down to investigate when two Mounted Infantrymen, Privates Evans and Whelan, rode up. They had been among the men Reynolds had seen from the summit of Shiyane, and they were dishevelled, wet from their swim across the river, and badly shaken, but Evans had dutifully brought the pencil note which Alan Gardner had scribbled perhaps half an hour before at Sothondose's Drift. It stated quite baldly that the camp had fallen, and that Gardner thought the Zulus were on their way to attack Rorke's Drift. When he heard the news, Dunne had a sudden sense of déjà vu; no doubt it was simply shock, for the news was so stunning, the import so enormous, that for a few minutes neither he nor Bromhead could take it in.

One of Dunne's subordinates, Acting Assistant Commissary James Dalton, snapped them out of it. Dalton was a mature man in his forties, a Londoner by birth, a career soldier with a good deal of service behind him who had formerly been a sergeant in the 85th Regiment. He had the quiet, authoritative manner of one long used to managing officers, and he had recent experience to back it up, as he had earned a good reputation serving with the Commissariat on the Cape frontier. It has become popular to suggest that he was the true hero of Rorke's Drift, and while that underestimates the contribution of others, there is no doubt that his influence at this crucial stage was telling. Dalton pointed out that there was in fact no option but to try to make a defence; if they tried to evacuate the post, they would be overtaken on the road and, as they were encumbered with the sick and likely to be heavily outnumbered, there was every chance that they would be slaughtered to a man. They stood a far greater chance of survival if they converted the two mission buildings into an improvised fort using the stores as barricades.

It is possible more lay behind Dalton's suggestion than simply cool logic and grit. Eighteen months earlier he had found himself in charge of a supply depot at a spot known as Ibeka on the frontier, during some of the most active British sweeps through Xhosa territory. Dalton had earned a mention in dispatches for his efficiency in keeping the mobile columns supplied with food and ammunition, but the Xhosa had quickly realized the importance of Ibeka and had isolated it and at one point threatened to assault it. The small garrison at Ibeka had fortified the post in preparation,

however, and that had been enough to discourage the Xhosa from launching a direct attack. It is quite likely that Dalton thought that simply by
placing the post at Rorke's Drift in readiness the Zulus might leave them
alone.

The final decision was Chard's, as senior officer, but while Bromhead
sent to inform him of the news he ordered that the post be made ready for
either fight or flight. B Company's tents, behind the storehouse, were
struck, a two-wheeled water-cart – part of Reynolds' hospital establishment
– was dragged closer to the buildings, fatigue parties began to drag the
mealie sacks and biscuit boxes out of the storehouse and pickets were
posted to give some warning of the Zulu approach.

All this was already under way by the time Chard rode up, a fact which
has been used to minimize Chard's role as commander and architect of the
defence. It is probably true that Chard was neither a particularly dynamic
nor ambitious officer; he was thirty-one years old and despite several
overseas postings had not seen action before, and he was notoriously
relaxed, much given to smoking his pipe. Indeed, his company officer,
Captain Walter Jones, judged him to be 'a most amiable fellow, and [an
asset] to the mess, but as a company officer . . . hopelessly slow and slack'.[19]
Much of the negative comment about both him and Bromhead, given a
good deal of publicity in recent times, can be traced back to the jealousies
and intrigues of senior officers at the end of the war, and in particular to
Evelyn Wood, who seems to have taken a dislike to Chard and influenced
the attitude of Chelmsford's successor, Sir Garnet Wolseley, who was
himself naturally inclined to resent those officers who had distinguished
themselves before he took command.

Whatever Chard's professional faults, he now found himself suddenly
and unexpectedly propelled into an extraordinarily dangerous situation,
and one in which any error of judgement on his part, any faltering of
resolve or failure of leadership, could lead to the deaths of everyone under
his command. To add further weight to his responsibility, the garrison of
course had no idea of the true Zulu intentions, but the general assumption
had taken hold immediately that an attack on Rorke's Drift was the prelude
to an invasion of Natal itself. John Chard did not falter. He agreed with
Dalton's assessment – the post would have to be defended.

It was by no means an ideal position to fortify. Jim Rorke had
constructed his buildings with no thought of security, and they were both
overlooked and hemmed in by cover that could neither be cleared nor

incorporated into the defences. The two buildings had been built about 30 metres apart, the house a little forward so that its rear wall was roughly in line with the front of the store, on a flat shelf of ground that jutted out from the base of Shiyane just 300 metres away. A wagon track wound up from the drift, branching about 50 metres in front of the buildings, one path continuing up towards the store, the other veering off across the front of the house, eventually to strike round behind Shiyane and meander towards the neighbouring farms downriver. The rocky shelf snapped off sharply just a few metres in front of the buildings and the ground level dropped, the exposed stump of the fracture forming a rocky ledge about 2 metres high which extended along most of the front of the post, giving way to a steep slope in front of the house. Neither Rorke nor Witt had done much to clear the strip of ground between the ledge and the tracks, and it was covered in bush matted with tall grass. In front of the house, below the slope, someone had started a stone wall but had never completed it, leaving a stretch 20 or 30 metres long and 1.5 metres high. Across the track beyond the house, however, was a fenced orchard containing some fruit trees, while just in front of the house stood two tall wattle trees. At the other end, to the right front of the storehouse, stood a well-built cattle pen, and further down, below the ledge, a bigger but less well-built cattle kraal. There were the usual scatter of outbuildings typical of frontier dwellings – a small cookhouse and cluster of clay ovens behind the store and a wooden-walled 'long-drop' toilet beyond the house.

The two main buildings were of typical border style, a few examples of which can still be seen in the Mzinyathi valley today, although most of them have long since fallen into disrepair. Both were long, low bungalows with walls made of shaped blocks of local dolerite, thatched roofs and open verandas. The store was the bigger of the two, about 25 metres by 7, while the house – Reynolds' hospital – was about 18 by 5.5 metres. The rear walls of the store were reinforced with buttresses; the interior was utilitarian, with a large shed on one side designed to garage a wagon and several big rooms with an attic above, accessed through an upstairs door by way of a wooden stepladder against the west wall. The interior of the house was more eccentric, Rorke's quirky sense of interior design having been further complicated by the amendments made by the Stockils and Surtees during their brief joint occupancy, to secure private living quarters. The rooms were small and cramped, and if they had ever been connected, they were not now, so that in some cases to get from one room to the next it was necessary to go outside and in again. The limitations of this from a military point of view would become desperately apparent over the next twelve hours.

There was not time or men enough to incorporate everything into a defensive perimeter, nor to cut down the bush to clear the field of fire. The out-buildings could not to be included within the lines and the close proximity of the calf pen to the storehouse was problematic. Chard, the Royal Engineer, paced out the line of barricades and decided to incorporate the calf pen, but the rough cattle kraal, just a few metres away below the ledge, would have to be left to the Zulus, as would the scattered outbuildings. It was easy enough to secure the back of the post, connecting the front left corner of the store by the shortest line to the right rear of the house. There were two ox-wagons on the site, and these were dragged into line, and biscuit boxes run together under the wagon-beds and right across the gap. These were then heaped up with mealie sacks to provide a solid wall about 1.2 metres high. The gap between the store and calf-pen was also plugged with mealie sacks.

Securing the front of the post was more problematic. Here a line would have to be built that stretched from the front corner of the calf pen, across the front of the storehouse and the yard between the two buildings, all the way to the far corner of the house. Here the garrison was certainly aided by the topography, and Chard was quick to spot that by running his line along the top of the rocky ledge he could make it a much more formidable obstacle. The finished barricade was no more than a metre high, but when added to the natural barrier of the ledge it meant that anyone assaulting it from the bush would be faced with a rampart 3 metres high. Even with the help of Stevenson's men, however, it took time to drag out the sacks and hump them across the yard, and there are suggestions that the line in front of the house was never completed. Dunne noted that 'there was nothing but a plank to close the opening at one point',[20] and the bags there may have been piled no more than half a metre high.

Once the work had begun, 'a breastwork of bags of grain, boxes of biscuit, and everything that would help stop a bullet or keep out a man. An ox-wagon and even barrels of rum and lime-juice were pressed into the service.'[21] Chard rode back to the drift to order the detachment he had left there to retire to the mission station. Sergeant Millne of the 3rd Regiment, a Mounted Infantryman who had worked on the ponts as a volunteer since the invasion began, and a civilian ferryman named Daniels, offered to moor the pont midstream and defend it, but since they would be completely exposed to Zulu rifle fire from the banks, and since there were not enough men to spare to guard the drift in any case, Chard declined, and both men made their way back to the post with the picket of the 24th. Driver Robson drove the Royal Engineers' wagon up and parked it below the cattle kraal; quite what happened to the mules, the draught oxen from the wagons and carts, and to the officers' horses is not clear, but since there are no references to them being penned in either of the corrals, they were presumably turned loose.

Since the hospital patients could not be evacuated in time, it was decided to leave them in the house. According to Reynolds, just eight of them were so incapacitated that they could not walk unaided, and the rest were issued rifles to defend themselves. In addition, six men from B Company were told to assist them, and several men were placed inside the storehouse, including in the attic. Chard 'tried to impress upon the men in the hospital the necessity for making a communication right through the building', but despite the fact that they took some pickaxes with them 'unfortunately this was not done – probably at the time the men could not see the necessity, and doubtless also there was no time to do it'.[22]

Throughout all this, a number of survivors from iSandlwana had ridden past. They were a depressing sight, most of them having lost hats, jackets and weapons in crossing the Mzinyathi, and all of them exhausted and shocked. Chard feared that they might demoralize the garrison since 'they stopped the work very much, it being impossible to prevent the men getting around them in little groups to hear their story'.[23] One said to Surgeon Reynolds '. . . no power on earth could stand against the enormous numbers of Zulus, and the only chance for us all was immediate flight'.[24] Frank Bourne recalled that one whispered to him 'Not a fighting chance for you, young feller.'[25] Harry Lugg of the Mounted Police, who had been in the hospital with an injured knee since his horse fell while crossing the Mzinyathi, recalled that 'Two of our men – Shannon and Doig – came in, excited and breathless. Upon my saying "What is it? Is it true" and so on, Doig replied "You will all be murdered." and then rode off with his comrade. Consolatory, certainly . . .'[26]

It was too much for Otto Witt, who had arrived down from the top of Shiyane to find soldiers barricading his home. Harry Lugg could not '. . . help laughing at [Witt's] gesticulations when [he] came back seeing their best parlour paper being pulled down and loopholes knocked out, whilst splendid furniture was scattered about the rooms'.[27] Witt was not only a civilian and a foreign national but a missionary, and he can hardly be blamed for thinking that he had no place in the coming battle. He was worried, too, about his wife and children in Msinga, who now seemed suddenly vulnerable, and he saddled his horse and rode off to find them. His friend August Hammar went too, and they took with them one of the patients in the hospital, a Lieutenant Purvis of the NNC who had been shot through the arm at Sirayo's stronghold and was suffering from dysentery, and who, according to Chard, 'was so sick he could hardly mount his horse'.[28] Reverend Smith was also tempted to go, but he found his African groom had ridden off on his horse, so he decided to throw in his lot with the defenders. The trader and the missionary had come and gone; now there remained only the red soldier.

Despite these desertions, the mood in the garrison remained firm. This was not so much bravado but rather an instinctive and realistic appreciation that defence was probably their only hope of survival. Given the option – the only option – between standing behind a good tangible barricade alongside friends and comrades who had fought together before, or of fleeing alone in a hostile environment with large numbers of fit and agile men in pursuit, flight must have seemed unattractive. 'The men knew what was before them', said Dunne, '. . . a struggle for life; but they one and all displayed the greatest coolness, though some of them were very young soldiers. On all faces there was a look of determination which showed that they meant to "do or die".'[29] Or as Harry Lugg put it simply, 'nothing remains but to fight'.[30]

It was now about 4 p.m., and the barricades were progressing rapidly, when Lieutenant Henderson and Hlubi Molife rode up with the Tlokoa. Chard had left the drift before they crossed so their arrival was a pleasant surprise, and when Henderson reported himself Chard asked if they would 'observe the movements, and check the advance, of the enemy as much as possible until forced to fall back'.[31] Since the observers had come down from the top of Shiyane, Chard had had no news of the Zulus' movements beyond the fact that they were approaching upriver from beyond the hill; Henderson agreed, and Molife and his men rode round the southern flank of Shiyane and took up a position just out of sight of the garrison.

They had not been gone long, however, when there was a splatter of shots and they came into sight again, a smear of brown horses and yellow corduroy against the green hills, riding fast for Helpmekaar. Henderson and Bob Hall rode past the front of the post and Hall called out, 'Here they come – as black as hell and as thick as grass!'[32] He and Henderson lingered for a while beyond the orchard, firing a few shots at targets still out of sight to the garrison, before they turned and rode after their men.[33] Even Chard found it hard to blame them – they were almost out of ammunition and after their experiences that morning they had no stomach for a further fight. He saw the same men perform well later in the war, but when he asked them about that day they merely replied 'that Durnford was killed, and that it was no use'.[34]

The sight of them going, however, snapped the tension that had so far held the garrison together, and Stevenson's NNC suddenly flung down the sacks and boxes they were carrying, vaulted over the barricades, and bolted in a rush. 'I am sorry to say', reported Chard, 'that their officer, who had been doing good service getting his men to work, also deserted us.'[35] So, too, did their NCOs, including a Corporal Anderson, a Scandinavian who spoke poor English and was quite probably confused by the sudden panic among his men. For the most part the regulars had held the auxiliaries in no very high regard, but the sight of their white officers running with the rest caused a sudden ripple of anger, and several men of B Company fired shots after them. Corporal Anderson was hit squarely through the head and fell forward onto his face, dead.[36] The first man on the British side had died – shot by his own men.

Whatever their fighting value, it was a serious blow for Chard to lose so many men with an attack seeming imminent. The exact number of white troops left at the post varies slightly on the different contemporary rolls and so will always be inexact, but there were now scarcely 150 men to defend a perimeter Chard had designed for 250. If the Zulus attacked on all sides at once, there would simply not be enough to go round. The only solution lay in providing a second line of defence, a fall-back position behind which the men could concentrate if they were driven out of any part of the perimeter, and Chard gave the order to start work on a new barricade. This started at the left front corner of the storehouse and cut straight across the yard to connect with the front barricade above the ledge. It was made of biscuit boxes piled two high, and gaps were left for the men to pass through. Once it was complete it meant that if either building had to be abandoned, the other could be turned into a self-contained redoubt.

Its construction was probably the single most important command decision Chard took that afternoon, and the lives of the garrison would depend upon it.

While the biscuit boxes were dragged into place, Private Fred Hitch from B Company, a Londoner known to his mates as 'Brickie' because of his former job as a bricklayer, was sent scrambling up onto the thatch of the storehouse to watch for the Zulus. This elevated position gave him a view over a few hundred metres of the flanks of Shiyane, and after a while he saw the Zulus come. 'I told Mr Bromhead that they were on the other side of the rise and was extending for the attack. Mr Bromhead asked me how many there were? I told him that I thought [they] numbered up to four to six thousand. A voice from below – "Is that all? We can manage that lot very well for a few seconds." There were other opinions . . .'[37]

A few minutes later the pickets posted by Bourne fell back to the buildings, and immediately afterwards 'a single Zulu appeared, standing out against the sky on top of a high hill which rose up about 100 yards [91 metres] in rear of the store'.[38]

A few kilometres away on the road to Helpmekaar, Reverend Otto Witt looked back and saw the first Zulus running towards the barricades. The Battle of Rorke's Drift had begun.

*

The iNdluyengwe were in the van, having pushed along the high ground upstream from Sothondose's Drift before the older men had caught them up. As they passed round the southern end of Shiyane and their scouts reported that the mission was defended, the iNdluyengwe halted to dress their ranks, sending out skirmishers and deploying into companies.[39] Probably they expected no great resistance and that the element of surprise was on their side for they made no effort to surround the post at first, simply coming on in a fast rush, most of them crouching low with their shields up in front of their faces in the stance Mlamula Matebula described the iNgobamakhosi adopting at iSandlwana. They made a cool and distinctly professional sight, not at all the wild savage charge the defenders had been expecting. One of the defenders of the hospital, Private Hook, noted that they 'took advantage of every bit of cover there was',[40] ducking behind anthills and boulders and weaving among the scant protection afforded by the long grass and a scattering of aloes on the otherwise bare slope. On the storehouse roof, Private Hitch fired a shot at them – the first, he claimed proudly, of the battle – then slid down off the roof and ran to join his friends in front of the hospital.

At about 500 metres' range, the men along the back wall manning the loopholes in the rear walls of the two buildings opened fire with a crashing volley that pushed out a cloud of white smoke, and the Zulus immediately began to return their fire. Trooper Lugg, who could hardly walk, had left the hospital and been posted in the attic of the storehouse:

> My carbine was broken or rather the stock bent. I found a piece of rein, tied it up and fell in with the soldiers. I thought, if I can get somewhere where I can sit down and pop away I shall be alright, because my knee was much swollen. I was told off in my turn to take a loophole and defend the roof from fire . . . I had the satisfaction of seeing the first I fired at roll over at 350, and then my nerves were as steady as a rock. I made sure almost before I pulled the trigger. There was some of the best shooting at 450 yards [412 metres] I have ever seen.[41]

According to one of Arthur Harness's gunners, Arthur Howard, who was in the hospital suffering from dysentery, the heavy Martini-Henry bullets caused havoc when they struck home and the Zulus 'would give a little spring in the air and fall down flat'.[42] Private Hook, a marksman in the company, spotted one man ducking behind an ant-heap,

> . . . about 300 yards [274 metres] off, popping his head out now and again to fire. I took careful aim, but my bullet just went over his head. I then lowered my sight, and fired again the next time he showed himself. I saw the bullet strike the ground in a direct line, but about ten yards [9 metres] short. I then took a little fuller sight, aimed at the spot where I knew his head would come out, and, when he showed himself, I fired. I did not then see whether he was struck, but he never showed himself again . . .[43]

This was the first time the iNdluyengwe had experienced such intense fire, but it slowed them not in the slightest, as Surgeon Reynolds noted. 'On they came at the same slow, slinging trot, their heads forward, their arms outspread, their bodies poised in a sort of aim at our mealie circus, and all in a dead silence. Here and there a black body doubled up, and went writhing and bouncing in the dust; but the great host came steadily on . . .'[44]

For a few moments, Chard was worried that they might simply charge home:

We opened fire on them, between five and six hundred yards [457 and 549 metres], at first a little wild, but only for a short time . . . The men were quite steady, and the Zulus began to fall very quick. However, it did not seem to stop them at all . . . It seemed that nothing would stop them, and they rushed on in spite of their heavy loss to within 50 yards [46 metres] of the wall, when they were taken in the flank by the fire from the end wall of the store building, and met with such a heavy direct fire from the mealie wall, and the hospital at the same time, that they were checked as if by magic.[45]

It was the one true charge of the battle, and it had been halted; James Dalton had been encouraging the men on the back wall, directing their fire, and when he saw the leading Zulus throw themselves down in the grass he climbed on one of the wagons and in his excitement threw his hat at them.

The iNdluyengwe were not finished, however, and numbers of them crawled forward to occupy the abandoned cookhouse and a low drainage ditch which lay no more than 30 metres from the British line and opened desultory fire at close range. The rest, coming up behind, shied away from the rear of the post, veering off to their left, passing close by the western end of the hospital, and pouring down the ledge, where they moved round to occupy the bush lying directly in front of the post. Although many of them were no more than 50 or 60 metres away, they were screened by the long grass and by the old stone wall, and here they regrouped for a few minutes before making a dash up the short, steep slope to the front of the hospital.

There was almost no physical barrier to stop them, no rocky ledge and only the flimsiest of barricades. According to Fred Hitch, they pushed right up the slope and across the barricade, so that the first of a series of violent hand-to-hand flurries broke out:

> . . . right up to the porch [and] it was only when the bayonet was freely given that they flinched in the least bit. Had the Zulus taken the bayonet as freely as they took the bullets, we could not have stood more than fifteen minutes. They pushed right up to us, and not only got up to the *laager*, but got in with us, but they seem to have a great dread of the bayonet, which stood to us from beginning to end. During that struggle there was a fine big Zulu – seeing me shoot his mate down – he sprang forward, dropping his rifle and assegais, seizing hold of the muzzle of my rifle with his left hand and [with] the right hand [got] hold of the

bayonet. Thinking to disarm me, he pulled and tried hard to get the rifle from me, but I had a firm hold of the small of the butt of the rifle with my left hand. My cartridges [were] on top of the mealie bags which enabled me to load my rifle and [I] shot the poor wretch whilst holding on to his grasp for some few moments.[46]

A private of the Army Hospital Corps had a similar close shave; a Zulu grabbed his bayonet and pushed his rifle aside and was just raising his spear to strike when Dalton, rushing over from the rear barricade, shot the Zulu dead. For a minute or two it looked as if the defenders' line would break but the Zulus could not sustain their position and they 'were driven back with heavy loss into the bush around the work'.[47]

It may seem curious that a people accustomed to fighting with stabbing weapons should develop such a respect for the British bayonets, but the Martini-Henry bayonet was indeed an impressive weapon, 47 centimetres of slim, sharp cold steel that the men had nicknamed 'the lunger' because it gave a soldier a reach of something over 2 metres, significantly more than the metre or so a Zulu needed to use his spear effectively. Nor could a bayonet thrust always be easily turned by the shield, because the weight concentrated on a very narrow point which was often enough to punch right through the hide, or snag it enough to pull it out of the Zulu's hands. Equally, the threat posed by bullets to men who believed themselves protected from them by ritual no doubt seemed a good deal less tangible than that of the all-too-obvious bayonets.

Nevertheless, the bayonets were not enough to discourage the iNdluyengwe from regrouping and mounting several small assaults in quick succession over the same ground. But each of these was driven back by squads under Bromhead and Bourne until the few metres of grass between the hospital veranda and the head of the slope was littered with a tangle of dead and dying men.

While this struggle was going on, the remaining amabutho, the u-Thulwana, iNdlondlo and uDloko, hurried forward, drawn by the sound of the firing. They followed in the wake of the iNdluyengwe around the foot of the hill, but seeing an attack stalled along the back wall in front of them, moved further to their left, past the hospital, before swinging round to join the men occupying the orchards, garden and bush. 'Up came their reserves,' said Harry Lugg succinctly, 'then they were on us.'[48]

As they came, several men on the back wall fired out at them, Privates

James Dunbar and George Edwards both shooting at an *induna* at the front who was riding a horse and wearing a distinctive shawl. The man was knocked out of his saddle, although it was impossible to know whose shot struck home. His death did not discourage the attack, however, and Chard noted ruefully that '. . . they occupied the garden, hollow road and bush in great force. The bush grew close to our wall, and we had not time to cut it down. The enemy were thus able to advance under cover close to our wall, and in this part soon held one side of the wall, while we held the other.'[49]

It was obvious that the weakest part of the British defences lay along the front of the hospital, and this the Zulus attacked unrelentingly. Elsewhere, between the buildings, the height of the rocky ledge made it impossible for them to get to grips with the defenders, whose heads and shoulders could only be glimpsed over the top of the barricades above them whenever they exposed themselves to fire. For the most part, the Zulus kept to the bush, pouring in heavy fire from their old trade guns until the front of the post was wreathed in smoke. 'Heavens!', said Reynolds, 'They rained lead on us at the distance of a cricket pitch or two . . . We stood up face to face, white men and black, and blazed at each other til nightfall.'[50]

By this time it had become impossible to hold the ground in front of the hospital veranda, and a few sacks and boxes had been dragged forward to improvise a new barricade which connected the right front of the hospital to the front barricade. During one of the lulls in the attacks Chard pulled the defenders back behind this; they effectively abandoned the slope to the attackers, but they could fire directly into anyone running up to attack the veranda at just a few metres' range. Even so, it became impossible to stop the Zulu attacks entirely, and as Chaplain Smith recalled, '. . . such a heavy fire was sent along the front of the hospital that, although scores of Zulus jumped over the mealie-bags to get into the building, nearly every man perished in that fatal leap; but they rushed to their death like demons, yelling their war-cry "Usuto! Usuto!" '[51]

Frank Bourne was certainly impressed: 'To show their fearlessness and their contempt for the red-coats and small numbers, they tried to leap the parapet, and at times seized our bayonets, only to be shot down. Looking back, one cannot but admire their fanatical bravery.'[52]

In fact, however, the numerical superiority of the Zulu soon proved to be of little use to them. The British front was so constricted, and the approach so hampered by bush, that it was impossible to bring the majority of their men to bear, and once the attacks had begun their commanders could do little apart from marshal small groups of them and try to direct them against British weak spots as they developed. It is quite likely that large numbers of Zulus spent most of the battle lying out in the bush further out, never getting the opportunity to become fully engaged.

From the beginning, however, numbers of them had moved up onto the Shiyane terraces and taken possession of the caves and crevices between the great slabs of fallen sandstone. Nestling in among them, they opened heavy fire on the British below. Their position was a commanding one, for although they could see little of the men directly in front of them beyond a line of dirty white helmets and red shoulders crouched behind the wagons and high rear wall, they looked down right onto the backs of the men fighting at the front. The range was between 300 and 400 metres, and had they been armed with effective modern rifles they could have made the British position untenable in a few minutes. The Zulu tragedy, of course, was that they possessed no such weapons. Although Frank Bourne was convinced that he heard the distinctive whiz of Martini-Henry rifles, there is no independent confirmation of this.[53] Having taken no part in the attack on iSandlwana, it is difficult to see how the reserve could have recovered more than a handful of British weapons, nor does it seem likely that they could have familiarized themselves with them so quickly – and as far as can be judged by the medical reports, none of the British casualties were hit by Martini-Henry bullets.

Instead, the Zulus on the terrace were firing weapons that had scarcely been accurate at ranges longer than 50 metres even when they were new, twenty or thirty years before. The British barricades were simply beyond their effective range, and although a certain amount of shot struck down into the yard, it did so at random, and probably a greater amount fell short, some of it onto the men of the iNdluyengwe occupying the ground around the kitchen outhouses. A fire-fight now developed in which the soldiers on the back wall had the upper hand. They were firing at an ideal range for the Martini-Henry, and they could steady themselves on the barricade, taking aim at targets that identified themselves with a puff of white smoke every time they fired, and were in any case increasingly picked out by the low evening sun which shone directly into the caves.

One man in particular had an extraordinary escape during this fire-fight. Chard's African wagon-driver – his name is not recorded – had led the Royal Engineer wagon up from the drift and had unharnessed the mules. He had then run away, fearing that to remain with the garrison was far more dangerous than simply hiding in the veld. He had hidden in one of the deepest caves on the terrace – none of them extend deeper into the mountain than a metre or two – to wait out the battle, but as Chard explained, this proved to be an error of judgement. 'He saw the Zulus run by him and, to his horror, some of them entered the cave he was in and lying down commenced firing at us. The poor wretch was crouching in the darkness, in the far depths of the cave, afraid to speak or move, and our bullets came into the cave, actually killing one of the Zulus. He did not know from whom he was in the greater danger, friends or foes . . .'[54]

There were, moreover, one or two good shots among the Zulus, and it is tempting to wonder whether they were members of Prince Dabulamanzi's entourage, some of whom had been taught to shoot by John Dunn. Certainly, the British got the better of the exchange, but several soldiers were hit in quick succession by musket balls which took them on their exposed shoulders – a remarkably small target at the distances involved. Corporal John Lyons was firing over the barricade near his friend, Corporal William Allan:

> I was determined to check this flank fire as much as possible. I became thus more exposed, and so did Corporal Allen [sic]. We fired many shots, and I said to my comrade, 'They are falling fast over there,' and he said 'Yes, we are giving it to them.' I saw many Zulus killed on the hill. About half-past seven, as near as I can tell, after we had been fighting between two and three hours, I received a shot through the right side of my neck. The ball lodged in the back, striking the spine . . . my right arm was partially disabled. I said, 'Give it to them, Allen. I'm done; I am dying,' and he replied 'All right Jack;' and while I was speaking to him I saw a hole in the right sleeve of his jacket, and I said, 'Allen you are shot,' and he replied, 'Yes, goodbye.' He walked away with blood running from his arm . . .[55]

Lyons staggered back and collapsed, twisting as he fell so that he landed in one of the gaps between the biscuit box barricade. Chard thought he was dead, but Lyons looked up and said, 'Oh, Sir! You are not going to leave me here like a dog?'[56] He was pulled through the gap and taken to Surgeon Reynolds, who had set up a casualty post on the veranda of the storehouse. Here he patched up the worst of the wounded, his pet terrier, a Jack Russell named Dick, yapping at his heels.[57]

Reynolds himself also had a lucky escape; once Chard had abandoned the veranda of the hospital, the only way to reach the men inside was through a solitary window in the east wall which opened into the yard. Reynolds volunteered to carry an armful of ammunition packets across the open yard to pass them to the eager hands reaching out from inside, but as he did so several Zulu bullets struck about him, one knocking a hole in his helmet.[58]

For the most part, however, Zulu fire coming from the front of the post, from the bush and orchard beyond, or fired point blank as the Zulus ran up to assault the barricades, was more destructive than that from the slopes of Shiyane, and several men had already fallen to it. A Private Thomas Cole had been posted to the hospital at the beginning of the fight. A claustrophobic, Cole soon found the cacophony of battle – the booming of the guns, the shouts of patients and screams of the wounded, the Zulu war-cries – unbearable in the dim, cramped rooms and rushed outside. He emerged onto the veranda at the height of the struggle there and was shot clean through the head, the ball passing out to break the nose of a Private Bushe nearby.

A Corporal Scammell of the NNC was hit in the yard, shot through the back of the shoulder. He collapsed and someone helped him off to Surgeon Reynolds, who patched him up, but Scammell refused to rest and instead crawled out into the yard again. Here he saw Chard and Dalton directing the men on the front wall, not far from the hospital. By this time the Zulus had occupied the whole of the bush in front of the post, and some had braved the curtain of fire to crouch down at the foot of the ledge, where they could only be reached by men leaning out over the barricades. According to Reverend Smith:

> Mr Dalton, who is a tall man, was continually going about the barricades, fearlessly exposing himself, and cheering the men, and using his own rifle most effectively. A Zulu ran up near the barricade. Mr Dalton called out, 'Pot that fellow!' and himself aimed over the parapet at another, when his rifle dropped and he turned round, quite pale, and said that he had been shot. The doctor was by his side at once, and found that a bullet had passed quite through above the right shoulder . . .[59]

Dalton passed over his rifle to Chard, who 'was standing near him at the time, and he handed me his rifle so coolly that I had no idea until afterwards of how severely he was wounded. He waited quite quietly for me to take the cartridges he had left out of his pockets.'[60] Chard fired off the cartridges, and Corporal Scammell saw him feeling in his pockets for more. Scammell crawled over and handed him his own cartridges, but the effort exhausted him, and he collapsed against the barricade calling for a drink. Louis Byrne, a civilian storekeeper attached to the Commissariat, bent over him to offer him a drink from his water bottle, but a bullet struck Byrne in the head and killed him.

This flurry of deaths and injuries was worrying. The post was now under heavy fire on all sides, and although no further rushes had been made against the rear wall, the pressure along the front was constant, and in several places groups of Zulus had reached the outside walls of the hospital and were battering against the doors or grabbing at the defenders' bayonets as they poked through windows or loopholes. The success of the defence depended on the integrity of the whole line – if it was penetrated at any point it would quickly collapse – and with gaps occurring through casualties there was a very real danger that the Zulus would be able to exploit a weak spot. Already, as Chard noted, there were not enough men to meet each new attack:

> Each time as the attack was repulsed by us, the Zulus close to us, seemed to vanish into the bush, those some little distance off, keeping up a heavy fire all the time. Then, as if moved by a single impulse, they rose up in the bush as thick as possible, rushing madly up to the wall (some of them being already close to it), seizing, when they could, the muzzles of our men's rifles, or their bayonets, and attempting to use their assegais to get over the wall. A rapid rattle of fire from our rifles, stabs with the bayonet, and in a few moments the Zulus were driven back, disappearing in the bush as before, and keeping up their fire. A brief interval, and the attack would be again made, and repulsed in the same manner. Over and over again this happened, our men behaving with the greatest coolness and gallantry . . .
>
> At about 6.00 p.m., the enemy extending their attack further to their left, I feared seriously would get in over our wall behind the biscuit boxes. I ran back with 2 or 3 men to this part of the wall and was immediately joined by Bromhead with 2 or 3 more. The enemy stuck to this assault most tenaciously, and on their repulse, and retiring to the bush, I called all the men inside our retrenchment . . .[61]

It was now that the wisdom of Chard's decision to prepare an interior line, the biscuit box wall, became apparent. The men scurried back, abandoning their positions along the barricades framing the yard, and crammed in to join those already holding the storehouse and the ground in front of it.

It was already evening – nightfall was little more than an hour away – and the garrison now held an absurdly small area of ground. But their position was more secure. So far Chard had lost no more than a handful killed and injured, so he had roughly the same men to defend a much smaller perimeter. Conversely, the British front was so small that the Zulus could not concentrate their strength against it effectively, while the store-house itself largely sheltered the defenders from fire from the Shiyane terraces. Furthermore, fire from behind the biscuit boxes could rake the yard at close range, and prevent the Zulus from entering it. Nevertheless, by abandoning the yard the garrison had largely freed the Zulus to manoeuvre without check around the whole of the western side of the post, and large numbers of them moved quickly forward to occupy the outside of the barricades. In particular, it became impossible to prevent the Zulus concentrating behind the wall at the foot of the slope in front of the hospital, or working their way along the rocky ledge, under the barricades, to pop up further along, nearer the storehouse, and fire or throw spears at the defenders above them.

The withdrawal had, indeed, left the hospital an isolated British island in a sea of Zulus. No one seems to have considered evacuating it when they fell back to the storehouse, and given the number of sick still inside that was probably in any case not possible. Nevertheless, the men inside were now completely surrounded by the enemy on three sides, and could rely on no one but themselves for their defence. Very soon the Zulus had burst through the outside doors, and they then drove the defenders from room to room.

The struggle for the hospital has become a mythic element in the Battle of Rorke's Drift, and deservedly so, but it remains surprisingly difficult to construct a comprehensive narrative. For much of the fight the defenders struggled in isolation in small rooms, the natural tunnel vision produced by combat exaggerated by a sense of walls pressing in on every side, by a hazy or non-existent understanding of the wider battle, by the growing darkness, and by a truly mesmerizing assault on the senses – of the booming of rifles in a confined space, so loud each time that it left ears ringing and hearing deadened, of the constant roar of voices, and of a breathless atmosphere saturated with gunsmoke and the smell of sweat and blood. Figures loom into sudden focus, appearing briefly out of the murk in vivid fragmentary accounts, only to disappear again as quickly, like pages torn from another battle story.

One of the most coherent accounts is that left by Private Hook, a Gloucestershire lad in his late twenties, a teetotaller who was making tea for the patients when the news of iSandlwana broke and was one of the six posted to defend the building. Hook's post-war career brought him into contact with many literary and curious people, and he would tell his story numerous times, learning to smooth out over the years the jagged edges of horror or confusion. Even so, his most vivid impression of the fight was of 'an extraordinary rattle as the bullets struck the biscuit boxes, and queer thuds as they plumped into the bags of mealies. Then there was the whizz and rip of the assegais.'[62]

Hook was posted in a small room – which he could not say – with Thomas Cole, but after Cole was killed found himself defending his post alone. There was only one patient in the room, an auxiliary of the NNC, one of Prince Mkhungo's iziGqoza who had been wounded in the attack on Sihayo's stronghold, and whose leg was heavily bandaged. The patient kept calling out '"Take my bandage off, so that I can come!" But it was impossible to do anything except fight, and I blazed away as hard as I could.'[63]

Hook had been defending his room for a while when he became aware that it was filling up with 'a thick, dense smoke' that hung heavily just below the rafters – the Zulus had set fire to the roof to drive the defenders out. The thatch had been damp after all the recent rain, but the Zulus had tossed into it spears bound round with grass and set alight, probably from the embers which were still smouldering in the cookhouse. It had taken some time to catch fire and burned slowly at first, and it was the heavy billows of smoke from the moisture-laden thatch as much as anything that suddenly made the building untenable. 'This put us in a terrible plight', said Hook, 'because it meant that we were either to be massacred or burned alive, or get out of the building.' Hook's room at least had a door – a 'frail' one, 'like a bedroom door' – and he quickly slipped through it into the next room. The patient called out to go with him, but 'It was impossible'; Hook heard the Zulus break in behind him, a terse conversation in isiZulu, then the sound of the patient trying to tear off his bandages to escape. He didn't manage to.[64]

Hook now found himself the only able-bodied man in a room occupied by several patients, some of whom were defending themselves. Suddenly a soldier burst in through another door; even in the smoke Hook recognized him as Private John Williams, who called out 'They've dragged Joseph Williams out and killed him!'

John Williams had been defending an outside room with Joseph Williams and William Horrigan. Joseph Williams was a good shot who took careful aim each time he fired, dropping a line of Zulus in front of his loophole – fourteen corpses were found there the next morning – but after a while all three began to run low on ammunition and they had decided that they could no longer hold their position. There was no internal exit so while John Williams and Horrigan had taken the pickaxes used to loophole the walls and knocked a hole through an interior partition, Joseph had held the Zulus at bay with his bayonet. He had not been able to hold them off for long, however, and had tried to make a run for it outside, hoping to get back to the yard but had stumbled and the Zulus had been onto him in seconds, spearing him to death. They had then burst into the room, killing the patients before Horrigan and John Williams had been able to drag them through the hole.

It's likely that by this stage the Zulus had already got into the building elsewhere. Two privates named Jones – Robert and William, not related – had defended the large front rooms that opened onto the veranda, crossing bayonets and stabbing at any Zulus who tried to break in, but once Chard's men had fallen back it had been impossible to prevent the Zulus crowding against the front doors and the Joneses had hurried into another room, leaving the Zulus to burst in behind them. It was now impossible to tell which rooms were held by the defenders and which by the Zulus, and a fierce tussle began from room to room. Several men died in the hospital, the details of their deaths unrecorded, their last desperate struggles known only to the Zulus who killed them.

John Williams and Henry Hook decided that they could not remain where they were indefinitely, so Williams again took the pickaxe and started to hack at one of the partition walls. Unlike the stone exterior walls, these were made of sun-dried mud brick plastered over and soon gave way under Williams' determined attack. 'Whilst he was doing this', said Hook,

> . . . the Zulus beat in the door, and tried to enter. I stood at the side and shot and bayoneted several – I could not tell how many, but there were five or six lying at my feet. They threw assegais continually, but only one touched me, and that afflicted a scalp wound which I did not

think worth reporting. In fact, I did not feel the wound at the time. One Zulu seized my rifle and tried to drag it away. Whilst we were tussling I slipped in a cartridge and pulled the trigger – the muzzle was against his breast and he fell dead.[65]

In one of his early accounts of the fighting, Hook included a detail which he later thought it discreet to leave out:

In the hospital I had my top coat and rug [greatcoat and blanket]. A young Zulu – he was only about twenty – stole this, and was making off with them when he was disabled, and I came and caught him with my things. I clubbed my rifle, brought it down with all my force on his head and smashed – not the Zulu's skull, but the stock of my rifle all to pieces. He lay quiet for about five minutes and then began to wink his eyes a bit, so I gave him the contents of the barrel in his head, and finished him off.[66]

Quite why a Zulu so young was involved in the fighting is not clear; perhaps he belonged to a young *ibutho* and had got mixed up with the uThulwana during the pursuit – or perhaps he was a mat-carrier, and considerably younger than twenty. The public adulation which followed the battle, the stirring newspaper engravings and dashing pictures by artists commissioned by the royal family, preferred not to acknowledge that the fight at Rorke's Drift was intense, brutal and bloody, a raw struggle for survival at close quarters, in which Hook found himself fighting at one point 'over the soles of my boots in blood'.[67]

As soon as John Williams had knocked through the wall, he began dragging the patients through. He left until last a Private John Connolly, whose left knee had been dislocated during a wagon accident on the road in Natal, and who was not easy to move. When the rest were shifted, Hook gave up his post, grabbed Connolly, who was a heavy man and wearing a greatcoat, and dragged him after him through the hole. 'His leg got broken again', said Hook philosophically, 'but there was no help for it.'[68]

Most of the defenders were now crowding into the rooms at the eastern end of the hospital towards the yard, but it was imperative that they escape the building as quickly as possible as the fire in the roof was taking hold. Some, however, had simply decided to take their chances on their own. Two privates, Beckett and Waters, were defending a small room opening to the outside where Witt stored his cloak and robes. Several Zulus had tried to enter the room but Waters shot them, and the two men then hid behind the hanging clothes. Despite the bodies lying on the floor they went unnoticed in the smoky gloom until Beckett could stand the tension no more. He ran outside, but it was not yet quite dark and he blundered into a Zulu who recognized his uniform and stabbed at him. Beckett staggered past, bleeding heavily from a stomach wound, and collapsed in the long grass where he lay unseen as night came on.

Private Waters' nerve held a little longer but the heat and smoke were becoming unbearable and as soon as it was quite dark he, too, ran outside. Before he went he pulled one of Otto Witt's black cloaks over him, and he was soon swallowed up by the night. He lay down in the grass to await events, and 'the Zulus must have thought I was one of their dead comrades, as they were all round me, and some trod on me'.[69] The prospect of lying in the open all night, awaiting discovery, did not appeal to him, so judging his moments when the Zulus were distracted he worked his way round the back of the hospital, trying to make for the storehouse and the new defensive perimeter. He got as far as the cookhouse, just a few metres from the storehouse, and crept inside, only to find to his horror that it was occupied by Zulus firing at Chard's men. The Zulus had their backs to him, however, and as it was too late to turn back he 'crept softly to the fireplace and, standing up in the chimney, blackened his face and hands with the soot. He remained there until the Zulus left.'[70]

It is a moment which defies imagination; in the darkness of that cramped little outbuilding, lit only by the guttering light of the burning hospital, Waters must have been close enough to touch the Zulus, and every time they fired the muzzle flash risked discovery. And no doubt, like Chard's servant in the Shiyane caves, the position attracted a good deal of return fire, too. Yet there Waters waited, still and silent, for the night to pass.

Waters and Beckett were not alone – a surprising number of men preferred to risk their lives in the open bush rather than try and work their way back to Chard's redoubt. In fact, of course, Zulu attention was focused throughout the night upon the storehouse, and if a man could make it into the long grass unseen there was an even chance, in that blackest of black nights, that they would not be spotted. Gunner Arthur Howard from N/5 battery, Arthur Harness's batman, certainly thought so – he '. . . ran out through the enemy, and lay down on the upper side of the wall in front of our N. Parapet. The bodies of several horses that were killed early in the evening were lying here, and concealed by these and by the Zulu bodies and the low grass and bushes, he remained unseen with the Zulus all round him.'[71]

'His greatest anxiety', Howard told someone afterwards, 'was to cover the red stripe of his overalls, which seemed to him to show up very clearly through the darkness. He was nearly discovered several times – once from the complaints and remonstrance of a stray pig, who had been struck down close to him by a chance bullet, and whose acclamations attracted attention.'[72]

Private Connolly, after his rough treatment by Hook, dragged a number of mealie bags under an outside window at the back and pulled himself up and through it. He landed on the ground in a heap, but pushed himself away in a sitting position, his feet out in front of him. He made it to about 50 metres from the building before he, too, lay down to wait. A number of bullets from the defenders whistled over him during the night, but he was not hit.[73]

Meanwhile, Hook, Williams and the Joneses and a number of patients found themselves in the far room, which opened through a small high window into the yard. The yard was now a no-man's-land, raked by fire from both sides, and lit up glaringly by the flames from the burning roof, and salvation, in the form of the biscuit box wall, lay 50 metres away. There was no choice, however, but to heave the patients through and hope to get them safely across somehow. The first man out was a comrade of Harry Lugg's, a trooper in the Mounted Police named Hunter; he got through the window safely, but was confused for a second by the chaotic sight which greeted him beyond. The nearest Zulus were just a few metres away, sheltering behind the abandoned dog-leg barricade on the hospital corner, and one bold individual darted out and speared Hunter through the kidneys. The Zulu was shot immediately by Chard's men lining the biscuit boxes, who, alerted to the escape attempt, put down a heavy suppressing fire on any possible Zulu positions.

While Hook and the two Joneses kept the Zulus back from inside, John Williams helped the patients to tumble out through the window, one after another, and they made their way across the yard until eager hands pulled them behind the biscuit boxes. Finally only one man remained, a promising young sergeant named Robert Maxfield. Maxfield was delirious with fever, however, and struggled against their help; '. . . although they dressed him, he refused to move. Robert Jones made a last rush to try and get him away, but when he got back into the room he saw that Maxfield was being stabbed by the Zulus as he lay on his bed.'[74]

As they crossed the yard, one of the patients, Private Roy, noticed that 'there were about thirty Zulus chasing us, but the men inside the fort shot them before they could harm us'.[75] Behind them, the roof of the hospital began to flare up fitfully, sending long plumes of sparks into the night sky, and showering the Zulus inside, and the dead and dying left behind, with burning debris.

There was scarcely more safety to be had by the defenders of the hospital once they had reached the new perimeter. While the struggle for the hospital had been going on, the Zulus had made a number of determined attempts in the failing light to seize the front wall.

Very little is known about Prince Dabulamanzi's command of the battle. There is a local legend that he stood on the slopes of the hill early on, below the rocky terrace, and given the occasional bouts of good shooting from that direction it is possible; however, he would have been greatly exposed to return fire, and it is unlikely he remained there long. In fact, due to the uncoordinated way the battle had begun, it was almost impossible to impose an overall structure on the Zulu attack, particularly as darkness came on, and it was left to junior commanders to direct the attacks whenever they spotted an opportunity. It was unusual for Zulu troops to fight at night – not only was command and control almost impossible in the darkness but the night was a time of *umnyama*, when evil influences might interfere in the plans of men. Yet that evening, there were many reasons why the Zulus were inclined to persevere. Their hopes of easy victory and loot had been thwarted, and to return home before they overran the place risked a greater humiliation than if they had never crossed the border at all. And victory did not seem so far beyond their grasp – they had captured one building, and the redcoats held only the smallest piece of land.

And so they attacked again and again – but luck was against them. As the hospital burned, it cast a pool of light around the post, lighting up the Zulus as they emerged from the bush. According to Harry Lugg, 'The thatch roof burst out into flames and made it as light as day, and before they had time to retreat we were pouring bullets into them like hail. We could see them falling in scores. Then you could hear suppressed British cheers.'[76]

At first, the corner inside the junction of the front mealie bag wall and the biscuit boxes proved to be a British weak spot. It was exposed to the fire from the front and from the abandoned barricades, and Zulus edging along the rocky ledge from the direction of the hospital could come up close completely sheltered from British fire, firing at the defenders above them at a metre or two's range, then ducking back to reload. Lieutenant Bromhead and seven men held this corner, Bromhead firing over the barricades, 'using his rifle and revolver with deadly aim'.[77] Several of the men were wounded one after another, and Private Edward Nicholas was shot clean through the head, spattering the men around him with his blood and brains. During one rush a Zulu leapt onto the barricade and was about to spear Bromhead; Fred Hitch had just fired a shot and his rifle was empty but he presented it anyway and the Zulu dropped back. Shortly afterwards, however, during the next rush, while Hitch was struggling with a man in front and below him, another Zulu managed to force his way through the line. 'I was just about to shoot down a Zulu in front', remembered Hitch,

> ... when the Zulu inside shot me through the right shoulder, carrying away the scapula. Turning round quickly, Bromhead at once shot down the man who had wounded me. I got up again and attempted to use my rifle, but it was no use; my right arm wouldn't work, so I strapped it into my waist band to keep it out of the way. Then Bromhead gave me his revolver to use, and with this I think I did as much execution as I had done before I was wounded.[78]

Hitch's endurance was extraordinary. When he could no longer fire the revolver, he took armfuls of ammunition packets with his good arm and distributed them along the barricades. Several hours later, weak from loss of blood and desperately thirsty, he slumped against the biscuit boxes, and a friend tore out the lining of one of Assistant Commissary Dunne's coats and strapped up his wounds. Hitch's mate, Private Deacon, asked him '... whether he should "put me out" when it came to the finish. He could see my strength was failing fast, and if the devils got through I would be quite unable to strike a blow myself. "No, I don't think I want any," I said ...'[79]

As long as the Zulus could shelter just a few metres away at the bottom of the ledge below the abandoned length of the barricade, the men defending that bloody angle were at risk, and one of the defenders, Corporal Schiess of the NNC, took it upon himself to deny them their refuge. Schiess, a short, broad dark Swiss who had probably once been a sailor,[80] had been a patient in the hospital suffering from blisters and he had been struck again during the fight by a stray bullet which tore open his instep 'which caused him great pain'. Nevertheless, according to Chard, he crept 'out a short distance along the wall we had abandoned, and slowly raising himself, to get a shot at some of the enemy who had been particularly annoying, his hat was blown off by a shot from a Zulu the other side of the wall. He immediately jumped up, bayoneted the Zulu and shot a second, and bayoneted a third who came to their assistance, and then returned to his place . . .'[81]

Shortly after this, the Zulus began to shift the direction of their attack, regrouping in the darkness beyond the eastern end of the post, as far away as they could from the burning hospital. From here they began a series of assaults at the far end of the stone calf pen. Hitherto the garrison had occupied the whole of the calf pen, but they were driven back first to an interior partition, and then out of it altogether, just holding the nearside of the wall inside the perimeter.

The remains of two huge piles of mealie sacks still stood in front of the veranda of the storehouse where they had been dragged out ready to be used for barricades. Partly to counter the new Zulu threat, Chard suggested that these should be dragged across to form one large pyramid with a hollow top. A few riflemen could be posted there, together with some of the worst of the wounded, and it would serve as a final redoubt, an additional layer of fire which could be directed over the heads of the men on the outside barricades just a few metres away.

Walter Dunne volunteered and 'worked hard at this, from his height, being a tall man, he was much exposed, in addition to the fact that the heaps were high above our walls, and that most of the Zulu bullets went high . . .'[82] A cloud of spears also fell about Dunne as he worked, but in one of those surreal moments that sometimes occur in the intensity of battle, Dunne most remembered that 'Overhead, the small birds, disturbed from their nests by the turmoil and smoke, flew hither and thither confusedly.'[83]

The outside of the new redoubt was about 2.5 metres high, and Harry Lugg, still in the attic of the storehouse, heard his comrades below pass Fred Hitch up to the slender protection it afforded. 'Poor old Brickie!' someone said; 'Never mind boys', Hitch replied with a thin chirpiness, 'better a bullet than an assegai.'[84]

The fighting continued sporadically against the wall of the cattle pen but, as Chard observed, it was impossible for the Zulus to clamber over the interior partition to reach the defenders without being shot down, 'it being so close', and the extra layer of fire from the redoubt proved decisive. After about 10 p.m., the Zulu attacks became noticeably less determined. According to Chard,

> . . . every now and then a confused shout of 'Usutu!' from many voices seemed to show that they were going to attack from one side and immediately the same thing would happen on the other, leaving us in doubt as to where they meant to attack. About midnight or a little after the fire slackened, and after that, although they kept us constantly on the alert, by feigning, as before, to come on at different points, the fire was of a desultory character. Our men were careful, and only fired when they could get a chance. The flame of the burning hospital was now getting low, and as pieces of the roof fell in, or hitherto unburnt parts of the thatch ignited, the flames would blaze up illuminating our helmets and faces. A few shots from the Zulus, replied to by our men – again silence, broken only by the same thing happening . . .[85]

In this way did the long and weary night pass. Both sides were now reaching the limit of physical and emotional exhaustion, pushed to the limits of endurance by the hours of visceral close-quarter killing and overwhelmed by the violent deaths all around them. According to Hook:

> . . . we did so much firing that [the rifles] became hot, and the brass of the cartridges softened, the result being that the barrels got very foul and the cartridge-chambers jammed. My own rifle was jammed several times, and I had to work away with the ram-rod til I cleaned it. We used the old three-sided bayonet, and . . . They were very fine weapons too, but some were very poor in quality, and either twisted or badly bent. Several were like that after the fight; but some terrible thrusts were given, and I saw dead Zulus pinned to the ground by the bayonets going through them.
>
> All this time the sick and wounded were crying out for water. We had a water-cart full of water, but it was just by the deserted hospital, and we could not hope to get it until the day broke, when the Zulus might begin to lose heart during their mad rushes. But we could not bear the cries any longer, and three or four of us jumped over the boxes and ran and fetched some water in.[86]

*Above* Captain Alan Gardner, 14th Hussars – one of only five Imperial officers to survive the battle.

*Above right* Major Edward Essex, 75th Regiment, the Centre Column's Director of Transport. Essex's narrow escape from iSandlwana – and from other later military disasters – earned him the nickname 'Lucky'.

*Right* Captain Theophilus Shepstone Jnr – 'Offy' – who commanded the Natal Carbineers during the iSandlwana campaign, and chased Matshana kaMondise at Mangeni.

Three officers of the
1/24th – Lt. Porteous (left),
Lt. Cavaye (standing) and
Captain William Degacher.
All were killed at iSandlwana.

Lt. F. J. Durrant Scott of
the Natal Carbineers (right),
who remained at iSandlwana
while his brothers, Sgt. Major
Dan Scott (left) and Trumpeter
C. Scott, rode out with Dartnell's
command; they survived the
day – but he did not.

Lieutenant Archibald Berkeley Milne of HMS *Active*, one of Chelmsford's ADCs and the man who climbed the Magogo hill with a telescope.

Collateral damage: Louis Dubois, a farmer from Helpmekaar, one of the many civilians who joined the invasion as wagon drivers – and were killed at iSandlwana.

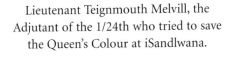

Lieutenant Teignmouth Melvill, the Adjutant of the 1/24th who tried to save the Queen's Colour at iSandlwana.

Lieutenant Nevill Coghill, who went to Melvill's assistance at Sothondose's Drift – and was killed beside him shortly afterwards.

Heroes of Rorke's Drift: a group of Royal Engineers photographed at the end of the war, with John Chard wearing his newly presented VC.

'Gunny' Bromhead, who commanded B Company, 2/24th at Rorke's Drift.

An unmistakable sense of relief shows in the faces of a group of the 2/24th, photographed at the end of the war.

The humiliation of the victors of iSandlwana: Zulu *amakhosi* formally surrender to Sir Garnet Wolseley near the ruins of oNdini in August 1879.

Imperial honours: the Colours of the 1/24th – including the Queen's Colour, left, recovered from the Mzinyathi – were presented to Queen Victoria at Osborne House on 28 July 1880. Colour-Sergeant Wilson (peering over the Regimental Colour) and Private Roy, DCM (far right) were both at Rorke's Drift.

The camp site at iSandlwana, photographed during one of the burial expeditions of June 1879, when wagons abandoned in the battle were still on the site.

Rorke's Drift, photographed in September 1879 from the foot of Shiyane. The original house – the British hospital – stood in front of the trees, but has been pulled down, and the surviving storehouse has been surrounded by the stout stone walls of Fort Bromhead. On the day of the battle the Zulu attack had come in from the left.

Melvill and Coghill's bodies were found on the rocky slopes on the Natal side of the Mzinyathi. Their bodies were collected and buried at the foot of this boulder, and a cross placed above it by Sir Bartle Frere. This shows the site as it was in late 1879.

Rorke's Drift, probably photographed in September 1879. Rorke's store still stands, but is surrounded by a stone fort built after the battle – the ruins of the house can just be seen on the right. Behind are the terraces of Shiyane from where Zulu marksmen harassed Chard's garrison; at the time of the battle the foreground was covered in bush and long grass.

*Above* A new order in Zululand: a photograph of Hlubi kaMota, who fought with Durnford at Bushman's Pass and at iSandlwana, and was rewarded with territory in Zululand after the war by the British. He is flanked by two members of the Royal House – Prince Ndabuko kaMpande (left) and Prince Shingana kaMpande (right).

*Right* King Cetshwayo kaMpande: a striking studio portrait taken during the King's visit to London in 1882 by the fashionable London photographer Alex Bassano.

*Left* Old wars, new world: an unknown Zulu veteran of the battle discusses iSandlwana with Dugald Macphail, who, as Quartermaster of the Buffalo Border Guard, also survived it. This photograph was taken on the battlefield in the 1930s.

Throughout the fight, Reverend George Smith had encouraged the men, pacing behind the lines, handing out ammunition packets from a soldier's haversack he had slung over his shoulders. During the lulls, he called out in a loud voice for salvation. 'All that night a minister was praying in the fort that they would go away,' remembered Private John Jobbins, 'God helped us and gave us the victory.'[87] Walter Stafford was told by Gert Adendorff that 'You will always find in a tight corner there is a hard case and there was one at Rorke's Drift. This man was cussing all the time. The Rev. Smith went to him and said, "Please, my good man, stop that cussing. We may shortly have to answer for our sins." The reply he got was, "All right, Mister, you do the praying and I will send the black Bs to hell as fast as I can."'[88] Someone else remembered Smith's exhortations simply enough; 'Don't swear men,' he admonished, 'don't swear, but shoot them boys, shoot them.'[89]

'It was no longer fighting,' admitted Munyu, 'they were now exchanging salutations merely.'[90] The Zulus lay among the long grass and bush in the inky blackness, the sputtering fire from the hospital painting dim swathes of light on the storehouse walls and barricades, the defenders invisible apart from the occasional glimpse of their helmets over the mealie bags and the sharp pinprick flashes of their firing. The sound of volleys rolled over them like sharp thunder-claps, and bullets whined randomly about them, less destructive than they had been during daylight, but undoubtedly more frightening. The bush that had sheltered them early on was now an obstacle, an unseen tangle to be blundered into or tripped over, and every rush forward meant treading on a carpet of dead and dying comrades. Still, at this hour, some were bold enough to try, and from their loopholes in the back of the storehouse the defenders now and then saw glowing circles of light dancing towards them as the Zulus tried to repeat their success of tossing spears tied round with burning grass onto the storehouse roof. Lieutenant Adendorff of the NNC and Corporal Attwood of the Army Service Corps, both shot down men who ran too close in the attempt. Harry Lugg saw one Zulu search out burning embers in the ovens to light his smoking horn, a quick toke of cannabis to stiffen his courage and dull his fatigue – Lugg shot him dead.[91]

Most, however, were at last giving way to exhaustion. They had begun the day 18 kilometres away at the Ngwebeni, and they had run much of the route to Rorke's Drift, crossing a flooded river along the way, and had fought for hours in a desperate hand-to-hand struggle. Some had managed a handful of cold roast corn that morning, but many had gone hungry all day. The early elation of storming the hospital had worn off, and the whites seemed as firmly ensconced behind their walls as ever. Some of the Zulus had probably begun to slip away as soon as it got dark, hoping at that late hour to find easier pickings down the valley, and by midnight they had begun to withdraw in large numbers.

And the long walk home still lay ahead.

# 26

# 'The subject of much astonishment'

## 22–24 January 1879

Major Spalding had taken a leisurely ride up to Helpmekaar. He had left Rorke's Drift late in the morning of the 22nd, and it had been late afternoon by the time he had wound his way up the steep slopes of the Knostrope Pass onto the Biggarsberg summit. Here, to his surprise, he had met a column of infantry marching in the opposite direction. These were the men he had come to find, D and G Companies of the 1/24th under Brevet Major Upcher and Captain Rainforth. The two companies should have moved forward to Rorke's Drift before now, but any fleeting relief Spalding may have felt on seeing them do so at last had soon been dispelled. Rainforth and Upcher had astonishing news – the first survivors from iSandlwana, cutting directly across country, had arrived at Helpmekaar about an hour before. The camp at iSandlwana had been overrun, Chelmsford's fate was unknown, and the Zulus were reportedly advancing on Rorke's Drift. Upcher and Rainforth had decided to march there as quickly as possible – and Spalding had turned about and gone with them.[1]

Their decision had left the depot at Helpmekaar entirely undefended. Three large corrugated iron sheds and two improvised huts full of supplies due to go forward to the column stood on the open grass ridge-top and, as at Rorke's Drift, no attempt had been made to entrench them. Survivors from iSandlwana straggled in throughout the evening and when Captain Essex arrived, having ridden up from the river crossing, he was surprised to find the place largely deserted and that,

> I was the senior officer present, so I took the command and caused some wagons to be drawn up at a short distance all round the storehouse, a zinc building, quite indefensible. I had sacks of oats placed under the wagons, and now had a barrier. We mustered, of those who escaped, about 25 Europeans; the others, about ten volunteers and camp

followers, continuing their retreat. A few others, such as owners of wagons, two or three farmers with their wives and children, now arrived, and my little garrison numbered 48 men, of whom, however, only 28 had rifles. We expected the approach of the Zulus every moment, but we had plenty of ammunition, and I told every one to fire away as hard as he could in the event of an attack, so as to deceive the enemy as to the number with whom he had to deal.[2]

Essex's determination does him credit, but few of the survivors had much fight left in them. Seeing several of them slip away, Essex ordered all the horses to be turned loose, and any that lingered near the camp to be shot. Quartermaster Macphail of the Buffalo Border Guard thought this a 'foolish order' which merely lowered morale still further; many of the Volunteers had more faith in their horses than they did in Essex, and they were anxious now about the fate of their families in the border settlements and *laagers*. The order 'cleared a lot of us out and left him to fight the Zulus by himself . . . You could hear a swear here and a swear there. Some muttered, "If the horses go, we go." We could hear many breaking away so we came along.'[3]

Macphail himself set off down the road that ran along the ridge-top towards Dundee. Others headed deeper into Natal; Lieutenant Higginson of the NNC had been surprised to find Captain Stevenson – whose men had deserted at Rorke's Drift – and the wounded Lieutenant Purvis already at Helpmekaar, and since he had no gun Higginson again excused himself and the three of them rode off towards Ladysmith.[4]

Typically, the regulars clung to their sense of duty to see them through. Captain Alan Gardner had been concerned that the victorious Zulu army might follow up its success by striking north across country to attack the nearest major concentration of British troops, Wood's column on the Ncome river. He had tried to find someone to take a message to Wood, but as no one would go he set off himself. Macphail passed him on the way, and thought the strain was beginning to tell – 'He was off his head . . . Poor fellow, any sort of noise made him start suddenly.'[5] It is unlikely any of the survivors were any steadier. Macphail persuaded one Millward to guide Gardner to Utrecht, where he finally found a volunteer to carry his message the last length of the journey.

Those that remained at Helpmekaar spent a tense night. The glow of fires rising in the Mzinyathi valley below suggested the progress of the Zulu army, and the sound of distant artillery fire – Arthur Harness's guns shelling the devastated camp at iSandlwana – hinted at heavy fighting going on somewhere in the darkness. Several times the garrison stood to at the barricades, the officers straining to hear the sound of any movement on the road from Rorke's Drift. At about 10.30 p.m. it came – but the defenders were surprised to hear not the thump of hundreds of naked feet through the grass but the sound of boots and wagon wheels. It was Major Spalding, returned with the two companies of the 24th.

Spalding, Upcher and Rainforth had not gone far down the road to Rorke's Drift that evening when they had met the first survivors – the men who had passed Chard's garrison – coming up. Spalding was disturbed to see them but pleased to note that they were 'chiefly Basutos and people in civilian clothes, but there were one or two Mounted Infantry'.[6] He ordered them to accompany him and fall in behind the infantry, 'but all except two slipped away when my back was turned'.[7] All of those he questioned assured him that Rorke's Drift had already fallen, and Spalding rode ahead with a man named Dickson, a local settler, to see for himself. By the time he reached the bottom of the pass it was getting dark and:

> At about three miles [4.8 kilometres] from same I came across a body of Zulus extended across the road. They were fifty yards [46 metres] off ... A deep donga ... was behind them capable of concealing a large force. They threw out flankers as if to surround the party. Mr Dickson agreed with me they were Zulu, an appearance borne out by the 'horns' which they threw out. So we trotted back to the troops some two miles in the rear.[8]

From a rise on the escarpment flames could clearly be seen rising from the burning hospital at the foot of Shiyane. The two companies turned about for Helpmekaar, convinced that the survivors were right, and that Rorke's Drift had fallen.

Smith-Dorrien was among those delighted to see them arrive. He had finally arrived at Helpmekaar after dark and at the end of a day which had tested his physical stamina and youthful endurance – not to mention his luck – to the limits. 'I had had a long enough day, having been on the move including a stretch of twenty miles [32 kilometres] on foot, much of it at a run, for forty-two hours, and directly Lieutenant Clements ... told me he had relieved me, I lay down then and there on two sacks of grain, and was fast asleep in a second.'[9]

News of iSandlwana rippled across the border with the flight of the survivors. On the far side of the Biggarsberg, sixteen-year-old Ruben Jones was leading a wagon and span up the road from Msinga when he met Jim Rorke's widow, Sarah, coming in the other direction. She had been living on a farm on the Knostrope Pass since selling the property at Rorke's Drift, but had left it as soon as one of the survivors brought her the news of the battle. She now passed the news on to Ruben – leaving him to ponder the fate of the Newcastle Mounted Rifles and his older brothers Sam and Fred.[10]

William Beaumont had returned from his foray across the border with Bengough's NNC to find the interpreter James Brickhill, who had not stopped since he crossed the Mzinyathi, breaking the news to Henry Francis Fynn's wife at the Msinga magistracy. The implications of the disaster were not lost on Beaumont – if the Zulus had overwhelmed Rorke's Drift and were coming for Helpmekaar, Msinga lay next in their path. Fortunately Fynn had insisted on fortifying the magistracy buildings before his depart-ure for the front, and the windows had been reinforced with steel shutters. Beaumont decided to stick to his post. He sent orders recalling the border levies who had supported Bengough's crossing of the Mzinyathi that morning – they did not respond – and set to work barricading the doors and windows. The only Europeans with him were Mrs Fynn who 'very pluckily said she would throw in her lot with me', her children, her sister, the jailer Mr Elkington and his family 'and two or three others who were strangers to me'.[11] That evening, however, as news of the disaster spread, he was joined by the first of a stream of refugees who abandoned their missions and farms and arrived seeking protection.

Otto Witt's family were among those fleeing. Witt lost his way up the Biggarsberg escarpment as night came on and, leaving Lieutenant Purvis to try to navigate to Helpmekaar, pressed on over the ridge with August Hammar. He arrived at the Gordon Memorial Mission in Msinga, not far from the magistracy, the next morning but found that his wife had already left. She had been told by panic-stricken refugees that Otto had been killed at Rorke's Drift. Witt rode on towards Pietermaritzburg where another survivor told him his family had been overtaken and massacred. The distraught couple were finally reunited somewhere on the road.

Colonel Bray of the 4th (King's Own) Regiment was on his way up the road from Greytown to Helpmekaar with a convoy of twenty-eight wagons, including fifteen loaded with ammunition, and just twenty-two men when he met the first people fleeing in the opposite direction. He decided his position was too exposed to attempt to *laager* in the open, so he made for the nearest buildings, which turned out to be Fynn's magistracy. 'I was greatly relieved at their arrival',[12] admitted Beaumont. Bray's men formed the wagons into a circle around the courthouse and set to work knocking holes through the interior walls and making loopholes. The preparations were completed by nightfall, and they all spent an anxious night listening to the distant gunfire at Rorke's Drift. But no Zulus came, and with the first grey light of dawn Beaumont rode out to see if he could find them. Searching the border with his binoculars, all he could see were 'men, women, children and cattle streaming inland from the border'.[13]

When Dugald Macphail reached Dundee he found the village deserted. The news had outpaced him, and most of the inhabitants had fled to the stone redoubt of Fort Pine. Families who had waved their menfolk off to war enthusiastically just a fortnight before were left to fend for themselves with no idea whether their husbands, lovers, sons and brothers were still alive.

Further north in Newcastle, a day or two before, Maud Bradstreet had helped her friend Mrs Hitchcock deliver a baby girl, Georgina. Now the news came that the Newcastle Mounted Rifles had fought at iSandlwana and that both their husbands were lying dead. The two women decided to set off for the safety of friends living across the mountains in Orange Free State; it would be a week before they found a safe refuge there. The baby survived on a diet of water strained through mealie meal.[14]

Dawn on the 23rd brought the usual heavy mist to the Biggarsberg heights, smothering the ridge in a damp white fug. As the sentries of the 24th stood on the barricades at Helpmekaar, lumpy in their greatcoats against the fierce pink of morning, they heard someone approaching up the road. Suddenly a body of men loomed out of the mist, and the sentries fired several shots before the men had time to cry out that they were members of the NNC.

The garrison was still digesting the significance of their arrival when, about 9.30 a.m., a black messenger ran up with a hastily scribbled note. It was from Chard; it informed them that Rorke's Drift had held, and requested their assistance.

\*

At iSandlwana, Chelmsford had roused his men before dawn that morning in the hope of getting them on the road before the full horror of the devastated camp became apparent. 'We were all out of camp on the road to Rorke's Drift before objects could be distinctly seen', remembered Lieutenant Maxwell,[15] but even so it was light before the rearguard started out and some of the officers found excuses to ride out briefly across the field. George Hamilton Browne was among them:

> I had just time to get to the door of my tent, inside of which I saw my old setter dog, with an assegai thrust through her. My two spare horses were also lying killed at their picket rope, with my Totty groom dead between them ... I saw the bodies of two of my officers lying dead with heaps of empty cartridge shells by their sides. Both had been splendid shots and I bet they had done plenty of execution before they went under. As I reined up I glanced out to the left and left front of the camp, and saw heaps and heaps of Zulu dead. Where the volleys of the 24th had checked them, they lay in lines, and the donga I had ridden over on the morning of the 21st was chock-full of them ...
>
> I had not time to dismount as I heard the bugle sound the advance and I galloped back to my men as fast as I could without trampling on the bodies of my poor comrades. On my way I reined up my horse sharply, for there lay the body of my old friend Lieut.-Col. Pulleine; I could do nothing for him, and it at once flashed through my mind our last words of chaff, so I saluted the poor remains and passed on as quickly as I could to my men.[16]

Others also had glimpses of the devastated camp. A civil surgeon named Thrupp, attached to the 24th, stumbled across the body of a Royal Engineer officer and, noticing his watch, took it from the body. Later, when he tried to trace the owner, he discovered it was Durnford's. Trooper Symons of the Carbineers noted a young black lad, apparently a *voorlooper*, 'on his knees with his face buried in his hands on the ground, dead and stiff'.[17] Just beyond the *nek* a wagon was found half overturned in a *donga*. The oxen were tied to it and were all apparently lying dead in their traces, but as the troops passed one of them suddenly staggered to its feet. The Carbineers cut it free, and it threw up its head 'cocked his tail in the air and ran off along the road to Rorke's Drift'.[18] Fynn heard later that it was rounded up and shot by the commissariat.[19] Trooper Clarke of the Mounted Police had left the camp on the morning of the 21st without his spurs; seeing the body of Trooper Stimson, he quickly dismounted to take his and was promptly chastised by Inspector Mansel for 'robbing the dead'. 'Why leave spurs to be looted by the Zulus?' grumbled Clarke.[20]

As the column passed down the Manzimnyama valley, stories of the horrors of the night circulated freely, growing in the telling. Some of the men fell out to drink at the stream, and Lieutenant Maxwell took the opportunity to wash the stale gore from his hands, 'and felt a good deal more comfortable'.[21] There were a few Zulu homesteads near the side of the road – they had been empty when the column had advanced three days before, but now there were men in several of them, amaQungebeni probably, returned from their attack on the fugitives at Sothondose's Drift. Symons noticed that one of them, when he suddenly spotted the column, ducked away, holding his shield over his back.[22] Chelmsford gave strict orders that the Zulus should not be touched, and soldiers and Zulus stared blankly at one another as the column went by. Fynn claimed to see spears propped up against the side of one hut, and an *inyanga* burning medicine over a fire.[23] The sight was apparently too much for the NNC, a few of whom, despite Chelmsford's prohibition, fired shots into the huts and killed a man.

There was certainly a dangerous atmosphere in the column; the dreadful night had produced a fierce anger, a burning for revenge that professional discipline could not quite contain. 'We saw red', said Trooper Fred Jones of the Newcastle Mounted Rifles, and here and there the outlying vedettes came across Zulu stragglers making their way back from the Mzinyathi and shot them.[24]

As the column emerged from the Manzimnyama, the soldiers began to notice groups of men coming up from the direction of the Mzinyathi to their left front, moving across the road and onto the higher ground on their left. Large masses could be seen further on moving out of the Batshe valley. Trooper Symons thought 'they looked just like a ten-acre [4-hectare] mealie field in blossom turned black'.[25] They were no more than a 'short cannon range away,' and Arthur Harness took the precaution of unlimbering his guns in case he were ordered to 'reap a few'. Charlie Harford was so surprised that, fearing that the column was walking into a trap, and thinking 'That perhaps the masses of Zulus in the valley below us had escaped the notice of the head of the column, [I] rode on as fast as I could, to report. But I found that the General was aware of their presence and that unless they attacked, the column was to push on with all haste to Rorke's Drift.'[26]

Henry Fynn recognized them by their shields and head-rings – they were the uThulwana returning from their attack on Rorke's Drift. They were exhausted, so utterly spent in some cases that a trader living near Elandskraal, downstream of Sothondose's Drift, had seen a band of them in the distance dragging their shields by the sticks through the grass, and they were mystified, too, at the sudden appearance of a white army which they had thought utterly destroyed.[27]

So neither side had the stomach to renew the fight, and in one of the most extraordinary incidents in those extraordinary twenty-four hours, the two armies, both in their way defeated, were content to watch each other pass by.

Lieutenant Maxwell found the whole affair surreal:

> ... they appeared in some places not more than 250 or 300 yards [229 or 274 metres] from us and far outnumbered us, and had they charged us, as we were on the line of march covering some half a mile [0.8 kilometres] in length, we must have been beaten. Our ammunition being, with the exception of a very few rounds, exhausted. I was at this time in the vanguard and suddenly from the enemy on the ridge there sprang out a young warrior to the front, who by his actions and speech was endeavouring to urge the others to attack. Failing in which, he madly rushed down the hillside towards the centre of the column and was shot dead at about 30 yards' [27 metres'] distance, not one having followed or even risen from their squatting position.[28]

The Mounted Police were in the rearguard and Sergeant Mason called across and 'exchanged words' with the Zulu army. 'They passed us by', said Trooper Clarke, 'shouting a few insulting remarks.'[29] Muziwento later heard reports of those conversations from his father's neighbour, Munyu of the uThulwana. 'Forthwith the [people] who served the white men shouted to them (the soldiers uttering not a word) saying, "Where do you come from?" They replied, "We come from the other side of the river there away." "You are telling lies!" said the others. The black men [NNC] wanted to fight with them – those Zulus; but the commander of the troops forbade it. So they just went on their way.'[30]

'The two columns advancing at angles', agreed Henry Fynn, 'soon became lost to each other.'[31] A little further on Fynn noticed some saddled horses wandering beside the road; if it occurred to him that they must have belonged to fugitives killed the day before, he did not say so.

As the column passed over a low *nek* and began to descend into the Batshe valley, not far from the spot where the men had dispersed *inkosi* Sihayo's followers just a fortnight before, they saw plainly the bulk of Shiyane, still several kilometres away across the Mzinyathi. There was no view of the mission station, but a heavy pall of smoke clung to the side of the hill, furthering the impression that the Zulus they had passed were a victorious army in retreat. '"What has become of messmates?" each inquired of the other', remembered Symons, 'as we marched dolefully along looking at the smoking ruins of the hospital. "All gone" we thought as we rode down the road we had traversed but three days before with fifteen days rations and enough ammunition to have brought half a dozen Cetywayo's and their armies to nought if properly applied. Vain boast! Where are they now?'[32]

'Those that had glasses', said Maxwell, 'eagerly scanned the place, but I was looking at the river which seemed to be a perfect torrent. The ponts appeared alright, so the Infantry would have no difficulty crossing. We received orders to march on a spot further up, and to cross in the best manner we could. After a very rough time of it in the river, we found ourselves across alright with the exception of a soaking . . .'[33]

As Chelmsford's men approached Rorke's Drift, Colonel Russell, commanding the mounted troops, ordered the Volunteers to dismount and line the Zulu bank to provide cover while the Mounted Infantry crossed at the drift downstream and advanced to scout out the post 'at the best gallop their weary and hungry horses could muster after having been under saddle nearly thirty hours'. Trooper Symons heard someone shout, '"What's that on the wall?" "It's a man waving a flag. There's another, look! The place is full of them! Are they friends or are they foes?" Perhaps they were Zulus and the waving of the flags a ruse to get part of our force across the river and then fall upon us. This suspicion was roused by the sight of a large force of natives on the spur of the Biggarsberg beyond the mission station . . .'[34]

Then Symons and the other Volunteers waiting above the river bank, sights fixed at 730 metres, suddenly saw a man galloping back towards the crossing on the other side, and Symons heard him call out 'All right! They're our men!'[35]

*

The battle for Jim Rorke's house had died away in the early hours of the morning. The fighting had gone on in the same pattern as before – shouts in the darkness, a flurry of shots, a volley or two in return – and several times Chard and Bromhead had had to climb up onto the mealie bags to listen for the sounds of an impending assault, but the last rush had come about midnight, and the heart had gone out of the sporadic firefights by 2 a.m. The final shots had been fired about two hours later, and a heavy silence settled over the post, broken yet by the groans and shrieks of the wounded, all the more disturbing in the still after hour upon hour of violent cacophony.

Shortly before 5 a.m. the all-consuming darkness began to give way and the landscape started to take form again, the black outlines of the hills showing the first contrast against the lightening sky, and the sun rose about 5.20.

Daylight fell on a scene of utter devastation. A great cloud of smoke hung along the foot of Shiyane, drifting up the valley. The roof of the hospital had fallen in and the fire was largely spent but here and there stubborn rafters or the larger pieces of Otto Witt's furniture were still burning, and the air was heavy with the smell of black powder, wood smoke, and roasted flesh. The yard was littered with the casual debris of war, shields, spears, crushed helmets, broken and discarded pieces of equipment. Behind the barricades, underfoot, thousands of spent cartridge cases had been trodden into a glittering yellow carpet with the dry kernels of mealies spilled from the stabbed and torn bags. Paper wrappings from cartridge packets lay in low drifts.

And the dead lay everywhere as they had fallen, stretched out, crumpled up, draped over the barricades, lying two or three deep on that small patch of ground in front of the hospital veranda where the fighting had raged back and forth, or piled up in heaps at weak points in the barricades, limbs sticking out at odd angles, dead hands reaching out as if clinging still to the living world. In the cool morning light, the passion of battle spent, their grisly presence was overwhelming, the bodies bearing the marks of injuries inflicted at close range, the barricades spattered with blood and brains. Some of the British dead had already been stripped, *hlomula*'d and disembowelled, while Chard noted dispassionately of the Zulus that, 'Some of the bullet wounds were very curious. One man's head was split open, exactly as if done with an axe. Another had been hit just between the eyes, the bullet carrying away the whole of the back of his head, leaving his face perfect, as though it were a mask, only disfigured by the small hole made by the bullet passing through.'[36]

Quite where the living Zulus had gone was by no means clear, but Chard sent out patrols to collect up the discarded weapons, to pull down the thatch from the storehouse, and to drag away the bodies from the barricades. As the men set out, stiffly, to begin their duties, a Zulu suddenly sprang up in the calf pen, right under their guns, fired a shot at close range – it missed – then vaulted the wall and set off at a run towards the river. 'Although many shots were fired after him as he ran', said Chard in frank admiration, 'I'm glad to say the plucky fellow got off.'[37]

As the troops began to pass over the field, those men who had spent the night lying out among the dead in the bush stood up to reveal themselves. Gunner Howard threw off his cloak and rejoined his astonished companions, and Private Beckett was found lying in a ditch nearby – 'the poor fellow was so weak from loss of blood that he could not walk, and he died shortly afterwards'.[38] At the very end, Private Waters' luck almost deserted him; emerging from the cookhouse, his hands and face blackened with soot, someone mistook him for a Zulu and nearly shot him.

Private Hook wandered about, marvelling at the terrible sights. He was surprised to see one of the 24th kneeling against the barricade in the yard, slumped forward against the bags as if dozing off. 'Hello,' Hook said, 'what are you still doing here?'[39] He tipped the man's helmet back to look at his face, and saw the bullet mark between his eyes – and as he did so the man's brain fell away into the helmet. Behind the post, he sought out the man he had sniped early in the fight – 'I found him lying dead, with his skull pierced by my bullet.'[40] Then:

> Going on a little further I came across a very tall Zulu, bleeding from a wound in the leg; I was passing him by when he made a yell and clutched the butt of my rifle, dragging himself onto his knees. We had a severe struggle which lasted for several seconds, when finding he could not get the rifle from me, he let go with one hand and caught me round the leg, trying to throw me. Whilst he was doing this I got the rifle from him, and drawing back a yard or two, loaded and blew his brains out.[41]

About this time a terrified African came into the post, claiming to be a member of the NNC who had survived iSandlwana. Chard passed him over to Mr Daniels, the civilian ferryman, who spoke some Zulu. Daniels had armed himself with Spalding's sword which 'he flourished in so wild and

eccentric a manner that the poor wretch thought his last hour had come'.[42]
At last Chard was convinced by the man's story and he scribbled a hasty
note and sent him off to Helpmekaar for assistance.

Shortly afterwards, about 7 a.m., a large body of Zulus came into sight
from the direction the first attacks had come but, keeping well out of rifle
range, they moved onto the lower slopes of kwaSingqindi hill opposite and
sat down in the grass. Chard immediately recalled his men – Hook says,
intriguingly, that they brought a few wounded Zulus in with them – and
they took up their positions once more behind the barricades. It was a
heart-stopping moment – Chard's men were drained, battered and bloody
and, despite his protestations that they were 'in excellent spirits', the
chances that they could withstand a renewed determined assault were slim.
They were also running out of ammunition – B Company had started the
battle with the usual seventy rounds in their pouches, and the company
reserve, 20,000 rounds, had been among the stores. Now, however, although
'each man had a good supply of ammunition in his pouches or pockets, we
had only a box and a half left besides'.[43] Nor was there any obvious hope
of relief, since there was no reason to suppose that Lord Chelmsford had
not died with the rest at iSandlwana.

The Zulus remained on the hillside for the best part of an hour. How
many there were of them is unclear, and small parties kept appearing from
the hills and squatting down to join them – certainly some in the garrison
thought they were the majority of the force that had attacked them overnight.
Perhaps they were a rearguard who had stayed to see their comrades away;
quite possibly, however, they were the men who had split off before the
attack to scour the countryside, and had now returned to regroup; many of
them may well also have been mat-carriers rather than fighting men, some
of whom had watched the battle from that same spot all night.

If they were hoping to retire by way of the drift, however, they could
not – for as Chard later realized, 'from there they could see the Column,
long before it came in sight of us'.[44] About 8 a.m. they rose up again, and
walked slowly back the way they had come. There was no energy now for
songs of victory or defiance.

The significance of the move was at first lost on the garrison, according
to Hook:

> Then came an awful time of suspense, two of our men had been on the
> roof of the storehouse signalling with flags when the Zulus meant to

attack us . . . The signallers were still able to stand above the ground, so that they could be seen at a good distance. We saw their flags going wildly. What was it? Everybody was mad with anxiety to know whether it could be friends to relieve us, or more Zulus to destroy us.[45]

A long column of men could be seen coming down to the river on the far side, and the word went round that shields and spears could clearly be seen among them, and that some appeared to be wearing the red coats taken from the dead at iSandlwana. Then, just as the defenders braced themselves for their destruction, Colonel Russell and Lieutenant Walsh came riding up from the drift. 'We broke into roar after roar of cheering,' said Hook, 'waving red coats and white helmets . . . we cheered again and again.'[46] Yet the reunion was a bitter-sweet one, according to Walter Dunne:

Approaching cautiously at first, a mounted officer, when re-assured galloped up and anxiously inquired if any of the men from the camp at Isandhlwana had escaped and joined us. Sadly we answered 'No!' Overcome by emotion at the terrible certainty conveyed by that short word, he bent down on his horse's neck trying in vain to stifle the sobs which broke from his overcharged heart. No wonder his grief had mastered him, for he had passed the night by that camp where hundreds of his brave comrades lay slaughtered, and the hope that some portion might have fought their way through was crushed forever.[47]

Chard was in his shirtsleeves and had just had time to 'wash my face in a muddy puddle', when Chelmsford and his staff, who had crossed by the pont, rode up. Chelmsford asked to see the officers and 'thanked us all with much emotion for the defence we had made'.[48]

And suddenly it was all over. Dunne broke open some of the biscuit boxes and issued a breakfast of sorts. 'We had bully beef', said Hamilton Browne, '. . . biscuit, tea and sugar in plenty but no cups, plates, knives, forks or spoons – not even a pot or kettle to boil water in. However we made shift to eat the bully and biscuits with our fingers, then boiled water in the empty bully tins, added tea and sugar and drank it with gusto.'[49]

Fatigue parties were ordered to clear the site, dragging away the Zulu dead and collecting the British dead together. The ruins of the hospital were unstable, and ropes were thrown around it to pull down some of the walls. Hook took the opportunity to search out the remains of Sergeant Maxfield; 'I was able to identify him after because I knew where he fell and he had a blue check shirt on; there wasn't much left to identify – only a small piece of his shirt as large as a lady's handkerchief, and a small part of his body, all the rest was burnt.'[50]

Chelmsford asked to hear the story of the battle from some of those who had distinguished themselves and while his staff sought them out the rest of the garrison wandered about, explaining details to the incredulous newcomers. Hook was preoccupied with making tea, and had gone off to the cookhouse and stripped off his tunic to start a brew when, 'A sergeant ran up and said "Come as you are, straight away!" . . . and with my braces hanging about me, I went into the midst of the officers. Lord Chelmsford asked me all about the defence of the hospital, as I was the last to leave the building. An officer took our names and wrote down what we had done.'[51]

As to Chard, he and Bromhead took a few moments' well-earned rest: 'In wrecking the stores in my wagon, the Zulus had brought to light a forgotten bottle of beer, and Bromhead and I drank it with mutual congratulations on having come safely out of so much danger.'[52]

Henry Fynn was awestruck by the 'multitudes of Zulu dead, chiefly of the Tulwana regiment heaped up high against the barricading and strewn all around'.[53] Walter Dunne found them lying 'in rows, as if literally mown down', and noticed that they were all 'ring kop, that is married men who alone wear a black ring woven into the hair'.[54] Hamilton Browne, who had 'been over a good many battlefields', noted the extraordinary number of Zulus who '. . . seemed to have dropped on their elbows and knees and remained like that with their knees drawn up to their chins. One huge fellow, who must have been, in life, quite 7 feet [2.1 metres] high lay on his back with his heels at the top of the parapet and his head nearly touching the ground, the rest of his body supported by a heap of his dead comrades.'[55]

In the bush in front of the ledge they found the body of Corporal Anderson of the NNC, who had been shot before the battle began by the men of B Company. His body had not been mutilated, perhaps because the Zulus had missed him in the dark. Trooper Symons thought primly that although 'his men fled at the approach of the Zulus, that was no reason for his deserting too'.[56] Lieutenant Mainwaring of the 24th was taken over the field by his old friend Gunny Bromhead, who:

> . . . told me afterwards he felt as if he was walking on air, as he never
> expected to see daylight again . . . In front of the verandah and outside

the hospital and near the two blue gum trees the Zulu bodies were lying three deep. Gonny especially pointed out one young Zulu *Induna* with a plume headdress, telling me that he was a very gallant man, and had headed a charge three times. 'But we got him the third time,' he added.[57]

In the middle of the morning Henry Francis Fynn and Colonel Russell set off for Helpmekaar, and on the escarpment they met Major Spalding and a small group of officers, including two survivors, Smith-Dorrien and Curling, on their way down in response to the note Chard had sent for assistance. When he arrived at the mission station – where he had been only the morning before, in very different circumstances – Smith-Dorrien could not believe the scene of utter destruction that greeted him: 'All round lay dead Zulus, between three and four hundred, and there was my wagon, some 200 yards [183 metres] away, riddled and looted ... Dead animals and cattle everywhere – such a scene of devastation! To my young mind it appeared impossible that order could ever be restored ...'[58]

The dead, indeed, could not be left where they were, especially as it promised to be another hot day. Captain Hallam Parr was given the job of superintending the burials. The men of the NNC were ordered to dig a large mass grave down the slope from the storehouse, but Hallam Parr found that such was their dread of being contaminated by the *umnyama* that clung to the dead like a miasma, the NNC could not be persuaded to touch the bodies:

> ... so the soldiers had to do this part of the work. If we had had a few carts, or even horses, our labours would have been much lightened, but the dead Zulus had either to be hauled by *reims* (ropes of hide) over the ground, or carried in rough stretchers. It was disagreeable work handling the dead, naked bodies, many with awful looking wounds. The men worked hard and cheerfully, and we soon got the immediate neighbourhood of the entrenchment clear of dead bodies.
>
> 'Come on, you black devil,' I heard a man mutter to a dead Zulu he was hauling over the grass, as the body caught against a stone, 'I'm blamed if you don't give more trouble dead nor alive.'
>
> 'It's your turn now, comrade, now we've cleared the rubbish out of your way,' said another 24th man to a dead soldier, who was found with two or three Zulus stretched almost upon him. 'I'm main sorry to put you away, mate,' continued he, laying the end of a torn sack gently over the dead man's face, 'but you died well, and had a soldier's end.'[59]

Trooper Symons noted that the Zulu weapons were also collected and dumped in a pit, and brush piled over them and set alight. Many of the firearms were still loaded and 'all day long these weapons were discharging in this hole. It is surprising no one got hit.'[60]

Just fifteen of Chard's men had been killed outright – Lieutenant Maxwell saw five of them lying in the calf pen, covered over with straw – and two more mortally wounded, but most of the rest had injuries of varying degree, from gunshot wounds like those of Hitch, Dalton, Allan and Lyons, to scrapes from spears, knocks, burnt fingers from hot rifle barrels and badly bruised shoulders. Maxwell was chatting to two men of the 24th when they 'bared their shoulders and I saw that they were black and blue and swollen, caused by the recoil or kicking of their Martinis, proving to what an extent they had been firing. In fact they told me that towards daylight they were unable to place the rifle to the shoulder, but held it out pointing to the front and firing. They had during the night to change shoulders constantly, which caused both being in this state . . .'[61]

The British dead were buried on the flat between the rear of the buildings and the foot of Shiyane, on the spot where the first rush of the iNdluyengwe had been halted less than twenty-four hours before. That there were not more of them is a testament to the effectiveness of their barricades and their elevated position, which protected all but their upper bodies from Zulu bullets and spears.

By contrast Chard counted 351 Zulu dead buried in the mass grave, but these were the bodies taken from close around the mission and later he admitted that, including those found dead where they had crawled, sometimes a long way off, the figure was much higher. All in all it seems that something like 600 Zulus were killed; the number of wounded is not known, and given that wounded men falling at the foot of the barricades were in great danger of being hit again – at least during the daylight hours – it is possible that the ratio of dead to injured was unusually high. Nevertheless, a large pile of bloodied shields was found near the drift, where the Zulus had dragged their wounded; how many they were able to evacuate successfully across the river, and how many drowned in the attempt, will never be known. Altogether a figure of 1,000 casualties – killed and wounded – does not seem unreasonable. Given that the number of those who attacked the post may have been as low as 3,000, it is conceivable that one in three of the attackers was hit – an extraordinarily high proportion which speaks volumes for their courage and tenacity.

And not all of them were killed in the fighting. No sooner was Chelmsford's column back on Natal soil than it proved impossible to contain the desire for revenge. According to Hamilton Browne:

> During the afternoon it was discovered that a large number of wounded and worn out Zulus had taken refuge or hidden in the mealie fields near the *laager*. My two companies of Zulus [i.e. the iziGqoza] with some of my non-coms and a few of the 24th quickly drew these fields and killed them with bayonet, butt and assegai. It was beastly but there was nothing else to do. War is war and savage war is the worst of the lot. Moreover our men were worked up into a pitch of fury by the sights they had seen in the morning and the mutilated bodies of our poor fellows lying in front of the hospital building.[62]

Later, when rumours of this incident circulated in Natal, Captain Hallam Parr was keen play down its significance, but he admitted, 'Only two or three wounded men were found, and these were taken care of and treated by the surgeons of the force. There were never probably many; but though strict orders were given on the subject, it was impossible to prevent the Natal natives, who were slipping away to their homes, killing, according to their custom, any wounded they came across on their way.'[63]

His protestation does not ring entirely true, for if Hamilton Browne was correct in his timing, those first killings took place when Chelmsford and his staff were still present – and there are no records of any attempt to prevent them. Trooper Clarke of the Mounted Police noted that several bodies tipped into the burial pit were still displaying vital signs.[64]

Certainly, the following day, six or seven prisoners who had been captured at Phindo on the 22nd and were still under the guard of the mounted men, 'were liberated at Rorke's Drift, but were fired upon and killed as they ran before they reached the river'.[65] Trooper Symons was shocked to hear that the wounded man he had captured 'was seen being shot by a mounted officer with a revolver'.[66] Most accounts again suggest that the NNC were responsible for the killings – Symons' 'mounted officer' may well have been Hamilton Browne. Over the following weeks, any Zulu – indeed, any African suspected of being a Zulu – stood at great risk of receiving the same treatment.

By late afternoon most of the burials were complete, and the barricades had been restored to some sort of order. Chelmsford had decided that pending a review of his strategy, most of the remnants of the column

would have to stay at Rorke's Drift to prevent the Zulus making another
strike into Natal. It would not be a pleasant experience. The entire
command was now low on ammunition, and the men 'Had nothing but
what they stood in, everything even to greatcoats, had been lost; there were
no tents, no covering of any kind; all that the officers and men had to
shelter from the bitterly cold sleet and rain which fell nightly converting
the enclosed space occupied into a slough of liquid mud were their thin
kersey frocks [tunics].'[67] A few empty mealie sacks were pressed into service
as greatcoats by cutting holes in them for the arms and head.

Despite the fact that a number of the NNC had already begun to slip
away, over 1,000 men would have to sleep that night around the post in
some sort of defensible order. There was not enough room to include them
even within a modified perimeter, and the NNC was told to sleep on the
slope of Shiyane. The NNC was not happy; not only did the men resent
being outside the *laager* but a good many Zulu dead still lay undiscovered
among the crevices between the boulders. The officers and NCOs were
reluctant to turn out for picket duty, and Lonsdale, Hamilton Browne and
Charlie Harford had to stand guard themselves. During the night there was
a false alarm when a rumour passed round that the Zulus had crossed the
Mzinyathi downstream and were coming to attack the post before dawn;
the NNC's officers promptly abandoned their men and hurried into the
perimeter.

Inside the perimeter it was cramped, dirty and smelly. The smell of
wood smoke and scorched flesh still hung over the post, with an extra
piquancy now from hundreds of damp uniforms and the waft from
undiscovered corpses. A few of the Carbineers were posted in the calf pen,
sleeping on straw that had been stripped off the storehouse roof. Their
bed was lumpy and the pen stank horribly; in the morning one of the
Carbineers reached into the straw to find a cartridge that had dropped out
of his belt and found his hand touching the swollen stomach of a dead
Zulu who had lain there, unnoticed, all night.[68]

One night at the post had been enough for Lord Chelmsford. The
afternoon of the 23rd he had sat down and written to the British High
Commissioner, Sir Bartle Frere. There had been no avoiding the central
issue: 'I regret deeply to have to inform you that No. 3 column has
maintained a terrible disaster', he began, before outlining the events of
the 22nd, and ending with an observation that, perhaps, explained what he

found so inexplicable. 'The desperate bravery of the Zulus', he said, 'has been the subject of much astonishment.'[69] The following morning, he and his staff rode off to Pietermaritzburg to face the consequences – whatever else, he did not lack courage – leaving Colonel Glyn in charge at Rorke's Drift.

Ironically, his departure meant that for the first time since the campaign began Glyn retrieved his independent command – and in circumstances which, with bitter irony, could hardly for him have been more desolate. As a major in 1866 he had been one of the officers who had received the new Colours of the 1/24th when they were presented to the battalion by the Countess of Kimberley at the curragh in Ireland. In the years since he had served with both the 1st and 2nd Battalions, and had commanded the 1st since 1867. The officers of the 24th had been the fabric of his professional and personal life; now, the Queen's Colour was lost, his adjutant Teignmouth Melvill was missing, and a score of officers he had served alongside for years lay unburied among the grass at the foot of iSandlwana.

Before he left, Chelmsford had asked Rupert Lonsdale to ascertain the state of the 3rd Regiment NNC. Lonsdale paraded the regiment. They were certainly demoralized, the black troops having been unnerved by the sight of British troops in defeat and by the fate of Gabangaye kaPhakade, while, after the various scares of the past few days, the white officers and NCOs had clearly lost faith in their men. Lonsdale addressed them, asking them whether they would be prepared to return to Zululand once British fortunes improved. After some discussion among themselves the iziGqoza came forward and said that they would – the rest seemed less inclined. Under the circumstances it is difficult to blame them; they had been hastily pressed into service, had received inadequate training, were poorly armed, were often abused and mistreated by their officers, and had been pitched into battle against a determined enemy who had old scores to settle. By now, however, Lonsdale had lost patience with them and he decided to dismiss the lot. He allowed Hamilton Browne to address a few choice remarks to them – from which the iziGqoza were specifically excluded – and then their rifles and red headbands were collected up.

Hamilton Browne spoke through an interpreter '. . . and guessed from his vehemence and impassioned gestures he was emphasizing my remarks with a few of his own. I told them that the Great White Queen would send them women's aprons when she heard of their cowardice and that they had better go home and dig in the fields with their wives. This is the greatest insult you can offer a warrior and they hung their heads in shame.'[70]

According to Charlie Harford:

> The matter of collecting arms and equipment from our men was taken in hand at once, and took some little time. They were all, of course, allowed to retain their blankets, much to their joy – and with as much beef as they could stuff themselves with ... were in fine spirits. I shall never forget the scene of their departure, we started them off soon after sunrise and the whole mass ... bounded gaily off, laughing and joking and performing all sorts of antics, then presently dividing into separate parties, making bee-lines for their homes, very soon presented the appearance of a swarm of ants covering the hillsides.[71]

Only the iziGqoza companies '... forming themselves into solid rings, marched past our troops of officers, raising their shields in the air, in salute, and rattled their assegais against them; then breaking into a war-song marched proudly away, every one of them a man and a warrior.'[72] It was an impressive display – and a deeply ironic echo of the calibre of men the British were up against.

Lonsdale himself rode off to Helpmekaar, leaving Hamilton Browne in charge of the European officers and NCOs. And so the 3rd Regiment of the Natal Native Contingent ceased to exist.

Chelmsford had taken Harness's battery and the mounted men with him, and he left them at Helpmekaar to shore up the wider defence of the border. The sight of the weary Zulu army retreating from Rorke's Drift had suggested there was no immediate danger of a Zulu counter-offensive, but word of the disaster was sure to sweep rapidly through the civilian population. He would need to act promptly to assuage the panic in the colony's white population and reassure its black. The plans he had drawn up for the defence of the colony would need to be implemented as quickly as possible. Worse still, he would have to inform the Government in London that a war it had not authorized had not only begun – but gone disastrously wrong.

# 27

# 'Wet with yesterday's blood'

## The aftermath, January–May 1879

At 2 p.m. on Wednesday, 22 January 1879, Sir Theophilus Shepstone, Administrator of the Transvaal, erstwhile Secretary for Native Affairs in Natal, one of the principal architects of the Anglo-Zulu War, was in the border town of Utrecht, in the heart of the disputed territory. He was walking with H.W. Struben, a member of the displaced Boer Volksraad (its parliament), a man of pro-British sympathies who had, nonetheless, opposed the 'underhand' way the British annexation had been carried out. Shepstone and Struben were discussing political affairs when suddenly 'it became dark, and for a moment neither of us realized it was a total eclipse of the sun'. Shepstone was uneasy, sensing that the eclipse was an ill omen; 'Struben,' he said, 'this may have a strange effect on the Zulus, who are superstitious.'

Later that same day, when Shepstone saw Alan Gardner arrive in town, exhausted and dishevelled after his long ride, he recalled the premonition he had had when first told that his son George had been attached to Durnford's staff. 'It is strange but true,' he said, 'that when I heard he had been appointed to serve Colonel Durnford, I felt as if I had heard his death warrant.'

Now he knew what the eclipse portended, and for a few minutes he could not bring himself to speak to Gardner, directing him to explain his story to Struben instead. As soon as the news began to circulate, a group of elderly Africans came to Shepstone to ask if it were true. '*Umtwanami ufile, uGeorge ugwazile*'; 'My child is dead,' Shepstone said, 'George is stabbed.'

'He was quite overcome' said Struben.[1]

*

On 25 January, at a homestead in northern Zululand, a young Dutch trader, Cornelius Vijn, was sitting inside a hut chatting to a messenger who had been sent by the king to ask after his welfare when he heard a commotion outside.

Vijn's story was an extraordinary one. He had been trading into Zululand regularly for years, and had crossed into the kingdom with a wagon-load of goods at the beginning of November 1878. He had been warned not to go because of the tense political situation, but having heard plenty of war scares over the years he had refused to listen, and so he had found himself in the country when war broke out. Feeling against the whites was strong, particularly among the young men, and at first he had feared for his life, but he had managed to send a message to Cetshwayo begging for protection, and the king had assured him of his safety. Vijn had been sent under care of royal *izinduna* to a secure part of the country, and his goods and cattle had not been touched. There he intended to wait out the war.

That morning, however, his attention:

> Was drawn to a troop of people, who came back from their gardens crying and wailing. As they approached, I recognized them as persons belonging to the kraal in which I was staying. When they came into or close to the kraal, they kept on wailing in front of the kraals, rolling themselves on the ground and never quieting down; nay, in the night they wailed so as to cut through the heart of anyone. And this wailing went on, night and day, for a fortnight; the effect of it was very depressing; I wished I could not hear it.
>
> The reason for this was that the headman of the Kraal, Msundusi, a trusty person and the husband of four wives, had fallen in the fight at Isandhlwana. It is true, on that day, the Zulus over-powered the Whites, and killed them in a way which my pen cannot describe, more than 1,200 Whites having been put to death in a dreadful manner. But also the Zulus, according to their account, many thousands had been left behind on the field – Dabulamanzi told me they had been buried – never more to return to their homes, and still more were wounded.[2]

It took just three days for news of the battle to pass across the kingdom. The same day that it reached Vijn in northern Zululand, a British vedette with the coastal column, at Eshowe in the south of the country, heard the cry being passed from hill-top to hill-top that a great victory had been won. As the army of national defence began to disperse, however, and men who had fought returned home, the cost of the victory became apparent, and the news was greeted not with celebration, as the triumph it undoubtedly was, but with outpourings of grief for the terrible losses.

How many Zulus were killed outright in the attack on the camp will never be known, but although some British accounts claimed optimistically that the figure was as high as 3,000, Mehlokazulu and others thought 'there might have been 1000 killed there'.[3] In addition, thousands more were wounded, some, like Mlambula Matebula, hit several times. The *amabutho* remained in the Ngwebeni valley for three days after the battle to allow the worst of their wounded to recover enough to face the journey home – or to die. Then the survivors began the long walk of many kilometres to get home.

At the end of the Anglo-Zulu War a British officer, Captain William Molyneux, would reflect on how the impact of the fighting reached into almost every homestead in the country:

One large kraal I visited ... was full of wounded men, who were as friendly as possible, and as merry as could be. One had lost two brothers at Isandhlwana, and had been wounded at Ulundi himself; his regiment was the Nkobamakosi ... How he got home in a fortnight he scarcely knew; it was very hard work, for he had been wounded in the thigh, but the other boys had helped him ... The many little mounds outside, covered with stones, told how many of the poor fellows had crawled home simply to die.[4]

Three years after iSandlwana, in 1882, the traveller Bertram Mitford would meet many veterans of the battle, some of them bearing impressive scars testifying to the fact that they had survived terrible injuries. Yet the obvious fact remained that they were the lucky ones, for, as Molyneux recognized, the return home was itself a brutal ordeal, and many made it only to succumb later to their injuries or to infection. Mitford met:

One young Zulu, a light-hearted, talkative fellow ... [who] had been shot in the leg at Isandhlwana soon after the fight commenced, and had lain on the ground until two of his brothers carried him out of harm's way, so was not able to see the end. I put in a suggestion to the effect that it was better to be shot through the leg at the beginning of the fight than through the head at the end of it, which aspect of the case seemed to vastly tickle his imagination, for he went into a fit of laughter and emphatically agreed with the idea ...[5]

There was nothing laughable about the return from the Ngwebeni as the *amabutho* began to drift away, carrying their wounded and their loot with them, those who had killed still wearing the tunics of their victims, splashes of red, blue, black and yellow among the mass of uneven browns and black-and-white shields. It was the custom that a victorious army should return to the king where the cleansing rites would take place, where the rights to the loot would be apportioned, and so that the king could discuss the battle with his commanders and apportion honours and blame. In that third week of January 1879, however, many of the veterans of the battle of iSandlwana were so exhausted that they had no time for custom – they simply went back to their wives and families to recover from the experience as best they could.

Ntshingwayo and Mavumengwana took the rest back to oNdini. Along the way, people were shocked by their appearance, for 'the warriors returned from battle carrying the fury of war on their backs. They were covered in blood and had tied up their wounds with grass.'[6] When the royal queens, the widows of King Mpande, saw the terrible state they were in they scolded the king, saying the losses were due to him leaving the *inkatha* now and then while the battle was in progress.

When they arrived, after several days' march, the *izinxweleha*, those who were 'wet with yesterday's blood' and still in a state of powerful ritual contamination, were separated off from the rest and taken to an appointed homestead nearby to be cleansed.[7] They could not report to the king until they had, 'on the ground that that would have been a source of evil influence on the king'.[8] The cleansing ceremonies took four or five days, and each day the *izinxweleha* went down to a nearby river, in groups according to their *amabutho*, singing the war-songs they had sung in the battle, wearing their captured uniforms and carrying their spears, which were still encrusted with dried blood, point upwards. At a point down-stream from wherever drinking water was drawn they bathed, washing off the taint and stain of battle. Some of them had brought their own medicines with them in their necklaces and could perform the necessary rituals without the guidance of an *inyanga*; for the rest, the specialist doctors again burnt special herbs on potsherds over a fire, as they had done at the start of the campaign, adding this time the contents of the stomach of a slaughtered beast. These were mixed with liquids into a pot and the *izinxweleha* came up in turn, dipping their fingers into the brew, sucking it off, then, jumping over the pot 'this way and that, squirting the medicine as he does so, this way and that, in the direction of the foe', and shouting 'Come out, evil spirit, come out, evil spirit, fall, evil spirit.'[9]

Once this ceremony was complete they formed together into a body, and were sprinkled with medicines and taken before the king. The king had also been prepared to meet them, his body smeared with strong medicines, and he had entered into that communion with the ancestors of the nation in a spiritual state the Zulu characterized as a deep rage. A man named Mtshayankomo kaMagolwane, who had fought at iSandlwana with the uKhandempemvu, described how the *izinxweleha*:

> ... went into the enclosure where the cattle from the open veld were kept ... the companies crossed one another's paths, one approaching from the east, another from the west. As we went we exclaimed, 'By us! [i.e. we did it!] By us! By us!' Others exclaimed 'What did we leave them? What did we leave them?' Others exclaimed 'It is war! It is war!' 'By us! By us!' Each man shouted his own cry. The king was now standing in his own enclosure ... He came out in a rage, his visage was awful; he could no longer be looked upon. He came out, and passed through us, coming down to the main enclosure. His chair was brought, and he sat down. We then stood and saluted, calling 'Bayede! You are the elephant! ... You of the innermost circle! You who devour men! Black lion!' The king said, 'Speak now. Tell me what you have experienced.'[10]

This was the time for the *izinduna* to step forward, reporting how their men had behaved in battle. Sometimes these discussions grew quite heated, the *izinduna* striding about, *giyaing*, growing fierce in defence of their men in the face of some implied criticism. The bets laid between the *amabutho* were recalled, and the performances assessed, although the wagers laid were never called in. It was a great point of honour among the *amabutho* to be recognized as the first to penetrate the enemy lines, to come to grips with them and 'stab' the enemy. All the *izinxweleha* had brought with them thin sticks of willow which they had cut and stripped of the bark themselves – if their *ibutho* was recognized as the first, they would have the right to cut the sticks to make a necklace of small interlocking beads, the *iziqu*, which was the public mark of the *iqawe*, the hero.

After iSandlwana, the debate was intense. The uKhandempemvu, iNgobamakhosi and uMbonambi all claimed to have stabbed the white soldiers first. Cetshwayo had discussed this privately with his generals, and had already decided who deserved the honour. At the assembly he called out Ntuzwa kaNhlaka, the commander of the uMbonambi. Ntuzwa was carrying his own willow stick and handed it to the king, and after a few moments teasing, in which Cetshwayo shook the stick like a spear and pretended to throw it towards the other candidates, he hurled it in the direction of the uMbonambi who had won the right by virtue of being the first among the tents. As it turned out, this would prove to be the last time the heroes were marked out before the assembled representatives of the nation as a whole, for in the future the willow-sticks would not be cut by those who had distinguished themselves fighting against foreign invaders but rather in wars fought against fellow Zulus.

Then it was time to recognize and reward individual courage and chastise cowardice. The right to all the loot taken in the battle was the king's, and although many men had taken and kept personal property, it was expected that the most important items, cattle and firearms, be presented to him. The custom was that a portion of the cattle would remain as part of the national herd while the rest would be distributed to men who had greatly distinguished themselves. These men were selected by discussion, again between the king and his councillors, called forward, and given beasts according to their deeds. Because of the nature of the battle at iSandlwana there were fewer cattle to go round than might normally be expected of a victorious campaign, and the names of those so honoured have not come down to us. There were more firearms, but so jealously were they guarded – and so sorely needed – that the king wisely decided to let all those who had taken a gun keep it.

Cowards, too, were named and shamed, although if there were any after iSandlwana their disgrace, too, has been forgotten. It was King Shaka's habit to make an example of cowards, to 'encourage the others' at a time when the rapid expansion of the kingdom was dependent on the resolve of his soldiers, and a bush still stands on the hills outside Eshowe, close to the site of his kwaBulawayo homestead, where he used to sit and judge his army on their return from a campaign. There the cowards were picked out, held fast, and small spears, used for slaughtering goats, were driven into their chests below the armpit. Shaka's successors had not been so strict, however, and by 1879 it had become the custom to 'name and shame' cowards, picking them out in front of the assembled *amabutho* and condemning their actions. The king would slaughter beasts from the royal herds and the meat would be roasted to feed his men and brought forth on wooden platters. Before distributing it, however, he would call out 'Put the cowards' meat in the water!', and it would be dunked, and served to them cold and wet so that 'the prime meat would go to the heroes alone'.[11] Sometimes one of the heroes would take the meat and dash it in the face of a coward himself, daring him to complain, and such was the stigma attached to this treatment that a coward's girlfriend would desert him rather than have it said that 'two girls go about together'. Only by distinguishing himself in a future battle might a man 'leave the potsherd of the cowards' and eat the meat of heroes once again.

Yet there were more pressing concerns that January than the alleged misdeeds of a few individuals. The level of casualties was deeply shocking. Although Ntshingwayo's handling of the battle had been competent, the king was deeply displeased that so many lives had been lost. Sishishili kaMnqandi, an officer of the uKhandempemvu and a royal favourite, whom Cetshwayo had asked to report on the army's performance, put the blame squarely on Ntshingwayo and Mavumengwana for having lost control of the *amabutho* and allowed them to fight before they were properly prepared. As a result, the commanders forfeited a good deal of the public acclaim that was due by right of their victory, although ironically the fault lay as much with the king's own policies; it was Cetshwayo's insistence that the engagement only take place when the British had been manoeuvred into the obvious position of aggressors that had allowed the *amabutho* to be caught unprepared.

The king was annoyed, too, that none of the British officers had been captured alive and brought to him as prisoners – he had hoped they might have intelligence of the British plans and he wanted them as a bargaining tool during any subsequent negotiations:

> ... [He] asked the induna when they reached Ulundi where the guns and plunder were, and also how it was that they had not taken any officers prisoners. They told him that the guns were left on the battlefield, and that one was capsized and broken; as for taking prisoners, that was impossible in the heat of the fight, and especially as the white men fought to the last, so could not have been taken prisoners; besides, they could not tell an officer from a soldier. Cetywayo replied that the officers were armed with swords, and the soldiers with rifles, and added 'Don't you see how useful it would have been to me to have some officers as prisoners?' He was altogether much displeased ...[12]

He was particularly furious about the attack on Rorke's Drift which had taken place in spite of his express orders that his army should not cross into Natal. Zibhebhu's discreet absence at the time – albeit looting on his own account – left Prince Dabulamanzi to take the blame for this alone. In the manner of unsuccessful commanders the world over, Dabulamanzi hedged his report by stressing his successes: 'Of the Rorke's Drift fight Cetywayo received the most imperfect news. Dabulamanzi reported that he had successfully stormed and taken "the house"; he attacked, and then retired, but admitted that he had suffered heavily.'[13]

The cost to the uThulwana – Cetshwayo's own *ibutho* – had, however, been obvious enough:

> The king, according to custom, received them in the grand kraal. He had only as yet received the news that the white man's camp had been taken, that 'Somtseu's' column had been eaten up. He had not heard of the repulse at Rorke's Drift, nor was he prepared for the terrible gaps made in his regiments. As the men began to file into the enclosure, he saw there had been very different fighting to that he had known in Amaswazi and Amatonga country [against African enemies].
>
> The Tulwana was the last regiment, and it filed in and saluted. 'Why don't the rest come in?' cried the king, impatiently. But the rest of the brave Tulwana could not hear him, for they were lying outside the mealie bags and biscuit boxes at Rorke's Drift.[14]

Dabulamanzi found it politic to retire to his homestead nearer the coast, away from the seat of government, but his attack was widely seen as folly by the kingdom at large and he served as a scapegoat for the frustration and anger felt by the people at their losses. Mehlokazulu remarked damningly that Dabulamanzi was not a good general – 'he is too hasty' – but according to Muziwento the unfortunate men of the uThulwana received the full force of the public's scorn: 'The Mbozankomo regiment was finished up at Jim's – shocking cowards they were too. Our people laughed at them, some said "You! You're no men! You're just women, seeing that you ran away for no reason at all, like the wind!" Others jeered and said, "You marched off. You went to dig little bits with your assegais out of the house of Jim, that had never done you any harm!"'[15]

It was a reaction in stark contrast to the public adulation that would steadily accrue to the defenders.

\*

The news had already reached Pietermaritzburg by the time Lord Chelmsford got there. Walter Stafford and Harry Davies had ridden into the colonial capital on the evening of the 23rd to find that a fellow survivor, Trooper Berning of the Newcastle Mounted Rifles, had beaten them to it by a few hours. Somehow rumours of iSandlwana had already reached the town's black population, and many white citizens awoke the following morning to find themselves without domestic staff. When the first list of casualties was produced a few days later and a return of colonial losses was posted the capital was stunned; many of the town's most prominent settler families were connected to the Carbineers dead, and it seemed that for a second time the name of Durnford lay at the heart of their grief.

Once news spread beyond the town confines, people began flocking in from the neighbouring countryside, and Lieutenant-Colonel Mitchell, the town commandant, hastily organized the construction of a town *laager*, ordering significant buildings to be loopholed and linking together blocks of houses and shops with barricades. When the news reached Durban volunteers were posted on the hills outside the town to watch for a Zulu approach, and a barricade was built across the Point to shelter civilians. The panic was mirrored the length of the colony, settlers abandoning their farms and converging on hastily prepared defensive *laagers*.

Bartle Frere, practised imperial administrator that he was, had taken the news on the chin. 'I had a long talk with Sir B. Frere this morning over the state of affairs,' wrote Chelmsford on the 28th, 'it is fortunate that there is one with so cool a head and so stout a heart at the head of affairs at the present juncture.'[16] Yet the state of affairs was undeniably grim – Chelmsford's invasion lay in tatters. The Centre Column – his main thrust, under his personal command – had been driven out of Zululand after less than a fortnight's campaigning, and the loss of men, supplies, ammunition and transport meant that what remained of it was immobilized until it could be resupplied.

Catching up on the news of the wider campaign at Pietermaritzburg, Chelmsford found that both his flanking columns – Wood to the north and Pearson on the coast – had also been heavily engaged. On the 22nd – a few hours before the attack on iSandlwana – Pearson had defeated the troops Cetshwayo had allocated to the defence of the southern border, and early on the 23rd, about the same time Chelmsford had arrived back at Rorke's Drift, Pearson had occupied his first objective, the mission station at Eshowe. As for Wood, he had set out to attack the abaQulusi around their strongholds at the Zungwini and Hlobane mountains; he had driven them off Zungwini – the Zulus there had interpreted the eclipse as a portent of their own disaster – and had been skirmishing along the foot of Hlobane when the message dispatched by Alan Gardner warning him of the disaster at iSandlwana reached him. At which point, commented a sergeant under his command, Wood had 'thought of his own small camp, 3 days in the rear of him. He ordered a return march at once and marched all night and day until he got to camp.'[17] Under other circumstances both reports might have been considered good news but, with the Centre Column between the two flanks gone, Chelmsford's original plan for a concerted advance had collapsed. There was little he could do but write to both commanders to halt their advance and tell them that, for the time being, they were on their own.

He also sent a telegram to Colonel Stanley, the Secretary of State for War in London. He hid nothing, and the bald facts seem all the more shocking for his cool and measured tone:

> I regret to have to report a very disastrous engagement which took place on the 22nd instant between the Zulus and a portion of No. 3 Column left to guard a camp about ten miles [16 kilometres] in front of Rorke's Drift – the former came down in overwhelming numbers and, in spite of gallant resistance made by six companies of the 24th Regiment, 2 guns, 2 Rocket-tubes, 104 mounted men and about 800 natives, completely overwhelming them . . .[18]

'The effects of this reverse have already been very serious', he added, somewhat unnecessarily, before adding plaintively 'additional reinforcements must be sent out'.

The telegram reached London on 11 February, and the effect on a government and public who had only the haziest idea they were at war in Zululand was electric.

\*

At Rorke's Drift life had remained miserable and strained, the unburied dead on the other side of the river an all-pervasive and unseen presence and the overwrought nerves of the garrison little assuaged by the slight improvement in security.

With the expulsion of the Centre Column from Zulu soil, and the survivors demoralized and reluctant to move far beyond the confines of the post at Rorke's Drift, the Zulus enjoyed unchallenged access to the battlefield at iSandlwana.

Once the British had gone, some of the amaQungebeni had begun to return to their homes nearby. The *amabutho* had had neither the time nor the capability to remove everything from the site on the afternoon of the 22nd, and a good deal remained strewn about and scattered in the grass, and the temptation to explore the ruined camp was strong. *Inkosi* Sihayo himself – who, since the army had disbanded and since the destruction of kwaSogekle, had been living at another of his homesteads, eZulaleni, on the eastern fringe of his territory, far away from the dangerous border – sent some of his men, and they dragged away four of the best wagons, while Matshana kaMondise took two.

Even so, the battlefield remained an awe-inspiring and terrifying space, and it took considerable courage to venture onto it, for the dead remained a fierce source of *umnyama* and the material benefits to be gained had to be weighed against the risk of misfortune to follow. There could be no question of the families who had previously lived on the battlefield returning to their homes, as many of them now contained Zulu dead in the grain-pits. Like boys the world over, however, young Muziwento and his friends could not resist exploring for themselves, despite their parents' disapproval, and Muziwento's description of the site just four days after the battle remains one of the most chilling eyewitness accounts to emerge from the whole iSandlwana saga:

> We went to see the dead people at Isandhlwana. We saw a single warrior dead, staring in our direction, with his shield in his hand. We ran away. We came back again. We saw countless things dead. Dead was the horse, dead too the mule, dead was the dog, dead was the monkey, dead were the wagons, dead were the tents, dead were the boxes, dead was everything, even to the very metals. We took some thread for sewing and a black pocket-book; we played with the boxes; we took the tent ropes and played with them. We thought to return home. As for Umdeni he took some biscuit, but I and my brother declined. We said 'We don't like them.' We went off, they carrying them . . . We asked for some. Said Umdeni, 'O! We don't choose, for you said you didn't like them.' We retorted, 'O! Sit there, if you please, with your little bits of bread smelling of people's blood!' This we said, being with envy. We then returned home.
>
> At daylight we came back again. We saw some boys who had died

in a tree, underneath it. They were dressed in black clothes. We saw white men dead (they had taken off their boots, all of them), and the people also who had served them, and fought with them, and some Zulus, but not many . . .

I took some boots for my part, and a satchel. I put on the black boots. Our brother also took some boots. He sat in a wagon and put them on. But no sooner had we put on the boots, than the people from home shouted 'You're dead! Look at the army away there!' We undid the boots; they refused. We burst them. We flung away our satchels. Our brother threw his away in a moment. I – I was a long time in taking mine off; he forsook me. I got mine off after a short time. I tore along with the utmost speed; I overtook our brother, and leaving him behind in my turn, arrived first at home. The people said, 'There is no army.'[19]

Watching through field glasses from the top of Shiyane, the British garrison could clearly see the abandoned wagons on the *nek*, and watched with frustration as the Zulus picked them over. Charlie Harford noted ruefully that '. . . for the first week or so small parties of Zulus could be seen clearly through our glasses, wandering about, searching the place all over, no doubt, for either full or empty cartridges. Several were dressed in white shirts, some of which were undoubtedly my property, as I had a dozen new ones in my portmanteau.'[20]

King Cetshwayo had been indignant that his commanders had not thought to bring him the cannons lost by the British at iSandlwana. They were important as tangible trophies of his success, and if the Zulus could work out how to use them they might add significantly to their war effort. A week after the fight he sent men down to recover them. One was found in front of the camp – whether it had fallen from the limber during the retreat or had been dragged there subsequently is unclear – while the other still lay in the *donga* in the Manzimnyama valley, where Curling had seen the limbers come to grief. Since they had no limbers of their own or draught horses, Cetshwayo's men dragged them all the way to oNdini by hand.

\*

On 29 January No. 5 Field Company Royal Engineers under Captain Walter Jones finally arrived at Helpmekaar. This was Chard's company, so long delayed on the road by the weather, and it was accompanied by Colonel F.C. Hassard, RE, who became the senior ranking officer. The same day four companies of the 4th Regiment arrived, increasing the number of available infantry companies to six.

Jones' sappers at once set to work to improve the border posts. Half of the company marched forward to Rorke's Drift, while the remainder dug a deep trench around the sheds at Helpmekaar, piling the earth up to form a rampart with a formidable parapet and bastions at the corners. In this fortification Hassard, according to Clery, 'shut himself up ... and strongly recommended everybody else to do the same'.[21] In fact Hassard did not feel up to the command and soon handed it over to Colonel Bray of the 4th – the man who had fortified the Msinga magistracy on the evening of the 22nd.

At Rorke's Drift the sappers pulled down the old mealie bag barricades – many of which were still bloodstained, and all of which were sodden, beginning to rot and giving off a foul smell – and laid out the profile of a new stone fort. Stones were taken from the Shiyane terraces – the bodies of several dead Zulus were found in the process, but a number of the 24th found time to carve their regimental numbers into exposed slabs of sandstone, where they can still be seen to this day – and a high loopholed wall constructed around the storehouse.

The new post was named Fort Bromhead, but life there was only marginally more pleasant than it had been among the old barricades. The survivors of Glyn's command slept every night within the fort's confines, and even without the rank and file of the NNC, the Artillery and mounted men, it was still cramped and unsanitary. 'To make matters worse', recalled Charlie Harford, '... we had a lot of rain, and the interior of the Fort became a simple quagmire from the tramping of so many feet. Fatigue parties were employed for the best part of the day in carrying liquid mud away and emptying the slush outside. In this state of filth we lived and ate and slept for more than two months, no-one being in possession of anything more than a blanket and the clothes that he stood up in.'[22]

The one exception to this were the men of B Company, who in recognition of their heroic defence were allowed to sleep in one of the few dry spots at the post – in the attic of the storehouse. The thatch had been stripped off but a tarpaulin had been thrown over the rafters to keep off the rain. 'However', said Harford,

... even they had their troubles in trying to keep dry, as the tarpaulin often bagged in between the rafters with a collection of water which had to be ejected, and I shall not easily forget one particular night when Dr. Reynolds ... and I met in the dark having been literally washed out of our sleeping place, and mooched about, endeavouring to find a more sheltered spot. Suddenly we hit upon the idea of lying down under the eaves of B Company's roof, so coiled ourselves up in our soaking wet blankets, thanking our stars that at all events there would be no river running under us, when presently swish came about half a ton of water clean on top of us. B Company were emptying their tarpaulin![23]

There were plenty of Zulu bodies still about the place too, their presence becoming all the more readily identifiable by the smell as each day passed. 'At various times for a period of six weeks', recalled Lieutenant Maxwell, 'bodies were found in the caves and among the stones on this mountain [Shiyane], and two months afterwards two brother officers and myself discovered in a cave near the summit three bodies, which were quite hard and sound. These had been wounded and managed to crawl thus far to die ...'[24]

Perhaps, indeed, they were rather the bodies of important men killed in the battle, who had been dragged into caves by way of burial by their comrades before the *impi* departed. Some weeks after the fight Harford was patrolling when he came across 'the body of a very fine specimen of a Zulu in the skeleton stage'. He took Surgeon Reynolds out to see it, and '... he too was impressed with the stature and splendid proportions, and brought away one or two bones of scientific interest, and the soles of his feet which had become detached and were just like solid pieces of horn. I also took the collar bones and the lesser bones of one of the arms, which I intended some day to give to the Durban Museum ...'[25]

Even under such trying circumstances, Harford, it seems, could not quite free himself from the allure of a good specimen. Some weeks later, when the situation at last began to ease, a Natal trader risked the proximity of the border to offer a wagon-load of goods to the garrison. Several times the officers of the 24th had shared their meagre rations with Hamilton Browne's NNC officers, and Browne was keen to return the favour. He discovered that the trader had a large bottle of gin with him, 'for his own use', and after offering various inducements persuaded him to part with it. That evening, Browne invited Major Black and several 24th officers to share this untold luxury with him.

'Harford', said I, 'where's the gin?' and at once my heart darkened with apprehensions. 'Oh, Commandant', quoth he, 'I have caught such a lot of beauties.' and he produced two large pickle bottles filled with scorpions, snakes and other foul creeping beasts and reptiles. 'Do look at them.' 'But the gin, Harford?' I murmured, so full of consternation that I could hardly articulate. 'I've preserved these with it,' said he, utterly oblivious to his horrid crime . . .[26]

In such conditions it is hardly surprising that the health of the garrison began to deteriorate, and many of the men who slept in the open, lying on mud and exposed to the rain at night, began to suffer from a variety of fevers and dysentery. Over the next few weeks, several of them were to die; they were buried in the growing cemetery behind the storehouse, alongside the victims of the battle. Even Chard was not immune, going down with fever and being sent down the line to Ladysmith to recover.

Inevitably, particularly for the first fortnight after the fighting, morale was very low and the garrison lived in expectation of fresh Zulu attacks. Several men, including Chard, were haunted by the events they had witnessed, dreaming of them, tossing and turning and crying out in their sleep. Colonel Glyn became withdrawn and listless, and with no sense of purpose to focus nervous energies on, false alarms became a frequent occurrence. Hamilton Browne described a typical incident:

We had attached to us a civilian doctor, a very good fellow, who had seen much service and who had distinguished himself in the Russo-Turkish War. He, however, had a bad go of fever and his nerves had all gone to pieces though he still did his duty. Well one night I was lying down fast asleep in the angle of the *laager* I was in charge of; the aforesaid angle, having been the ancient pig-pen of the farm, was by no means a pleasant bedroom, although airy enough, and we had just had our usual rain-storm, when I was suddenly woken up by the doctor who in an excited tone said 'For God's sake, Commandant, get up, the Zulus are on us.' I was up in a second and the muttered order, 'Stand to your arms,' was answered by a rustle as the men rose from their mud beds and manned the parapet. The pig-kraal angle was the most exposed portion of the *laager* and being the nearest the river was the most likely to be attacked first. A sharp click as the breeches of the rifles were opened and shut, a sharper rattle as the 24th stood to arms and fixed bayonets and every man was at his post.

Not a further sound. Not a word spoken.

I got into the most advanced spot and peered out into the darkness but could see nothing.

A bit of a moon and the stars gave a glimmer of light that would have flashed on the Zulu spears and given them away had they been there, but I saw not a spark nor a flash.

I could see the white range markers that I had had put up and had any large body of men been between them and me they would have been obscured, so evidently my corner of the *laager* was not in danger of immediate attack.

Just then Colonel Glyn (the O.C.) came round. 'What is it, Commandant Browne?' he said to me. 'I don't see anything, sir.' I replied, 'There can be no large number of the enemy on this front.' 'Who gave you the alarm?' 'Doctor—' The Colonel turned sharply round. 'What is it Dr—? Why did you give the alarm sir?' 'Good God, don't you hear them sir?' Said the medico, excitedly. 'Hear them? Hear what sir?' snorted the enraged Colonel. 'Why, the frogs, sir', ejaculated the doctor. 'The Zulus are waking them as they advance.'

A dead man could have heard the frogs. Anyone who has ever been in Natal or further north knows the diabolical row the frogs kick up, after rain . . .[27]

Conditions up the road at Helpmekaar were no better. Lieutenant Curling had returned there with Harness's battery on the 24th, and wrote to his mother a few days later:

Those who have escaped have not a rag left as they came away in their shirt-sleeves. We always sleep at night in the fort or *laager* as it is called and in the open air. It is very unpleasant as it rains nearly every night and is very cold. None of us have more than one blanket each so you can see we are having a rough time. The first few days I was utterly done up but have pulled round all right now. What is going to happen no one knows. We have made a strong entrenchment and are pretty safe even should we be attacked. The only thing we are afraid of is sickness. There are 50 sick and wounded already who are jammed up at night in the fort. The smell is terrible . . .[28]

Among those sick and wounded were survivors of iSandlwana and Rorke's Drift. Poor Trooper Hayes, who had so troubled his tentmate Trooper Dorehill by crying out in the night that the Zulus were coming was still tormented in his dreams in the comparative safety of the *laager* at Helpmekaar. He died of fever on 20 March, and was buried alongside others in a small walled cemetery on the heights.

The wounded from Rorke's Drift were transported on 26 January to Helpmekaar, where they came under the care of a dedicated and conscientious surgeon of the Army Medical Department, D. Blair-Brown. The facilities were scarcely any better than those at Rorke's Drift, but Blair-Brown improvised beds in one of the zinc storage sheds by laying empty mealie sacks on rows of biscuit boxes, and on these he did his best for his patients, washing Dalton's wounds with quinine – 'I had no antiseptic' – applying poultices to reduce the swelling on Hitch's and Scammell's shattered shoulders, washing and 'sloughing' Allan's flesh-wound. Corporal Lyons' injuries troubled him the most since Lyons had been largely paralysed by the shot that struck him in the neck, and could not move or feel his arms. Blair-Brown put Lyons out with chloroform and made a prolonged attempt to find the bullet, tracing its course down the spine; he could not, and Lyons was still in a bad way when Blair-Brown sent him down the line to the base hospital at Ladysmith. A month later he came under Blair-Brown's care again, and on examining him Blair-Brown found a lump beneath the muscle that had not been there before. He cut it open and extracted the bullet, a roughly hammered piece of lead, which had been working its way through Lyons' body – and Lyons' health immediately began to improve. Lyons kept the bullet as a souvenir and later wore it on his watch chain. Despite the seriousness of their wounds, despite the agonizing haul in a springless wagon up the Knostrope Pass from Rorke's Drift to Helpmekaar, despite the lack of proper medical facilities and the desperately unhygienic conditions in which they were treated, and despite the prevalence of disease, all of the wounded from Rorke's Drift who came under Blair-Brown's care survived.[29]

Under such difficult conditions, a spirit of strong hostility against the Zulus prevailed among the fragile outposts on the border, which found expression in acts of retribution that the officers, for a few weeks, did little to check. With stories of disembowelled drummer boys circulating widely and the troops living in nightly fear of attack, there were unfortunate consequences for any lone Zulus who fell into British hands – 'Our only cry now is revenge, revenge',[30] wrote Sergeant John Tigar of the 2/24th to his mother from Rorke's Drift on 20 February. Although most of the Zulus found on the battlefield at Rorke's Drift had been killed on the 23rd, and in the sweeping up operation afterwards, some of them, as Hamilton Browne had admitted, in cold blood, it is likely that a number of wounded were found further off over the following days, and the records are discreet concerning their fate. As early as the 23rd, when he first visited Rorke's Drift from Helpmekaar, Lieutenant Curling claimed to see 'a spy ... hanging on one of the trees in the garden'.[31] 'One morning,' admitted Charlie Harford,

> Major Black and I were sitting outside, warming ourselves in the sun and chatting, when we saw the most extraordinary-looking object suspended on the scaffold, and wondered what on earth it could be. Presently, a Private of the 24th came up from that direction, and Black and I asked him what the thing was, and he said that it was a Kaffir spy that had been hanged. 'Good Heavens' said Black, 'By whose orders was he hung?' 'Captain Harford, sir,' was the reply, so we went down at once to look into the matter. The poor wretch, who was an old, wizened-up, grey-headed native, had apparently been dead for some hours, and must have been hung some time during the night, but by whom it was never discovered. Every possible inquiry was made, but not a soul knew anything about it and nothing was known of the native or where he had come from . . .[32]

Smith-Dorrien, describing what seems to have been the same event, was horrified to see an elderly Zulu hanging from a framework he had erected to stretch *reims*; 'It was found that it was a case of lynch law performed by incensed men, who were bitter at the loss of their comrades. Other incidents of the same sort occurred in the next few days before law and order were re-established.'[33]

Hamilton Browne cheerily admitted to ordering one 'spy' to be hanged – a scout he had captured on patrol, who had, Hamilton Browne said, put on a red headband to pass himself off as a member of the NNC; Hamilton Browne excused himself on the grounds that when a sergeant had asked him what to do with the prisoner, he had been in a temper, having just barked his shin, and replied 'Oh, hang the bally spy!'[34]

Conditions at Helpmekaar were, if anything, worse. Here Simeon Nkambule and the Edendale men had rallied after their flight on the 22nd, and stayed to take an active part in the patrolling over the following weeks. They regularly returned with Africans captured in the vicinity, and any who could not adequately explain themselves were likely to be shot. 'All spies are shot,' wrote Curling, 'we have disposed of three or four already.'[35] 'A prisoner who was taken yesterday was tried by court-martial today,' wrote Civil Surgeon Lewis Reynolds on 27 January, 'and found to be a spy, and was shot by 10 Basutos. He jumped into his grave to try and escape the bullets, but without avail.'[36]

*

That same day, 27 January, the inquest into the disaster had begun. At Chelmsford's request a Court of Inquiry had been convened from among the senior officers present at Helpmekaar. The president was Colonel F.C. Hassard, Royal Engineers, and its members were Lieutenant-Colonel Law, Royal Artillery, and Colonel Arthur Harness, who had been in command of N/5 Battery. Its brief was to inquire into 'the loss of the camp'.

The purpose of this court has been much misunderstood; it was not an impartial body looking into the conduct of the iSandlwana campaign as a whole but rather an intelligence-gathering exercise on Chelmsford's behalf, intended to shed light on the crucial decisions which had occurred at iSandlwana during his absence. By definition Lord Chelmsford's own role fell outside its remit, nor did it attempt to apportion blame. It took evidence from the surviving imperial officers – Essex, Gardner, Cochrane, Smith-Dorrien and Curling – as well as from Crealock, Clery and Cracroft Nourse. None of the survivors had of course been privy to command decisions during the battle, and Harness deliberately chose not to record a wealth of anecdotal evidence from other survivors since it was not relevant to the central issue. Later, the choice of Harness – who had himself played a significant part in the story – was criticized in some quarters, but in truth Harness was not a man to let his personal interests compromise his duty. He did, however, interpret the court's brief in a very literal sense – much to the chagrin of modern historians:

> I am sorry to find that it is thought that more evidence should have been taken. Of course, I know Lord Chelmsford thought so, for he sent an order that it should be done: but he does not know, nor does the general public know, that a great deal more evidence was heard, but it was either corroboratory of other evidence already recorded or so unreliable that it was worthless. I wrote it all myself, and indeed I think I managed the thing entirely and might have recorded or rejected what I liked; it seemed to me useless to record statements hardly bearing on

the loss of the camp but giving doubtful particulars of small incidents more or less ghastly in their nature. We were assembled to inquire into the loss of the camp and I still think that the evidence we took was the very best living evidence, and that nothing more was necessary. I am sure that no more light will be thrown on the matter. I am glad to think that I stuck out most determinedly against giving an opinion, for you will hardly believe that Hassard and Law really thought it should be given. I said, 'You may give an opinion but I decline to do so, and I will not sign the proceedings unless it is recorded that I have not given an opinion.' However, it ended by no opinion being given, as you know. The duty of the court was to sift the evidence and record what was of value; if it was simply to take down a mass of statements the court might as well have been composed of three subalterns or three clerks . . .[37]

Given the narrowness of Harness's interpretation of the brief – which the other members of the court do not seem entirely to have shared – and the fact that most of the witnesses were peripheral to the decisions taken on the day, it was perhaps inevitable that the inquiry actually shed little light on what had caused the loss of the camp. Indeed, it is difficult now to see what useful purpose it did serve, beyond making it painfully obvious once again just how few officers in positions of command had survived the day.

It did, of course, facilitate the rapidly emerging need of those involved to distance themselves from any responsibility for the defeat – and to find someone upon whom it could be blamed. In the aftermath of the Court of Inquiry old resentments resurfaced. The obvious lack of evidence from colonial troops prompted Curling to comment in a private letter that 'most of those who escaped were volunteers and Native Contingent officers, who tell any number of lies'.[38] Curling's family passed the letter on for publication – a curious decision, probably prompted by the wish to pre-empt any colonial criticism of imperial officers – but when it appeared in the *London Standard* his comments outraged settler society and Harness was forced to advise Curling to apologize.

The court's report was also hugely influential in shaping understanding of the battle. It formed the basis of a confidential report compiled in March 1879 by Lieutenant W. James, Royal Engineers,[39] which in turn influenced the official history of the war. This official view has itself had a significant impact on modern histories of the battle, although in fact James's report is not entirely consistent with the broader range of evidence from survivors –

those eyewitness accounts Harness chose to ignore – and it may indeed have misinterpreted some of the recorded evidence. Crucial to the James version was the position of J.F. Lonsdale's company of the NNC, which James placed in the middle of the 24th's line, and whose collapse was represented as being responsible for the overwhelming of the line. In fact Essex's evidence does not support this view – but the NNC, having black faces, were perfect scapegoats; by implying that the tactical defeat was due entirely to the failings of the auxiliaries, the regulars, by contrast, emerge without reproach.

But the NNC weren't the only possible scapegoats and in fact it was in the early part of February, as Harness's inquest was under way, that the cracks which had always existed between Headquarters and No. 3 Column staff widened to a formidable gulf as a sudden and subtle war of words broke out between the two. It was the first round in what would prove to be an enduring search to find someone to blame for the iSandlwana disaster.[40] It began when Glyn submitted his report of the day's events to Chelmsford's Deputy Adjutant-General, Colonel Bellairs. Bellairs replied with a seemingly innocent query asking Glyn to clarify how he had followed the standing orders with regard to the establishment of the camp there. Glyn, then in the depths of his depression, merely passed the note to his staff officer, Major Clery, with no more comment than 'Odd the general asking me to tell him what he knows more about than I do.'[41] Clery, however, at once spotted the trap: if Glyn replied, he was tacitly accepting responsibility for the defence of the camp. A flurry of correspondence ensued in which Glyn 'accepted all responsibility for details, but declined to admit any responsibility for the movement of any portion of troops in or out of camp'. Chelmsford, in an otherwise odd breach of the principles of chain of command, suggested that it was Glyn's duty to protest any decisions with which he did not agree; Glyn replied that it was his duty to follow his commanding officer's instructions. And there that particular fox went to ground.

Clery – who had discreetly avoided any mention of the part he had played in positioning the camp – thought John Crealock was behind what had been a surprisingly subtle attempt to shift any element of blame away from Chelmsford and onto Glyn. Clery had never liked Crealock – few of his colleagues did – but he was probably right. Over the following months Crealock would work hard behind the scenes to ensure that the blame for the disaster fell anywhere but upon him and his 'chief'.

Another ideal scapegoat was Anthony Durnford. Durnford had always been an outsider, tainted by the messy affair at Bushman's River Pass, and involved in the complex and contradictory world of colonial Natal in a way that most regulars – who were merely passing through – were not. He was also a Royal Engineer – the regimental history of the 24th noted sniffily that he was 'unable to see the correct tactics to be pursued',[42] ignoring the fact that he had exercised no control over Pulleine's garrison, and despite the fact that, though undeniably the senior officer present, he had only arrived at iSandlwana an hour before the attack. Durnford was also dead – and so could not answer back.

As early as 3 February the High Commissioner Sir Bartle Frere wrote to the British Government back home referring to 'poor Durnford's disaster', while on the 10th he wrote blandly to the Queen herself that the orders Chelmsford had left to Pulleine 'were not obeyed, owing apparently to Colonel Durnford . . . coming up and either taking command of the camp or inducing Colonel Pulleine to divide his forces'.[43] Indeed, when the findings of the Court of Inquiry were passed to the Deputy Adjutant General, Colonel William Bellairs, en route to Lord Chelmsford, Bellairs did not feel constrained by Harness's scruples regarding a judgement, and added an opinion of his own: 'From the statements before the court . . . it may be gathered that the cause of the reverse suffered at Isandhlwana was that Lt. Col. Durnford, as senior officer, overruled the orders which Lt. Col. Pulleine received to defend the camp, and directed that the troops should be moved into the open, in support of a portion of the Native Contingent which had been brought up and which was engaging the enemy.'[44]

There was an element of truth in this, of course, and certainly Durnford had asked Pulleine for support, but the extent to which Pulleine provided it at the expense of his own orders is not at all clear. It was a position which largely exonerated everyone else, however – and which conveniently ignored the fact that whatever mistakes Durnford had made they were committed within a framework of ambiguity and shoddy staff work created by Lord Chelmsford himself. It is also a view, of course, that entirely omits the Zulus, their superior generalship, courage and determination, from the history of their greatest victory.

But if the opinion that Durnford was solely to blame for the disaster was soon to become the official line, it was not to go unchallenged.

*

It was two weeks after the disaster before the garrison at Rorke's Drift began to recover its nerve enough to mount the first extended patrols away from the mission buildings. Colonel Glyn was still lost in depression but the ever-resourceful Major Black took it upon himself to organize a scratch mounted force from volunteers among the officers of the disbanded NNC. For the most part these patrols were merely intended to watch for signs of Zulu movements on the other side of the river and they ranged along the Mzinyathi valley. On one occasion Charlie Harford found a battered portmanteau lying in the grass. It turned out to belong to Reverend Smith, having been looted from Rorke's Drift during the battle; the bag itself was waterlogged and beyond repair but Harford found a bible inside, and returned it to its owner.

The new patrols were a boon to Hamilton Browne, who had soon become restless cooped up at Rorke's Drift:

> My orders were that I was not to cross the river unless I considered it was fairly safe to do so or unless I considered there was something to be gained by my running the risk in crossing it. Well of course there was a great deal to be gained by doing so. The Zulus had kraals on the other side of the river – were they not hostile? And therefore to be plundered and destroyed. They had cattle, goats, fat-tailed sheep and fowls – were not these something to be gained? They had our big camp to plunder – might we not have a little loot to repay us?[45]

Hamilton Browne and his companions took to crossing a short distance over the river, foraging among the homesteads. On at least two occasions they rode down Zulu scouts who had been watching them – one was wearing a red headband, the 'bally spy' destined to be hanged. They became so troublesome to the amaQungebeni that specialist *izinyanga* were brought in to counter them. The doctors built a fire on the Zulu bank and, when the wind was blowing in the right direction, burned medicine on it that drifted across the border, in the hope of driving the British away. Hamilton Browne's response was to sneak out early one morning with Captain Develing and hide in a fold in the ground on the Zulu bank. When the *izinyanga* appeared and began their ceremonies, Hamilton Browne and Develing took aim and fired together:

> My man spun round and round and then fell into the fire, getting a taste thereby of what was in store for him later on. Develin[g]'s one

collapsed in a heap and never moved. We strolled up to them. My fellow had been hit through the throat, as I had taken rather too full a sight, but kicked the bucket when we reached him. Develin[g]'s one had been shot through the heart and on turning the body over we found it was a woman. We neither of us expressed any regret . . .[46]

On 4 February, one of these patrols made a discovery which was to significantly lift the garrison's spirits. Since Walter Higginson's story of crossing the Mzinyathi with Melvill and Coghill had become common knowledge, Glyn had been under pressure from the officers of the 24th to search for the lost Queen's Colour. He had been reluctant at first, fearing perhaps the confirmation that it was lost forever, but he finally allowed Major Black to lead a small patrol towards Sothondose's Drift. On 3 February Black and Harford rode out to scout the ground in preparation for the patrol. They paused on the heights above the drift on the Natal side, and since it was still only early afternoon they chanced their arm and descended a little way down towards the river, guided by a track in the grass,

> . . . the path by which, it is said, the fugitives had made their way. Suddenly, just off to the right of us, we saw two bodies, and on going to have a look at them, found that they were those of Lieutenants Melvill and Coghill! Both were clearly recognizable. Melvill was in red, and Coghill in blue, uniform. Both were lying on their backs about a yard from each other, Melvill at right-angles to the path and Coghill parallel to it, a little above Melvill with his head uphill. Both had been assegaid, but otherwise their bodies had been left untouched.
>
> Major Black at once said, 'Now we shall see whether they have the Colours on them,' and proceeded to unbutton Melvill's serge, while I opened Coghill's patrol jacket, but there were no Colours. Presently Major Black said, 'I wonder if Melvill's watch is on him! He always carried it in the small waist-pocket of his breeches!' and, on looking, there was his gold watch, which was subsequently sent to his widow. Nothing was found on Coghill, but his bad knee was still bandaged up. Undoubtedly Melvill must have stuck to him and helped him along, otherwise he never could have got so far over such terrible ground . . .[47]

Black and Harford covered the bodies with stones until a proper burial could be arranged, and returned to Rorke's Drift. The news caused a good deal of excitement and there was no shortage of volunteers for the next day's patrol. It was to be commanded by Black and Commandant Cooper

of the NNC, and accompanied by Harford and several subalterns of the
NNC. The interpreter James Brickhill, who had rejoined the garrison a few
days before from Msinga, went along, as did Chaplain Smith who would
read the burial service over Melvill and Coghill.

Watched by pickets from the top of Shiyane, the party rode downriver
towards the drift, and Black halted to post a covering party on the heights.
They then went down to Melvill and Coghill's graves, where Smith read the
burial service. Black then told Harford, together with Captain Harber and
Lieutenant Wainwright, to go down to the river to search the banks and
shallows. It was a steep descent through long grass and bushes to reach the
river, and there were more bodies along the way, the remains probably of
the men killed by Zulu fire from across the river. When they reached the
banks they found that the river had dropped considerably since the 22nd;
Brickhill was astonished to see that where his horse had struck a submerged
obstacle midstream there now stood a large boulder 2 metres clear of the
water. The rocky bed of the river was exposed in the shallows on either
side and among the usual tangle of uprooted bushes and snagged driftwood
there was all manner of military debris.

The three officers posted themselves at intervals and began to walk
downstream. A steep bluff rises up on the Natal side, and just below it the
river at low water flows over a large patch of exposed stones. Harford was
nearing the foot of the cliff when he:

> ... stumbled on the Colour case mixed up with a heap of other things,
> and picking it up I said to Harber, who was closest to me, 'Look here,
> here's the case! The Colours can't be far off!' We all three then had a
> look at it, put it on a conspicuous boulder, and went on. Then, as
> Harber was returning to his position, I noticed a straight piece of stick
> projecting out of the water in the middle of the river, almost in line
> with us, and said to him, 'Do you see that straight bit of stick sticking
> up in the water opposite to you? It looks to me uncommonly like a
> Colour pole.' He waded straight in, up to his middle, and got hold of it.
> On lifting it out he brought up the Colour still adhering to it, and on
> getting out of the water handed the standard to me, and as he did so
> the gold-embroidered centre scroll dropped out, the silk having more-
> or-less rotted from the long immersion in the water.[48]

And so, in a fitting end to a story ripe with portents and symbolism, the
Queen's Colour of the 1/24th, the emblem of its commitment to Crown

and Empire, was found in the waters of the Mzinyathi river, as if Zululand itself had cast it out – upside down, the crown on top of the pole snagged between the rocks. The finders let out a cheer which brought Major Black, the only 24th man present, scrambling down the steep hillside. 'I handed him the Colour', said Harford, 'amidst ringing cheers in which he joined', and Black led them back up the slope, 'he carrying the Colour.'[49]

The party rode back to Rorke's Drift with the Colour carried erect, so that the pickets on top of Shiyane could not mistake it. To Harford's surprise they found a guard of honour waiting for them, 'and the whole garrison turned out to give them an ovation'. Black presented the Colour to Glyn; it was an emotional moment, and Glyn thanked the party 'with tears in his eyes'. At Glyn's insistence the party escorted the Colour up to Helpmekaar the following day where it was formally handed back to the surviving companies of the 1/24th. Glyn himself rode up to receive it. At Black's suggestion, Harford, who had first spotted the Colour in the river, was allowed to carry it for the last part of the journey: 'It was the proudest moment of my life, and I shall ever consider it so. I very much doubt whether such another case has ever occurred that an officer on duty and belonging to another Regiment has been given the honour of carrying its Queen's Colour.'[50]

Arthur Harness witnessed the ceremony that followed. 'Poor Glyn, in speaking to the two companies under Major Upcher, fairly broke down. He said that fourteen years before, he and Upcher were the officers to receive that Colour, and they were again receiving it being almost the only officers left with the regiment.'[51]

*

When the news of iSandlwana reached London on 11 February, it burst like a bombshell in the corridors of power. Prime Minister Disraeli's administration had only discovered a fortnight before that Frere had sanctioned the invasion of Zululand without the express authority of the Colonial Office. The defeat at iSandlwana had made a busted flush of Frere's gamble that he could mask the significance of the move by sleight of hand, assuming that Chelmsford could bring the war to a successful conclusion before the Government had time to object and that the benefits to confederation would be so obvious that, as had happened over his blockade of Zanzibar a few years before, he would then be commended for his decisive action.

There was no question now of slipping the war beneath the political radar, and within a few days it would become the dominant story in the British press. At a time when British troops were heavily committed in Afghanistan, a war in southern Africa was a fresh and unnecessary drain on imperial resources, and the folly of embarking upon an aggressive campaign of conquest seemed all the more conspicuous. Yet clearly it was crucial for Britain's future interests in the region to restore her prestige; in due course awkward questions would need to be asked of both the High Commissioner in southern Africa, Sir Bartle Frere, and Lord Chelmsford, but in the meantime it was necessary for the Government to restore Britain's tarnished honour.

Within days of the news arriving, officers commanding infantry, cavalry and artillery regiments on garrison duty in Britain were ordered to recall their officers from furlough, make up any deficiencies in the ranks from the pool of recruits in training, and make ready for departure to the Cape. iSandlwana could not be allowed to go unavenged.

*

As early as 1 February Chelmsford had written from Pietermaritzburg to Glyn expressing the 'hope that you have sent off Lt. Chard's report of the defence of Rorke's Drift post – I am anxious to send that little gleam of sunshine home as soon as possible'.[52] While it would be unduly cynical to suggest that Chelmsford magnified the significance of Rorke's Drift to distract attention from the debacle at iSandlwana, there is no doubt that it was a piece of very good news at the end of a very bad day and that – like Prince Dabulamanzi before him – he was anxious to temper his serious failures with a small token of success.

In that he was following the lead set by popular opinion in Natal. The Zulu victory at iSandlwana had seemed to confirm the deep-seated settler fear of 'the Zulu menace', and the white population had reacted with the same mix of fear and hatred which had emerged among the troops along the border. While settler society mourned its dead and went into *laager* in panic, its press clamoured for revenge. In such a context, the victory at Rorke's Drift seemed not only to have saved Natal from the imagined horrors of a Zulu invasion, but to offer a glimmer of hope for success to come; and the fact that the true Zulu intentions on that day were unknown was largely irrelevant. As a result, the press in Natal from the first made much of the defence, an example taken up – as Chelmsford had hoped – by their counterparts back home when the story broke there.

The military, on the whole, were taken by surprise by this interest. The true significance of the day's events was all too obvious to them – they had endured a serious defeat and been repulsed from Zululand, and Rorke's Drift was little more than an afterthought. 'The fact is', Major Clery wrote home, 'that until the accounts came out from England nobody had thought of the Rorke's Drift affair except as one in which the private soldiers of the 24th behaved so well. For as a matter of fact they all stayed there to defend the place because there was nowhere else to go, and in defending it they fought most determinedly.'[53]

In fact, of course, Clery had missed the point that Rorke's Drift was to strike a chord then – and ever since – precisely because it was not the action of a great general, a flamboyant leader or a hand-picked elite squad, but rather one in which ordinary soldiers, none of them ranked above a lieutenant, had found themselves in an extraordinary situation – and had risen spectacularly to the occasion. It engaged with a particular part of the British psyche that saw itself at its best when faced with impossible odds; in the victory at Rorke's Drift, the population at large discerned something they hoped lay deep in themselves, that, despite all the faults of the Victorian era, at their heart, too, they were just as courageous and proud and would always do their duty.

Yet there was a problem in the lionization of Rorke's Drift, in that the obvious candidates for heroic enshrinement, Chard and Bromhead, did not seem natural hero material. In response to requests from above, and probably with Clery looking over his shoulder, Chard had produced a workmanlike report of the battle, but the effect of the sudden attention seemed to drive Bromhead further into his shell. According to Clery:

> Well, Chard and Bromhead to begin with; both are almost typical in their separate ways of what would be termed a very dull class. Bromhead is a great favourite in his regiment and a capital fellow at everything except soldiering. So little was he held to be qualified in this way from unconquerable indolence that he had to be reported confidentially as hopeless. This is confidential, as I was told it by his commanding officer. I was about a month with him at Rorke's Drift after Isandhlwana, and the height of his enjoyment seemed to be to sit all day on a stone on the ground smoking a most uninviting-looking pipe. The only thing that seemed equal to moving him in any way was any allusion to the defence of Rorke's Drift. This had a sort of electrical effect on him, for he would jump up and off he would go, and not a word could be got

out of him. I used to find him hiding away in corners with a friend helping him to complete his account, and the only thing afterwards that helped to lessen the compassion I felt for all this, was my own labour when perusing this composition – to understand what on earth it was all about. So you can fancy there was not one who knew him who envied his distinction, for his modesty about himself was, and is, excessive.

Chard there is very little to say about except that he too is a 'very good fellow' – but very uninteresting.[54]

As public acclaim broke over Chard's head, his company commander, Captain Walter Jones, found his reaction similarly frustrating. 'Chard makes me angry, with such a start as he got, he stuck to the company doing nothing. In his place I should have gone up and asked Lord Chelmsford for an appointment, he must have got one, and if not he could have gone home soon after Rorke's Drift, at the height of his popularity at home. I advised him, but he placidly smokes his pipe and does nothing. Few men get such opportunities.'[55]

Yet their shortcomings as personalities were not at all apparent to the press, for whom actions had spoken distinctly louder than words, and for whom ordinary heroes were the stuff that sold papers. Indeed, as the searching gaze of the public spotlight began to fall on the conduct of the iSandlwana campaign at a more senior level, the achievements of junior ranks began to stand out all the more in contrast to the shortcomings of their seniors. The defence of Rorke's Drift was soon celebrated with a host of dramatic engravings in the illustrated papers, some based on drawings sent home by officers from Natal, and displaying a fair degree of accuracy – and others not. While portraits of Chard and Bromhead appeared in the upmarket broadsheets, dramatic pictures of Private Hook defending the hospital doorways were published in the more popular editions. A *Punch* cartoon depicted Chard and Bromhead sitting among the mealie bags and biscuit boxes receiving the thanks of the nation.

It was inevitable that the garrison would be showered with awards. Some of these were of immediate and practical benefit. Sergeant George Smith of B Company wrote home that:

... the people of Pietermaritzburg are so well pleased at the manner in which my company kept the stores from being taken by the enemy that they cannot do enough for us. They have subscribed £150 for us to buy the troops a lot of clothing, and pens, ink, and paper, matches, pipes, and a lot of everything, and sent them to us to be given to the troops at Rorke's Drift. They have also sent word that they consider we have been the means of saving the whole of the colony from being taken by the Zulus, and I don't think they are far wrong . . .[56]

Chard, Bromhead, Dunne and Reynolds all received promotions valid from the day after the battle. This was only the beginning: on 2 May the *London Gazette* announced the award of eight Victoria Crosses, the supreme British award for gallantry. They were given to Chard and Bromhead and six men of B Company – Corporal Allan, Privates Hitch, Hook, Robert Jones, William Jones and John Williams. The choice of these individuals is interesting; Chard and Bromhead were obvious candidates, two had displayed considerable gallantry despite terrible wounds, and the rest were all defenders of the hospital who reflected Clery's view that the ordinary men of B Company had behaved so well. Nevertheless, the award ignored the important contribution made by representatives of other corps, and a certain amount of behind the scenes lobbying took place as influential parties argued for the recognition of their favoured candidates. Eventually a further three VCs were authorized – to Corporal Schiess of the NNC, Surgeon Reynolds – whose citation gave as the reason for the award his delivery of ammunition to the hospital, rather than his treatment throughout the battle of the wounded – and finally James Dalton. Dalton was to prove a popular choice with B Company, many of whom remembered his stirling efforts to encourage them throughout the fight. Walter Dunne had also been put forward for the award, but the Commander-in-Chief, the Duke of Cambridge, was becoming troubled by the number authorized, and called a halt before Dunne was approved.

It has been suggested that the high number of awards was deliberately sanctioned to distract public attention from the failure at iSandlwana. This is a simplification. It is certainly true that the War Office and Government as a whole were happy to indulge the public's need for heroes, and it is worth noting that in 1879 there were no other awards available to recognize gallantry, apart from the Distinguished Conduct Medal, which was not available to officers. Nevertheless, each of the men honoured had done more than enough to justify his Victoria Cross – and, in fact, given the desperate nature of the fight and how long it lasted, more than a few of the rest might reasonably be considered at some point to have done so too.

It was far more difficult, however, to pick out from the general mess of iSandlwana any individual acts worthy of public recognition. For one thing, the criteria for the award of the Victoria Cross stipulated that recipients had to be alive to receive it – there was no provision in 1879 for it to be awarded posthumously – and that the deed itself had to be vouched for by a senior officer. No doubt many heroic deeds had been performed by men who were then killed, or were witnessed by officers who did not live to report them. And others who might have done something worthy of consideration and had survived, had, by definition, at some point run away – a fact which many in the military establishment were uneasy at recognizing. There was, moreover, a general and unspoken reservation about celebrating even individual bravery in what had already become the most shocking and humiliating defeat of the age.

Once again, however, the public had other ideas. From the first, the press had identified one aspect of the battle which had the same elements of individual courage and lowly rank that had so appealed about Rorke's Drift, and all wrapped up with an obvious symbolic glamour – the attempt by Melvill to save the Queen's Colour. Characterized usually as 'the dash with the Colours', the scene was imagined on the front cover and centre pages in half a dozen forms, more often than not entirely inaccurately. Melvill and Coghill were shown escaping the camp together, often cutting their way through the horses of Zulus surrounding them, sometimes with the Colour wrapped around Melvill's body – never cased – and in at least one example riding through an exotic jungle.

It made for heroic imagery – but within the terms of any viable awards, was it heroic? Since both Melvill and Coghill had been killed, they could not be awarded the Victoria Cross, although it was possible for an announcement to be made that they 'would have received it, had they lived'. The problem was, however, that despite Melvill's undoubted courage – and it took extraordinary courage to carry the Colour on horseback under such circumstances – the fact is that he was taking the Colour to safety, and in doing so inevitably increased his own chance of survival when all his fellow officers remained upon the field to die. What was at issue was not his decision to try to save the Colour – which was applauded – nor even his failure to do so; it was implicit in the warrant for the Victoria Cross that the extraordinary degree of bravery it recognized involved a deliberate decision, cool or reckless, on the part of the individual concerned to place himself in a degree of danger which went above and beyond the call of duty. Was a deed worthy of the Victoria Cross if the heroic deed itself increased the subject's chance of survival, rather than risked it? In the end, the War Office conceded the point and on 2 May the *London Gazette* officially announced that Melvill and Coghill 'would have been recommended to Her Majesty for the Victoria Cross had [they] survived'. Asked his opinion on the decision, Chelmsford wrote to General Sir Alfred Horsfold at the War Office:

> As regards poor Melvill and Coghill the case is even more difficult. The latter was a Staff Officer attached to Col. Glyn, and had every right to leave the camp when he realized the fact that nothing could be done to save it. It is, however, most probable that Melvill lost his life endeavouring to save Coghill, rather than vice versa.
>
> Coghill had strained his knee and remained in camp on the 22nd as a consequence. He could hardly walk, and any exertion such as walking or riding would have been likely to render him helpless. He could not have assisted, therefore, in saving the colours of the 1/24th, and as I have already said I fear he was a drag to poor Melvill.
>
> As regards the latter, . . . I feel sure that Melvill left the camp with the colours under orders received. He was too good a soldier to have left without. In being ordered to leave, however, he no doubt was given the best chance of saving his life which must have been lost had he remained in camp. His ride was not more daring than that of those who escaped. The question, therefore, remains had he succeeded in saving the colours and his own life, would he have been considered to have deserved the Victoria Cross?[57]

Privately, Chelmsford's successor, Wolseley, complained at the idea of 'officers escaping on horseback when their men on foot are killed',[58] but he was out of tune with public opinion, and in 1906, when the Victoria Cross statute was amended to allow for posthumous awards, and after considerable petitioning from both Melvill's widow, Sara, and Coghill's father, both were officially awarded the Victoria Cross. The award was gazetted on 15 January 1907.

A number of the survivors did, apparently, receive some consideration. Alan Gardner was a possible candidate because after escaping from Helpmekaar, and despite being exhausted, he had ridden to Utrecht to warn Wood's column. Chelmsford felt, however, that while Gardner 'deserved recognition' the ride itself had been 'not one of danger but of fatigue, and consequently could not be construed as a gallant act deserving the VC'.[59] Horace Smith-Dorrien understood that his name was mentioned for stopping to help the wounded Mounted Infantryman above Sothondose's Drift – he did not receive it, however, because the 'proper channels for correspondence had not been observed'.[60] Since the recommendation for the award had to be approved by the candidate's commanding officer, it might be that Smith-Dorrien paid the price for securing a post in the war without his colonel's consent. As late as 1881, Evelyn Wood recommended Trooper Barker of the Carbineers for having given up his horse to Lieutenant Higginson; the War Office again replied that while it commended Barker's action, it did not consider it worthy of the VC. No one thought to recommend Walter Stafford, who on several occasions during the retreat had stopped to help away wounded men.

In the event only one Victoria Cross was actually awarded to a living recipient for an act committed at iSandlwana. In Utrecht on 11 September 1879 Chelmsford's successor, Sir Garnet Wolseley, presented Samuel Wassall with the medal for saving the life of Private Westwood at Sothondose's Drift.

It is interesting to note that at no point were any of the officers killed at iSandlwana, other than Melvill and Coghill, singled out for recognition of any sort, either public or official, despite the fact that the apparently heroic nature of Durnford's death was known early on. Indeed, most contemporary pictorial impressions of the battle tend to stress the courage and resolution of ordinary soldiers rather than their officers – officers are often marginalized in the composition or entirely omitted. This reflected a general sense of public unease about where the responsibility for the disaster lay, a feeling that the courage of the other ranks had been squandered by the folly of their officers – although who was to blame, exactly, remained unclear. It is a feature of Charles Fripp's famous painting *The Last Stand at Isandhula* – a picture greeted with some public indifference when exhibited in 1885, but now widely reproduced as an icon not merely of the Anglo-Zulu War but of Victorian adventurism and folly generally – that, unusually for a Victorian battle painting, it includes no officers in the central composition, but an entirely fictitious drummer boy instead – while the highest rank of any soldier depicted is that of a lance-sergeant. R.T. Moynan's painting *The Last of the 24th, Isandula* similarly depicts a single private soldier, in a heavily symbolic composition based on the story of the man who defended the cave. Only Melvill and Coghill survived the trend to artistic anonymity, appearing in two dramatic, and almost entirely inaccurate, paintings by the French battle painter, Alphonse de Neuville, and a rather more authentic colour illustration by Fripp.

It is notable, in particular, that, despite the rich variety of visual interpretations of the battle, there were no contemporary pictures eulogizing Durnford's last moments – and there have been precious few ever since. History, it seems, still cannot quite decide whether Durnford is the hero of the piece – or the villain.

While the British sought to make heroes of the survivors, their dead still lay out on the field at iSandlwana in such concentration that the natural processes of decay, of scavengers and the elements, could not readily absorb them. The battle had taken place in an area of comparatively dense human population, and with little big game around scavengers were few in the open grassland; jackals in small numbers certainly, perhaps a few spotted hyenas still living in the wilder parts of the Mzinyathi valley, the odd Cape Vulture or pied crow. Dogs from the homesteads nearby, or the soldiers' pets which had been left behind and had to feed on whatever they could find, as well as the destructive Bush Pigs may also have played their part in breaking down the remains.

Yet there were just too many corpses. So they lay there, slowly desiccating in the sun, their body cavities opened by Zulu custom, their skin drying and withering on their bones, hair, moustaches and beards often intact, their features grotesquely familiar – a macabre reproach to the living.

# 28

# 'Melancholy satisfaction'

No Zulu attack into Natal followed in the weeks after the Zulu victory at iSandlwana. While the Natal press speculated on the reasons for this, most attributing it to the state of the Mzinyathi and Thukela rivers – the levels continued to fluctuate, according to the rainfall – it had, in fact, never been King Cetshwayo's intention to invade. The king could not in any case have launched an invasion of Natal that February even had he wanted to. His army was exhausted by its victory, and after the cleansing ceremonies and the apportioning of honours and blame, the *amabutho* had dispersed to their homes to recover from their wounds and to rest, to clean and re-haft their spears and to make new loin-coverings, to be ready should the fray be renewed.

At the beginning of March Cetshwayo sent the first of what would prove by the end of the war to be a stream of messengers to British outposts hoping to open negotiations for a peaceful settlement. If he had thought that by his victory he might force the British to the negotiating table, however, he had misjudged their mood; while he sat at oNdini hoping that the British would abandon the invasion, his enemies were preparing to renew their offensive.

By the end of March Chelmsford's reinforcements had begun to arrive in Durban, and he was in a position to reassess his strategy. While Evelyn Wood's Left Flank Column was still active from its new base at Khambula hill – it had moved there to offer more protection to Utrecht at the end of January – Pearson's column had dug in at Eshowe. King Cetshwayo was irritated that Pearson appeared to have settled in his country, as if it were already defeated, and had ordered that the British line of communication with the Thukela border be cut with no supplies or messengers able to make it through. For two months Pearson had been largely cut off from the outside world, but his column was at least maintaining a forward British presence on Zulu soil. Chelmsford would have to start his invasion from scratch – but first he needed to extricate Pearson.

Chelmsford had accumulated sufficient reinforcements at the Thukela to begin operations to relieve Eshowe by the beginning of April. Both the British Government and the colonial administration in Natal were bent on revenge – and they were now in a position to start exacting it.

Here and there a voice in the wilderness spoke out against the prevailing mood. Bishop Colenso, inevitably perhaps, continued to challenge the official British line whenever the opportunity presented itself. When the Natal administrator Sir Henry Bulwer nominated Wednesday 12 March a Day of Humiliation and Prayer to honour the losses at iSandlwana, Colenso held a service in St Peter's Cathedral in the colonial capital in which he systematically reviewed the injustice of British policies:

> Wherein in our invasion of Zululnd have we shown that we are men who 'love mercy?' Did we not lay upon the people heavily, from the very moment we crossed the border, the terrible scourge of war? Have we not killed already, it is said, 5,000 human beings, and plundered 10,000 head of cattle? It is true that, in that dreadful disaster, on account of which we are this day humbling ourselves before God, we ourselves have lost many lives, and widows and orphans, parents, brothers, sisters, friends, are mourning bitterly their sad bereavements. But are there no griefs – no relatives that mourn the dead in Zululand? Have we not heard how the wail has gone up in all parts of the country for those who have bravely died – no gallant soldier, no generous colonist, will deny this – have bravely and nobly died in repelling the invader and fighting for their King and fatherland? And shall we kill 10,000 more to avenge the losses of that dreadful day? Will that restore to us those we have lost? Will that endear their memories more to us? Will that please the spirits of any true men, any true sons of God, among the dead? Above all, will that please God who 'requires of us' that we 'do justly' and 'love mercy?'[1]

Curiously, Colenso found some unexpected support from the pen of Otto Witt. Witt had always been a supporter of the war, but in the aftermath of the destruction of his property he, too, found himself out of step with public opinion:

> Who wins your warmest sympathy – the Captain, who, knowing that he is lost, stops a moment to spike the canon and die; or the Zulu who, in his excitement, leaves his fellow soldiers behind, and alone makes the attack on the hospital at Rorke's Drift, resting his gun on the very

barricade, and firing at those inside? Is your admiration greater for the ninety-five who entered the commissariat stores at Oscarsberg and defended it against 5,000 Zulus than for those 5,000 who fought outside the whole night, trying to overpower the whites, and who withdrew, leaving 1000 dead, hundreds of whom were lying even on the very veranda of the house? Indeed, your admiration ought to be as great for the one as for the other. Where did you find greater courage or contempt for death than theirs?[2]

It was as well neither Colenso nor Witt expected an honest answer.

*

The arrival of reinforcements, and the failure of the Zulu to mount a counter-attack, led to a tangible shift in the fortunes of war, and a gradual relaxing among British garrisons along the border. Rorke's Drift benefited from the arrival of skilled personnel more than most; at the beginning of March a new entrenchment had begun to be erected on the rise overlooking the pool above the drifts. It took several weeks to complete, but by a combination of Royal Engineers expertise and NNC muscle – some of Major Bengough's troops were brought up from Msinga for the purpose – a solid stone fort was constructed, a long oblong with impressive bastions at the corners and covered shelters to protect those sleeping from the rain. The Royal Engineers wanted to call it 'Fort Revenge' but Chelmsford instructed them to think of a more appropriate name and they chose instead Fort Melvill. At the end of the month the old garrison below Shiyane was finally broken up, and most of the men marched down to the new fort, leaving the old post, with all its dramatic and terrible memories, abandoned and empty.

There had already been changes in personnel. When Rupert Lonsdale had disbanded the 3rd NNC after the battles, Charlie Harford's appointment as staff officer had come to an end. He had been content to remain at Rorke's Drift after the adventure with the Colours, but shortly afterwards he was ordered to Helpmekaar where the most exciting duty that fell to Harford was wrangling with Boer farmers over the price of cattle. He was relieved a few weeks later to receive a message from the colonel of his own regiment, Colonel Welman of the 99th, asking him if he would like to resume his old appointment as adjutant. Lieutenant Davison, with whom he had exchanged a lifetime ago at Chatham, before the war began, had died of disease during the siege of Eshowe. Harford was delighted to accept, and his departure from Helpmekaar for Durban brought an end to a remarkable chapter in his career, one which he would look back on later as the defining experience of his life.

William Cochrane and the Edendale men had also left Helpmekaar. With the arrival of reinforcements from home, Lord Chelmsford began to reorganize his forces, creating a new column from scratch – the 2nd Division – and redistributing some of his existing troops. Simeon Nkambule and the Edendale men had been attached to Evelyn Wood's column and brigaded with other survivors of Durnford's mounted troops, including Hlubi's Tlokoa, into a new unit known as the Native Horse. Cochrane, who had been on attached duty to Durnford's column – which officially no longer existed – found himself transferred to the new unit, and they left together for Wood's column at Utrecht. The Mounted Infantry under Lieutenant-Colonel Russell were also sent to join Wood.

Hamilton Browne had also left Rorke's Drift. Lonsdale had been sent to the Cape to raise a new unit of Irregular Horse, and once the work had begun he had sent for Hamilton Browne and a number of his old officers to join him. It was a bitter-sweet moment for Hamilton Browne, who was delighted to be free of the unpleasant confines of Rorke's Drift, yet torn at being parted from the men with whom he had shared such extraordinary times. Towards the end of February he had organized one last raid across the river – ambushing a homestead at dawn, tossing burning brands into the thatch and shooting down the occupants as they emerged – and then taken his farewell of the garrison. 'The feeling towards a comrade is very strong in the Lost Legion, and as I rode away after a handshake all round the air seemed to burn blue and smelt like a cart-load of Tandstickor matches on fire. However, the last hand-grip, the last cheer, in which the men of the 24th join, is given and we ride away. I with a hump on me as big as a baggage camel.'[3]

*

The war broke suddenly and violently into life again at the end of March.

It had been clear to King Cetshwayo for some weeks that the British build-up on the southern front portended a new offensive. He had tried at the end of February to re-assemble the *amabutho* but they had been reluctant to come, asking for more time to rest; they eventually responded to the muster in the third week of March. Wood's column in the north had begun raiding aggressively again as a diversion against Chelmsford's planned expedition to relieve Eshowe, and once again the king and his council were faced with having to defend the kingdom on two fronts.

The situation was further complicated by the defection on 10 March of Prince Hamu. Hamu's relationship with the king had been difficult long before the war had begun, and Evelyn Wood had made concerted diplomatic overtures to seduce him away with promises of British favour after the war was over. Hamu had eventually taken the bait and had arrived at Wood's Khambula camp with 1,300 of his followers. His retinue included two white men who had enjoyed – exactly as John Dunn had with Cetshwayo – a privileged position at Hamu's court. One of them turned out to be James Michael Rorke, the son of Jim Rorke himself, who had crossed into Zululand some years before the war began and taken up a Zulu lifestyle, marrying several wives. The other, a Mr Calverley, was riding a horse someone recognized as a spare belonging to Nevill Coghill. It transpired that many of Hamu's fighting men had fought at iSandlwana, and that the horse was among Prince Hamu's share of the loot.

The defection of Hamu – the only one of the great regional barons of any note, apart from John Dunn, to abandon the king during the course of the war – was a serious blow, not merely threatening the unity of the kingdom, but also abandoning a large part of northern Zululand to British influence. It was a deciding factor in shaping the council's military response, and it opted to repeat the strategy which had worked so successfully in January. The troops in the coastal sector would once again be reinforced by detachments from oNdini, but this time the main army would strike against Wood's column in the north.

The Zulu army set out on 24 March. It consisted of the same *amabutho* who had triumphed at iSandlwana, and once again command was given to Ntshingwayo kaMahole, but this time the king's senior councillor, Mnyamana Buthelezi, would accompany it as a measure of the importance Cetshwayo placed in the expedition. On 28 March, as it drew near Wood's base at Khambula, the *impi* stumbled upon a British foray in progress. In response to a request from Chelmsford to mount a diversionary attack, Wood had launched an assault upon the abaQulusi stronghold at Hlobane mountain. The attack had begun before dawn on the 28th, and was well under way when the royal *impi* arrived. Several *amabutho* – the uKhandempemvu, uVe and iNgobamakhosi – were detached to help the abaQulusi, and the British were driven off the mountain with heavy losses.

Although most of the *amabutho* were not deployed at Hlobane, the victory there greatly enhanced the feeling of self-confidence which had prevailed since iSandlwana, and when the *impi* went on to attack the hill-top camp at Khambula the following day it did so in defiance of the king's instructions, in the wake of the bitter lesson learned at Rorke's Drift, not to attack fortified positions. 'We are the boys from iSandlwana' shouted the iNgobamakhosi as they rushed to the attack; but this time there were no open-order formations and no exposed flanks, just a chain of entrenched wagon *laagers* and redoubts. After fighting which lasted from late morning until late afternoon, the Zulus were driven off with heavy losses, and as they began to withdraw British irregulars pursued them and shot them down mercilessly.

At least 1,000 Zulu were killed at Khambula, and perhaps a similar number wounded. Mehlokazulu had taken part, and was grazed on the head by a bullet, and many of those who died were heroes who had distinguished themselves at iSandlwana. Worse still, the battle had emphasized on a grand scale an obvious truth first revealed at Rorke's Drift: that against a European army fully equipped with modern firepower and securely entrenched behind barricades, tactical flair and raw courage was not enough.

This defeat was followed by another just a few days later on the coast. Lord Chelmsford crossed the Thukela at the Lower Drift at the end of March. The easy swagger of the iSandlwana campaign had given way to an obsessive caution, and Chelmsford's advance averaged just a few kilometres each day, in part because every evening his wagons were drawn into a protective *laager*, and every morning that *laager* was broken up. It was an approach that paid dividends, however, and when, on 2 April, the Zulu forces at Eshowe moved out to attack Chelmsford's *laager* near the old royal homestead of kwaGingindlovu they were easily defeated. Prince Dabulamanzi, the unsuccessful commander at Rorke's Drift, who lived locally, commanded the right horn during the battle, and received a flesh wound in his thigh. Among those facing him inside the square was George Hamilton Browne, newly returned from the Cape, who further vented his revenge for iSandlwana by slaughtering exhausted Zulus during the pursuit.

The following day Chelmsford relieved the garrison at Eshowe, and began to withdraw his forces back to the border. After three months he had suffered heavy losses, gained almost no Zulu territory, and he was largely back where he was before iSandlwana. Yet any impression that the war was developing into a stalemate was deeply misleading. British reinforcements were still arriving in Durban on a regular basis and, if need be, they would continue to do so almost indefinitely. Among the Zulu, however, there were no fresh reserves and already there was scarcely a family in the land untouched by loss. After Khambula and kwaGingindlovu King Cetshwayo knew in his heart what he had suspected from the beginning – that he and his people were engaged in a war that they could not hope in the long run to win.

*

The victories at the end of March and early April freed Chelmsford to face up to a duty he had shied away from over the previous months. It had been quite impractical on the night of 22 January to attempt any burial of the dead at iSandlwana, but as the weeks went by and the strategic position began to improve, Chelmsford found himself under increasing pressure both from the colonial press and from London to bury the dead.

It was not a task he relished. The sheer quantity of the remains made collecting and interring them a daunting task, and he had quietly decided that it was best left until the worst stages of decomposition had passed. With the spectre of the battle already looming large in the consciousness of both the settler community and the newly arrived troops – old hands took great pleasure in telling young soldiers fresh out from England of the horrors inflicted on the 24th's 'young drummer boys' – he was reluctant to risk a fragile morale still further by exposing his men to the sight of the stricken field.

Yet the job could not be avoided forever, and in March he had instructed the garrison at Rorke's Drift to make a foray across the river to investigate the state of the battlefield. The patrol was led by the indefatigable Major Black and consisted of three officers and a sergeant of the 24th, Commandant Cooper, twelve officers of the NNC, and ten Mounted Police under Major Dartnell. Two companies of Bengough's NNC were brought forward from Msinga to support the move.

The patrol crossed by the pont, and cautiously followed the old road through the Batshe valley. There was no sign of life in *inkosi* Sihayo's old fields but when they drew near iSandlwana a handful of Zulu scouts were seen. These fired a few shots, then ran off, lighting two signal fires which brought a body of men running to cut the patrol off. Black's patrol ventured no further than the *nek*, and stayed only long enough to experience the awful smell rising from the battlefield and to notice that many of the bodies were only partially decomposed before turning back towards Rorke's Drift. On the return journey they were again fired upon and they returned to the river at the gallop; the amaQungebeni, it seemed, were as determined to defend their territory as ever.

Black had planned another patrol for 28 March, in response to Chelmsford's request that his commanders along the border mount diversions to distract the Zulus from the departure of the Eshowe relief column. This time the move was planned to coincide with a large incursion by Bengough's NNC but the water level proved to be too high for the black infantry to get across the river and the raid was aborted. As British garrisons along the border began to operate with more confidence, however, they made an intriguing discovery. In a deserted farmhouse on the Natal bank 6.4 kilometres downstream from Rorke's Drift a wood-cutting party discovered a crown finial from one of the poles for the 2/24th's Colours which had been lost at iSandlwana. How it came to be dropped there remained a mystery, but it seemed to have been unscrewed by someone familiar with such things.

On 9 April Major Dartnell led the largest patrol yet towards the old battlefield, a combined force of nearly 2,300 auxiliaries, Carbineers and Mounted Police – the biggest force to have crossed at Rorke's Drift since the invasion of 11 January. The force moved through the Batshe valley, destroying the abandoned homesteads it found there, but rumours that a large Zulu force was gathering to oppose them at iSandlwana forced it to retire by way of Sothondose's Drift that afternoon without having reached the main battlefield.

So far the amaQungebeni had been remarkably successful in defending their territory, seeing off a succession of patrols. Yet by April the war in the local theatre was turning against them. Chelmsford had decided a new strategy; the victories at Khambula and kwaGingindlovu meant that it was no longer necessary to invade on so many fronts. Instead of his original five columns – three offensive and two defensive – Chelmsford planned two new thrusts. A column made up from Pearson's old command and the Eshowe relief column combined, the 1st Division, would advance up the coast, destroying the royal homesteads there, while a new, more powerful thrust would advance through the centre of the country towards oNdini. This would be formed by combining Wood's column – under a new name, the Flying Column – with a column made up of fresh troops from Britain, and be known as the 2nd Division. Still faced with the same lack of roads that had shaped his strategy in January, Chelmsford intended to start the 2nd Division from a point north of Rorke's Drift and strike across country to join his original intended route towards oNdini near Babanango mountain. The advantage of this amended route was that he would not have to take his fresh, untested troops past iSandlwana.

As the new build-up began, patrols were regularly sent out eastwards across the Ncome, which had the effect of driving those amaQungebeni who had returned to the disputed territory further away, thereby facilitating another move towards iSandlwana. It was now becoming increasingly imperative that the burial of the dead be attempted, and not merely for questions of decency. The expansion of his forces meant that Chelmsford was critically short of transport – and the wagons of the entire Centre Column were still out on the old battlefield.

Before dawn on 15 May Major Black set off with a fresh patrol from Fort Melvill, reaching iSandlwana at dawn. It was not opposed and Black allowed the men twenty minutes to wander the battlefield – not time to see much, as the grass had already grown long and hid most of the dead, but enough to see that the Zulus had taken away few of the wagons. The party then followed the fugitives' track, marked by debris and bodies, through the Manzimnyama and up over the crest of Mpethe. Here they descended by the easiest route before dividing, one group crossing the river and the other doubling back along the flat to the bottom of the slope where Smith-Dorrien, Curling, and the last of the fugitives had been driven down during the battle. At the foot of the slope they found Major Smith's body, still clearly identifiable by the uniform, and Captain Penn Symons of the 24th, who scrambled up alone through the rocks to the top of the hill, noted with awe the skeletons of men and horses jumbled up among the rocks.

The party was just covering Smith's body with stones when suddenly a ragged volley burst out above them and they looked up to see about thirty Zulus on the crest. According to pickets watching from the summit of Shiyane, the Zulus had shadowed them all the way from iSandlwana. Fortunately Bengough's battalion had been ordered up to the Natal bank in case of just such an eventuality and they opened a heavy suppressing fire from the heights opposite which drove the Zulus to cover and allowed Black's men to get safely across the drift.

This patrol was the final prelude to a much bigger expedition, timed to recover those 'serviceable wagons' before the start of the new invasion.

Over the next week an unprecedented mounted force was assembled at Fort Melvill. Designated the Cavalry Brigade and commanded by General Frederick Marshall – one of five generals sent out in response to a request from Lord Chelmsford for senior officers to assist him – it consisted of two newly arrived regular cavalry units, the 17th Lancers and 1st (King's) Dragoon Guards, together with the Volunteer units which had fought at iSandlwana – the Natal Carbineers, Natal Mounted Police, Buffalo Border Guard and Newcastle Mounted Rifles. The Buffalo Border Guard brought along a local settler, Dr Prideaux Selby, who knew many of the local farming families, to identify the colonial dead. Arthur Harness was also present with two guns from N/5 Battery, together with a detachment of mounted auxiliaries as scouts and a newly raised local Irregular unit, Carbutt's Rangers. Two companies of the 24th under Major Black and a battalion of Bengough's NNC were to provide infantry support.

It was almost an invasion force in itself, and for the first time in the war the operations would be fully reported by the mainstream British press. Norris-Newman had scooped his rivals with his eyewitness reports of the iSandlwana campaign, but news of the disaster had placed the Zulu campaign squarely in the centre of London news editors' desks and the prominent papers of the day had hurried their reporters to Natal. They included Archibald Forbes of the *Standard*, a peppery Scot who had served in the Army himself and had earned a reputation as the leading war correspondent of the day, and Francis Francis of *The Times*. Also present was Melton Prior, a 'special artist' for the *Illustrated London News*.

The expedition set off early on the morning of 21 May. It was a far cry from the old carefree days of January; the cavalry set off first, advancing in two divisions and throwing out scouts far ahead to watch for any Zulu movements, while the 24th and NNC took up a position at the southern end of the Batshe to support them. There was no opposition – although reports soon circulated that Matshana had gathered a force of 2,000 men at Mangeni to oppose them – and the troops set fire to any amaQungebeni homes that had escaped the previous sweeps, the column's progress marked by pillars of smoke rising up from the hills as they went. General Marshall himself led the way, and the column passed through the Manzimnyama valley and over the *nek*. Archibald Forbes' account of its arrival on the battlefield remains one of the most powerful dispatches of his career – and one of the most eloquent eyewitness accounts to emerge from the campaign:

Already tokens of the combat and bootless flight were apparent. The line of retreat towards Fugitives' Drift, along which, through a chink in the Zulu environment, our unfortunates who thus far tried to escape, lay athwart a rocky slope on our right front, with a precipitous ravine at its base. In this ravine dead men lay thick, mere bones, with toughened, discoloured skin like leather covering them, and clinging tight to them, the flesh all wasted away. Some were almost wholly dismembered, heaps of yellow clammy bones. I forbear to describe the faces, with their blackened features and beards bleached by rain and sun. Every man had been disembowelled. Some were scalped. And others had been subject to yet ghastlier mutilations. The clothes had lasted better than the poor bodies they covered, and helped to keep the skeletons together. All the way up the slope I traced the ghastly token of dead men, the fitful line of flight. Most of the men hereabouts were infantry of the 24th. It was like a long string with knots in it, the string formed of single corpses, the knots clusters of dead, where (as it seemed) little groups might have gathered to make a hopeless, gallant stand and die. I came on a gully with a gun limber jammed on its edge, and the horses, their hides scored with assegai stabs, hanging in their harness down the steep face of the ravine. A little further on there was a broken and battered ambulance wagon, and around lay the corpses of the soldiers, poor helpless wretches, dragged out of an intercepted vehicle and done to death without a chance for life.

Still following the trail of bodies through long rank grass and amongst stones, I approached the crest. Here the slaughtered ones lay very thick, so that the string became a broad belt. Many hereabouts wore the uniform of the Natal Police. On the bare ground itself, among the wagons, the dead were less thick; but on the slope beyond, on which, from the crest of which we looked down, the scene was the saddest, and more full of weird desolation than any I had yet gazed upon. There was none of the stark blood-curdling horror of a recent battlefield. A strange calm reigned in this solitude of nature. Grain had grown luxuriously round the waggons, sprouting from the seed that dropped from the loads, falling in soil fertilized by the life-blood of gallant men. So long in most places had grown the grass, that it mercifully shrouded the dead, whom four long months tomorrow we have left unburied.

As one strayed aimlessly about, one stumbled in the grass over skeletons that rattled to the touch. Here lay a corpse with the bayonet jammed into the mouth up to the socket, transfixing the head and mouth a foot into the ground. There lay a form that seemed cosily curled up in calm sleep, turned almost on its face, but seven assegai stabs have pierced the back. Most, however, lay flat on the back, with arms stretched widely out, and the hands clenched. I noticed one dead man under a waggon, with his head on a saddle for a pillow, and a tarpaulin as if he had gone to sleep, and died so.[4]

Fred Symons was in the ranks of the Carbineers, the first time he had seen the camp since that dreadful return on the night of the battle. 'I cannot describe my feelings', he wrote, 'upon entering the field and seeing the remains of men, cattle and wagons lying in strange confusion.'[5] Norris-Newman, too, had personal memories and

> Had the melancholy satisfaction of discovering my own tent, or rather the disjecta membra of what had once been mine; and immediately behind it were the skeletons of my horses, with the bodies of my servants, just as I had left them, picketed on 22nd January, when I accompanied the reconnoitring force of Lord Chelmsford. But I could find nothing of value remaining: my papers, letters and books were lying about, torn up. I found, and brought away with me as mementoes, some of my wife's letters, a book and some of my ms. stories, and a photograph that had reached me just two days before the massacre.[6]

Forbes, wandering about the campsite sickened by the 'sour odour of stale death',

> ... chanced on many sad relics – letters from home, photographs, journals, blood-stained books, packs of cards, Lord Chelmsford's copying book, containing an impression of his correspondence with the Horse Guards, was found in one of his portmanteaus, and identified in a kraal two miles [3.2 kilometres] off Colonel Harness was busily engaged in collecting his own belongings. Colonel Glyn found a letter from himself to Lieutenant Melvill, dated the day before the fight. The ground was strewn with brushes, toilet bags, pickle bottles, and unbroken tins of meat and milk. Forges and bellows remained standing ready for the recommencement of work.[7]

Melton Prior hastened about drawing pencil vignettes of the destruction in his notebook, a group of Lancers gently pushing the grass aside with their lances to look upon a crumpled heap of weathered clothes from which limb bones still protruded, boots still on feet, a right hand still with the flesh upon it. On the *nek* he drew General Marshall and his staff gazing down at a group of skeletons among the wagons, the grinning empty-eyed skulls subtly out of perspective, their size subconsciously reflecting their terrible impact. When his sketches reached London they were too shocking to be engraved as they stood, and Prior's editors discreetly removed all but the most genteel remains from the published versions.

In a homestead 3 kilometres from the camp, a patrol of Dragoons under Lieutenant Sadler found one of the 2/24th's Colour poles, apparently the one from which the finial had been removed; he returned it to the regiment, but to its men's disappointment no one had thought to look for the Colour itself before the huts were put to the torch.

Durnford's body was found lying in the long grass on the outskirts of the 1/24th camp where he fell, easily recognizable with 'the long moustache still clinging to the withered skin of the face'.[8] Round him were a cluster of Volunteer dead and some men of the 24th. The Carbineers were particularly keen to identify their own dead. They found the body of Trooper Swift, who had apparently 'died hard; they killed him with knobkerries.'[9] Lieutenant Scott was found near Durnford 'hidden partially under a broken piece of wagon, evidently unmutilated and untouched. He had his patrol jacket buttoned across, and while the body was almost only a skeleton, the face was still preserved and life-like, all the hair remaining and the skin strangely parched and dried up, though still perfect.'[10] Nineteen-year-old James Adrian Blaikie was recognized by the size of his particularly large skull – his brother had brought one of his hats along and gently placed it over his head to be sure. In the same clump of dead were Troopers Borrain, Dickinson, Tarboton, Lumley, Davies and R. Jackson; Troopers Swift, Moodie and F. Jackson were lying further towards the *nek*. Earlier reports had suggested that Tarboton had been decapitated, but if so the burial detail did not mention the fact – perhaps it was hard to tell. Nearby lay the body of Captain Bradstreet of the Newcastle Mounted Rifles.

The state of preservation varied – some bodies were immediately identifiable while others, said Melton Prior,

... could only be recognized by such things as a patched boot, a ring on the finger-bone, a particular button, or coloured shirt, or pair of socks in a few known instances. And this could only be done with much difficulty, for either the hands of the enemy, or the beaks and claws of vultures tearing up the corpses, had in numberless cases so mixed up the bones of the dead that the skull of one man, or bones of a leg or arm, now lay with parts of the skeleton of another . . .[11]

Colonel Glyn had begged that the 24th be allowed to bury their own dead, and with some misgivings Marshall had agreed. Archibald Forbes did not approve: 'One has some sympathy with the claim of the regiment to bury its own dead; but why postpone the interment till only a few bones can be gathered? As the matter stands, the Zulus, who have carefully buried their own dead, who do not appear to be very numerous, will come back tomorrow and find that we visited the place, not to bury our dead, but to remove a batch of wagons.'[12]

He had a point. The Artillery and Volunteers roughly covered over their own dead, mostly by piling loose stones over them, but all those in a red coat were left where they fell. Before Durnford's body was buried Offy Shepstone searched through his pockets for personal effects to send to his family. He found a penknife in his pocket, and gently took two rings from the withered fingers.

And then the practical work of the expedition began. About forty wagons were selected as worth salvaging, and Arthur Harness recovered the limber which had got stuck in the *donga* – the other one could not be found. The Zulus had not challenged the expedition at all – Matshana's *impi* had never materialized, if it ever existed – and the column was assembled and began the return march to Rorke's Drift. It had been on the battlefield for just a few hours. It was back on the other side of the river by early afternoon, leaving iSandlwana once more to the dead.

The following day Harness set out with Melton Prior and a squadron of Lancers to Sothondose's Drift to properly bury the remains of Harness's colleague Major Smith. Melton Prior sketched the burial; his sketch was never published, and the site of Smith's grave is today lost amid the dense bush that covers the final reaches of the fugitives' trail.

*

With the ghosts of iSandlwana laid at least temporarily to rest, the war moved quickly on. The wagons were taken to a new border depot at Landman's Drift on the Ncome to become part of the 2nd Division, and it was from here that the second invasion began eleven days later, on 1 June.

Whatever Lord Chelmsford's faults, he was not a general who failed to learn from his mistakes. His new advance was screened by cavalry vedettes to a degree simply not possible with the limited resources available in January, and he continued every night to protect his camps with entrenched *laagers*. Even so, fear of the Zulu army, of the terrible blood-stained bogeymen of iSandlwana, was so prevalent, particularly among troops fresh out from England, that false alarms were common, particularly at night. Worried that King Cetshwayo might still have the power to surprise him, Chelmsford authorized his mounted troops to strike at the bases of civilian support for the war, burning any homesteads they came across and destroying grain stores, and the progress of his columns was marked by broad swathes of destruction. Once again the amaQungebeni bore the early brunt of this; *inkosi* Sihayo's eZulaleni homestead lay directly in the path of Lord Chelmsford's advance and, despite a gallant attempt by his retainers to defend it, it was burned after a skirmish on 5 June.

At each homestead along the way the British were eager, before they put the huts to the torch, to seek out relics of iSandlwana, and when they found them they felt vindicated in their destructiveness. Saddles, portmanteaus, boots, tins, brushes, boxes and items of uniform, all were found in homesteads scattered along the way, a fair indication, too, of how men from every part of the country had fought in the battle. Arthur Harness had the last laugh on those who had teased him when he had meticulously ordered every piece of his battery's equipment to be marked – when two artillery wagons were found they still bore the designation 'N/5'.

In fact, however, Cetshwayo's army had the capacity to mount only one last challenge to the British advance. By the end of June the combined 2nd Division and Flying Column had reached the banks of the Mfolozi Mhlope, on the threshold of the great cluster of royal homesteads which constituted the Zulu capital. The king made a last ditch attempt to 'ward off the falling tree' by attempting with increasing desperation to open negotiations, but the moment for this, if it ever existed, had long since passed. Lord Chelmsford had by then been informed by London that he was to be superseded – a replacement, General Sir Garnet Wolseley, was already on his way to Natal with full civil and military powers, in effect taking command of both Frere and Chelmsford. Ironically, it was not the disaster at iSandlwana which had finally caused the Government to lose faith in its local representatives, it was the escalating cost of the war and the increasingly strained relationship between the military and the civil authorities in Natal. Chelmsford's one hope was to defeat the Zulus before Wolseley arrived – he needed the political and personal closure of a final victory, and he was in no mood to talk.

On 4 July 1879 Chelmsford crossed the Mfolozi with more than 5,000 troops, including several batteries of artillery and Lancers, as well as two hand-cranked Gatling machine-guns. Ironically, the 1/24th were not among his forces; the battalion had been hastily reconstituted with raw recruits drafted from eleven different battalions back home, but the troops had not yet found time to settle in under their officers and had behaved badly during one of the scares on the final approach – as punishment Chelmsford left them to guard his camp, denying them the opportunity to revenge themselves for iSandlwana.

The battle at oNdini – Ulundi, as the British called it – lasted less than an hour. Chelmsford drew up his troops in a hollow rectangle, the infantry lining the sides four deep and guns in the angle. For the last time the *amabutho* attacked in defence of their king and country, but the rushes lacked their earlier verve. As Mehlokazulu, who was there with the iNgobamakhosi, put it, 'at the Ondine battle, the last, we did not fight with the same spirit, because we were then frightened. We had had a severe lesson, and did not fight with the same zeal.'[13] Even so, Melton Prior noted that one charge from the left horn, led with typical aplomb by Zibhebhu ka-Maphitha, reached within nine paces of the British line before being chopped down. Elsewhere, however, few of the rushes were able to penetrate the terrible curtain of fire, and most of the attacks stalled at 300 or 400 metres. Chelmsford, sitting upright on his horse throughout the fight, John Crealock and Berkeley Milne by his side, saw the Zulus falter, and then ordered his cavalry to chase them from the field. The 17th Lancers – who had last charged an enemy at Balaclava in the Crimea – drove through the retreating *amabutho*, turning the retreat into a rout, and the Irregular Horse followed behind shooting survivors and stragglers. No sooner had the Zulus been driven over the hills than the cavalry took a grand tour of the Mahlabathini plain, setting fire to each of the great *amakhanda* in turn.

Several of those who had been through the flames on the British side were in at the kill. The Native Horse were there, with Cochrane in command, and both Essex and Gardner were inside the square. Chard – who had recovered from his bout of sickness after being treated in Ladysmith with a traditional Boer remedy, being sewn in a wet goat's skin to draw the fever – had rejoined his company, which was in reserve in the middle of the square. Private Wassall was present in the ranks of the

Mounted Infantry, and Arthur Harness had the satisfaction of commanding N/5 during the battle, and although disappointed that the enemy did not come within close range of his position nevertheless congratulated himself that 'my seven pounders made excellent shooting'.[14] The Natal Volunteers – the Carbineers, Newcastle Mounted Rifles, and Buffalo Border Guard had not been allowed to accompany the advance and to their disgust spent the end of the war guarding the supply lines, while Smith-Dorrien, still in the transport department, could get no further than Chelmsford's camp on the Mfolozi Mhlope, though he heard the boom of the guns.

No attempt was made to occupy oNdini, and the entire British force was back across the river by late afternoon. They had left more than a thousand Zulus dead, scattered in the long grass in a great arc around the position of the square, and as dusk came on the families of the dead and wounded emerged from hiding in search of their loved ones. The great royal homesteads would burn for several days.

King Cetshwayo had not stayed to watch the final humiliation. He had retired beyond the hills, and he left his attendants to sit on a rock alone to listen to the sound of the guns. When, an hour later, the first of his soldiers appeared, streaming past carrying badly wounded men, he threw a corner of his cloak over his head, for he could not bear to look at the fall of his kingdom.

*

There were small adventures still to come for Charlie Harford. He had missed the end of the war, spending his time between Durban and Pieter-maritzburg, but one day,

> ... being an honorary member of the Maritzburg Club, I ... was told that a Kaffir had been there daily for weeks past, enquiring for me, not saying what he wanted except that he wished to see me. I left word as to when I should be at the Club again, and when I did, found my friend squatting patiently waiting on the doorstep for my arrival. Getting up and greeting me with the usual salutation of *Inkosi*, and evidently very pleased at having unearthed me at last, judge my surprise when from an old bundle he produced the left boot of my favourite pair of Dean's field boots, in which was stowed away two pocket handkerchiefs with my name on them, relics from the camp at Isandhlwana which he had picked up at Ulundi, on the battlefield not far from Cetewayo's kraal.

He had belonged to our Contingent, and on the disbandment of the
Natives had made his way to No. 1 Column on the coast, whence he
apparently attached himself to the 2nd Native Contingent (in which no
doubt he had pals), and came in for the fight there. Isandhlwana was
fought on the 22nd January, and Ulundi on the 4th July, so the Zulus
had ample time to carry off the Isandlwana loot to Ulundi, and no
doubt in the confusion of the distribution my pair of boots had got
separated, and this single boot thrown away. It is quite safe to say no-
one else in the whole of the Forces had boots of a similar cut and my
friend, like all other Kaffirs being an observant individual, knew directly
he saw it who it belonged to, and at once brought it away in the hope
of being able to find me again and hand it back . . . the Zulu army had
the honour of carrying my boot over 150 miles [241 kilometres], and
this good chap had tramped with it another 200 miles [322 kilometres]
on the off-chance . . .[15]

Although the fighting in Zululand was over, King Cetshwayo was still at
large, and Chelmsford's successor, Sir Garnet Wolseley, organized new
columns to sweep through the country to pacify it. Harford was offered a
staff appointment in a column commanded by Colonel Mansfield Clarke
which operated in the northern coastal district. Since Harford spoke isiZulu,
he was employed in negotiations with local *amakhosi*, trying to persuade
them formally to surrender although the king himself had not. In particular,
Harford was sent to meet with a powerful *inkosi*, Somkele kaMalanda,
whose Mpukonyoni people dominated the north of the coastal plain south
of Lake St Lucia. After a tense meeting, the *inkosi* finally agreed to submit,
and:

> . . . during this time one of Somkele's warriors came up and asked if
> any of us had been at Isandhlwana, and on telling him that I was out
> with the Contingent at Isipezi at the time of the fight, he caught hold of
> both my hands and shook them firmly in a great state of delight, saying
> it was a splendid fight. 'You fought well, and we fought well', he
> exclaimed, and then showed me eleven wounds that he had received,
> bounding off in the greatest ecstasy to show how it all happened.
> Rushing up to me he jumped, fell on his stomach, got up again, rolled
> over and over, crawled flat, bounded on again, and so forth and came
> right up to me. His movements being applauded by the warriors
> squatting in the centre of the kraal with a loud 'Gee!'
>
> I now had a look at his wounds. One bullet had gone through his

hand, three had gone through his shoulder, and had smashed his shoulder-blade, two had cut the skin and slightly into the flesh right down the chest and stomach, and one had gone clean through the fleshy part of the thigh. The others were mere scratches in comparison with these, but there he was, after about eight months, as well as ever and ready for another set-to. Could anything more clearly show the splendid spirit in which the Zulus fought? No animosity, no revengeful feeling, but just sheer love of a good fight in which the courage of both sides could be tested, and it was evident that the courage of our soldiers was as much appreciated as that of theirs . . . [16]

It was in such meetings with ordinary Zulus, now that the *amabutho* had been safely defeated, that the British first began to move away from the impression of the Zulu as bloodthirsty savages that had prevailed after iSandlwana, and recast them as noble warriors in a form which flattered both their own military achievements and their sense of cultural superiority. As John Chard put it, 'Those Zulus were an enemy that it was some credit to us to have defeated. Their bravery and courage could not have been excelled, and their military organization and their discipline might have given a lesson to more civilized nations. Cruel and savage as they were, the Zulus were, however, a gallant enemy.'[17]

Yet, while a genuine mutual respect had undoubtedly been fostered on the battlefields of 1879, it was not one based on any kind of equality of experience. In finding common ground with individual Zulus, British soldiers could reassure themselves that the war was indeed over, and assuage any lingering feelings of guilt about the causes of the conflict. Yet the Anglo-Zulu War had not been a cricket match in which evenly matched sides had met in fair play and the best side had won – it had been an unequal struggle between an industrialized nation with the best weapons the technology of the age could provide and a people fighting for their country with little more than raw courage to sustain them. The defeated lost not only the lives of thousands, their indigenous political institutions, the centres of their political administration, many, many ordinary homes and thousands of head of cattle, but also their independence and the very fabric of their way of life. Nothing for the Zulu would be the same again.

The British, however, walked away from the consequences of the war. In London the Disraeli administration had fallen – given a shove in part by Gladstone's tub-thumping in the Midlothian by-election, in which he had thundered 'What was the crime of the Zulus?' – and the new Conservative Government set its face against imperial expansion. Sir Garnet Wolseley's political brief was on no account to accept the financial burden of annexing Zululand. Instead – with Theophilus Shepstone's advice – he decided to divide the country up among thirteen *amakhosi* nominated by the British. The criteria for selecting them was that they be sympathetic to British interests – and opposed to the Zulu royal house. Among those who gladly accepted the posts were John Dunn, Prince Hamu, Zibhebhu kaMaphitha and the Tlokoa *inkosi* Hlubi. These negotiations were already under way when King Cetshwayo was finally captured by British Dragoons on 28 August. For weeks, since Ulundi, he had wandered with a small entourage through northern Zululand, from the homestead of one loyal supporter to another, avoiding increasingly desperate British attempts to capture him, until he was eventually surprised early one morning and taken without a fight. He was brought under guard to Wolseley's camp near the ruins of oNdini, and from there taken to the coast where he was put on board a steamer destined for exile in the Cape Colony.

Charlie Harford saw Cetshwayo brought into Colonel Clarke's camp under guard, and his account hints at a touch of regret at the awareness that an old order was passing, with just the faintest trace of guilt that he himself had been part of the process:

> After alighting from the cart (and with his wives hanging on to him as if they thought he was doomed to immediate execution, and absolutely terrified), [he] strode in with the aid of his long stick, with a proud and dignified air and grace, looking a magnificent specimen of his race and every inch a warrior in his grand *umutcha* [loin covering] of leopardskin and tails, with lion's teeth and claw charms around his neck. Well over six feet [1.8 metres], fat but not corpulent, with a stern, severe and cruel countenance, he looked what he was, a savage ruler.[18]

*

For Lord Chelmsford the war had ended with a concerted rearguard action to protect his reputation from growing criticism of his handling of the iSandlwana campaign. Ironically, the Natal press had been among the first to suspect that Chelmsford's staff had been making an orchestrated attempt to shift the blame for the defeat onto Durnford's shoulders. On 29 May the *Natal Witness* reported that it was common knowledge that 'certain members of Lord Chelmsford's staff ... came down to 'Maritzburg after the disaster, prepared to make Colonel Durnford bear the whole responsibility, and it was upon their representations that the High Commissioner's telegram about "poor Durnford's misfortune" was sent'.[19] There was an irony in this, of course, in that the Natal press had been no friend to Durnford in the past, and yet it sensed in the thrust of the staff's attacks that the military establishment was closing ranks. If Durnford was at fault, the colonial press recognized that, by implication, so too were the settler gentry, whose sons had, after all, died beside him.

Several people rose up to champion Durnford in Natal, among them Bishop Colenso, and – of course – his daughter Frances, to whom Durnford had become attached when his own marriage was failing. It was under Colenso's influence that Durnford's body was exhumed in September 1879, and re-interred – with a surprising degree of pomp and ceremony – in the military cemetery at Fort Napier in Pietermaritzburg. Frances Colenso, her love for Durnford validated now in a way it could never have been in life, formed an alliance with Durnford's brother, Edward, and between them they waged a long campaign in his defence. Edward Durnford produced pamphlets challenging point by point Lord Chelmsford's explanation of events, and together they wrote a strongly polemical history of the war, fiercely critical of both Chelmsford and Bartle Frere.

There is no doubt that Chelmsford struggled to understand much of the criticism levelled against him. In his mind, he had made proper arrangements for the safeguarding of the camp, and it seemed to him unjust that he was accused of shortcomings which had occurred during his absence.

It was a battle he would fight for the rest of his career. Although he had returned to England – as he had hoped – as the victor of Ulundi rather than as the vanquished of iSandlwana, his superiors were not unaware of his failings. In a confidential memo the Commander in Chief, the Duke of Cambridge, had pressed him to answer a number of points about his handling of the campaign, and Chelmsford's replies had been uncertain and evasive. The duke saw through them, and his conclusions were sharply critical of the sense of over-confidence and propensity to underestimate Zulu capabilities that pervaded the Centre Column. He criticized, too, Chelmsford's decision to split his forces, his inadequate reconnaissance and his failure to ensure that the camp was properly defended. Only in one area did he let Chelmsford off the hook – in apportioning some blame to an unnamed officer (he meant Durnford) who had further divided the camp's garrison on the eve of attack rather than drawing them together.

Chelmsford was a member of the old Victorian military establishment, and he had a network of influential contacts built up over a lifetime of soldiering. The Queen herself admired him and rallied to him, considering much of the criticism of him unjust. And yet the Duke of Cambridge had, in a very real sense, marked his card. Although Chelmsford enjoyed a number of prestigious military appointments throughout the rest of his career – Commander of the Tower of London, Gold Stick[20] – he was never allowed to command troops in action again.

He died on 9 April 1905, following a collapse during a game of billiards at the United Services Club.

*

The Battle of iSandlwana destroyed both the confederation policy which had provoked it and the glittering career of Governor General Sir Henry Bartle Frere. The spotlight of public scrutiny which had flooded British policies in southern Africa in the aftermath of iSandlwana, and the embarrassment this had caused the Disraeli administration, had brought an immediate halt to further hopes of expansion in the region, and with Gladstone's election as Prime Minister they collapsed completely. When, in late 1880, there was a republican uprising among the Boers in the Transvaal which led to a series of British military defeats, Gladstone scrabbled to make peace on terms which effectively abandoned almost all British claims to the territory, shrugging off completely the political strategies which had led Frere to confront the Zulu kingdom in the first place.

Frere's reputation had withered in the spotlight, the qualities of independence and resolve which had made him seem such an ideal imperial proconsul just a few short years before, now, against the sight of that devastated field at iSandlwana, seeming no more than arrogance and folly. Perhaps he deserves the blame that has accrued to him – he had, after all, pursued the confrontation in the teeth of opposition from London – but the war was not his alone. Theophilus Shepstone, the man who had shaped so many of Natal's policies, and Secretary of State for the Colonies Lord Carnarvon must take their share of the guilt, although perhaps in their way they were all victims of those historical forces which had first propelled European empires into Africa.

Effectively demoted by the appointment of Sir Garnet Wolseley as

Chelmsford's successor in June 1879, with civil as well as military powers, Frere was finally recalled to London once the dust had settled in August 1880. Called upon to defend his policies inside Parliament and out, he spent much of his time vigorously defending his actions, but his career was ruined. He died in Wimbledon in May 1884.

\*

For the professional soldiers who had served under Lord Chelmsford, the end of the war meant a move to pastures new. Edward Essex served as a staff officer throughout the Transvaal Revolt of 1881, and narrowly escaped death twice more, in the Battles of Laing's Nek and Ingogo; his capacity for hair's-breadth survival earned him the nickname 'Lucky Essex'. He went on to become an instructor at the Royal Military Academy at Sandhurst, and commanded the Gordon Highlanders.

John North Crealock's later career, like his chief's, was successful but undistinguished. He commanded his regiment, the 95th, in Gibraltar and India before accepting a series of home appointments. His rival, Cornelius Clery, went on to serve under another Zulu War veteran, Redvers Buller, in the Natal campaign during the Anglo-Boer War in 1899; for all his theoretical knowledge he proved an uninspired commander and he resigned his command in 1900.

Rupert Lonsdale, who had narrowly escaped the victorious Zulu army that hot Wednesday afternoon, was less lucky in West Africa. He served briefly in the BaSotho 'Gun War' of 1880, and in 1881 took up an appointment on the staff of Sir Samuel Rowe on the Gold Coast. He remained there for seven years but in 1888 he returned to England, apparently in poor health. He died in Liverpool on 28 February 1888, the cause of his death being given as 'acute spinal paralysis'.

George Hamilton Browne continued the life of a hard-bitten adventurer. He knocked about southern Africa, commanded the Diamond Fields Horse for a while, and followed Cecil Rhodes' private enterprise conquest of Zimbabwe. He married twice, the second time late in life to a lady of means at a time when he was in dire financial straits; he died in a nursing home in Jamaica in 1913. After his death his widow found that he had spent all her money; when she petitioned the New Zealand Government for some assistance in the light of her husband's distinguished service there, she was informed they had no record of anyone of his name serving in their forces.

Of that small 'band of brothers' who sailed out on board the *Edinburgh*

*Castle* in 1878, Lieutenant George Williams was the only one to die in the campaign, killed in the debacle at Hlobane. William Cochrane had fought at three major engagements – iSandlwana, Hlobane and Khambula – and survived them all. He went on to serve with the Cape forces during the BaSotho 'Gun War' of 1880–81 and later the Anglo-Egyptian Campaign. During the reconquest of the Sudan in 1898 he commanded the line of communication towards Omdurman. He retired with the honorary rank of brigadier-general and died in 1927. Henry Charles Harford remained with his regiment, the 99th, and served in India and Malta and rose to the rank of colonel, at various times commanding both battalions, but he saw no further active service and was eventually deemed by a medical board to be both physically and mentally unfit for duty. He eventually retired to Sussex and died in 1927.

Horace Smith-Dorrien eclipsed them all. He enjoyed a long career which saw service in almost every theatre in which the late Victorian Army was engaged. He fought on the North-West Frontier, in Egypt and the Sudan, returned to southern Africa for the Anglo-Boer War, and as a general commanded II Corps during the retreat from Mons in the First World War. His successful defence of Le Cateau in 1914 against orders earned him the resentment of his commanding officer, Sir John French, and in May 1915 he lost his command. He was offered an appointment in East Africa, but ill-health intervened, and his career was effectively over. He had by then become something of a national hero, and was in regular demand as an after-dinner speaker, and of all the many anecdotes of his long and adventurous life, the one he enjoyed telling perhaps the most was that of his encounter with Quartermaster Bloomfield at iSandlwana on 22 January 1879.[21] He died on 12 August 1930 of injuries received in a car crash near Chippenham, Wiltshire.

Of the men who rose briefly to public celebrity for their part in the defence of Rorke's Drift, John Chard perhaps enjoyed the role of hero the most. When he returned to England in October 1879 he was honoured with a series of presentations, addresses and invitations to dine, many of which he accepted in his usual modest and relaxed manner. He was invited to dine with Queen Victoria – she liked him, he was invited back – and posed for his portrait in at least two paintings of the battle. Inevitably, his later career offered little to compare with Rorke's Drift and he passed through a succession of peacetime appointments. In the autumn of 1896 he was diagnosed as suffering from cancer of the tongue, the result of his lifelong passion for the pipe, and in August 1897 he went on the sick list. He went to live with his brother, vicar of the village of Hatch Beauchamp in Somerset, and Queen Victoria wrote of her concern. He died on 1 November 1897, aged forty-nine.

Gunny Bromhead, in contrast, struggled with the demands imposed by fame, and was content to slip back into the routine of life in the regimental family. He followed the 2/24th in their postings to Gibraltar – he too was invited to an audience with the Queen – and then India. He was present in the 3rd Burma War of 1886 but died of typhoid in Allahabad on 9 February 1892.

For the other ranks who fought at Rorke's Drift, the honour of bearing the Victoria Cross offered only slight mitigation against the hardships which typically beset old soldiers in Victorian times. 'Harry' Hook left the Army in 1880 and found a job working at the British Museum, where the VC ribbon on his attendant's tunic aroused considerable interest over the years – he was interviewed a number of times and became so adept at telling the story of the battle that he became one of the best-known ordinary soldiers of his day. He died in March 1905. Fred Hitch survived his terrible injuries but was invalided out of the Army and found work in London with the Corps of Commissionaires. In 1901 his VC was stolen and he applied for a replacement; he was eventually presented with a new one by Lord Roberts in 1908. With the advent of the motor car, he established a small motor business and later secured a job as a taxi driver in Chiswick, south London; he died in 1913 and was buried with full military honours in Chiswick Old Cemetery in a funeral attended by over a thousand cabbies.

At least two of the VC winners display clear signs, in retrospect, of posttraumatic stress. Robert Jones left the Army in 1888 and worked as a groundsman on an estate in Herefordshire. In later years he suffered headaches – his medical reports mention a head injury which does not seem to have been inflicted at Rorke's Drift, and may have been the result of a hunting accident – and on 6 September 1898 he borrowed his employer's gun on the pretext that he needed to shoot crows and shot himself in the mouth. William Jones, who had crossed bayonets with Robert on the bloody threshold of Otto Witt's house, was discharged from the Army as unfit due to rheumatism – the effects of years of cold nights spent sleeping on wet ground – in February 1880. He settled in Manchester and took what work he could, appearing as himself on occasion in travelling shows. In 1893 he was forced to pawn his VC. He became plagued by nightmares which drove him to rush out of his house, on one occasion carrying his young granddaughter with him. In 1912 he was found wandering the steets confused and distressed. He died in April 1913.

Perhaps the saddest fate befell Chistian Ferdinand Schiess, the Swiss-born corporal in the 3rd NNC who had so impressed Chard by leaping over the barricades at Rorke's Drift to bayonet Zulus sheltering beyond. When the NNC was dissolved at the end of the war he struggled to find work, and by 1884 he was living unemployed and destitute in Durban. His plight aroused some sympathy and the Navy agreed to ship him to England free of charge while a public subscription kept him in food. His health was broken, however, and he succumbed to pneumonia on 14 December 1884. His death certificate gave his age as 'not known – about 36 years'; he was in fact twenty-eight years old. He was buried at sea off the coast of West Africa.

*

The 24th had finally buried their dead at the end of June 1879, once the war had moved safely away from the Mzinyathi border.

On the 20th Wilsone Black led a party of 30 mounted and 50 dis-mounted men of the 1st Dragoon Guards, 140 men of the 2/24th, 360 Border Guards and 50 men of an auxiliary unit, Tetelekhu's Horse, across from Rorke's Drift. They were accompanied by Major Dartnell and repre-sentatives of the Mounted Police and Volunteer units, including the Carbineers.

By this time the grass had grown long all over the battlefield, and the debris scattered across the campsite was becoming weathered by the sun and rain. Already some of the burials completed in May were being washed open, while even their units found it difficult to recognize the unburied dead. Even so, Black noted that seventy dead of the 24th lay in a clump behind their officers' tents, while further down, where the tents once stood, lay another sixty, among whom Black recognized Captain Wardell and Lieutenant Dyer. A similar number lay at the foot of iSandlwana – Black thought Younghusband was among them – while down the slope the site of Durnford's stand on the road was also evident. Many of the dead lay on the Manzimnyama side of the *nek*, and here and there the bodies of soldiers and Zulus still lay entwined together.[22]

Black's party dug shallow graves in the hard soil and covered over the remains. There were too many to inter in one day, and the party returned to Rorke's Drift that night. They came back again on the 23rd, and again on the 26th, to finish the job.

Yet the dead at iSandlwana have determinedly refused to stay buried. Most of the remains – particularly those buried with such haste in May – were only a couple of centimetres below the surface, and the first heavy rains began inexorably to expose them. As early as September 1879 Sir Garnet Wolseley ordered Brevet Major C.J. Bromhead – Gunny's brother – to visit the site and carefully clean up the field, reburying any exposed remains. Bromhead camped on the battlefield on the night of 19 September with F and H Companies of his battalion, and the next day his men swept across the battlefield.[23] Many of the damaged graves were repaired, and a number of bodies located in the outlying areas and buried. Bromhead authorized three large cairns of stones to be built on the spots where he thought the resistance had been toughest. One of these was constructed on the shoulder of iSandlwana where Younghusband had made his stand, and another below it on the *nek*.[24] The third stands across the *nek*, at the foot of the Mahlabamkhosi *kopje*.

Despite Bromhead's endeavours, Wolseley complained in early 1880 that travellers – the site was already receiving attention from adventurous tourists – had reported that remains were again exposed. A party of one NCO and ten men of the 60th Rifles was sent out under a Lieutenant O'Connell, accompanied by a Sub-Inspector Philips and seven troopers of the Natal Mounted Police. They camped on the battlefield for five days from 14 March, and O'Connell did his best to ensure the graves were fully repaired. His methods were nothing if not practical – he lined his men up, gave each man a sack, and walked them across the battlefield. Once two or three bags were full, they dug a hole and buried the remains together.[25]

Even so, at the end of 1880 a Fellow of the Royal Geographical Society, R.W. Leyland, made a brief visit to the site and saw 'The most unpleasant sight . . . many unbleached human bones. They had been washed by heavy rains out of the shallow graves in which they had been interred – We noted some bodies partially exposed, portions of skeletons visible. In one instance the leg bones, encased in leather gaiters, protruded at the bottom of a grave, and close by were the soldier's boots, containing what remained of his feet.'[26]

Finally, in 1883, a Natal civil servant, Alfred Boast, was instructed by the lieutenant-governor to take a work party to the site and bury the dead once and for all. Boast camped on the battlefield from 12 February to

9 March and exhumed all but those graves individually identified. The remains were buried in graves 1 metre deep and 0.75 metres wide and stones piled up on top. Boast's meticulous report lists a total of 298 graves, each containing the remains of between two and four men.[27]

It is Boast's stones that form the basis of the cairns which characterize the site today. In 1929, however, a small portion of the battlefield – on the *nek* – was fenced off and while this served to protect the main monuments from casual damage, many of the outlying cairns fell into disrepair, damaged by the rain or by straying cattle. By the 1940s many were in danger of being lost, and in 1958 a local curator flattened some of the rest. While many of these were replaced and rebuilt in the 1960s, the location of some of those now on the site was fixed by memory alone.

*

For all their opposition to it, the Colenso family never really escaped the war, any more than Frere or Chelmsford could. The defeat of the Zulu army and the capture and exile of King Cetshwayo only intensified Bishop Colenso's campaigning on their behalf. He poured forth a series of pamphlets deriding Frere's policies, pointing out the absurdities of the propaganda campaign waged to justify the invasion, and highlighting the injustices inflicted on the Zulu people afterwards. The first of a steady stream of royalist supporters walked all the way from Zululand to Pietermaritzburg to appeal to him for a sympathy and support they found entirely lacking in the colonial officials who now exercised the ultimate control over their lives. Colenso strove heroically on their behalf but, increasingly isolated from mainstream settler society, and particularly from all influence over Theophilus Shepstone and his influential clique, his efforts were ultimately in vain. Refusing to be daunted, Colenso gave himself up to Zulu affairs, to the detriment of his health – in June 1883 he was taken ill and died; he is buried in front of the altar of St Peter's Church in Pietermaritzburg.

The burden of his work was taken up by his eldest daughter, Harriette, and his youngest, Agnes. Both became tireless champions of the Zulu cause throughout the difficult years towards the end of the century which marked the breaking up of the old kingdom.

Frances Ellen Colenso – Durnford's friend, Nell – found comfort in his death in a hopeless fight to restore his reputation. In 1880 she published a fictionalized and rather cloying account of his involvement in the Langalibalele affair under the pseudonym Atherton Wylde, and, along with her ally Edward Durnford, she continued tirelessly to pursue any clues that might expose the extent to which she believed Chelmsford's supporters had deliberately shifted the blame to Durnford. When an officer present during the burial expeditions mentioned to Edward Durnford that he had seen Offy Shepstone remove something from Durnford's body, Edward seized on the hope that it might have been Chelmsford's orders of the day. Believing they might exonerate Anthony from the charge that he had been specifically ordered to 'take command of the camp', Edward wrote to Shepstone to demand an explanation. Shepstone replied that he had only removed a ring from Durnford's dead fingers and Edward was inclined to let the matter drop, but Frances pursued it with such determination that in the end Shepstone demanded an inquiry to clear his name. It found no evidence that he had removed or suppressed any papers from Durnford's body, and ironically, when Durnford's orders were found on the battlefield, they included no such phrase. Frances Colenso died in 1887 from tuberculosis she had contracted while nursing a sick soldier in 1878.

Sir Garnet Wolseley's post-war settlement of Zululand was largely shaped by Theophilus Shepstone's belief that the Zulu kingdom should be reduced to its constituent parts, thus breaking down the unity imposed by Shaka. With the collapse of confederation, Shepstone decided to retire from public life and lived quietly in retirement in Pietermaritzburg until his death in June 1893, but his influence continued to shape colonial policies towards the African population until at least the 1920s. He left behind him, moreover, a family deeply imbued with his attitudes and beliefs, and placed at the very centre of Natal governmental affairs. His brother John – who had failed to capture Matshana kaMondise in 1857 and who had read Frere's ultimatum to the Zulu delegates in December 1878 – continued to dominate the Natal Native Affairs department throughout the 1880s, using his considerable influence to block any attempted resurgence by the Zulu royal house. As late as 1904 he provided evidence to the South African Native Affairs Commission arguing against allowing black Africans a right to vote in colonial elections; he died in 1916. During much of that time, from 1884 to 1893, the post of Secretary for Native Affairs was held by Theophilus' son, Henrique.

Theophilus Shepstone Junior, 'Offy' – who had followed the family tradition by failing to capture Matshana at Mangeni on the day of iSandlwana – served throught the remainder of the war, and in 1884 accepted an offer from the Swazi King Mbandzeni to represent his affairs. Shepstone's role was to act as an intermediary between the Swazi king and white concession hunters, but Shepstone failed to draw a clear distinction between his own interests and those of his patron; according to the historian Huw Jones, he 'failed to represent their interests during the eight years in which they had relied upon him for advice and guidance. Largely through his interest in personal aggrandisement, the Swazi had effectively lost their independence'.[28] Offy Shepstone died in March 1907.

For the junior colonial officials and Volunteer Corps troopers whose lives were touched by the war, the end of hostilities marked the return to the everyday hardships of life in the colony. James Brickhill, the Centre Column's interpreter, continued to work as a translator, though not again with the military; he died in Durban in 1892. Fred Symons went back to his life as a farmer, although his friend Ted Greene continued his interest in the Volunteers and rose to become a colonel in the Natal Carbineers. Henry Fynn returned to his post as magistrate at Msinga, where he spent most of the rest of his career; he died in Pietermaritzburg in 1915.

Otto Witt had left Natal in 1879 for England and Sweden, but in 1880 he returned to his mission, Oscarsberg. On landing in Durban he was surprised to find that the interviews he had given citicizing settler attitudes had made him unpopular in colonial society, and he and his family were compelled to take a circuitous route back to their property. They found it much as the military had left it – the house long gone and the store fortified – and Witt pulled down the remains and built a new church resting, at least in part, on the store's foundations. Witt subsequently applied to the British Government for compensation for the destruction of his property; after careful consideration, the Government decided that, while the Army had indeed assumed responsibility for the site during the war, all damage inflicted there had been the result of enemy action rather than its own and it declined. Witt remained at Rorke's Drift until 1890, and in 1891 he returned to Sweden; he lived until August 1923.

In the immediate aftermath of the war, the Tlokoa *inkosi*, Durnford's old friend Hlubi kaMota, had reaped the rewards of being on the winning side. Under the Wolseley settlement he was given a slice of land along the eastern bank of the Mzinyathi, effectively displacing Sihayo, and providing a loyal buffer zone on behalf of British interests on the Zulu side of the border at Rorke's Drift. During the upheavals that followed he was frequently called upon to raise his followers in support of British interests, and he always did so, his men fighting in a number of skirmishes throughout the 1880s. In the end, though, he learned a hard truth, for with the extension of British interests over Zululand late in the century, he found his own powers limited no less than those of his Zulu counterparts. The British triumph had proved inimical to the aspirations of all traditional African leaders – whether collaborators or no. Hlubi died in October 1902.

A similar lesson had been learnt in short order by the iziGqoza princes, Mkhungo and Sikhota, whose followers had fought at iSandlwana. Once the war was won and King Cetshwayo captured, the British saw no real reason to replace one member of the royal house with another, and their support for the iziGqoza cause was quietly dropped.

# 29

# 'The day that I die'

## Mehlokazulu, 6 June 1906

And the Zulus?

Mehlokazulu was recognized when the *amakhosi* and their followers came to formally submit to Wolseley at oNdini in August 1879. He was arrested under the terms of the Frere's ultimatum, photographed in captivity between white and black guards – an imperial trophy of conquest – and sent down under guard to Pietermaritzburg where he was put on trial. Under questioning he gave a long, detailed and accurate account of the role he had played in the war, and only in one area was he evasive; he stated that the action in which he had crossed into Natal and arrested his 'mothers', MaMtshali and MaMthethwa, had been authorized by both his father, Sihayo, and the king. Since neither were on hand to contradict him his statement went unchallenged – the whites preferred to believe in any case in Cetshwayo's aggressive intent. Yet his trial was something of a fiasco, for he had committed no crime under Natal law, offered no insult to Natal citizens, and had punished Zulu citizens on Zulu soil under Zulu law. He was released with nothing more than a sanctimonious ticking-off from the judge.

Mehlokazulu returned to Zululand late in 1879 to find it a very different place, however. Wolseley's settlement had quite deliberately sought to erode the influence of the royal house and its supporters, and the amaQungebeni were high on his hit list. Their territory had been given to Hlubi Molife, who built his own Sotho-style stone-walled huts close to the ruins of kwaSogekle in an obvious act of displacement. Sihayo himself continued to live in the eastern borders of his old domain, close to Babanango mountain, but his old affluence had gone – the war had killed two of his sons and left him impoverished. Many influential *amakhosi* continued to blame him for bringing the ruin of the British invasion upon their heads.

King Cetshwayo, after his capture, was lodged in the old Dutch castle at

Cape Town. Here he became something of a curiosity to well-heeled British tourists working their way around the Empire, and he was astute enough to receive visitors courteously, building a groundswell of support in England among liberals who were beginning to question the justice of the invasion.

Wolseley's settlement had, in any case, proved too successful for its own good, unleashing deep divisions within the country. Both Zibhebhu ka-Maphitha and Prince Hamu worked assiduously to repress all expressions of support for the old regime in their area and in doing so found themselves categorized as traitors by the majority of Zulus who had fought loyally in support of their king. By 1881 friction was beginning to spill into open violence, raising the spectre that a post-war Zululand might prove more of a threat to the stability and security of Natal than the pre-war one. Confused that events were not unfolding as its advisers, chiefly Shepstone, had predicted, the Colonial Office toyed with the idea of restoring Cetshwayo to part of Zululand under British authority. In July 1882 the king was allowed to visit London to argue his case. Large crowds curious to see the victor of iSandlwana, the ape-like savage depicted in the down-market press at the time, were astonished to find a tall, regal man impeccably dressed in European clothes. Cetshwayo was introduced to Queen Victoria at Osborne House – the meeting was apparently a little cool, she had friends among the 24th, but she presented him with a silver mug and instructed her portrait painter, Carl Sohn, to paint him anyway. He was taken to the theatre and had his picture taken at Bassano's, the fashionable London photographer, and after a day or two he was followed everywhere by good-natured crowds who gathered outside his lodgings and gave three cheers whenever he appeared.

It was a masterly display of rehabilitation, and the king returned to the Cape under guarantee to return to Zululand. Only at the last minute was he informed that large chunks of his kingdom would be kept from him to shelter those who had waxed fat in his absence.

He landed again on Zulu soil in February 1883, and ironically it fell to Theophilus Shepstone to escort him to oNdini. All his old royal homesteads had been destroyed, and the king built a new oNdini close to the ruins of the old. Henry Fynn was appointed magistrate and adviser to the king. Cetshwayo was strictly prohibited from reviving the *amabutho* system, but many of his old adherents flocked to pay him their respects. Among them were Sihayo and his son Mehlokazulu, Ntshingwayo – the victor of iSandlwana, Mnyamana Buthelezi and Vumandaba kaNthathi, who had received the British ultimatum on his behalf and prevented the iNgobamakhosi crossing into Natal at Sothondose's Drift.

Yet his return was a disaster. It polarized opinion within the country between royalist and anti-royalist factions, and his followers not unnaturally took the opportunity to avenge themselves upon those who had oppressed them during his absence. In May a large force of his supporters launched an attack against *inkosi* Zibhebhu, but Zibhebhu, who was poised to emerge as the greatest Zulu general since Shaka's day, lured them into a trap and destroyed them in an ambush in the Msebe valley. Fearing for his own safety, Cetshwayo called up his old *amabutho* – in flagrant defiance of the conditions imposed by the British – to oNdini. Here he met with his old council to discuss what to do next.

Zibhebhu beat them to it. On the night of 20 July 1883 he made a daring march across country from his homestead in the north and at dawn on the 21st his men appeared on the ridges overlooking oNdini. The royal *amabutho*, the same groups who had triumphed at iSandlwana – the iNgobamakhosi, the uMbonambi, the uKhandempemvu – went out to meet him in some disarray and collapsed before Zibhebhu's triumphal advance. A detachment of the uThulwana, survivors of Rorke's Drift, were surrounded in the royal homestead and wiped out, and for the second time in its history oNdini went up in flames. Cetshwayo was wounded by a spear and only just managed to escape; many of his old councillors were run down and killed before they could get away. Among them was Ntshingwayo kaMahole of the Khoza, left lying sprawled on the field across his great war-shield, killed not by a foreign enemy, but by a fellow veteran of iSandlwana. So, too, was Sihayo kaXongo Ngobese, who had owed his rise to royal patronage, whose son had brought disgrace on the royal house – and who had now paid the ultimate price.

The king himself took refuge under British protection at Eshowe. For several months he tentatively tried to rebuild his authority then, on 8 February 1884, he collapsed suddenly and died. A doctor who examined him officially attributed the cause of death to heart disease, but suggested privately that he may have been poisoned.

The death of Cetshwayo ushered in dark years for Zululand, and the civil war spluttered on with varying degrees of intensity until Cetshwayo's son, Dinuzulu, defeated Zibhebhu and, in 1888, orchestrated one last uprising against British rule. He was easily defeated and sent to that traditional political prison of the British Empire, St Helena.

The final defeat of the royal house in 1888 paved the way – at last – for British annexation and the opening up of Zululand to white settlement. As Africans in Natal had discovered over the previous decades, this meant that the population of Zululand now lost their best grazing lands, often those containing the graves of their ancestors, to white settlement. Their *amakhosi* became dependent on the support of the white authorities and were now in effect agents of imperial control.

In 1906 a new tax was levied across Zululand and Natal, a poll tax to be paid by every man, regardless of status or wealth. It caused considerable hardship in Natal where the black population was already heavily taxed, and several groups refused to pay. A young *inkosi* of the amaZondi people, living in Msinga not far from the amaChunu, Bhambatha kaMacinza, took to the bush and when Mounted Police were sent to arrest him in June he attacked them. He then fled across the Thukela into Zululand and tried to raise the *amakhosi* there to rebellion.

The outbreak of the rebellion threw into the same sharp relief for the Zulu *amakhosi* the dilemmas that living under colonial rule had posed for the Natal Africans during the previous half-century. Bhambatha tried to harness the prestige of the old Zulu order to his cause by drawing on the heroic mystique of the royal house – deliberately choosing King Cetshwayo's remote grave in the Nkandla forest as a rallying point – but Dinuzulu, having learned a bitter lesson in 1888, remained aloof, leaving individual *amakhosi* to ally themselves as best they could. Some, like Sishishili kaMnqandi, who had fought with the uKhandempemvu at iSandlwana, opted to place their faith in the new order, and declared for the colonial government. Most simply sought to avoid trouble, caught between the attentions of the colonial authorities and the resentment felt by their young men.

Among those *amakhosi* trapped by this dilemma was Matshana ka-Mondise. Matshana's second escape from the Shepstones had clearly left him feeling uncomfortable, and throughout the 1880s and 1890s he had lived quietly at Nsingabantu, although the missionary, Reverend A.W. Lee – who met him in 1904 – thought that he had lost none of his strength of character. He was, said Lee, 'an elderly man of immense dignity ... a tall, spare man, who regarded lesser folk with a considerable hauteur and demanded from them full recognition of his importance'.[1] With the outbreak of the rebellion, however, Matshana came under considerable pressure from his followers to join the rebels, but clearly worried at the fate that would befall him if he did, he refused; in the end, his son slipped away to join Bhambatha.

For Mehlokazulu the situation was even worse. He had spent twenty years harried by the colonial authorities, fearful of his reputation as an *iqawe* and of the role he played in 1879 – Lee thought him 'a Zulu of the old school, a fighting man with a distinguished record ... he glared at me out of rather prominent, blood-shot eyes'.[2] If there is a hint of strain in that description, Mehlokazulu was undoubtedly feeling it, for when the rebellion broke out the amaQungebeni were targeted and colonial troops moved into their area. Mehlokazulu fled to take refuge on Malakatha mountain, near iSandlwana, and while he was gone the troops burned his homestead.

It is difficult to avoid the impression that Mehlokazulu had had enough. His youthful act of family pride had brought about the destruction of Zululand – now all he had left, so it seemed, was his reputation as a warrior. He decided to throw in his lot with the rebels, yet he had few illusions about the outcome. One of his wives was pregnant and before he left for war he instructed her to name the child when it was born Mhlawosuku – 'the day that I die'. He then took those of the amaQungebeni who were willing to stand beside him and set off into the dense bush along the central Thukela for a rendezvous with Bhambatha.

But the colonial forces got wind of his movements, and at dawn on 6 June they ambushed Mehlokazulu's and Bhambatha's combined forces at the entrance to the narrow Mome Gorge. The rebels were trapped in the gorge and shot down without mercy. Bhambatha was killed – and so too was Mehlokazulu. Over the following weeks the colonial authorities ruthlessly suppressed any lingering traces of defiance in both Zululand and Natal.

\*

In 1914 the novelist, Sir Henry Rider Haggard, visited Zululand for the first time.

In 1877 Haggard, then a very junior imperial bureaucrat, had been a member of Theophilus Shepstone's staff on the expedition to annex the Transvaal. Haggard had admired and respected Shepstone and regarded him as a mentor, and he had been in favour of both the annexation and of the British intervention in Natal – his first published book, *Cetewayo and his White Neighbours*, published in 1881, was a rather ponderous defence of Shepstone and critique of King Cetshwayo. He had left Africa that same year, but those formative years had made a deep impression on him, and in particular he remembered the extraordinary camp-fire stories he had heard during his time there about the Zulu people. In 1885, challenged by his brother to write a novel 'half as good' as Robert Louis Stevenson's *Treasure Island*, Haggard had produced *King Solomon's Mines*, a stirring tale of Boy's Own adventure which encapsulated many of the prevailing Victorian myths about an Africa that was at once savage, alien, exotic and alluring. It was a huge commercial success, and Haggard's career as a novelist was set. Ironically, although the Zulus featured heavily in his works – he wrote a trilogy which charted the rise of the kingdom under Shaka to its fall in the war of 1879[3] – Haggard did not set foot in the kingdom in the 1870s.

When he returned to southern Africa in 1914 it was under very different circumstances. Africa itself had changed – there had been a great war between the British and the Boers in 1899–1902, but the various colonies and Boer republics had been brought together in the Union of South Africa – while Haggard himself had become a secure member of the imperial establishment. Recently knighted, he had been appointed to sit on a Royal Commission to report on the state of Britain's overseas dominions. During his official trip to South Africa, he took time off to visit many of Zululand's historic sites – places which had haunted his imagination, but which he had never seen. He travelled with two early settler authorities on Zulu affairs, James Stuart and J.Y. Gibson, in an American-made Overland car. At iSandlwana they picked over relics of the battle displayed by a 'Mr Parr', who had built a store near the Nyogane stream, and Haggard pondered the fate of the men he had known personally who had died in the battle.

Yet something nagged at Haggard throughout the expedition. His entire career had been shaped by his commitment to imperial beliefs, his firm conviction of the righteousness of Christian British values and of the enlightenment and beneficence of British rule. He admired and respected the Zulu people, but in 1877 he had believed implicitly that the invasion of Zululand was a just war, fought to free the Zulu from the tyranny of their own political systems and spiritual beliefs and to bring stability, progress and civilization. Now, thirty-five years on, he began to suspect that what truly lay beneath the conflict was a clash of cultures which had proved catastrophic for the Zulu:

> This afternoon I went to Mr Gibson's office and inspected a large map of Zululand. So far as I could make out about two thirds of the country as I knew it in 1875 has since that date been appropriated by Boers and other white men. If this goes on what is to become of the poor Zulus. What will happen if they are continually crowded together ... Truly their case is sad and they have been ill-treated. First, an unnecessary war in which 10,000 were killed, and then their recent troubles.[4]

Haggard certainly had few illusions about the violence inherent in much of the history of the Zulu kingdom – indeed, since the pages of his books are awash with blood it is probably fair to say that as a novelist he relished it – and he was realistic enough to recognize that 'cruelty bred of fear is no new story in South Africa'. Yet the ruthlessness with which the colonial militias had suppressed the recent rebellion seemed difficult to reconcile with the ideology of his youth, and while he struggled to dismiss the savage retribution meted out to the uprising as an aberration and to suppress doubts about the historical process of which he had been a part, he glimpsed in one particular death something of the overlapping layers of tragedy that had befallen the Zulu people:

> I had an interesting conversation with Sir Charles [Saunders, chief magistrate for Zululand] about the Zulus, a race in which he takes the deepest and most sympathetic interest. He spoke feelingly of the harsh treatment they have received and are receiving and declared that the 'constant pin-pricks', such as land-snatching and the poll-tax were the direct cause of the 1906 'rebellion'. He added that this was suppressed with the greatest cruelty notably in the last affair ... Mome I think the place was called, where all quarter seems to have been refused even to those who threw down their arms and pleaded for mercy, as did the old chief Mehlokazulu, who held up his hands and said 'please' before they shot him ...[5]

# Glossary

## IsiZulu

*Abamnumzana* – see *umnumzana* (sl.)

*abaqawe* – see *iqawe* (sl.)

*abelungu* – see *umlungu* (sl.)

*amabutho* – see *ibutho* (sl.)

*amadlozi* – see *idlozi* (sl.)

*amahawu* – see *ihawu* (sl.)

*amahubo* – see *ihubo* (sl.)

*amakhanda* – see *ikhanda* (sl.)

*amakhosi* – see *inkosi* (sl.)

*amaklwa* – see *iklwa* (sl.)

*amasoja* – soldiers

*donga* – an erosion gully, dry for most of the year but flooded after heavy rains

*giya* – a solitary display of martial prowess, a war-dance including elements of mock-combat performed by an individual to demonstrate and enhance his reputation as a warrior

*hlomula* – the practice by which the corpse of a powerful animal killed in the hunt or a brave enemy killed in battle is stabbed after death by men not directly involved in the killing but who were nonetheless closely involved in the event (i.e. the hunt or battle). It is a means of acknowledging the group participation in the act; a degree of honour still attaches to those who *hlomula*, even though they have not killed the victim themselves

*ibandla* – the full royal council of senior men which advises the king

*ibeshu* (pl. *amabeshu*) – the rear part of a male loin covering, a square of dressed hide worn over the buttocks

*ibutho* (pl. *amabutho*) – a guild or regiment recruited according to the common age of the members

*idlozi* (pl. *amadlozi*) – the spirit of a dead ancestor

*ihawu* (pl. *amahawu*) – a general term for a shield made from cow-hide

*ihubo* (pl. *amahubo*) – sacred songs sung in honour of the ancestors on ceremonial occasions

*ikhanda* (pl. *amakhanda*) – a homestead maintained by the Zulu king containing a barracks for the royal *amabutho*. From 'head', meaning of royal authority

*iklwa* (pl. *amaklwa*) – a long-bladed short-hafted spear used for stabbing – the archetypal Zulu close-combat weapon

*impalimpala* – a signal-horn

*impi* (pl. *izimpi*) – a group gathered together for military purposes, an armed force; matters pertaining to war

*impondo zankhomo* – 'the horns of the cow/bull', a characteristic Zulu encircling tactic

*indoda* (pl. *amadoda*) – an adult man, by implication married

*induna* (pl. *izinduna*) – a state official or appointed functionary, officer etc.

*ingomane* – a loud rhythmic challenge or celebration produced by a group of men drubbing their spears and sticks against their shields

*ingxotha* – a single brass armband bestowed by the king on his favourites as a reward for military or civil service

*inhlendla* – a spear with a large barbed or curved blade carried in the manner of a sceptre by men of rank and authority

*inkatha ye sizwe ya'kwaZulu* – the 'sacred coil of the Zulu nation', a coil of grass rope mixed with powerful mystical substances and embodying the strength and unity of the nation

*inkosi* (pl. *amakhosi*) – a hereditary ruler, chief, king

*insizwa* (pl. *izinsizwa*) – a young man not yet entered into full adult state by way of marriage, a youth

*inxweleha* (pl. *izinxweleha*) – those 'wet with yesterday's blood', men who are in limbo having killed an enemy but not yet been ritually cleansed of the powerful supernatural taint caused by shedding blood

*inyanga* (pl. *izinyanga*) – a herbalist

*iqawe* (pl. *abaqawe)* – a renowned and acknowledged warrior, a hero

*isangoma* (pl. *izangoma*) – a spirit diviner; one who is able to intercede with the ancestral spirits

*isibhalo* – the system of compulsory labour levied by the colonial government on Africans living in Natal

*isicholo* – a top-knot of hair coloured with red ochre adopted by a woman on marriage

*isicoco* – a ring of fibre twisted into the hair and plastered with gum worn by married men

*isigodlo* – the screened-off section at the top of a royal homestead, the private quarters of the king; the word is also applied to the unmarried women who attend the king in those quarters

*isihlangu* (pl. *izihlangu*) – a full-sized war-shield protecting a man from chin to knees and favoured during the early period of the Zulu kingdom; the property of the state, it was issued to the young men when they assembled to serve with their *amabutho*

*isikhulu* (pl. *izikhulu*) – a powerful regional magnate, the 'great ones' of the Zulu kingdom

*ithonya* – a supernatural ascendancy over an enemy achieved through the offices of a practised diviner

*iwisa* (pl. *amawisa)* – a neatly worked stick with a large round head carried for everyday protection in peacetime and used as a club in battle. Often translated as 'knobkerrie'

*izangoma* – see *isangoma* (sl.)

*izibongo* – the praise poem commemorating the deeds of a great man and recited upon formal occasions by his *imbongi* (praise singer)

*izinduna* – see *induna* (sl.)

*izinyanga* – see *inyanga* (sl.)

'*Ji!*' – a shout of exultation, often used when striking an enemy in battle

*ka* – of, usually 'son of', e.g. Shaka kaSenzangakhona

*muthi* (pl. *imithi*) – medicines possessing either physiological or spiritual properties and used both for spiritual preparations or for treatment of injuries

*qaqa* – to cut the stomach of a fallen enemy as part of a process of post-combat spiritual cleansing *ukuxoxa* – the ritual challenge offered by one *ibutho* to another during a national ceremony

*umbhumbhulozu* – a war-shield, smaller than the *isihlangu*, introduced by Prince Cetshwayo during the succession crisis of 1856, and by 1879 generally preferred by men in the younger *amabutho*

*umkhonto* (pl. *imikhonto*) – a spear

*umkhosi* – the annual ceremony, held in December or January, to secure the blessings of the ancestors upon the new harvest and to renew the ties of the people to their king and institutions

*umkhumbi* – a circle, a formation adopted by the *amabutho* to undergo ritual preparations for war, or to receive instruction from their commanders

*umlungu* (pl. *abelungu*) – the name for a person of European descent

*umnumzana* (pl. *abamnumzana*) the head of the homestead, family patriarch

*umnyama* – literally 'blackness', a time of ill omen when dark spiritual forces might upset the equilibrium between the ancestors and the living and bring about misfortune

*'uSuthu!'* – the Zulu royalist war-cry, first adopted as the name of Prince Cetshwayo's followers during the 'War of the Princes' in 1856, used thereafter by those who fought for the Zulu kings

*zila* – to ritually adopt or restrain from certain practices as part of a rite of purification

## Afrikaans/Dutch

*Afrikaans* – the language spoken by the descendants of the first Dutch East India Company settlement at the Cape – principally Dutch but with words incorporated from slaves imported to the Cape from Malaysia and from other European and local African languages

*aasvogel* – a vulture

*assegai* – a spear. Originally thought to be of Portuguese origin, the term was widely used in Afrikaans and has passed into common South African usage

*Boer* – literally a farmer or country-person, often used specifically to refer to an Afrikaans-speaking settler

*commando* – a group of farmers gathered together as a military unit

*knobkerrie* – a stick with a large round knob on the end (the equivalent of *iwisa* in isiZulu)

*kop* – literally a 'head', but used to describe an isolated rounded hill

*kopje* – a small *kop*

*kraal* – an enclosure or corral, usually for livestock but often used to describe African settlements

*laager* – wagons drawn together for defence, also applied to defensive fortifications generally

*nek* – a saddle of land between two higher hills

*spruit* – a stream

*reim* – a length of cured hide used as a rope.

*voorlooper* – an African boy who controls a team of oxen

*Voortrekker* – those who wander or move to the fore such as a pioneer or a semi-nomadic farmer; often abbreviated as Trekker

# Select Bibliography

The literature of the Anglo-Zulu War is immense. Since I have footnoted all direct quotes within the book, I have decided not to attempt an exhaustive bibliography here; it would in any case soon be out of date if I did. Instead I have opted for a largely subjective selection; I have listed below a number of books which, within their particular fields, shed important light on many different aspects of the war and its impact on popular consciousness. In some cases – most notably when dealing with iSandlwana – they provide opposing viewpoints within the framework of continuing debate. As such, they do not always offer consistent interpretations of the same events – and indeed some of them reflect views very different to my own.

Ballard, Charles, *John Dunn: The White Chief of Zululand* (A.D. Donker, Craighall, 1985).

Bancroft, James, *Rorke's Drift* (Spellmount Publishing, London, 1988).

Barthorp, Michael, *A Pictorial History of the Zulu War* (Blandford Press, Blandford, 1979).

Baynham Jones, Alan, and Stevenson, Lee, *Rorke's Drift By Those Who Were There* (Stevenson Publishing, Brighton, 2003).

Bennett, Lt. Col. I.H.W., *Eyewitness in Zululand: The Campaign Reminiscences of Colonel W. A. Dunne, South Africa 1877–81* (Greenhill Books, London, 1989).

Binns, C.T., *The Last Zulu King: The Life and Death of Cetshwayo* (Longman, London, 1963).

Brown, R.A., *The Road to Ulundi: The Water-Colour Drawings of John North Crealock* (University of Natal Press, Pietermaritzburg, 1969).

Bulpin, T.V., *Shaka's Country* (Howard Timmins, Cape Town, 1956).

Castle, Ian, *Zulu War – Volunteers, Irregulars and Auxiliaries* (Osprey Publishing, Oxford, 2003).

Castle, Ian, *British Infantryman in South Africa 1877–81* (Osprey Publishing, Oxford, 2003).

Castle, Ian, and Knight, Ian, *Fearful Hard Times: The Siege and Relief of Eshowe* (Greenhill Books, London, 1994).

Child, Daphne (ed.), *The Zulu War Journal of Col. Henry Harford* (Shooter and Shuter, Pietermaritzburg, 1978).

Clarke, Sonia (ed.), *Invasion of Zululand 1879* (Brenthurst Press, Houghton, 1979).

Clarke, Sonia (ed.), *Zululand at War 1879* (Brenthurst Press, Houghton, 1989).

Colenso, F.E., assisted by Durnford, Lt. Col. E., *A History of the Zulu War and its Origin* (Chapman and Hall, London, 1880).

Cope, R., *The Ploughshare of War: The Origins of the Anglo-Zulu War* (University of Natal Press, Pietermaritzburg, 1999).

Coupland, Sir Reginald, *Zulu Battle Piece: Isandhlwana* (Collins, London, 1948).

Drooglever, R.W.F., *The Road to Isandhlwana: Colonel Anthony Durnford in Natal and Zululand* (Greenhill Books, London, 1992).

Duminy, A., and Ballard, C. (eds), *The Anglo-Zulu War: New Perspectives* (University of Natal Press, Pietermaritzburg, 1981).

Duminy, A., and Guest, B. (eds), *Natal and Zululand from Earliest Times to 1910: A New History* (University of Natal Press, Pietermaritzburg, 1989)

Emery, Frank, *The Red Soldier: Letters from the Zulu War 1879* (Hodder and Stoughton, London, 1977).

Filter, H. (compiler), and Bourquin, S. (trans. and ed.), *Paulina Dlamini: Servant of Two Kings* (University of Natal Press, Pietermaritzburg, 1986).

French, Maj. The Hon. G., *Lord Chelmsford and the Zulu War* (Bodley Head, London, 1939).

Gibson, J.Y., *The Story of the Zulus* (Longman, Green and Co., London, 1911).

Gon, Philip, *The Road to Isandlwana: The Years of an Imperial Battalion* (Donker, Johannesburg, 1970).

Greaves, Adrian, *Rorke's Drift* (Cassell, London, 2002).

Greaves, Adrian (ed.), *Redcoats and Zulus: Myths, Legends and Explanations of the Anglo-Zulu War 1879* (Pen and Sword, Barnsley, 2004).

Greaves, Adrian, and Best, Brian (eds), *The Curling Letters of the Anglo-Zulu War*, (Pen and Sword, Barnsley, 2001).

Greaves, Adrian, and Knight, Ian, *Who's Who in the Zulu War 1879: Vol. 1 The British* (Pen and Sword, Barnsley, 2007).

Greaves, Adrian, and Knight, Ian, *Who's Who in the Zulu War 1879: Vol. 2 Colonials and Zulus* (Pen and Sword, Barnsley, 2007).

Guy, J. *The Destruction of the Zulu Kingdom: The Civil War in Zululand 1879–1884* (Longman, London, 1979).

Haggard, H. Rider (Coan, Stephen, ed.), *Diary of an African Journey* (Hurst, London, 2002).

Hall, Sheldon, *Zulu; With Some Guts Behind It: The Making of the Epic Movie* (Tomahawk Press, Sheffield, 2005).

Hallam Parr, Capt. H., *A Sketch of the Kafir and Zulu Wars: Guadana to Isandhlwana* (C. Kegan Paul, London, 1880).

Hamilton Browne, Col. G., *A Lost Legionary in South Africa* (T. Werner Laurie, London, c. 1913).

Holme, Norman, *The Noble 24th* (Savannah Publications, London, 1999).

Humel, Chris, (ed.), *The Frontier War Journal of Major John Crealock, 1878* (Van Riebeck Society, Cape Town, 1988).

Jackson, F.W.D., 'Isandlwana, 1879: The Sources Re-examined', *Journal for the Society for Army Historical Research*, XLIX, 173, 175, 176 (1965).

Jackson, F.W.D., *Hill of the Sphinx* (Westerners Publication, London, 2003).

Knight, Ian, *Brave Men's Blood* (Greenhill Books, London, 1990).

Knight, Ian, *British Forces in Zululand 1879* (Osprey Publishing, London, 1989).

Knight, Ian, *Zulu: The Battles of Isandlwana and Rorke's Drift* (Windrow and Greene, London, 1992).

Knight, Ian, *Nothing Remains But to Fight: The Defence of Rorke's Drift, 1879* (Greenhill Books, London, 1993).

Knight, Ian, and Castle, Ian, *The Zulu War: Then and Now (After the Battle)*, (London, 1993).

Knight, Ian, *The Anatomy of the Zulu Army* (London, Greenhill Books, 1995).

Knight, Ian, *Go to Your God Like a Soldier: The British Soldier Fighting for Empire 1837–1902* (Greenhill Books, London, 1996).

Knight, Ian, *Great Zulu Battles 1838–1906* (Arms and Armour Press, London, 1998).

Knight, Ian, *Great Zulu Commanders* (Arms and Armour Press, London, 1999).

Knight, Ian, *Isandlwana 1879* (Osprey Publishing, Oxford, 2002).

Knight, Ian, *With His Face to the Foe: The Life and Death of Louis Napoleon, The Prince Imperial, Zululand 1879* (Spellmount, Staplehurst, 2003).

Knight, Ian, *The National Army Museum Book of the Zulu War* (Sidgwick and Jackson, London, 2003).

Knight, Ian, *Rorke's Drift 1879: 'Pinned Like Rats in a Hole'* (Osprey Publishing, Oxford, 2003).

Knight, Ian, *British Fortifications in Zululand 1879* (Osprey Publishing, Oxford, 2005).

Laband, John, *The Battle of Ulundi* (KwaZulu Monuments Council, Ulundi, 1988).

Laband, John, *Rope of Sand: The Rise and Fall of the Zulu Kingdom in the Nineteenth Century* (Jonathon Ball, Johannesburg, 1995).

Laband, John, *The Atlas of the Later Zulu Wars 1883–1888* (University of Natal Press, Pietermaritzburg, 2001).

Laband, John (ed.), *Lord Chelmsford's Zululand Campaign 1878–1879* (Army Records Society, Manchester, 1994).

Laband, John, and Knight, Ian, *The War Correspondents: The Anglo-Zulu War* (Sutton Publishing, Stroud, 1996).

Laband, John, and Thompson, Paul, *Kingdom and Colony at War* (N & S Press, Pietermaritzburg and Constantia, 1990).

Laband, John, and Thompson, Paul, *The Illustrated Guide to the Anglo-Zulu War* (University of Natal Press, Pietermaritzburg, 2000).

Laband, John, and Thompson, Paul, with Henderson, Sheila, *The Buffalo Border 1879: The Anglo-Zulu War in Northern Natal* (University of Natal, Durban, 1983).

Laband, John, and Wright, John, *King Cetshwayo kaMpande* (KwaZulu Monuments Council, Ulundi, 1983).

Lock, Ron, and Quantrill, Peter, *Zulu Victory: The Epic of Isandlwana and the Cover-Up* (Greenhill, London, 2002).

Mitford, Bertram, *Through the Zulu Country: Its Battlefields and Its People* (Kegan, Paul, Trench and Co., London, 1883).

Molyneux, Maj. Gen. W.C.F., *Campaigning in South Africa and Egypt* (Macmilan & Co., London, 1896).

Montague, Captain W.E., *Campaigning in South Africa* (William Blackwood, London, 1880).

Morris, Donald R., *The Washing of the Spears* (Jonathan Cape, London, 1966).

Mossop, George, *Running the Gauntlet: Memoirs of Adventure* (Nelson, London, 1937).

Norris-Newman, Charles L., *In Zululand with the British throughout the War of 1879* (W.H. Allen and Co., London, 1880).

Paton, Col. G., Glennie, Col. F., and Penn Symons, W. (eds), *Historical*

*Records of the 24th Regiment* (Simpkin, Marshall, Hamilton, Kent, London, 1892).

Payne, David, and Payne, Emma (eds), *Harford: The Writings, Photographs and Sketches* (The Ultimatum Tree Publishing, Kent, 2008).

Rattray, David, *A Soldier Artist in Zululand* (Rattray Publications, KwaZulu-Natal, 2007).

Samuelson, R.C., *Long, Long Ago* (Knox Publishing, Durban, 1929).

Smail, J.L., *From the Land of the Zulu Kings* (A.J. Pope, Durban, 1979).

Smith, Keith I., *Studies in the Anglo-Zulu War* (D.P. and G. Publishing, Doncaster, 2008).

Snook, Lt. Col. Mike, *How Can Man Die Better: The Secrets of Isandlwana Revealed* (Greenhill Books, London, 2005).

Snook, Lt. Col. Mike, *Like Wolves on the Fold: The Defence of Rorke's Drift* (Greenhill Books, London, 2006).

Stevenson, Lee, *The Rorke's Drift Doctor: James Henry Reynolds, V.C. and the Defence of Rorke's Drift* (Stevenson Publishing, Brighton, 2001).

Taylor, Stephen, *Shaka's Children: A History of the Zulu People* (HarperCollins, London, 1994).

Thompson, P.S., *The Natal Native Contingent in the Anglo-Zulu War* (Brevitas, Pietermaritzburg, 1997).

Vijn, Cornelius, *Cetshwayo's Dutchman* (Longmans, Green and Co., London, 1880).

Webb, C. de B. and Wright, John (eds), *The James Stuart Archive of Recorded Oral Evidence Relating to the History of the Zulu and Neighbouring Peoples*, 5 volumes (University of Natal Press, Pietermaritzburg and Durban, 1976, 1979, 1982, 1986, 2001).

Webb, C. de B. and Wright, John, (eds), *A Zulu King Speaks: Statements Made by Cetshwayo kaMpande on the History and Customs of His People* (University of Natal Press, Pietermaritzburg and Durban, 1978).

Whitehouse, Howard (ed.), *A Widow-Making War: The Life and Death of a British Officer in Zululand, 1879* (Paddy Griffith Associates, Nuneaton, 1995).

Wood, Sir Evelyn, *From Midshipman to Field Marshal* (Methuen, London, 1907).

Yorke, Edmund, *Rorke's Drift 1879: Anatomy of an Epic Zulu War Siege* (Tempus, Stroud, 2006).

Young, John, *They Fell Like Stones: Battles and Casualties of the Zulu War, 1879* (Greenhill Books, London, 1991).

# Notes

## Prologue

1 Haggard, *Diary of an African Journey*.
2 Rian Malan interview by Tim Adams, *Observer Magazine*, 25 March 2007.

## 1. Mehlokazulu's fury: The killing of MaMtshali

1 The language spoken historically – with some regional variations – by the African people living in the area of modern KwaZulu-Natal in South Africa. The reference to 'Zulu' of course post-dates the emergence of the Zulu kingdom as the dominant power in northern KwaZulu-Natal in the nineteenth century.

2 The supernatural ascendancy of men in battle was called *ithonya*, and the best diviners who specialized in warfare were said to be able to conjure mist. At dawn on 25 June 1879, at the height of the British invasion of Zululand, Zulus living on the left bank of the Thukela river launched a raid on African settlements and colonial outposts on the Natal side. The Zulu attack was masked by a dense mist which was said to have been conjured by one of the groups participating in the attack, the amaChube. Conversely, when a concentration of troops resisting the imposition of a poll tax in Natal, and led by the *amakhosi* Bhambatha and Mehlokazulu, was surrounded by troops at the mouth of the Mome Gorge on the morning in June 1906, the rebels attributed their complete failure to spot the approaching troops to the superiority of the Colonial forces' *ithonya*. See C. de B. Webb and J.B. Wright (eds), *The James Stuart Archive of Recorded Oral Evidence Relating to the History of the Zulu and Neighbouring Peoples*, Vol. 3 (Pietermaritzburg and Durban, 1982), testimony of Mpatshana kaSodondo.

3 *Inkosi*, pl. *amakhosi*. The word 'chief' is usually avoided by modern historians because it is associated with nineteenth-century colonial usage, when the position of chief was entirely dependent upon the recognition and support of the colonial administration. Many traditional *amakhosi* were not recognised

as 'chiefs' by the Government because they were thought to be hostile to the white administration; others were artificially created 'chief' for administrative purposes. This effectively distorted and subverted the role of the *amakhosi*, since 'chiefs' were ultimately responsible to the Government rather than their own people, and became agents of colonial administration. The tensions this produced were particularly evident in the 1906 Poll Tax Rebellion, when many 'chiefs' felt obliged to side with government forces against rebels from their own communities. See Jeff Guy, *Remembering the Rebellion* (Pietermaritzburg, 1906).

4　Statement of 'Umpahla', a witness, 29 July 1878; British Parliamentary Papers (hereafter BPP), C 2220, 6 December 1878.

5　J.Y. Gibson, *The Story of the Zulus* (London, 1911). Most accounts place the attacks on consecutive days; Gibson's is unusual in suggesting that they took place a few days apart.

6　H.C. Lugg, *Historic Natal and Zululand* (Pietermaritzburg, 1949). Lugg identifies the location of the killings and is adamant that Mehlokazulu had the two women strangled, not shot as is sometimes claimed, because he 'did not wish to shed the blood of his mothers'. Mehlokazulu himself admitted while in Pietermaritzburg jail in late 1879 that 'he had strangled the two women'; E. Harding Steward, *Royal Engineer Journal*, 2 February 1880.

## 2.　Charlie Harford's luck

1　Daphne Child (ed.), *The Zulu War Journal of Col. Henry Harford* (Pietermaritzburg, 1978). Hereafter *Zulu War Journal*.

2　In June 1667 Dutch ships had successfully raided an English fleet anchored in the Medway; as late as the 1860s the ports were considered a possible target for French attacks in the light of perennial British suspicions of a Bonaparte ascendancy – in this case Napoleon III – in Paris.

3　Child, *Zulu War Journal*.

4　Child, Ibid.

5　Ibid.

6　Memoir of Lieutenant Arthur Clinton Baskerville Mynors, 3/60th Regiment (Privately published, 1880).

7　Child, *Zulu War Journal*.

8　Ibid.

9　An exception being Pioneers in infantry battalions who were directed to grow beards in peacetime.

10　Child, *Zulu War Journal*.

### 3. Snagged in the tree of the kings

1 The story of Jobe's meeting with King Shaka is given in A.T. Bryant, *Olden Times in Zululand and Natal* (London, 1929). Bryant adds the caveat that various versions of the story place the encounter either at Hlazakazi, at Siphezi, or on the spurs of Qhudeni itself. Siphezi seems to me too far away from the Mzinyathi to offer commanding views, and since Shaka's army was contesting a ford below Hlazakazi – perhaps even Rorke's Drift itself – this remains to me the most likely site.

2 The definitive – and very beautiful – work on the Zulu names for indigenous Nguni cattle is *The Abundant Herds* by Marguerite Poland and David Hammon-Tooke, illustrated by Leigh Voigt (Cape Town, 2003).

3 For a detailed description of Zulu ceremonial dress see Ian Knight, *The Anatomy of the Zulu Army: From Shaka to Cetshwayo* (London, 1995).

4 A.T. Bryant, *The Zulu People: As They Were Before the White Man Came* (Pietermaritzburg, 1949).

5 On the influence of generational conflict on Zulu history, see Benedict Carton, *Blood From Your Children* (Pietermaritzburg, 2000).

6 It was common during the heyday of the Zulu kingdom, *c.*1816–79, for the Zulu kings to appoint older female relatives – often the widows of their fathers – to administer important royal homesteads. Shaka, for example, set his aunt, Queen Mnkabayi, to rule the ebaQulusini homestead near Hlobane mountain.

7 For a post-modern analysis of the myths surrounding Shaka see Dan Wylie, *Myth of Iron* (Scottsville, 2006). Carolyn Hamilton's *Terrific Majesty: The Powers of Shaka Zulu and the Limits of Historical Invention* (Cape Town, 1998), attempts to place those myths within a historical context.

8 White Mfolozi.

9 For example, the amaChube people, who lived in the Nkandla forest on the lower reaches of the Thukela river, had strong ties to the Zulu royal house, but were never conquered by Shaka. *Inkosi* Mvakela married a sister of Shaka's mother, Nandi, and the amaChube considered themselves allies of the Zulu rather than their subjects. Mvakela's grandson, *inkosi* Sigananda, was to play a prominent part in the 1906 Poll Tax Rebellion.

10 The king distributed feathers and furs – many of them collected as tribute from the Thonga peoples in the wildlife-rich flats of Maputhaland – to each *ibutho* when it was enrolled. There were insufficient for each man, however, and the king's bounty went largely to his favourites; the remaining men were expected to acquire these items themselves. War-shields made from the

king's cattle were the property of the individual rather than the state, and the natural colour of the hair on the face of the hide formed part of the uniform. Young *amabutho* carried predominantly black or brown shields; new shields were issued every few years, each bearing more white on the hide, until senior *amabutho* were equipped with white shields. For a detailed description of the Zulu army, see Ian Knight, *The Anatomy of the Zulu Army.*

11 Traditions are not entirely clear regarding the fate of the ruling *inkosi* of the Sithole at that time, who seems to disappear from the record with Jobe's rise to prominence.

## 4. 'When I am gone'

1 This is not, of course, a name that would have been familiar to its indigenous inhabitants. Nor indeed is it one that might last indefinitely – in recent years, the Zulu monarch, King Goodwill Zwelithini, has questioned the relevance in the new South Africa of a province retaining the name given it by outsiders and conquerors.

2 The role of the locusts varies in different versions of this story. They are absent from some altogether; in others Shaka is said to have referred to 'white men *and* locusts'. Given that the African followers of Henry Francis Fynn Jnr – one of the prominent settlers whose famous *Diary* (edited by J. Stuart and D. Malcolm, Shuter & Shooter, Pietermaritzburg, 1950) chronicles those early meetings – were known as *izinkhumbi*, locusts, my interpretation is that Shaka intended to use the imagery of one to represent the other.

3 In fact, in the modern sense, the cultural identity of the Afrikaner people is largely a product of reaction to defeat in the Anglo-Boer War (1899–1902) and of the Afrikaner nationalist movements of the 1930s. Before that the geographical separation of Afrikaner communities, and their sense of individuality and self-reliance, meant that they were more culturally and linguistically diverse.

4 As a test of their fidelity Dingane asked Piet Retief, the Boer leader, to recover Zulu cattle which had been appropriated by the *inkosi* of the Tlokoa Sotho, Sekonyela, across the uKhahlamba mountains; Retief retrieved the cattle by tricking Sekonyela into letting him place handcuffs on his wrists, and refusing to release him until he agreed. Despite the friction between Dingane and Sekonyela, this disrespect for the person of an *inkosi* was deeply unsettling in Zulu eyes. According to Zulu sources, Retief then compounded his presumption by taking a percentage of Dingane's cattle as payment for his services before returning the rest to Dingane (Zulu etiquette demanded

that he should have returned all of them to the king, and allowed Dingane to apportion him a reward). There are also Zulu traditions which suggest that during his visit to the Zulu capital, some of Retief's young men may have attempted to sneak into Dingane's private quarters at night; although they were presumably seeking the company of the hundreds of royal ladies living in seclusion there, when their tracks were discovered in the morning it was widely assumed they had intended the king some harm. It should be noted, however, that the death of Retief and his followers remains an emotive issue, and some aspects of the story are still contested.

5  The Battle of the Thukela provides an interesting contrast between contemporary British and Zulu tactics. Prominent among the settler forces was Robert Joyce, whose knowledge of British tactics of the Napoleonic era came from time spent in the ranks of the 72nd Regiment, from which he had deserted – Joyce was one of those responsible for training the settlers' African auxiliaries in musketry drill. On the Zulu side, the field commanders included Zulu kaNogandaya, who had learned his profession as a favourite *iqawe* of King Shaka. During the battle the Zulu centre was checked by settlers' musketry, but the settler forces collapsed when outflanked by the Zulu horns. The battle offers a number of interesting parallels with iSandlwana forty-one years later.

6  The Biggarsberg were named by the Boers in honour of one of the Port Natal settlers, Alexander Biggar. Biggar accompanied the Ncome expedition and fought in the battle; his wagon broke down on the long haul over the ridge, and the feature was named by his companions to remember the incident.

7  *Graham's Town Journal*, 21 August 1871, quoted in Bill Guest, 'The War, Natal and Confederation', in Andrew Duminy and Charles Ballard (eds), *The Anglo-Zulu War: New Perspectives* (Pietermaritzburg, 1981).

8  In doing so he restored his authority over a good deal of territory north and east of this line which the Trekkers had claimed by right of their support to his crown, but had never in fact occupied. While the Thukela and Mzinyathi between them provided a clear boundary for much of the border, however, the line became imprecise along its upper reaches, above the confluence of the Ncome and Mzinyathi, and towards the uKhahlamba foothills.

## 5. 'Better move before them'

1  After the British arrived at the Cape in 1806 they steadily found themselves drawn into conflict with African groups on the eastern Cape frontier, chiefly

the Xhosa. There were nine wars with the Xhosa altogether, although a couple of these were fought by the Dutch before the British arrived.

2   As an administrative district of the Cape, Natal did not warrant a governor of its own; the lieutenant-governor was therefore the senior colonial administrator in the colony.

3   The choice of words is curious – or deliberate. The Zulu King Dingane is said to have ordered his men to seize Piet Retief's party in 1838 with similar words.

4   For a colonial perspective on the Matshana incident see D.C.F. Moodie, *The History of the Battles and Adventures of the British, the Boers and the Zulus in Southern Africa* (Cape Town, 1888). For an African perspective see the account of Lunguza kaMpukane in Webb and Wright (eds), *The James Stuart Archive*. Vol 1. Bishop Colenso collected a number of statements in connection with the incident which are to be found in the Colenso Papers, Pietermaritzburg Archives. See also Thomas McClendon, 'You Are What You Eat Up: Deposing Chiefs in Early Colonial Natal 1848–1856', *Journal of African History*, Vol 47. (2006).

5   Many among the Zulu elite despised those who had too closely associated themselves with settler society. Cetshwayo once reproached Mpande himself as a *khafula* on the grounds that he had secured his throne by crossing into Natal to seek the support of the Boers. The term *khafula*, of course, had a pleasing resemblance to the dismissive and derogatory word widely used in colonial Natal to refer to the African population – *kaffir*.

6   Report by J.W. Shepstone, 3 January 1877, BPP, C 1776.

7   My thanks to Anthony Coleman for this point.

8   Quoted in Edward Durnford's memoir of his brother, *A Soldier's Life and Work in South Africa* (London, 1882).

9   Information from Andries and Lindizwe Ngobese, descendants of Mehloka-zulu kaSihayo, interviewed in October 2006.

10   And not kwaSoxeghe, 'the maze', as it has sometimes been given; I am grateful for the opinions of Lindizwe and Andries Ngobese on this point.

11   Ibid.

12   Bertram Mitford, *Through the Zulu Country: Its Battlefields and Its People* (London, 1883).

13   Rorke was actually born on the Eastern Cape in 1827. His father had come to the Cape from Galway as a soldier in a British regiment.

14   *Umutsha*, the front part of a loin covering, consisting of strips of fur worn hanging from a belt around the waist.

15   'Bluchers' were a type of boot made popular during the Napoleonic Wars by the Prussian Field Marshal Prince Gebhard von Blücher.

16   Mitford, *Through the Zulu Country*.

## 6. 'The Power to control the Zulus'

1  There are suggestions that British troops tried to exhume King Mpande's body in the aftermath of the Battle of Ulundi on 4 July 1879. See Cornelius Vijn (Bishop Colenso) (ed.), *Cetshwayo's Dutchman* (London, 1880). The bones of a large individual, still wrapped in several layers of rotting hides and blankets, were removed and carried away; it is likely, however, that these were the remains of Mpande's attendant, Nhlangano kaLubaca Ntuli, who was of a similar build, rather than the king. What became of the remains that were removed is unclear.

2  Colenso to the Society for the Propagation of the Gospel, 8 August 1857.

3  Frank Emery, *The Red Soldier* (London, 1977).

4  The most meticulous and detailed account of these disputes can be found in Huw M. Jones, *The Boiling Cauldron: The Utrecht District in the Anglo-Zulu War 1879* (Shermershill, Gloucestershire, 2007), which is broadly sympathetic to the Boer position.

5  The details of Prince Mbuyazi's death were not known. There is no truth in the rumours repeated in the Natal press at the time that he was captured alive and flayed on Cetshwayo's orders; John Wesley Shepstone believed he was run down and killed in the confusion of the pursuit.

6  Secretary for Native Affairs Papers (hereafter SNAP), 1/7/6, Pietermaritzburg Archives Depot.

7  Memorandum, 3 March 1873, SNAP, Archives Depot.

8  By far the most perceptive study of Anthony Durnford's life and career can be found in Robin Drooglever, *The Road To Isandhlwana: Colonel Anthony Durnford in Natal and Zululand* (London, 1992).

9  Durnford, *A Soldier's Life*.

10  The pattern of long-established hostility with the French was so ingrained with the British commander, Lord Raglan – who had been wounded in the left arm at the Battle of Buçaco, and lost his right arm at Waterloo – that he famously had a habit of referring to the enemy in the Crimea not as Russians but as 'the French'.

11  Durnford, *A Soldier's Life*.

12  An intellectual with a sharp and questioning mind, Colenso familiarized himself with isiZulu, and published books on Zulu grammar. His re-examination of Old Testament texts, published in a series of treatises from 1862, greatly offended High Church elements within the Anglican community, causing a bitter scandal. The row became so intense that in December 1863 Bishop Robert Gray, the senior Anglican cleric in the British

colonies in southern Africa, deposed Colenso for heresy and appointed a rival bishop in Natal in his place. Although the legality of the deposition was found to be unsound – and Colenso in any case ignored it – the incident created a deep rift within the Anglican community in settler Natal, and this was further exacerbated by Colenso's critical attitude towards the racist and exploitative attitudes which underpinned the administration of Natal's black majority.

13  Durnford, *A Soldier's Life*.

14  The advantages of such an exercise became readily apparent in the Anglo-Zulu War in 1879 when the British military relied heavily upon Durnford's maps.

15  Durnford, *A Soldier's Life*.

16  D.F.C. Moodie, *John Dunn, Cetywayo and the Three Generals* (Pietermaritzburg, 1886).

17  The name oNdini was applied to three different Zulu royal homesteads. The first was established by King Mpande on the Mhlatuze river, and Cetshwayo spent much of his youth there. When he moved to central Zululand on his accession, Cetshwayo took the name and applied it to the new homestead he built there (the British generally referred to this complex by an alternative name, Ulundi) – the old oNdini continued in existence but was generally known thereafter as kwaHlahlangubo. The main oNdini homestead was destroyed by the British on 4 July 1879 after the Battle of Ulundi. On his restoration in February 1883 Cetshwayo built a new, and slightly smaller complex just a few kilometres from the old one. This final version was destroyed during the Zulu civil war of 1883.

18  John Ackerman to J.E. Carlyle, 5 October 1876. Wigram Papers, Society for the Propagation of the Christian Gospel Archives, London.

## 7. 'Will no one then stand by me?'

1  It is generally agreed that the amaHlubi were driven out of the Mzinyathi valley around 1819 by the amaNgwane of Matiwane kaMasumpha, who had himself been attacked by the Ndwandwe *inkosi*, Zwide kaLanga. See John Wright and Andrew Manson, *The Hlubi Chiefdom in Zululand-Natal* (Ladysmith, 1983).

2  *Papers Relating to the Late Kaffir Outbreak in Natal*, 1874, BPP, C 1025.

3  Durnford, *A Soldier's Life*.

4  During the disturbances in the highveld in the 1810s and 1820s, the Tlokoa had been at the centre of a formidable coalition led by Queen Manthatisi on

behalf of her son Sekonyela, a minor. When Sekonyela came of age, a section of the Tlokoa led by his brother Mota had refused his authority and crossed the mountains into Natal.

5  Account of one of the Carbineers, quoted in Drooglever, *The Road to Isandhlwana*.
6  Durnford, *A Soldier's Life*.
7  The accounts of the surviving participants in the Bushman's River Pass incident, both colonial and amaHlubi, are collected in R. O. Pearse et al., *Langalibalele and the Natal Carbineers* (Ladysmith Historical Society, 1973), published on its centenary.
8  Quoted in Drooglever, *The Road to Isandhlwana.*
9  Ibid.
10  Durnford, *A Soldier's Life*.


## 8. 'Neither justice nor humanity'

1  Colonial Office Papers, in A. Duminy and C. Ballard (eds) *The Anglo-Zulu War: New Perspectives* (Pietermaritzburg, 1981). July/August 1874, quoted in Etherington, *Anglo-Zulu Relations*.
2  The uKhamdempenvu were raised in 1868, during the last years of King Mpande's reign, but under Cetshwayo's influence; the iNgobamakhosi were raised in 1873 and the uVe in 1875.
3  Quoted in John Martineau, *The Life and Correspondence of Sir Bartle Frere* (London, 1895).
4  Frere to Carnarvon, April 1877, quoted in Damian O'Connor, *The Zulu and the Raj: The Life of Sir Bartle Frere* (Knebworth, 2002).
5  Frere to Carnarvon, 19 July 1877, Carnarvon Papers, National Archives (hereafter NA), London.
6  Shepstone to Carnarvon, 11 December 1877, Colonial Office Papers, NA, London.
7  Frere to Carnarvon, 19 December 1877, Colonial Office Papers, NA, London.
8  Carnarvon to Frere, 27 April 1877, Colonial Office Papers, NA, London
9  Hicks Beach to Frere, 25 July 1878, quoted in O'Connor, *The Zulu and the Raj.*
10  Joseph, a Christian convert from the Hermannsburg mission, was murdered on 4 March 1877, although the exact motives for it are not clear. Maqhamusela Kanyile, a convert from the Norwegian mission at Eshowe, was murdered on 9 March 1877 because of his Christian faith. In fact it seems that the killings were not sanctioned by the king, but were carried out by members of the local

community – in Maqhamusela's case, including some of his own family – because the converts had disgraced their ancestors. See Professor Tony Cubbin, *Maqhamusela Khanyile: First Christian Martyr of the Norwegian Lutheran Mission Society* (Zululand Historical Society, 1988).

11  Bulwer to Shepstone, 16 January 1878, Shepstone Papers, KwaZulu-Natal Archive.

12  For a detailed analysis of the boundary dispute broadly sympathetic to the Boer cause, see Jones, *The Boiling Cauldron*.

13  Correspondence between Bulwer and the Commissioners, Report of 16 July 1878, BPP, C 2220.

14  Edward Fairfield, Minute, 12 September 1878, 179/127, Colonial Office Papers, NA, London.

15  Cetshwayo to Bulwer, 16 September 1878, SNAP, Pietermaritzburg Archives Depot.

16  Mitford, *Through the Zulu Country*.

17  Information from Mehlokazulu's descendants, Andries and Lindizwe Ngobese.

18  Ibid.

19  Information from uMnukwa, a household official in King Cetshwayo's court, quoted in Vijn, *Cetshwayo's Dutchman*.

20  Information from uMnukwa.

### 9. 'A very serious evil'

1  Chelmsford was a near contemporary of Thomas Hughes, author of *Tom Brown's Schooldays* (1857). Hughes' novel was inspired by his time at Rugby school between 1834 and 1842 (Chelmsford entered the Army in 1844) and championed the values which shaped the attitudes of the (male) ruling elite in the second half of the nineteenth century.

2  Sir John Henry Newbolt's poem 'Vitaï Lampada', in which a broken British regiment on a colonial battlefield – 'the sand of the desert is sodden red, red with the wreck of the square that broke' – is steadied by a schoolboy's rallying cry, 'Play up! Play up, and play the game!' makes explicit the link between public school values and imperial attitudes.

3  At a time when the Army was still influenced by the opinions of the Duke of Wellington – not least that the terms 'officer' and 'gentleman' were synonymous – there seemed little wrong in achieving rank through purchase when a significant private income was considered as good an indicator of social standing as any. The abuses to which the system was prone – particularly

unofficial sweeteners demanded by those selling ranks in popular regiments – led throughout the Victorian era to a sustained attack upon the system, however, and it was finally abolished as one of Minister of War Cardwell's famous reforms in 1871.

4  The term Caffre or Kaffir was in general use among Europeans throughout the eighteenth and nineteenth century to describe a black South African. It is derived from *kafir*, the term for unbeliever used by early Muslim traders, and the British found it preferable to Xhosa which they could not pronounce. Although undoubtedly dismissive, the word does not then seem to have implied the degree of bitter contempt with which it has become loaded in more recent times.

5  Sir John Michel, three letters written at the end of January 1878, quoted in Major the Hon. Gerald French, *Lord Chelmsford and the Zulu War* (London, 1939).

6  Chelmsford to Sir Archibald Alison, 19 December 1878, quoted in Sonia Clarke (ed.) *Zululand At War 1879* (Johannesburg, 1984).

7  Thesiger to Shepstone, 8 July 1878, Chelmsford Papers, National Army Museum London (hereafter NAM), quoted in John Laband, *Lord Chelmsford's Zululand Campaign 1878–1879* (Stroud, 1994).

8  Hicks Beach to Frere, 17 October 1878, BPP, C 2220.

9  Quoted in Duncan Moodie (ed.), *John Dunn, Cetywayo and the Three Generals* (Pietermaritzburg, 1886).

10  Thesiger to Shepstone, 21 July 1878, Chelmsford Papers, NAM.

11  Melton Prior, *Campaigns of a War Correspondent* (London, 1912).

12  Chelmsford to H.E. Wood, 23 November 1878.

13  Message from King Cetshwayo to Sir Henry Bulwer, 30 August 1878, Government House Papers, KwaZulu-Natal.

14  A flat-bottomed ferry pulled across the water by means of a cable fixed on either side.

15  For a detailed analysis of the causes of the war, and in particular of Frere's manipulation of the border dispute and the drafting of the ultimatum, see Richard Cope, *Ploughshare of War: The Origins of the Anglo-Zulu War of 1879* (Pietermaritzburg, 1999).

16  John Shepstone, report dated 19 December 1878 in BPP, C 2308.

17  Quoted in Gibson, *The Story of the Zulus*.

## 10. 'An uncommonly rough road'

1 This was the figure arrived at by F.B. Fynney in his pamphlet *The Zulu Army and Headmen* ('Published by order of the Lt. Gen. Commanding', 1878). In fact, this rather overestimates the strength of some of the older *amabutho*, some of whose members were too old to fight, and a good number of whom were always needed to watch the border or to remain at home to protect cattle and homes at the behest of their *amakhosi*. Cetshwayo was never able to muster more than 30,000 men at a time, of whom no more than 25,000 were concentrated into one single striking force.

2 Williams was later attached as a staff officer to an auxiliary unit, Wood's Irregulars; he was killed at the Battle of Hlobane on 28 March 1879.

3 Sir Horace Smith-Dorrien, *Memories of Forty-Eight Years' Service* (London, 1925). Smith-Dorrien's memoirs were not drafted until twenty years after the battle.

4 Daphne Child (ed.), *Zulu War Journal*. See also David and Emma Payne (eds), *The Writings, Photographs and Sketches of H.C. Harford* (Tenterden, 2008).

5 Since the future of Zululand after conquest was not at this stage decided Chelmsford had no right to make such promises – but a number of Volunteers confirm that they were indeed made.

6 Dunford, *A Soldier's Life and Work*.

7 Chelmsford, Memorandum from Pietermaritzburg, 30 October 1878, Chelmsford Papers, NAM, quoted in Laband, *Lord Chelmsford's Zululand Campaign*.

8 Child, *Zulu War Journal*.

9 Harford to his mother, 14 January 1879, quoted in Payne, *The Writings, Photographs and Sketches of H.C. Harford*. It is interesting to note some discrepancies between Harford's immediate impression of events, conveyed at the time to his family, and the more coherent version worked up afterwards into his journal.

10 The name was not originally hyphenated.

11 R.S. Baden-Powell, *The Matabele Campaign 1896* (London, 1897). Baden-Powell met Hamilton Browne during this campaign.

12 The case against Hamilton Browne's own account of his adventures in the New Zealand Wars is outlined by Barbara Cooper in 'George Hamilton Browne: An Investigation into his career in New Zealand', in *Historical Review: The Bay of Plenty Journal of History*, Vol. 33, No. 2, November 1985. It is certainly true that there is an almost total lack of evidence to confirm

his own participation in the stories outlined in Browne's book *With the Lost Legion in New Zealand* (London, 1911).

13 George Hamilton Browne, *A Lost Legionary in South Africa* (London, c. 1913).

14 Ibid.

15 Child, *Zulu War Journal*. In a letter written to his mother on 14 January 1879, reproduced in Payne, *The Writings, Photographs and Sketches of H.C. Harford*, Harford tells the same story but gives the man's name as Jacob.

16 Newman Noggs is a character in Dickens' *Nicholas Nickleby*.

17 Child, *Zulu War Journal*.

18 C.L. Norris-Newman, *In Zululand with the British throughout the War of 1879* (London, 1880).

19 Ibid.

20 Ibid.

21 Hat band or head-cloth.

22 Norris-Newman, *In Zululand with the British throughout the War of 1879*.

## 11. 'A Dreadful Sameness'

1 Captain W.E. Montague, *Campaigning in South Africa* (London, 1880).

2 The incident is described in the Colonels Paton, Glennie and Penn Symons, *Historical Records of the 24th Regiment* (London, 1892).

3 The 24th became the South Wales Borderers on 1 July 1881, as part of an extensive re-organization of the Army's territorial associations. The new title reflected the fact that the 24th had established an administrative depot at Brecon, south Wales, in 1873. The regiment has gone through several incarnations since – from the Royal Regiment of Wales to today's Royal Welsh – each of which has celebrated a Welsh connection which was only just beginning at the time of the Anglo-Zulu War.

4 Lt N.J. Coghill, Diary, 12 May 1876, quoted in Patrick Coghill (ed.), *Whom The Gods Love: A Memoir of Lieutenant Nevill Josiah Aylmer Coghill*, compiled by his nephew (Gloucestershire, 1966).

5 Frere, quoted in Martineau, *The Life and Correspondence of Sir Bartle Frere*.

6 Sir A.T. Cunynghame, *My Command* (London, 1879).

7 Ibid.

8 Recruits were required to sign up for a minimum of six years with a further six in the reserve, rather than the twelve years which had been compulsory previously. It was hoped that by shortening the minimum period of service,

enlistment would seem less of a commitment for life and appeal to a more intelligent class of recruit.

9  J.N. Crealock, Journal entry, 6 April 1878, quoted in Hummel (ed.), *The Frontier War Journal of Major John Crealock*.

10  Letter in the *Dover Express*, 25 April 1879, quoted in Emery, *The Red Soldier* (London, 1977).

11  Fred Symons, Talana Museum, Dundee, KwaZulu-Natal. Fred Symons left a long account of his experiences in Zululand in the form of a journal. I have relied on a typescript copy held in the Talana Museum, Dundee, KwaZulu-Natal. However, the original manuscript together with other documents is held by the Natal Carbineers Archive, Pietermaritzburg, while the Campbell Collections, University of KwaZulu-Natal, Durban, have copies of material apparently expanded and reworked later from parts of the journal. See also Mark Coghlan, *Trooper Fred Symons, Natal Carbineers: Enthusiasm and Misgivings* (no date or publisher; Natal Carbineers Archive, c. 2009).

12  Ibid.

13  Clery to Sir Archibald Alison, 11 March 1879, quoted in Clarke (ed.), *Zululand at War 1879*.

14  Ibid.

15  Bulwer, quoted in Sonia Clarke, *Invasion of Zululand* 1879 (Johannesburg, 1979).

16  Wolseley held dismissive views of most of the officers under Chelmsford's command; in fairness he may have been prejudiced as he had served with Crealock's elder brother, H.H. Crealock, and clearly disliked him intensely.

17  Clery, quoted in Clarke, *Zululand at War 1879*.

18  Crealock to Sir Archibald Alison, Helpmekaar, 9 January 1879, quoted in Clarke, *Zululand at War 1879*.

19  Clery, 11 March 1879, quoted in Clarke (ed.), *Zululand at War 1879*.

20  Symons papers, Talana Museum. Mealies is the local name for corn.

21  Ibid.

22  Ibid.

23  Sam Jones, account in the *Natal Mercury*, 22 January 1929.

24  Report dated 6 January 1879, 'From Our Helpmekaar Correspondent', *Natal Mercury*, 11 January 1879.

25  From *giya*, a solitary war-dance involving shadow-fighting imaginary enemies.

26  Symons Papers, Talana Museum.

27  Norris-Newman, *In Zululand with the British throughout the War of 1879*.

28  Letter to Sir Archibald Allison, Helpmekaar, 9 January 1879, quoted in Clarke, *Zululand at War 1879*.

29  Norris-Newman, *In Zululand with the British throughout the War of 1879*.

## 12. 'The shadow of the Great White Queen'

1  Durnford, *A Soldier's Life.*

2  Ibid.

3  Ncwadi's grandfather – Zikhali's father – was the famous Matiwane ka-Masumpha, who had been driven out of Zululand sixty years previously by the Ndwandwe, and who had eventually returned, only to be put to death by King Dingane.

4  The amaZondi lived astride the main road from Greytown to Keate's Drift. Cramped and impoverished, they had suffered significantly under colonial rule; in 1906 the *inkosi* of the amaZondi, Bhambatha kaMancinza, had been the first to lead armed resistance against the imposition of the Natal government's poll tax.

5  At least until stocks ran out; some late arrivals were issued with Sniders.

6  Revd Owen Watkins, 'They Fought For the Great White Queen', in *The Methodist Recorder*, quoted in G.A. Chadwick and E.G. Hobson (eds), *The Zulu War and the Colony of Natal* (Pietermaritzburg, 1979).

7  Anecdote quoted by Sir Garnet Wolseley in Adrian Preston (ed.), *The South African Diaries of Sir Garnet Wolseley, 1879–80* (Cape Town, 1973).

8  Theophilus Shepstone, quoted in Drooglever, *The Road to Isandhlwana.*

9  Durnford, *A Soldier's Life.*

10  Chelmsford to Frere, 1 January 1879, Chelmsford Papers, NAM, quoted in Laband, *Lord Chelmsford's Zululand Campaign.*

11  Presumably to give him sufficient rank to act as a column commander. A brevet rank was a temporary promotion allowing an officer to hold a rank one above his substantive rank. It was sometimes issued in the field, often to give officers sufficient authority for a particular duty or as a reward for gallantry. As a brevet colonel Durnford would have ranked above substantive lieutenant-colonels, but below a substantive colonel.

12  Durnford, *A Soldier's Life.*

13  Norris-Newman, *In Zululand with the British throughout the War of 1879.*

14  Chelmsford to Frere, 10 January 1879, Chelmsford Papers, NAM, quoted in Laband, *Lord Chelmsford's Zululand Campaign.*

15  Norris-Newman, *In Zululand with the British throughout the War of 1879.*

16  Child, *Zulu War Journal.*

17  Account of Lugubu Mbata, Carl Faye Papers 8/16, KwaZulu-Natal Archive.

18  Capt. H. Hallam Parr, *A Sketch of the Kafir and Zulu Wars* (London, 1880).

### 13. 'A big fuss over a small matter'

1  Report 'From our Biggarsberg Correspondent, 11 January', *Natal Mercury*, 17 January 1879.
2  Hallam Parr, *A Sketch of the Kafir and Zulu Wars*.
3  Child, *Zulu War Journal*.
4  Norris-Newman, *In Zululand with the British throughout the War of 1879*.
5  Child, *Zulu War Journal*.
6  Ibid.
7  Hamilton Browne, *A Lost Legionary in South Africa*.
8  Child, *Zulu War Journal*.
9  *Natal Mercury*, 17 January 1879.
10  Hamilton Browne, *A Lost Legionary in South Africa*.
11  H.G. Mainwaring, 22 January 1895, quoted in Norman Holme, *The Noble 24th* (London, 1999).
12  Hallam Parr, *A Sketch of the Kafir and Zulu Wars*.
13  Hamilton Browne, *A Lost Legionary in South Africa*.
14  Child, *Zulu War Journal*.
15  Hamilton Browne, *A Lost Legionary in South Africa*.
16  Child, *Zulu War Journal*.
17  Hamilton Browne, *A Lost Legionary in South Africa*.
18  Child, *Zulu War Journal*.
19  Hamilton Browne, *A Lost Legionary in South Africa*.
20  Child, *Zulu War Journal*.
21  Hamilton Browne, *A Lost Legionary in South Africa*.
22  Presumably *'Ji!'*, a cry of exultation or triumph.
23  Hamilton Browne, *A Lost Legionary in South Africa*.
24  Ibid.
25  Child, *Zulu War Journal*.
26  Hamilton Browne, *A Lost Legionary in South Africa*.
27  Child, *Zulu War Journal*.
28  Ibid.
29  Payne, *The Writings, Photographs and Sketches of H.C. Harford*.
30  Symons Papers, Talana Museum.
31  Paton, Glennie and Penn Symons, *Historical Records of the 24th Regiment*.
32  Hamilton Browne, *A Lost Legionary in South Africa*.
33  Norris-Newman, *In Zululand with the British throughout the War of 1879*.
34  Chelmsford to Frere, 'Camp in Zululand near Rorke's Drift 12 January 1879', Chelmsford Papers, quoted in Laband, *Lord Chelmsford's Zululand Campaign*.

35  Crealock to Sir Archibald Alison, 'Rorke's Drift, 14 January 1879', reproduced in Clarke, *Zululand at War 1879*.

36  Symons Papers, Talana Museum.

37  Harford to his mother, 14 January 1879, quoted in Payne, *The Writings, Photographs and Sketches of H.C. Harford*.

## 14. 'Quite red with soldiers'

1   Personal interview with Mdiceni Gumede, 24 April 1996. Mr Gumede's grandfather, iZitha Gumede, was an *udibi* (mat-carrier) who carried mats and raw meat for kinsmen in the iNgobamakhosi during the iSandlwana campaign.

2   Bishop Wilkinson, 14 January 1871, quoted in 'E. and H.W.', *Soldiers of the Cross in Zululand* (London, 1905).

3   Ibid.

4   King Cetshwayo, letter from captivity in Cape Town to Sir Hercules Robinson, Governor of the Cape, 29 March 1881, BPP C 2950; quoted in C. de B. Webb and J.B. Wright (eds), *A Zulu King Speaks* (Pietermaritzburg, 1978). Hereafter, King Cetshwayo, letter to the Governor of the Cape.

5   Dymes' account quoted in Durnford, *A Soldier's Life*.

6   Chelmsford to Durnford, 14 January 1879, Chelmsford Papers, quoted in Laband, *Lord Chelmsford's Zululand Campaign*.

7   Durnford, *A Soldier's Life*.

8   Chelmsford to Frere, 'Camp in Zululand near Rorke's Drift, 12 January 1879', Chelmsford Papers, NAM, London, quoted in Laband, *Lord Chelmsford's Zululand Campaign*.

9   Crealock to Sir Archibald Alison, Rorke's Drift, 14 January 1879, quoted in Clarke, *Zululand At War 1879*.

10  Chelmsford to Frere, Rorke's Drift, 13 January 1879, Chelmsford Papers, NAM, quoted in Laband, *Lord Chelmsford's Zululand Campaign*.

11  Chelmsford to Wood, Rorke's Drift, 16 January 1979, Chelmsford Papers, quoted in Laband, *Lord Chelmsford's Zululand Campaign*.

12  Spelt over the following months in a variety of ways according to the impressions of the writer.

13  Manuscript of Captain W. Penn Symons, Regimental Museum, Brecon.

14  'From The Witness Correspondent, Headquarters Camp, Near Rorke's Drift, 18 January 1879', *Natal Mercury*, 24 January 1879.

15  Chelmsford to Frere, Rorke's Drift, 16 January 1879, quoted in French, *Lord Chelmsford and the Zulu War*.

16 'From The Witness Correspondent, Headquarters Camp, Near Rorke's Drift, 18 January 1879', *Natal Mercury*, 24 January 1879.

17 Chelmsford to Frere, 16 January 1879, quoted in French, *Lord Chelmsford and the Zulu War*.

18 Hamilton Browne, *A Lost Legionary in South Africa*.

19 Ibid.

20 Ibid.

21 Ibid.

22 Henry Francis Fynn Jnr, 'My Recollections of a Famous Campaign and a Great Disaster', *Natal Witness*, 22 January 1913.

23 Ibid.

24 'Bashee Valley Camp, Jan 20 1879', *Natal Mercury*, 28 January 1879.

## 15. 'Give the matter to us!'

1 'Cetywayo's Story', *Macmillan's Magazine*, February 1880, reprinted in Webb and Wright, *A Zulu King Speaks*.

2 Account of Mpashana kaSodondo, in Webb and Wright, *The James Stuart Archive*, Vol. 3.

3 The *ibutho* selected in January 1879 was either the uVe – the youngest in the army – or the iNgobamakhosi, with which the uVe were incorporated.

4 Account of Mpashana kaSodondo.

5 Ibid.

6 R.C. Samuelson, *Long, Long Ago* (Durban, 1929).

7 Account of Mpashana kaSodondo.

8 King Cetshwayo, letter to the Governor of the Cape.

9 Account of Mpashana kaSodondo.

10 Account of Mahlahlana Ngune, *Natal Mercury*, 22 January 1929.

11 Account by a Zulu deserter of the uNokhenke, translated by Chelmsford's interpreter, the Hon. William Drummond, published in the *Natal Witness*, 24 February 1879. It is interesting to note that this account includes the phrase '. . . and drive it back into Natal; and, if the state of the river will allow, follow it up through Natal, right up to the Drakensberg'. The implication that the king instructed his army to invade British territory is flatly contradicted by a mass of evidence from other Zulu sources; it seems that either the deserter told his interrogators what he thought they wanted to hear, or Chelmsford's staff inserted this phrase to stress King Cetshwayo's alleged aggressive intent.

12  Account of Nzuzi Mandla of the uVe, *Natal Mercury*, 22 January 1929.

13  Ibid.

14  Account of Mhlahlana Ngune, *Natal Mercury*, 22 January 1929. The choice of these phrases is significant – Mantshonga and Ngqelebana were the Zulu names for two white men, Rathbone and Walmsley, who had been caught up in the 'Battle of the Princes' in 1856 when Cetshwayo destroyed his rival Prince Mbuyazi. The whites were widely blamed on that occasion for encouraging Mbuyazi's defiance, and a number of black Border Policemen, commanded by John Dunn, had fought on Mbuyazi's side. The choice of these phrases therefore reflects popular support for Cetshwayo's perceived defiance of the whites.

15  Account of Gumpeka Qwabe, *Natal Mercury*, 22 January 1929.

16  Account of Mtshapi kaNoradu, in Webb and Wright, *The James Stuart Archive*, Vol. 4.

17  Symons Papers, Talana Museum.

18  Hamilton Browne, *A Lost Legionary in South Africa*.

19  Child, *Zulu War Journal*.

20  Hamilton Browne, *A Lost Legionary in South Africa*.

21  Symons Papers, Talana Museum.

22  Fynn, 'My Recollections of a Famous Campaign and a Great Disaster'.

23  Hamilton Browne, *A Lost Legionary in South Africa*.

24  Child, *Zulu War Journal*.

25  Symons Papers, Talana Museum.

26  Hamilton Browne, *A Lost Legionary in South Africa*.

27  *Regulations for Field Forces in South Africa, 1878* (Pietermaritzburg, 1878).

28  Manuscript, Penn Symons.

29  Hamilton Browne, *A Lost Legionary in South Africa*.

30  Paton *et al.*, *Historical Records of the 24th Regiment*.

31  Symons Papers, Talana Museum.

## 16. 'We laughed and parted'

1  George H. Swinny, *A Zulu Boy's Recollections of the Zulu War and of Cetshwayo's Return* (London, 1883), reprinted in C. de B. Webb (ed.), *Natalia*, No. 8, December 1978.

2  F.B. Fynney, *The Zulu Army and Zulu Headmen*, 2nd edition (Pietermaritzburg, 2 April 1879).

3  On 25 January 1879.

4 Chelmsford to Frere, 'Head Quarters Camp, Insalwana Hill', 21 January 1879. Chelmsford Papers, NAM, quoted in Laband, *Lord Chelmsford's Zululand Campaign*.

5 Fynn, 'My Recollections of a Famous Campaign and a Great Disaster'.

6 Coghill, quoted in Coghill, *Whom the Gods Love*.

7 This camp was never made, of course, but it is interesting to note that, even if the lip of the gorge was exploited as a defensive feature, visibility is considerably limited on all sides by comparison with the iSandlwana site.

8 Fynn, 'My Recollections of a Famous Campaign and a Great Disaster'.

9 Coghill, *Whom the Gods Love*.

10 Chelmsford to Frere, 21 January 1879, Chelmsford Papers, NAM, quoted in Laband, *Lord Chelmsford's Zululand Campaign*.

11 Clery to Colonel Harman, 17 February 1879, quoted in Clarke, *Zululand at War 1879*.

12 Child, *Zulu War Journal*.

13 Symons Papers, Talana Museum.

14 Norris-Newman, *In Zululand with the British throughout the War of 1879*.

15 Child, *Zulu War Journal*.

16 Account in *Natal Mercury*, 22 January 1929.

17 Symons Papers, Talana Museum.

18 Norris-Newman, *In Zululand with the British throughout the War of 1879*.

19 Hamilton Browne, *A Lost Legionary in South Africa*.

20 Fynn, 'My Recollections of a Famous Campaign and a Great Disaster'.

21 *Report of Proceedings of 21st, 22nd, 23rd and 24th January 1879, from Lt. Milne R.N*, Lugg files, Campbell Collections, University of KwaZulu-Natal, Durban. Hereafter, Milne Report.

22 Ibid. The 'highest hill' is presumably the Mkwene high-point, above where the Isandlwana Lodge now stands.

23 Ibid.

24 W.C.F. Molyneux, *Campaigning in South Africa and Egypt* (London, 1896).

25 Account by unidentified Zulu man (describing the practice of the army) in Leslie, *Among the Zulus and Amatongas*.

26 Account in *Natal Mercury*, 22 January 1929.

27 The most complete version of Mehlokazulu's account, taken at Fort Napier, Pietermaritzburg on 28 November 1879, while he was on trial, was published in the 'War Supplement' to the *Natal Mercury*, c. December 1879. Variations on this text – all apparently drawn from the same interview – appear in Norris-Newman, *In Zululand with the British throughout the War of 1879* and the *Royal Engineers Journal*, 2 February 1880. Hereafter, Mehlokazulu, Interview.

28 Norris-Newman, *In Zululand with the British throughout the War of 1879*.

29  Ibid.
30  Child, *Zulu War Journal*.
31  Symons Papers, Talana Museum.
32  Norris-Newman, *In Zululand with the British throughout the War of 1879*.
33  Child, *Zulu War Journal*.
34  Hamilton Browne, *A Lost Legionary in South Africa*.
35  Symons Papers, Talana Museum.
36  Ibid.
37  Ibid.
38  Ibid.
39  Ibid.
40  Hamilton Browne, *A Lost Legionary in South Africa*.
41  Norris-Newman, *In Zululand with the British throughout the War of 1879*.
42  Symons Papers, Talana Museum.
43  Ibid.
44  Ibid.
45  Ibid.
46  Child, *Zulu War Journal*.

## 17. 'Did you hear that?'

1  Milne, *Report*.
2  Clery to Colonel Harman, 17 February 1879, quoted in Clarke, *Zululand at War 1879*.
3  Typescript of radio broadcast by Colonel Lewis, 1939, 'From Broadcast Reminiscences of Natal 1937–1939', Killie, Campbell Collections, University of KwaZulu-Natal, Durban. Lewis was told this anecdote by Dorehill himself. Hayes' grave is in the military cemetery at Helpmekaar.
4  Symons Papers, Talana Museum.
5  Ibid.
6  Leoni Twentyman Jones (ed.), *Reminiscences of the Zulu War by John Maxwell* (Cape Town, 1979).
7  Child, *Zulu War Journal*.
8  Hamilton Browne, *A Lost Legionary in South Africa*.
9  Symons Papers, Talana Museum.
10  Maxwell reports hearing this story. Twentyman Jones, *Reminiscences of the Zulu War by John Maxwell*.
11  Symons Papers, Talana Museum.
12  Hamilton Browne, *A Lost Legionary in South Africa*.

13  Norris-Newman, *In Zululand with the British throughout the War of 1879.*

14  Child, *Zulu War Journal.*

15  Symons Papers, Talana Museum.

16  Hamilton Browne, *A Lost Legionary in South Africa.*

17  Child, *Zulu War Journal.*

18  Ibid.

19  Symons Papers, Talana Museum.

20  Hamilton Browne, *A Lost Legionary in South Africa.*

21  Ibid.

22  Ibid.

23  Ibid.

24  Ibid.

25  It must be admitted that evidence of the Zulu movements in the Mangeni area is thin, and that any reconstruction of events must include a degree of speculation. My interpretation is based on the evidence of one of Bishop Colenso's informants, Magema Fuze, who stated that 'Matyana was ordered to meet the big army', by Henry Francis Fynn Jnr's comment that 'the Zulus were ascending the Mangeni on the eastern side', by Muziwento's assertion that Chelmsford attacked Matshana's men on the 22nd, not the main army – 'we heard it said that Matshana, the son of Mondisa, had just been slaughtered' –and by the complete absence of any Zulu tradition that royal *amabutho* were engaged in the skirmishing in the Mangeni hills.

26  Child, *Zulu War Journal.*

27  Clery to Colonel Harman, quoted in Clarke, *Zululand at War 1879.*

28  Ibid.

29  Paton *et al.*, *Historical Records of the 24th Regiment.*

30  Clery to Harman, quoted in Clarke, *Zululand at War 1879.*

31  Clery to Sir Archibald Alison, 28 April 1879, quoted in Clarke, *Zululand at War 1879.*

32  Hallam Parr, *A Sketch of the Kafir and Zulu Wars.*

33  Newnham-Davis, interview in *Chums* magazine, 1900.

### 18. 'The valour of ignorance'

1  Coghill, *Whom the Gods Love.*

2  Probably Clery.

3  Smith-Dorrien, *Memories of Forty-Eight Years' Service.*

4  Swinny, 'A Zulu Boy's Recollections'.

5  There is no 'Bongoza' listed among the names of King Cetshwayo's *amabu-*

*tho;* in fact, this force may well have been men of the Mpungose chiefdom, which lay to the south-east of Babanango mountain, making their way to join the royal army.

6 The king's supporters were known by the name 'uSuthu'; 'horned' suggests that they were in battle array (i.e. deployed as 'chest and horns').

7 Swinny, 'A Zulu Boy's Recollections'.

8 Curiously, this site was chosen as the location for the battle scenes in the 1979 movie based upon iSandlwana, Douglas Hickox's *Zulu Dawn*.

9 Fynn, 'My Recollections of a Famous Campaign and a Great Disaster'.

10 UMhoti, *Isandhlwana: As Related by one of the Zulus*, Symons Papers, Campbell Collections, University of KwaZulu-Natal.

11 Symons Papers, Talana Museum.

12 Child, *Zulu War Journal*.

13 Twentyman Jones, *Reminiscences of the Zulu War by John Maxwell*.

14 Clery to Colonel Harman, 17 February 1879, quoted in Clarke, *Zululand at War 1879*.

15 Hamilton Browne, *A Lost Legionary in South Africa*.

16 Information gathered by Bishop Colenso's informant, Magema Fuze, in Bishop Colenso's notes, quoted in Cornelius Vijn (trans. Colenso), *Cetshwayo's Dutchman* (London, 1880).

17 Symons Papers, Talana Museum.

18 Ibid.

19 Norris-Newman, *In Zululand with the British throughout the War of 1879*.

20 Child, *Zulu War Journal*.

21 Twentyman Jones, *Reminiscences of the Zulu War by John Maxwell*.

22 Child, *Zulu War Journal*.

23 Ibid.

24 Twentyman Jones, *Reminiscences of the Zulu War by John Maxwell*.

25 Ibid.

26 Ibid.

27 Child, *Zulu War Journal*.

28 Norris-Newman, *In Zululand with the British throughout the War of 1879*.

29 Symons Papers, Talana Museum.

30 Ibid.

31 Ibid.

32 Ibid.

33 Russell, Report, WO32/7731, National Archives, London.

34 Hamilton Browne, *A Lost Legionary in South Africa*.

35 Clery, report to the Deputy Adjutant-General dated 7 February 1879, W033/34, National Archives.

36 Clery to Colonel Harman 17 February, quoted in Clarke, *Zululand at War 1879*.

37 Paton *et al.*, *Historical Records of the 24th Regiment*. Captain William Penn Symons was present with the battalion that day and was presumably the source of this information.

38 Clery to Colonel Harman, 17 February 1879, quoted in Clarke, *Zululand at War 1879*.

39 Today Milne is chiefly remembered as the man who, as commander of the Mediterranean fleet at the very moment the First World War broke out, allowed the German warships *Goeben* and *Breslau* to escape to Constantinople, indirectly drawing Turkey into the war as a German ally. Milne served the remainder of the First World War on half-pay, although the Admiralty exonerated him of any error of judgement; he had been wrong-footed by the German movements and had only lighter, slower ships with which to stop them. He retired in 1919 and died in 1938.

40 *Cussonia spicata*, in English the Common Cabbage Tree, in Afrikaans the Kiepersol Boom and in isiZulu the Umsengembuzi ('Goat Food'), can attain a height of over 10 metres.

41 Milne, *Report*.

42 Hamilton Browne, *A Lost Legionary in South Africa*.

43 Russell, Report.

44 Gardner, evidence to the Court of Inquiry, Helpmekaar, 27 January 1879, BPP, C 2260.

45 Paton *et al.*, *Historical Records of the 24th Regiment*.

46 Ibid.

47 Symons Papers, Talana Museum.

48 Arthur Harness, Helpmekaar, 25 January 1879, quoted in Clarke, *Invasion of Zululand 1879*.

## 19. 'We commence work in earnest'

1 Vause to 'Miss Katie', published in the *Natal Witness*, 21 January 1967.

2 Stafford, *Natal Mercury*, 12 March 1924. Stafford lived a long and adventurous life and left a number of accounts of iSandlwana, many of them written in old age and varying slightly in detail.

3 Vause to 'Miss Katie', published in the *Natal Witness*, 21 January 1967.

4 Quoted in Durnford, *A Soldier's Life*.

5 Cochrane, Report, Helpmekaar, 8 February 1879, published in the *London Gazette*, 21 March 1879.

6  Ibid.

7  Corporal Gamble, Sappers Cuthbert, Maclaren and Wheatley and Driver Robson. Robson returned to Rorke's Drift with Chard and fought in the defence; the others were killed at iSandlwana.

8  Chard's movements are detailed in a long letter he wrote at Queen Victoria's request and submitted to Windsor Castle on 21 February 1880. Quoted in Norman Holme, *The Noble 24th* (London, 1999).

9  Ibid.

10  The family name is apparently pronounced 'Brumhead' rather than 'Bromhead', and similarly 'Gonny' (from Gonville) pronounced 'Gunny' – so Gonville was known to his colleagues as 'Gunny Brumhead'. My thanks to Brigadier David Bromhead for this point.

11  Quoted in Coghill, *Whom The Gods Love*. The note is transcribed from a handwritten original. The reference to rations is intriguing, since the 2/24th carried with them a day's rations, and there is no mention elsewhere of more being sent out to them. Rations for all the men out with Chelmsford would require more than one light wagon – and Coghill himself mentions that the NNC were expected back in camp to be fed. I have assumed it is either a mistranscription or a careless reference to the reserve ammunition, which Clery mentions was specifically ordered to be ready to send out at short notice.

12  Quoted in Philip Gon, *The Road to Isandlwana* (Johannesburg, 1979).

13  Paton *et al.*, *Historical Records of the 24th Regiment*.

14  There is some confusion about the positioning of the mounted vedettes. According to the account of Trooper W.W. Barker – published in John Stalker, *The Natal Carbineers* (Pietermaritzburg, 1912) – the vedettes were posted 'from three to five miles away'. Barker himself was posted with Trooper Hawkins 'on a hill to the extreme front, quite six miles away'; unsurprisingly, he does not name the feature, and attempts to identify such a spot have compounded the confusion. However, the map in the official history of the war, J.S. Rothwell, *Narrative of Field Operations Connected with the War in Zululand* (London, 1881), shows no vedettes posted beyond the amaTutshane conical hill and the iThusi highpoint on the iNyoni escarpment. It is worth noting that Inspector Mansel of the Mounted Police was told by an unidentified staff officer not to post vedettes too far out as they would be 'of no use' (quoted in Durnford, *A Soldier's Life*). Vedettes posted out of sight of the camp would not be able to signal information visually, which Barker mentions doing; in my view it is more likely Barker simply confused the distance and was referring to the post on iThusi – but it should be noted that the evidence is open to other interpretations.

15  Barker, in Stalker, *The Natal Carbineers.*

16  The Hon. Standish William Vereker, the third son of Lord Gort, was a gentleman adventurer who had come to southern Africa, apparently for the sport, in 1878. Instead he had joined the Frontier Light Horse, and had taken part in the Sekhukhune campaign in 1878 before transferring to the 3rd NNC in time for the new campaign.

17  Higginson, Official Report, W0 32/7726, National Archives, London.

18  Barker, in Stalker, *The Natal Carbineers.*

19  Higginson, Official Report.

20  Account of Malindi, who was serving in this company; Chelmsford Papers, NAM.

21  Curling to his family, 2 February 1879, quoted in Adrian Greaves and Brian Best (eds), *The Curling Letters of the Anglo-Zulu War* (Barnsley, 2001).

22  Brickhill, account in the *Natal Magazine*, September 1879.

23  Ibid.

24  Ibid.

25  Cochrane, evidence to the Court of Inquiry, Helpmekaar, 27 January 1879, BPP, C 2260.

26  Higginson, Official Report.

27  Cochrane, Report, *London Gazette.*

28  Ibid.

29  Smith-Dorrien, *Memories of Forty-Eight Years' Service.*

30  Cochrane gave several versions of this conversation – in his evidence to the Court of Inquiry (Helpmekaar, 27 January 1879, BPP, C 2260), his report, and to Edward Durnford, which is included in Durnford, *A Soldier's Life.* He is also the anonymous 'special service officer' quoted by Paton *et al., Historical Records of the 24th Regiment.*

31  Higginson, Official Report.

32  Davies, Report, WO 32/7726, National Archives, London.

33  Raw, Report, WO 32/7713, National Archives, London.

34  Davies, Report.

35  Nourse, evidence to Court of Inquiry, Helpmekaar, 27 January 1879, BPP, C 2260.

36  'Going at a canter ... between 5 and 6 miles'. Cochrane, Report, *London Gazette.*

37  Davies, Report.

38  A manuscript copy of Jabez Molife's account is among the Durnford Papers at the Royal Engineers Museum, Chatham. It is reprinted in F.W.D. Jackson and Julian Whybra, 'Isandhlwana and the Durnford Papers', *Soldiers of the Queen* (Journal of the Victorian Military Society), No. 60, March 1990.

39  Ibid.

40  Davies, Report.

### 20. 'The king's day!'

1   Sir William Beaumont, account in the *Natal Mercury*, 22 January 1929.

2   Sir H.M. Bengough, *Memories of a Soldier's Life* (London, 1913).

3   Beaumont, *Natal Mercury*.

4   Bengough, *Memories of a Soldier's Life*.

5   Beaumont, *Natal Mercury*.

6   J.Y. Gibson, *The Story of the Zulus* (London, 1911).

7   In recent years there has been some debate about the site of the Zulu bivouac. Of contemporary commentators, only Muziwento mentions the 'Ingwebini' by name, but it is worth noting that no other spot was suggested by other eyewitnesses. The site is marked as such on the map produced by Captain Anstey and Lieutenant Penrose, RE, and published in the official *Narrative of Field Operations Connected with the War in Zululand*. Their source was an (unnamed) son of Sihayo who, after the war, gave them 'assistance and information with great readiness and good will' so that 'accurate information, respecting the ground occupied by the Zulus, both before and during the battle has been obtained by them' (introductory comments to Mehlokazulu's account, *Royal Engineers Journal*, 2 February 1880). The Ngwebeni is, moreover, the only feature in the vicinity both large enough to provide shelter for the Zulu army and with sufficient access to water. That the bivouac took place there has been well known to local residents, both black and white, across 130 years.

8   King Cetshwayo, letter to the Governor of the Cape.

9   Ibid.

10  Mehlokazulu, account in the *Royal Engineers Journal*, 2 February 1880.

11  Account in the *Natal Mercury*, 22 January 1929.

12  Ibid.

13  Gibson, *The Story of the Zulus*.

14  L.H. Samuelson, *Zululand: Its Traditions, Legends, Customs and Folk-lore* (Durban, 1974; includes material originally published in 1912).

15  Account of Mpashana kaSodondo.

16  Mehlokazulu, Interview.

17  Mitford, *Through the Zulu Country*.

18  Account in the *Natal Mercury*, 22 January 1929.

19  On the role of Zulu foragers see Ian Knight, *The Anatomy of the Zulu Army*.

20 Legend has credited Zibhebhu with almost superhuman achievements in securing intelligence that morning, for it was said after the war that he had penetrated the British camp, passing himself off as a man of the NNC, then had worked his way up the mountain itself until, from the summit, he had been able to look right down among the tents and study the British defences – or lack of them – at his leisure. Such feats were not beyond the capacities of Zulu scouts, but on this occasion the story is probably apocryphal – it is difficult to see what Zulu scouts might have learned from inside the camp that they could not plainly see from the escarpment – and no doubt reflects the absolute mastery of the terrain attained by Zibhebhu and his scouts. The story is given in C.T. Binns, *The Warrior People* (London, 1975).

21 Mehlokazulu, Interview. The footnotes to this article suggest that the 'moving about' referred to the vedettes riding in a circle, the signal for 'enemy in sight'. If nothing else, this suggests the vedettes were on the lip of the iNyoni escarpment, close enough to be seen by the camp, rather than on hills further out with no direct line of sight.

22 Ibid.

23 Ibid.

24 *Natal Mercury*, 22 January 1929. The reference to cooking fires is intriguing; either these were the remains of the aborted meal of the night before, or the men had taken the chance to light fires under cover of the mist.

25 The uKhandempemvu were also known by the name uMcijo, although uKhandempemvu seems to have been preferred by most Zulu sources.

26 Account in Frances E. Colenso, assisted by Lt. Col. E. Durnford, *A History of the Zulu War and its Origins* (London, 1880).

27 'Zulu Deserter'.

28 Both the Battle of Nyezane (22 January 1879) and the Battle of Khambula (29 March 1878) began with spontaneous Zulu attacks.

29 uGuku, in Colenso and Durnford, *A History of the Zulu War and its Origins*.

30 'Zulu Deserter'.

31 Barker in Stalker, *The Natal Carbineers*.

32 *Natal Mercury*, 22 January 1929.

33 King Cetshwayo, letter to the Governor of the Cape.

34 The early movements of the *amabutho* on 22 January have led to theories in recent years that the Zulu attack was already under way before Durnford's detachments stumbled upon the *impi*. It is certainly possible to posit alternative scenarios in which Ntshingwayo reacted to Lord Chelmsford's absence by seizing the initiative and launching an attack on the reduced garrison. However, if this is so not one eyewitness source made a clear and unambiguous statement to that effect, and there is a significant raft of evidence to the

contrary – for example, Mehlokazulu's comment that the Zulu high command were unaware of Chelmsford's absence, and Ntshingwayo's remark that he would wait on British movements. In fact, the Zulu sources – gleaned over many years from men from many different *amabutho* – are remarkably consistent and reflect a general understanding that the attack was not to be made on the 22nd, and that they reacted to being fired upon by British patrols rather than the other way around. Whilst some *amabutho* had clearly left the Ngwebeni earlier that morning, it seems equally clear to me that they had returned again, and that the vast majority of the *amabutho* were still in the valley when the encounter took place. The deserter of the uNokhenke specifically states that his *ibutho* had 'returned to our original position' and 'sat down again', while both Mehlokazulu and Mhlahlala mention that they were attempting to breakfast when the encounter took place – and not already deploying for an attack. It is also important to note that the final ritual preparations for combat had not taken place among the majority of the *amabutho* when the fighting began; such preparations were extremely important to bolster the ceremonies which had taken place at kwaNodwengo the week before. The potency of those rituals was believed to dilute with each passing day (see Knight, *Anatomy of the Zulu Army*, on the significance of these rituals) and it was vital to top them up last thing before entering combat. Indeed, so important were they that Ntshingwayo insisted on performing them upon the reserve *amabutho* – the only ones he could restrain for long enough – even as the attack developed. King Cetshwayo noted that his commanders were still in conference when the battle began, and not present with their *amabutho*; Muziwento (whose father Zibane was present) commented that the *amabutho* 'mutinied' against attempts by their own officers to restrain them. As to whether the Zulu were still in the Ngwebeni at the time of the encounter or had for some reason already begun to emerge from it, all the British eyewitness testimony – Raw, Hamer, Nyanda – stresses that only small groups of foragers could be seen on the heights, and that the main body of the army was not discovered until the patrols ascended a geographical feature – a ridge or hill – and saw the *amabutho* in the valley beyond. The deserter of the uNokhenke notes that the British patrol 'appeared on the hill to the west', Mhlahlala commented that his *ibutho* first advanced 'up the hill' (*after* the first shots had been fired) and even King Cetshwayo – who of course debriefed his generals – said that his 'troops then moved up a little hill'. All these references imply a feature more significant than the undulations that lie along the upper reaches of the Ngwebeni in the direction of iSandlwana. I am firmly of the opinion that no attack had been deliberately launched before the encounter with Raw's men, that the Zulu army was largely concealed behind Mabaso, and that Raw's men, pursuing foragers, had ridden up onto the south-western slopes of the hill before spotting the army below them.

35  Raw, Report.
36  James Nathaniel Hamer was a civilian hired by Durnford to work in No. 2 Column's commissariat department. His account is in the Chelmsford Papers, NAM, London.
37  Nyanda, WO 33/44, National Archives, London.
38  Higginson, Official Report.
39  Raw, Report.
40  Gibson, *The Story of the Zulus*.
41  'Zulu Deserter'.
42  Mehlokazulu, Interview.
43  Quoted in Mitford, *Through the Zulu Country*.
44  Account of Mhlahlala, *Natal Mercury*, 22 January 1929.
45  Swinny, 'A Zulu Boy's Recollections'.
46  An account of iSandlwana by Lee appeared in the *Natal Witness*, 19 January 1929. It is written in the first person, as if spoken by Mehlokazulu, but this seems to be a dramatic device; Lee had met Mehlokazulu when he first arrived at iSandlwana, but Mehlokazulu was killed in the 1906 rebellion, just a few years later. Rather, this account is Lee's dramatic and imaginative impression of the battle, influenced by conversations over the years with Zulu participants.
47  'Zulu Deserter'.
48  Account of Ndukwana kaMbengwane, in Webb and Wright, *The James Stuart Archive*, Vol. 4.
49  *Natal Mercury*, 22 January 1929.
50  'Zulu Deserter'.
51  'The chiefs, knowing that the work of death was being executed, broke up the meeting and went to their several regiments.' King Cetshwayo, letter to the Governor of the Cape.
52  'Mabope is chewed by the Zulus when going into battle, the *induna* giving the word "Lumani (bite) umabope!", which they do for a few minutes and then spit it out again, saying "Nang'umabope" (here is the *umabope*). The notion is that the foe will be bound in consequence to commit some foolish act (the verb *bopa* means "tie")'. Samuelson, *Zululand*.
53  Nyanda, Report.
54  uGuku, in Colenso and Durnford, *A History of the Zulu War and its Origin*; Nyanda, Report.

## 21. 'The lightning of heaven'

1  There is some confusion regarding where the sacred *inkatha* was kept. Most sources agree that it was kept under the watchful eye of Queen Langazana, a widow of *inkosi* Senzangakhona who lived until 1884, in the esiKlebheni royal homestead near Senzangakhona's grave in the emaKhosini valley (see H.C. Lugg, *Historic Natal and Zululand*). However, one of the girls in Cetshwayo's private quarters, Nomguqo 'Paulina' Dlamini was adamant that that it was kept in a special hut in the most private part of the oNdini homestead (see H. Filter and S. Bourquin, *Paulina Dlamini: Servant of Two Kings* (Pietermaritzburg, 1986)). The most likely explanation is that the *inkatha* was brought to oNdini from esiKlebheni when required for important rituals. On 26 June 1879, during the last stages of the invasion, the British mounted a foray into the *emaKhosini* valley and destroyed a large number of royal homesteads; Zulus retreating before them destroyed several more. Among those set ablaze was esiKlebheni and, unknown to the British, the sacred *inkatha* was then among the huts. It was destroyed with the rest.

2  Filter and Bourquin, *Paulina Dlamini.*

3  Ibid.

4  Ibid.

5  Brickhill, *Natal Magazine.*

6  Gardner, Report, WO 33/34, National Archives, London.

7  Glyn's copy of these orders was found on the battlefield by one of the burial details later in the war and passed to Major J.W. Huskisson, 56th Regiment, who was appointed Commandant of Durban during the war. The original orders are still with Huskisson's descendants. One can only speculate why they were at iSandlwana; perhaps they were simply left by Glyn with the rest of his effects when he rode out that morning, or perhaps he passed them over to Pulleine for guidance during his absence.

8  Curling, 11 February 1879, quoted in Greaves and Best, *The Curling Letters of the Anglo-Zulu War.*

9  Essex, letter in *The Times*, 12 April 1879.

10  Ibid.

11  Ibid.

12  Ibid.

13  Cochrane, Report, *London Gazette.*

14  'What Lieutenant Davis Says', *Natal Mercury*, 31 January 1879.

15  Davies, Report.

16  Jackson and Whybra, 'Isandhlwana and the Durnford Papers', *Soldiers of the Queen*. This account, with a few minor variations, also appeared in the *Natal Mercury*, 28 February 1879.

17  *Natal Mercury*, 22 January 1929.

18  Stalker, *The Natal Carbineers*.

19  Nourse, Account in the *Natal Witness*, 19 January 1929.

20  Mitford, *Through the Zulu Country*.

21  Lee gave two slightly different versions of this chant, one of which appeared in the *Natal Witness* of 19 January 1929, the other in Captain H. Wilkins, *The Story of the Blood Drenched Field of Isandhlwana*, produced for the sixtieth anniversary of the battle (Vryheid, 1939). See also Lee's *Once Dark Country* (London, 1949).

22  Nourse, *Natal Witness*, 19 January 1929.

23  Johnson, quoted in Holme, *The Noble 24th*.

24  Trainer, ibid.

25  Davies, Report.

26  Holme, *The Noble 24th*.

27  Vause, Diary, Campbell Collections, University of KwaZulu-Natal, Durban. Part of it is reproduced in the *Daily News*, 22 January 1969.

28  Ibid.

29  Account in the *Natal Mercury*, 12 March 1924.

30  Statement dated 1939, copy in Talana Museum, Dundee.

31  Ibid.

32  Essex, evidence to the Court of Inquiry, Helpmekaar, 27 January 1879, BPP, C 2260.

33  Vause, Diary.

34  Ibid.

35  Nyanda, Report.

36  Essex, evidence to the Court of Inquiry, Helpmekaar, 27 January 1879, BPP, C 2260.

37  Nyanda, Report.

38  G.A. Chadwick, 'The Anglo-Zulu War of 1879: Isandlwana and Rorke's Drift', *South African Military History Society Journal*, January 1979.

39  Essex, evidence to the Court of Inquiry, Helpmekaar, 27 January 1879, BPP, C 2260.

40  Ibid.

41  Manuscript, Penn Symons.

42  Gardner, evidence to the Court of Inquiry, Helpmekaar, 27 January 1879, BPP, C 2260.

43  *Natal Mercury*, 12 March 1924.

44  Letter from an unidentified 'Officer attached to Col. Glyn's Column', *The Times*, 10 April 1879.

45  Smith-Dorrien, *Memories of Forty-Eight Years' Service.*

46  Letter from 'Officer attached to Col. Glyn's Column', *The Times*, 10 April 1879.

47  Smith-Dorrien, *Memories of Forty-Eight Years' Service.* The noise may have been the royalist war-cry 'uSuthu!', or the cry of exultation, 'Ji!' It is possible that some of the *amabutho* may have sung the sacred songs of the ancestors as they advanced; others chanted the songs of their *ibutho*, or improvised cries such as that inspired by the rockets. There are suggestions that the *amabutho* likened themselves in attack to bees and may even have made a buzzing noise to heighten the allusion. At a distance of some hundreds of metres these sounds clearly merged together, and the effect, probably as intended, was deeply menacing.

48  Higginson, Official Report.

49  Essex, letter in *The Times*, 12 April 1879.

50  Curling, evidence to the Court of Inquiry, Helpmekaar, 27 January 1879, BPP, C 2260.

51  Captain W. Penn Symons makes an ambiguous remark about men defending the *dongas* in his unpublished manuscript; it is not clear whether he is referring to the 24th, amaNgwane or Durnford's men.

52  Nyanda, Report.

53  Brickhill, *Natal Magazine.*

54  Ibid.

55  Mehlokazulu, Interview.

56  Gardner, evidence to the Court of Inquiry, Helpmekaar, 27 January 1879, BPP, C 2260.

57  Stalker, *The Natal Carbineers.*

58  Edwards, account in the *Natal Advertiser*, 22 January 1929.

59  Mehlokazulu, Interview.

60  *Natal Mercury*, 22 January 1929. Zimema was actually describing his experiences at the Battle of Nyezane on the coast earlier that same day, but the intensity of the fire at iSandlwana was if anything greater.

61  *Natal Mercury*, 22 January 1929.

62  Wilkins, *The Story of the Blood Drenched Field of Isandhlwana.*

63  Account in *Ilanga Lase Natal*, 20 June 1936.

64  Brickhill, *Natal Magazine.*

65  Mehlokazulu, Interview.

66   Brickhill, *Natal Magazine.*

67   Essex, evidence to Court of Inquiry, Helpmekaar, 27 January 1879, BPP, C
     2260.

68   Holme, *The Noble 24th.*

69   Shepherd's notes were published posthumously by the St John's Ambulance
     Brigade as *A Pocket Aide-Memoire Compiled for the Instruction of Troops in
     Zululand* (London, 1880).

70   Shepherd, *A Pocket Aide-Memoire.*

71   Essex, evidence to Court of Inquiry, Helpmekaar, 27 January 1879, BPP, C
     2260.

72   Sir Evelyn Wood, *From Midshipman to Field Marshal* (London, 1906).

73   Sir Bartle Frere, quoted in J. Martineau, *The Life and Correspondence of Sir
     Bartle Frere* (London, 1881).

74   Essex, letter in *The Times*, 12 April 1879. In his Court of Inquiry report
     (Helpmekaar, 27 January 1879, BPP, C 2260) he says 'The companies 1st
     Battalion 24th Regiment first engaged were now becoming short of ammu-
     nition, and at the request of the officer in charge I went to procure a fresh
     supply, with the assistance of Quartermaster 2nd Battalion 24th Regiment
     and some men of the Royal Artillery. I had some boxes placed on a mule
     cart and sent it off to the companies engaged, and sent more by hand,
     employing any men without arms. I then went back to the line, telling the
     men that plenty of ammunition was coming.'

75   Smith-Dorrien, *Memories of Forty-Eight Years' Service.*

76   Smith-Dorrien's letter was passed on by his family and published in a
     number of newspapers at the time; it is reproduced in French, *Lord
     Chelmsford and the Zulu War* and Emery, *The Red Soldier.*

77   Essex, letter in *The Times*, 12 April 1879.

78   My thanks to Lieutenant-Colonel Mike McCabe RE for this point. In
     desperate circumstances, the back of an axe head or the butt of a rifle might
     also have done the trick.

79   A number of screws from the lid panel have been found on the battlefield
     over the years, bent in a manner which can only realistically be attributed to
     the opening of the boxes in such a way. Some surviving examples still have
     the brass housing from the box top in place, indicating that the wood was
     broken away while the screw was still fixed. In order to bend the screws one
     end would need to be firmly fixed and the other struck with considerable
     violence.

80   Essex, letter in *The Times*, 12 April 1879.

81   Account of Malindi, Chelmsford Papers, NAM.

82   Raw, Report.

83  Essex, evidence to Court of Inquiry, Helpmekaar, 27 January 1879, BPP, C 2260.

84  Molife in Jackson and Whybra, 'Isandhlwana and the Durnford Papers', *Soldiers of the Queen.*

85  Henderson to his father, 28 January 1879, quoted in Peter Haythorn and Amy Young (eds), *Henderson Heritage* (Pietermaritzburg, 1972).

86  Quoted in Colenso and Durnford, *A History of the Zulu War and its Origin.*

87  Brickhill, *Natal Magazine.*

88  Davies, Report.

89  Brickhill, *Natal Magazine.*

90  Personal information from Isaac Dlamini whose great-grandfather fought at the battle.

91  *Natal Mercury*, 22 January 1929.

92  Account of 'Untabeni and Uhlowani, two scouts', WO 32/7713, National Archives, London.

93  Some of the unattached men may have been in camp, however.

94  Quoted in Mitford, *Through the Zulu Country.*

95  Smith-Dorrien, *Memories of Forty-Eight Years' Service.*

96  Quoted in Colenso and Durnford, *A History of the Zulu War and its Origin.*

97  Account in Symons Papers, Campbell Collections, University of KwaZulu-Natal.

98  *Natal Mercury*, 22 January 1929.

99  Curling quoted in Greaves and Best, *The Curling Letters of the Anglo-Zulu War.* In his evidence to the Court of Inquiry (Helpmekaar, 27 January 1879, BPP, C 2260), Curling stated that the Zulus 'advanced slowly, without halting'.

100 Quoted in Frank Emery, 'Isandlwana: A Survivor's Letter', *Soldiers of the Queen*, No. 18, September 1979.

101 Higginson, Official Report.

102 'Zulu Deserter'.

103 Letter in the *Times of Natal*, 26 February 1879.

104 Ibid.

105 Essex, letter in *The Times*, 12 April 1879.

106 Davies, Report.

107 Ibid.

108 Quoted in Jackson and Whybra, 'Isandhlwana and the Durnford Papers', *Soldiers of the Queen.*

109 Watkins, 'They Fought For the Great White Queen'.

110 Davies, Report.

111 *Natal Advertiser*, 22 January 1929.

112 Gardner, evidence to Court of Inquiry, Helpmekaar, 27 January 1879, BPP, C 2260.

113 Essex, letter in *The Times*, 12 April 1879.


## 22. 'Kill me in the shadows'

1 Hamilton Browne, *A Lost Legionary in South Africa*.

2 Hamilton Browne, Official Report, Rorke's Drift, 2 February 1879, WO 32/ 7726, National Archives, London. Hamilton Browne's reports confine themselves rather more to facts than his memoirs, written years later; on the whole, however, the two are largely consistent regarding the sequence of events.

3 Hamilton Browne, *A Lost Legionary in South Africa*.

4 Ibid.

5 Ibid.; Hamilton Browne, Official Report.

6 Hamilton Browne, *A Lost Legionary in South Africa*.

7 Ibid. This passage implies that the Zulu right horn entered the camp first, although this is contradicted by both Zulu and British eyewitnesses. The probable explanation, as Trooper Symons of the Carbineers noted, is that when the uMbonambi first struck the tents, sweeping round Pulleine's right, there was a rush to the rear of draft animals and non-combatants; many of these animals passed over the *nek* only to turn back into the camp when they met the right horn, causing further chaos among the troops trying to retreat. From a distance the movements on the *nek* may well have been clearer to Hamilton Browne than those on the flats below the tents, giving the impression that the right horn had entered the tents before it actually did so. In fact the two events must have taken place within minutes of each other – in the time it took for frightened animals to run over the *nek*, and back again.

8 Hamilton Browne, *A Lost Legionary in South Africa*.

9 Ibid.

10 Account of a member of the uMbonambi, in Mitford, *Through the Zulu Country*.

11 'Mantshonga' Walmsley was the Natal Border Agent at the Lower Drift of the Thukela at the time of the battle, who Cetshwayo's party believed encouraged their rival Prince Mbuyazi. 'Ngqelebana' Rathbone was a trader who was trying to flee Zululand with his cattle, but was prevented from escaping to Natal by the state of the river.

12 Account of a member of the uMbonambi, in Mitford, *Through the Zulu Country*.

13 The story of Mkhosana is mentioned in a number of contemporary sources (see for example Lugg, *Historic Natal and Zululand*), and I had the great good fortune to be told family traditions relating to his death by his grandson, the late Prince Gilenja Biyela. Mkhosana's body was covered over by his brother, Mthiyaqwa, who survived the battle and family traditions are strong on a number of points – notably that Mkhosana was wearing his regalia, and with regard to the gaping wound in the back of his head. Prince Gilenja was of the opinion that Mkhosana must have been accidentally shot by one of his own men during the charge; while this is possible, the injury sounds more consistent to me with the notorious exit wounds inflicted by Martini-Henry rounds. The warrior of the uMbonambi who fought in the battle thought that Mkhosana was shot 'clean through the forehead'.

14 Mehlokazulu, Interview.

15 Ibid.

16 Swinny, 'A Zulu Boy's Recollections'.

17 Ibid.

18 Account of Mpashana kaSodondo.

19 *Natal Mercury*, 22 January 1929.

20 Mitford, *Through the Zulu Country*.

21 *Natal Mercury*, 22 January 1929.

22 Brickhill, *Natal Magazine*.

23 Hamer, Chelmsford Papers, NAM.

24 Higginson, Official Report.

25 Account in Symons Papers, Campbell Collections, University of KwaZulu-Natal.

26 Essex, evidence to Court of Inquiry, Helpmekaar, 27 January 1879, BPP, C 2260.

27 Account of Malindi, Chelmsford Papers, NAM.

28 Swinny, 'A Zulu Boy's Recollections'.

29 Letter published in the *Times of Natal*, 26 February 1879.

30 Swinny, 'A Zulu Boy's Recollections'.

31 Information from Lindizwe Ngobese.

32 Account of Malindi, Chelmsford Papers, NAM.

33 Greaves and Best, *The Curling Letters of the Anglo-Zulu War*.

34 Nyanda, Report.

35 Vause, letter in the *Natal Witness*, 21 January 1879.

36 Raw, Report.

37 Brickhill, *Natal Magazine*.

38 Hamer, Chelmsford Papers, NAM.

39 *Natal Witness*, 19 January 1929.

40  Greaves and Best, *Curling Letters of the Anglo-Zulu War*.

41  Quoted in Mitford, *Through the Zulu Country*.

42  Stalker, *The Natal Carbineers*.

43  Account of a member of the uMbonambi, in Mitford, *Through the Zulu Country*.

44  Colenso and Durnford, *A History of the Zulu War and its Origin*.

45  Essex, evidence to the Court of Inquiry, Helpmekaar, 27 January 1879, BPP, C 2260.

46  Stafford, Account, January 1938, Campbell Collections, University of Kwa-Zulu-Natal, Durban.

47  Notes on interviews conducted by Denys Bowden with survivors of the Anglo-Zulu War, Bowden Papers, KwaZulu-Natal Museum, Pietermaritzburg, quoted in Ian Knight, 'Kill Me in the Shadows', *Soldiers of the Queen*, No. 74, September 1983.

48  Brickhill, *Natal Magazine*. This is the only reference to the 1/24th Quartermaster, James Pullen, during the battle. There are very few survivors' accounts of activity in the 1/24th camp during the battle; it is highly likely that Pullen had at some point been involved in distributing supplies from his battalion's reserve ammunition supply.

49  Quoted in Knight, 'Kill Me in the Shadows'.

50  *Natal Witness*, 19 January 1929.

51  Davies, Report.

52  Local time was two hours later than Greenwich Mean Time; in GMT the eclipse began at 11.00 a.m. and ended at 1.30 p.m.

53  *Natal Mercury*, 22 January 1929.

54  Mitford, *Through the Zulu Country*.

55  Report by an unidentified survivor of the Carbineers, newspaper cutting, Old Court House Museum, Durban.

56  Stalker, *The Natal Carbineers*.

57  *Natal Advertiser*, 22 January 1929.

58  Ibid.

59  Quoted in Edward Durnford, *A Soldier's Life*.

60  Mehlokazulu, Interview.

61  Ibid.

62  Brickhill, *Natal Magazine*.

63  Account in W.H. Clements, *The Glamour and Tragedy of the Zulu War* (London, 1936).

64  *Natal Mercury*, 12 March 1924.

65  Stafford, Account, 1939.

66  *Natal Witness*, 19 January 1929.

67  *Natal Advertiser*, 22 January 1929.

68  *Times of Natal*, 31 January 1879. It seems likely however that the time was a little after this, as fighting went on for some time after the Zulus penetrated the camp.

69  Watkins, 'They Fought For the Great White Queen'.

70  Higginson, Official Report.

71  Smith-Dorrien, *Memories of Forty-Eight Years' Service*.

72  Smith-Dorrien to his father, quoted in Smith-Dorrien, *Memories of Forty-Eight Years' Service*.

73  Davies, Report.

74  Ibid.

75  Greaves and Best, *Curling Letters of the Anglo-Zulu War*.

76  Ibid.

77  The excavation was officially sanctioned by the KwaZulu-Natal heritage body, Amafa KwaZulu-Natali, and the remains re-interred once the grave had been repaired, in accordance with its policy.

78  Colenso and Durnford, *A History of the Zulu War and its Origin*.

79  Norris-Newman, *In Zululand with the British throughout the War of 1879*.

80  Mehlokazulu, Interview.

81  Quoted in Colenso and Durnford, *A History of the Zulu War and its Origin*.

82  Mitford, *Through the Zulu Country*.

83  *Natal Witness*, 19 January 1929.

84  Unnamed eyewitness quoted in J.P. Mackinnon and S.H. Shadbolt, *The South Africa Campaign of 1879* (London, 1879).

85  H. Rider Haggard, 'The Tale of Isandhlwana and Rorke's Drift', in Andrew Lang (ed.), *The True Story Book* (London, 1893).

86  Swinny, 'A Zulu Boy's Recollections'.

87  UMhoti describes how one group of the 24th was driven down the Manzimnyama; papers in the Anstey family confirm the body of Edgar Anstey was found there. Edgar's brother, Captain T.H. Anstey, Royal Engineers, completed a survey of the battlefield in November 1879 during the course of which, according to family sources, he recovered a blood-stained handkerchief from Edgar's remains. A cluster of cairns on the banks of the Manzimnyama is believed to mark the spot today.

88  Mehlokazulu, Interview.

89  *Natal Mercury*, 22 January 1929.

90  Mitford, *Through the Zulu Country*.

91  UMhoti, Account in Symons Papers, Campbell Collections, University of KwaZulu-Natal.

92  Knight, 'Kill Me in the Shadows'.

93  *Ilanga Lase Natal*, 20 June 1936.

94  Wilkins, *The Story of the Blood Drenched Field of Isandhlwana*.

95  Swinny, 'A Zulu Boy's Recollections'.

96  Hallam Parr, *A Sketch of the Kafir and Zulu Wars*.

97  Knight, 'Kill Me in the Shadows'.

98  *Natal Mercury*, 22 January 1929.

99  Ibid.

100 Knight, 'Kill Me in the Shadows'.

101 Ibid.

102 Account of a man of the uVe, quoted in Colenso and Durnford, *A History of the Zulu War and its Origin*.

103 Ibid.

## 23. 'Do you hear that?'

1  Chard, letter to Queen Victoria, 21 February 1880, quoted in Holme, *The Noble 24th* (London, 1999).

2  Ibid.

3  Davies, Report.

4  Brickhill, *Natal Magazine*.

5  Stafford, Account, January 1938.

6  Brickhill, *Natal Magazine*.

7  Ibid.

8  James Hamer, in 'Copy of Part of My Son's Letter', Chelmsford Papers, NAM, London.

9  Stalker, *The Natal Carbineers*.

10 Brickhill, *Natal Magazine*.

11 As well as detailing the incident in his own account, Brickhill told the story to Lieutenant Maxwell of the 3rd NNC. See Twentyman Jones, *Reminiscences of the Zulu War by John Maxwell*.

12 Davies, Report.

13 Stafford, Account, January 1938. Lieutenant L.D. Young of the 2/3rd NNC was killed in the battle. Young's brother, Lieutenant H.C. Young, wrote a letter published in the *Echo* on 24 February 1879 in which he claimed to have been in the camp and to have seen his brother shot through the head before he escaped; Walter Higginson refuted this version in the *Natal Mercury* of 16 May 1879, claiming that H.C. Young had never been present at iSandlwana, but had been sick at the Sandspruit on the day of the battle.

14 Hlubi, Account, Secretary for Native Affairs Department Papers, 1/1/34, No.

159, KwaZulu-Natal Archive. See also Hallam Parr's *A Sketch of the Kafir and Zulu Wars*: 'The Basutos ... fired two or three rounds at a point where the Zulus seemed weakest, and then charged, and many of them managed to escape.'

15  Wilkins, *The Story of the Blood Drenched Field of Isandhlwana.*

16  Anecdote in Amy Helen Young, *Hathorn Family History* (Pietermaritzburg, c. 1970).

17  Quoted in Shepherd's biography in Mackinnon and Shadbolt, *The South Africa Campaign of 1879.*

18  Smith-Dorrien, *Memories of Forty-Eight Years' Service.*

19  Ibid.

20  Ibid.

21  Quoted in Holme, *The Noble 24th.*

22  Ibid.

23  At the Battle of Maiwand in Afghanistan on 27 July 1880 the 66th Regiment found itself in a similar predicament to the 24th at iSandlwana, and to rally his men Colonel James Galbraith ordered one of the Colours to be uncased. About 200 men rallied to them, but Galbraith was killed shortly afterwards and the stand largely broken up.

24  Brickhill, *Natal Magazine.*

25  Ibid.

26  Knight, 'Kill Me in the Shadows'.

27  Ibid.

28  Ibid.

29  Brickhill, *Natal Magazine.*

30  Captain Church's report, quoted in Durnford, *A Soldier's Life.*

31  Anonymous letter in the *Daily News*, 7 April 1879.

32  Clery to Colonel Harman, quoted in Clarke, *Zululand at War 1879*. The reference to 'curious reports' is intriguing, for Chelmsford denied receiving either of Hamilton Browne's earlier messages, and it is difficult to know to what other reports Clery might have been referring.

33  Norris-Newman, *In Zululand with the British throughout the War of 1879.*

34  Ibid.

35  Russell, Report.

36  Paton *et al., Historical Records of the 24th Regiment.*

37  Mansel, Report, quoted in Durnford, *A Soldier's Life.* Mansel's account seems credible enough but, as F.W.D. Jackson points out (in *Hill of the Sphinx* (Bexleyheath, 2002)), it seems likely that the Mounted Police only patrolled towards the camp after the worst of the fighting was over (3–4 p.m.). Either Mansel has confused the chronology, and his return was earlier, or the

flashes he saw were not those of the 7-pdrs firing. Note that he heard no sounds of battle – another manifestation perhaps of the treacherous acoustics of the countryside around iSandlwana.

38 Mitford, *Through the Zulu Country*.
39 *Natal Mercury*, 22 January 1929.
40 Ibid.
41 Mitford, *Through the Zulu Country*.
42 H.V. Morton, *In Search of South Africa* (London, 1948).
43 *Ilanga Lase Natal*, 20 June 1936.
44 Knight, 'Kill Me in the Shadows'.
45 Mehlokazulu, Interview.
46 Ibid.
47 Ibid.
48 Knight, 'Kill Me in the Shadows'.
49 Captain W.E. Montague, *Campaigning in South Africa* (London, 1880).
50 Interview with the author, March 1991.
51 *Natal Mercury*, 22 January 1929.
52 Webb and Wright, *The James Stuart Archive*, Vol. 3.
53 *Natal Mercury*, 22 January 1929.
54 Trooper Richard Stevens, letter first published in *Colchester Mercury and Essex Express*, 15 March 1879, quoted in Frank Emery, *The Red Soldier: Letters from the Zulu War 1879* (London, 1977).
55 Mehlokazulu, Interview.
56 Webb and Wright, *The James Stuart Archive*, Vol. 3.
57 *Natal Mercury*, 22 January 1929.
58 Account in Symons Papers, Campbell Collections, University of KwaZulu-Natal.
59 Mehlokazulu, Interview.

## 24. 'Get on man!'

1 Hamilton Browne, *A Lost Legionary in South Africa*.
2 Ibid.
3 Quoted in Frank Streatfield, *Reminiscences of an Old 'Un* (London, 1911).
4 Norris-Newman, *In Zululand with the British throughout the War of 1879*.
5 See for example Gosset, quoted in French, *Lord Chelmsford and the Zulu War*.
6 According to the intelligence booklet published at Lord Chelmsford's behest in November 1878, F.B. Fynney's *The Zulu Army and the Zulu Headmen*, the

iNdluyengwe carried black shields with large white spots on the lower half. This information clearly pre-dates their incorporation into the uThulwana, however, and it is possible that by January 1879 they were both wearing the head-ring and carrying white shields.

7　Account 'By an Eye-Witness' (Reverend George Smith), *Natal Mercury*, 7 April 1879.

8　Davies, Report.

9　Watkins, 'They Fought For the Great White Queen'.

10　Stafford, Account, January 1938.

11　Ibid.

12　Watkins, 'They Fought For the Great White Queen'.

13　Colonel Lewis, radio talk.

14　The cloak is now in Firepower, the Royal Artillery Museum, Woolwich, London.

15　Colonel Lewis, radio talk.

16　Ibid.

17　Smith-Dorrien, *Memories of Forty-Eight Years' Service*.

18　Ibid.

19　Greaves and Best, *Curling Letters of the Anglo-Zulu War*.

20　Brickhill, *Natal Magazine*.

21　Greaves and Best, *Curling Letters of the Anglo-Zulu War*.

22　*Times of Natal*, 26 February 1879.

23　Account in the *London Magazine*, No. 38, Vol. XXXI.

24　Smith-Dorrien to his father, quoted in Smith-Dorrien, *Memories of Forty-Eight Years' Service*.

25　Stalker, *The Natal Carbineers*. The crossing spot has been known as Fugitives' Drift ever since the battle.

26　*Times of Natal*, 26 February 1879.

27　Brickhill, *Natal Magazine*.

28　Higginson, Official Report.

29　The rock was apparently identified in an engraving in the *Illustrated London News* as a large coffin-shaped boulder which lies close to the Zulu bank, and it is a popular marker for visitors to the site today. In fact, however, a close reading of the evidence suggests that the rock to which Higginson and Melvill clung was close to the Natal bank (the Colour case was found among the rocks on the Natal side). The coffin rock may actually have been the submerged feature which Brickhill says almost unhorsed him when he first entered the water.

30　*Natal Mercury*, 22 January 1929.

31　Vause, letter in the *Natal Witness*, 21 January 1967.

32  Account in the *London Magazine*.

33  Account in Bishop Colenso's notes, in Vijn, *Cetshwayo's Dutchman*.

34  Gibson, *The Story of the Zulus*.

35  Higginson, Official Report.

36  'Told to Mr Jas. Chadwick by Mbulwane Mdime at Qudeni, about 1919', Notes in Talana Museum, Dundee.

37  Paton *et al.*, *Historical Records of the 24th Regiment*.

38  Stalker, *The Natal Carbineers*.

39  *Natal Mercury*, 22 January 1929.

40  Statement 'Taken by H.C. Shepstone, 3 February 1879', BPP, C 2260.

41  Child, *Zulu War Journal*.

42  Twentyman Jones, *Reminiscences of the Zulu War by John Maxwell*.

43  Ibid.

44  Child, *Zulu War Journal*.

45  Charles Fortescue-Brickdale (ed.), *Major-General Sir Henry Hallam-Parr, Recollections and Correspondence* (London, 1917).

46  Symons Papers, Talana Museum.

47  Paton *et al.*, *Historical Records of the 24th Regiment*.

48  Symons Papers, Talana Museum.

49  Fynn, 'My Recollections of a Famous Campaign and a Great Disaster'.

50  Symons Papers, Talana Museum.

51  Fynn, 'My Recollections of a Famous Campaign and a Great Disaster'.

52  Symons Papers, Talana Museum.

53  Symons Papers, Talana Museum.

54  Symons Papers, Campbell Collections, University of KwaZulu-Natal.

55  Symons Papers, Talana Museum.

56  Newnham-Davies, Interview, *Chums* magazine.

57  Twentyman Jones, *Reminiscences of the Zulu War by John Maxwell*.

58  Symons Papers, Talana Museum.

59  Ibid.

60  Child, *Zulu War Journal*.

61  Fynn, 'My Recollections of a Famous Campaign and a Great Disaster'.

62  Twentyman Jones, *Reminiscences of the Zulu War by John Maxwell*.

63  Family history; interview with Tim Coghlan.

64  Account in the *Natal Mercury*, 22 January 1929.

65  Symons Papers, Talana Museum.

66  *Natal Mercury*, 22 January 1929.

67  Fynn, 'My Recollections of a Famous Campaign and a Great Disaster'.

68  Twentyman Jones, *Reminiscences of the Zulu War by John Maxwell*.

69  Hallam Parr, *A Sketch of the Kafir and Zulu Wars*.

70 Child, *Zulu War Journal.*

71 Ibid.

72 Newnham-Davies, Interview, *Chums* magazine.

73 Child, *Zulu War Journal.*

74 Hallam Parr, *A Sketch of the Kafir and Zulu Wars.*

75 Twentyman Jones, *Reminiscences of the Zulu War by John Maxwell.*

76 Symons Papers, Talana Museum.

77 *Natal Mercury*, 22 January 1929.

78 Private William Meredith, 2/24th, letter in the *South Wales Daily Telegram*, 24 March 1879, quoted in Emery, *The Red Soldier.*

79 Fynn, 'My Recollections of a Famous Campaign and a Great Disaster'.

80 Paton *et al.*, *Historical Records of the 24th Regiment.*

81 Mitford, *Through the Zulu Country.*

82 A Private Dennis Harrington was also killed in the battle, and may have been Thomas's father.

83 Twentyman Jones, *Reminiscences of the Zulu War by John Maxwell.*

84 Hamilton Browne, *A Lost Legionary in South Africa.*

85 Clery to Colonel Harman, quoted in Clarke, *Zululand At War 1879.*

### 25. 'We stood up face to face, white men and black . . .'

1 Dunne's account was originally published in the *Army Service Corps Journal* of 1891 (hereafter Dunne, Account, *Army Service Corps Journal*). It is reproduced in Colonel Ian Bennett, *Eyewitness in Zululand* (London, 1989), and Alan Baynham Jones and Lee Stevenson, *Rorke's Drift By Those Who Were There* (Brighton, 2003), which remains an extremely useful compendium of the eyewitness accounts of the survivors, including most of those listed below.

2 My thanks to Joe Stockil for sharing family research on this point.

3 Gonville was one of four sons of Edmund de Gonville, 3rd Baronet Bromhead.

4 A variety of childhood ailments, a lifestyle lived in the open, often in hot climates and exposed to tropical diseases, plus the occupational hazards of regular proximity to loud bangs, meant that many distinguished Victorian soldiers were hard of hearing, including Evelyn Wood, who commanded Chelmsford's Left Flank Column, and whose career was not affected by it in the least, rising as he did to the rank of field marshal.

5 Transcript of an interview Bourne gave to the BBC series *I Was There*, *Listener*, 20 December 1936.

6 Bourne, *Listener.*

7   Gibson, *The Story of the Zulus.*

8   'Return of Natives (not on Active Service) killed or captured by the Zulus on or since 22 January', BPP, C 2367.

9   Gibson, *The Story of the Zulus.*

10  Witt's account was published in a number of UK papers, notably the *Illustrated London News*, 8 March 1879.

11  Account 'By an Eyewitness' (Reverend George Smith), *Natal Mercury*, 7 April 1879.

12  Quoted in Captain W.R. Ludlow, *Zululand and Cetewayo* (London, 1882).

13  Stafford, Account, 1939.

14  Ibid.

15  Swinny, 'A Zulu Boy's Recollections'.

16  Dunne, Account, *Army Service Corps Journal.*

17  Chard, letter to Queen Victoria, 21 February 1880, quoted in Holme, *The Noble 24th..*

18  Fort Melvill was later built on this site.

19  Jones, quoted in Emery, *The Red Soldier.*

20  Dunne, Account, *Army Service Corps Journal.*

21  Ibid.

22  Chard, letter to Queen Victoria, 21 February 1880, quoted in Holme, *The Noble 24th.*

23  Ibid.

24  Account in *Army Medical Department Annual Report*, Appendix for 1878 (AMD, 1879). See also Lee Stevenson, *The Rorke's Drift Doctor* (Brighton 2001), and Baynham Jones and Stevenson, *Rorke's Drift By Those Who Were There.*

25  Bourne, *Listener.*

26  Lugg, letter in the *North Devon Times*, 24 April 1879.

27  Ibid.

28  Chard, letter to Queen Victoria, 21 February 1880, quoted in Holme, *The Noble 24th.*

29  Dunne, Account, *Army Service Corps Journal.*

30  Lugg, *North Devon Times.*

31  Chard, letter to Queen Victoria, 21 February 1880, quoted in Holme, *The Noble 24th.*

32  Lugg, *North Devon Times.*

33  Letter from Bob Hall, *c.* 1906, Campbell Collections, University of KwaZulu-Natal, Durban.

34  Chard, letter to Queen Victoria, 21 February 1880, quoted in Holme, *The Noble 24th.*

35  Ibid.

36  George Smith, who buried him on 23 January, noted the wound. Smith delicately attributed his death to the Zulus. Note in KwaZulu-Natal Archive, quoted in Baynham Jones and Stevenson, *Rorke's Drift By Those Who Were There.*

37  Hitch, Regimental Museum, Brecon, quoted in Baynham Jones and Stevenson, *Rorke's Drift By Those Who Were There.*

38  Dunne, Account, *Army Service Corps Journal.*

39  Hitch mentions that he saw from the hospital roof the Zulu *amabutho* halting to deploy.

40  Hook, Account in the *Royal Magazine*, February 1905.

41  Lugg, *North Devon Herald.*

42  Howard, letter in the *Daily Telegraph*, 25 March 1879.

43  Hook, Account in the *Strand Magazine*, Vol. 1, January–June 1891.

44  Reynolds, Account in *The VC, c.* 1903; see Baynham Jones and Stevenson, *Rorke's Drift By Those Who Were There.*

45  Chard, letter to Queen Victoria, 21 February 1880, quoted in Holme, *The Noble 24th.*

46  Hitch, Regimental Museum, Brecon, quoted in Baynham Jones and Stevenson, *Rorke's Drift By Those Who Were There.*

47  Chard, Official Report, WO 32/7737, National Archives, London.

48  Lugg, *North Devon Times.*

49  Chard, letter to Queen Victoria, 21 February 1880, quoted in Holme, *The Noble 24th.*

50  Reynolds, Acccount, *The VC.*

51  Account 'By an Eyewitness' (Reverend George Smith), *Natal Mercury*, 7 April 1879.

52  Bourne, *Listener.*

53  Bourne's account in *Listener* is heavily influenced by Colonels Paton, Glennie and Penn Symons' regimental history; Bourne admits that he knew nothing of the details of iSandlwana at the time, but it may be that the realization that the Zulus had captured so many Martini-Henry rifles at iSandlwana shaped his impressions of Rorke's Drift after the event.

54  Chard, letter to Queen Victoria, 21 February 1880, quoted in Holme, *The Noble 24th.*

55  Account in the *Cambrian*, 13 June 1879.

56  Chard, letter to Queen Victoria, 21 February 1880, quoted in Holme, *The Noble 24th.*

57  A photograph of the dog appears in Stevenson, *The Rorke's Drift Doctor.*

58  Reynolds, Account, *The VC.*

59　Account 'By an Eyewitness' (Reverend George Smith), *Natal Mercury*, 7 April 1879.

60　Chard, letter to Queen Victoria, 21 February 1880, quoted in Holme, *The Noble 24th*.

61　Ibid.

62　Hook, Account, *Royal Magazine*.

63　Ibid.

64　Ibid.

65　Hook, Account, *Strand Magazine*.

66　Account in *Rare Bits*, c. 1883; quoted in Barry C. Johnson's thorough biography of Hook, *Hook of Rorke's Drift* (Birmingham, 2004).

67　Account from an unknown West Country newspaper, 21 May 1881, believed to be Hook's first interview; quoted in Johnson, *Hook of Rorke's Drift*.

68　Hook, Account, *Royal Magazine*.

69　Account in the *Cambrian*, 13 June 1879.

70　Chard, letter to Queen Victoria, 21 February 1880, quoted in Holme, *The Noble 24th*.

71　Ibid.

72　Hallam-Parr, *A Sketch of the Kafir and Zulu Wars*.

73　Statement made by Connolly on being invalided home, RA VIC/O34/64, Royal Archives, Windsor Castle.

74　Hook, Account, *Royal Magazine*.

75　Account in an unidentified Dundee newspaper, 1879, quoted in Baynham Jones and Stevenson, *Rorke's Drift By Those Who Were There*.

76　Lugg, *North Devon Times*.

77　Hitch, Regimental Museum, Brecon, quoted in Baynham Jones and Stevenson, *Rorke's Drift By Those Who Were There*.

78　Hitch, Account, *Chums* magazine, 11 March 1908.

79　Ibid.

80　Note by Harford, in Payne, *The Writings, Photographs and Sketches of H.C. Harford*.

81　Chard, letter to Queen Victoria, 21 February 1880, quoted in Holme, *The Noble 24th*.

82　Ibid.

83　Dunne, Account, *Army Service Corps Journal*.

84　Lugg, *North Devon Herald*.

85　Chard, letter to Queen Victoria, 21 February 1880, quoted in Holme, *The Noble 24th*.

86　Hook, Account, *Royal Magazine*.

87　Account in the *Monmouthshire Beacon*, 29 March 1879.

88 Stafford, Account, 1939.
89 Sir Garnet Wolseley, Diary, 21 August 1879, quoted in Professor Adrian Preston (ed.), *Sir Garnet Wolseley's South African Journal* (Cape Town, 1973).
90 Swinny, 'A Zulu Boy's Recollections'.
91 H.C. Lugg, *A Natal Family Looks Back* (Durban, 1970).

## 26. 'The subject of much astonishment'

1 Spalding's movements are outlined in his Official Report, WO 32/7738, National Archives, London.
2 Essex, letter in *The Times*, 12 April 1879.
3 *Natal Mercury*, 22 January 1929.
4 Higginson, Official Report.
5 Macphail, *Natal Mercury*, 22 January 1929.
6 Spalding, Official Report.
7 Ibid.
8 Ibid.
9 Smith-Dorrien, *Memories of Forty-Eight Years' Service*.
10 *Natal Mercury*, 22 January 1929.
11 Ibid.
12 Ibid.
13 Ibid.
14 Sheila Henderson, 'The Turbulent Frontier: Biggarsberg and the Buffalo at the Crossroads', in G.A. Chadwick and E.G. Hobson (eds.), *The Zulu War and the Colony of Natal* (Mandini, 1979).
15 Twentyman Jones, *Reminiscences of the Zulu War by John Maxwell*.
16 Hamilton Browne, *A Lost Legionary in South Africa*.
17 Symons Papers, Talana Museum.
18 Ibid.
19 Fynn, 'My Recollections of a Famous Campaign and a Great Disaster'.
20 W.J. Clarke, 'My Career in South Africa', manuscript in the Campbell Collections, University of KwaZulu-Natal, Durban.
21 Twentyman Jones, *Reminiscences of the Zulu War by John Maxwell*.
22 Symons Papers, Talana Museum.
23 Fynn, 'My Recollections of a Famous Campaign and a Great Disaster'.
24 *Natal Mercury*, 22 January 1929.
25 Symons Papers, Talana Museum.
26 Child, *Zulu War Journal*.
27 Family information from Mr Dedekind at Elandskraal.

28  Twentyman Jones, *Reminiscences of the Zulu War by John Maxwell.*
29  Clarke, 'My Career in South Africa'.
30  Swinny, 'A Zulu Boy's Recollections'.
31  Fynn, 'My Recollections of a Famous Campaign and a Great Disaster'.
32  Symons Papers, Talana Museum.
33  Twentyman Jones, *Reminiscences of the Zulu War by John Maxwell.*
34  Symons Papers, Dundee.
35  Ibid.
36  Chard, letter to Queen Victoria, 21 February 1880, quoted in Holme, *The Noble 24th.*
37  Ibid.
38  Ibid.
39  Hook, Account, *Royal Magazine.*
40  Hook, Account, *Strand Magazine.*
41  Ibid.
42  Chard, letter to Queen Victoria, 21 February 1880, quoted in Holme, *The Noble 24th.*
43  Ibid.
44  Ibid.
45  Hook, Account, *Royal Magazine.*
46  Ibid.
47  Dunne, Account, *Army Service Corps Journal.*
48  Chard, letter to Queen Victoria, 21 February 1880, quoted in Holme, *The Noble 24th.*
49  Hamilton Browne, *A Lost Legionary in South Africa.*
50  Hook, first interview, quoted in Johnson, *Hook of Rorke's Drift.*
51  Hook, Account, *Royal Magazine.*
52  Chard, letter to Queen Victoria, 21 February 1880, quoted in Holme, *The Noble 24th.*
53  Fynn, 'My Recollections of a Famous Campaign and a Great Disaster'.
54  Dunne, Account, *Army Service Corps Journal.*
55  Hamilton Browne, *A Lost Legionary in South Africa.*
56  Symons Papers, Talana Museum.
57  Mainwaring, quoted in Holme, *The Noble 24th.*
58  Smith-Dorrien, *Memories of Forty-Eight Years' Service.*
59  Hallam Parr, *A Sketch of the Kafir and Zulu Wars.*
60  Symons Papers, Campbell Collections, University of KwaZulu-Natal.
61  Twentyman Jones, *Reminiscences of the Zulu War by John Maxwell.*
62  Hamilton Browne, *A Lost Legionary in South Africa.*
63  Hallam Parr, *A Sketch of the Kafir and Zulu Wars.*

64 Clarke, 'My Career in South Africa'.

65 'Statement of a Natal Volunteer', Bishop Colenso's notes, in Vijn, *Cetshwayo's Dutchman*.

66 Symons Papers, Talana Museum.

67 Paton *et al.*, *Historical Records of the 24th Regiment*.

68 Symons Papers, Talana Museum.

69 Chelmsford to Frere, Rorke's Drift, 23 January 1879, Chelmsford Papers, NAM, quoted in Laband, *Lord Chelmsford's Zulu Campaign*.

70 Hamilton Browne, *A Lost Legionary in South Africa*.

71 Child, *Zulu War Journal*.

72 Hamilton Browne, *A Lost Legionary in South Africa*.

## 27. 'Wet with yesterday's blood'

1 H.W. Struben, *Recollections of Adventures* (Cape Town, 1920).

2 Account in Bishop Colenso's notes, in Vijn, *Cetshwayo's Dutchman*.

3 Mehlokazulu, Interview.

4 Molyneux, *Campaigning in South Africa and Egypt*.

5 Mitford, *Through the Zulu Country*.

6 Filter and Bouquin, *Paulina Dlamini*.

7 Although these ceremonies were entirely dictated by Zulu spiritual belief, it is interesting to note that they had much to offer in terms of modern approaches to post-traumatic stress conditions – they provided a framework of psychological support which recognized the emotional damage caused by combat, attributing it to the evil influence of shedding blood, and recast feelings of horror, shame and guilt into forms that were deeply rooted in Zulu culture, allowing sufferers not only to externalize them, but to exorcize them.

8 Account of Mpashana kaSodondo.

9 Ibid.

10 Mtshankomo kaMagolwana, in Webb and Wright, *The James Stuart Archive*, Vol. 4.

11 Mtshapi kaNorado, in Webb and Wright, *The James Stuart Archive*, Vol. 4.

12 'Cetywayo's Story', in Webb and Wright, *A Zulu King Speaks*.

13 Ibid.

14 Hallam Parr, *A Sketch of the Kafir and Zulu Wars*.

15 Swinny, 'A Zulu Boy's Recollections'. 'Mbozankomo' was an alternative name for the uThulwana.

16 Chelmsford to Wood, 28 February, Pietermaritzburg, Chelmsford Papers, NAM; quoted in Laband, *Lord Chelmsford's Zululand Campaign*.

17 Corporal Andrew Guthrie, 90th Regiment, Diary, quoted in Andrew Guthrie Macdougall, *The Guthrie Saga* (Bishop Auckland, 1998).

18 Chelmsford to Colonel F.A. Stanley, telegram, 27 January 1879, Chelmsford Papers, NAM; quoted in Laband, *Lord Chelmsford's Zululand Campaign.*

19 Swinny, 'A Zulu Boy's Recollections'.

20 Child, *Zulu War Journal.*

21 Clery to Sir Archibald Alison, Wolf's Hill Camp, 25 May 1879, quoted in Clarke, *Zululand At War 1879.*

22 Child, *Zulu War Journal.*

23 Ibid.

24 Twentyman Jones, *Reminiscences of the Zulu War by John Maxwell.*

25 Child, *Zulu War Journal.*

26 Hamilton Browne, *A Lost Legionary in South Africa.*

27 Ibid.

28 Greaves and Best, *Curling Letters of the Anglo-Zulu War.*

29 Blair-Brown's observations can be found in his 'Surgical Notes on the Zulu War', *Lancet*, 25 July 1879, and his book *Surgical Experiences in the Zulu and Transvaal Wars* (London, 1880).

30 Regimental Museum, Brecon.

31 Greaves and Best, *Curling Letters of the Anglo-Zulu War.*

32 Child, *Zulu War Journal.*

33 Smith-Dorrien, *Memories of Forty-Eight Years' Service.*

34 Hamilton Browne, *A Lost Legionary in South Africa.*

35 Greaves and Best, *Curling Letters of the Anglo-Zulu War.*

36 Dr Lewis Reynolds, *The Diary of a Civil Surgeon Serving with the British Army in South Africa during the Zulu War* (Duntroon, 1997).

37 Harness, Camp Dundee, 26 April 1879, quoted in Clarke, *Invasion of Zululand.*

38 Published in the *Standard*, 27 March 1879. See Clarke, *Invasion of Zululand* and Greaves and Best, *Curling Letters of the Anglo-Zulu War.*

39 Lieutenant James, RE, Report on the *The Isandlana Disaster*, published by the Quartermaster-General's Department in March 1879 and marked 'Confidential'; a copy annotated by Major Gossett is in the Chelmsford Papers, NAM.

40 On this subject see Keith Smith, 'The Blame Game', in Keith Smith, *Studies in the Anglo-Zulu War* (Doncaster, 2008).

41 Clery to Alison, 11 March 1879, quoted in Clarke, *Zululand at War 1879.*

42 Paton *et al.*, *Historical Records of the 24th Regiment.*

43 Quoted in Drooglever, *The Road to Isandhlwana.*

44 Ibid.

45  Hamilton Browne, *A Lost Legionary in South Africa.*

46  Ibid.

47  Child, *Zulu War Journal.*

48  Ibid.

49  Ibid.

50  Ibid.

51  Harness, Helpmekaar Camp, 19 February 1879, quoted in Clarke, *Invasion of Zululand.*

52  Chelmsford to Glyn, Pietermaritzburg, 25 January 1879, Chelmsford Papers, NAM.

53  Clery to Alison, Wolf's Hill Camp, 16 May 1879, quoted in Clarke, *Zululand At War 1879.*

54  Ibid.

55  W.P. Jones, letter, quoted in Emery, *The Red Soldier.*

56  Smith, letter in the *Brecon County Times*, 29 March 1879, quoted in Baynham Jones and Stevenson, *Rorke's Drift By Those Who Were There.*

57  Chelmsford to General Sir Alfred Horsfold, 14 May 1879, Chelmsford Papers, NAM.

58  Wolseley, Diary, 3 August 1879, quoted in Preston, *Sir Garnet Wolseley's South African Journal.*

59  Chelmsford to General Sir Alfred Horsfold, 14 May 1879, Chelmsford Papers, NAM.

60  Smith-Dorrien, *Memories of Forty-Eight Years' Service.*

## 28. 'Melancholy satisfaction'

1  Quoted in Jeff Guy, *The Heretic* (Pietermaritzburg, 1983).

2  Witt, *Illustrated London News*, 8 March 1879.

3  Hamilton Browne, *A Lost Legionary in South Africa.*

4  *Illustrated London News*, 12 July 1879.

5  Symons Papers, Talana Museum.

6  Norris-Newman, *In Zululand with the British throughout the War of 1879.*

7  *Illustrated London News*, 12 July 1879.

8  Forbes, ibid.

9  Letter, *Natal Mercury*, 11 February 1879.

10  Norris-Newman, *In Zululand with the British throughout the War of 1879.*

11  Melton Prior, *Campaigns of a War Correspondent* (London, 1912).

12  Forbes, *Illustrated London News*, 12 July 1879.

13  Mehlokazulu, Interview.

14 Harness, Camp Mtonjaneni, 6 July 1879, quoted in Clarke, *Invasion of Zululand 1879.*

15 Child, *Zulu War Journal.*

16 Ibid.

17 Chard, on receiving a presentation sword of honour in Plymouth, reported in the *Western Daily Mercury*, 17 November 1879, quoted in Baynham Jones and Stevenson, *Rorke's Drift By Those Who Were There.*

18 Child, *Zulu War Journal.*

19 *Natal Witness*, 29 May 1879.

20 Gold Stick is a position in the Queen's Household.

21 A book of cuttings in the Smith-Dorrien Collection of the Imperial War Museum in London includes numerous reports of his speaking engagements, and his iSandlwana story is mentioned frequently.

22 Black's reports are quoted in Norris-Newman, *In Zululand with the British throughout the War of 1879.*

23 Bromhead, Report, BPP, C 2676.

24 The original cairn stood just behind the 24th memorial; the large circular base can still be seen, and a small cairn has recently been built on top of it. Most of the original stones seem to have been used to fill the base of the 24th memorial during its construction in 1914.

25 Lieutenant M. O'Connell, 60th Rifles, Report, Pietermaritzburg, 16 April 1880, in BPP, C 2676.

26 R.W. Leyland, *A Holiday in South Africa* (London, 1882).

27 Boast, Report, KwaZulu-Natal Archive Depot, Pietermaritzburg.

28 Huw M. Jones, *Biographical Register of Swaziland* (Pietermaritzburg, 1993).

## 29. 'The day that I die'

1 Lee, *Once Dark Country.*

2 Ibid.

3 *Marie* (1912), *Child of the Storm* (1913) and *Finished* (1917).

4 H. Rider Haggard (Stephen Coan (ed.), *Diary of an African Journey* (London, 2000).

5 Ibid.

# Index

# Picture acknowledgements

### Section one

Page 1 – *top* author's collection; *bottom* Private Collection. 2 – *top, both* author's collection; *bottom, left* Ron Sheeley; *bottom right* Campbell Collections, UKZN. 3 – *top left* author's collection; *top right and bottom* Ron Sheeley. 4 – *top* Ron Sheeley; *bottom left* Campbell Collections, UKZN; *bottom right* Bodlian Library. 5 – *both* author's collection. 6 – *top* Private Collection; *bottom, both* author's collection. 7 – *top and bottom right* author's collection; *bottom left* Local History Museums, Durban. 8 – *top left and bottom right* author's collection; *top right and bottom* left Rai England/MOD.

### Section two

Page 1 – *top left* Private Collection; *top right* author's collection; *bottom left* KwaZulu-Natal Archives Depot; *bottom right* Local History Museums, Durban. 2 – *top* Museum Afrika; *bottom* David Jackson. 3 – *top* author's collection. 4 – *top* author's collection; *bottom* Private Collection. 5 – *top and bottom right* author's collection; *bottom left* Campbell Collections, UKZN. 6 – *both* author's collection. 7 – *both* author's collection. 8 – *top* Mary Evans Picture Library; *bottom* author's collection.

### Section three

Page 1 – *top left* David Jackson; *top right* Rai England/MOD; *bottom* National Army Museum. 2 – *top* Campbell Collections, UKZN; *bottom* Local History Museums, Durban. 3 – *top, both, and bottom left* Ron Sheeley; *bottom right* author's collection. 4 – *top* author's collection; *bottom left* Ron Sheeley; *bottom right* Michael Graham-Stewart. 5 – *top* Mary Evans Picture Library; *bottom* Regimental Museum, Brecon. 6 – *both* author's collection. 7 – *top* Michael Graham-Stewart; *centre* Ron Sheeley; *bottom* author's collection. 8 – *top* author's collection; *bottom* Local History Museums, Durban.